LETTERS
OF
AYN RAND

LETTERS
OF
AYN RAND

EDITED BY MICHAEL S. BERLINER
INTRODUCTION BY LEONARD PEIKOFF

A DUTTON BOOK

DUTTON

Published by the Penguin Group
Penguin Books USA Inc., 375 Hudson Street, New York, New York 10014, U.S.A.
Penguin Books Ltd, 27 Wrights Lane, London W8 5TZ, England
Penguin Books Australia Ltd, Ringwood, Victoria, Australia
Penguin Books Canada Ltd, 10 Alcorn Avenue, Toronto, Ontario, Canada M4V 3B2
Penguin Books (N.Z.) Ltd, 182–190 Wairau Road, Auckland 10, New Zealand

Penguin Books Ltd, Registered Offices:
Harmondsworth, Middlesex, England

First published by Dutton,
an imprint of Dutton Signet,
a division of Penguin Books USA Inc.
Distributed in Canada by McClelland & Stewart Inc.

First Printing, June, 1995
1 3 5 7 9 10 8 6 4 2

LIBRARY OF CONGRESS CATALOGING-IN-PUBLICATION DATA:
Rand, Ayn.
[Correspondence]
The letters of Ayn Rand / Michael S. Berliner, editor ;
introduction by Leonard Peikoff.
p.   cm.
Includes index.
ISBN 0-525-93946-6
1. Rand, Ayn—Correspondence.   2. Women novelists, American—20th
century—Correspondence.   3. Women philosophers—United States—
Correspondence.   I. Title.
PS3535.A547Z48   1995
813'.52—dc20   94-23646
[B]   CIP

Printed in the United States of America
Set in New Times Roman

Designed by Steven N. Stathakis

Information about other books by Ayn Rand and her philosophy, Objectivism, may be obtained by
writing to Objectivism, Box 177, Murray Hill Station, New York, New York 10157 USA.

This book is printed on acid-free paper. ∞

ACKNOWLEDGMENTS

The following individuals and copyright holders have generously given permission to print material from previously unpublished correspondence: Christopher Cerf, the Estate of Cecil B. DeMille, Sen. Barry Goldwater, John Hospers, the Estate of Rose Wilder Lane, Ira Levin, Elizabeth T. Ogden, the Estate of Isabel Paterson, Robert Stack, and the Estate of Barbara Stanwyck.

The quoted letters of Frank Lloyd Wright are Copyright © 1994 The Frank Lloyd Wright Foundation and are used with the permission of the Foundation. All rights reserved.

Excerpts from the letters of H. L. Mencken are quoted by permission of the Enoch Pratt Free Library in accordance with the terms of the will of H. L. Mencken.

CONTENTS

INTRODUCTION

I was a student and friend of Ayn Rand's for thirty-one years, from 1951 —when she was 46 and writing *Atlas Shrugged*—until her death in 1982, at the age of 77. So people always ask me: "What was she really like?"

My standard answer is: "Read her novels; she was everything their creator would have to be." But now I have a follow-up answer: "Read her letters."

When Michael Berliner handed me the manuscript of this book a month ago, I did not know much about the letters, and I proceeded to read them through. I started out coolly, as an editor, but I was soon hooked; I became emotionally involved and even rapt. I ended in tears.

It is almost eerie to hear her inimitable voice again, so many years after her death, but this book *is* Ayn Rand, exactly as I knew her. It captures her mind—and also her feelings, her actions, her achievements, her character, her soul. An authorized biography of Ayn Rand will appear in due course. But these letters will remain unique. Through them you can see her thinking and choosing and judging and reacting day by day, across decades, in virtually every aspect of her professional and personal life.

These letters do not merely tell you about Ayn Rand's life. In effect, they let you watch her live it, as though you were an invisible presence who could follow her around and even read her mind.

The person you will meet in this book has several essential attributes.

The first thing you will see is that Ayn Rand does not merely agree or disagree with the ideas of her fans or associates; if she undertakes to answer someone, she methodically explains her conclusions; she offers a patient—and often brilliant—sentence-by-sentence analysis. She does not merely accept or reject a practical proposal; she works to identify its merits and drawbacks, then weighs them dispassionately. If a friend in trouble solicits her advice, she does not give a glib answer; she identifies the basic problem, often down to its philosophical roots, so that the individual can see for himself how to decide.

Ayn Rand not only says or does—she says *why*; she always gives her *reasons*. Like the person I knew, therefore, her letters are the opposite of casual or purposeless. They are focused, deliberate, and bracingly logical. In a word, they display in lifelong practice the quality extolled as the top virtue by her own philosophy of Objectivism: rationality.

As a result of her method of thinking, Ayn Rand knew exactly what ideas and values she endorsed in every field and why. Hence her individualism and her integrity—her refusal to sell out to any establishment, to contradict her own conclusions, or to compromise her work. "I am not brave enough to be a coward," she once said. "I see the consequences too clearly." In this respect, she was not like her hero, Howard Roark; on the contrary, *he* was like her, as these letters make clear. In 1934, for instance, when she was an impoverished beginner, an editor at an important publishing house suggested that she rewrite her first novel (*We the Living*) with the help of a collaborator. She replied, in part: "If anyone is capable of improving *that* book—he should have written it himself. I would prefer not only never seeing it in print, but also burning every manuscript of it— rather than having William Shakespeare himself add one line to it which was not mine, or cross out one comma." Was she, then, a prima donna? Here are her next two sentences: "I repeat, I welcome and appreciate all suggestions of changes to improve the book without destroying its theme, and I am quite willing to make them. But these changes will be made *by me*."

Because Ayn Rand's value judgments, like her ideas, were products of her mind, they, too, were absolutes to her. Hence her unique intensity as a person—made of her unbreached commitment to her values, her pride in them, and her consequent complete openness about her feelings. She saw no more reason to repress her emotions than her convictions.

When Ayn Rand liked or disliked something, her friends knew it, as you will know it when, through these magically eloquent letters, you all but reexperience her passions: her enchantment with America; her bitter disappointment over the country's slow deterioration (which, virtually alone, she saw in the '30s); the joy and agony of her creative work; her fierce battle against every obstacle, including poverty; her pleasure in her growing success, first as a screenwriter, then as a novelist; her childlike delight at an unexpected gift from a friend; her unforgiving anger at injustice or betrayal; her desperate kisses on paper to her parents and sisters trapped in Russia; her lifelong love for her husband, Frank O'Connor; and the fundamental element conditioning all these emotions: her capacity to make moral judgments, that is, to condemn the evil and, above all, to revere the good, specifically, the greatness possible to man. As to this last: In 1934, she wrote a letter to thank an actor she did not know, whose performance onstage "gave me, for a few hours, a spark of what man could be, but isn't. . . . The word *heroic* does not quite express what I mean. You see, I am an atheist and I have only one religion: the sublime in human nature. There is nothing to approach the sanctity of the highest type of man possible and there is nothing that gives me the same reverent feeling, the feeling when one's spirit wants to kneel, bareheaded. Do not call it hero worship, because it is more than that. It is a kind of strange and improbable white heat where admiration becomes religion, and religion becomes philosophy, and philosophy—the whole of one's life."

If Ayn Rand's religion (speaking metaphorically) was admiration, then she expressed it in the ultimate fealty: *action*. Ayn Rand not only thought and valued; she acted accordingly. She was not content merely to desire ideals, to aspire, to dream; she hated the notion that "man's reach must exceed his grasp." She struggled ceaselessly to bring her dreams into the world, actually to achieve her values, here and now, on earth. She felt nothing but contempt for the Platonic contempt for this life. She demanded of men something much harder: the integration of mind and body—that is, idea expressed in behavior, theory in practice, ideal in reality.

The letters capture this aspect of Ayn Rand in two main areas: in regard to her own creative work and in regard to politics.

When Ayn Rand finished a play or novel, the new creation was, in effect, the "spiritual" part of her work, but it was not the end of the job; it was the beginning. Thereafter, like the *practical* idealist she was, she worked diligently to launch her creations into the world and then to watch over them vigilantly, taking responsibility for every "materialistic" detail of their progress, giving every detail her full mind and attention. Among other things, as you will see, she herself devised sales arguments for her agents to use and plans for promotional campaigns; she deliberated over the choice of publishers, the phrasing of contracts, and the conditions of her media appearances; and she weighed permissions requests and (for plays) casting, and even the print styles and colors of book jackets. Needless to say, she also labored on the exact wording of ads and blurbs—always with detailed reasons to the advertising and publicity departments.

As to politics, the letters indicate her many efforts not merely to argue for man's rights, but also, in action, to advance the pro-capitalist cause. One of the earlier efforts, prominent in these letters, was her attempt to unite and arm the better conservatives—that is, to gather them together into a fighting national organization with a clear-cut individualist credo. As you read about the vicissitudes of this project, you will, perhaps, understand more clearly why Ayn Rand was doomed to fight an unending battle: not only against leftists and moderates, but, worst of all, against "rightists"— in other words, the pitiful compromisers and anti-intellectual temporizers who made up the so-called "free enterprise" segment of the American spectrum. In the end, Ayn Rand decided that such men were not an asset in the fight for freedom, but a liability. She decided that it was too early for political action, that philosophical reeducation of the country had to come first. Her letters indicate by what series of painful shocks she reached this decision.

Despite her many disappointments, Ayn Rand did not make collective judgments; she did not become malevolent about people as such. To the end, she felt goodwill toward newcomers and gave them the benefit of the doubt—for as long as they could prove they deserved it. When, as an ignorant and confused teenager, I met her for the first time, she answered my philosophical questions urgently, for hours, struggling to help me clarify my thinking. To her, ideas were the decisive power in life, and a functioning intelligence, however confused, was of inestimable value. The same generosity is evident in many of her letters—lengthy letters of philosophical explanation and analysis sent to complete strangers who had written her their ideas or asked a question. When Ayn Rand thought that an intellectual letter was honest and intelligent, her attitude, especially in the early years, was "price no object"; in the name of full clarity, she could be extravagant in pouring out on paper her time, her effort, her concentration, her knowledge.

As to the people whom she knew personally and cared for, the sky was the limit, as you will see (and as I was lucky enough to learn firsthand). To her friends, Ayn Rand gave unwavering support, in every form possible—intellectual, emotional, and material—from all-night philosophical sessions to editorial advice to food packages (for friends stranded in postwar Europe) to an apartment she herself furnished and decorated (for her sister Nora) to immigration assistance (for her old nanny) to gifts of money.

In this respect, too, *The Fountainhead*'s Howard Roark was made in her image: using character Peter Keating's words, she was the original example of the "kindest egoist" in history. As the letters reveal, she also knew when to stop being kind. She drew the line according to the principle of justice. She would not give someone the unearned; she would help a friend in need, but she turned away the would-be moochers (as soon as she recognized them).

Because Ayn Rand so consistently practiced the rational principles she preached, she experienced and enjoyed the psychological reward: an un-breached self-esteem. She had no doubts about her own mind or value; she knew exactly who and what she was. Anyone who knew her can testify to this, though she rarely spoke about her virtues; the letters reveal the same quality. Here, for instance, is her answer to a fan in the '40s: "You asked me why *The Fountainhead* is a bestseller. Do you want my sincere answer? Because there are more people of intelligence and good taste in the United States than I expected to find. I don't think of it as 'I have lived up to the public.' I think: 'The public has lived up to me.' "

The letters are a treasure trove of material in regard to this unique woman, including many further aspects, even down to her attitude toward cats (charmingly expressed in an answer to *Cat Fancy* magazine in 1966: "You ask: 'We are assuming that you have an interest in cats, or was your subscription strictly objective?' My subscription," Ayn Rand replies, "was strictly objective *because* I have an interest in cats").

Besides the portrait of Ayn Rand, this book has other values to offer. Intellectually, the letters are, in essence, an introduction to Objectivism, because of their lengthy discussions of a wide range of philosophical, eth-ical, and political questions (there are many passages that will be illumi-nating even to adepts in her ideas).

The letters are also a minicourse in creative writing, because Ayn Rand often gave literary advice and analysis to young writers. And the letters are a study in some depth of the plots and characters of her own novels, es-pecially *The Fountainhead*, about which there is the most correspondence. Finally, they are a provocative cultural commentary on American life from the '30s on, with striking insights still germane and resonant decades later.

Dr. Berliner has done an excellent, conscientious job of locating and assembling all the documents. He has organized the abundant materials, culled the best passages, provided an explanatory framework, and, where appropriate, edited with a deft and unobtrusive hand. For all this work, fans of Ayn Rand are in his debt.

Here then is Ayn Rand talking privately—to agents and lawyers, to actors and writers, to relatives and columnists, to friends and antagonists, to industrialists and teenagers and philosophers and priests, to her favorite radio announcer, her "boss" Hal Wallis, her first American employer, Cecil

B. DeMille—talking to Frank Lloyd Wright and H. L. Mencken and Alexander Kerensky and her long-lost sister and astronaut Michael Collins and Barry Goldwater and Bennett Cerf and Mickey Spillane and many others, some famous, some obscure, some unknown. These last include a legion of fans bursting with provocative questions from all over the country and the world.

Here is Ayn Rand talking about everything under the sun—and now we have the privilege of listening in. I hope you, too, find it inspiring.

—LEONARD PEIKOFF
Irvine, California
June 1994

PREFACE

Answering a letter in 1943 from her friend, well-known political writer Isabel Paterson, Ayn Rand wrote: "I got a special thrill out of your letter —all my life, reading the published correspondence of famous people, I have envied them because they received personal letters on important and abstract subjects, I mean from friends, not just professional correspondence." At the time, Ayn Rand was just on the verge of fame, her novel *The Fountainhead* having been published six months previously. Now, fifty-two years later, in the sort of dramatic development she loved, her own correspondence is being published.

In the many cartons of photographs, papers, and mementos left by Ayn Rand at the time of her death in 1982 was correspondence dating from 1926 to 1981. Out of more than 2,000 letters by her, I have included approximately 35 to 40 percent of the total, omitting repetitious material and many routine business letters.

Ayn Rand arrived in the United States in February 1926, having obtained a six-month visa from the USSR to visit her relatives in Chicago. She had no intention of returning to Russia, instead securing a letter of recommendation through a relative to the Cecil B. DeMille Studios in Hollywood. Her intention was to begin her writing career in the movies, having taken a film-writing course at the State Institute of Cinema in Leningrad shortly before her departure. She arrived in Hollywood in early September 1926 and remained there until moving to New York City in 1934. Unfortunately there is almost no extant correspondence prior to her move to New York, but there is no doubt that she wrote extensively to her family in Russia. Her effects contain more than a thousand letters from her parents, sisters, and cousins sent to her during this period, but her letters to them were surely handwritten in Russian, and no copies remain. Her correspondence gradually increased as she began to sell her plays and novels, and it virtually exploded after publication of *The Fountainhead*, when she often wrote dozens of letters a day, occasionally fifteen to twenty pages long. In 1951, her letter writing came almost to a complete stop for six years. The most likely explanation is that this was the period of her most intense work on *Atlas Shrugged*, which was published in 1957. In addition, she had now returned permanently to New York, living in the same city as most of her friends and colleagues; this made extensive correspondence unnecessary.

Readers of this book will quickly realize that Ayn Rand's letters seem more like polished documents than casual conversations. This is no accident. For one thing, she took letter writing very seriously, once commenting at the top of page five of a letter to Isabel Paterson that she had already been writing it for four hours. Ayn Rand was uninterested in "small talk," either in person or on paper. So her letters—even to friends—are not full of the nonchalant, almost stream-of-consciousness writing that makes up so much general correspondence. But there is an additional reason for the relative formality of her letters, a reason which she explained in another letter to Isabel Paterson: So as not to endanger her family in Stalin's Russia, Ayn Rand had to be extremely meticulous in self-censoring her letters to her relatives and thus became unable to write spontaneously, without careful editing. So although her letters are generally missing some spontaneous touches, her practice of editing means that the content of her letters is a reliable guide to her intellectual development. The letters, however, are *letters* and not formal statements of her philosophic positions; hence they should not be taken as definitive. Consequently, the reader should not exaggerate the importance of (a) possible ambiguities caused by her using informal rather than more precise language or (b) seeming conflicts with her published views. In all cases, her published statements are definitive.

Although I have not edited Ayn Rand's writing itself, I have deleted some of the less interesting material within letters and also the routine opening and closing material. She characteristically began her letters by thanking her correspondents for their letters, often apologizing for her delay in responding, and expressing pleasure that they had found her philosophy helpful. She routinely concluded her letters with a short paragraph, sometimes expressing hope that she would see the correspondent soon—if he or she was a friend or acquaintance. In letters to fans, she would often recommend one of her articles, such as her letter "To the Readers of *The Fountainhead*" (reprinted in the Appendix). I have omitted these introductions and conclusions. I have also deleted closings such as "Sincerely yours" or "Yours truly" but have retained those which indicate something about her relationship to the correspondent.

The letters have been arranged chronologically, in order to provide some sense of the development of Ayn Rand's life and thought. There are, however, three exceptions, chapters containing her letters to Frank Lloyd Wright, Isabel Paterson, and philosopher John Hospers. These letters are relatively self-contained and have special intellectual or historical interest.

I have kept the explanatory notes to a minimum, because this is a collection of Ayn Rand's writings and not a biography. Although I have provided background or follow-up information when needed and available, I have resisted the temptation to try to fill in every blank, answer every question, and generally place every fact and comment within the context of her life.

The material in square brackets constitutes either words I have added for clarity or to provide particularly significant background information.

Correspondents are identified when first mentioned in the text. Readers should refer to the Index at the end of the book.

I wish to thank Leonard Peikoff for his editorial advice and for giving me access to Ayn Rand's materials. Thanks also to Donna Montrezza for research and—with David Bombardier—for meticulous proofreading; to Dena Harman for production assistance; and to Harry Binswanger for sharing my excitement about the history surrounding Ayn Rand's life and for filling in many of the details. And finally, thanks to my wife, Judy, for her constant enthusiasm for the letters and especially for encouraging me to undertake the project of cataloging the Ayn Rand material, which led directly to this project.

—Michael S. Berliner

CHRONOLOGY OF AYN RAND'S LIFE

YEAR	AGE	EVENTS
1905	—	born September 2 in St. Petersburg, Russia
1911	6	finds her first image of a heroine; teaches herself to read
1913	8	reads story about detective; begins inventing her own stories and movie scenarios
1914	9	summer trip abroad; reads *The Mysterious Valley* and discovers her first fictional hero; decides to be a writer
1915	10	begins trying to write novels
1917	12	summer in Finland; begins "thinking in principles"; discovers *Ivanhoe*
1918	13	discovers writings of Victor Hugo; family leaves Petrograd for Crimea
1921	16	graduates from gymnasium; returns to Petrograd; enters university
1924	19	graduates from Univ. of Leningrad; works as museum guide; enrolls in State Institute for Cinema Arts
1925	20	studies English; travels to Latvia to obtain US visa
1926	21	leaves Russia January 26; celebrates 21st birthday in Berlin; departs France for US February 10, arrives New York City February 18; after six-month stay with relatives in Chicago, moves to Hollywood in September; works for Cecil B. DeMille as movie extra and script reader; on set of *The King of Kings*, meets Frank O'Connor

1928	23	works at odd jobs, including waitress
1929	24	marries Frank April 15 in L.A.; gets job in the RKO wardrobe department; on weekends, plots *We the Living*
1931	26	becomes naturalized citizen of US March 13
1932	27	becomes office head at RKO wardrobe; sells *Red Pawn* story and screenplay to Universal; writes *Penthouse Legend*
1933	28	sells *Penthouse Legend* to MGM
1934	29	begins planning *The Fountainhead*; writes *Ideal*; *Penthouse Legend* produced in Hollywood (as *Woman on Trial*) and sold to Broadway producer; moves to New York City in November and works as script reader when *Penthouse* postponed
1935	30	sells *We the Living* to Macmillan; *Penthouse Legend* opens on Broadway (as *Night of January 16th*) for six-month run
1936	31	*We the Living* published in the US, then in England
1937	32	writes *Anthem*; works at architect Ely Jacques Kahn's office to do research for *The Fountainhead*
1938	33	*Anthem* published in England only; begins writing *The Fountainhead* June 26
1939	34	*The Unconquered* (stage version of *We the Living*) produced by George Abbott on Broadway
1941	36	after its rejection by twelve publishers, sells *The Fountainhead* to Bobbs-Merrill
1942	37	finishes *The Fountainhead* and delivers it to publisher December 31
1943	38	*The Fountainhead* published May 6; gets first ideas for *Atlas Shrugged*; sells *The Fountainhead* movie rights to Warner Bros. and returns to Hollywood in December to write screenplay
1944	39	signs as screenwriter with Hal Wallis; purchases house designed by Richard Neutra; writes screenplay for *Love Letters*
1945	40	first US edition of *Anthem* published by Pamphleteers
1946	41	begins writing *Atlas Shrugged* September 2
1947	42	testifies before the House Un-American Activities Committee regarding Communist influence in the movies; does research in Colorado for *Atlas Shrugged*

1948	43	production begins on *The Fountainhead* movie; writes final screenplay
1949	44	*The Fountainhead* movie released
1951	46	in October, returns permanently to New York City; begins full-time work on *Atlas Shrugged*
1957	52	finishes *Atlas Shrugged* in March; novel published October 10
1958	53	gives private lectures on fiction writing; helps write "Basic Principles of Objectivism" for newly formed Nathaniel Branden Lectures
1961	55	*For the New Intellectual* published
1962	57	starts *The Objectivist Newsletter*
1964	59	*The Virtue of Selfishness* published
1966	61	*Capitalism: The Unknown Ideal* published; "Introduction to Objectivist Epistemology" appears in *The Objectivist* (successor to *The Objectivist Newsletter*)
1968	63	Nathaniel Branden Institute closes
1969	64	gives private lecture course on nonfiction writing and workshop on Objectivist epistemology for philosophy professionals
1970	65	*The Romantic Manifesto* published
1971	66	*The New Left: The Anti-Industrial Revolution* published; *The Ayn Rand Letter* begins publication upon close of *The Objectivist*
1974	69	delivers "Philosophy: Who Needs It" to the graduating class of West Point
1976	71	*The Ayn Rand Letter* closes
1977	72	Ford Hall Forum in Boston (for which she had spoken annually since 1961) holds luncheon in her honor
1979	74	*Introduction to Objectivist Epistemology* (1st ed.) published; Frank O'Connor dies
1981	76	gives last public speech ("Sanction of the Victims") in New Orleans
1982	77	works on screenplay for projected miniseries of *Atlas Shrugged*; dies at home March 6

ARRIVAL IN AMERICA TO
WE THE LIVING (1926–1936)

Ayn Rand arrived in America on February 18, 1926. She stayed with relatives in Chicago for six months, writing the following letter—the earliest discovered—just before she left for Hollywood. It is written to Leo (last name unknown), who represented her idea of a romantic hero at that time and became the model for Leo Kovalensky, a main character in *We the Living*. This much-edited letter was written in Russian and presumably recopied and then sent to Leo in Leningrad.

August 28, 1926

Hello [written in English] Lyolya,

There was a time when I loved that American expression of yours [referring to "hello"], and now I am using it myself, because they don't have any other expression here. Thank you for your letter. Though a little late, I am fulfilling my promise to you. You said you wanted to have an American to correspond with. I am writing to you as a real "American resident."

I am so Americanized that I can walk in the streets without raising my head to look at the skyscrapers; I sit in a restaurant on very high chairs like in futuristic movie sets and use a straw to sip "fruit cocktails," brought to me by a real Negro; I have learned to cross the street without getting hit by a car, while traffic cops yell "come on, girl" to me.

[Paragraph crossed out:] Not taking anything too seriously is the chief rule Americans adhere to. Everybody makes fun of everybody else, not maliciously, but very wittily, and that is the essence of America. The language here is not English at all, and is all "jokes" and "wisecracks" as they are called here.

As you can see, not only have I reached Riga [many family members expected her to abort her trip and return to Russia], I reached further still. The only thing that remains for me is to rise, which I am doing with my characteristic straight-line decisiveness. I hope you will be impressed once more when you hear that I didn't back down from a much harder path. I heard you were told that I returned. I am getting used to America. I had gotten used to all kinds of adventures even before I got to Riga.

Even though I speak English now and even think in English, I would be very happy to have "a Russian to correspond with," if you want to write to the faraway city of Chicago. Regarding your coming to Chicago, I will meet you at the train station, even if you arrive in 1947; even if I am by then the greatest star in Hollywood; I just hope you have nothing against photographers and reporters following me and all my friends around, as is customary with stars—at least I hope that will be the case. But since it will be a long time until that happens, I will be very happy to have "a Russian to correspond with."

■　■　■

The following was written in English on a postcard and probably translated into Russian and sent to her family in Leningrad. Although AR kept hundreds of letters from her family, there are no copies of the letters she wrote to them. AR had a chance meeting with Cecil B. DeMille on September 4, 1926, when she went to his studio with a letter of reference. He subsequently hired her as an extra, then as a junior screenwriter.

June 18, 1927

Hello, everybody!

I would like to write a long letter, but I have not a second to spare. Am very, very busy—writing. So I am sending this to say that I am perfectly all right, very much so. Am very happy with my work and my scenarios. Many, many kisses to all of you, until I will have time for a long letter.

Yours, A.

P.S. That's the house I saw when I was driving with C. B. DeMille, as I wrote to you in my last letter.

■　■　■

Unfortunately, no other letters remain until 1934, when AR purchased a type-writer and began to make carbon copies of her correspondence. The intervening years were busy ones for her, both personally and professionally. She met actor Frank O'Connor in 1926 on the set of *The King of Kings* and married him in 1929. She became a naturalized citizen in 1931. Working first at odd jobs, then at the RKO wardrobe department, she wrote numerous screenplays and short stories, as she strove to master the English language. In 1931 she began her first major novel, *We the Living* (then called *Airtight*). In 1932 she sold a story, *Red Pawn*, to Universal, and in 1933 sold to MGM a play, *Penthouse Legend* (later retitled *Night of January 16th*). In 1934 she began planning *The Fountainhead* (then called *Second-Hand Lives*), although her first formal notes are dated December 4, 1935. The following letter was written to Jean Wick, her agent for *We the Living*.

March 10, 1934

Dear Miss Wick,

I must confess that I am a little anxious to hear some news about my book. I have not written to you sooner, realizing that you were very busy, but I would appreciate it very much if you would let me know what publishing houses have had the book to date, what are the reactions and opinions of it, and if there have been rejections—what reasons were given. You understand that this is of great importance to me in connection with my work on the second part of the book. I am glad to say that this work is progressing rapidly and I would appreciate your help in the matter.

■ ■ ■

To the Commissioner General of Immigration

March 10, 1934

Dear Sir,

I am an American citizen and I would like to bring my parents to this country, from Russia. But before filing the proper "Petition for issuance of immigration visa," I would like to know whether they would come under the classification of quota preference immigrants and, if found to qualify for that classification, how long would they have to wait for their turn for a preference quota from Russia.

I would also like to know how long would a Russian citizen have to wait for a regular quota immigrant's visa (not a preferred quota) to enter this country, whether the Russian quota is exhausted and how far in advance does one have to reserve one's turn.

> *More than three years later, on May 31, 1937, she received a telegram from the Soviet government, stating only: "Cannot get permission."*

■ ■ ■

To Jean Wick

March 23, 1934

Dear Miss Wick,

I have just finished the second part of *Airtight*. There are still revisions and a little polishing to be done, but I will be able to send the script to you within a few weeks.

During our conversation here, I mentioned some of my views in regard to the selling points of my book and you said that you would like me to write them down for you. So, if I may, I would like to mention them here, in the hope that they may appeal to you, if you have not thought of the book from that particular angle.

When I first began work on *Airtight,* the quality which I hoped would make it saleable, quite aside from any possible literary merit, was the fact that it is the *first* story written by a Russian who knows the living conditions of the new Russia and who has actually lived under the Soviets in the period described. My plot and characters are fiction, but the living conditions, the atmosphere, the circumstances which make the incidents of the plot possible, are all true, to the smallest detail. There have been any number of novels dealing with modern Russia, but they have been written either by emigrés who left Russia right after the revolution and had no way of knowing the new conditions, or by Soviet authors who were under the strictest censorship and had no right and no way of telling the whole truth. My book is, as far as I know, the first one by a person who *knows* the facts and also *can tell* them.

I have watched very carefully all the literature on new Russia, that has appeared in English. I do not believe that there has been a work of fiction on this subject, which has enjoyed an outstanding and wide popular success. I believe this is due to the fact that all those novels were translations from the Russian, written primarily *for* the Russian reader. As a consequence, they were hard to understand and of no great interest to the general American public, to those not too well acquainted with Russian conditions.

Airtight, I believe, is the first novel on Russia written *in English by a Russian.* Throughout the entire book, I have tried to write it *from the viewpoint of and for the American public.* I have never relied on any previous knowledge of Russia in my future readers, and I have attempted to show a panorama of the whole country as it would unfold before the eyes of a person who had never heard before that such a country as Russia existed. It is not, primarily, a book for Russians, but a book for Americans— or so I hope.

I have also attempted to show, not the political struggles, theories and ideals of modern Russia, of which we have heard so much, but the everyday human lives, the everyday tragedies of human beings who are not or try not to be connected with politics. It is not a story of glamorous grand dukes and brutal Bolsheviks—or vice-versa—as most of the novels of the Russian Revolution have been; it is the story of the middle class, the vast majority of Russian citizens, about whom little has been said in fiction. It is not the usual story of revolutionary plots, of GPU spies, of secret executions and exaggerated horrors. It is the story of the drudgery of life which millions have to lead day after day, year after year. Our American readers have been crammed full, too full, of Russian aims, projects and slogans on red banners. No one—to the best of my knowledge—has spoken of what goes on every day in every home and kitchen behind the red banners.

In connection with the present interest in Russia, I hoped that the book would be of value to the American reader, for no essay, no travelogue can give one so vivid a picture, so complete a feeling of a foreign country as a fiction story can.

The above may all sound quite presumptuous and immodest, coming from the author herself, but I did not intend it as self-praise and self-publicity. I do not presume to assert that my book has accomplished all the desirable qualities mentioned above. I have merely stated what I have tried to accomplish. But if I have succeeded, then I do think the considerations I have outlined should arouse an interest in the book on the part of publishers and readers. Or am I mistaken?

I would like to mention that the qualities I have described are not the aim, theme or purpose of the book, but I have gone into them in such detail only because I believe they are valuable sales points. I may be quite mistaken and these suggestions may have no value. But since you were kind enough to express the desire to hear them and since these "sales points" have been in my mind all through the writing of the book, I felt that I should share them with you and let you judge their worth.

I have not written about this sooner, for I wanted to finish the book first and to see whether my intentions had been carried out in the final shape of the story. I believe they have. However, I shall leave the decision on that to your own judgment.

■ ■ ■

To Kenneth MacGowan, a film producer and director whose credits included *Little Women* (1933) and *Anne of Green Gables* (1934). In 1947, he became chairman of the UCLA theater department.

May 18, 1934

Dear Mr. MacGowan,

Having heard that you are interested in my story—*Red Pawn*—I am taking the liberty of writing to you a few words in connection with it. There are a few ideas which I had in mind when I wrote that story and I have been very anxious to express them to someone in a position to understand them. It is not so much in regard to the value of the story itself, as to a certain new theory of mine about motion pictures, which this story exemplifies and which, I believe, would be valuable and worth trying out.

In brief, my theory relates to making motion pictures appeal to *all* types of audiences. I know that it has been tried. I know also that it has not been tried successfully.

We have all heard a great deal about the fact that motion pictures in their present form do not appeal, as a rule, to the higher or so-called intellectual type of audiences. Without a doubt, there is a large and valuable public which does not patronize motion pictures at present, for we must admit that few pictures have, or intend to have, any intellectual appeal. On the other hand, the majority of so-called purely "artistic" films have been inexcusably dull. The unfortunate opinion is still prevalent that to be artistic a picture has to be so vague and plotless as to become insufferable even to the highest of audiences. I am firmly convinced that no amount of the best acting, directorial "touches" and camera work alone will ever hold *anyone*.

There is only one common denominator which can be understood and enjoyed by all men, from the dullest to the most intelligent, and that is plot.

Everybody goes into a theatre to enjoy primarily *what* they are going to see and not *how* it is going to be presented to them. If they are not interested in what they see, they do not care how it is shown. The best manner of presenting nothing still makes it remain *nothing*.

That much is not new. The novelty of what I propose to do—and I believe it is a novelty, for I have never seen it done deliberately—consists in the following: in building the plot of a story in such a manner that it possesses tiers or layers of depth, so that each type of audience can understand and enjoy only as much of it as it wants to understand and enjoy, in other words so that each man can get out of it only as much as he can put into it. This must be done in such a manner that one and the same story can stand as a story without any of its deeper implications, so that those who do not care to be, will not be burdened with any intellectual or artistic angles, and yet those who do care for them will get those angles looking at exactly the same material.

If the plot of a story is simple and understandable enough to be interesting, alone, by itself, to even the lowest type of mentality, if it has the plain elements that can appeal to all, and if, at the same time, that plot carries a deeper meaning, a significance which can be reached only by the highest, then the problem is solved. I must emphasize once more that it is not merely a matter of a plain story—for the sake of the "lowbrow"—artistically presented for the sake of the "highbrow." It is a matter of the plot, the story, the very meat of the film arranged ingeniously enough to satisfy both. Is there any reason why a story cannot be built in such a way that it is convincing and interesting to those who cannot analyze it and yet just as convincing to those who can?

Let me illustrate just exactly what I mean on the example of *Red Pawn*. If you recall its plot, it is, on first glance, merely the story of a woman who comes, at the price of a great sacrifice, to rescue her husband from a life sentence in prison and of her worst enemy's great, unhappy love for her. There is nothing very intellectual or difficult to understand about that. All the incidents of the plot are motivated by reasons and emotions which are common and sympathetic to all men. It does not require a great deal of intellectual effort to be held by the suspense, first, of the woman's mystery, then of her growing predicament, then of her solution of the problem. Those who cannot go any further will be held merely by these physical facts of the plot as it develops, merely by the most primitive suspense of the story, by the quality they would enjoy in a plain serial.

But those who can see further, will have before them the spectacle of a rather unusual emotional crisis involving the three characters of the story, and the picture of a life and conditions which they have not seen very often.

Those who want to go still further, will see the philosophical problem of the main figure in the story—the Commandant of the prison island—, the clash of his belief in a stern duty above all with the belief in a right to the joy of living above all, as exemplified in the woman. And this clash is not merely a matter of details and dialogue. It is an inseparable part of the very basic plot itself.

As a rule, a consideration such as this last one would be enough to kill the chances of a story right then and there and to frighten everyone away from it. It does sound odd, to say the least, an attempt at philosophy in a motion picture. But if that philosophy is there only for those who want it, if it does not intrude for a single moment to bore those who do not care for any thinking in their entertainment, if the story is still there, intact, unchanged, for those who will never suspect any breath of thought in it, then it can only add to the ranks of people enjoying the picture a vast, untouched, unsuspected number of men who *do* ask something besides puns and seduced virgins from their entertainment, those countless people who have been, so far, neglected and forgotten by the movie world. This higher type of public may not be as numerous as the average kind, and I admit that one could not make pictures for their tastes alone. But if a picture can be made to satisfy them as well as the average audience, well then, why not?

Most pictures have some kind of an idea behind them. Only, usually, the idea is inferior even to the plot. But if we can make a plot for everyone and an idea for the "highbrows"—well, again, why not?

Such is my theory of building a story in "tiers." It is, in a way, the same principle as that of an airplane carried by three motors. If two of them fail, the third one is still enough to carry the plane safely. But how much safer the plane is, starting out with the three! As a matter of fact, in the example in question, I am more than sure that neither of the three motors would fail.

This is a principle which I have applied to every story I have written so far, but I have never developed it as plainly and obviously and, if I may say so, as skillfully, as in *Red Pawn*. Also, I've never had a chance to attempt to explain my theory to anyone, as I have done it here. I have no doubt that it will work. No doubt, but also no proof, for I have not seen it tried yet. It is my anxiety to see it tried which prompted me to write this letter. It is, of course, difficult to have any new theory tried, for there is always an element of chance in the attempt. But in this case, it occurs to me that there is hardly any chance at all, for disregarding all my considerations, the story, I believe, is good enough to stand on its own just as any movie. I can go on, as all pictures, with just the one motor. What the other two motors, which it carries, will do—that is what the experiment will show.

I have not the slightest doubt that this story will be made eventually, and that it will be one of the greatest hits ever made, and that it will give an entirely new field to motion pictures. I do not say it merely because it is my story, for I would not dare to say it about all the things I've written. But I have such faith in this one, that I am willing to stand for any accusations of presumptuousness, arrogance or bad taste making this statement.

I have no doubt that this story will be made. But it is only natural that I would like to see it made soon.

I must apologize for something that does approach bad taste in writing to you all this which may sound merely as an involved "sales talk" in favor of my story. In a way, of course, it is a sales talk. But I intended it to be and have tried to make it more than just that. It is not a sales talk for a story, but for a story *and* for an idea. If you find that the story lives up to the idea, so much the better. If not—perhaps the idea itself may be of value to you.

And, speaking for a moment of the story alone, I would like to bring to your attention one fact which may, but should not, be considered against the story. It is the political angle, the fact that it may be considered as anti-Soviet and thus, perhaps, unsuitable for production at the present moment. I would like to say that it is *not* a political story. The fact that it is led on a prison island could offend the Soviet government no more than pictures of Devil's Island offended the French government, and such pictures have been made successfully. All the political implications can be softened or removed from the story entirely. And, if even then there remain doubts on the subject, the story can be transferred to any other island in any other country or part of the globe. For the story, essentially, is neither Russian nor political.

AR's synopsis of Red Pawn, *edited by her into novelette form, was reprinted in* The Early Ayn Rand. *Neither her sixty-page treatment nor her complete screenplay has been published, nor was a movie ever made.*

■   ■   ■

To Jean Wick

June 19, 1934

Dear Miss Wick,

Mr. [Gouverneur] Morris [a writer friend] has received a letter from Mr. Mencken [H. L. Mencken, editor of *American Mercury* magazine] in regard to my book *Airtight*. I am quoting from his letter: "I agree with you thoroughly that it is a really excellent piece of work, and I see no reason whatever why it shouldn't find a publisher readily. The only objection to it, of course, is the fact that it is anti-Communist in tone. Most of the American publishers who print Russian stuff lean toward the Trotskys. However, that is an objection that is certainly not insuperable."

In view of this, Mrs. Morris has suggested that we try to submit the novel to Dutton, for they have just published a nonfiction book entitled *Escape from the Soviets*, which is violently anti-Soviet and, from what I hear, a great bestseller. Evidently, Dutton are not pro-Communist and I am very happy to know that neither is the public, and therefore an anti-Soviet book has a chance of success.

In his letter, Mr. Mencken has offered to send the book to any other publisher we name, if Knopf have not taken it, and Mrs. Morris has written to him, suggesting Dutton. If it is convenient for you, you may get in touch with him about this.

I have been waiting to hear about Knopf's decision and, if they have rejected the book, I will appreciate it if you would let me know the reasons they gave.

I realize that we have to take into consideration the publishers' political views when submitting the book. But, if Mr. Mencken is right and the political angle is the only one that stands in the way of a sale, I certainly refuse to believe that America has nothing but Communist-minded publishers. I will appreciate it if you will let me know the reactions to the book from this angle.

If it is not imposing on your time, and I realize that you are very busy, I would also appreciate a few lines about your opinion of the second half and the book as a whole, for I have not heard it yet and I am quite naturally interested to know it.

■ ■ ■

To Cecil B. DeMille

July 3, 1934

Dear Mr. DeMille,

This letter is primarily to express my gratitude to you—at the distance of so many years. I have always wanted to tell you how much I appreciated your kindness and interest in me at a time when—if you remember—I was a very inexperienced, very bewildered and frightened little immigrant from Russia. I have waited all these years to show you that I had justified your interest in me, that I had something which you were kind and farsighted enough to see so far in advance.

If I have achieved any kind of success, I owe it to your instructions which I have remembered and tried to follow all these years. I have always hoped that I would not drop out of sight entirely, that the day would come when I would be successful enough to show you that you had not wasted the attention you had given me at my start in Hollywood.

I cannot say that I have accomplished a great deal yet, but at least I am a writer and I feel that I can now thank you from the bottom of my heart, without asking you for help or for a job, just thank you and tell you that you have always been the person for whose sake I have wanted most to succeed, if you will excuse my presumption in this.

I am taking the liberty of sending you a synopsis of my story *Red Pawn,* which I had sold to Universal some time ago and which Paramount has just bought from them as a probable vehicle for Marlene Dietrich. I am now working here on the screenplay. I would appreciate it very much if you would read this synopsis—not because I want to try and sell it to you, since it is already sold, but because I am very anxious to show you what I have accomplished, particularly since it is accomplished in accordance with your ideas as to story construction and situations. I am a little proud of this story and I feel that it is, in a way, the best manner I know of to thank you for your help to me many years ago.

If you will be kind enough to read it, I would be very grateful if you would grant me a little time to see you afterwards.

> *After her signature, AR wrote "('Caviar'—if you remember),"*
> *"Caviar" being DeMille's pet name for her.*

■   ■   ■

To Jean Wick

In a letter of June 29, Wick told AR that she would make a major name for herself, though it would likely be a slow process. She encouraged AR to move to New York from Hollywood in order to meet publishers and other book people.

July 19, 1934

Dear Miss Wick,

I am most grateful for your letter and for the kind interest with which you analyzed the problem of my career. I must say that your letter really made up for my slight disappointment in Knopf's decision about my book.

I quite agree with your suggestion about my coming to New York. I do believe it would be advisable and very much to my advantage. But as I mentioned in my last letter, I am at present working at the Paramount Studio on an original story of my own and I do not know how long I will be held here. As soon as I finish this assignment, I will try to arrange to go to New York, if I find it possible. Frankly, the financial angle is the only circumstance that is keeping me from it, for I have been anxious to move to New York for a long time.

As to the opinion of Mr. Abbott at Knopf's, I can see his point of view and I can understand his hesitation, particularly in regard to the length of my novel. However, if I had a chance to do it, I would like to point out to him that he is greatly mistaken on the subject of the book being "dated." In the first place, the book does not deal with a "temporary" phase of Russian life. It merely takes place in the years 1922–1925, instead of the immediate present, but it deals with the birth of conditions which are far from gone, which still prevail in Russia in their full force, which are the very essence of the revolution. In the second place—and this may sound paradoxical—*Airtight* is *not* a novel about Russia. It is a novel about the problem of the individual versus the mass, a problem which is the latest, the most vital, the most tremendous problem of the world today, and about which very little has been said in fiction. I have selected Russia as my background merely because that problem stands out in Russia more sharply, more tragically than anywhere on earth.

However, I quite agree with you that it would not be advisable to press that point with Knopf's at present, and I mention this only in case you find yourself confronted again with the same objection.

■ ■ ■

To H. L. Mencken

July 28, 1934

Dear Mr. Mencken,

Gathering all my courage, I am writing to thank you for your kindness and interest in my novel *Airtight*. I am still a beginner with very much of a "fan complex," so I hope you will understand my hesitation in writing to one whom I admire as the greatest representative of a philosophy to which I want to dedicate my whole life.

I am sure you understand that my book is not at all a story about Russia, but a story of an individual against the masses and a plea in defense of the individual. Your favorable opinion of it was particularly valuable to me, since I have always regarded you as the foremost champion of individualism in this country.

This book is only my first step and above all a means of acquiring a voice, of making myself heard. What I shall have to say when I acquire that voice does not need an explanation, for I know that you can understand it. Perhaps it may seem a lost cause, at present, and there are those who will say that I am too late, that I can only hope to be the last fighter for a mode of thinking which has no place in the future. But I do not think so. I intend to be the first one in a new battle which the world needs as it has never needed before, the first to answer the many too many advocates of collectivism, and answer them in a manner which will not be forgotten.

I know that you may smile when you read this. I fully realize that I am a very "green," very helpless beginner who has the arrogance of embarking, single-handed, against what many call the irrevocable trend of our century. I know that I am only a would-be David starting out against Goliath—and what a fearful, ugly Goliath! I say "single handed," because I have heard so much from that other side, the collectivist side, and so little in defense of man against men, and yet so much has to be said. I have attempted to say it in my book. I do not know of a better way to make my entrance into the battle. I believe that man will always be an individualist, whether he knows it or not, and I want to make it my duty to make him know it.

So you can understand why I appreciate your kindness in helping me to put my book before the public, for—if you will excuse my presumption—I consider myself a young and very humble brother-in-arms in your own cause.

Gratefully yours,

■ ■ ■

To H. L. Mencken

In his July 31 letter to AR, Mencken wrote: "I sympathize with your position thoroughly, and it seems to me that you have made a very good beginning in *Airtight*. I see no reason whatever why it should not find a publisher and make a success. Certainly the time has come to turn back the tide of Communist propaganda in this country."

August 8, 1934

Dear Mr. Mencken,

I am profoundly grateful for your letter and very happy to know that you share my viewpoint on the philosophy of my novel. Frankly, I was a little afraid that you might consider it presumptuous on my part to hope that you would agree with me.

Since you are kind enough to offer to send the book out, I would like to ask you to send it to Dutton's, for I understand that they are not pro-Soviet and will have no objection to the political angle of my novel.

If this is not an imposition on your kindness, I would appreciate it very much, frankly because I know that the book will receive more attention if it comes from you.

■ ■ ■

To Jean Wick

August 20, 1934

Dear Miss Wick,

Under separate cover I am mailing to you a copy of a novelette I have written from my screen story *Red Pawn*. If you recall, this is the story which Paramount has bought and which will, probably, be Marlene Dietrich's next or second vehicle. Paramount has the screen rights, of course, but I have the serial rights and I have rewritten the story in novelette form, hoping that it may be suitable for a serial publication in a magazine. The fact that it is going to be produced on the screen may prove of some help in selling it.

If you like it and find that you are interested in handling it, please let me know and I shall mail you additional copies of it. I would like very much to give it a try at the *Saturday Evening Post*, if you do not find that impossible, because the *Post* seems to have a very decided anti-Soviet attitude.

I do not want to give you the impression that I can write nothing but Russian stories. My first ones were Russian merely because it is the background I know best and because I found in it material that has not been overdone. *Red Pawn,* incidentally, was written before *Airtight.* But I am working, at present, on a new novelette with a strictly American background. It is laid in Hollywood and does not have a single Russian in it.

The new novelette, Ideal, *was published in its initial, theatrical script form in* The Early Ayn Rand *and first produced on the stage in 1990 in Hollywood.*

■   ■   ■

To Colin Clive, stage and film actor

This letter to Clive was undated but written just after AR had seen him on stage in *Journey's End,* by R. C. Sheriff. Clive's answer is dated October 23, 1934.

Dear Mr. Clive,

I do not know whether you read "fan" mail, but I hope you will read this, and I hope—most anxiously—that it will interest you, though I am not at all sure of that. There have been times—not many—when I wanted to express my admiration for some achievement of rare beauty, but I have never done it, because I did not believe that the one who achieved it would care or understand. And I am not certain of that now, but I am making the attempt just the same, my first one.

I want to thank you for a little bit of real beauty which you have given me, a little spark of something which does not exist in the world today. I am not speaking of your great acting nor of the great part which you brought to life so expertly. Others have done great acting before, and there have been many great parts written. I am speaking of something which, probably, was very far from the mind of the author when he wrote *Journey's End*, and from your own when you acted it. Perhaps that which I saw in you exists only in my own mind and no one else would see it, or care to see. I am speaking of your great achievement in bringing to life a completely heroic human being.

The word *heroic* does not quite express what I mean. You see, I am an atheist and I have only one religion: the sublime in human nature. There is nothing to approach the sanctity of the highest type of man possible and there is nothing that gives me the same reverent feeling, the feeling when one's spirit wants to kneel, bareheaded. Do not call it hero-worship, because it is more than that. It is a kind of strange and improbable white heat where admiration becomes religion, and religion becomes philosophy, and philosophy—the whole of one's life.

I realize how silly words like these may sound today. Who cares about heroes any more and who wants to care? In an age that glorifies the average, the commonplace, the good, stale "human values," that raises to the height of supreme virtue the complete lack of it, that refuses to allow anything above the smug, comfortable herd, that places the life of that herd above all things, who can still understand the thrill of seeing a man such as you were on the stage? It is not your acting that did it, nor the lines you spoke, nor even the character you played, because the character was far from the type of which I am speaking. It was something in you, in the whole of the man you were, something not intended by the play at all, that gave me, for a few hours, a spark of what man could be, but isn't. I do not say that you were that man. I say only that you let me see a first spark of him, and that is an achievement for which one has to be grateful.

This is what I wanted to say to you, when I met you a few days ago, but I could not say it to you in person. That is why I am writing this. Perhaps it will only make you smile. But if your work means more to you than just a way of making your living, then, perhaps, you will want to hear that among the hundreds who watch you every night, there was one to whom your work meant more than just spending an evening in the theater.

Gratefully yours,

(In case you do not remember—as, of course, you don't—this is the Russian writer who Mr. E. E. Clive introduced to you a few nights ago. The "vodka" may remind you.)

Clive responded that AR's letter meant a great deal to him and that he would always keep it. He told her that he'd toasted her play Woman on Trial, *later retitled* Night of January 16th, *with vodka that night.*

■   ■   ■

To Jean Wick

October 27, 1934

Dear Miss Wick,

I owe you an apology for my long silence. Perhaps you understand that it was caused by the matter of my stage play—*Woman on Trial*. It has just been produced here, at the Hollywood Playhouse. I am enclosing two clippings of reviews—from the *Los Angeles Times* and the *Hollywood Citizen-News*. I am very happy about the production and it looks as though it is going to be quite successful. Mr. Woods [A. H. Woods, Broadway producer] has not accepted it for production as yet, but he is negotiating about it with E. E. Clive, the local producer, I believe.

I have had a hectic month and all my time has been taken up by the supervision of rehearsals. During the last few weeks we have been rehearsing day and night. Please excuse me for not writing to you sooner.

I have received your letter today and I have thought it over carefully from every angle. I greatly appreciate all the details of the matter which you have given me. Here is what I have to say: I certainly would not go so far as to demand the book [*We the Living*] be published exactly as it is or not at all. I am quite willing to make all the cuts and changes that may be required to improve it. But I do insist that the theme and *spirit* of the book be kept intact. Therefore, I must explain in detail exactly what I mean.

I am afraid that I cannot agree with Mr. Benefield's [an editor at Appleton-Century-Crofts] idea of the book. It is *not* a love story. It never could be. In fact, I believe, personally, that the love story is the least interesting thing about it. Mr. Benefield may be right about the fact that I have too much background in it and I am willing to cut it some. But that background is more essential than the plot itself for the story I want to tell. Without it—there *is no* story. It is the background that creates the characters and their tragedy. It is the background that makes them do the things they do. If one does not understand the background—one cannot understand them.

And Mr. Benefield is completely mistaken about the fact that the American reader "has a fair knowledge of existence in Leningrad during the time covered by the novel." The American reader has no knowledge of it whatsoever. He has not the slightest suspicion of it. If he had—we would not have the appalling number of parlor Bolsheviks and idealistic sympathizers with the Soviet regime, liberals who would scream with horror if they knew the truth of Soviet existence. It is for them that the book was written.

The principal reaction I have had from those who have read the book is one of complete amazement at the revelation of Soviet life as it is actually lived. "Can it possibly be true? I had no idea that that's what it was like. Why were we never told?"—those are the things I have heard over and over again. Those are the things I wanted to hear. Because the conditions I have depicted *are* true. I have lived them. No one has ever come out of Soviet Russia to tell it to the world. That was my job.

I repeat, I may have too much of it in the book and I am willing to cut it down some. But I also repeat that it must stand as a most important part of the novel—*not* merely as a setting for a love story. I have never heard one person say that he was *bored* while reading the book. I have tied my background firmly to the structure of the plot. But that background *has to* be there.

Furthermore—and here we come to the most important point—has Mr. Benefield understood the idea of the book? *Airtight is not* the story of Kira Argounova. It is the story of Kira Argounova *and* the masses—her greatest enemy. Those masses—and what they do to the individual—are the real hero of the book. Remove that—and you have nothing but a conventional little romance to tell. The individual against the masses—such is the real, the only theme of the book. Such is the greatest problem of our century—for those who are willing to realize it.

I feel I must explain one point to Mr. Benefield—a point of the greatest importance. Mr. Benefield wonders why I stop in the last chapter to present the biography of the soldier who kills Kira Argounova. That stop, in my opinion, is one of the best things in the book. It contains—in a few pages—the whole idea and purpose of the novel. After the reader has seen Kira Argounova, has learned what a rare, precious, irreplaceable human being she was—I give him the picture of the man who killed Kira Argounova, of the life that took her life. That soldier is a symbol, a typical representative of the average, the dull, the useless, the commonplace, the masses—that killed the best there is on this earth. I believe I made this obvious when I concluded his biography by saying—quoting from the book: "Citizen Ivan Ivanov was guarding the border of the Union of Socialist Soviet Republics." Citizen Ivan Ivanov *is* the Union of Socialist Soviet Republics. And that Union killed Kira Argounova. Kira Argounova against citizen Ivan Ivanov—that is the whole book in a few pages.

I am willing to do some cutting and I believe I could cut out about fifteen thousand, perhaps even twenty-five thousand words. That would be the most. Cutting it down to 100,000 words would be impossible. [The published book is approximately 175,000 words.]

I agree that the title may not be a good one and I am entirely willing to change that.

If this is acceptable to Mr. Benefield, I shall get down to work on the cutting at once. However, since the offer is only conditional, I must insist that you do not withdraw the book from other publishers, but continue to submit it, until—and if—we reach a definite agreement with the Appleton-Century company.

As to the matter of a suggested collaborator, I give you full authority to refuse at once, without informing me, any and all offers that carry such a suggestion. I do not care to hear of such offers. I consider them nothing short of an insult. Anyone reading my book must realize that I am an individualist above everything else. As such, I shall stand or fall on my own work. I hope you do not consider this as a beginner's arrogance. It is merely the feeling of a person who takes pride in her work. At the cost of being considered arrogant, I must state that I do not believe there is a human being alive who could improve that book of mine in the matter of actual rewriting. If anyone is capable of improving *that* book—he should have written it himself. I would prefer not only never seeing it in print, but also burning every manuscript of it—rather than having William Shakespeare himself add one line to it which was not mine, or cross out one comma. I repeat, I welcome and appreciate all suggestions of changes to improve the book without destroying its theme, and I am quite willing to make them. But these changes will be made *by me.*

The time is certainly ripe for an anti-Red novel and it is only a question of finding the right party to take an interest in it. I do not believe that we will get very far with publishers who disapprove of or try to diminish the political implications of the book. These implications are its best chance of success. If you remember, Mr. Morris in his letter to Mr. Mencken, referred to the book as the *"Uncle Tom's Cabin* of Soviet Russia." That is exactly what the book was intended to be and exactly the angle under which it must be sold. It was suggested to me that I get in touch with some of the senators who objected to the recognition of Soviet Russia, with some political interests who are fighting Communism in this country—and get them to launch the book. I do not believe that it would be advisable for me to approach them myself. Would it be possible for you? Please let me know what you think of this angle.

■ ■ ■

To Jean Wick

November 24, 1934

Dear Miss Wick,

I am leaving for New York today. I have signed a contract with A. H. Woods for the production of my play and he is planning to open it by the beginning of January.

I am motoring to New York and expect to be there by December 2nd. I am looking forward to seeing you. I do not know yet where I will stop, but I shall telephone you as soon as I arrive. I hope this opportunity to come to New York will help me with my book, as you have suggested.

AR lived in New York City until 1943.

■   ■   ■

To Mary Inloes, agent for *Night of January 16th*, which opened on Broadway on September 16, 1935, and closed in April 1936

December 10, 1934

Dear Miss Inloes,

I owe you many apologies for my long silence. I hope you will excuse me, when you hear of all the troubles I've had—on my way here. Everything went wrong with our car—from the license plate getting loose to the brakes burning out *three* times. To top it all, you came very near to having on your hands a crippled Russian writer—if any. We had an accident in Virginia and the car almost overturned. Fortunately, we were not hurt, but we left the car there and finished the trip by bus. The Auto-Courts [motels] are awful. You may use me as a reference to discourage ambitious authors from motoring across the continent.

To make up for it, everything seems to be going very nicely here in New York. I found Mr. Satenstein thoroughly charming and he seems to be a very good businessman. As to Mr. Woods, he is perfectly lovely and very easy to work with. I do not believe that I will have any trouble with him about the play. The suggestions he had to make so far were mostly the same cuts that we did in Hollywood, and also some grand things about the presentation of the play, which will improve it a great deal and are only details of production that do not affect the play itself. He plans to produce it on a grand scale which Hollywood could never approach. I do hope that you will be able to come here for the opening.

I have been very busy making the changes in the script, which he wanted to have as soon as possible. That is why I have not written to you sooner. I have not even actually unpacked, as yet. I have just delivered the script to him today.

New York is grand. I love it. I am very happy to be here. Of course, I haven't even begun to see it. It is quite cold, but I don't mind, and I *do not* miss California sunshine.

I would appreciate it very much if you could send me any clippings you may have from the Hollywood papers—if they haven't forgotten me entirely.

■ ■ ■

To Mary Inloes

March 16, 1935

Dear Miss Inloes,

I owe you many apologies for my long silence. I hope you realize that its reason has been the long string of continuous delays I have encountered with *Woman on Trial*. The matter is still unsettled. Mr. Woods is still searching for a leading lady. All these months I have been waiting to hear that he has found one, every hour of every day. I have heard many promises that it would be settled "not later than Monday," then "not later than Thursday" and so on, for over three months. I have delayed writing to you in the hope that, at any moment, I may have definite news to tell you. Unfortunately, the matter is still where it stood in December, so I am writing without waiting any longer. I hope you will forgive my delay.

Frankly, I am very bitterly disappointed in the way Mr. Satenstein has handled our contract. If you remember, I wanted to insist on a definite *short* option in the contract, but waived it aside on Mr. Satenstein's assurance that Mr. Woods had every intention to produce the play immediately and no specified time was necessary. As it stands now, Mr. Woods has a legal option of *six months*, which I would have hesitated to grant him for the little advance I received.

I am convinced that both Mr. Satenstein and Mr. Woods acted in good faith and that the delay is an unfortunate, unforeseen circumstance. Nevertheless, it has put me in the most impossible situation and I am carrying the hardest end of a matter for which I was least responsible. I consider it a great mistake on Mr. Satenstein's part to have taken anyone's word in a legal matter, which should have been specified on paper. As circumstances stand, with Mr. Woods obviously anxious not to lose the play, I would have received a second option, by now, had we specified a shorter time in the contract. As it is, Mr. Woods actually does not have to hurry, having legally six months in which to produce the play.

Needless to say, my situation is desperate, not to say a catastrophe. I could hardly have been expected to live in New York for six months on two hundred and fifty dollars, on less than that when one considers that to reach New York was impossible on the hundred dollars allowed for the purpose. Mr. Satenstein has tried to help me, but the only job he could get for me is that of a reader for RKO here, at which I am earning an average of ten dollars a week, working ten hours a day. Mr. Satenstein has undertaken to get another advance for me from Mr. Woods, but up to now nothing has happened. I can hardly be blamed for considering the whole situation rather unfair.

I do not like to complain about it and that was another reason for my delay in writing to you. I had hoped that the situation would be solved any minute, but as it stands, it still may be solved tomorrow—or in another three months. So I had to tell you the whole truth.

■   ■   ■

To A. H. Woods, Ltd., producers of *Night of January 16th*

October 14, 1935

Dear Sirs:

Walter Pidgeon having withdrawn from the cast of *Night of January 16th*, his last appearance being Saturday evening, October 19th, my understanding is that you intend to replace him in the cast by William Bakewell. While Mr. Bakewell may well be good in parts to which he is suited, he certainly is not suited for the part which is now being relinquished by Mr. Pidgeon. He is much too young and has not the required strength of personality for the character portrayed, which requires "guts," as the name of the character in the play, Guts Regan, implies. The character implies menace, aggressiveness and sinister force. I am not alone in my opinion that Mr. Bakewell does not measure up to these characteristics. The character in the play is the head of the New York underworld and Mr. Bakewell can not at his age and with his appearance measure up to that type of man. I am not unreasonable in objecting to the employment of Mr. Bakewell. I have no desire to hold up the performance of this play, but time being limited, I am making the following alternate suggestions for this part: Mr. Morgan Conway, who played the part of Regan in the Hollywood production and Mr. Robert Shayne, who knows the part.

My objection and request is made under the terms of the Minimum Basic Agreement, under the fourth paragraph of section 7 which reads as follows:

> If, after the opening of the play, the Manager shall make any change in the cast, and objection thereto is made by the Author, then the Manager agrees forthwith to replace the person or persons so substituted by an actor or actress who shall be approved by the Author.

■　■　■

To Gouverneur Morris, a screenwriter at Universal, whose credits included many silent films in the early 1920s, such as *Anybody's Woman* (1930) and *East of Java* (1935)

November 29, 1935

Dear Mr. Morris,

My only excuse for my long silence is that of a person who has just emerged from Hell. The year which has passed has been so terrible, with the constant disappointments, the indefinite waiting and the struggle, that I did not want to let anyone hear from me, for all I could say would have been complaints. I had to reach some success before I could feel like a human being again—and write like one.

I am just beginning to raise my head—more or less. Not because of my play—although that is doing rather nicely—but because of my book. Selling it has been the greatest thing in my life so far. I had been so bewildered and discouraged by the long delay on the book, that I felt I would never be able to write again. Now that's over. Whether the book fails or succeeds, it will at least have been published.

The book was sold during the first weeks of my play and I have been terribly busy, giving it a final editing. Macmillan, who are going to publish it, did not want any changes made, no cuts or alterations of any kind. But I wanted to revise it once more and make a few minor changes which, I think, improved it. I have delivered the completed script about a week ago and I expect galley proofs of it in about two weeks. The book will come out in February or March. So I am free now to relax and begin to enjoy life. And also to think of my next novel, which I have in mind already and over which I feel very enthusiastic—so far. It is *not* another Russian story, but a strictly American one.

I do not know whether you knew that I have had to withdraw my book from Miss Wick, some time ago. I found that we disagreed too much on the book and that it was difficult for Miss Wick to handle it, since she did not feel in sympathy with it. The book was sold by Miss Ann Watkins who is now my agent. You may know of her—she is the agent of Sinclair Lewis and one of the grandest persons I have ever met.

The only important change in my book is the title. It is now going to be called *We the Living*. Remembering that you have never liked the title *Airtight,* I hope that you may approve of this one.

I do not know how to express my profound gratitude to you for your interest in my book and for your kindness in writing about me to the press. You have seen, undoubtedly, the nice mention which O. O. McIntyre gave me in his column on your recommendation. Now that my worst struggle is over, I find many people interested in me, but I shall never forget that you had faith in me at the time when I was just beginning and needed it most.

There is not much that I can tell you about my play. It is doing very well, it seems very popular and successful. But I get no satisfaction whatever out of it, because of the changes which Mr. Woods insisted on making. I find them so inept and in such bad taste that the entire spirit of the play is ruined. I have never considered it as a particularly good play and was fully prepared to allow any changes to improve it. But I do not think that bringing it down to the level of cheap melodrama and destroying its characters, which was the best thing it had, constitutes an improvement. And that is exactly what Mr. Woods has done. I am trying to look at the whole thing philosophically, consider it a necessary sacrifice to make a beginning and forget about it, while I try to write something better.

Since I frankly lacked the courage to write to you sooner, I have never had the chance to ask you what you thought of my novelette *Ideal*, which I left with you when I departed from Hollywood. If it is not too late and if you still remember it, I would greatly appreciate your opinion of it. I have rewritten it into a play, which I have finished recently.

I do not know when I shall come back to Hollywood. I would like to stay here a little longer and I do not plan to return, unless the screen rights to my play are sold and I am brought back to work on the adaptation. I love New York. It is a city, and I suppose that I am one of those decadent products of civilization that do not feel at home outside of a big city. With the exception of a few friends, I do not miss Hollywood at all. If and when I have to return, the pleasure of seeing you again will be my chief compensation. That prospect does make me wish to come back sometime soon.

AR's final, reedited version of Night of January 16th *was published by New American Library in 1968 and is still being regularly performed, particularly in summer stock and in high schools.*

■ ■ ■

To Gouverneur Morris

January 23, 1936

Dear Mr. Morris,

Thank you ever so much for the fascinating little book you sent me for Christmas. Needless to say, I enjoyed it tremendously and laughed aloud while reading it. I think it is a beautiful work and most timely and most decidedly needed at the present moment. You probably know that I quite agree with your viewpoint. I can sympathize all the more since you seem to feel as strongly about the subject as I do about another—and not dissimilar problem—that of Soviet Russia. I feel that something has to be done about this modern tendency toward the Red and all forms of Red. And the more voices are raised against it—the better. We certainly hear more than enough from the opposite side. Therefore—my thanks and congratulations for your work.

My novel is announced for publication on April 14. But I expect to have finished copies of it earlier. I have just completed the final corrections on the page proofs and am looking forward anxiously to the day of publication.

As to my play, I am having nothing but endless troubles and lawsuits with my producer. The whole matter is so complicated and so revolting that it is not worthwhile to bother you with its details. I would like to ask you, however, *not* to see the play when it comes to Los Angeles. I am sincerely ashamed of it in its present form, owing to changes which I could not prevent Woods from making, and I would prefer that you remember the play as it was, with all its faults, rather than to see the disgraceful burlesque it has become.

■ ■ ■

To Ev Suffens, the stage name of announcer Raymond Nelson

April 6, 1936

Dear Announcer,

(Please excuse me, but I haven't been able to catch your name yet.) Thank you for the nice welcome you gave me on your program Saturday night. But I'm not really a new customer. I'm a very old and faithful one. I have been listening to your program for months. I must admit that you've made a radio fan out of me. And you were wrong when—in answer to my wire about your being my favorite announcer—you said that I "probably say it to all the announcers." If you'll excuse me, I hate radio announcers. But you are a most amazing exception. My husband and I started by listening to your program for the classical music you played and we used to turn the radio down while you talked. Now—we wait impatiently through the music just to hear you talk. You probably know that the secret of your charm is in the fact that you don't sound as if you were talking to morons. And I want to thank you for the real treat that your program and your wit are for us. We listen to you faithfully every night, rain or shine, guests or no guests. When we have guests, we make them listen, too.

Of course, we would like to hear as many classical recordings as you can give us. For the life of me, I can't understand why people should intrude with their senseless jazz requests upon the only classical program we have, when every other station plays plenty of jazz night and day. Can't we, the badly neglected minority that possesses a trace of good taste, be allowed *one* good program out of a hundred trashy ones? Particularly since I don't think that we are a minority. However, I know it's not your fault. But if we have to compromise, please enter my vote for as many classics as possible. Your recordings of *Faust* were grand and I would like to hear more of it.

As to special requests, I would like very, very much to hear the *Phaedra* Overture by Massenet. Of course I don't mean to rush you and nag you about it. But if it is possible to get the record, I would appreciate it very much. Also—do you have "Serenade" by Drdla? I would love to hear it. And are you allowed to play any of the Viennese operettas of Emmerich Kalman? If they are not restricted, I would like to hear selections from *Countess Maritza* and *Czardas Fürstin*. (I hope I have spelled it correctly. If not—excuse me.) As you see, I don't ask for heavy classics, but only for what is called "light concert classics." They are really the most delightful form of music and the one most seldom heard.

Please give my love to Oscar and Oswald.* I think they are one of the cutest things on your program. (Just between you and me, did you really lose Oscar or did you lose the machine that barks for Oscar? I don't care, because I like to think that there *is* an Oscar. Anyway, I'm glad he came back.)

Thanking you again for your delightful work.

Sincerely yours,

P.S. You were right about my name the first time. It's pronounced "I-n." If you noticed it, I sent you my first wire on Saturday, when *Night of January 16th* closed. I didn't want you to think that I was after some free advertising.

■ ■ ■

To Gouverneur Morris

In a March 27 telegram, Morris wrote that AR's inscription in his copy of *We the Living* "filled his eyes with tears" and that the book "is a splendid performance."

April 14, 1936

Dear Mr. Morris,

I do not know how to express my gratitude to you for the telegram you sent me and for your interest in my book. But I would like you to know how much I appreciate the wonderful things you have said about me. Your kindness and praise have given me the greatest encouragement and I hope that my future will not disappoint you. I shall do my best to live up to your prediction.

I was very happy to know that you liked my book and its appearance in a printed form. The book is released now and I can only hope for the best. However, I expect plenty of hell from our good Red reviewers. The question in my mind is only whether they will succeed in keeping the book from the public. If they don't, if the book reaches America and makes at least a few pause and question their Communist theories, I shall be satisfied, no matter what they say about me. If the book turns a few potential Reds

---

* Oscar and Oswald were dog characters on Suffens's show. The names were given to two stuffed lion cubs given to AR by her husband, and they became like family members. Forty years later, they were still being brought out at Christmastime, with Frank doing the talking for them.

away from the cause—I will know that I have accomplished something worthwhile. How tragically the book is needed here I am realizing more and more every day. New York is full of people sold bodies and souls to the Soviets. The extent of it almost frightens me. But I've done all I could. The future will tell the rest.

And—no matter what happens now—my deepest gratitude to one great man who understood me.

■   ■   ■

To Marjorie Williams, director of the Hollywood Studio Club, a residence for young women aspiring to careers in the film industry. AR lived there her first three years in Hollywood.

April 27, 1936

Dear Miss Williams,

Thank you ever so much for your letter. I was very happy to know that you remember me and that you liked my play. I am sending you a copy of my first novel which has just come out. I think that it is a much better piece of work than the play—and I hope you will like it. I would appreciate it very much if you would write to me and tell me what you think of it.

The novel describes Soviet Russia in the years when I lived there. So if you still remember what a crazy, temperamental person I was when I lived at the Club, you may understand it now, when you read about the kind of country I had just left.

I would like to take this opportunity to thank you and the other officers of the Studio Club for all your kindness and help at a time when I needed it so badly. I am happy that I have reached some degree of success to justify your interest in me and to prove that your help has not been wasted. It has taken me a long time, as careers usually do, but I am happy to be, in some measure, among those "graduates" of your splendid organization who justify the wonderful work which you are doing and which is needed so very badly—because there is nothing more helpless and tragic, I am convinced, than a beginner with ambitions for an artistic career and without money or experience. I want you to know that I have not forgotten and that I am grateful to the Studio Club from the bottom of my heart.

■   ■   ■

To Ev Suffens

May 19, 1936

Dear Mr. Suffens,

You asked for it. I have never told you about my book because, as you will see, it is definitely anti-Soviet and I was under the impression that your station—not your program, but station WEVD—is somewhat "pink." However, since you are interested in my novel and have mentioned it over the air, I am happy to send you a copy of it as a little token of gratitude for your lovely program and the many requests you have played for me.

I want only to warn you that I do not know whether you should mention the book by its title over the air, because I certainly wouldn't want the Red "comrades" to "liquidate" you for it. You are free to mention it if you wish. But use your own judgment.

Whatever your personal political convictions may be, I do hope that you will enjoy the book and that, after you've read it, I shall still be able to get a request played on the *Midnight Jamboree.*

■ ■ ■

To Ev Suffens

May 24, 1936

Dear Mr. Suffens,

Since I am an old, faithful admirer of your program, you know how I feel about it. But you are conducting a poll among your listeners and I want to register my vote formally. On the first question you asked over the air: do we want the *Midnight Jamboree* continued through the summer, I answer: *YES!!!* Most emphatically *yes.* Your program has become a household institution with us, like a visit with a friend each evening. If you were to discontinue it, it would leave a void no other program could fill. I don't exaggerate when I say that I would simply be heartbroken, because the *Midnight Jamboree* is the best, the most charming, the most amusing program on the air and the *only one* to which we listen regularly.

On your second question: do we want the program conducted as it is now or made more formal, I answer: *by all means keep it as it is now.* Its whole charm is the informality and your peculiar, inimitable sense of humor. The *Midnight Jamboree* is really Ev Suffens. You do play excellent music, but any other station can play the same records. If you were to turn into a formal, stuffy announcer, I would be bored to death. And I don't believe that anyone would listen to three solid hours of formality. Artificial, pretentious, fawning pomposity is precisely what is wrong with most radio announcers and what gives the radio its slightly silly, inane aspect. Since there is no one on the air quite like you—why even consider giving up your charm and originality to become like hundreds of others?

We love "Oscar," "Oswald," "Rasputin," and your whole family. They have become real characters to us, real friends whom we would miss terribly. My suggestion would be to have more of them, not less. As to the music, my vote is: *more classics*, particularly light concert classics such as you have been playing lately. Personally, I would say: all classics, but I don't mind suffering through a jazz number once in a while if it's necessary and if your audience demands it.

To sum up, I say: WE WANT THE *MIDNIGHT JAMBOREE* CONTINUED FOREVER AND JUST AS IT IS NOW. And I add a vote of thanks and a salute to the best program on the air and the man who created it.

■　■　■

To Ev Suffens

June 10, 1936

Dear Ev,

Do we miss the *Midnight Jamboree*? Well, "you have *no* idea!" Oh, yes, the Jamboree is still there, but "she ain't what she used to be." "Don't look now," but we are not very happy about the announcer who is understudying you. He is not bad, as radio announcers go, but he is just that— a radio announcer, and with a leaning toward jazz music besides. Such old, faithful fans of the *Midnight Jamboree* as we are have actually stopped listening and missed several evenings.

Oscar and Oswald the Firsts are sitting dejectedly by the radio, waiting for your return. They don't like this vacation and want their jobs back. Petunia's back is arched, her fur is ruffled and she is mad at you. She wants to know why you disgraced her publicly by announcing over the air that you didn't like her? But she'll forgive you when she hears the "Grasshoppers' Dance" again. We haven't had any "Grasshoppers' Dance," any "Down South," not even a single "Toonerville Train" for ages.

Our regards, best wishes and love to Oscar, Oswald, Rasputin and— well, all right, and Ev Suffens.

■　■　■

To Mary Inloes

June 18, 1936

Dear Mary Virginia,

I have just sent you a copy of my book, for I certainly do not want you to wait for it at a lending library. However, I am grateful for your being interested in it and trying to get it from a library. Needless to say, I am quite happy and proud about the book, much more so than about the unfortunate *Night of January 16th*.

Speaking of *Night*, I must report that it is doing very well in summer stock. There are several companies doing it now and many more planned. The London production is tentatively scheduled for September. I understand also that a road tour of the big cities is planned for this fall.

You asked me what I am working on at present. For the last month I have not been able to do any work at all. I have had to give lectures and speeches about Soviet Russia—and of course I couldn't refuse the opportunity, feeling as strongly as I do about the subject. I have even been interviewed over the radio. It is all a rather nerve-wrecking experience, but quite enjoyable. However, I have two new plays and a long novel outlined, and I shall settle down soon to some serious work. I don't know as yet when I will return to Hollywood; my plans are quite indefinite for the summer.

■ ■ ■

To Marjorie Williams

Approximately half of this letter was later used as a fund-raising appeal for the Studio Club, and a shorter selection is reproduced in the one-page history of the Club in the display case of the building at 1215 N. Lodi Place, Hollywood.

June 18, 1936

Dear Miss Williams,

I can only thank you for the compliment you paid me in wishing to use my letter as part of a drive for the Studio Club. You certainly may use my letter, or any part of it, for so splendid a purpose and I shall be only too happy if it will help, even in the slightest degree, the cause of other potential writers who are going through what I have been through.

I would also like to point out to all those people, who are in a position to help the Studio Club, the following—if you find it of any value: millions are given each year to charities which help crippled children, old people, blind people and all kinds of disabled unfortunates; which is a perfectly worthy cause. But, on the other hand, has anyone given much thought to the crying, desperate need of helping the exact opposite type of human beings—the able, the fit, the talented and unusual ones crushed by purely material circumstances? That idea of hardships being good for character and of a talent always being able to break through is an old fallacy. Talent alone is helpless today. Any success requires both talent and luck. And the "luck" has to be helped along and provided by someone. A talented person has to eat as much as a misfit. A talented person needs sympathy, understanding and intelligent guidance *more* than a misfit. And the question arises: who is more worthy of help—the sub-normal or the above-normal? Who is more valuable to humanity? Which of the two types is more valuable to himself? Which of the two suffers more acutely: the misfit, who doesn't know what he is missing, or the talented one who knows it only too well? I have no quarrel with those who help the disabled. But if only one tenth of the money given to help them were given to help potential talent—much greater things would be accomplished in the spirit of a much higher type of charity.

Talent *does not* survive all obstacles. In fact, in the face of hardships, talent is the first one to perish; the rarest plants are usually the most fragile. Our present-day struggle for existence is the coarsest and ugliest phenomenon that has ever appeared on earth. It takes a tough skin to face it, a very tough one. Are talented people born with tough skins? Hardly. In fact, the more talent one possesses the more sensitive one is, as a rule. And if there is a more tragic figure than a sensitive, worthwhile person facing life without money—I don't know where it can be found.

The Studio Club is the only organization I know of personally that carries on, quietly and modestly, this great work which is needed so badly: help for young talent. It not only provides human, decent living conditions which a poor beginner could not afford anywhere else, but it provides that other great necessity of life: understanding. It makes a beginner feel that he is not, after all, an intruder with all the world laughing at him and rejecting him at every step, but that there are people who consider it worthwhile to dedicate their work to helping and encouraging him. Isn't such an organization worthy of everyone's support? What if out of every hundred whom the Studio Club helps, ten will prove that they had something worth saving, something which might have perished without help at the most dangerous time of the first steps? Isn't it worth the gamble? So many gamble on roulette, and slot machines, and horses. Why not gamble for a change on human beings and human futures?

I have gone into all this at such length because it is a question for which I have felt a kind of crusading spirit for a long time. I have always hoped to be able to express these things some day and to be heard. If it can be of any assistance to the Studio Club, you may quote it all or any part of it you find valuable. And you know that my best wishes and gratitude are with the Club always.

I would like to be entered as a contributing member of the Club and I am enclosing a check for it. When I become more firmly established, I hope to be able to contribute a more substantial membership.

In closing, I want to thank you for your kind opinion of my novel. I am very happy to know that you liked it. And I was delighted to read your opinion on individualism. That one word—individualism—is to be the theme song, the goal, the only aim of all my writing. If I have any real mission in life—this is it. And you know how badly it is needed at present!

■ ■ ■

To John Temple Graves, syndicated newspaper columnist from Birmingham, Ala.

July 5, 1936

My dear Mr. Graves,

Please accept my sincere and profound gratitude for your opinion of my book *We the Living*, as expressed in your column of June 8. I appreciate it all the more, not only because you wrote it, but because you were kind enough to send it to me.

I am particularly grateful to you for calling the public's attention to my book from an angle which is more important to me than any possible literary accomplishment of mine, namely for mentioning the fact that my book is not merely an argument against Communism, but against all forms of collectivism, against any manner of sacrilege toward the Individual. It would be easier for me to conceive of tolerance toward a theory preaching a wholesale execution of mankind by poison gas than to understand those who find any possible ethical excuse for destroying the only priceless possession of man—his individualism. After all, any form of swift physical annihilation is preferable to the inconceivable horror of a living death. And what but a rotting alive can human existence be when devoid of the pride and the joy of a man's right to his own spirit?

All the crimes of history have always been perpetrated by the mob. And if any of our various modern forms of proclaiming the mob's superiority over everything in life are allowed to triumph, we are headed for another era of Dark Ages, darker than any the past has known. It seems tragically obvious that a great many representatives of our press—and the press is the only real dictator of public opinion—have succumbed to one version of collectivism or another—mainly to the Soviet variety. Consequently, I felt a particular gratification in discovering in you one of the few remaining champions of what seems to be almost a lost cause. How badly these champions are needed at present I do not have to tell you, you must realize it yourself.

I can only thank you and tell you that my every good wish is with you and your work. We seem to be fighters in the same camp—and, perhaps, if it is not too late, we may still win.

Part of the second paragraph above was quoted in Graves's column of July 10, 1936.

■ ■ ■

To John Temple Graves

August 12, 1936

Dear Mr. Graves,

Thank you ever so much for your most interesting letter. I must confess that I have not answered it sooner because I wanted to read the book *Who Owns America*, which you mentioned in your letter. However, I have been so rushed with urgent business that I have not been able to do it yet, and I am writing with a promise that I shall read it in the very near future. It has been on my list for a long time, but I haven't been able to catch up with the many books I intend to read.

I must thank you also for your column which you sent me, with the quotation from my letter. I am very glad that you found it interesting enough to quote.

However, [your use of] the term "umpired individualism" frightens me a little. I admit that I do not know the exact meaning in which it is used. It comes down to the question of "umpired" by whom, how and to what extent? To my strictly layman and perhaps not very scientific viewpoint, it seems that the whole question of individualism or collectivism rests primarily on the choice between two basic principles: either we believe that the State exists to serve the individual or that the individual exists to serve the State. It may be an abstract, general principle, but generalities of this kind have a way of producing infinite consequences in practical reality. I believe more firmly than in any Ten Commandments that the State exists only and exclusively to serve the individual. I see no conceivable logical or ethical excuse for the opposite belief, nor any possible compromise between the two. If the role of the State as a servant, not a master, is taken as a basic, immutable sort of Constitution—then "umpiring" is safe and desirable; provided that the "umpiring" is done precisely to protect single individuals, *not* society as a whole or the state as a whole; provided that each act of the "umpires" is definitely motivated by and does not clash with the above sort of Constitution.

"Society" is such a dangerous abstraction. As a rule, what can pass for a benefit to "society" is actually a disaster to all and any single individuals composing it. As witness Soviet Russia. I cannot get away from the idea that "society" as such does not exist, apart from its members. It is not a separate, mystical entity. It is only a shorter way of saying "a million" or "a hundred million people." Yet all collectivist schemes use the word State or Society as a complete, single entity and demand that all individual citizens sacrifice everything for it. If we have a society where everyone sacrifices—just exactly who profits and who is happy? A happy collective composed of miserable, frustrated members is an absurdity. Yet that is precisely what collectivist Russia claims to be. And any theory which substitutes carelessly the word "society" for the word "men" runs the same danger. You cannot claim that you have a healthy forest composed of rotting trees. I'm afraid that collectivists cannot see the trees for the forest.

I admit that I am not an economist, but I cannot get away from the feeling that pure, abstract economics, particularly the Marxist kind, forget the human element for the sake of the economic one. And again: do economics have to fit man as he is or does man have to be ground to a pulp to fit into a preconceived economic mold?

Do we agree now or not quite?

■   ■   ■

To Frank O'Connor, then appearing in a Connecticut summer-stock production of *Night of January 16th*

August 19, 1936

Cubby Sweet!

Well, here is the first love letter I ever had a chance to write. And I have nothing to say, except that I miss you terribly. As a matter of fact, I don't really miss you, it's the funniest feeling: on the one hand, I feel so blue that I could cry any minute, and on the other hand I feel very proud and virtuous that I've actually done it: let you go away and stayed to do "my duty."

The worst thing was coming home from the station. It was terrible and I enjoyed it, because it was a completely new feeling, something I've never felt before: the whole city seemed empty, and that's not such a cliché as it sounds, it was the certainty that no one, not anywhere, on any street, really mattered to me. I felt free and bitter and I wanted to cry. I didn't look back at your train once. How did you feel?

There's one good thing, however: the absence of my "inspiration" inspires me more than anything else. I've really done grand work and I feel like working. I think mainly because I feel terribly guilty if I stop for a moment, because I have no right to be here if I'm not working. So I am. I just reread the last scene of the first act and it still seems grand. Hope I'll like it tomorrow.

No news of any kind, except that the script arrived from Reeid. I haven't read it yet. Marjorie stayed here last night and I saw her dance yesterday. It was really magnificent. I had some nice dialogue with the housekeeper: "My husband is away and I have a friend staying with me, will you please change the bed linen?" She brought it up herself, and was probably disappointed to see that it was only Marjorie.

Be sure and listen to me on the radio Sunday, if I don't come up before then. I think it's going to be good. It's station 101 on the dial, at 5:30. Have you a radio there anywhere?

Tweetness, I miss you! This is fun, writing to you, but it seems silly and unreal. I'm waiting for your letter to see how you do it. I'm a poor little feline with a can tied to my tail. And my tail is down, and my fur up, and I'm a Siberian blue "kittan." Oscar and Oswald are no help, they're moping about and won't talk to me.

Do I have to tell you that I love you?

Here's a picture of us all and how we look here:

(tears)

(drawn from nature)

Good night, Tweet!

XXXXXXX

Your
Fluff

P.S. Lions is felines!

■ ■ ■

To Frank O'Connor

August 21, 1936

Cubby darling!

I received *two* letters from you, together—this morning. It was swell, and thanks, you did write after all. I couldn't quite believe that you ever would.

You "catched" me on the "first, most and foremost." All right, it was for Thursday and Friday. But you're King of Beasts, Prince of Cubs, Thing of Beauty, and lions is felines! (*Mainly* dandelions ain't!)

I have had a very exciting day today. Saw Jerome Mayer and it's all settled. This contract [for a stage version of *We the Living*] will be signed probably Thursday. He didn't make any funny demands for any collaborators, after I explained my point. He was very nice. We discussed the play at great length and I showed him my outline, which he liked very much. We also discussed casting. He does have Brian Aherne in mind, but for *Leo*, not Andrei. He also mentioned Francis Lederer for Leo, which may be all right; he admitted, however, that he is not sure of what Lederer would be like in a tragic role. I told him about Katharine Hepburn turning down the Guild play, and he said he would find out right away whether we could have her. He mentioned Dorothy Gish, a vague possibility. Pat said she looks very young and is grand. I'm going to Westport tomorrow to see her in *Russet Marble*. She does the part of a young girl in that, so I'll see what she's like.

I'm way in the first scene of the Second Act and it goes swell—so far. And I don't miss you at all. (Well, you know that's a lie.) How do you actually feel without me? I feel funny. I still am not used to being alone. I try not to think about it when I'm working, but I feel awfully blue when I write this. And I can't bear to look at Oscar and Oswald, since they won't talk to me. They're putting all their answers in cold storage. Cubbyhole, how do you really feel? Try to put it on paper. I can't. I love you and it's terrible to have such a hold on me, you can sit there and gloat, if you want to. There's no one here to "bait" a poor, defenseless kittan (they're the best kind to bait) and I miss it terribly.

I'll come Monday, so don't be too low and too tired until then. Watch your "vitality." And *eat*. But plenty! Even Emily misses you. Faith called to find out how I was bearing up under it. I'm ashamed to say that I sleep well and feel fine, except that I could have a "fit" any moment— and you can't blame me for that.

Love from Oscar and Oswald, but *mainly* from Fluff.

Good night, Tweetest.
XXXXXXX

■ ■ ■

2

WE THE LIVING TO
THE FOUNTAINHEAD (1937–1943)

To John Temple Graves

January 30, 1937

Dear Mr. Graves,

My sincere, if belated, gratitude for the nice things you have said about me in your column. I hope you will forgive my long delay in writing to you when I tell you that since summer I have been in what amounted to a solitary confinement due to urgent work on the dramatization of my novel *We the Living*. A New York theatrical producer bought the play before it was written and I had to work on it for solid days and nights, trying to finish it in time for this season. You can understand what a difficult job it was. I have just completed it, but it is now too late for a production this winter and we plan to open it early in the fall. The play is being cast now—and that is a tremendous difficulty, considering the part of "Kira."

Speaking of plays, I hope against hope that you have *not* seen *Night of January 16th*, when it played in Birmingham. I am very grateful for the advance notice you gave it in your column, but I felt, when I read it, as if I had betrayed the confidence of a friend. I must admit that I am somewhat ashamed of *Night of January 16th* in its present form. This is due to the fact that, the play being my first one, I had a very unfortunate contract with the producer, which allowed him to make such cuts in the manuscript that all sense has been eliminated from the play. Only the plot and the characters have been kept, but every abstract or psychological implication has been destroyed, so that it is now nothing but a rather vulgar melodrama. It has

been successful in New York last winter, but it is not at all the kind of success I wanted. I am afraid that the play must have been a shock to you, if you saw it, coming as it did after my novel. I know that there can be no comparison between the two. My only consolation is that I have learned a lesson and never again will I entrust any work of mine to a producer whose artistic standards are so different from mine.

I *have* read, at last, *Who Owns America*. I think it is a splendid book and I thank you for calling my attention to it. In principle, I agree with its authors completely and could subscribe to almost everything they said. I am not sufficiently versed in economics to judge the practical value of their recommendations, but I was delighted to read such a rarity as a sane criticism of our present system, which did not turn into Communistic drivel. I am glad to know that there still are people and a mode of thinking that can be opposed to Communism in a true, sensible democratic spirit. I have met so many people who declared bluntly that anyone criticizing Soviet Russia is automatically a fascist and a capitalistic exploiter. And it was gratifying to hear a voice in refutation of that preposterous nonsense.

■ ■ ■

To Mr. Craig, a fan

January 30, 1937

Dear Mr. Craig,

Your letter inquiring about the origin of my name has been forwarded to me by my publishers Cassell & Co. In answer to your question, I must say that "Ayn" is both a real name and an invention. The original of it is a Finnish feminine name which is spelled in Russian thus: "Айна." Its pronunciation, spelled phonetically, would be: "I-na." I do not know what its correct spelling should be in English, but I chose to make it "Ayn," eliminating the final "a." I pronounce it as the letter "I" with an "n" added to it.

■ ■ ■

To Gladys Unger, a friend from the Hollywood Studio Club

July 6, 1937

Dear Gladys,

I have thought of you often and I have also thought about the "Serf-Actress." I quite agree with you on it. I had the same fear, that the outline as we had it, was not quite modern enough for the Broadway I have seen and know better than I did before I came here. I still think it is a good idea and a very interesting theme that has a good play in it. But you are quite right, there is nothing I could do about it now. It isn't that I have lost interest, but that I do not see even a remote possibility of when I could come back to Hollywood.

So it is only fair if I release any interest I may have had in the "Serf Actress" and do not hold you up on it any longer, since you want to proceed on it yourself. No, I do not want to take any percentages or royalties on it, because I don't feel that I have put enough time and work into it to warrant a percentage. If you remember, I was busy on other things when we were working on our outline and I never could devote to it the time I would have liked to devote. Besides, it is your own idea and you may put a great deal of work into it before it is ready as a play.

My play which Ivan [Lebedeff, a Russian-born actor whom AR knew in Hollywood] mentioned to you must be the adaptation of my novel *We the Living*. Jerome bought it for the stage, before it was written as a play, and I dramatized it myself. It was a terribly hard job—took me all winter. I don't think I ever want to do another dramatization. It's much harder than writing two new plays. It will be produced this fall, if all goes well. We have great difficulties in casting the leading part of "Kira."*

I am now working on another play, because two producers are tentatively interested in it, at least in the idea of it. I am also working slowly, at nights, on my next novel. The publishers here and in England are already asking questions as to when, what and how soon it will be ready. I am really trying to cover two fields, or as my editor at Macmillan said, riding two horses, and I want to try not to let either one of them throw me.

We have moved for the summer to Stony Creek, Connecticut. There is a nice summer stock theater here and Frank is acting in it. It will be very

---

* A theatrical version of *We the Living* was produced in 1939 by George Abbott under the title *The Unconquered*. Closing after five days, it was later described by AR as "a total flop."

good experience for him. And the place is so quiet, that I seem to be doing the best work I've done for months. It's an ideal place for a writer.

■　■　■

To Alexander Kerensky, premier of Russia before the 1917 Bolshevik revolution. This undated letter has been translated from the handwritten Russian.

Dear Aleksandr Fyodorovich,

If you remember me being among the crowd in the "Town Nutt" this morning, I am taking advantage of the permission you gave me to send you my book [*We the Living*] which I had mentioned to you.

Of all the great Russian people in the world, your opinion is the most valuable to me, and I have waited for an opportunity to send you this book for a long time: since I started writing it. It was printed here, in America, two years ago; last year, in England; and is now being prepared for print in several European countries.

I lived in Russia for many years under the Soviet regime, and I think that a depiction of daily Soviet life will probably be of interest to you. If you do not consider it stupidity on my part, I would like to ask you to let me know your opinion when you finish reading the book. I would be very grateful if you wrote me a few words about it when you find a convenient time. I am asking this for myself personally, and, if you like the book, I promise not to abuse your name and opinion for the purpose of literary advertising.

Please pardon my Soviet orthography. I was brought up in a Soviet university, and now do not know how to write otherwise. I am not at all confident in my Russian style, because in the recent years I have written, thought, and worked in English, and I hope you forgive me.

With deep respect,

■　■　■

To Wera Engels, a European actress

March 22, 1938

Dear Wera,

I have just received a letter from Ivan, in which he tells me that you would like to offer *Ideal* to Marcel L'Herbier, to be produced as a French picture with you in the lead. Needless to say, I have always wanted to see you play "Gonda," and I appreciate very much your interest in this story and the fact that you have never forgotten it.

I am very much interested in the possibility of a screen production in France, starring you. . . . If a deal can be made, I would like to go to France and do the screen adaptation.

Ivan thinks it is "Fate" that you should finally appear in *Ideal*. I am beginning to think so myself. The story was really intended for you, so let us hope that it will do great things for both of us.

■　■　■

To Maj. Gen. John F. O'Ryan of Fighting Funds for Finland. Finland was engaged in a war with the USSR.

February 15, 1940

Dear Sir,

Enclosed please find my contribution to your fund for the purchase of armaments for Finland.

Allow me to express my admiration for your work in behalf of a great cause.

■　■　■

To Dashiell Hammett, detective novelist

AR's letter is in response to Hammett's form letter offering $3.50 tickets to a social event supporting his magazine *Equity*.

August 1, 1940

Dear Mr. Hammett,

And here I thought that you were a detective and a brilliant one, because *The Maltese Falcon* has always been one of my favorite mystery stories.

Don't you know who I am? This is not to say that everyone should, but I think you should. And if you do, you ought to know better than to send me an invitation like this. Well, you're half right, at that. I do welcome anyone fighting against Coughlin's "Social Justice" [a pro-fascist organization]. But when you give a party to fight *both* "Social Justice" and *The Daily Worker,* count me in and I'll give you $7.00 per ticket, let alone $3.50. Not until then, Comrade, not until then.

■ ■ ■

To Channing Pollock, drama critic and author of novels and plays, including *The Ziegfeld Follies of 1915*

"To All Innocent Fifth Columnists" was AR's unpublished, 5,000-word critique of those whose silence aids collectivism. ("The totalitarians in this country do not want your active support. . . . All they want from you is indifference.")

March 7, 1941

Dear Mr. Pollock:

I was very glad to hear that you approved of my "To All Innocent Fifth Columnists." And I shall be only too happy if you find that you can use any of it in your lectures—with or without credit. I do not care at all about credit, but I care tremendously to have these ideas spread in every possible manner.

I realize the difficulties that would confront you if you headed a national organization [upholding individualism] such as I have in mind. But my plan would not necessarily burden you with a big administrative job. Your contribution would be "ideological" or intellectual guidance, at the head of a committee somewhat on the order of the Advisory Board which you suggest in "What Can We Do For Democracy?" Since our "ideology" (I hate the word, but it's the most expressive one to convey my meaning) would be very much in line with that of your lectures, your work on such a committee would demand some time and thought, but no additional writing or research or slackening of your own writing and lecturing activities. The executive and administrative side of the organization could be turned over to other men—under the guidance of the committee.

The first problem, of course, would be to select the members of this committee. If, upon further consideration, you find that you are willing to make an attempt toward an organization of this kind, I would ask you to think over the names of those whom you consider the right people for the

directing committee. I am firmly convinced that if we could get together
—as you suggested in our conversation—about fifty men of good reputation and standing in their various professions, who share our political
convictions—the most important step would be accomplished right there.
I am still enthusiastic and, perhaps, naive enough to believe that the groundwork for the entire program of the organization could be laid out at one
such meeting (probably a long one).

If you find time on your lecture tour to write to me and send me the
names of these men, I will go to see them, and I am very willing to do all
the explaining, contacting, arranging and general running around. I can get
any number of young people to do all the "ground" work. But if I proceed
with these young people on our own, you realize what a long time it would
take to achieve the effectiveness which a committee of prominent men
would give us.

■   ■   ■

To Channing Pollock

*"The Individualist Manifesto" was an 8,000-word statement of AR's ethical/
political philosophy, which has not been published. She also wrote a 1,500-
word version entitled "The Individualist Credo," published in the January
1944 issue of Reader's Digest as "The Only Path to Tomorrow."*

April 28, 1941

Dear Mr. Pollock:

The "Manifesto" took twelve hours Saturday and fifteen yesterday—I go
at it with interruptions only for meals. I shall have it finished tomorrow
and mail it to you as soon as it is typed. It will be quite a bit longer than
2,500 words, because it must present the whole groundwork of our "Party
Line" and be a basic document, such as the *Communist Manifesto* was on
the other side. However, I think the problem can be solved by having *two*
manifestos; that is, a very short declaration of our principles and aims—
for the purpose of recruiting members, and the complete text for those who
join. I shall have them both ready to submit to you within the next few
days.

I do not think that recruiting will prove to be a major problem. Once
started, it will go on its own momentum. The need is there. So is the
audience. Just let people know what we are doing and we won't have to
go after them—they will come to us. As far as rank-and-file membership

is concerned, I believe I can get hundreds within a few days. The major step, I think, is to get our Committee together.

And I can't tell you how happy I am that we have started.

■ ■ ■

To Channing Pollock

May 1, 1941

Dear Mr. Pollock:

Here it is [the "Manifesto"]. This may not be the final version, but it includes all the basic issues which, I think, should be stated to make our "ideology" clear and consistent.

This is what I have been waiting for years to see someone do. I really never intended to do it all alone. I can tell you now that I was plain scared when you asked me to do it. And also flattered. I had thought that our Committee would undertake the writing of some such document as its first action. But I suppose I was contradicting myself there—one can't do those things collectively. Someone has to start. However, this is the point where I need all the "collective" help possible. I think that after you have read it and we make such changes as you suggest, we will have to submit it to our Committee, get their reactions and advice and then formulate the final shape before it is published or made public. When it is released, I think it should bear the signatures of our Committee—let us be the signers of a new Declaration of Independence.

I hope you won't find that I am too much of an Intellectual Egotist in this "Manifesto"—which, of course, I am. Frankly and proudly, not apologetically. Some people might say that we should not come right out with such a doctrine. But I think we must. Evasion and compromise have killed all pro-capitalist movements so far. I think the tragedy of Capitalism from the beginning has been the lack of a consistent ideology of its own. It moved on the strangest mixture of Collectivist-Christian-Equalitarian-Humanitarian concepts, the worst mental hodgepodge in history. Are we to be the ones who will clear it up? I don't know. It sounds presumptuous. But that is what I would like to see us do. And since I preach that all public good comes from individuals—we have to attempt it.

■ ■ ■

To Channing Pollock

                                                              May 27, 1941

Dear Mr. Pollock:

I was terribly sorry to hear of the hardships which our organization work
has imposed upon you. I realize fully how busy you are and I can only
express my admiration for the idealism which caused you to undertake this
extra work. Of course, you should not be forced to continue to do so much
single-handed. My most earnest suggestion is that we do not wait much
longer for our "names." We can proceed with those we have. They are
prominent enough to ensure the prestige of the organization and to remove
from it any suspicion of "racket." If we now call a meeting of those who
have agreed to join us, we can take out our incorporation papers, raise the
necessary funds—and remove detail, routine work from you. I really do
not believe that a large number of prominent men is absolutely necessary
at the beginning. What we need most is quality, not quantity—as in all
social matters. The other "names" will join us when they see us going
ahead on a concrete program of action.

    If you prefer to wait a little longer for the latest answers, I would
suggest that we meet at least with those of our "names" who are here in
New York. They could suggest other names—and take over some of the
work and correspondence which you are carrying alone at present. I can
help on that, of course, but my name is not prominent enough to sign alone
to the original invitations.

    I would be afraid to go through *Who's Who* in search of new names,
because names as such are not what we want; we want people who are
widely known as representing our principles; and we must be *very certain*
of the political viewpoint of those we invite to serve on our Committee; a
prominent person whom we might invite merely for the sake of his prominence could do us more harm than good.

    I think Mr. Nicholas Roosevelt's opinion that our organization "would
be just one more of the same" is a very important criticism for us to
remember. We must make it very clear that we intend to *formulate and
propagate* a basic *IDEOLOGY* of Individualism and Capitalism, a complete
philosophy of life restated in the terms of the twentieth century. No organization is doing *that*. If we don't make this our first and clearest aim—
we will be nothing but "just one more of the same." Also, we must avoid
all generalities, compromises, "softening up" and attempts to pacify or
appeal to too many different viewpoints. They all do that—and fail. Unless

we stick very clearly, militantly and decisively to our basic principles—and keep these principles clear-cut—we *will* become another ineffectual patriotic organization.

■ ■ ■

To Channing Pollock

June 8, 1941

Dear Mr. Pollock:

I have waited to write to you until after I had read "Life's Too Short," which I have just finished. This is going to be a long letter, because the subject deserves it.

Let me say, first, that I felt very honored by your wanting my opinion of it. Since you challenged my "honesty," I tried to bend backwards in being honest; I tried to forget my admiration for all your other works and to read it as severely and unsympathetically as I could, just hunting for flaws and for things to dislike. And—I couldn't find any. I think "Life's Too Short" is one of the most charming, gracious, clever and entertaining things I have ever read.

There's my *honest* opinion—and I have to say it, even though you might distrust my honesty from now on. In all sincerity, I would have preferred to find something to criticize in it. But I read it with delight—and I only wished there were more of it. I told my husband some of the charming little incidents from it, and we laughed over them together, and he said: "Why, it's wonderful!"

Well? You wanted to know why it has not been published? I think I know it—and it's not a cheerful reason. It has not been published—not because of faults, but because of its chief virtue. It reads like the conversation of a very intelligent man. You feel a clear, bright, cheerful mind behind every sentence. There is no mush, no portentous platitudes, no vague, loud generalities of the kind that sound deep and mean just exactly nothing. The writing has such remarkable economy—nothing said but what has to be said and not an adjective over. Also, the writing is simple—with the most deadly simplicity of all: the simplicity of intelligence. I say "deadly" because that is just what *intelligence* represents to the contemptible second-raters who are mainly in charge of our literary life at present.

I don't think that most editors are conscious of it or deliberately vicious about it. But I do think that their instinct—they'd call it their

"Taste"—objects automatically to any manifestation of pure intellect, of *brains*. It is not even a question of subject matter. The subject matter of "Life's Too Short" is simple and human enough; it can be understood by and would appeal to the most un-intellectual, average reader; there is nothing "difficult" or "highbrow" about it. The intellectual quality is in the writing. It appeals to the emotions *through the mind*. The effect it creates in the reader is this: what a wise, charming man there is looking at us from between the lines. But the process of reading between the lines is an *intellectual enjoyment*. It is subtle. It requires intelligence to create it and to appreciate it. Not necessarily an abstract, ponderous, "philosophical" intelligence. But a simple, easy, cheerful mental process accessible to any mind, provided that mind wishes to be exercised. *There* is the secret. The minds of our present-day "intellectuals" do not wish to function. They dread it. And they resent it above all else. What they want is emotion, but not intelligent emotion. Just plain, cheap, sodden emotion that requires no thinking, that would vanish the instant thought was applied to it.

I can best make this clear by an illustration. I have read, appalled, the kind of autobiographies that are being published today. Autobiographies of nobodies full of nothing at all. Great big life stories of second-rate newspapermen who use world events as a background for their nasty little personalities. Like this: "And when I saw the fall of Vienna, it reminded me of a day seven years earlier when I met Jimmy Glutz in a dive in Singapore, and over a glass of absinthe I said: 'Jimmy, what is the meaning of life?' and Jimmy answered: 'Hell, who knows, you old bastard?' " You see what I mean? Is there any point, reason or excuse for this sort of thing? Yet it is being published every day and blown up into bestsellers. An accident? I don't think so. A deliberate intention. The intellectual revolution of the second-rater. The best method of destroying superiority is not to denounce it. It is to establish standards of superiority that destroy all standards. It is to hail as superiority its very antithesis: the small, the meaningless, the average. And they can get away with it only on one condition: that intelligence not be allowed to function, that a good, healthy, questioning mentality not be allowed to speak anywhere. Because one single "Why?" or "What the hell?" would destroy the whole hysterical tribe of glorified nonentities.

Our literature, our theater and all our arts are now one gigantic conspiracy against the mind. Not even merely against the great mind, but against any mind, against the mind as such. Down with thought and up with the emotions. When thought is destroyed—anything goes. Thought is the privilege of the superior few. In emotions we're all equal, even the

animals. Look at such a phenomenon as Gertrude Stein. She is being published, discussed and given more publicity than any real writer. Why?
There's no financial profit in it. Just as a joke? I don't think so. It is
done—in the main probably quite subconsciously to destroy the mind in
literature.

It is not surprising, therefore, that most of our editors and other literary
authorities are Red. I don't believe that they are all in the pay of Moscow.
The trouble is deeper and more vicious than that. We are living in the
century of the Second-Rater. The second-rater is always pink—by sheer
instinct. He has to glorify equality and he has to push his own equals to
the front. If this is not so—why, then, are all those dashing heroes of the
current autobiographies, such as Vincent Sheean, Walter Duranty, Negley
Farson, why are they all pink? If there is no deliberate plan behind it all
—wouldn't it be reasonable to suppose that at least one of those heroes
would be conservative or neutral? But there is not a single one.

And there, I think, is another reason why "Life's Too Short" is not
published. Not only are you a famous conservative, but you are a man of
achievement. *That*, monstrous as it may sound, is the reason why editors
are not interested in your autobiography. They want the autobiographies of
men who have never achieved anything and never will. There are some
exceptions to this rule, but not many. Of all the autobiographies published,
the number of those whose lives are really worth recording is far inferior
to the number of those whose lives weren't even worth living. *That* is the
ghastly reversal of all values that we are now facing.

So, if I have to demonstrate my honesty by criticizing you, I would
rather criticize your editorial in *This Week* magazine where you wrote on
"knowing the time to quit." If you remember, I objected to it—and you
cited "Life's Too Short" as an example of a case where an author should
accept the negative verdict of several editors. I said then that I didn't believe
this—and I say it more strongly now. I am afraid that you are thinking of
the time when editors were still men of integrity, discernment and achievement, and their opinion could be considered respectfully. We are long past
that time. There are still a few editors of that caliber left, but very, very
few. The rest? Well . . .

What makes me want to scream in this case, is the insidious injustice
of the whole process. Our Red "intellectuals" and our editors play upon
the best instincts of our authors in order to destroy them. It is only the
completely mediocre writer who never entertains any doubts on the value
of his work. The man of talent is always more severe with his own writing
than any outside critic could ever be. A good writer's first instinct is always

to blame himself. His own scrupulous honesty makes it difficult for him to accuse others of dishonesty or injustice. And thus, if his work is rejected repeatedly, he accepts the verdict, even when, in all sincerity, he can find no fault in his work; he simply accepts that he must have failed somewhere. He prefers to doubt his own standards rather than the ethics of editors. Thus, in his own mind, he completes for them their dirty work.

So what I want to criticize is not "Life's Too Short," but its author's attitude towards it. I think this work should be completed and published. I cannot advise you to undertake the struggle—because I know it will be a hard one. But if you are too busy with other work to complete "Life's Too Short"—then, I think, you owe to it at least the acknowledgment of its value in your own mind. You must consider it a victim of the immense injustice of our century. You must not help the second-raters in power by granting them the benefit of the doubt at the expense of your own work, at the cost of vindicating their bad judgment by questioning your own. Of course, personally, I wish you would finish "Life's Too Short" and make them publish it.

And—I think it is best not to advise young people to learn when to quit. They could learn it in a society of honest men, where the positions of authority and decision are held by men whose judgment can be respected. The kind of society we had yesterday. That is not what we have today. Today—young people have to go through a living hell and rely on nothing but their own faith in themselves. At the price of a thousand self-deluding mediocrities, I would like to save the genuine few—who have a very, very hard battle to fight today. And if you hold "Life's Too Short" as an example of "when to quit"—you're defeating your own point. You're proving mine. The case of "Life's Too Short" sets the time, not to quit, but to begin fighting in very grim earnest.

Well, am I honest?

Forgive me if I made you read such a long letter, but you asked for my opinion and I wanted to give it in full. If you don't agree with it—you can give me hell Tuesday.

Pollock's autobiography was published by Bobbs-Merrill in 1943 with the title Harvest of My Years. *He inscribed a copy: "To Ayn Rand, without whose insistence this book would not have been written."*

■　■　■

To Channing Pollock

Pollock inscribed his book *The Adventures of a Happy Man*: "To Ayn Rand—the best mind and most inspiring personality I have encountered in many years."

June 14, 1941

Dear Mr. Pollock:

Thank you from the bottom of my heart for *The Adventures of a Happy Man*—and for your inscription. I have been trying for years to become hard-boiled and to let nothing affect me too much. But this did. I read your inscription and I feel encouraged for the rest of my life—the kind of encouragement that only a creative person needs or understands.

I was delighted to learn that you had written to Little, Brown about "Life's Too Short." If I helped in any way to reawaken your interest and make you finish that book—I am most selfishly flattered.

I have met DeWitt Emery and have seen him *three* times while he was here. I don't know whether this was due to his enthusiasm for our cause or to his being impressed by me—and I am vain enough to hope it was both. I really did not find him hard or tough at all—he was very charming and very sincerely interested in our cause. He promised definitely that he is with us, and will do everything he can. He did say that he cannot give it his full time until after the passage of the Labor Bill on which he is working, but that would not be necessary, I think, until our organization actually gets going. He pointed out very emphatically that we should have financial backing first of all—and he will help us to get in touch with the right people.

■ ■ ■

To Channing Pollock

In Pollock's previous letter, he wrote that *Anthem* was "obvious" and "artificial" and that "you are bigger than your book—and you can do better." The edition he read was the 1938 British edition, not the rewritten (and current) edition published in 1946.

June 23, 1941

Dear Mr. Pollock:

No, I have no desire to kill you. I am sorry, of course, that you did not care for *Anthem*, but I appreciate your honesty in stating your opinion.

Last Thursday, when I received your wire, I telephoned at once to Dr. Ruth Alexander and saw her the same day. We had a most interesting conversation. She was quite enthusiastic about our project, and she said that she will join us—but on one condition: that our organization remain as direct and uncompromising in its "ideology" as I outlined it to her. She explained that she will not belong to any group which evades or pussyfoots on major issues, such as the issue of defending capitalism. I assured her that this was precisely our own attitude.

I have finished reading *The Adventures of a Happy Man*—and enjoyed it tremendously. It is such a bright and cheerful book. I agreed with almost everything in it—except the chapter on faith. That is because I think that there is nothing on earth more important than knowledge. Someday, when you have the time, I should like to have a nice long argument with you about that.

■   ■   ■

To Channing Pollock

July 7, 1941

Dear Mr. Pollock:

I got in touch with Miss Gloria Swanson and I am to see her soon, probably this week. She is interested in our cause and could be very helpful. This is all the news I have to report for the present. I am waiting for Mr. Emery —and I am really waiting for his instructions as to our next steps in securing financial backing.

I do hope that you will be able to come to New York soon and I am looking forward to seeing you. I must reproach you for just one sentence in your letter to Mr. Emery—the one about "Miss Rand is either disgusted with my inertia or . . ." You really should know better than that. After all the time and effort you have put into our organization, I hope you are not really doubting my appreciation.

■   ■   ■

To Channing Pollock

July 20, 1941

Dear Mr. Pollock:

Here is the letter of Mr. Eames which you sent me. I am afraid that Mr. Eames missed the point and did not understand the nature of our proposed organization at all. We would not compete with or duplicate any other organization. What we want to do is not being done by anyone, and the need for it is desperate.

Here are the main points:

1. Our side has no "ideology," no clear-cut, consistent system of belief, no *philosophy* of life. Merely to claim to be defenders of the "American Way" is not enough. It is a generality which is being used by everybody and anybody for all sorts of purposes. What organization of our side has defined a concrete ideology of Americanism? None. The first aim of *our* organization will be *intellectual* and *philosophical*—not merely political and economic. We will give people a *faith*—a positive, clear and consistent system of belief. Who has done that? Certainly not the N.A.M. They—and all other organizations—are merely fighting for the system of private enterprise and their entire method consists of teaching and clarifying the nature of that system. It is good work, but it is not enough. We want to go deeper than that. We want to teach people, not what the system of private enterprise is, but *why* we all should believe in it and fight for it. We want to provide a *spiritual, ethical, philosophical* groundwork for the belief in the system of private enterprise.

The Communists do not owe their success merely to booklets on the economics of Communism. They provide, first, an intellectual justification —a faith in collective action, in unlimited majority power, in a general, levelling equality, in "unselfishness," "service," etc. What are the intellectual justifications for our side? What are our moral values? Who has defined it? Who is preaching *philosophical* individualism? No one. And if it is not preached, economic individualism will not survive. Who could possibly acquire a new faith, a sense of spiritual security, of idealism and dedication out of N.A.M. literature? No one—least of all the N.A.M. That is not the purpose of their work. Their propaganda is strictly and exclusively economic, and they are doing a very good job—as far as it goes. But *we* must go farther.

2. There is no mass membership organization of our side. All of them—including the N.A.M.—merely ask people to contribute *money*. That

is why the average citizen takes no interest in any of them. People want to be active, to do something concrete for our cause—and no one gives them anything to do. You recall the almost desperate plea in the letters you received in answer to your lectures. "Please tell us what to do!"—*that* is the mood of the people. When it is answered merely by "send us a check," no wonder that people turn away, indifferent and disheartened. The subversive organizations, the Communists and the Nazis, go out after mass membership, enroll people and give them a concrete program of activity for their cause. Who is doing that on our side? Yet *that* is what the people need and want. As witness—the tremendous response of volunteers in the Willkie campaign. The people are with us, but they must have leadership that offers them a concrete program of personal, individual *activity*. *That* is what our organization would do.

3. There is no organization of our side in the intellectual field. And there are hundreds of Leftist groups. As witness—the collectivist trend in all the arts and in all the avenues of public expression. Who has done anything to stop it? Our organization would make it possible for anti-collectivist thought, art and literature to be presented and heard—which is practically impossible now.

These are only the main points. As to the N.A.M.—Mr. Gall, who is one of its most influential leaders, did not think that we would duplicate their work. Quite the contrary. He told me he has known for a long time that the program I proposed to him, the program of *our* organization, is precisely what is needed and needed desperately, but the N.A.M. itself, by its very nature, could not undertake it. He realized that it must be an *intellectual organization*—not one exclusively of manufacturers. And he is working now to help us get financial backing. He sent me most of their literature. It is excellent material—for schoolchildren interested in economics. No more than that.

■   ■   ■

To Channing Pollock

August 5, 1941

Dear Mr. Pollock:

Thank you for the copy of your letter to Mr. Emery which you sent me. I think that Mr. Emery's idea to have the National Small Business Men's

Association publish the "Manifesto" might be an excellent one—and I have written him a long letter about it.

Thank you very much for the nice things you said about me in that letter. Only, may I make one correction? I haven't "nearly lost faith in myself." Do I really impress you as so tragic a Russian? I often lose faith in other people—if there's any left to lose—but never in myself. You know that I believe in egotism. And I know that you approve of such an attitude.

■   ■   ■

To DeWitt Emery, head of the National Small Business Men's Association. Emery wrote AR that he had stayed up half the night reading *We the Living.*

August 5, 1941

Dear Mr. Emery:

Thank you for your letter about my book. I can't tell you how grateful I am for it. It was worth writing the book—just to receive a letter like yours. You say that you're "probably not doing a very good job of telling you what I want to express." It was a beautiful job. It's my turn now not to know how to express what I would like to say to thank you—but I hope that you, too, can read between the lines.

I received today a copy of Mr. Pollock's letter to you in regard to the "Manifesto"—and I must say I feel like warning you that our friend Mr. Pollock is inclined to exaggerate a little. I've never "lost faith in myself." I don't do that. If I do any faith-losing, it's in other people, not in myself. You know that I'm a "hard and ruthless woman." At least, I'd like to be.

■   ■   ■

To DeWitt Emery

August 14, 1941

Dear Mr. Emery:

Thank you for recommending me as a speaker in Chicago. I should be very glad to speak there—provided I'm really allowed to say something important and uncompromising. I'm no good at all as a polite speaker to an audience that agrees with me. During the [Wendell Willkie 1940 presidential] campaign, I was at my best among hecklers, on street corners and on 14th Street. I suppose that's my fighting instinct.

I have quite a few things to report to you. A few days ago I saw Gloria Swanson and had a nice long talk with her. She is really a splendid person. She feels as strongly about our cause as she did during the campaign—but she feels as we do, that our side is not doing enough. She said that she was not interested in another one of those "preserve democracy" organizations. So I was delighted to explain to her that that's precisely what we *don't* intend to organize, and I gave her a copy of my "Manifesto." Next morning, she telephoned me very early—and I can't repeat what she said about the "Manifesto," it would sound too much like boasting on my part. The important thing is that she said it was precisely what she believed, and she would fight for a cause and an organization like ours. Now we can count her in on our Committee—and she said she will introduce me to several prominent men who can be useful to us, as Committee members and as backers. So I'm very happy about it and hoping for the best.

■ ■ ■

To Gloria Swanson, actress and later AR's colleague in pro-individualist causes

September 8, 1941

Dear Miss Swanson:

I have seen *Father Takes a Wife* and I want to congratulate you on your magnificent performance. It was a delight to see you again on the screen. The audience cheered when your first close-up came on, so I know that everybody felt as I did.

I think RKO did not do you justice in the story they gave you. There was not enough of you—and too much of the minor characters. And your personality deserved a much more startling, original kind of part. You *are* an individualist in every best sense of the word—and your part should have been that of some exceptional character, not of a conventional one. Your greatness lies in being so *different*—and your part should have matched your talent. I hope the studio will realize this in your next picture for which all of us will be waiting impatiently.

Until then—thank you for giving us a chance to see again the kind of artistry that most pictures can no longer offer us today.

■ ■ ■

To DeWitt Emery

September 10, 1941

Dear Mr. Emery:

I was quite simply thrilled to hear that you had spoken about me to Henry Ford and read to him parts of my "Manifesto." I am a natural-born hero worshipper, but I find damn few heroes to worship—and he's one of my last few, because he is a symbol of the capitalist system at its best. Did you read to him the last part of the "Manifesto"—the part about the collectives of capitalists that destroy capitalism? I think that's the part that should appeal to him and that he, above all people, would understand.

Is there any possible way for me to see him? Could you arrange that perhaps? If it were possible, I'd travel to Dearborn or to the bottom of hell. I am perfectly certain that if I could speak to him for half an hour (uninterrupted), I could get him to back us and we wouldn't need anything or anybody else. I may be wrong and too sure of myself, but I don't think so. I would not be so certain of my ability to convince any other man, but I *am* certain about Ford, if he is what I think he is, judging by his public record.

If you cannot arrange this, could you arrange to have him read a letter I'd write? I think I could make it brief and convincing—but I won't bother if it has to go through half a dozen secretaries. If we could get it to him personally and if he would give us just the attention necessary to read it— we might be able to accomplish a lot.

As to my working for P & E—I'd be delighted, if I can really go ahead with the cause. No, I'm not going to get "damned mad" about being offered a salary. I told you that I had to have a salary if I were to give the work my full time, and I won't be any good unless I give it my full time. The job I have now takes more than eight hours a day—sometimes it's twelve and more—so I couldn't do any real work until I quit this. If I were a capitalist, I'd much rather work for the cause as a volunteer—but, unfortunately, I am only a proletarian defender of Capitalism, than which there is no worse thing to be. If I were a defender of Communism, I'd be a Hollywood millionaire-writer by now, with a swimming pool and a private orchestra to play the Internationale. As it is, I have to work for my living. So I'm quite definitely for sale—all of me above the neck—to anyone on our side who really intends to work for our side. This is the best way I know to say "thank you." Seriously, though, I'd be very happy to work for you—and I hope you will really start soon on the kind of campaign we need.

I spoke to Mr. Gall on the phone—he said that he has sent the "Manifesto" to the vice president of the N.A.M.—for his okay on arranging to finance us. I wish you could help me there—I don't know just how one goes about pushing people for financing, and I think the N.A.M. crowd could be made to finance us, but they need pressure and reminders. They seem terribly slow, at least about this—and yet they still profess great interest and desire to help us.

There is no evidence of either a meeting with or letter to Henry Ford.

■   ■   ■

To DeWitt Emery

October 4, 1941

Dear Mr. Emery:

Here is the outline of the Organization Plan which we discussed. This is only a brief, general plan, covering the most important points. You will notice the main precautions which I mention to keep the organization from being kidnapped by the wrong element, in particular the absence of general elections. This is most essential—or the whole thing will be snatched right from under our feet as soon as it shows signs of succeeding.

I read your Memorandum of September 24 with great interest. There is only one suggestion I should like to make here: I think the tentative name you propose for the organization, "American Neighbors," is very wrong. The name of an organization is its trademark and its slogan. It must suggest some idea of what the organization stands for. It must have a certain ring, an inspiring quality. "American Neighbors" is wrong because: 1. The first thing it brings to mind is the "Good Neighbor" Policy; people's first impression will be that it has something to do with South America. 2. It is actually meaningless—because it could mean anything; it doesn't convey any suggestion of our cause. 3. It is too deliberately prosaic; it's not inspiring; personally, if I heard of an organization by that name, I would not join it—I'd distrust it. Whatever name we decide upon, it must not be anywhere in these categories.

Now, as to the article "The Evolution of Freedom" which you sent me for comment, I think it is extremely bad. It is so confused, so involved that it's impossible in places to understand what the author is talking about. It seems to be written by an amateur determined to sound like a professor, with all the worst qualities of a pseudo-academic style. Of one thing I am certain: *the person who wrote it is not on our side.* Trust the nose of a good bloodhound on this subject—I can always *smell* the quality of a person's convictions. The author might believe (might, but I doubt it) that he is a defender of capitalism, but his thinking is muddled and his real inclinations show through.

For instance:

1. The idea that Nazism is worse than Communism. That's pure Communist Party Line nowadays. Any sincere defender of capitalism must oppose both these "isms" as equal evils. And of the two, Communism is much the greater menace in this country. Anyone who doesn't realize this is tainted with a great big dose of New Deal germs, whether he knows it or not.

2. The author's definitions of the ideologies of Communism and Fascism are so grossly unfair that out of a whole mess of semi-incomprehensible sentences only one thing stands out clearly: a defense of Communism. I quote: "Communistic aims have been: to equalize opportunity, to make men free under representative government, to assure abundance for all, and to eliminate private profits." Oh yeah? This is as beautiful—and dishonest—a sales talk for Communism as I've ever read. The rest of that sequence is practically double-talk, so its only purpose seems to have been the above glowing definition—introduced "objectively." Is that ineptitude? Or intention?

3. The author's argument against Communism is reduced to that old, old one about "the-ideals-are-noble-but-the-practice-is-evil." Well, *THAT'S* precisely the Party Line of all pinks and New Dealers. They all hate Stalin, but love Communism. This kind of propaganda is no service to our system of free private enterprise. It's the surest and quickest way to undermine it. Communism must be fought *not* on the grounds of its practice, but *precisely* on the grounds of its *theoretical ideals.*

4. The author talks about evaluating ideologies—and hasn't the faintest idea of what constitutes an ideology. He doesn't know how to think down to fundamentals. Such a sentence as: "Religious freedom has to come first—historically, as in our Bill of Rights—for without the assumption that men strive towards the good, such political concepts as 'the betterment of society' and 'the general welfare' would be entirely meaningless"—such a

sentence is pure drivel. It sounds big and means just exactly nothing. What is "good"? Are "good" and religion synonymous? Can't one strive for "good" outside of religion? Where's the meaning—and so what, if any? One doesn't found ideologies upon a great big vague assumption like that. If one were to present such a sentence as an argument to the young intellectuals who are leaning to the left nowadays because they are desperately seeking an honest faith—they'd laugh.

5. The author has got his history all mixed up. *Where* on earth did he get the idea that religious freedom preceded political freedom in history? That's simply rubbish. There's never been a society that had religious freedom before it had political freedom. There's no such case in history. When the pilgrim fathers came here, they had political freedom, but no religious freedom; the Puritans had plenty of religious restrictions and persecutions. England had the Magna Charta in 1215—and the Inquisition under Bloody Mary in the XVI century. No country, nowhere, at no time, had any "freedoms" until political freedom was given reality by the economic freedom of capitalism. Again, this made me wonder about the author: was it sheer ignorance—or a subtle little job of boring from within—with the object of assuring people that it might be all right to lose our political freedom since it would not interfere with the freedom of our souls? (Note Mr. Roosevelt's latest on "religious freedom" in Soviet Russia.)

6. The author's conclusion—a demand for "economic democracy"—is more than dubious. Just what does he mean by the "right to labor"? If he means the right of a worker to work in spite of a strike—it's one thing. But if he means that the government must guarantee a job to every man—that's quite another. No good propagandist could allow himself to be vague and muddled on a big point like that—unless the muddle is intentional. And the only sentences that seem to stand out clearly (all through page 6) point to the second meaning—jobs guaranteed by the government. See the vague something on top of page 6 about "abuse of economic power through technological advancement or the reduction of enterprise." What is being defended and what is being attacked here, for heaven's sake? See the mention of Soviet Russia as seeking "economic freedom." But, above all, see the very last paragraph of the article: "When democracies fail to evolve the economic democracy that is required of them, they endanger the political freedoms that they have long established." Boy, oh boy! If this isn't collectivist Party Line, I'll eat *Das Kapital* unabridged. The loudest hue and cry of all pinks, reds and liberals is now "Economic Democracy." That's the standard polite term for Communism. Thomas Mann has been yelping for the last four years about "economic democracy." Another word

for it is "Extended Democracy." What in hell are we asked to *evolve*? Capitalism does not need to "evolve" economic freedom—it has it, or did have. It's the whole heart of the capitalist system. But you notice the author does not speak of "economic freedom"—he speaks of "economic democracy." Such a little difference! An innocent one? Not on your life!

Of course, the standard technique of good "Trojan Horses" is never to come all-out for Communism. It's always to be "objective." It always goes like this: muddle the issue, throw a few bones to the "right," but be sure the bones are pretty lean, then bear down heavily on the "left" and make certain that the "left" is what stands out best in the reader's mind after he's through. Read Walter Duranty, Harold Laski, Dorothy Thompson and the rest of the experts. It's a set formula. And this author has followed it faithfully. That is why the paragraphs which were marked in red (on page 4) do not impress me. Just to say "Men desire freedom" means nothing. All the pinks talk about "freedom." (Even four freedoms.) To conduct a subversive campaign under the cover of a few capitalistic-sounding slogans is an old, old trick.

This article has no author's name and I know nothing about the organization that released it. If the author is honest and well-meaning, then he is one hell of a poor propagandist for our side. But my guess would be that he is clever—too clever. My guess is that he's a Trojan thoroughbred.

You did not say why you were interested in this article. If you are considering using it—or hiring its author—or collaborating with this organization in some manner—then my opinion is: *NO!!!* (I wish I knew how to reproduce a scream on paper, for that's what I'd like it to be.) Perhaps you sent it as a test for me—or just sent it casually, and I took much too long in discussing it. But I was frankly worried when I read it—worried about the nature of your connection with these people or your planned connection—and I felt that I must give you as complete a report on it as I could.

Enough for one letter?

By the way, do you read my letters? I wrote to you in the last one that I had moved, but you sent me a letter to my old address. So I'll repeat myself: the new address is: The Bromley, 139 East 35th Street, New York City. My new phone number is: Murray Hill 6-6549.

Hope you didn't have as hard a time moving as I did. I'm just beginning to get settled now. All this and moving too is almost more than a human being can handle. But I guess I'll survive—and hope you will, too.

Of the subsequent letters from Emery in AR's files, none refers to AR's criticism of "The Evolution of Freedom." The proposed organization discussed with Emery and Channing Pollock was never established.

■   ■   ■

To Archibald Ogden, her editor for *The Fountainhead* at Bobbs-Merrill

Second-Hand Lives was the original title of *The Fountainhead.* It was Ogden who convinced his employers to publish the book, telling them: "If this isn't the book for you, then I'm not the editor for you."

December 8, 1941

Dear Mr. Ogden:

I should like to have included in our contract for the publication of my novel at present entitled *Second-Hand Lives*, the following paragraph which appeared in my contracts with the publishers of my first novel:

"It is understood and agreed that no changes of any nature whatsoever will be made from the copy as submitted without the approval of the Author."

I shall, however, welcome the editorial suggestions which you might care to make, and give them earnest consideration.

■   ■   ■

To Archibald Ogden

February 19, 1942

Dear Mr. Ogden:

You made me feel terribly guilty by your nice letter while I owed you one. Of course I shall be delighted to have lunch with you on the 24th and then I'll ask you to forgive me in person.

But to prepare my defense, I must explain that I have not written to you sooner because I have been (and still am) in an orgy of writing the novel. It has been a day and night job, literally. The record, so far, was one day when I started writing at 4 p.m. and stopped at 1 p.m. the next day (with one interruption for dinner). I can not do that often, but that time I did my best writing. I have gone for two or three days at a time without undressing—I'd just fall asleep on the couch for a few hours, then get up and go on. But I'll make myself clean and respectable by Tuesday.

I wanted to surprise you with the completed second part. I am not quite finished with it yet, but will be in a week or so. That will be a big load off my mind, because it gets easier to write further on. If you are not one of those people who think that an author is the last judge of his own work, I will say that I think the book is going very well so far.

Thank you very much for your most intelligent criticism of *We the Living*. I think you are right in everything you said about it. This is the second time that you have analyzed my work better than I could have explained it myself. As an editor, you seem to be the answer to an author's prayer. I knock on wood—but I don't think the precaution is necessary.

> *Among Ogden's comments on* We the Living*: "In* Second-Hand Lives *you have hit on something more fundamental—more universal—than in* We the Living*. . . . Andrei [Taganov] was no Roark. We could sympathize with his ideal, perhaps, but not his ideas. . . . If it were a manuscript coming to my desk by an unknown author, I would say, 'Here's a gal who is going places, let's take a chance on her.' With the new manuscript you know my feeling: 'Here's a gal who has arrived, we can't afford to miss her.' "*

■ ■ ■

To Gerald Loeb, vice president of E. F. Hutton and Co.

Loeb was a budding writer and a friend of Frank Lloyd Wright. The origin of Loeb's six-year correspondence with AR is not known.

January 15, 1943

Dear Mr. Loeb:

I suppose you won't trust me at all now—because I like your story "He and She" very much. I think it is a very good story, but it has one major technical fault. It is not written in short story form.

The characterizations are excellent and it is amazing how much you have told about the two characters in such a brief space. I loved your indirect method of characterization—by small, objective, eloquent facts, rather than by explicit statements from the author. You did not *say* that the woman was no good and that the man was an admirable character—you *showed* it. I don't know whether you noticed that this is my own method of writing. I think it is a difficult method and you have used it extremely well.

The technical fault lies in the fact that you never brought the story down to the present, that is, to a concrete incident taking place in detail before the eyes of the reader. You have told it all in the general narrative, in the manner of a synopsis. So that after one finishes it, one has the feeling of having read the outline of a novel, not a short story. The first requirement of a short story is that it must be built around one single incident. It can be an incident which is complete in itself, or it can be an incident which summarizes and climaxes a long development of events, but it must be a single incident, like a sharp focus. Otherwise it is not the construction of a short story, but of a novel, no matter what the length. Length is *not* the standard by which one differentiates a short story from a novel; the method of construction *is*. One cannot take a broad view of a subject, such as one takes for a novel, and say: "I will make it a short story by telling it briefly." One must take a subject which can be brought into one focus, *one concrete incident*, and build the narrative around it. If the material cannot be treated in such a way, then it is not material for a short story.

Now, "He And She" *can* be treated in the proper short story form. To do that, you must show one scene between your characters in detail, with action and dialogue. That scene must be a crucial one, *not* just an incidental one chosen at random, but a scene that climaxes the rest and resolves the theme of the story. By these requirements, you can see for yourself what scene it must be. What is the theme of your story? It is in the last two lines: "Well, women are women and it is useless to try to change them. He had found out once more." The scene in which he finds it out, the scene where the woman shows her real character and the man receives a dreadful, tragic disappointment—the scene which takes place between the paragraphs of Part Five and Part Six—*that* scene must be written and presented in detail. Then you'll have a proper short story form.

I suspect that you won't like this suggestion because having that scene unstated is very effective. I got a jolt when I read it. But it is the effect produced by an eloquent pause in an intelligent conversation. It is not right in a short story—because the reader has been reading a long general narrative, getting acquainted with the characters and waiting for the climax when he would see them in action. That unwritten scene is the logical climax. If the reader does not see it—nor any other specific scene—he feels cheated. And you cannot choose another scene for a focus, because in a short story it is the crucial scene that must be featured.

If you make this change, I think you will have an excellent story that will sell. The situation is tragic and very human, the characters are excellently presented, the man is most appealing and will hold the interest and sympathy of the readers.

I do not object at all to the method of using the "he" and "she," and giving the characters no names. It underscores the theme—by saying, in effect, that it is not a matter of just this one man and this one woman, but that they are the symbols of a deep tragedy which will always take place between men and women of this nature. I did not find it confusing—except in one minor instance: on page 2, line 4. The sentences read: "But she said yes. So they met and she went to the delicatessen to buy some ready things." The first "she" refers to the girlfriend, the second to the heroine, and it is confusing for the moment. I would suggest that you change it to: "But the girl said yes." Keep the "she" exclusively for the heroine—and you will achieve the effect you want without confusion.

I would suggest that you eliminate the subtitles of "Part One," "Part Two," etc., and also the numbering of paragraphs. It is not done in a short story—and it only stresses the impression of the outline of a novel broken into parts and chapters. A short story must be treated as a single unit. You will achieve the same effect by simple paragraph breaks.

As a minor compliment, let me congratulate you on some of your very good sentences. They have the quality of a calm, penetrating intelligence, and a nice kind of bitter, humorous wisdom. For instance: "He wanted to start at the bottom and work to the top—not start with illusion and work down to reality." I think this is very well put—considering what that sentence covers.

In conclusion, just as a personal remark, I want to say that it was very interesting to me to discover how you judge people. You place competence above all, as the test virtue which determines the whole character of a person. So do I. But I don't know anyone else who does, or who understands how and why it *is* the test virtue. Howard Roark does.

■ ■ ■

To D. L. Chambers, president of Bobbs-Merrill

March 30, 1943

Dear Mr. Chambers:

Now that the last page proof [of *The Fountainhead*] is done and I am back on this earth, I want to thank you for the many valuable suggestions which you marked on the proofs, and for the careful attention you have given my novel.

Will you give my thanks to Mr. Van Riper for the report he wrote on my book, and to the two young ladies whom I know only as "Libbets" and "Pat" for their notes on the copy. I have not always agreed with the notes, but I found many of them valid, and I appreciate all the work they put into this job.

I have found it very pleasant to deal with your New York office, and I must report to you, most gratefully, that working with Mr. Ogden has been extremely helpful and valuable to me. I do think he is a miracle as an editor. I hope *The Fountainhead* will be successful—for the sake of all of us.

■ ■ ■

To Archibald Ogden

May 6, 1943

Dear Archie:

Thank you for your letter. It was very nice of you to wish to cheer me up—and that is why your letter was heartbreaking to me. If I were up against malice, I could fight it. When I'm up against genuinely good intentions—not backed up by facts—I'm licked.

Apparently your genius *is* that of an editor and lies in the printed word—not in any other form of reality. So I'm going to put it all down on paper. Maybe you'll understand. Please try to.

You say: "I guess it's your faith in others I sometimes worry about." I don't know what that word means. If you mean "faith" in a religious sense—in the sense of blind acceptance—I don't have any faith in anything or anybody, I never have had and never will have. I go by facts and reason. I had neither faith nor nonfaith in you when I first met you. I formed no opinion of you until I had some concrete evidence on which to base an opinion. I trust and admire you as an editor, because of the intelligent judgment you exhibited while we were working on the novel. This is not "faith." It is much sounder. It is my reasonable conviction.

What evidence has the firm of Bobbs-Merrill given me of its competence to handle the business side of a book's publication?

Whom is it that I must have faith in, and on what grounds?

You have said that I don't know the business side and must let those in charge handle it. I shall list what I know about the methods I have observed other publishers using.

When a book is supposed to be a "lead" and a "special":

1. It is publicized months in advance. There has been no mention of my book anywhere.

2. The author is given publicity. I was given nothing.

3. Posters and display material are prepared. I've had none.

4. Window displays are arranged. I've had none.

5. Circulars are sent to mailing lists. I've had none.

6. A party of some sort is arranged for the trade. I've had none.

7. Ads are taken in both Sunday papers and in the dailies. I have one ad coming.

8. The book is issued in time to get reviews on publication. Mine was rushed through in a manner that gave nobody but an ass like Harry Hansen time to read it. I hold Bobbs-Merrill responsible for that review. It is obvious that Hansen hasn't even read the book—he's skimmed through it. And our publication date was chosen because the firm wanted bills to come in one month in advance!

Now I don't say that I advocate necessarily all of those methods or any one in particular. I only know that those are the methods used. *You've used none of them.* Perhaps you have better methods of your own. Very well. *TELL ME WHAT THEY ARE.* Name them. I don't want compliments, I don't want consolations, I don't want any talk about anyone's "faith." I want facts.

If you can tell me what Bobbs-Merrill have done for the book, I shall be delighted to be proved wrong.

I use the word "you" in the above as meaning Bobbs-Merrill as a business firm, not you as a person. In your own specific job, that of editor, you have proved yourself superlative. I have not changed my opinion on that. I repeat that I think you are a genius as an editor. I know how much you have done for the book in that respect and how much I owe you.

But I am not at all clear about your position or authority on the business side of the firm. So when I criticize that, you will have to decide whether it applies to you or not. I honestly don't know. I am criticizing the behavior of the firm. If you had authority in those matters, then the fault is yours. If you hadn't, then my words are no reflection upon you. In either case, they are not a reflection upon you as an editor.

You are too intelligent and honest a man to say the sort of things you said in your letter. Archie, doesn't reason and logic mean anything to you at all? Why do you say things like that? *WHY?* Won't you tell me, as a gesture of charity, if nothing else? I'm actually begging you to give me an explanation. Why do you ask me to have faith in a publicity department that forces reviewers to call in and inquire whether the author of your "important" book is a man or a woman? Is that a proof of competence? Is that what one does to promote a new "discovery"? I suppose *faith*—the blind faith of a moron—is all one can feel for publicists who do this. Certainly not respect or confidence. Is that the kind of faith you ask me to feel? To me, that performance on the part of a publicity department is either criminal negligence or plain lousy incompetence. In the name of all logic and honesty, I don't see any other alternative, or explanation. If I'm wrong—tell me what the publicity department has done for me.

I did have faith. That's where *I'm* guilty. Since the first of January, when I delivered my script to you, I never asked what your publicity department was doing. I didn't interfere, I didn't hint, I didn't ask for anything. Observe the results.

Now we come to the beautiful ad I'm getting on Sunday. I have told you, every indication has told you, advance reactions have told you and you have agreed that the book must be sold as an important, challenging, intellectual novel on a great modern issue—and *not* as a cheap story on architecture. Until I annoyed you by tactlessly butting in into what you said was none of my business—you didn't even take the trouble to read the first and only ad for the book you're stacking your reputation on! When you read it, you saw that I was right to worry. Don't talk to me about my book "not depending on one line in an ad." It doesn't. It doesn't depend on any one of the other things which Bobbs-Merrill haven't done. But what, in Christ's name, *does* it depend on? My wonderful genius? Is that what you expect to sell books for you? Do you believe that publishers succeed or fail on mere luck—the luck of getting or not getting good books? Do you believe that it's the books that do it? Then what are publishers for? What is it that good publishers do for their authors? Just set up the print? Take the credit if the book succeeds and blame the author if it doesn't?

I don't mind the fact that your advertising appropriation is limited. But precisely when an appropriation is limited one must weigh the tone and nature and every word of an ad most carefully, to get the utmost good out of it. The horrible crap you read to me over the phone wouldn't sell a book to a half-wit. It is not intellectual appeal, it is not commercial appeal, it is not even good blurb-writing. It is just simply dull and meaningless. It says nothing. It's just wasted space, wasted words, wasted money.

Don't talk to me about people who must be good because they make their living in advertising. There are incompetents and fools making a living for a while in any profession. The fact of holding a given job at a given time does not prove that one is good at it. Judge by the product and the results. Successful publishers don't employ advertising copy writers who put out stuff like that. It's not only the overemphasis on architecture, it's not only such dreadful words as "Fakers and Prophets"—which certainly wouldn't arouse anyone's interest—it's the fact that the main idea has not even been hinted at, that your one good line about the ego has been dropped, that nothing in the whole goddamn mess gives any indication of the book's theme, importance or seriousness.

To make things nicer, all you have to show the public so far is one ghastly kind of review. And your ad will merely support it. Your ad will tell the public, in effect: "Yes, that's right, this is just a pretty novel about architecture." It couldn't have been planned better if it had been done on purpose. There's the good start you've given the book. If the book goes, it will have this handicap to overcome. You've begun by placing an obstacle in its way. Now you have a period of ten days (until whatever reviews we get on the 16th) during which the book will be dead. At the end of the ten days, Mr. Chambers will decide that it's not worth advertising, because it is not selling.

This could have been prevented if you had taken the time to look at that ad. You didn't. The advertising agency, the publicity department, the sales department are all sensitive people whose feelings must not be hurt by outside curiosity or advice. An advance inquiry would be rude interference. Only an author is the kind of person who must listen politely to everyone and anyone, never get offended, accept every suggestion and consider every criticism made by copy readers and writers of popular novels of the light fiction type. I suppose that's because an author deals in such dry, routine stuff as creative writing which does not make a person emotional or sensitive. Archie, if this sounds like nasty sarcasm, remember that this is what *you* told me. Not so crudely, but in effect.

Now let me do you justice. You *did* convince your salesmen of the book's merits, so that the sale has been good, or so I'm told. It was because *you* talked to them personally. (But that sale won't do us any good if the books are returned.) You *did* send out excellent letters about the book. It's because *you* wrote them personally. You *did* give me an excellent ad in the two trade sheets. It was good because *you and I* rewrote it. It was pretty awful originally. Why couldn't you take the time to do that again on the much more important and expensive matter of our first Sunday ad? Why couldn't you bring me the copy and let me express an opinion? You didn't have to take my opinion, only to consider it—and I had proved myself helpful once. I know it wasn't indifference or laziness on your part. It was your goodwill, politeness and "faith" in your advertising agency. That's what makes it much worse than intentional negligence. There's your best example of the results of "faith." Everything you've done on your own has been good and able. You turn aside at the most important moment—not for any good cause, not on any logical reason—but for the sake of courtesy to a lot of worthless people. I know your career depends on this book as much as mine. You're sacrificing it—for the sake of humanitarian kindness to other people. There's a rather tragic illustration of the fact that I really wrote the truth in my book. It was not just a story, Archie. It works that way—in international politics, in private life or in the publishing business. It's good intentions that are murdering all of us.

Archie, darling, *goodwill* is no proof or guarantee of anything whatsoever on earth. So it's perfectly pointless to assure me how much you want my book to succeed. I know it. I believe you. What I don't believe is that the firm of Bobbs-Merrill knows how to sell a book. If desire were all, then any writer would have a bestseller. If an author came to you and said: "Here's a manuscript, it's good because I want it so very much to be good," you'd throw him out. You don't buy novels because their authors are sincere in *wanting* them to be good. You buy on the basis of performance. You judge by concrete and reasonable standards. *NOT* by anybody's faith, sincerity, hope, desire or the fourth dimension.

And yet you ask me to feel confidence that my book is being properly handled merely because you all want so much to have it succeed. Bobbs-Merrill have made a mess of my book's release in every way that I can detect. JUST EXACTLY ON *WHAT* BASIS must I have confidence? If I'm wrong, tell me. But don't speak of "faith."

Do you wonder now why Bobbs-Merrill don't get any good books? Do you wonder why authors rush to Simon & Schuster? Is this the way you hope to establish a reputation, to acquire prestige and a good list? In exchange for what?

Bobbs-Merrill have paid me—for a year and a half of unspeakable and unbelievable work—less than the amount they paid in that year to their cheapest stenographer. Our contract reads that they have the right to publish the book in any way they please. There is an implication of honor in such a clause. It is presumed that the publisher will exert his honest best effort to publish and sell a book in the best way possible to him. So honor is all I have to rely on now. Honor, honesty and integrity are matters of intelligence, reason and action, not of goodwill, emotion, sentiment, desires, instincts and mush. Let the conscience of whoever is concerned—yourself,

Mr. Chambers, Mr. Baker, Miss Reynolds and all others—tell you what must be done now.

All I can add is that my life is at stake. Also yours.

■ ■ ■

To DeWitt Emery

May 17, 1943

Dear Mr. Emery:

I am enclosing a review of the book from yesterday's Sunday *Times* [Lorine Pruette's review of *The Fountainhead*]. It explains, better than I could do it myself, what connection there is between a story of architecture and our political cause. It shows why I consider my book important for our side. This review is the first one to state my theme clearly and honestly. The other New York reviewers (four of them, in the daily papers) have ignored the theme completely and spoken of the book only as a story about architecture. Since the theme is overstated (it's practically in every line of the novel) such an omission could not be accidental. One case could be ascribed to stupidity. Four of them can be explained only by intention.

That is why I thought of the plan I discussed with you over the phone. If the Reds and some of our own cowardly "conservatives" do not want to let it be known that a book has come out on the theme of the Individual against the Collective, I want to break through and make it known, in a very loud manner, in spite of them. There is a vast audience for such a theme. The mood of the whole country is going our way. The people are with us—only the intellectuals remain Pink-New Deal-Collectivist. It's a blockade and it must be broken.

In the last ten years, the Reds have done a good job of building up literary celebrities for their own purposes, such as Orson Welles, Clifford Odets, John Steinbeck, etc. These celebrities then appear on Red committees, endorse Red causes, build up other Red names, and the racket works as the radicals' best propaganda method. It's a monopoly now. *Not one* new novelist or playwright of our side has been allowed to break through in the last decade. I think it's time our side took some action. It's time we realized—as the Reds do—that spreading our ideas in the form of fiction is a great weapon, because it arouses the public to an *emotional*, as well as intellectual response to our cause. Call it a sugarcoating—though I don't like to say that. It works. Look at the Reds to see how it works. Look how savagely they have defended the art field from all intrusions of conservatives. They know its value.

So I think that my book will give our side the opportunity we need—if there are any intelligent "reactionaries" willing to stand by me. I want to find an organization or, preferably, a private person who would undertake to finance a campaign to publicize my book *from the political-ideological angle* on a large scale—as the books of Willkie, Quentin Reynolds, Vincent Sheean, Steinbeck and the rest of the comrades have been publicized. My publishers are doing quite well with the book, but they can't undertake the kind of campaign I have in mind and they can't make it political.

Of course, I have a selfish motive in this—such a campaign would give me a name on a national scale. But I believe in selfish motives—and so do you, and so does any intelligent supporter of the capitalist system. However, you know me well enough to know that my financial gain is not my first concern in this case. I want the book and the ideas of this book to be spread all over the country. When you read it, you'll see what an indictment of the New Deal it is, what it does to the "humanitarians" and what effect it could have on the next election—although I never mention the New Deal by name. People who've read it told me that, without any prompting on my part. And to prove to any potential backer that I'm not after his money to swell my own royalties, I am willing to give him such share of my rights in the book as he would consider proper to cover his risk.

I would still profit by the buildup. That will be my gain—and *that* will also be the gain of our side. You know what a good propagandist I am and what I can do, as witness that little manifesto I wrote in five days. Let our side now build me up into a "name"—then let me address meetings, head drives and endorse committees. I think I can do better than the Steinbecks and Orson Welleses—and God knows they've done plenty for their side. I can be a real asset to our "reactionaries," and I say it as a matter of fact, not of conceit. I have always thought that the reactionaries should discover me. But I had nothing concrete to offer them. Now I have. Let them get behind me. I performed a miracle in getting a book like this published in these times, when the whole publishing world is trembling before Washington. Now let the reactionaries help me spread the book. If the book goes over big, it will break the way for other writers of our side. If it's allowed to be killed by the Reds—our good industrialists had better not expect anyone else to stick his neck out in order to try to save them from getting their throats cut.

That is why I would be most grateful if you could help me find an intelligent "Tory" to back the book in this way. I saw Mr. Edmunds on the day after I spoke to you—he was about to leave for Washington, so I don't know whether he has written to you about our conversation. He was very nice and he gave me two leads: one to reach the Du Ponts, the other to reach Senator Hawkes. I am following them up and will hope for the best. But I am particularly anxious to approach Henry Ford and Helen Frick, and I wonder whether it would be possible for you to help me with that.

As to the commercial aspects of the book's future right now, it looks very promising. We have had considerable reorders already and I've had a movie offer, which I am not in a hurry to accept. I want to see how things go and I haven't even seen the out-of-town reviews as yet. But none of that is important at the moment—it's the political side of it that I am anxious to push, and the publishers or booksellers can't help me with that. They all have to be neutral and they're all scared of controversy. It's our side—if there is such a thing—that should help me now.

■   ■   ■

To Lorine Pruette, reviewer of *The Fountainhead* for the *New York Times*

In her review on May 16, Pruette wrote: "[Ayn Rand] has written a hymn in praise of the individual. . . . you will not be able to read this masterful book without thinking through some of the basic concepts of our times."

May 18, 1943

Dear Miss Pruette:

You have said that I am a writer of great power. Yet I feel completely helpless to express my gratitude to you for your review of my novel.

You are the only reviewer who had the courage and honesty to state the theme of *The Fountainhead*. Four other reviews of it have appeared so far, in the daily papers—and not one of them mentioned the theme nor gave a single hint about the issue of the Individual against the Collective. They all spoke of the book as a novel about architecture. Such an omission could not be accidental. You have said that one cannot read the book "without thinking through some of the basic concepts of our times." You know, as I do, that the theme is actually overstated in my novel, that it's in every line. If one reviewer had missed the theme, it could be ascribed to stupidity. Four of them can be explained only by dishonesty and cowardice. And it terrified me to think our country had reached such a state of depravity that one was no longer permitted to speak in defense of the Individual, that the mere mention of such an issue was to be evaded and hushed up as too dangerous.

That is why I am grateful to you in a way much beyond literary matters and for much more than the beautiful things you said about me and the book, although they did make me very happy. I am grateful for your great integrity as a person, which saved me from the horror of believing that this country is lost, that people are much more rotten than I presented them in the book and that there is no intellectual decency left anywhere.

If it is not considered unethical for an author to want to meet a reviewer, I would like very much to meet you. I have met so many Ellsworth Tooheys that it would be a relief to see a person of a different order.

THANK YOU.

■   ■   ■

To Benjamin DeCasseres, syndicated columnist for the *New York Journal-American*

In his review of *The Fountainhead* on May 16, DeCasseres praised AR's hero Howard Roark as "an uncompromising individualist" and "one of the most inspiring characters in modern American literature." In his May 23 column, he termed *The Fountainhead* "the most original and daring book of fiction written in this country" and "a bull in the Socialistic-Communistic china shop."

June 13, 1943

Dear Mr. DeCasseres:

Thank you very much for your review of my novel *The Fountainhead*. I was glad that you liked Howard Roark. When I wrote the book I thought that Roark would become a testing-stone for people—they would betray their own nature by the way they'd take him. And it has proved to be so. Those who understand Roark are men with a sense of human dignity. Those who find him "unsympathetic" are secondhanders, rotten at the core, rotted by collectivism.

I have been a reader of your column for years—in fact, my husband and I take the *Journal-American* because of its columnists. We got angry at the *Journal* just once and dropped it, then had to go back because we missed you. So it was thrilling to me, in a personal, non-professional way, to see you writing about me.

I have wanted to meet you for a long time. If *The Fountainhead* can serve as an introduction, would you let me know and give me an appointment to see you?

■　■　■

To Samuel B. Pettengill, a former congressman and head of the Transportation Association of America

June 13, 1943

Dear Mr. Pettengill:

I received your letter with the copy of your column referring to me, and on the same day I got a clipping of your column from the *Hartford* (Conn.) *Times*. I can't tell you how much I appreciate it. I am very grateful to you, not only in a personal, but in a wider sense: it was encouraging to see a prominent figure of our side willing to help a new fighter. The indifference of most of our conservative national leaders to young beginners who wish to serve our cause, has ruined us and delivered the whole intellectual field to the Reds. A new "conservative" writer, these days, is left in the position of having his throat cut by an organized Red gang, while the leaders of his side look on, faintly bored, or turn away. That is what drives all the young intellectuals to Communism. Thank you for being an exception.

Incidentally, I thought your column was excellent. It is time someone stopped all that nonsense about Soviet Russia's "achievements." What achievements?

Thank you also for your little leaflet "The Welfare State," which you enclosed. I have given it to a few friends. It works.

I shall be eager to hear your opinion of *The Fountainhead*. It is actually an illustrated message, in fiction form, of my "Individualist Manifesto." I have taken the basic principles of the "Manifesto" and shown them in concrete action and in human terms, how they work, what they do to people, what are their psychological roots and their practical consequences. If you liked the "Manifesto," I think you will like and understand the book. I know, however, that it is a very long book. If you find yourself pressed for time, I would like to call your attention to two passages: Roark's speech (it starts on page 736) which is a complete statement of the moral philosophy of our side—and Toohey's speech (it starts on page 689) which is an exposition of the collectivist mind and of the humanitarian "world of the future." This is not to say, of course, that I am not anxious to have you read the whole novel. But these two passages will give you an idea of the nature of the book.

I think that the book can be of value to us in 1944. I am getting letters from readers who say that the book aroused them to fury against the "humanitarians" and made them want to "get the Tooheys out of Washington."

■ ■ ■

To George Bruce, a screenwriter, whose credits included *The Man in the Iron Mask* (1939) and *Two Years Before the Mast* (1946)

In Bruce's letter to AR, he called *The Fountainhead* "the most beautifully conceived and exquisitely executed work of fiction I have ever read."

June 19, 1943

Dear Mr. Bruce:

"Thank you" is an inadequate thing to say in exchange for a letter such as yours. Look at page 318-319 of *The Fountainhead*, the first meeting of Roark and Mallory. I am not a sculptor nor broke and jobless, but what Mallory felt in that scene is what I felt when I received your letter. Let that scene tell you how grateful I am to you. As a writer, you know what a letter like yours means to a writer.

May I ask where you found out my full name [Ayn Rand O'Connor] and address? I am deeply grateful that you cared for *The Fountainhead* enough to inquire about its author.

You say that you regret having to pursue "pure commercialism." I do not think there is anything wrong in that. To earn one's living is an honorable motive. Commercial writing becomes offensive only in those who hold it as the highest form of art, on the ground of majority appeal, and are incapable of doing anything else. You are obviously not one of those. It is my turn to envy you the ability to be commercially successful while preserving your own vision and standards.

■ ■ ■

To John C. Gall, prominent conservative attorney and later AR's attorney

July 4, 1943

Dear Mr. Gall:

You have really made me speechless and helpless. I do not know how to thank you for your letter. A reader's response such as yours is one of the real and rare rewards for being an author, a reward of which an author can feel legitimately proud. I have accepted very long ago and very sadly the fact that the people of our political side seldom back up our ideas with any action. That you did so and that you chose my book to do it makes me more than grateful.

I sent you *The Fountainhead* because I remembered our conversations here and knew that you were one of the few "conservatives" who would understand the philosophical roots of our cause, beyond the surface political slogans. A great many Republicans would be scared to death to recognize that altruism is the curse of the world and that as long as we go on screaming "service" and "self-sacrifice" louder than the New Deal we will never have a chance. In any encounter with collectivists it is always the acceptance of altruism as an ideal not to be questioned that defeats us. I wrote *The Fountainhead* to show, in human terms, just what that ideal actually means and where we must stand if we want to win. If we can make the word "altruism" become a shameful term, which it actually is, instead of the automatic trademark of virtue which people think it to be—we will get the Tooheys out of Washington someday.

As a kind of return present for all these copies of my book which you bought, I am sending you a copy of a book that came out recently—*The God of the Machine* by Isabel Paterson. I think it will interest you. It is the best and most complete statement of the basic principles of our side, and the greatest defense of capitalism I have ever read. It does for capitalism what *Das Kapital* did for the Reds, if such a comparison is not too offensive.

■   ■   ■

To Sylvia Bailey, a fan

July 5, 1943

Dear Mrs. Bailey:

Thank you for your fine letter. Perhaps I am not too far ahead of my time if I can find a reader such as yourself.

On the evidence of your letter, I don't think that you can be one of the "little people." Not if you respond as you did to Howard Roark. He is really a test for people—in my story and in real life. Only those with a sense of human dignity can and will like him.

I know that it is usually the most honest people who accept the doctrine of self-sacrifice as an ideal—with the most tragic consequences. If my book has helped you in any way to discard that doctrine and to find a different, positive faith in humanity, I am grateful to know that the book has accomplished its purpose.

By the way, perhaps your mistake is really a compliment—I am not "Mr." Rand, but "Miss." But I am glad if my writing sounds like that of a man.

■ ■ ■

To Leah T. Jones, a fan

July 5, 1943

Dear Mrs. Jones:

Thank you for the great compliment of your letter, not only as a compliment but for the understanding back of it.

It does mean a great deal to an author when a reader wants to read a book twice. I should, perhaps, apologize if my book kept you up till daylight, but I will do no such thing, because I am selfishly glad that it did.

I don't know whether I shall be in Cincinnati or Dayton, but if I am I wish you would call me up—I would be very happy to meet you.

■ ■ ■

To Thilo Schreiber, a fan

July 5, 1943

Dear Mr. Schreiber:

I am glad that you consider my book as I wanted to see it considered—as *American* literature. That is what Howard Roark meant—the American spirit. *The Fountainhead* is my contribution to keeping America what it was and must remain—the country of individualism.

I deeply appreciate your good wishes, and I can say that any book I shall ever write will always be in defense of the cause of the individual.

■ ■ ■

To Franklin Brewer, a longtime friend

July 6, 1943

Dear Franklin:

Thank you for your letter. I should add thank you for the things you said about my book, but that seems inadequate. You say that it is difficult to write about *The Fountainhead*, so you will understand me when I say that it is extremely difficult for me to thank those who like it. Both the book and those capable of responding to it mean too much to me. I will say only that I appreciate particularly your saying that *The Fountainhead* was to you "in the nature of a revelation and reaffirmation." I don't know how many people will understand the kind of reaffirmation that book is, but thank God for those who do, I firmly believe that they are the ones who will save the world—if it can be saved. I still think it can.

I had heard that you were in the Army, and I had been thinking of you, wondering whether you will discover that the book is out. So I was rather thrilled to get a letter from you beginning with "I have finished it!" You might remember that you practically witnessed some of the birth pangs of this book—it was in Stony Creek that I was going through the worst agonies, trying to work out the plot and outline. I suppose I may assume that you agree with me that it was worth it.

Now to answer your questions: yes, Dominique is entirely a brain-child. I have never met anyone from whom she could have been copied. No, I don't know Gloria Braggiotti, but I should be delighted to meet her if she reminds you of Dominique in any way. "Francon" is pronounced *Fran*-kon, with the accent on the first syllable, without a cedilla, it's a "k" not a "c" sound.

To answer your personal questions: Frank and I are very much the same as usual, or so it seems to me, I don't know that we ever change. We're still here in New York, and our apartment is as messy as ever—my fault—and it's full of cat hair from Tartallia. (This is Tartallia II, if you remember, not the same one we had in Stony Creek.) I am more or less taking a rest now, after the terrible rush I had to finish the book. No future plans at the moment, and no definite idea of what I'll do next. It is really wonderful to feel a right to be lazy for a while. Nick [Carter, Frank O'Connor's brother] is here in New York. Yes, he is writing and doing quite well; he's had several political booklets published, and has sold a short story to a magazine. Faith [Hersey, a longtime friend] is still working for the opera company; she is their press agent and doing excellently, they have grown into quite a big organization. She has been travelling all over the country and I have seen her only a few times in the last year. She was here recently and looked wonderful. She has acquired a new kind of assurance and cheerfulness—it made me very glad to see that.

As to your being in the Army, I would like to say that you have all my admiration. I don't mean that in the usual flag-waving way, I mean only that of all the classes of people in this war, I feel a true respect and a sense of loyalty only to those in the armed forces, and a great deal of very bitter contempt for all other groups of society. If you remember my views, you'll understand what I mean.

Since you say that you live on letters in the Army, I hope this will serve as one meal and as my small contribution.

■   ■   ■

To Tom Girdler, founder and chairman of Republic Steel and Vultee Aircraft

July 12, 1943

Dear Mr. Girdler:

I have just read the galleys of your book *The Right to Work*. They were given to me by a person who knew my political convictions and knew how much I would appreciate your book.

Allow me to express my deepest admiration for the way in which you have lived your life, for your gallant fight of 1937, for the courage you displayed then and are displaying again now when you attempt a truly heroic deed—a defense of the industrialist. Your book is an excellent document, beautifully written, exciting and challenging. Please accept my congratulations for it.

But as I read your book I could not help feeling that you came within an inch of the basic principle you wanted to state and missed it. All the facts to support it are there, but the statement is not. Please do not consider it presumptuous if I felt I must point it out to you. This is not in the nature of criticism, but of a tribute to the tremendous importance of your book's subject.

You wished to defend and justify the industrial manager as the true mover of civilization. All through your book one hears a bewildered indignation that society has failed to recognize him as such. May I tell you the reason of that failure? It is because the industrialist has never found the moral principle on which he must stand. He has stood on it in fact, he has built our entire civilization upon it—but what he has preached and believed has been its exact opposite. It is a terrible kind of reversal and the results have now caught up with us. The results are destroying the world.

The basic falsehood which the world has accepted is the doctrine that altruism is the ultimate ideal. That is, service to others as a justification and the placing of others above self as a virtue. Such an ideal is not merely impossible, it is immoral and vicious. And there is no hope for the world until enough of us come to realize this.

Man's first duty is not to others, but to himself. He can survive only through the function of his reasoning mind directed toward the conquest of nature. Which means—his productive work. This is his primary concern. His creative capacity is his highest virtue. But we have been taught that the highest virtue is to give, not to achieve. Yet one cannot give that which has not been created. Creation comes before distribution—or there will be nothing to distribute. The need of the creator comes before the need of any possible beneficiary. The creator stands above any humanitarian.

It is true that the real benefactors of mankind have been the creative, productive men. No humanitarian ever has or can equal the benefits men received from a Thomas Edison or a Henry Ford. But the creator is not concerned with these benefits; they are secondary consequences. He considers his work, not love or service of others, as his primary goal in life. Thomas Edison was not concerned with the poor people in the slums who would get electric light. He was concerned with the light. You were not concerned with the poor people who benefit from better and cheaper steel. You were concerned with steel work. This is eloquent in every word of your book. It is the best, noblest thing in your book and in your life. You were never moved by any altruistic motive of service—and more honor to you for that—when you created Republic Steel or Vultee Aircraft. You were moved by a simple, personal, *selfish and noble* love for your own work. That is the only truly moral motive and the greatest virtue. The profit motive is merely its expression—the physical means by which one gains the freedom of one's work and function. Why then should you have to justify yourself on any grounds other than the truth? Why should you apologize for it with moral excuses borrowed from the parasites? You seek your justification in the fact that the industries you created are now saving civilization. That is true. They are. But it must never be offered as a prime justification. The prime justification is the right of creative genius to create. *Not* service to humanity.

You say in your book: "I dispute with anyone who holds that men such as Mr. Taft—or President Roosevelt—are necessarily more honorable men, more kindly men, less selfish men, because they were born under no obligation to make a living." I say you have not gone far enough. I dispute with you or anyone who holds that politicians or social workers are not necessarily *less* honorable, *less* kindly then the men who make their own living. I say that humanitarians are parasites, in principle and in fact, since they are primarily concerned with distribution, not with production, that is, with distributing what they have not produced. Parasites are neither honorable nor kindly. So it shocked me to read you, a great industrialist, saying in self-justification that you are just as good as a social worker. You are not. You are much better. But you will never prove it until we have a new code of values.

You say in your book: "Tolerance for socialistic propaganda has increased in this country because Americans who know better have not sufficiently resisted the idea that a man with payroll responsibilities is necessarily less of a humanitarian than people of prominence without such responsibility." No, that is not true. It was because the men with payroll responsibilities felt it necessary to apologize for themselves as "humanitarians." It was because we accepted altruism as an ideal and the title of "humanitarian" as a brand of virtue.

You speak of "a conception that is the rotten core in all of the New Deal thinking: that because a man is obliged to *make* his own living, he therefore becomes somewhat less honorable than people who do not have to make a living." If we accept altruism as an ideal, this "rotten core" is completely logical: since it is nobler to "serve" than to produce, the man free to dedicate himself to some sort of humanitarian "serving" is nobler than the man who is producing. Where is the basic and vicious error? In the conception of service to others as a primary virtue.

We cannot save the system of free enterprise while we ourselves hold the moral beliefs of its enemies. We cannot save it without a complete and consistent philosophy of individualism. A militant and inspiring philosophy, not an apologetic one. Altruism by its very nature is a collectivist principle. If we accept the moral law that man must live for others—we have accepted collectivism, and all the practical consequences will follow inevitably.

You have come very close to the truth in your book, when you chose the Right to Work as your basic theme, as the thing to be defended. It is the creator's first right. But it cannot be defended, except as an individual right to be exercised for the individual's own sake. If collectivism is our moral code—why shouldn't society tell a man how he must work? If service to others is his motive—why shouldn't those others tell him how they wish him to serve? And this is the reason why collectivists "never seem to understand why other men so highly prize the right to work," as you say in your book. They are consistent philosophically. We are not.

There is no hope for the world unless and until we formulate, accept and state publicly a true moral code of individualism, based on man's inalienable right to live for himself. Neither to hurt nor to serve his brothers, but to be independent of them in his function *and in his motive*. Neither to sacrifice them for himself nor to sacrifice himself for them in selfless service—but to deal with them in free exchange among equals, each with a legitimate right to his own benefit, and *not* in the spirit of any kind of altruistic service of anyone by anyone.

But I realize that the cowardly hypocrites among our so-called conservatives would be scared to death by such a doctrine. That is why I am writing this to you. You had the courage to stand on your rights and your convictions in 1937, while others crawled, compromised and submitted. You were one of the few who made a stand. You are doing it again now when you come out openly in defense of the industrialist. So I think you are one of the few men who will have the courage to understand and propagate the kind of moral code we need if the industrialists, and the rest of us, are to be saved. A new and consistent code of individualism.

You might say that this is a job for writers and intellectuals. I imagine you must have felt disgusted, when you wrote your book, that you had to undertake the task of defending yourself, that your own great achievement had not aroused defenders among those whose job it is to do public thinking and writing. Well, that job has been done, only I am certain that you have never heard of it, in the present state of our intellectual world. Two books have been published recently on the basic philosophy of individualism. One is *The God of the Machine* by Isabel Paterson. The other is *The Fountainhead* by me. *The God of the Machine* is a political treatise that presents a complete and consistent credo of individualism in social and economic relations. It is a basic document of capitalism, as *Das Kapital* was that of communism, with the difference that *The God of the Machine* is an honest and brilliant book. *The Fountainhead* is a novel that presents the conflict of individualism and collectivism in personal and moral terms, in the realm of man's spirit. Its hero is the kind of man you appear to be, if I can judge by your book, the kind of man who built America, the creator and uncompromising individualist. I have presented my whole thesis against altruism in this book. It cannot be stated completely in a letter.

I am anxious to call these two books to your attention, because they were written for and in defense of men like you. But that I should have to do it myself is the same evil commentary on our society as the fact that you should have to defend yourself. You must know how completely our intellectual field is controlled by the collectivists. I am sure you don't know that there are a few writers of your side who are struggling alone against an impossible blockade. If you think of what you felt in 1937, you will understand the kind of siege in which we, the conservative writers, are being choked to death. Only it's much worse, because it's done in silence. You had at least the advantage of an open, public fight. We are not allowed to be heard and the country at large does not even know that we exist, fight and are being murdered by methods much dirtier than those used against you by the thugs of the CIO. You were facing a firing squad. We are being choked in a cellar. Our communication lines have been cut by our own side. The literary editors of all important conservative publications are pinks, "liberals" and actual Communists. The proof? That you have never heard of *The God of the Machine* or *The Fountainhead*. If books of equal importance had come out in defense of collectivism, you and the whole country would have seen it announced in neon lights.

Our capitalists and industrialists own, control and support the press. Yet they have it staffed with the worst pinks in existence. They pay fabulous salaries to people engaged in cutting their throats. They support their own murderers, then wonder why they are being destroyed, and who's doing it, and why the public is so socialist-minded. The public is allowed to hear nothing else. Our conservatives read only what Clifton Fadiman or Lewis Gannett have recommended. Then they wonder why all current literature is pink.

I am very anxious to have you read my book and *The God of the Machine*. But I do not like to send books out to be forgotten on a desk or given to a secretary. If this letter makes you think that the subject is worth your attention, please let me know that you do want to read them and I shall be more than happy to send you copies of both books. I think that all supporters of free enterprise should get together. I think that you industrialists should give us writers at least a hearing. It is later than we all think.

With my deep admiration for your achievement and for that which you represent,

■   ■   ■

To Archibald Ogden

July 29, 1943

Dear Archie:

(also, dear Walter, dear Ross, dear Jo, dear Janet and dear everybody else!)

This is what happens when you give an author such a shock as the ad in last Monday's *Times*. You can't spring such surprises on authors—their morale goes to pieces. The ad is grand (it's the size that stunned me), and Bobbs-Merrill are a wonderful publishing house, and I love you all.

I don't know which way one gets more out of publishers—by being a holy Russian terror or a happy Pollyanna, but at the present moment I'm not thinking of proper diplomacy. I'm just simply happy and grateful to all of you, and I hope this idyll will last for both sides.

Seriously, I think the ad was excellent, wording and all, even the nude statue. (*Third* big printing, huh? Well, it looked grand in print anyway.) Also, the proof of the new jacket you sent me has my approval, compliments and thanks. I could have wished not to burden a clean book like ours with quotes from someone as dirty as Albert Guerard, but I suppose it doesn't matter and I know you wanted three important rags to quote. The heading you wrote redeems the rest and does tie it into a good whole. Didn't I say that whenever you put out any copy about this book it is always right? Thank you once more.

I am having a grand time here [in Ridgefield, Conn., visiting Isabel Paterson], as you can see by the tone of this letter. I'm turning into a humanitarian and loving the world. That's a natural result of doing nothing but loafing. Will be back in the city some time next week and will bring along a nice suntan and some of this mood (I hope). Until then, my collective love to the whole of Bobbs-Merrill—

and to you individually—

P.S. This letter is to remain in force up to, but not including the next time I get mad at Bobbs-Merrill.

■ ■ ■

To Archibald Ogden:

August 16, 1943

Dear Mr. Ogden:

I am now working on a short nonfiction book which I should like to have Bobbs-Merrill publish. Its provisional title is *The Moral Basis of Individualism.* We might find a better one, but this title will give you an exact idea of the book's theme and purpose.

The book will present, in simple, concrete terms, the thesis of *The Fountainhead*—the statement of man's essential integrity and self-sufficiency, the exposition of altruism as a fallacy and a moral evil, the definition of a proper moral law which is to be found neither in self-sacrifice for others nor in domination over others but in spiritual independence. And (which is not in *The Fountainhead* except by implication) an outline of the proper social, political and economic system deduced from and based on man's moral nature—the capitalist system, its meaning, principles and actual working as the only *moral* system of society.

Capitalism has never found the moral principle on which it must stand. We have stood on it in fact, we have built our entire civilization upon it —but what we have preached and believed has been its exact opposite. The results are now destroying the world. There is no other explanation for the confusion, the helplessness, the intellectual silliness, the total insanity of mankind at present.

Contrary to the vulgar belief that men are motivated primarily by materialistic considerations, we now see the capitalist system being discredited and destroyed all over the world, even though this system has given men the greatest material comforts and benefits ever achieved on earth. The reason is that men "do not live by bread alone" and that the capitalist system has stood in their eyes for nothing but bread. They have been taught to consider it as a practical, realistic system, but not an ethical one. A system without an ideal. Every defender of capitalism, so far, has found nothing better to say than, in effect, "Men are imperfect, so they'll never work for anything but money, so capitalism is best, isn't this sad?—communism is really the moral ideal, but human nature can never live up to it, etc., etc." Say that to men—and they will kill themselves and others and destroy the world in order to reach the ideal. Look at them. They are doing a thorough job of it at this moment.

I find—in the horror of the present time and in the horror of man's past history—*not* a proof of man's essential evil, but a great and tragic proof of his essential morality, that is, his determination to act according to what he considers as right. Altruism (the conception of living for others as a virtue) has been preached as mankind's moral ideal for centuries. And all the great horrors of history have been committed in the name of an altruistic purpose. After each disaster men have said: "The ideal was right, but Robespierre was the wrong man to put it into practice," (or Torquemada, or Cromwell, or Lenin, or Hitler, or Stalin) and have gone on to try it again. At the price of incredible suffering and rivers of blood, mankind has stuck to the pursuit of its alleged moral ideal—surely a demonstration of men's moral instinct.* But we look on and say: "This noble ideal is beyond human nature, because men are imperfect and evil."

Isn't it time to stop and to question that noble ideal instead?

America has been living on a kind of double standard, a terrible basic contradiction. We have functioned, in economics, on the principle of individualism—and achieved miracles. We have held, in spirit, a collectivist ideal—and achieved world disaster. Altruism is collectivism by definition. (You must live for others. Others are the State, the class, the race or whatever. You must live for the collective. You must live for the State.) We could go on with this contradiction for a while, but since man *is* a moral being the consequences were bound to catch up with us. They have.

Men grew prosperous, happy, successful under our system of individualism. But since they held as virtue the ideal of living for others, their own success gave them a feeling of guilt. The richer they grew, the guiltier they felt. They could not find the proper spiritual pride, peace and sense of fulfillment—which an act of virtue gives us—in their own achievement. Achievement was not a moral act. Self-sacrifice was. The more they achieved, the more they felt a need to apologize and atone for it in some way. Their own success drove them to their own destruction.

We must define, understand and accept Individualism as a *moral* law, and Capitalism as its practical and proper expression. If we don't—capitalism cannot be saved. If it is not saved—we're finished, all of us, America and the world and every man, woman and child in it. Then nothing will be left but the cave and the club.

Look at the tempo of destruction around us. An idea is responsible for that—a fatally erroneous idea. An idea can stop it—a true one. How fast or how well will depend on the quality of the men who understand it and

* "Moral instinct" is metaphorical. AR was an opponent of the deterministic view that man possesses instincts, i.e., innate ideas.

on what they do about it. But humanity cannot start to recover until the idea and direction of recovery become clear to them. Men *do* live through their minds. Everything we are and have comes from men's thinking. Only an idea can save us.

This, briefly, will be the content and purpose of my book.

It will be a short book, actually a booklet, the kind that would sell for a dollar, I suppose. About fifty thousand words or less. The idea of *The Fountainhead* must be stated in non-fiction form—to stand on its own as an idea—more completely than it could be stated in a novel, without the distraction of a story and a plot. It will not, of course, interfere with *The Fountainhead* in any way. In fact, I think it would help the sale of *The Fountainhead*. Take notice of the reviewers who said that *The Fountainhead* could "change the life of anyone who read it." I am now getting fan letters to that effect—readers speak of the difference *The Fountainhead* has made in their entire view of life. But the idea must be given the complete statement—particularly as applied to the sociological and economic realm —which most readers cannot make for themselves. And those who have not read *The Fountainhead* might be prompted to read it once they hear and understand the idea on which it is based. They might be baffled by the conception of a non-altruistic man as a noble, virtuous and heroic being. They might not be able to visualize him for themselves. Well—let them read about Howard Roark. In this way the novel and the booklet will complement each other.

Two years ago, I wrote a thirty-two page article called "The Individualist Manifesto." It was not written for publication, but as an appeal to all individualists to unite for the preservation of our capitalist system. It stated briefly the ideas outlined above. I sent a few typewritten copies to prominent men. The response amazed me. Everyone who read it asked my permission to make copies and circulate it. I received two offers to have it published—from conservative political organizations. I refused at the time, because the "Manifesto" was not written in a form proper for publication, it was an appeal, not a book. I intended to rewrite it, but have not done so, because just then Bobbs-Merrill "came into my life" with the contract for *The Fountainhead* and plunged me into a year and a half of the kind of work that made it impossible to attend to anything else. All this time I have been receiving inquiries about and requests for the "Manifesto." So now that *The Fountainhead* is done, I decided to undertake the task of rewriting the "Manifesto" for publication.

I could have it published as a pamphlet by one of the organizations that are interested in it, but I would prefer, of course, to have it done by Bobbs-Merrill. The organizations concerned will give us a ready-made field of distribution and will more than cover the cost of publication, apart from the sale to the general public. I have not discussed the matter with them—I believe Bobbs-Merrill would have to discuss it and make the proper arrangements—but I know that these organizations would act as distributing agents for the booklet.

I am going on a lecture tour this fall and winter, to speak on the ideas of this booklet and of *The Fountainhead.* I believe it will help the sale of both.*

I should like to sign a contract for the publication of the booklet now, in order to be free to refuse other offers. I shall have the booklet written in about a month. I am interested in a quick publication and would like to see it out this fall.

■   ■   ■

To Tom Girdler

August 17, 1943

Dear Mr. Girdler:

Thank you for your letter of July 27th. I was deeply impressed and very grateful to learn that you had purchased *The Fountainhead* and Isabel Paterson's *The God of the Machine.* I had not really intended my letter to be a sales talk to make you buy books—I would have been glad to send them to you and wanted only an assurance that they would be read, since I don't believe in forcing books on busy people nor in sending out books that will remain unwanted. But since you showed an interest great enough to make you *buy* them—(I guess you do believe in the capitalist system)—an author can only feel the deepest appreciation.

I shall be more than happy to have a chance to meet you and talk to you—and I am frankly delighted if my letter made you wish to do so.

■   ■   ■

* Although AR signed a contract with Charles Pearson Lectures, she did not go on a lecture tour.

To Benjamin DeCasseres

August 28, 1943

Dear Mr. DeCasseres:

Thank you very much for the San Francisco clipping of your column on Howard Roark. It was thrilling for me to see it, and it was very nice of you to think of sending it to me.

I liked your leaflet "I Am Private Enterprise" which you enclosed. I remember reading that in your column and I am glad that it has been reprinted for distribution to the public.

I do hope that you will regain your health soon—so that I will have a chance to meet you, a purely selfish reason. (That's an example of how selfishness leads one to benevolence toward our fellow men.)

■ ■ ■

To Charles Larson, MGM screenwriter

August 28, 1943

Dear Mr. Larson:

Thank you for your beautiful letter. You say that you do not know whether I need "praise or gratefulness" for my work. Yes, I do—and I want to tell you frankly that your letter meant a great deal to me.

If you understood *The Fountainhead*, you will understand and not take it as vulgar conceit when I say that the reaction of readers is, to me, not a test of my book's worth, but of the reader's worth. When I hear praise of *The Fountainhead* it reaffirms my faith in men, my conviction that they are not all secondhanders, that the spirit of Howard Roark exists and finds response among them. If this is "needing praise," make the most of it— and accept my deepest gratitude.

■ ■ ■

To Lilian Koch, a fan

August 28, 1943

Dear Miss Koch:

I appreciate it very much that you wish to discuss *The Fountainhead* in your professional work. As a personal note from the author, I should like to say that *The Fountainhead* represents my tribute to the heroic in man, to the creator, the individual who stands against the collective.

As for your questions about Dominique, I am afraid that I cannot explain her any better than I did in the book. I could add only that the greatness of her love for Roark made her want to destroy him because she could not bear the thought of his existence in a world dominated by second-handers. Her love was worship and it is not easy to see sacrilege against one's god committed every day by every person around. She wanted to prevent incidents such as the Stoddard Temple. Why did she marry Wynand? To make him pay for the destruction of the Stoddard Temple. She lost her fear of the world when she understood that it has never been and can never be dominated by the secondhanders nor by any collective, that the world lives, grows and is moved by the genius of the creators, of the single, clean, exceptional men such as Howard Roark.

■ ■ ■

To Helen Blodgett, a fan

August 28, 1943

Dear Mrs. Blodgett:

You ask why I chose architecture as the profession of my hero. I chose it because it is a field of work that covers both art and a basic need of men's survival. And because one cannot find a more eloquent symbol of man as creator than a man who is a builder. His antithesis, the collectivists, are destroyers.

■ ■ ■

To Matilda Alford, a fan

August 29, 1943

Dear Mrs. Alford:

I was happy to hear that you understood so well the theme and principles of *The Fountainhead*. Few people would have the courage really to understand these principles, and fewer still to apply them to their own lives.

I suppose almost everyone has some touch of the secondhand in him, but on the evidence of your letter I do not believe that you can be classified as a secondhander. If my book can help you to develop in the way you wish, in the way of integrity and independence, I shall be deeply gratified.

I am working at present on precisely the kind of book you suggest—a nonfiction treatise on the principles of *The Fountainhead*, on the moral bases of the creative man, of individualism as opposed to the vicious doctrine of altruism preached by collectivists.

No, I am not a secondhander, nor "still struggling." A secondhander could not have written *The Fountainhead*. I do not say this as a boast, but merely because I have had a very hard time through refusing to be a secondhander, so I think I have the right to say it.

Thank you for saying that you know I didn't write my book for anyone, but wrote it because I wanted to. This is true, as it is true of any work done by any decent human being, and it showed me that you understood the whole point of my book. But there is a great difference between writing for an audience and writing as one believes, then finding an audience able to respond. In this sense, I am very happy to have readers such as yourself, and very grateful.

■ ■ ■

To H. W. Miller, a fan

September 1, 1943

Dear Mr. Miller:

I will not attempt to thank you for the things you said about *The Fountainhead*. I am very happy, not merely that you liked it, but that you liked it for the right things.

You write of yourself as belonging to those who "haven't the slightest idea what a large number of people think they're doing." That has always been my own problem. I can write about the secondhanders. I am baffled when I come up against them. I wonder whether you and I mean the same thing, the same feeling—and, anyway, I grant my respect immediately to anyone who cannot understand the behavior of people at present. To understand them completely is to be part of them—and that is not an honorable distinction in the world of today.

I am frankly curious and should like to meet you in person. Would you telephone me at Murray Hill 6-6549? I would like to discover what you are like—and, if you're interested, I'll tell you "how in Hell anyone has the strength to do so much hard work, all of it good." Thank you for that lovely sentence.

■ ■ ■

To Monroe Shakespeare, a manufacturer of fishing tackle in Kalamazoo, Michigan

October 10, 1943

Dear Monroe:

I don't quite know how to answer your letter. When I read, in the copy of the letter you sent out, the paragraph about your putting up money of your own [to advertise *The Fountainhead*], I wanted to cry. It was the kind of emotional shock I've never experienced before. I didn't think or ever expect you to offer your own money for this campaign. One reads about beautiful gestures like that in books, but they never happen in real life and I never thought anything like it would happen to me. All I can say now is that if you should ever need my help in any way, you can have it—in anything short of advocating collectivism and two other crimes I wouldn't commit. I told about you to a friend of mine who is very embittered about our conservatives in general—and she said you were a miracle and "nature's nobleman." She meant it. So do I.

Thursday afternoon, Mr. Aaron E. Carpenter telephoned me long distance from Philadelphia. He has read half of my book so far, is most enthusiastic and asked me to have lunch with him Tuesday when he is coming to New York. I have never met him before—so look how your name is working. This is a greater magic than William Shakespeare ever worked. (I've never cared for him too much anyway—from now on *my* first Shakespeare is Monroe.)

The book is doing very well at the moment—it has risen on the *Herald-Tribune* bestseller list in today's issue. It has appeared as bestseller in San Francisco for the first time—which is very unusual this long after publication, and most encouraging. It means word-of-mouth advertising and genuine response from the readers, which means that the book does have popular appeal. If your project goes through now, the book and I will be made in a big way.

I am enclosing a copy of a little debate in print I did for "Wake up, America!" [a syndicated debate sponsored by the American Economic Forum]. It's not much, but it goes into 870 papers, so it's good publicity and at least a few points hammered home against the collectivists. Notice how Mr. Villard [Oswald Garrison Villard, former editor of *The Nation*] was afraid to admit that he's for collectivism. I think we can make that word stick and use it as they used "capitalism."

Regards from both of us to Mrs. Shakespeare and yourself. You know

I am not a religious person in the conventional manner, but I want to say in my own sense and in every best sense men have ever said it: God bless you!

Gratefully yours,

■   ■   ■

To DeWitt Emery

October 16, 1943

Dear DeWitt:

Thank you for your letter. I was glad to get such a long one from you, particularly with political discussions. You know how I love discussions. So I'm going to match it.

First—for God's sake, you don't have to give me an accounting of everything you read, by way of apology for not having read *The Fountainhead*. Skip it, as you always say, skip it. It's all right, and I won't hint about it again. The loss is yours, not mine. I've read it.

Second—what on earth are you talking about when you wonder whether I believe in "absolute individualism, disregarding the interdependence which is a necessary part of any capitalistic or industrial society"? (?!?) Of course I believe in absolute individualism. Yes, I mean laissez-faire. Yes, absolute laissez-faire. I don't know what is meant by any sort of blasted "interdependence." I do know that the word began to be used a couple of years ago—by the pinks, for a very specific purpose. I hope to God our side hasn't adopted it—along with "democracy."

I don't see any kind of "interdependence" in a capitalist society. Everything a man gets is paid for by his own labor. He trades his products for the products of others—to the extent he has earned, and no more. A man who feeds himself by his own labor is not a dependent. Traders are not dependents. Only poor relatives, slaves and imbeciles are.

If the word means that I, for instance, depend on the farmer for my bread while he depends on me for his books—that is nonsense. He does not give me the bread free—and I do not give him my book free. I do not help him to grow wheat—and he does not help me to write a book. He depends on nothing but his own work and ability—and so do I. Then we exchange our products—through voluntary action, to mutual advantage— if we both want the exchange. If we don't—I buy a box of soda crackers —and he buys a novel by William Saroyan. We *don't have to* deal with each other. Where the hell's the "interdependence"? Now, of course, in a Communist society, I would be given a bread ration and I'd gobble it up, because I'd have nothing else—and the farmer would have my novel rammed down his throat (if [radio commentator] Elmer Davis liked it). Then, of course, if the Cambodians need milk—we've all gotta rush out and sacrifice and get milked, because we need the totem poles which the Cambodians produce—our economy couldn't possibly survive without totem poles—we're all "interdependent." *That*, my dear conservative president of the National Small Business Men's Association, is what the word was pushed into use for.

You write: "Of course, there was a time in the evolution of mankind when each individual was absolutely dependent upon himself for everything, but that time was prior to the advent of the use of capital." *When* was there such a time? No exact knowledge is available on prehistorical man. But every theory ever presented on the subject—on the basis of archaeological evidence—shows that man began with a *collectivist* society. Every recorded description of savages describes collectivism. Every contemporary savage society leads a tribal, communal, *collectivist* existence. The whole progress of mankind has been away from the collective toward individualism. Toward the *independent* man. This had been generally recognized and accepted. But about a year ago, for the first time to my knowledge, the newspaper *PN* came out with an article claiming that savages lived in a state of individualism and that we, the conservatives, were reactionaries who wanted to go back to the caveman; while they, the collectivists, represented progress. Surely we haven't fallen for that one, too? If we accept the premise of an individualistic savage (who never existed)— then of course Communism is progress. And there's no way for us to argue ourselves out of that one. Then let's close shop and go to Soviet Russia.

■   ■   ■

To Isabel Turner, a fan

October 17, 1943

Dear Miss Turner:

Of course I was "interested in knowing what one medium library is doing with my book," as you put it. And I was very glad to hear what you thought of my book.

Yes, I am happy if *The Fountainhead* is rising on pure merit, as you say. But I believe that it takes a person of merit to recognize merit and to let the general public know it. It takes a person capable of independent judgment. I knew that *The Fountainhead* would need someone like yourself wherever it went. No help given to me personally would mean as much to me as any help given to my book. So if you were able to build it from two copies to thirty—I am very grateful to you.

I was pleased to hear that you found many people who are in complete sympathy with my ideas of individualism. That is encouraging and hopeful for the future of our country. I have always believed that Americans were individualists, but one can't help doubting it occasionally when one sees the solid stream of collectivist books that have been dumped on us for the last ten years. I hope this trend is changing.

Please give my best regards to those in your library who took an interest in *The Fountainhead*. If you hear any reader praising it and understanding its ideas—please give him my personal gratitude. I shall be in Hollywood in December—and I'll come to the Bullock's Book Club to thank you in person.

■   ■   ■

To Furwen Ann Thomas, a fan

October 18, 1943

Dear Miss Thomas:

I am glad if *The Fountainhead* was the first book that made you want to write to its author.

I am gratified that it has given you "a better understanding and perhaps more respect for buildings." I had hoped that one of the effects of my novel would be to infect some readers with my own love for New York. I can say that I am actually in love with skyscrapers—and with the magnificent talent that made Americans capable of constructing them.

■   ■   ■

To Dorothy Elzer, a fan

October 18, 1943

Dear Miss Elzer:

I am glad that you liked *The Fountainhead*—and that you liked it enough to ask for a sequel.

You say: "How about it?" Well, friend, it can't be done. I have said everything I had to say about these particular characters—and I have nothing left to add. You see, I believe that a book which is intended to have a sequel must be written differently from a book intended to be complete in itself.

But I do appreciate your desire to read about "the life of Mr. and Mrs. Howard Roark." If you want to know what their life will be like—look at their last scene together. It will give you the key.

I will, of course, write other books—only don't expect them "on the market real soon." It took seven years to write *The Fountainhead*. No, I won't take that long on the next one, but give me a little time. This is not a reproach to you—an author can only be grateful to an impatient reader.

■ ■ ■

To Gwen Davenport, a fan and novelist

October 21, 1943

Dear Miss Davenport:

Thank you very much for the copy of *A Stranger and Afraid* and for your lovely inscription. I enjoyed your novel immensely. The suspense in it did get to be almost unbearable. That is a beautiful job of construction. I believe that good plot construction is the most important part of a good novel, and the most difficult part.

Archie Ogden has told me of what you wrote to Bobbs-Merrill about *The Fountainhead*, and that your "missionary work" for it put it on the bestseller list in Louisville. As an author, you know that nothing one can do would mean more to an author than this. So you will understand how deeply I appreciate it.

■ ■ ■

October 22, 1943

Dear Ruth:

I have some news to tell you, confidentially, since it has not been publicly released as yet: I have sold the screen rights to *The Fountainhead* to Warner Brothers, for $50,000. This has made me a capitalist overnight, which is a wonderful feeling. I shall have to go to Hollywood in December to stay there for a few months. I am sorry that I'll miss you when you'll be in New York this winter.

AR stayed in California until October 1951.

■ ■ ■

To Ruth Alexander

November 7, 1943

Dear Ruth,

Thank you for your nice letter about my big event. We will leave for Hollywood by the end of this month, and we intend to stop in Chicago for a few days.

Thanks for showing me Mr. Queeny's [Edgard M. Queeny, author of *The Spirit of American Enterprise*] letter, which I am enclosing. It was very interesting. Would you ask him for me to sit down and think a little about the connection between philosophy and reality? He might discover that true philosophy is derived from reality, and that our actions must be governed by abstract philosophical principles whenever we act as human beings and expect to achieve any rational goal. Or where does he think philosophy comes from—and how does he propose to act in practical reality without conception of whether he is acting on the right or wrong principle? By guesswork? By hit-and-miss? Does he conduct chemical research by ignoring or *directly opposing* the laws of nature? If a philosophy is inapplicable to reality, it is simply not a philosophy. If, however, he accepts a philosophy as correct and true, then acts against it—he can only bring disaster upon himself and achieve the exact opposite of what he is after. (As he has done in his book.)

This is in reference to the incredible sentence of his letter that: "we should make the best compromise we can with the opposing philosophy, who right or wrong have the votes." The "opposing philosophy" does not admit of compromise. The "opposing philosophy" is collectivism—which is death and destruction. One cannot choose a compromise between life and death. There ain't no such in-between. And does he still think that the opposition "have the votes"? God save capitalism from capitalism's defenders! Nobody can defeat us now—except the Republicans. If Mr. Roosevelt gets a fourth term, it will be the conservatives, such as Mr. Queeny, who will have given it to him. By *"compromising."*

I hope you don't mind being the innocent bystander in this lecture. I just couldn't return a letter like Mr. Queeny's unanswered.

Our best regards to Ray. Frank sends you his love—without asking your or my permission.

My love as always,

■   ■   ■

To Monroe Shakespeare

November 16, 1943

Dear Monroe:

Thank you for all the thought you have given to my problem. Your analysis of the situation was very valuable to me and I think you are entirely right. I shall not undertake to risk any money until I am certain of what results a publicity man can offer for it, and in any event I shall not do it without consulting you or being sure that it does not conflict with any action you decide to undertake.

I have been checking up on publicity men with a great many people here—and the general opinion is that $10,000 is too much to spend, that no such sum should be necessary for the purpose. So you were correct on that. But it seems extremely difficult to find a reliable press agent of the proper political standing. I am still looking for one.

I am afraid that my publishers cannot be of help in this, precisely for the reason you mentioned: they do no promotion except of the most conventional, routine, strictly literary-market style, and they would neither venture nor understand a campaign of political promotion. They would not know how to reach the public from that angle. Since advertising is very helpful to a general sale of the book, and they do know how to handle that, their own promotion is more effective in that medium. I discussed the question with them and they were eager to have me organize my own campaign, but they could offer no practical suggestions, since it is out of their experience.

Frank and I are leaving New York on the 28th and will be in Chicago on the 29th, where we will stay for four days. We will leave our things in Chicago, then make a trip to Kalamazoo from there—it will be better than descending upon you with all our hand luggage, a typewriter and a cat. Will you let me know which day you would like us to come and how long you care to endure our company? I will make no other engagements in Chicago, until I hear from you. I am looking forward most eagerly to seeing you again.

■   ■   ■

To Mrs. Frank Curlee, a fan

November 16, 1943

Dear Mrs. Curlee:

I was very glad to hear from you again and shall be pleased to meet you in person. Would you come to have tea with me at my home, on Saturday afternoon, November 20, at 5 p.m.? Drop me a note to let me know if this is convenient for you—or telephone me at Murray Hill 6-6549, any morning before noon.

No, of course your letter was not wrong or presumptuous. I am very much interested in young writers and I would be glad to discuss your husband's work with you. I must warn you, however, that I am not an authority on poetry and I know very little about the procedure of placing poems with publishers, which is a special field, different from that of book publications. So I could give you only a general opinion or advice. I might be a little more helpful on short stories.

■   ■   ■

To Earle H. Balch, editor at G. P. Putnam's Sons

November 28, 1943

Dear Mr. Balch:

To supplement our recent conversation, I am writing this to urge upon you my conviction on the tremendous historical importance and the great commercial possibilities of *The God of the Machine* by Isabel Paterson.

The God of the Machine is the greatest book written in the last three hundred years. It is the first complete statement of the philosophy of individualism as a political and economic system. It is the basic document of capitalism.

No historical movement has ever succeeded without a book that stated its principles and gave shape to its thinking. Without a formulated system of thought, no consistent human action is possible; such action can result only in self-contradictory confusion and ultimate tragedy. Capitalism has never had this basic statement. That is why the American system, which gave mankind the greatest, unprecedented, miraculous blessings, is now in the process of destroying itself. Men do not know what they had, what they are losing and how they are losing it. They had no book to tell them.

But they have the book now. *The God of the Machine* is a document that could literally save the world—if enough people knew of it and read it. *The God of the Machine* does for capitalism what the Bible did for Christianity—and, forgive the comparison, what *Das Kapital* did for Communism or *Mein Kampf* for Nazism. It takes a book to save or destroy the world.

There is a tremendous market for *The God of the Machine*, a vast audience, waiting and ready—but it must be reached in the proper way. As you can see now—and most particularly since the last election—the American people are desperately anxious to preserve the system of free enterprise. But they are bewildered and confused. They would grab a book that would give them the arguments and ammunition they need. But they must be told that *this* is the book.

During the presidential campaign of 1940, I worked as head of the Research Department at the National Headquarters of the Associated Willkie Clubs. It was my job to find and spread literature in support of capitalism. At that time I saw the desperate public need for intellectual ammunition. We received letters by the thousands, begging us for information. People said in effect that they wanted to defend free enterprise, but did not know how to do it; they got stumped by collectivist arguments and had no answers. They begged us for answers. More than that: whenever we sent out some mild, ineffectual, compromising piece of campaign literature, we got no response. Whenever we sent out a clear, strong, consistent piece of writing—we got requests for thousands of reprints, we could not keep up with the demand from local clubs and private individuals.

The same situation is true now—only more so. There is a huge public demand for ammunition against collectivism, an actual public hunger—

which no one tries to satisfy. There is a market which is simply going begging. *The God of the Machine* is the answer—and a potential gold mine for its publishers, if properly exploited.

But to do this, you must inform the public that:

a) It is *not* just another book on free enterprise. So many of them have been published and they were so bad, weak, muddled, unconvincing and ineffectual that the public has been disappointed too often and is now wary.

b) It is *not* another "middle-of-the-road" mess, but a clear, strong, fighting document. (Don't soften the nature of the book—*stress* it.)

c) It is *the* book on capitalism and individualism, the book that will give readers ammunition in any argument with collectivists, the book that will answer their every question and tell them everything they want to know about Americanism—philosophically, historically, economically, morally.

If *this* were told to the public through a clear, well-thought-out campaign of publicity backed by a few intelligent ads—such a campaign would not even need to be too costly, merely well-planned and through the right channels—there would be no stopping the sale of the book. The response would astonish you—not merely response from "important" men and intellectuals, but from average people and the general public. Let me assure you of this. I know.

As a minor illustration, let me mention the fate of my own book *The Fountainhead*. It is a novel on individualism. Ten publishers rejected it— because it was "too strong," "too intellectual," and they said it would not sell. Look at it now. It has sold about 25,000 copies at this writing, has had seven printings in six months, and the sales are growing every week. The original exploitation campaign of my publishers was not large—but they did inform the public of the nature of my book. The public did the rest. From the fan mail I am getting, I know that it is not the story or any particular literary merit of mine, but the *idea* of the book, the philosophy of individualism, that is selling the book. The idea answers a public need. *The God of the Machine* would answer it much more effectively—*precisely* because it is not fiction.

Incidentally, don't let anyone tell you that *The God of the Machine* is "too difficult to understand" or "above the head of the average reader." I have given copies of it to many people, most of them men and women without formal education. They had no trouble reading and understanding the book. They were enthusiastic about it.

As a practical suggestion, I would like to urge you to make mimeographed publicity releases along the lines of this letter—and send them to editors, columnists, political commentators all over the country, as well as to industrial leaders, and even to bookstores. But *not* just to book reviewers and the usual trade channels. These alone will not do the job.

I would suggest that you take a few ads—they don't have to be large, but they must be most carefully worded along these lines, for full effect.

I would suggest that you discuss the book and enlist the help of the [conservative business leaders] listed. It would be most helpful if you met them in person. I have spoken to them about *The God of the Machine*, but a conversation with the publisher could have better practical results. These men represent organizations with thousands of members. If you make the proper arrangements, they would send out circulars and publicity to their memberships—a ready-made field of readers most interested in the subject. They are doing this for my book.

In conclusion, let me say that *The God of the Machine* is a book that will live forever and will have a great influence on the thinking of mankind. But if you, as a publisher, take advantage of it now and stand behind it, it can also become a great commercial asset—which is a proper reward for its author and publisher.

AR's final assessment of The God of the Machine *was expressed in her 1964 review of the book in* The Objectivist Newsletter, *vol. 3, no. 10.*

AR and her husband returned to California in December.

■   ■   ■

To Archibald Ogden

December 18, 1943

Archie my darling:

Yes, that's still how I feel about my one editorial genius. I guess distance does that—and slight homesickness. By the time I crossed the continent, you became a kind of shining legend in my mind. Now you and Isabel Paterson stand for New York and for all the best that's happened to me in New York—and I miss you terribly.

Everything has gone wonderfully so far, I hope it continues this way, and I hope I don't get spoiled for battles, if there are to be battles—but so far it's grand. The trip was sheer luxury—I simply sat and gloated all the way—I'm not quite used yet to the mink coat standard of living—but travelling in a private compartment will teach anyone the pleasure of capitalism. Just look at all the wonderful gadgets next time you're on a train, see how cleverly designed they are—and see if you don't feel like blessing private enterprise, as I did for three thousand miles. (And forever.)

My grand surprise in Hollywood was Henry Blanke, the producer who is to do *The Fountainhead*. Now I don't want to be rash, but I could almost say that I think maybe he is almost an Archie Ogden—only I don't use that comparison promiscuously. It was Blanke who discovered the book, that is, he read the book itself, not a synopsis, then he went to the heads of the studio and demanded that they buy it. Doesn't that remind you of another man in my past? You know, it is very strange how *The Fountainhead* keeps illustrating in real life its own thesis. It will be my fate, like Roark's, to seek and reach the exceptions, the prime movers, the men who do their own thinking and act upon their own judgment. The Tooheys and the Clifton Fadimans don't count—and may God damn them. One man out of thousands is all I need—all any new idea needs—and these men, the exceptions, will and do move the world. Whatever I do in my future career, I will always have to seek and reach an Archie Ogden. You were the first and the most eloquent symbol of what I mean. So whenever I come upon that wonderful miracle among men, I'll give it your name.

Of course I know it's too early for me to judge Blanke, my producer, I won't know until the script is finished. I fully realize that I may be terribly disappointed, that he may not have my ideas at all. It's possible, but it does not look that way right now. He loves *The Fountainhead*, he admires my style of writing, and he is crazy about Roark. He says there's no one in Hollywood who can write dialogue as I do. Whatever he decides to do with the story later, this much I can hold to his credit. He told me that he fell in love with the book, that he started reading it and couldn't put it down and dropped all his other business until he had finished it. I heard a corroboration of this from one of his other writers. Five days after he finished the book, Warners had bought it.

I am to write my own screen version as I please. This doesn't mean that it will be the final version—and the battles will probably start after I finish it—but at least I'll have a chance to present my version. Blanke has given me no objections and no restrictions, except on the sex side—we'll have to be careful of the Hays office and treat such scenes as my famous rape scene through tactful fade-outs.

As to the working conditions of a Hollywood writer's life—they are exactly as one would imagine a Hollywood writer's life, with all the trimmings. I have an office the size of a living room, with another office outside and a secretary in it. Nobody can come in without being announced by my secretary and she answers my telephone. The grandeur and the glamour and the pomp and circumstance are simply wonderful. Of course I love it —for the moment. But I won't exchange it for the pleasure of writing as I please. I haven't gone Hollywood yet.

As to sunny California—I have a miserable cold and it's pouring outside. It's cold, wet and nasty. I hate Hollywood as a place, just as I did before. It's overcrowded, vulgar, cheap and sad in a hopeless sort of way. The people on the streets are all tense, eager, suspicious and look unhappy. The has-beens and the would-bes. I don't think anything in the world is worth this kind of struggle.

I miss New York, in a strange way, with a homesickness I've never felt before for any place on earth. I'm in love with New York, and I don't mean I love it, but I mean I'm in love with it. Frank says that what I love is not the real city, but the New York I built myself. That's true. Anyway, I feel the most unbearable, wistful, romantic tenderness for it—and for everybody in it.

And this means you, to a greater extent than most, since you were the man who let me build my New York. So—all my love to you, also to Betty, "little Dominique" and little Archie. Since this will have to serve as a Christmas card—Merry Christmas and a happy New Year from both of us to all of you. Love,

■　■　■

To Walter Hurley, an executive at Bobbs-Merrill

December 18, 1943

Dear Mr. Hurley:

Just a greeting from a happy author—knocking on wood. Everything is wonderful so far, and I hope it will continue this way, for the sake of *The Fountainhead*, which means for the sake of all of us.

Mr. Henry Blanke, who is to produce *The Fountainhead* for Warner Brothers, is one of the most brilliant and distinguished producers in Hollywood. He is very enthusiastic about the book and intends to make a big picture from it. I give you one guess as to what my first thought is. Yes, that it will help the sale of the book. I'm a one-track mind.

The Warner Studios have been grand to me. Boy, how they treat authors out here! I have a huge office, a secretary and all the usual grandeur. No, I don't think I've gone Hollywood yet, but what a temptation! Only I do miss New York, and the Empire State Building, and even the Bobbs-Merrill office (or should I name that first?).

Please drop me a line and let me know how things are going with the book at your end, how are the sales, what happened on the Literary Guild deal which Mr. Baker mentioned to me, and everything and anything else. I feel like an exiled mother and you are the guardian of my child—so let me know all the news.

Look up my article ["The Only Path to Tomorrow"] in the January *Reader's Digest*. I hope you can use it as publicity for *The Fountainhead*. Please do so—in any manner that it could tie in.

Here's to a prosperous New Year for *The Fountainhead*, which means for Dobbs-Merrill and me. (I still hold no other wish.)

■ ■ ■

3

LETTERS TO FRANK LLOYD WRIGHT

Though not extensive, Ayn Rand's correspondence with Frank Lloyd Wright covered twenty years, from 1937 to 1957. The two met a number of times, and Ayn Rand and her husband spent a weekend at Wright's summer head-quarters, Taliesin East, in Spring Green, Wisconsin. Two major projects involving Rand and Wright never materialized: Wright's designing the buildings for the 1949 movie of *The Fountainhead* (his price was too high), and Wright's building a home for the O'Connors, cancelled when the O'Connors decided not to move out of Manhattan. Wright's drawing of the "Ayn Rand house" appears in several Wright collections, including the cover of the 1994 weekly calendar produced by the Taliesin Associates.

December 12, 1937

Dear Mr. Wright,

I am writing a novel about the career of an architect; not an essay or historical treatise, but a novel. I should like to have the privilege of meeting you and discussing it with you. I do not seek your help or collaboration, nor do I wish to impose any work upon you in connection with it. I would like only to see you and to hear you speak. If you do not consider this request a presumption on my part, please grant me permission to come to Wisconsin for an interview with you.

I do not suppose that you have heard my name, since I am not that famous—as yet. My first novel, *We the Living*, was published in 1936. My second [*Anthem*] will be published this coming spring or fall. My third—

the one about architecture—is contracted for by Macmillan in America and by Cassells in England. I am mentioning this only to show that I am not a beginner who proposes to take up your time on a dubious undertaking.

My new novel, to put it very briefly and dryly, is to be the story of an architect who follows his own convictions throughout his life, no matter what society thinks of it or does to him. It is the story of a man who is so true to himself that no others on earth, nor their lies, nor their prejudices can affect him and his work. A man who has an ideal and goes through hell for it.

So you can understand why it seems to me that of all men on earth you are the one I must see. My hero is not you. I do not intend to follow in the novel the events of your life and career. His life will not be yours, nor his work, perhaps not even his artistic ideals. But his spirit is yours— I think.

His story is the story of human integrity. That is what I am writing. That is what you have lived. And to my knowledge, you are the only one among the men of this century who has lived it. I am writing about a thing impossible these days. You are the only man in whom it is possible and real. It is not anything definite or tangible that I want from an interview with you. It is only the inspiration of seeing before me a living miracle— because the man I am writing about is a miracle whom I want to make alive. I think I can do it alone. I know I will do it better after having seen you.

My novel is not really about architecture, or rather it is not *only* about architecture. I have chosen architecture merely as the medium through which my theme can be expressed best. And my theme—if it can be stated briefly—could be explained, perhaps, in these words:

"The natural man, the natural way is no longer the desirable way. Man power itself is becoming vicarious. Culture itself a vicarious atonement; academic education in its stead, destroying native powers. Remittances have taken the place of earnings. Criticism takes the place of creation. Life is more and more a vicarious matter of subsisting existence—no subsistence existing as organic. Therefore life is no longer really living."

I think the man who said this will understand what I am trying to say. And if we find that we speak the same language, as I sometimes think we do, then my book will be what I would like it to be—a monument to you, in a way, to the spirit in you and in your great work.

May I come?

Sincerely,

On December 31, Wright's secretary at Spring Green, Wisconsin,
wrote to AR: "I am sorry for this late reply to your letter of the
12th which arrived while Mr. Wright was in the East. He has now
left for a several month sojourn in the Arizona desert so there will
be no opportunity for you to see him."

■ ■ ■

November 7, 1938

Dear Mr. Wright,

It is quite likely that you do not remember my name, so may I reintroduce
myself by reminding you that I am the writer who was introduced to you
by Ely Jacques Kahn at the dinner of the National Association of Real
Estate Boards in New York, where you were the speaker. I told you at that
time about the novel on architecture which I am writing, and you were kind
enough to say that you would give me an interview in New York where
you expected to be in November, on your way to England.

Forgive me for taking advantage of an after-dinner introduction, I
know how stupid such occasions must seem to you, only you see, it's
much more difficult for me, because I have been trying desperately for a
year to get in touch with you in some way. The novel I am writing
is not about you, but it is the life story of a great architect who defies all
traditions. I am afraid that the public will connect your name with it,
whether you and I intend it or not. That is why I am anxious to discuss
it with you before publication, in order to make certain that you will
not disapprove of the things I may say in it; and because I feel that you
must be informed of a book that comes as close to you as this one will, I
believe.

I do not seek any help from you in any literary or financial sense, nor
do I want to put you to any effort or inconvenience. But I should like, most
eagerly, to have one interview with you—only to tell you about it and to
ask you a few questions. If your time in New York shall be too limited
and you will find this impossible, I am prepared to go to Taliesin for an
interview with you, at any time that you will find convenient.

I am taking the liberty of sending to you my first novel, *We the Living*,
which was published two years ago, and also the first three chapters of my
novel on architecture, which is contracted for and to be published by Knopf.
These, I think, will be the best references that I can offer you. If you will
glance through them, you will be able to decide whether I am a writer good

enough to deserve any further consideration from you. I think the script of these first three chapters will give you an idea of what I am driving at in my architectural novel. If you find then that it interests you and if you see *why* I am anxious to speak to you—please let me know when you could give me an interview. If you do not approve at all—please let me know that, because then I'll stop torturing myself with attempts to reach you and I will have to proceed on the novel without the thing I would like to have—your blessing on my undertaking.

Sincerely yours,

Wright answered on November 18: "No man named 'Roark' with 'flaming red hair' could be a genius that could lick the contracting confraternity. Both items obtrude themselves disagreeably on the imagination, and he is not very convincing anyway. Will try to sometime see you in New York and say why if you want me to do so."

■ ■ ■

An undated telegram presumably sent shortly after AR's receipt of the preceding letter from Wright:

WOULD YOU OBJECT SERIOUSLY IF I CAME OUT TO TALIESIN FOR A TWENTY MINUTE INTERVIEW IF ONLY TO PERSUADE YOU THAT MY HERO HAS NOT GOT FLAMING RED HAIR AND TO LEARN FROM YOU WHAT YOUR OBJECTION IS TO THE NAME ROARK. THIS BOOK MEANS MORE TO ME THAN A TOUR DE FORCE, SEEKING AS I AM TO INTERPRET THROUGH THE MEDIUM OF FICTION THE SIGNIFICANCE AND BEAUTY OF MODERN ARCHITECTURE. PLEASE DON'T HESITATE TO BE AS BRUTAL AS YOU LIKE IN EXPRESSING YOUR WISH IN REGARD TO MY TRIP AND I WOULD APPRECIATE IT IF YOU'D WIRE ME COLLECT.

SINCERELY

On November 22, Wright's secretary wired AR: "Sorry. Mr. Wright has already left for the Arizona desert."

■ ■ ■

More than three years later, AR received the following letter from Wright:

Scottsdale, Arizona
April 23, 1944

My Dear Miss Rand:

I've read every word of *The Fountainhead*. Your thesis is *the* great one. Especially at this time. So I suppose you will be set up in the marketplace and burned for a witch.

Your grasp of the architectural ins and outs of a degenerate profession astonishes me. There is a lot of intelligent research visible back of this work of yours: a very real passion for your very real Cause. The Individual *is* the Fountainhead of any Society worthwhile. The Freedom of the Individual is the only legitimate object of government: the Individual Conscience is the great inviolable.

Well—the theme is as old as civilization but now buried under aeons of rubble in the upward struggle of Man, in spite of our experiment in the USA. You are digging in that rubble for our salvation as a people. And while you sensationalize your digging, what else is a "novel" for?

Your novel is Novel. Unusual material in unusual hands and, I hope, to an unusual end.

So far as I have unconsciously contributed anything to your material you are welcome.

We can now watch the usual performance of omitting the message while gaudifying the pictures. Hollywood ruined *The Devil and Daniel Webster*, knocked the lesson out of *The Remarkable Andrew*, missed the real idea in *The Pied Piper*, etc., etc., ad libitum, ad nauseam. I am afraid you are down the same street.

Thanks for Ellsworth Toohey. A great portrait. His time is up.

Sincerely yours,
Frank Lloyd Wright

■ ■ ■

May 14, 1944

Dear Mr. Wright,

Thank you. Your letter was like the closing of a circle for me, the end of ten years of my life that began and had to end with you. I felt that *The*

Fountainhead had not quite completed its destiny until I had heard from you about it. Now it is completed.

Thank you for your very gracious sentence: "So far as I have unconsciously contributed anything to your material you are welcome." You know, of course, that you have contributed a great deal, and I think that you know in what way. I have taken the principle which you represent, but not the form, and I have translated it into the form of another person. I was careful not to touch upon anything personal to you as a man. I took only the essence of what constitutes a great individualist and a great artist.

I have thought that you might resent Howard Roark, not for the things in which he resembles you, but precisely for the things in which he doesn't. So I would like to tell you now that Howard Roark represents my conception of man as god, of the absolute human ideal. You may not approve of it and it may not be the form in which you see the ideal—but I would like you to accept, as my tribute to you, the fact that what I took from you was taken for the figure of my own god.

Am I really "sensationalizing" my material? If I am, I think it is in the same way in which your buildings are "sensationalized." Your buildings are not designed for sloppy, "homey" living, not for flopping around in bedroom slippers, but for standing straight and making each minute count. I felt, whenever I entered a building of yours, that one could never relax here—relax in the sense most people do all their lives, that is, feel small, mean, slothful and comfortably insignificant. I felt that here one had to be a hero and lead a heroic life. Most people live in a kind of disgusting everyday stupor, and they experience a higher sense of existence only on very rare occasions, if at all. In your buildings one would have to experience it all the time. I think that is the way you build. Well, that is the way I write. No, my characters and events are not of the "century of the common man." They are not little people nor average people nor "just like the folks next door." You don't build for the way people live, but for the way they should live. I don't write about people as they are, but as they could be and should be. There are no such people in real life? Why, yes, there are. I am one of them.

You said, when I met you here, that I was too young and couldn't have suffered enough to write about integrity. Do you still think so?

I *have* been "set up in the market place" (the review of my book which you read in the *Architectural Forum* is just a little sample of that), but I can't be "burned for a witch," because I think I am made of asbestos.

I am not too afraid of what Hollywood might do to my book. So far, it looks as if I will win the battle, and the book will be preserved on the screen. I am willing to take the chance, because my producer's enthusiastic. But should others interfere and succeed in ruining the story, even a ruined screen version will attract the attention of some proper readers to my book. And that is all I want. I have stated my complete case in the book. I want those who can hear me to hear me. [After the movie came out, the book returned to the bestseller list.]

Now, would you be willing to design a house for me? You said you had to be interested in a person before you accepted him or her as a client. I don't know yet when and whether I will be able to go East to buy the land—but if I can go, would you care to design the house? I should like to know that before I buy the land.

Will you forgive me now for Roark's long legs and orange hair?

Gratefully—and always reverently,

■ ■ ■

June 22, 1944

Dear Mr. Wright:

Here is the final script of the screen version of *The Fountainhead*, which I have just finished. I would like very much to have you read it and see for yourself whether the theme, message and spirit of the book have been preserved. It is, of course, much shorter than the book, but I think you will agree with me that Hollywood has not ruined it.

This is the story as it will be produced, and it will give you an idea of the studio's approach to the picture and the earnestness of their purpose. My producer, Mr. Henry Blanke, has asked me to ask you whether you would consider working with us on the picture, to act as architectural supervisor and to design Roark's buildings, if the script meets with your approval. Mr. Blanke is as anxious as I am to prove to the world that an honest picture with a great message *can* come out of Hollywood.

You have told me that an honest picture on man's integrity and on architecture would be a miracle worth watching. If you find that we are on the right road so far, would you help us with the miracle? Would you help us to carry out the idea properly to the end? Since I am undertaking to make the whole world conscious of great architecture, you will understand how anxious I am to show truly great architecture on the screen. You know, and I know, that there is nobody but you who can design Roark's buildings to achieve the purpose we want the picture to achieve.

If you find the script acceptable to you, will you let me know whether you would be willing to take part in an experiment that might prove to be an unusual achievement? Selfishly (I believe in selfishness), as well as for the sake of my cause, I hope you will.

Reverently yours,

Wright answered on July 8: "I've read the manuscript and it does not betray you." He said that he would be glad to do a house for her but could not undertake to do the sets.

■ ■ ■

The next year, Wright sent AR a copy of his book *When Democracy Builds* and inscribed it: "To Ayn Rand, who seems so much more successful with fiction than I am with tact."

August 20, 1945

Dear Mr. Wright:

Thank you. I would like to think that you know how much it meant to me—receiving a book of yours from you. I look at your signature—and think that life is seldom as properly and wonderfully dramatic as this. You told me once that I couldn't have suffered enough to write about integrity. I think I have—and this was one of my nicest rewards.

As to your inscription, I would like to say that I have never known any *facts* as magnificently successful as Frank Lloyd Wright buildings. So that if I succeeded with fiction, it was in great measure because these facts helped me to believe in man's creative faculty.

I am leaving for New York on September 5th, for a month's vacation. While there, I intend to buy land for a Frank Lloyd Wright house of my own. May I come to see you and to discuss it with you while I am in the East? If you will be at Taliesin at that time and if it is convenient for you, I should like to make the trip there. I should like very much to see you again.

Gratefully and reverently yours,

■ ■ ■

November 30, 1945

Dear Mr. and Mrs. Wright,

Thank you for the days we spent at Taliesin. It was an exciting experience which I had looked forward to for years and shall always remember.

I am sorry that we did not have a chance to see you in person [in the hours] before we left—so I shall have to let a letter thank you for both of us.

Under separate cover, I have sent you *The God of the Machine* by Isabel Paterson. I hope you will find it a most important key to the solution of the questions we discussed.

With best regards and sincere appreciation from my husband and myself—

Cordially,

In his response of January 14, 1946, Wright thanked her for The God of the Machine, *which he said he "learned from." He included some personal news and closed with the hope that he would soon be in Los Angeles.*

■　■　■

September 10, 1946

Dear Frank Lloyd Wright:

I am sending you a copy of *Anthem*, a short novel of mine which is to be published this fall. I wrote it while I was working on *The Fountainhead*. I think you might like it.

I have hesitated to bother you with any questions or reminders about my future house—but Gerald Loeb tells me that a client should show his interest by pestering the life out of you. I think you know my interest— and I'm not good at expressing personal things which I feel very strongly. So I can only ask: Do I get my dream house?

I will not be able to come East this year to look for the land—and I don't want my choice of the land to be rash, since that will be my permanent home. So are you still willing to grant me the exception of a house designed ahead of the site?

I am working now on my next novel, so I'm dead to the world, and that is why I cannot make the trip. I plan to come East when I finish this novel, which will be a big event in my life. I hope I can then celebrate by actually starting the building of my house—if it becomes possible to build, by that time.

Incidentally, have you seen the comment in *Life* magazine of September 2, about my "public silence"? Would you like me to send them an answer, or would you prefer that I make no comment? As you see, I have kept my word—I have not tried to use your name for publicity.

I would like to hear your opinion of *Anthem*—and whether it's good or bad, I won't use it publicly, either.

Reverently, always—

In response to a printed letter alleging a resemblance between Wright and Howard Roark, Life *magazine wrote: "Miss Rand has not admitted any connection between [them]. But both are complete individualists, unallied with any group or school. Wright studied under Functionalist Louis Sullivan. . . . Roark's master was Henry Cameron, designer of functional skyscrapers. And both Roark and Wright lead very complicated lives."*

■ ■ ■

October 10, 1946

Dear Frank Lloyd Wright:

Thank you.

The house you designed for me is magnificent. I gasped when I saw it. It is the particular kind of sculpture in space which I love and which nobody but you has ever been able to achieve.

Most personally: Thank you for the fountain. That was as if you had autographed both my house and my book. This house is one of the greatest rewards an author can ever receive.

I was not very coherent when I told you what kind of house I wanted—and I had the impression that you did not approve of what I said. Yet you designed exactly the house I hoped to have. The next time somebody accuses you of cruelty and inconsideration toward clients, refer them to me.

I love the version with the top studio floor—and that is the one I want to have. My workroom alone on the top floor is my ideal of a place to write in. The double-corner-windows of glass are wonderful.

There are many things I would like to ask you about the details of the house. My first two practical questions are:

1. Is the stairwell in the studio an open one, or is it closed? It would have to be closed for me, because I need absolute privacy, silence, and the feeling of being cut off from everything, when I write.

2. Are you harsh on our future servants? The servant's room seems too small for anyone to live in. If I read the plans correctly, it looks like a

bedroom and bathroom combined. So I wonder whether the space marked for a den can be used for the servants' quarters?*

I should like to discuss the details with you in person. When you come west, may I come to see you in Arizona? Or, if you are in Los Angeles, I should love to invite you to visit us—if this is convenient for you.

What is the next step in the birth of a house? Can one start on working drawings—or does that have to wait for the site? Is there a particular kind of hill with a particular kind of grade which I must find to fit the dimensions of the house? (I want it to be in Connecticut.) What will the house actually cost to build—and what do I owe you so far?

There are many, many things I want to ask you. (Just practical questions—*not* esthetic ones. I want the house to be as you want it. I really practice what I preach.) Please let me know when I may see you.

Gratefully and reverently,

P.S. No, I have not read *The Tragic Sense of Life* by Unamuno, but I shall get it and read it.

■   ■   ■

December 30, 1946

Dear Frank Lloyd Wright:

I am enclosing my check for the preliminary drawings of my house.

I would like very much to have a preliminary drawing of the opposite elevation of the house—the side of the main entrance. I am eager to see what it will look like.

There are a great many questions I want to ask you about the details of the house, before we start on the working drawings. May I come to see you in Arizona, to discuss it? I would like to come sometime in late January or February. Please let me know whether this would be convenient for you.

With all my gratitude for this house,

As ever,

---

* In response, Wright sent a floor plan of a revised servants' quarters.

On January 21, Wright wrote: "Thanks for the check. Come when you are ready." But AR did not visit him in Arizona.

■   ■   ■

On September 19, 1957, Wright wrote to AR, thanking her for a copy of *Atlas Shrugged* she had sent him and wondering "why this long silence." He hoped she had not rejected her former thesis and that John Galt was still "the uncommon man!" "We look forward," he wrote, "to just what you have designed." At that time, he had read only the first chapter.

October 5, 1957

Dear Mr. Wright:

Thank you for your letter. I will be very interested to hear your reaction to *Atlas Shrugged* and I hope that you will write to me, at the above address, when you will have read it.

Cordially,

■   ■   ■

4

RETURN TO HOLLYWOOD (1944)

To Lenora M. Patton, a fan

January 14, 1944

Dear Miss Patton:

Thank you for your letter and your kind invitation [to dinner]. I am terribly sorry that I can't accept it—my letterhead will tell you why. I have sold the movie rights to *The Fountainhead* and am now in Hollywood, writing the screenplay.

I should have liked to meet you and your friend. If you read *The Fountainhead*, you must know that I am "accessible to a budding Assistant Treasurer" and to anyone who likes and understands my book, either at the Twenty-One Club or at the Automat. I don't know when I'll be back in New York, but when I am I'll drop you a line and I'll hope to meet you on your next visit to New York, if you will give me a rain check until then.

■ ■ ■

To William Mullendore, executive vice president and later president of Southern California Edison

January 17, 1944

Dear Mr. Mullendore,

Please forgive me the delay in acknowledging your note and the excerpts from Toohey's speech which you sent me. Allow me to thank you now and to tell you that I appreciated it very much.

I was rather thrilled by the excerpts you chose—it was very interesting for me to see what impressed you out of that speech. I note that you picked several which were my own favorite lines, such as: "Suspend reason and you play it deuces wild."

I hope that I will have an opportunity to see you again and to talk to you. You were one of five guests at that dinner who, I felt certain, were true and intelligent conservatives. Unfortunately, I was not so sure about some of the others—and I should have liked to hear more from you.

In 1961, AR described Mullendore as "the only businessman that I know of—then or in fact now—who was completely uncompromising. He was for free enterprise, laissez-faire, with no middle of the road, none of that conservative compromising."

■   ■   ■

To Walter Hurley

January 23, 1944

Dear Walter Hurley:

Thank you very much for your two letters. Needless to say, I am very happy if *The Fountainhead* is selling and I hope it will sell more and more.

Please give my very special thanks to Mr. Baker for the Literary Guild deal—and include a kiss to him from me across the continent. Mr. Chambers has just sent me a proof of the Guild ad—and it's pretty lurid, but not as bad as it could be. The main thing is the size and the splash, which will help our sales, so I was very happy to see it.

Thank you also for the *Omnibook* deal. I regret only that their digest was not submitted to me for editing. It's not too awful, but I could have improved it within the same space. I don't want to write to Mr. Chambers about it, not to make it an official complaint at this late date, but will you remind him tactfully that this digest was supposed to be submitted for my approval according to our contract? I want only to make sure that this will be done on any other digests we may sell.

Everything is still going wonderfully here. Mr. Blanke is most pleased with the first sequence of the screenplay which I have turned in. I am working as I used to work for Bobbs-Merrill, which means—like a dog, but I love it. Warners' plans for the picture are really tremendous—and I hope it will work out that way.

My best regards to you and all my friends at Bobbs-Merrill, whom I still miss very much in spite of sunny California, which *is* beautifully sunny right now.

Omnibook *was a pocket-size monthly magazine devoted to abridgments of current bestsellers and aimed primarily at men and women in the armed forces. The 46,000-word version of* The Fountainhead *was published in January 1944 in both the English and Spanish editions.*

■ ■ ■

To D. L. Chambers

January 23, 1944

Dear Mr. Chambers:

I am sorry that I cannot tell you for certain when I will finish *The Moral Basis of Individualism.* I will try to have it done by April—if my screen work will be finished in time for that, but I cannot promise it, because I have no way of telling how long Warner Brothers will need me on the picture. You must realize what a tremendous job it is to condense *The Fountainhead* into a screenplay. It is more than a full-time job, and I can do no other writing until it is finished.

I trust I am not letting you down, since I am still working indirectly for Bobbs-Merrill. A good picture will help the sale of *The Fountainhead* tremendously—and that is much more important for me, as well as for you, than a new book. *The Fountainhead* has sold well, but not yet as well as it could and should, so I will not rest until I have done everything that is in my power to put it into top sales as, I think, it deserves.

■ ■ ■

To Richard Mealand, screenwriter and novelist, who recommended *The Fountainhead* to Bobbs-Merrill

January 23, 1944

Dear Dick:

I think I am still keeping my head, but Hollywood is doing its best to turn it—by being unexpectedly and unbelievably good to me. Maybe I shouldn't praise a rival studio, but Warners have been grand so far. Henry Blanke is a miracle of a producer—it's a pleasure to work with him.

I have turned in the first sequence of my screenplay—and Mr. Blanke was enthusiastic about it. He even said that he was surprised—he had not expected such a professional job. I realize that I can't tell what will happen later, but so far everything has been wonderful for me.

I don't mind if all this sounds like boasting—*The Fountainhead* is your godchild, so you should be informed. Are you proud of the godchild? I mean specifically that it was mentioned as one of the "notable" books of the year in *Time* magazine, that it had a scrambled-up digest made in *Omnibook*, and that you will soon see the most lurid ads of it put out by the Literary Guild which picked it as a "dividend book." I like to watch all this and to think of the day when you stopped me in the hall and asked where I would like to submit my book.

Once more and always: thank you.

■ ■ ■

To Richard Mealand

February 20, 1944

Dear Dick:

Good God! This is in relation to the postscript of your letter—about your having lunch with "an ardent admirer" of mine—Hugh MacLennan, author of *Barometer Rising*. Look up your synopsis of *Barometer Rising* and see who covered it for Paramount. If you keep them, see my comment on it.

My ardent admirer? I have been Hugh MacLennan's ardent admirer for three years. I have been selling him to everyone I know. In all the time I was a reader for Paramount, I found only two books which I liked so much that I wanted to buy them, and did. The mystery story *Grim Grow the Lilacs* [by M. F. Rodell] and *Barometer Rising*. I even wanted to write Hugh MacLennan a fan letter at the time, but I didn't, because of the Paramount rule that readers mustn't communicate with authors. I think *Barometer Rising* is one of the best novels I have ever read and certainly the best first novel.

So you can imagine how your postscript affected me. I gasped aloud when I read it. You'll understand why this would appeal to my sense of the dramatic. It's so beautifully right—things like that happen in books, but very seldom in real life. Offhand, I can't think whom I would like to see "profoundly influenced by *The Fountainhead*" rather than Hugh MacLennan.

Will you do me a favor? It seems to be your fate always to be the source of good things for me. Will you tell this to Hugh MacLennan—or show him this letter, if you wish—and ask him to write to me. I would like to hear from him about *The Fountainhead*. Or give me his address and I'll write to him—now that I'm no longer a Paramount slave.

However, I think of my period of slavery with tenderness and gratitude—and I miss you all very much. I won't come back with "Rolls-Royces and a new hairdo," but I will come back with the same old sloppy haircut—and a Packard. Yes, that's what I bought. Don't get frightened, it's only a 1936 Packard, though in perfect condition and magnificent-looking—black, half-a-block long and drips with chromium.

I haven't seen anyone, but I will, now that I have a car. I'll get in touch with Mr. Dozier and Miss Reis, as you suggest. Only I don't want to be "snatched" out of Warner Brothers, at least not right now. I know it sounds incredible for Hollywood, but things are going wonderfully for me so far. I fully realize that maybe it won't go like this to the end—but up to the present it has been perfect. I have just signed a contract with them to remain until I finish the script (they had me only for ten weeks, if you remember)—at a salary of $750 a week.

I don't know when I'll be back in New York, but in spite of all this grandeur, I'm quietly dreaming of the day when I'll get back and start work on my next novel. The thing haunts me already.

■ ■ ■

To Hugh MacLennan, an author

March 19, 1944

Dear Mr. MacLennan:

Thank you. I have admired your book and wondered about you for almost three years—so I was more than happy to hear from you. I read *Barometer Rising* in galleys, when I was a reader for Paramount, and I stayed up all night, to do the best synopsis I ever did for them. I certainly tried my best to have them buy it for the screen—but you know that readers have very little influence on a studio's decision.

Since you read *The Fountainhead*, you must know that I admire nothing in people—except the quality of genuine originality, the ability to do one's work in an unborrowed way of one's own. That, to me, is the only virtue. That is the quality which *Barometer Rising* had—and that's why I loved it and why I'm very interested in you as an author and a person.

The two things I liked above all in *Barometer Rising* were: beautiful writing, completely *un-trite*, and a brilliant plot structure. Contrary to the cheap highbrows who scorn plot, I think that a good plot is the most important part of any literary work, and the hardest part to do well. A sense of plot structure is the rarest one of all the qualifications of a writer. I don't mean a mechanically contrived sequence of events with some thriller-action. I mean a truly integrated story. And the only modern novel I've read in years that showed a beautiful skill of plot integration was *Barometer Rising*.

If you want to know what particular sequences stand out in my mind, for sheer beauty of writing and treatment, it's: the scene between Penelope and the doctor on the train, the scene when Neal returns and meets her again, the description of the explosion. These were great—my compliments to you. I loved the *strength* of your characters—Neal, Penelope and even her father. I'm so sick of noble humanitarians who serve everybody and intellectuals who seek the meaning of life and find it by going off to fight for Loyalist Spain—which is about all we've had in novels for twenty years (oh yes, and "the little people with hearts of gold")—that characters like yours had to be admired, if only as contrast.

The thing that did not seem to fit the rest of *Barometer Rising* was the final sequence where you reverted to the "and so he solved his personal problems by losing himself in unselfish service" pattern. That didn't ring true. It never does, anyway, but it seemed particularly out of place in your book because all your characters were too strong and too good for that.

When I finished your book, my guess about the author was: here's a brilliant writer, with the natural talent and instincts of an individualist, who felt that he had to apologize for himself by sticking in some "social significance" at the end of his book. Here was an interesting story about interesting people—and suddenly, the author seemed to feel that interesting people couldn't be an end in themselves, that they and their story had to be "justified" by "something higher." At that point, the story lost conviction. So I thought: here's something the author doesn't really believe.

That is why, when Dick Mealand wrote to me that you said you were "profoundly influenced by *The Fountainhead*," I was thrilled and I thought you were the one man who needed that particular influence. I thought, in effect: Hugh MacLennan should go on writing about men of Roark's type, and not attempt to apologize for it with any kind of a Toohey philosophy.

And if he hasn't yet realized that Neal was a better man when he fought for himself than when he "served the community"—maybe *The Fountainhead* will show him how and why.

Has it?

Your letter contains the same kind of contradiction. You say you oppose statism but approve of the ends of socialism. What *ends*? What *is* socialism—except Statism? When the State (the community, the nation, the race, the class, the *collective*, it's all one) owns the means of every man's livelihood, the product of his labor, his energy, his time and his life—what in hell can that possibly be except Statism? The *ends* of socialism are all listed in Ellsworth Toohey's speech on pp. 689–695 of *The Fountainhead* (as well as the reasons which make people accept such ends). But that isn't what you want, is it?

You can't really think that Ellsworth Toohey is a "bad" socialist, a hypocrite, but that there are "good" socialists, who are "good" yet preach the very same things. Toohey is the completely good socialist—the honest one—because he doesn't fool himself and really desires what he preaches, with his eyes open. What he says in his speech represents the real, logical, consistent, naked *ends* of socialism. Once we say that man must live for others (which is the basic premise of socialism), we have accepted all the ideas of Toohey's speech. There can be no "good" way of living for others or "bad" way of living for others (who, incidentally, would decide what constitutes such a distinction, and by what standards?)—just as there can be no "good" slavery or "bad" slavery. Living for others is slavery—and nothing else whatever—and no names, ends or excuses can alter the fact. The issue is simply: does man live for others or does he live for himself? Slavery or freedom. Not one version of slavery against another.

No, I certainly don't think that Henry Wallace is a good person. I think he means, proposes and desires exactly what he says and writes. It was Henry Wallace who said (I quote it as exactly as I can remember) that instead of stressing rights, liberties and all the things which keep people apart, we should stress duties, responsibilities and all the things which bring people together. Don't you realize what is meant and intended here? So we shouldn't "stress rights" at a time when the whole world is perishing from the destruction of human rights?

If you are disappointed in all the socialists you know—are you fooling yourself by thinking that they betray their ideal? Don't you realize that they are *produced by* their ideal, that they are its logical, consistent exponents —and the only types who could be? Do you really think that all the horrors perpetrated by altruists and socialists were due to the mistakes or hypocrisy of their leaders? Look at the premises, leaders and results of the French Revolution and the Russian Revolution. "The worst butchers were the most sincere." Robespierre and Lenin were completely sincere in their devotion to their ideas. So, for that matter, is Hitler sincere in whatever ghastly nonsense it is that he believes. Can you name anyone anywhere who can equal the record of horror achieved by just these three? They were not hypocritical, nor were they "mistaken." They were frighteningly consistent—in true accordance with their idea. That idea could produce no other results. Once you accept the idea of man as servant for or tool of others—once you reject the total and sacred inviolability of the individual—the guillotine, the GPU and the Gestapo will follow automatically and inevitably—no matter what other trimmings you put on the idea and no matter who is the great altruist in charge. The guillotine is implicit in the idea of altruism.

Do you think it is a mere coincidence that all the Fascist leaders are ex-socialists? Mussolini, Hitler, Laval, Oswald Mosley and all the lesser ones. Fascism, Nazism, Communism and Socialism are only superficial variations of the same monstrous theme—collectivism.

If you care to continue the discussion, please write to me and tell me what it is you really believe and why. I want to discuss it because I am interested in you and your talent. I hate to see another talent choked, twisted, ruined and turned upon itself by the Toohey philosophy. I've seen many tragic instances of that.

Thank you for the things you wrote about *The Fountainhead*. I was glad to hear them from you. You were the second of only two men who understood that *The Fountainhead* was a dramatization of abstract principles—and a very difficult one to do.

I am very interested in your new book. When will it be available—and do you care to tell me more about it? I'd like to know.

I should like very much to meet you and Mrs. MacLennan—but I'm afraid that I won't be back in New York before May. If this type of letter doesn't frighten you, let's correspond until we meet—as I hope we will some day.

With my best and most real regards,

MacLennan's four-page response on March 26 combined praise for The Fountainhead *and opposition to capitalism. There is no record of another letter from AR to him.*

■ ■ ■

To Ralph E. Lewis, of Preston & Files, her attorneys

March 22, 1944

Dear Mr. Lewis:

I am enclosing the bestseller lists which you requested. Please *do not* send them off to Mr. Chambers, as these are the only copies I have. Please return them to me after taking the dates and such information as you may need.

These lists are from the Sunday Book Magazines of the *New York Times* and the *New York Herald-Tribune*. They are considered *the* bestseller lists of the publishing business, the ones by which a book's success is judged. They differ from each other in that they are taken from different stores; the *Times* list represents an average drawn upon all the stores of a given city; The *Herald-Tribune* list gives individual stores. This last is the oldest such list in the country and is, I believe, considered as the most indicative one and the most important.

You will notice that *The Fountainhead* first appeared on the *Herald-Tribune* list on June 11—it is listed on the side, among "books reported by two stores." It stayed there for three weeks, then vanished, and reappeared on July 16, when it rose to the list proper, with four stores reporting. *This* is the time when the first disastrous break occurred—because the book sold too well and Bobbs-Merrill were caught out of print. The book reappeared on August 13 and stayed on the list steadily, week after week, until October 1, when it rose to the highest number of stores reporting that it had ever reached—5 stores. This is where it had really hit its stride and was climbing steadily. And *this* is where Bobbs-Merrill killed it. They were out of print in October—and you have Mr. Chambers's letter admitting this.

The *Times* list is less steady for all books (except top bestsellers). You will notice that the breaks in the *Times* list coincide with those of the *Herald-Tribune*. July and October were the months when the book vanished from both lists.

The lists I am sending you are the only ones on which the book appeared. I did not save those where it was not listed. You may check on them in the library, if you wish to see whether this is so. Since I came to California, I have not been buying the New York papers, but I have watched the lists from the copies here at the studio—and the record is as follows:

The book appeared on the *Times* list on: December 12, December 19, January 16, January 23, February 6. It appeared once on the *Herald-Tribune* list—two weeks ago (I did not take down the date), listed on the side, by two stores. I have not seen last week's lists yet.

Now in regard to Mr. Chambers's letter—I think that we should now ask a written and official statement from him, a letter of agreement to the effect that since the plates are made they will be kept for me to buy at *whatever time* Bobbs-Merrill decides that they need the plates no longer; that such plates will not be destroyed under any circumstances and at any time, but will be preserved for my purchase. This, I believe, will put Mr. Chambers on the spot; if he really has the plates, he will be legally obliged to keep them.

I think we must also question at once his statement that the *Omnibook* matter is "closed." If he thinks we don't know it, we must let him understand that we know it is up to me to decide whether this is closed, not up to him.

■ ■ ■

To Charles S. Pearson, of Charles S. Pearson Lectures

April 16, 1944

Dear Mr. Pearson:

Please excuse my delay in writing to you. I have not written sooner, not because of indifference or negligence, but because I have been going from week to week without knowing how things would develop for me here and without being able to make my future plans. I had thought that I would be back in New York this spring, but I could not tell how long my writing assignment would keep me here.

Now, however, it appears that I will have to remain here at least for the rest of this year—as the studio will want me during the actual shooting and production of my picture. So I will not be able to do any lectures at all during 1944, and cannot renew our agreement.

If you will send me an itemized statement of the money you have spent on press material for me, I will reimburse you for it—as I appreciate your interest and do not want you to suffer an actual financial loss on my account.

Promotional material had been produced for lectures entitled "The Moral Basis of Individualism," "Only One Freedom," and "The Evil of Altruism."

■ ■ ■

To William Mullendore

Mullendore sent AR a long comment by Thomas F. Woodlock, quoted in the *Wall Street Journal* of May 1, 1944. The quoted material began: "Every despotism has a specially keen and hostile instinct for whatever keeps up human dignity and independence."

April 16, 1944

Dear Mr. Mullendore:

Thank you ever so much for your letter with the quotation from Amiel's *Journal*. It was very interesting and startling to read it—it *is* so very close to my own philosophy.

I cannot help wondering how mankind allowed itself to be dragged down to the present state of depravity—when there were clear-headed thinkers a hundred years ago, who saw the nature and meaning of collectivism. I hold the doctrine of altruism responsible for it. So long as nobody denounced that doctrine as positive evil, so long as men continued to regard it as an ideal, it had to work its way down to its ultimate consequence— collectivism. The two *are* inseparable, and the altruist *is* the collectivist. But—what a job to make people understand this!

Your quotation gave me one more proof of my contention that altruism is the real issue and our real enemy, that our side must make a stand on this, and that we have no chance on a long-range historical scale until we make this stand. The issue cannot be evaded or ignored any longer. Altruism has reached its logical climax—and we cannot fight the effects without blasting the cause.

■   ■   ■

To Gerald Loeb

April 23, 1944

Dear Mr. Loeb:

I hope you will forgive me for my long silence—the length of this letter will serve as explanation and, I hope, as apology. You said in one of your letters that you have no ability for small talk. My trouble is that I have no ability for small letters—that is, I cannot answer casually and carelessly, particularly when there is a serious subject such as writing to discuss. I must always make a thorough job of it. So I delayed answering you until

I could do it right. Please forgive me if I took too long. It was not indifference on my part—but a miserable struggle against the California climate. After coming home from work I could do nothing but go to sleep and my mind simply refused to function. I am better now—and getting slowly used to it.

I am ashamed to say that I have seven letters of yours to answer. I was selfishly glad every time I heard from you—but failed in my part of it. Now I shall attempt to answer everything, in the order received. Before I come to the literary discussion, let me say right now that your dialogue scene is very good, much better than I expected from a first attempt.

Thank you very much for the booklet "The Battle for Investment Survival" which you sent me. It is really excellent and helped me a lot to understand the situation. I was deeply touched by your offer to give me advice on investments. I appreciate it more than I can say. When I'll know what my financial future is to be, I would like to ask your advice in a general way and would be very grateful for any suggestion you can give me. But I would not think of asking you to open an account for me and handle it and do all the work, on a friendly basis. When and if I can venture into Wall Street, I would like very much to become a regular, business client of yours—if, however, I am not too small an investor for that. I frankly know nothing about the stock market—and I suspect that your firm handles only large accounts. My situation is very peculiar—I don't know to what financial class I belong, whether I am a small "nouveau riche," with more riches coming, or a big "old poor" who got just one major break and will get no more. As things look for me in Hollywood at the moment, it seems that I'll make more money than I ever expected or would know how to handle. I'll have to get used to the situation. And I simply have not had the time to think it over carefully.

Now, to your next letters. "Life in a Tower" is very charming and witty—in a peculiar way of your own which I can't quite define—you probably know what I mean. It has a kind of dry humor that can't be classified, it's not quite like any other manner of writing. That, precisely, might be its commercial drawback; an editor might be baffled and not know how to classify it—it is not an essay nor an article. I think it would be good for *The New Yorker*, in manner and intention, but it might be too short. As it stands, it is just a brief vignette, like a speech by a witty man giving his general impression. I think that *The New Yorker* would want it expanded into a more complete essay. I know I'm late with this opinion—so let me know what you have done with it. Have you tried it on *The New Yorker*? If not, I think it would be definitely worth trying.

Thank you for going after Greta Garbo for me. I was glad to hear that she has read my book. Mr. Blanke, my producer, knows her personally—and I asked him what he intended to do, after I received your letter. He said he would speak to her—but that it is too early for us to begin any business negotiations with her. He cannot start on the casting until my script is finished—because when he talks to actors he must give a definite shooting date, and this cannot be set, even tentatively, until the script is done. No, we have not decided on a leading man either—and have no one definite in mind. The whole casting will be a difficult problem—a bad cast could ruin the story.

I'm glad you agree with me about the review of my book in the *Architectural Forum*. Do you see what was disgusting about it? Not that they condemned the book, but that they did it in such hooligan, corner-lout manner—which is the present manner of all the pink intellectual vermin. It's not the reviewer I blame, but the editor. A reviewer might be a minor punk—but an editor should have some sense of intellectual decency, which Mr. Nelson does not have. I think he has lied to you—any magazine always keeps track of who wrote what in its pages. Such a record is always kept on file. If Mr. Nelson said they could not trace it now—I believe he was simply afraid of you and trying to save his own face.

I was amused to hear about your conversation with Frank Lloyd Wright. A few weeks ago, he came to Los Angeles—and I got to see him. I spent a whole hour talking to him, and was very much impressed. I may be wrong, but he seemed to be a very sincere kind of man. At least, sincere in his devotion to architecture. No, he hasn't read my book as yet—I had the feeling that he resented an outsider's attempt to treat of his subject. But he said he wanted to read it, so I sent him a copy. I haven't heard from him yet. I mentioned to him his conversation with you—and he laughed about the "orange hair," he said that I owed it to him because if he had seen the book in advance, he wouldn't have let me give my hero orange hair—it was unnatural. He's wrong there, and I'm sure he couldn't have talked me out of it.

Thank you for sending me your article on "A Layman Looks at Building." It is excellent—thorough, complete and very clearly presented. I enjoyed reading it. And I agree with everything you said, except for one point. You are right when you say that so-called modern architecture is "too bare and too cold. If persisted in, this tendency will kill off modernism and functionalism altogether in time." But I do not think that the solution is, as you say, to preserve "the attractive features that have lived through the years and can be adapted to inclusion in the postwar functional building." That would mean a modern building trimmed with simplified Greek pilasters, flattened-out pediments, semiclassical ornament and so forth. There are quite a few such buildings—and they are worse than anything else. They're neither fish, flesh nor fowl. Like all compromisers, they're inferior to both types which they're trying to mingle—inferior to the strictly period house and to the bare modern house. There is a housing project here that is a simply ghastly example of just such an adaptation. And all the worst kinds of cheap-priced apartment buildings in New York are such adaptations—look at the Bronx modern on the Grand Concourse.

But you are right that plain "shoe-box" modernism is cold, boring and has no human appeal whatever. I like your term for what the moderns lack—"human functionalism." The solution, however, is in an architecture such as Frank Lloyd Wright's—that is, buildings which are not plain and bare, but with a complicated, ingenious pattern and an ornament of their own, but an ornament designed for that particular structure, strictly original and not borrowed from any established historical style. Buildings do need beauty and ornament for their human appeal—but why must the ornament be an eternal repetition of and variation upon old Greek trimmings? There is such a field open for true creative originality. But—with the exception of Wright—I don't know any architect capable of creating it. The trouble, I think, is still the same as it always was: before the advent of modern architecture, mediocre architects simply copied what had been done before; now, they simply put up shoe boxes of concrete, which require no more originality or imagination than the copying did. What we need is more Wrights or Howard Roarks. But where to find them? I have no solution for that. It's the same in every line of endeavor. The original talent is the rarest thing in the world. But in architecture, mediocrity is more glaringly obvious than in other lines—because there's a huge, physical object such as a building to demonstrate it.

Now—to your dialogue scene. You said in your letter that it seemed amateurish to you. It is anything else but. Your approach to dialogue is thoroughly professional. Apparently, you have done it unconsciously, not knowing the rules, which proves that you do have a talent for writing. The rule is simply this: an amateur writing dialogue will go on with it forever and will have his characters talk lengthily, pointlessly, at random—under the mistaken impression that it must sound exactly the way people talk in real life. The fact is, of course, that if anyone attempted to transcribe real-life dialogue in shorthand and then put it into a story, as is, the result would be the worst kind of writing imaginable. People do talk at random, and seldom make a clear point in a few words, simply because nobody can make a brief formulation of a thought in conversation. So a lot of words are naturally wasted in real-life talking. Therefore, the problem of a dialogue writer is a subtle one: he must make his dialogue sound as if this is the way people really talk—and yet write it with a brevity, clarity and economy of words never achieved by anybody in real-life talk. He must never allow an extra line which has no specific purpose. He must have every line carry either exposition or characterization—and usually both. But he cannot allow his characters to talk so precisely that they will sound stilted. The trick is to select out of people's normal expressions those lines that are representative, that can give you—in one flash—the whole idea of the person or subject discussed, while sounding completely natural. It is a very difficult trick—and I was surprised to see how well you've done it.

I can clarify this best on the example of your own dialogue. Take your first line. When Tom enters, Olivia says: "Well, I never." That is all—and it's perfect for its purpose. It shows surprise, and rudeness, and a woman who talks in bromides. In real life, she would have said that and a great deal more. But you omitted the "more"; that line was enough, it said everything, yet was natural. You could have selected another popular bromide—but most of them would have been meaningless—you picked the one that was characteristic. This is true of all your dialogue in the scene. All of it is the natural expression of a person and suggests a lot beyond the actual words used. "Come over now and sit on the bed and watch me dress but be a good boy"—is a swell line. It gives you the complete picture of a sloppy little tart without taste or manners.

I could see that you were afraid of dialogue—because you ventured only a few lines, with explanatory narrative in between. I would like to see you try a whole page of dialogue—straight conversation without explanations. It would not be necessary for your short story—but when you come to writing your novel, you will have to do it. Don't be afraid of it—you'll do it all right, I can tell that by the sample. Did you notice that in your scene there are very few places where the characters exchange talk? Most of it is just one line, then a narrative interruption. Only on pages 4 and 5 do you have a straight exchange of line and answer—and it's very good. So why were you afraid of it? I would suggest that you forget all self-consciousness about dialogue—and just write it as you did here. Follow your natural feeling about it. It's good. You don't have to run from it back to narrative all the time.

Incidentally, this little scene does more to bring your short story alive than any amount of narrative could do. I remember the story itself—and this one scene gave it more color, gave it a reality it did not have. Now I would suggest that you go over the story, select the key spots and present them in dialogue, like this scene, and with less hesitation. I believe the result would astonish you. You will have a complete, professional short story.

Well, I think I've covered all the objective, businesslike answers I owed you—now to a personal remark. I liked what you wrote about competence. You said that you love competence as Howard Roark does—and as I do. I can't tell you how much I love it. It's the only thing I love or admire in people. I don't give a damn about kindness, charity or any of the other so-called virtues. (Besides, I've never encountered them in the form they're supposed to exist, the way they do in books.) Competence, talent, efficiency, ability are the only values I recognize. Plus the first and most important one—integrity. But I'm profoundly convinced that integrity is a quality possessed only by competent human beings. A man doesn't have to be a genius—he may be only a good bricklayer—but if he's good at his work, any work, he will have spiritual integrity. A kindly, mushy, sloppy individual who loves everybody, but cannot do a good day's work at whatever it is he's doing—will never have any kind of integrity, and will prove himself to be a weakling and a coward in any crisis.

Why did you write that you are "poor at games, at social small talk, at telling jokes, at heavy drinking" as if this were a defect in you? I think you ought to be proud of being poor at those things. The people who're good at that are usually very worthless human beings. And as to small talk—that's the particular abomination of my life. I hate it, am utterly no good at it and have given up the attempt to put up with it or tolerate it in others. I've been too busy all my life to want to waste time on listening to or uttering small talk. And so have you, I suspect. Incidentally, the Sunday when you visited us here, you talked a great deal and all of it was very interesting—but it was not small talk. So why should you wish to acquire a small-talk talent?

This letter is already abominably long, so I'll add only a few words about myself. Everything is going very well for me at the studio. I will have my script finished soon—and then I'll know more about the actual plans of production, the casting, etc. I would have finished by now—only I was interrupted by being taken off my script for three weeks and assigned to rescue another picture already in production. They had started shooting a picture with such dreadful dialogue that the director refused to do it. I was given the job of re-dialoguing the main scenes—and had to do it while running a race with the camera. I liked doing it, and they were all very pleased with my work. But that, among other things, kept me in such a rush and nervous tension that I could not do anything else, had no time for any private life at all—or any of the letters I wanted to write (that's for a hint of apology).

If you get tired of reading this letter—forgive me that I had to do it all at once, like this. At least, you'll know that I was not indifferent. I am deeply grateful for one sentence in your letter written from your country house: "I will be very happy if all this doesn't disturb you, as I enjoy writing to you." No, it does not disturb me—and I'm glad if you like writing to me—and I enjoy very much hearing from you. The length of this letter will show you that I enjoy writing to you, too. Will you please overlook this one long delay—and write to me again? Now that I have caught up with things, I will try not to be so slow again, and will answer more "competently."

■ ■ ■

To Gerald Loeb

June 3, 1944

Dear Mr. Loeb:

Thank you very much for your very interesting letters. Now I have to answer four—and I'm glad that you are understanding enough to excuse my irregular answering habits. I am better this time than last, am I not? Someday I might catch up with myself.

First, about "He and She." The last version you sent me is a great improvement on the previous one. It is not yet in the right short story form, but much nearer. I think you have grasped the idea of the form now—and you need some practice to master the technique. The main flaw in your story, as it stands now, is that the climax is not strong enough. It does not quite give the story the completeness and finality which a short story requires.

The best thing in the story is that it sounds real, alive, the characterizations are clever, the observations subtle—and the whole carries a great deal of conviction. True, there are grammatical errors and awkward sentences, but that is not important. That comes merely from your uncertainty in the use of a fictional form. The virtues of the story, however, are important and show that you have writing ability. The rest you will get with practice. If you are getting tired of this story, I would suggest that you let it rest for a while, try another one, and then come back to this one. You cannot really learn except by writing and you cannot do it on one and the same story. If you rewrite it too much, you will go stale. After doing another short story, and maybe two or three, you would come back to this one with a fresh approach and much more assurance—and you will see what it needs, much better than if you attempt to practice on it over and over again.

No, I don't agree with your friend who said that your story reads "like it was written by someone who is an amateur at life." It does not read like that—but your friend's remark sounds like the remark of someone who is an amateur at literature. Writing has *nothing* to do with an author's personal life or experiences in the direct, factual sense your friend implied. It has to do with an author's thinking—not with the actual events of his life. A book does reveal the author's inner self, but not the superficial, accidental circumstances of his existence. You ask, in connection with this friend's remark, whether the fact that you have never been in love will prevent you from writing about love. Of course not. Writing has nothing to do with factual experience. Only with creative imagination. To be exact, I would say: 10% observation, 90% imagination. If the subject of love is not the one you want to write about—you don't have to. It is not literature's exclusive and compulsory subject. If you do want to write about it, you can write without actual experience. Write of it as you imagine it. If you stick to a consistent idea of your own—it will come out real and alive, whether you've actually experienced it or not.

Incidentally, someone once said that ninety percent of the people would never have been in love if they hadn't read about it. I am under the impression that your friends make too much of the fact that you've never been in love. Chances are they haven't been either. What most people call love is anything else but. I would think—this is just surmise—that you haven't been in love simply because you're more particular and more honest with yourself than other people.

You ask, is anybody in *The Fountainhead* in love, beside Roark and Dominique. Oh my, yes. You ask, are Roark and Dominique in love. Most definitely. THAT is real love—it is not just physical, the physical is only the expression of the spiritual, or it could never have that much force and violence. Who else is in love? Why, Wynand is truly in love with Dominique. But above all, and greater, I think, than any other emotion in the book, is Wynand's love for Roark. Wynand is in love with Roark—in every way except the physical. It is not a homosexual feeling—but it *is* love in the romantic sense and in the highest sense. Not just affection or admiration. As to Keating—no, he didn't love anybody. Catherine is the nearest he ever came to it—but even then it wasn't much, because—being actually selfless—he was not capable of any real and complete emotion.

You ask, what is Roark's attitude toward women. Apart from Dominique "is he cold and virginal otherwise"? Yes, he is. Most cold and totally virginal. Because he is too highly sexed. Just as Dominique is. The highly sexed person is extremely selective. He, or she, can respond only to a special and great attraction. The lesser ones will have no effect on him. It is a mistake to think that the promiscuous person is the highly sexed one. Quite the contrary. It is the person of a sexually lower order who will respond to anything and anybody. It is the same difference as between a gourmet and a glutton. Which one of the two has the higher sense of food?

I am a little shocked at your supposing that Roark would "indulge commercially." How could he? His whole nature is in the fact that he has a tremendous reverence for himself. That means—for anything pertaining to his life, actions and personality. And since sex is a most personal, most important matter, how could he degrade himself with a woman he despised? He would consider it a degradation. It is Keating and Toohey, in the book, who were cheap and promiscuous about their love lives. Incidentally, so it is in real life too. A person betrays his own valuation of himself in his attitude on sex. If the attitude is cheap and sloppy, the person has no real self-respect, whether he knows it or not. He usually does know it. As to Roark, I can imagine him having other mistresses, beside Dominique, but they would have to be very high types of women and his relation to them would never be casual. Since he could not find many such women, he simply didn't care—and didn't have time to care.

Your next question is: what picture did I re-dialogue? It was *The Conspirators*. But I did it for Hal Wallis—and he has left Warners—and another producer has taken the picture over, and changed everything in it, including the title. So I don't think there will be much of mine left in it. Please don't go to see it. I'd hate to have you accuse me of somebody else's mess.

Now THIS is your $64 question: "What's the idea for your next novel? A bestseller? Or a propaganda story to please you?" Are you baiting me or is this serious? Do you really think anyone can sit down and say: "Now I'm going to write a bestseller?" Why, of course it's going to be "a propaganda story to please me." Just like *The Fountainhead*. And if it becomes a bestseller—*that* is what will make it sell—that it pleased me.

I mean this seriously and literally. NOBODY ON EARTH CAN WRITE DOWN. Unless a book pleases its author—it will not please anyone. If it pleases its author—that is no guarantee that it will sell. But if its author has written it down, to make money—*that* is a sure guarantee that it will not sell at all. Don't pay any attention to and don't believe the people who tell you that they despise their own works, that they write "just for money." Such people are successful with trash—because that is the true level of their own minds. They don't write down—they write on their real level. To be exact, actual trash is never successful, even commercially. There are many awful writers that are successful—but that is because they do well the job they choose, that of popular writing. Even pulp stuff has to be good on its own terms and requires its own skill. This cannot be simulated. The writer has to be on the level of his writing. Some authors have a gift in both fields—for serious books and for popular fiction. In such cases, their popular fiction is not trash. They write it because they like it, and they do it well. But any writer who attempts to "go popular" always fails, always has failed and always will fail. There have been good, serious writers of a high literary style, who tried and couldn't write an acceptable *Liberty* magazine serial, while much lesser writers could and did. This is simply because no man can sink beneath himself. It is really easier to surpass oneself than to degrade oneself. A man can make an effort up—to improve himself—but God help the man who makes an effort down. The conception of pulling oneself up by one's bootstraps is more logical and feasible than the vicious popular fallacy that a man of talent can make himself sink below his own shoe soles—that is, disregard his talent, his taste, his judgment, his literary standards, and write down to "the public" for financial reward.

Of anything I may tell you, which you might find of value—this is the most important: DO NOT SET OUT TO WRITE WITH YOUR EYES ON THE BOX OFFICE. IT CAN'T BE DONE.

You must write that which *you* consider good, to the best of your judgment, taste and ability. There is no other rule or standard to go by. If you commit the above popular error—it is a fatal error and your writing effort will be doomed in advance.

Above any minor technical advice which I might give you, I should like to straighten out your general approach to writing—which, I think, is terribly wrong, as indicated in many of the questions you ask. The above is one of them. I shall come to several others later. You seem to represent a peculiar combination: when you write a story, your approach is honest, direct and fresh, you write what you see and think, as you see it and as you think it—and therefore it is good. When you discuss writing in general, you seem to labor under several popular delusions, which are not your own, but something you heard. You must think these general questions over for yourself—and get rid of the popular misconceptions as quickly as you can. It would be no use to master grammar, style, plot construction, etc., while you're laboring on erroneous and confused premises. That would be like attempting to build a motor car without any knowledge or understanding of the laws of physics. You must have a clear conception of what writing is, in essence and in principle, before you attempt to write. And of all the things which writing *isn't*, box-office-chasing is the foremost.

To come back to your questions, in the order received, I never thought of any sales when I wrote *The Fountainhead*—and I was told by an awful lot of so-called experts that it would not sell. Well, I knew it would—but I didn't aim at sales, I didn't give it any thought beyond the general thought that if I made it a good book it would have a chance to sell. I did not think of any box-office rules, nor popular trends, nor public taste, nor Gallup polls of any nature whatsoever. I don't suppose you realize how many established rules of the literary marketplace I blasted to hell in that book; how many popular notions I ignored or reversed. Well, it sold—didn't it? So I'm the last person on earth to whom anybody should say that writing according to one's own conscience and standards is the opposite of commercial success. Or, as the populace puts it, "idealism is not practical." I say—nothing is practical, except idealism. I could write you volumes to expound this particular point, but I suppose you understand. This idea that "idealism" and "practicality" are opposites is another vicious popular fallacy—and not only in the field of literature. It shows merely that those who say it do not really know what makes things work in practical reality—and do not know what constitutes idealism.

You asked me why *The Fountainhead* is a bestseller. Do you want my sincere answer? Because there are more people of intelligence and good taste in the United States than I expected to find. I don't think of it as "I have lived up to the public." I think: "The public has lived up to me."

Now to your second letter. Here is your second dangerous popular fallacy about writing. You say that a friend discouraged you about "He and She," by making you realize that you wrote of events which had not actually happened. If I understood your point correctly. Don't ever, ever think that you must write only of things which literally happened, and that if you do, your writing will be good. THIS is the foremost sign of the amateur. If you tell an amateur that his story is not good, he always declares indignantly: "Oh, but it really happened just like this!" The writer who doesn't understand that this is beside the point is not a writer at all. It is ENTIRELY beside the point whether you copied the incidents of "He and She" from reality or invented them. Neither proves anything and neither has any relation to the value of your story. What matters is only how well you have presented the material and to what degree you have made it convincing on its own terms—not where you got it from. A story has to create and carry its own truth—not truth to actual facts. There is a tremendous difference here, which you must grasp thoroughly if you want to write fiction. It is the difference between literature and journalism, writing and reporting. Or—the difference between painting and photography.

There is a story told about Michelangelo which illustrates this beautifully: on one of his statues (that of David, I believe) he made a muscle which never existed on a real human body; when he was told that nature never created such a muscle, he answered that nature should have. *That* is the true artist.

In this connection, I want to mention a point out of your first letter. You said that some people told you that much of *The Fountainhead* couldn't happen. Tell them for me that it happened in *The Fountainhead* —and if they don't know what I mean, they have no business reading books at all. They don't know the difference between a book and yesterday's two-cent tabloid.

Now to your third letter. Your third popular fallacy is your submitting "He and She" to a psychiatrist for literary criticism. I was sort of aghast at this. I cannot imagine what made you do it—unless it is the popular delusion that psychiatrists understand human nature, and so should writers, and one can help the other. In the first place, psychiatrists don't understand human nature. In the second place, if they did, on their own terms and methods it would be an understanding totally different from that of a writer. The approach is different, the basic premise is different—and the mixture of the two fields is totally fantastic. If you do not believe me, just look again at the advice this psychiatrist gave you—as you list it in your letter. I can say nothing about it, except that it was total nonsense. All of it. My opinion, on every point you listed, is the exact opposite of what he said.

Next time someone tells you about a character in your story that "Women do not do such things," just answer: "This one does." That's all there is to it.

No, I don't think that you should go to a school of journalism. Certainly not if your aim is fiction writing. If you had a literary school in mind, even then I wouldn't know whether it would be wise. You might find it of some help—not in learning how to write, but in stimulating your interest in writing, and in judgment upon the writing of others, in general appreciation. If you feel you need that. You might try such a school, see if it's interesting. But I wouldn't give it too much time. Personally, I don't believe in such schools. I never heard of a good one nor of any writer whom it had helped. I don't believe that writing can be taught. The method I would recommend, and the one by which I learned is this: whenever you read any book or story, analyze it and ask yourself what makes it work. If you read a good passage which you enjoy—ask yourself what precisely makes it good, what is the technique used, how was the effect achieved. It is never accidental. If you read a bad passage, ask yourself what is the mistake, what makes it bad. Then, of course, don't ever copy what you find good, don't imitate—only learn the principle and apply it in your own way.

But I want to stop for a moment here and ask you: *why* do you want to write a book which *must* be a bestseller? I think it's important that you answer that question to yourself. It will clarify your whole attitude toward writing. Certainly, you don't want it in order to make money. If money is your only objective, why learn a new trade when you have been so successful at your present one? Let me try here to think for you—I hope you won't consider this presumptuous, since you ask my sincere and serious advice. Obviously, it is not the money from a bestseller or from movie rights that you want. And it is not fame, in the sense of seeing your name in the papers or signing autographs among the cafe society. You are not that type of man—and I don't think you would even enjoy that. And it is not prestige—you have prestige, of a more solid kind than that of best-selling authors. And it is not the desire to be "successful," in the vulgar sense of the failures who want to justify themselves and convince themselves of their own value—through popular acclaim. You *are* successful, in the best sense of the word, you made your own way in a very difficult profession. You don't need to convince yourself of your own ability and competence as a human being—you *have* convinced yourself, you have objective proof of that. Well, all the above are the usual reasons that make people want to write bestsellers—and none of these reasons apply to you. Now let me tell you what I think is your reason—I would be very much interested to know whether I guessed right.

You want to write because you feel attracted to that form of expression, because you have writing ability and many things you'd like to express. But—being a competent man, devoted to the idea of competence and contemptuous of inefficiency—you want to make sure that you do a good job in anything you undertake. And you got the idea that competence in writing is to be gauged by financial returns. That the only standard by which you can learn whether you've done a good job is in the bestseller lists and in the movie rights. Actually, you want success, in the real and proper sense of the word, the success of a competent workman—but the standard by which you propose to judge such success is the standard of the fakes and the phonies.

Now, to go a step further. I think I know the reason which led you to this mistake. The reason makes the mistake understandable and excusable. Your profession—Wall Street—is the only one in which making money is a proper primary goal, in which it is legitimate and honest and right to set one's standards by the aim of making money. Because—that is the proper primary purpose of a stock exchange—to make money through exchange. Secondarily, this exchange provides the lifeblood of industry, helps to develop it, finds backers for new ventures—etc. But—this is the important point—only *secondarily*. By the very nature of the activity, stockbrokers and investors deal in stocks in order to make money. Not in order to develop industries. If you went into Wall Street for the purpose of, say, building up the stock of Chrysler as against the stock of Ford, you would fail. Chrysler, on the other hand, if he engaged in stock market activities as a manufacturer, for the purpose of building up his company—would have to be successful in that—not successful in mere exchange. His primary purpose would be his company. Yours—the activity of exchange. Now, don't make the mistake here of saying: ah, but the overall aim of any activity and any profession is to make money. It might be and it might not be. That is irrelevant. The point is that when you choose any activity, you must act according to the nature and terms of that activity—if you want to succeed. Chrysler's aim might be to make money. But since he has chosen to make it through the activity of an automobile manufacturer—his first concern, within that activity, must be the one proper to it. What? TO MAKE GOOD AUTOMOBILES.

Do you see what I am driving at? The most greedy industrialist would not succeed if he told himself in effect: "People like lousy cars, let's figure out what sort of lousiness appeals to them and then let's manufacture it." He *must* tell himself constantly that his *primary* job is to make good cars. Everything else—exploitation, advertising, any kind of clever sales campaigns—is secondary. The first thing is to have a good product. Sure, fakers have succeeded in selling water as patent medicine. But this is not the proper, nor the solid, nor the lasting formula of success. The proper formula is: make a good product, then sell it cleverly. The product comes first, the financial rewards second. Even if the money is the manufacturer's first aim—precisely in order to make it, he cannot place money first.

How does he decide what is good? By his own standards, knowledge and judgment. He might take into consideration what the public seems to like. But he would be insane to follow public taste, if he knew that the public is mistaken or foolish in its preference. He would not manufacture a car he thought to be crazy, if at the moment there existed a public fad for it. Now, in material things, such as industry, an objective common standard of what is good can be reached—approximately. (And even then —never without a long struggle. Just think what a battle it was to convince people that the automobile or the airplane or the movies were a good, sound invention.) Still, in material things, true worth is demonstrable. A car is good if it runs well. In the field of art—this cannot be done. There are no obvious standards. Oh yes, there are objective standards, too—but not obvious and not immediately nor easily perceived by all. Here, public taste is no criterion at all. Not one way or the other. If a book sells—it does not prove that it is good. Nor that it is bad. It proves exactly nothing—as far as the actual, intrinsic merit of the book is concerned.

But that, too, was only a side explanation. The main point is that both the industrialist and the artist have to place the quality of their product first. The financial reward is only the consequence. BUT, to come back to Wall Street, the stock market is the ONLY activity in which financial rewards are the first, direct, immediate and proper consideration. I say this not as reproach or criticism, but quite the contrary. A good stockbroker must, to be practical, think only of that which will make money. This is his function—and the direct, complete test of whether he has succeeded or not. He would be foolish if he decided to plug pink securities with gold edges, in preference to blue securities with silver edges—for artistic reasons. That is not his function. Buying and selling securities that will make money—is.

Now, to embark upon a writing career and to be guided by the idea that money comes first and financial reward is the test of success—is foolish, because it is contrary to the nature of writing as a profession. The nature of it is to write good books. There are no common, popular standards of what makes a good book. *You*, the writer, must set the standards. You have no other choice. You might make money at it and you might not. What difference does this make to you? You want real success, not money to live on. Real success is not, cannot, never has and never will be determined by money in the field of literature. WRITE THAT WHICH YOU THINK IS GOOD. If, by your own honest standards, you find your writing good—you *are* a success. The rest is secondary and incidental.

I didn't intend to write at such length about it, but this subject interests me very much—and I wanted to make it as clear as I could.

Well, now to the theme which you outlined for your novel. I think it is a very interesting theme—and an extremely difficult one to handle. It would require such a subtle handling of psychology and characterization that you would have to be in complete control of your technique before you attempted it. It seems to be an almost impossible undertaking for a first novel. However, if the subject appeals to you and you feel you can handle it—that is the main test. If you think you can do, do it. If you're not sure of your means, of the technique—then, I would say, try an easier subject first. The idea, as such, is extremely interesting. I even think that it would interest many people (if you care about that)—because sex is surely a subject of interest to all—and the view upon sex of a mature man who is adolescent physically could throw a new light on the whole question. A new angle on an old and general problem is always interesting.

But, as you outline it, I don't think your theme is finished or completed. You realize this yourself—you say that your $64 question is— "how does it end?" Why, certainly not the way you outline it. That is, not on the hopeless despair of the hero—nor on any artificial solution. As you describe the case, it seems to me that you've stopped right in the middle of a process. The mental state of the hero—the idea that man is a slave to sex and to nature, that there is an irreconcilable conflict between the mind and the sex urge—is a perfect description of the mental state of an adolescent. Not of a mature man. In the case of your hero—this mental state would be intensified tenfold, because he is developed intellectually, he is an intelligent man in every other way, and an experienced man—but in the matter of sex he is still a youth. That mental state, however, is NOT caused by his particular predicament. Only intensified by it. It is the normal mental state of very many adolescents when they discover sex. Not of all, but of many. The tragedy of your hero is not that he gets into such a state—but that it will take him longer to outgrow it than it would in the case of an actual adolescent. And the most interesting part of the process would be that he can outgrow it while consciously watching his own spiritual growth. And he will outgrow it. He has to. That, too, is a law of nature.

Why is man a slave to sex? Because he needs it so strongly? Well, his need of food is even stronger, and more urgent and more immediate. But nobody thinks of himself as a slave to food. We simply take for granted that we need it—and we are in complete control of the means by which we get it. We keep on inventing new means all the time—we find new pleasures in food—and the whole matter is not tragic at all. In fact, in a normal, modern civilization, to a normal, average man the problem of getting food is no problem at all. Yes, he does need food, he is not free to decide not to eat—but why should he decide that? He is free to satisfy his need in an endless number of ways, he controls his means of production

—he is a free man. (I am speaking of a civilized, capitalistic society—not of a collectivist slave pen.) The basic fact about sex—its overpowering necessity—is the same. So the mere fact that man needs it does not make him a slave. Now, of course, his means of satisfaction are not as simple as in the matter of food. But still, he is in control of them. The thing that seems to terrify your hero is the fact that his satisfaction depends upon another human being, upon some woman. There is nothing so dreadful in that. Not if he found the right woman. It can appear terrible to him—only until he does find her. But if he doesn't—well, as he matures and grasps the subject, he would learn that he can find a second-best substitute. Let's say, not a wife, but an attractive mistress. It would not be sex at its best and highest—not the perfect union of the spiritual and the physical—but it would not be terrifying or degrading or enslaving. That typically adolescent feeling comes, I think, only from physical impatience—a strong physical desire that drives the man to women he despises, for lack of anything better, while his mind naturally objects. Why should his mind object if he found a woman he did not despise?

I don't know whether you have copied your theme from an actual case or merely imagined it in the abstract. For the purposes of a novel it would not matter which. But, I think, in either case, you stopped halfway. If you have imagined it—starting with the conception of: what would be the fate of such a man if he existed?—you have not followed him far enough. Though he does sound very real indeed as far as you went. If you have taken him from an actual case which you observed—you have caught him in the middle of the process of growing up. This is not the end of your theme or your novel. Such a man would grow up. This would not be his final attitude on sex.

Now, could such a subject be treated in the movies? Of course not. Movies cannot treat of physical sex as such at all. It must always be disguised as love or called love. That is an absolute rule of the Hays office. But this would not prevent a studio from buying the screen rights to such a novel, if it were a good story. They never buy anything for the theme, only for story value. In the case of such a novel, they would not mention —on the screen—that the hero had a physical disability from which he recovered. They would treat it as the story of a mature man who is unhappy in his love for a woman—or for several women. They would simplify the issue to that, make it "respectable"—and use only the plot events of the story, if they liked the plot. Of course, the theme would be a detriment in their eyes. It would count against buying the novel. But they could buy it —if the story were good enough.

Well, this covers every point of every letter. I'm afraid I'm a little too conscientious this time. Now, only your last note—about Frank Lloyd Wright. Yes, I know he liked *The Fountainhead*—he wrote me a beautiful letter about it—and it made me very happy. I'm not even sure that he really likes the story or Roark, but he was most enthusiastic about the thesis and the treatment of architecture. His letter was very lovely.

No, I haven't bought the Storer house—I am thinking of buying it and have consulted his son, Lloyd Wright, about its condition. The trouble is that it requires a small fortune to put it in good repair—the present owners have let it go to pieces. So I'm not sure I'll be able to buy it. But I love it. It's a magnificent house.

If this reaches you at Taliesin—please give Mr. Wright my very best regards. Maybe you can tell him—if my letter to him and my book haven't told him—how much I admire him.

Loeb responded that she was correct about why he wanted to write a bestseller, but he didn't agree that financial success is not a measure of literary success or that automakers produce the best cars possible. Success, he wrote, is getting people to buy your product, whether it's a car or a book.

■ ■ ■

To Jack Warner, of Warner Bros. Pictures

June 21, 1944

Dear Mr. Warner:

I am sorry that I have not had the opportunity to meet you in person, but I would like to tell you that after working here I feel very happy it was Warner Brothers who bought *The Fountainhead*, and not anyone else.

Mr. Blanke has told me how enthusiastic you were about the book and I am glad I was able to carry it out in the adaptation as it was, preserving its theme and spirit, without being asked to make bad taste concessions, such as a lesser studio would have demanded. It was a pleasure to work for you and Mr. Blanke—and I hope some day to have the opportunity of meeting you and thanking you in person.

I am very sorry that we could not get together on a deal, due to my six-months limitation request, but I shall always be on call to help you in any way you may wish with *The Fountainhead*. I should like to see this child of mine through to its birth, and knowing that it is in good hands, I am certain that its birth will be the day of a great achievement for Warner Brothers, as well as for me.

■   ■   ■

To Archibald Ogden

July 19, 1944

Dear Archie:

I owe you an apology for my long silence—and such a long account of events that I don't know where to begin. So much has happened to me here, but I'll have to skip all the details now, and start with the most important and urgent. The letterhead will explain part of what happened. I have finished the script of *The Fountainhead* at Warners (with great success, as I'll tell you later—and with the whole story kept intact, theme, message, Roark's speech and all; it will go into production this fall) and I have signed a five-year contract with Hal Wallis. The best part of the contract is that I'll work for pictures only six months out of each year and will have six months for my own writing and my next books. So, I hasten to say, I haven't sold myself to Hollywood. That kind of a contract was hard to get—picture people don't like it, but I got it. It was that—or I would have gone back to New York. I wouldn't take a full-time contract and I won't give up books for anything. Hal Wallis was a big producer at Warners and has just left them to start his own independent company. He will release pictures through Paramount, but he will make them independently, with his own separate staff. I'm the first writer he has signed. The second one is, incidentally, Lillian Hellman, of all people. Nice contrast, isn't it? Well, anyway, Wallis is *the* big man of Hollywood right now and this is the most important new company and the talk of the town, etc.

But all this is only by way of explanation and buildup for what follows. I told you I would try to get you into the movies and here it is. Hal Wallis needs a good story editor—and I've sold you to him. That is, if you're still available, willing and interested. I don't even know where you are and what you are doing. But I suspect that if you're still with the Council on Books in Wartime, you may be open to temptation and lured away from them. Here is the exact situation: Wallis has hired a story editor, but sort of on approval—and, *confidentially*, I don't think that the man is very good. I told Wallis about you—and Wallis was most impressed and said he would like to have you in addition to his present editor. So he asked me to write to you at once, find out whether you are available—and if you are, Wallis will be in New York at the end of this month, and he would like to see you then, and discuss it with you.

There's your Hollywood break, darling. Now do you want it? I hope you do.

A story editor's job here is this: he has to cover the field of everything written, like a bloodhound; he has to find stories that would make good movies, and be able to tell which future novels and plays have the possibilities of big hits; he has to hire writers to do the screenplays—he has to negotiate contracts and the buying of stories. The final say on all these activities is up to the producer (Wallis, in this case), but the story editor is the one who has to find the stories and the people for Wallis to buy or hire. The most essential part of the job, of course, is that they need a man who knows good stories and good writing. The shortage of material here is dreadful. You wouldn't believe what trash they consider, for lack of anything better. Wallis needs stories desperately right now—and he needs a man whom he could trust to cover the field, so that he wouldn't have to read everything himself, but could rely on his story editor to discover good and unusual things for him. Well, you discovered *The Fountainhead*, didn't you? In other words, the man they need must have story sense and literary judgment, above all—and in all the world I don't know anyone better qualified than you for this kind of a job.

I don't know what they pay story editors, but by the general rate of salaries here, it is much, much more than they pay in publishing houses. I don't know how you feel about working for the movies and whether it would interest you—but I thought this: If you have found the kind of publishing house you wanted, then it probably wouldn't be wise to give it up for Hollywood, because I do believe that you are to be *the* big man of book publishing, the breath of fresh air, the godsend to all writers and the new day of book publications. If you are advancing toward a house of your own—then I don't want to be the one to sidetrack you and I don't think you should be sidetracked. But if the situation is still the same as when I left New York, that is, if there is no clear way towards a publishing house of your own until after the war and if you haven't found a firm that could be a proper stepping-stone towards that goal—if you are still wasting your superlative talent on committees, councils and glorified press-agentry for very inglorious stuff—then why not try Hollywood, at least for the duration? You could make much more money and you might find it exciting and interesting.

Of course, everything in Hollywood is uncertain, and everybody's future is uncertain, even that of the biggest names and stars. I wouldn't advise you or anyone to plan on a Hollywood career as a life future. Some people have lasted here for years and years. Others didn't—and there are no rules, chances or probabilities to go by. It certainly is not a matter of ability, it is not entirely a matter of luck—it is just something that one can't figure out at all. The only way to look at it is like one looks at horse racing: the financial stakes are tremendous and it is worth taking the chance if one looks upon it strictly as a chance that can fail at any moment. If you are free to take the gamble, it's certainly worth taking. If it would mean losing valuable contacts, the reputation you built up in the publishing business or a position that can lead you to what you want—then you shouldn't take the chance. You can judge this better than I can. If your immediate job in New York is important—don't leave it. But if you can risk a year or two out here, to see how you like it, at least until the war is over and we do have publishing again, as it should be—then take this, because it could mean something very big. There is a terrible shortage of good editors here. And there are many vacancies, in other studios.

Well, I've tried to tell you the objective side of it as much as I know. The personal side—do I have to tell you how selfishly happy I would be to have you here—and as editor in the same company with me? Personally, I don't like California—but for a family, it is really the ideal place. I think Betty would love it—and it would be wonderful for little Dominique and Archie Jr. As an added attraction: we have just bought a house—actually an estate, 13½ acres, in the country, twenty miles from Hollywood—and it is so lovely here that even I am relenting towards California. It's a big house—ultra modern—by Richard Neutra—and we have a huge garden, an orchard with every possible kind of fruit tree, our own chickens and everything. (No swimming pool yet, but a tennis court of our own.) Well, you could live with us until you get used to Hollywood and decide where you want to live (or for the duration, as far as I'm concerned). Housing conditions are unbelievably dreadful here, the place is overcrowded, no houses or apartments available at all, but now you wouldn't have to worry about that. Your children would really love this house—and as for the sunshine and the air and the fruit, it is really like an advertisement of the Hollywood Chamber of Commerce. It's unbelievably wonderful just now. I'm not quite used to it myself. If you do come here, this is just an added bribe.

I think you would like Hal Wallis. So far, I've found it grand to work for him. I say "so far," because one must always add this in Hollywood. He is intelligent, outspoken, direct, very energetic and ambitious, extremely competent—and he wants to make better movies, serious ones, not arty phonies, but really good stories well done. But you can judge for yourself when you speak to him. Will you write to me *at once* and tell me whether you're interested and where Wallis can reach you when he comes to New York? I must be able to tell him before he leaves—and that will be in about a week. So write me air-mail, as quickly as you can. My address is:

> 10,000 Tampa Avenue
> Chatsworth, California.

(Yes, the street number is just plain ten thousand.) That's my new home —our own—I'm now really a capitalist and a proud owner. Archie, darling, who made this possible for me? I don't forget that, I think of it more and more violently every day with every new thing that happens to me—and I'm not religious but I say: God bless you.

Well, I haven't much time to tell you all the news of us—this was to be a rush note, and it's late and I haven't had any sleep last night, nor will have tonight—early conference tomorrow. So I'll just give you a brief synopsis.

Everything went wonderfully with *The Fountainhead* at Warners. My producer, Henry Blanke, held out to the end as he had started, that is, with complete enthusiasm and understanding of the story and no intention of changing it, ruining it or vulgarizing it. I wrote the whole script—and he made no changes whatever, except minor technical ones, which were very valuable—but no story changes at all. It is still possible that the studio heads might interfere when we go into actual production and might start ruining things—one must always expect it in Hollywood until the moment the picture is released—but so far it does not seem probable, and as things stand now my script will go into production as I wrote it. It is the complete story of *The Fountainhead*, as it is in the book, only, of course, much shorter. I couldn't put everything in—I had to take only the essence and the highlights. All the minor characters had to be dropped, even Katie. I had to skip Dominique's marriage to Keating—she only marries Wynand. The characters, in order of importance, stand like this: Roark, Dominique, Wynand, Toohey. Keating is a somewhat minor part, entering the story only when Roark's story needs him. We start actually at the end of part one—on the scene when Roark, already a struggling architect, refuses his last chance at a commission and goes to work in the quarry. From then on, it's just like the book, condensed. Well, I didn't mean to give you all the details, but I couldn't help telling you about *our* story. I won't repeat the compliments I got on the script—but it was really wonderful. Blanke was crazy about it. No cast or director will be chosen until this fall—the actual shooting probably to start the first of the year. The cast is a big problem —and Blanke doesn't want to rush on it, we must have the right people. No Roark in view at all—there just aren't any men to play him, so that will be the toughest problem. But I must tell you that we are trying to get Frank Lloyd Wright to do the buildings. I met him when he was here, I gave him a copy of the book—and, Archie, here is another miracle of my life, perhaps the one that makes me happiest: Wright was enthusiastic about the book! Remember what I told you about my previous encounter with him? Well, the book won him over. I had a beautiful letter from him about it—next time I'll send you a copy of it. Of all the compliments to the book, this is the one I wanted most and expected least.

I finished at Warners—and started working for Hal Wallis, without a pause in between. That is, I had two weeks off—during which time I had to buy a house, because it is impossible to live in apartments here, and also I had to invest the money from the movie sale into something, and do it quickly, because money is dropping in value every day. So you can imagine that I almost went crazy with all this. I was so exhausted that I went to a doctor and had a check-up—but he found I was all right. I am now writing the adaptation of a novel which Wallis bought—it's to be his first picture, and I'm rushing like mad. This will give you some idea why I haven't written to you—haven't had a moment for rational thought or for composing a letter to make sense. I'm not sure this one does. Will you forgive me and answer me?

With all our love, from both of us—to the four of you, and with all my gratitude, always,

On August 8, Ogden replied: "I really cannot leave here at this time. I'm not only under a certain moral obligation to see this thing through; I really want to. . . . So don't feel sorry for me, and above all, don't think I'm ungrateful for your kindly efforts on my behalf. Possibly my small reluctance to going to Hollywood, if the chance really came, would be the fear of failing you—or failing to live up to your buildup."

■ ■ ■

To Gerald Loeb

August 5, 1944

Dear Mr. Loeb:

Your letters are always so interesting that I cannot drop just a short note in reply. To start with the last one, which I have just received—your problem of how to meet a worthwhile woman is a problem that I have faced all my life, though not in the same terms. I was fortunate enough to meet Frank early in life, so my quest was not of a romantic nature, but all my life I have been troubled by the fact that most people I met bored me to death and I wondered where and how one can meet interesting people. I knew such people existed, I didn't believe that all of humanity was like the dreadful, wishy-washy, meaningless specimens I saw around me—but I seemed to have terrible luck in meeting the kind I could have liked. I am enough like Roark to be able to exist quite happily in solitude, and I had Frank, which is the greatest mercy God has ever granted me (and I feel that without being religious), but I do like people—when they are really human beings—I love to meet interesting minds and exchange ideas and feel an interested affection, not contempt, for those around me. So, you see, in a way, it was the same problem as yours—though I wanted only to find friends, and you seek more than that. The practical steps, however, would be the same, the question—how to go about meeting the right people and where to go. I think I have found the answer—so maybe it will be of help to you.

First of all, let me say most emphatically that money or social position have nothing to do with it. I have always had a very mixed circle of acquaintances, some extremely wealthy, some of the poorest kind of struggling young intellectuals and non-intellectuals—and I find that, as far as human quality goes, money and social status make no difference whatever. Don't let yourself fall for that awful nonsense of Karl Marx about economics determining human nature. They don't. Neither in general historical events—nor in specific human instances. Economic position affects only the form, the surface details of a person—his clothes, his grammar, his manners. *NOT* his essence as a human being. And what you and I are interested in is the essence, not the surface polish. I have found that the rich, as a rule, are more boring than the poor, only because they have a standardized line of patter and behavior which makes them awfully dull. The poor, at first glance, may seem more colorful. But when you get to know either of them better, you see that there is no essential difference. There is the same emptiness, pettiness, malice and general slothfulness of the spirit. The fact that a man earns his money by physical labor does not make him a superior human being. That is as silly a fallacy as the opposite one—that a man is superior because he does no labor, but sits on his rear on inherited money. Both facts are beside the point. The idea that working women are more "real" or interesting than society women is, I think, plain nonsense. I know them both. The majority of the working women will be like the girl in your story "He and She." They work badly, grudgingly, sloppily, only because they have to. They are preoccupied with the same nonsense as the society women, only they have less time for it. That is why I disagree most emphatically with Frank Lloyd Wright when he says, "Look in the tearooms for the real women of America." Ayn Rand says: Bosh! The only difference between the women in the tearooms and the women in the Waldorf-Astoria is the price list on the menus.

But the truth of the matter is that one finds worthwhile men and women among *people who work*. Follow me here very carefully, forgetting the cheap generalities which all our modern minds have been stuffed with. I do not mean LABOR. I do not mean people who have to earn their living. I do not mean proletarians. I do not mean tearooms. I mean what you and I understand by the term of "competent people." People who love to work, who are good at it, serious about it and concerned primarily with it. Bright, creative, productive, ambitious people. People who get money for their work, but who do not work primarily for the money—whether it's a weekly pay envelope or a thousand dollar bonus. People who are ambitious—not to climb socially, not to get wealth and titles—but ambitious to do more and more work of a better and better kind. It's among such people that you'll find the woman you want, if I have understood you correctly.

Of course, such people are very rare. But they do exist. Now, how does one find them? There may be one or two in any business, any profession, but the wading through the other kind of people would be too long and the chances too small. So the only shortcut I have found is to go to places where people go because they are attracted by the specific purpose of the place. For instance: I have met a greater number of interesting men and women, within a few months, than I did in my whole life, during the Willkie campaign of 1940, when I worked as a volunteer in the National Headquarters of the Willkie Clubs. Don't misunderstand me, God knows I am not endorsing Willkie now, and I don't mean that those people are to be found in politics. As a matter of fact, that is the last profession in which they would be found. But what I mean is that the Willkie Clubs, at the time, were a rallying point for people who wanted to serve a certain principle. Those people came there for one purpose only—to work for a cause they believed. And among the great numbers of hangers-on, phonies, ward-heelers and fat clubwomen, there was a surprising number of wonderful men and women, people of intelligence, integrity, character. They came— to work.

The same would apply to any place or organization that has a legitimate purpose; it would attract the same kind of people. Not all of them, of course. There will always be a preponderance of the usual and dumb, as there is everywhere. But the chances of meeting interesting people would be far greater than at parties, purely social gatherings, resort hotels or tea-rooms. In practical terms, I would suggest this: select a place whose purpose attracts and interests you—then go there regularly; if the place is legitimate, it will attract other people like yourself, the people you want to meet. For instance: a literary club—or a literary college course (though most of those are phony, one would have to be careful)—it would have, among hopeless aspirants, some men and women sincerely interested in the subject and working hard at it. An architectural club—though here there wouldn't be many women. A volunteer political organization is always good—though I don't know what's become of them now. It would be hard to choose the specific place. But in a general way, that is the advice I'd give you: look for places where sincere people are working hard—and go there. Choose by the nature of the work. Going incognito into a convention of ditch-diggers would do you as little good as going to the swankiest Wall Street party.

Incidentally, people are always at a disadvantage at a party. You may have met some very interesting women at parties—and never known it, because it is the custom not to raise any serious subject socially, but to be trite, trivial and so-called gay. Many nice women would struggle like hell to put on a silly, overpainted front, even though they hate it, and would talk hopeless drivel only because it's socially expected of them. But if you meet people at work, the nature of the work will make them talk seriously and you will have a better insight into their real characters.

Now in regard to the brief story you outline about a man and woman meeting on the train, and you ask: True or False? I'd say False. In every way. It could happen, but it's a deadly thing to count on—if I understood the point correctly. It is wrong to wait for the woman to do the chasing— though many men do that, and many let themselves be dragged into marriage even though they didn't really want it. A great many men take their love life passively—the way one conventionally supposes women do—they take what comes along and make the best they can. That's wrong for both sexes. I would say—find what you want and go after it openly, whether you're a man or a woman. A little less openly if you're a woman. But go after it. Don't wait for the other party to make the overtures.

I believe that our mind controls everything—yes, even our sex emotions. Perhaps the sex emotions more than anything else. Although that's the opposite of what most people believe. Everything we do and are proceeds from our mind. Our mind can be made to control everything. The trouble is only that most of us don't want our minds to control us—because it is not an easy job. So they drift and let chance and other people and their own subconscious decide for them. I believe firmly that everything in a man's life is subject to his mind's control—and that his greatest tragedies come from the fact that he willfully suspends that control.

The only danger is to succumb to some such fallacy as that "the heart is more important than the brain." (By "heart" they actually mean here a less polite anatomical organ.) NOTHING IS MORE IMPORTANT THAN THE BRAIN. *NOTHING.* And no man can find any lasting happiness, any kind of satisfactory existence in any part of his life—professional, mental, emotional, sexual—not in any part, unless the primary choice and decision and action proceeded from and with the consent of his brain.

You ask: "Is not a man's thinking conditioned by his life?" My answer is: *NO!!!* (I'm sorry I had no bigger caps to use on this machine, or I would have used them.) This is THE crucial fallacy of our century, and one deliberately fostered to destroy all thinking, fostered, incidentally, by the Marxists. I could write volumes on this point (and intend to some day), but right now I would like only to point out briefly that the whole statement shows a complete destruction of the mere conception of what constitutes thinking. A simple example will do: a man who is happy and living in luxury in a penthouse will think that two and two make four; the same man, miserable, starving and homeless, is not going to think that two and two make six. If he does, he is not thinking at all. You might only say that adversity will make it harder for him to think correctly—but even that is not true, certainly not of an intelligent man. The rational process is as cold and exact as mathematics. It has nothing to do with a man's emotional life, his background, experience or conditioning. He will think in a slum or in a palace, if he can think at all. If he can't, nothing will make him, luxury or no luxury, conditioning or no conditioning.

Thinking has nothing to do with emotions. That most people let their emotions interfere in their rational processes is true. But what does that mean? That means only that they cannot think properly. That does not mean that thinking is emotional.

You say: "Any story I might write would reflect my observations of life." True. But your observations, if they are at all rational, will not be "conditioned" by your life. Only the *material* of your observations will be conditioned, if you want to call it that. That is, you may choose to write about Wall Street, because the circumstances of your life led you to work in Wall Street and you know that background. But the background is not important. *What you think of it is.* And what you think of Wall Street is not conditioned by Wall Street, but by the nature of your own mind. Had you been, let's say, a lawyer, you might decide to write a novel about law. But what you would think of it would be, in essence, what you would think of Wall Street—that is, it would show the same mental quality, the same ability to draw correct conclusions from given facts, the same ability to understand the given material and illuminate it with a view of your own. THAT is thinking. That which you bring to your material—that which comes from you. Not the material. Another man from Wall Street, writing a novel about it, would not write the same novel you would. Men shape their material—physically and intellectually. *Not* the material—the men. Man builds a house out of stone—the house doesn't shape itself and then invite the man to live in it. Man writes a novel about Wall Street—Wall Street does not dictate a novel to him. No, there is no Economic Determinism. And may the Marxists be thrice damned!

Now, once more on our pet subject—commercial writing. You ask me what is the difference between ads aimed at "classes and masses"—and stories written in the same way. In the first place, the difference in the purposes of the two things. An ad is aimed *"primarily"* at people—its purpose is to make people do something, buy something. So it has to consider the nature of the people to whom it is addressed. A story is not written to accomplish any purpose beyond itself. (Not even a propaganda story— and I'm the chief living writer of propaganda fiction, I think—at least I think I'm the only one who knows how to do it properly—and I still say that: the propaganda is not the purpose of the story.) A STORY IS AN END IN ITSELF. It is not written to teach, sell, explain or destroy anything. It is not written even to entertain. It is written as a man is born—an organic whole, dictated only by its own laws and its own necessity—an end in itself, not a means to an end. Therefore, a story cannot be concerned with its future readers. That is a different consideration entirely. A story must be written for itself, for its own sake. I mean, of course, a good story. God knows, any amount of tripe is written the other way—with an eye on the readers. And it does sell, but it remains—tripe.

You ask, would I write the same story for *Harper's* as for *Click*? I would never set out to write a story for *Harper's* or for *Click* or for anything. You don't write stories that way. I would write *a story*—and then I would decide whether it fits *Harper's* or *Click* and submit it accordingly. And if I find that it fits no magazine at all, I will keep it in my desk. But I will write it just the same. What you refer to there, is an agent's job. An agent's job comes after the writer's, not before. First you write, then you decide where to submit it. Never, never, never vice versa.

Now this leads us to the question of propaganda stories and to a point on which you are most terribly wrong about *The Fountainhead*. You say about it: "The sex is the ginger ale that gets the castor oil of individualism and architecture across." It is nothing of the kind. It is as much and as important a part of the story as the individualism and the architecture. And it is in the story because the story required it—not because it would make readers swallow the other passages. Do you realize that sex, as such, cannot sell a story any more than architecture can? As witness—the tons and tons of sexy novels that fail, and particularly Broadway shows, full of nothing but sex, that close after one performance. NOTHING SELLS A STORY BUT THE STORY. A story sense is the one and only and first and foremost and paramount requisite of any good writer. Everything else—style, description, characterization, propaganda—is secondary. Important, but secondary.

It's like building a house. You must have doors and windows and trimmings. But if your foundation and your steel skeleton do not stand—nothing will stand. And when you lay a foundation, you are concerned only with what that foundation requires. Nothing else. You know the kind of house you want—you plan your foundation and skeleton accordingly. Now, a *story* is a sequence of events, around a central line, with a definite beginning and end, concerning definite people. Your central line determines your events *and* your characters. Now take *The Fountainhead* as an example. In the briefest statement, it is the story of a man of integrity. Everything pertaining to the integrity of that man, in every aspect, had to be included. And it had to be shown—not in abstract discourses (that would be the method of nonfiction)—but in *concrete events*. Therefore, there had to be a romance—and the events of that romance had to present the man's strength, ruthlessness, directness and honesty. That's how it's done—not by thinking that a stenographer reading the book would like to imagine herself as Dominique. You might ask, what's the difference, if it's only in the writer's mind? A tremendous difference. If I thought of what the stenographer would like—I would never devise a romance that had power and conviction. When I think of the requirements of my theme and story, I arrive at a romance that has strength and conviction. And because it has conviction, the stenographers like it. BUT YOU CANNOT REVERSE THAT PROCESS.

But more than that. I did not write *The Fountainhead* to sell individualism or architecture. It is a dreadful fallacy to think that fiction can be written to sell anything. If that were my purpose, I would have written a nonfiction treatise on individualism, and another one on architecture. It is true that fiction is a much more powerful weapon to sell ideas than nonfiction. But why? Precisely because it is not a *sales weapon*. It tells a story—the story has the reality of life—and so abstract ideas acquire reality. Abstract ideas *are* a part of real life—and so we can grasp them better, more closely, when we meet them in the living background of fiction. But abstract ideas are proper in fiction *only* when they are subordinated to the story. Not when the story is artificially devised to expound some thesis. That is why propaganda writers fail. That is why propaganda stories are always so false and dull. That is why I am the only writer of ideas in fiction that I know of at the present time. I mean, the only one who does it properly—and gets away with it. Forgive me for this little boast—I think I've earned it.

I cannot help thinking that just before *The Fountainhead* came out, there were two long, big novels published on themes selling Communism. They both got glowing, raving reviews. They both had a tremendous publicity campaign—and a nationwide, organized, enthusiastic support of a beautifully trained pink click that controls our press and has succeeded in putting over many pieces of Red junk in the nonfiction field. And they both flopped miserably. No amount of pushing could sell them to the public— and what expert pushing! And this, when our whole intellectual atmosphere is collectivistic and right in line with what those authors were preaching. Well, *The Fountainhead* came out—with as vicious a campaign of opposition against it as any book ever had. You may not know the details— take my word for it. *The Fountainhead* came out against every odd possible. Well—look at it. Ask some bookseller. It is the only novel of an intellectual character that has been a bestseller for many, many years. The only novel with an abstract or "propaganda" idea in the serious sense. So I think I know how to sell ideas in fiction.

You may ask, why do I write "propaganda" stories if I say that the propaganda is not my purpose. Because I want to write stories that are real—and "propaganda" is the whole meaning of life and reality. That is, ideas are the meaning of life, the only things that make a human life, as distinguished from an animal one. I believe that man determines his own life, that he sets his own purpose—and that his ideas give it meaning. Consequently, if I want to write of men, I want to write of the meaning of their lives—the field of ideas. Just as a man's life is never purposeless (if he is a true man, not a conditioned beast), so a story about men must never be purposeless. That is why I have abstract themes in my stories. Do I want to sell individualism to people? Why, certainly. And if *The Fountainhead* sells it to them—fine. But that is only a secondary consideration, a side-issue, "pure gravy" as my Ellsworth Toohey said. I'm glad if people can grasp the idea of my story. I'm glad if they like the sex. I'm glad if they buy the book at all. But none of this has anything to do with my book. All of this is a personal indulgence which I can permit myself *after* the book is written and published. I can then permit myself to enjoy all those secondary things, if they happen. I cannot think of them when I write the book. Do you know something else? I cannot even think of them when I reread the book now. I cannot read it and say to myself: "Isn't it wonderful that this was successful?" I can't. Not while I'm reading it. What there is between an author and his book is more personal—and well, yes, sacred —than the privacy of a romance between a man and a woman. Nobody else can enter. No readers, publishers, critics or box offices. I don't know how I can impress this upon you any stronger.

When you are ready to write your novel, I would like to discuss this with you concretely—and show you just how to go about integrating ideas into a story. It's a long, difficult process and cannot be explained in a letter. I would like to do it in person—when you really want to do it. But don't take *The Fountainhead* as an example of propaganda fiction. It *is* an example and it does show the correct way—but you won't be able to apply it if you misinterpret the way it was written. Just remember only that NOTHING in *The Fountainhead* was put in for the sake of an audience. EVERYTHING was put in because the story, the subject, required it.

It is true also that any good book may be read from many angles and the readers will get out of it only as much as they're able to get. BUT the author cannot deliberately plan a book with some "high" angles and some "low" angles, to please all tastes. Again, that is not the way it's done. You must *never* use in your own mind such expressions as "coat it with the sugar of popularity" (in regard to a serious theme). You *don't* "coat" anything in a good story, and most certainly not with "Sugar."

Re General Motors and the millions they spend on tests of public opinion—well, I know nothing whatever about the details of running an automobile business, but I will venture to say that these millions are wasted, purely and entirely, that General Motors would do better without any such tests and that the whole idea of making the tests is the product of some college punks who have got to do something to earn a salary they don't deserve. Now correct me if I'm wrong on that.

I think this answers everything.

I have signed a contract with Hal Wallis, who, as you probably know, was a big producer at Warners, but just left to start his own independent company. He discovered me at Warners—and I am the first writer he signed. At present, I am already hard at work on an adaptation of a novel called *Love Letters*, which will be Mr. Wallis's first picture. The novel is not too good—so don't read it—but it has a good idea and I will have to make a good story out of it.

Right at the moment, my boss, Mr. Wallis, is your closest neighbor— he's in New York, in the Waldorf-Tower. He will be there only this coming week. I would like very much for you to meet him. He's our kind of man. I mentioned you to him—and he has heard a great deal about you, he spoke of you in very flattering terms. So, if it's convenient for you, would you telephone him and meet him? I'd like you to get a firsthand account of my activities in Hollywood—and take a look at the man who owns me for the next five years. (Or half of the next five years.) I think you will like him —and I would like to hear your impressions.

I won't go into too many details about my new house—that in itself would take a volume of descriptions. It is a wonderful house. Not as good as a Frank Lloyd Wright one—but there are none of Wright's here that would have suited our purpose, the one we found was too old and needed too many repairs. This one is all steel, glass and concrete—with a big garden, orchard and field of alfalfa. I never thought I'd become a farmer —but that is what Frank wanted—and I find I love living in the country. It is so much more peaceful and free—and I write better. We have a tennis court, two moats (that is, big lily ponds), the master bathroom is solidly lined with mirrors—it is fantastic and very beautiful. The feeling of being a capitalist and a landowner is grand. But then, I defended capitalism when I didn't have enough to pay my rent. This place is twenty miles from Hollywood—but Mr. Wallis allows me to work at home, so I don't have to go to the studio every day.

Last of all, I want to thank you from the bottom of my heart for telling me that you saw *The Fountainhead* on a table in Frank Lloyd Wright's bedroom. I can't tell you how much that sentence meant to me. More, I think, than any other thing I heard about the book from anyone. I suppose you will understand why. If my literary discussions have been of help to you, will you do me a big favor in return? When you have the time, will you write to me *everything* that Wright said to you about *The Fountainhead* and about me. Everything that you can remember. You see, I don't care so much about readers—but about this one reader I do. And not only as a reader. I'd like to know what he thought of me in person—if he thought at all. You know what I think of him.*

I notice one more question in your long letter—a question in the nature of a compliment. You ask where I get my general knowledge—whether it's instinct, ability, reading or experience? No. Do you know the answer? Honesty. The fact that I look at everything through my own eyes—like Roark.

■   ■   ■

To Harry C. Scott, of the Southern California Telephone Co.

September 4, 1944

Dear Mr. Scott:

This is to explain my urgent need of telephone service.

I am a writer employed by Hal Wallis Productions, Inc., at the Paramount Studios, 5451 Marathon Street, Hollywood, California. Writers are expected to report at the studio every day, and my employer can demand that I do so. However, in view of the great distance and the gas shortage, he has permitted me to work at my home, provided he can reach me by telephone for any instructions he has to give me or for notice to come to the studio within an hour, when my presence is required.

The Paramount Studios are located twenty-one miles from my home. Under present regulations, I can not obtain sufficient gas to drive forty-two miles a day, six days a week, if my employer demands that I work at the studio, which he would have to do if I have no telephone in my home and he has no means of reaching me when he needs me. To make the situation worse, I am not able to drive a car—so my husband would have to drive me to the studio and call for me each day, which would mean eighty-four miles (four trips of 21 miles each) to drive every day—an impossible undertaking for which no gas could be obtained.

* Loeb answered that he would not repeat Wright's comments about AR, saying that they were confidential.

My husband is engaged in farming on our property. We have 13½ acres—10 acres in alfalfa, the rest occupied by the house, an orchard and livestock (chickens and rabbits). My husband has recently undergone an operation and is still under a doctor's care. (Dr. S. A. Thompson, 6715 Hollywood Boulevard, Hollywood, California.) Should anything happen to my husband so that immediate medical help is required, I would have no way to call for help, since I cannot drive a car. The nearest house of neighbors is about 1,000 feet away. These neighbors occupy their house only on weekends, so that I could not count on the use of their telephone in an emergency.

Our house being isolated, we would have no way, without a telephone, to call for the police in case of personal danger—and we are not within hearing distance of neighbors, should we attempt to call for help.

In view of this situation, I hope you will find it possible to give me the telephone service which I do need desperately.

A phone line was not extended to the O'Connors' ranch until February 1947.

■ ■ ■

To Dr. Edward Spencer Cowles, a fan

September 24, 1944

Dear Dr. Cowles,

I was frankly and pleasantly stunned to hear of Maurice Maeterlinck's compliment to my work. Would you thank him for me and give him my most respectful regards? It was strange that your letter reached me just when I was trying to interest a studio here in making a new screen version of *Monna Vanna*, which I consider one of the greatest plays in all world literature.

Monna Vanna *was first performed in 1902, and an English translation was first published in 1903. An English-language edition is published by Second Renaissance Books.*

■ ■ ■

October 5, 1944

Dearest Nick,

Thanks a million! Officially and correctly—thanks for the shipping of our furniture, which I have not yet formally acknowledged. But even though that was the biggest trouble for you—my personal, unofficial and most enthusiastic thanks are for the little bunch of records that arrived yesterday. You don't know how much they meant to me—or do you? I had no chance to write to you sooner and remind you, so I just waited—and did I dance last night when they arrived! They arrived in perfect condition—except for one, which was cracked; it can still be played—and I think the crack was there before you shipped it, probably caused by Volodia or Peter, it doesn't look like a shipping crack. Anyway, please take the chance and *send the rest of them on.* Just put an extra pad of cotton, if you can get it, around "Canadian Capers."

The furniture all arrived in good condition—except the glass tabletop and bottom, the tall glass vase and one red goblet. These were busted. But it doesn't matter—the insurance company is going to replace them or pay us for them. All the precious antiques, such as the blue cigarette box, arrived intact. Thanks again. And will you please thank Faith for me for her assistance. We were really touched by her and your efforts to clean the chairs. Sorry that you had to attempt it—it was really a dirty job for Jesus. They look halfway decent now, but, of course, will have to be recovered soon.

Now what about you and your trip to California? You know how I always said that you write the most brilliant letters and have a wonderful knack for not saying anything, when you don't want to. So now you're exercising that particular talent on me. You have specifically refrained from informing us on that point. Are you planning to come? When? We're really most anxious to know. Frank guessed some time ago that you will not leave New York until after the election. Is that what's holding you there? If so, have a good time, but for God's sake start for California in November. Do I have to tell you how bad another winter in New York will be for you? I cannot even gather from your letters what is the state of your health now. You referred once to your "former and *continued* T.B." Does that mean that your last examination showed active T.B.? You never told us what that last report was. Also, you write about having a job in order to earn money. Well, if you're allowed to hold a job, aren't you allowed to travel? If you still need bed rest, but are working only for the money—please let me know and I'll send you the money, and you take the bed rest. It is insane to take such a chance. If you are better and are working because you want to, for the cause, that is different. But in either case, I do wish you would start making plans about coming here. You can't afford another winter of New York. Why take such a chance—when it isn't even a chance, but a certainty—you know that every winter breaks you down and destroys whatever recovery you achieved in the summer. How many times do you want to go through that? I note with fiendish glee that you write about being bored in New York and about missing us. Well, what are you waiting for? I admit, without any cover-up, that we both miss you dreadfully. Yes, even self-sufficient as we are. Yes, even Oscar and Oswald want to get you here. They are now asking cautiously when Cousin Moe is coming. *PLEASE* start making train reservations now—I understand one has to do it long in advance, to get on a train at all. If you need the money for the ticket when making reservations—let me know and I'll wire it. Do you get any discount as a veteran? Anyway, let me know how much you need—and please do start. Now, if you don't want to come for any reason, then let us know and I'll stop pestering you about it—but oh! how we wish you'd come!

Of course, I wish you luck on "Three on a Bone." If that goes through, you'll have to stay—but then, collect your royalties and go to Florida for the winter, or something. It would be thrilling if you had a play produced now—and I'd hate not to be there. What about "Dynasty"? I was interested to hear that you were working on it again. I always thought that should make a good novel. AND I'm still waiting to hear of you working on "A very blunt instrument." You know that's been my personal and enthusiastic favorite among your projected opuses. Or, still not in a mood for that? Well, of course, "don't force yourself, my good man." I received your and Joe's [brother of Frank and Nick] pamphlet on the CIO—thanks—I haven't read it yet, but read the last chapter, and it is excellent.

As to news about us—well, there is so much to tell that that's what has delayed my correspondence, I couldn't undertake even to begin. But a synopsis is better than nothing—so I'll give you a synopsis. Everything is going wonderfully for us—so well that I'm bewildered. Frank is taking it all in his stride, as our rightful due, and his attitude is only "Well, it's about time." He doesn't seem at all surprised—but I am. I can't get quite used to it all. I won't attempt now to describe the house—you must see it for yourself. It's wonderful. Frank has gone wild about working the soil— he is out with his chickens and rabbits all day, I hardly even see him. I don't remember ever seeing him chronically and permanently happy—and ardently enthusiastic—and busy, and glowing—as he is now—and it's wonderful to see. As for my work, well, you know that I'm with Hal Wallis on a long-term contract. Have just finished my first screenplay—and it's going into production in about two weeks. It was even in the papers here —about it being a record of speed in Hollywood, Wallis's setting up his company, and me writing the screenplay. It was a record. I worked as usual, like a dog, and since he lets me work at home, I worked day and night. But I finished the thing in record time—and it's to be Wallis's first production. I'd like to tell you all the compliments I received and how enthusiastic Wallis is about me—but it will sound silly in a letter, I'll tell you when I see you in person, I hope. Anyway, things are going wonderfully with the job so far. I just got a few days off (on pay) as reward for my speed—so I'm dutifully writing to you, this being actually the first free day I've had here. The screenplay is an adaptation of a dreadful novel called *The Love Letters*. It's coming out soon—the novel, I mean. Don't read it. It's awful. We only took the general idea from it—and the screenplay is practically an original by me. It's a vast improvement, if I do say so myself. Actresses whom Wallis wanted to get for the movie, refused to do it, when they read the galleys of the novel—but on the strength of my script Wallis got the girl he wanted most and she was the hardest to get, because every studio is after her—Jennifer Jones. She'll play the lead, and Joseph Cotten the male lead. William Dieterle is the director.

I don't know yet what my next assignment is to be. Will know in a few days. As to *The Fountainhead*, it will go into production early in 1945. The casting will begin about the first of the year. No one set for it as yet. The problem is still to find a Roark. Did you see that *The Fountainhead* is back on the bestseller lists? I hear it is selling more than ever before. Isn't that amazing—a year and a half after publication? I'm terribly happy about it, because that shows word-of-mouth appeal, a real response from the readers themselves, not from organized plugging.

Haven't any personal gossip to tell—we hardly go anywhere or see anyone—we just sit on our ranch like isolationists and are very happy. I could stun you with a lot of "Buckinghaming"—I'm a real celebrity here now—and so far, it's both amusing and thrilling—I'll tell you the flattering details when you come.

Joe has gone on a theatrical tour—with a small company that plays one-night stands in schools and colleges. We had one letter from him—he seems very happy, feels well and is doing well. I sent him to a hospital here, for a general checkup, before he left, because he wasn't actually sure whether his health would permit the trip. But it was found that he's in better condition than he himself thought—and the doctors allowed him to go.

Well, that's all the news in a general way. Now to bother you with some minor requests. You said once that you would be willing to get us kitchen gadgets in New York and mail them to us. If you can—here are the things we need, which are unobtainable here:

Pots and pans. We got some junky ones here, and we're getting along, but I would like to get what is probably the impossible—stainless steel pre-war pots and pans. If they can still be found in the better stores, please get us some—any size or shape.

A good-sized tea-cattle.

A good drip coffeepot—preferably for six cups. (Don't bother replacing the glass one which you gave away—it wasn't much good—we don't need it.)

A good flour sifter (with a ring that turns—you can't find them here at all).

A big cake pan (with a hole in the middle) preferably aluminum.

A gadget for poaching eggs—(like the one you had—or, as I've seen, one that poaches four eggs at once—they used to be made, but can't be found here now).

None of this is "obligatory," but would be a tremendous favor if you could get all or part of it. I'll send you the money for it in advance, if you need it and if you think those things can be had.

AND, coming back to my pet subject, could you try to get for me the record that broke in the shipping? It's a recent one, so I think you would be able to get it at the Gramophone Shop (it's on 48th or 49th Street, between Madison and Park). The name is: "Water Pebbles" by Claude MacArthur, Victor Record No. 24107-B. THANKS A LOT in advance for this—that's more important for me than the pots and pans. Incidentally, the Capehart is wonderful—and what a pleasure!—it means more to me than any other luxury we've had, much more than the mink coat.

Love from: Oscar, Oswald, Pop, Mom, Turtle-Cat, Cubbyhole and me—

P.S. There were some minor household things which didn't arrive and are not on your list. If they're lost or broken, never mind, but if you gave them away, thinking they're of no value, I'd like to get them back from whoever got them: Frank's big breakfast cup; one white horse head (the other was broken); one white pigeon (we had two, only one arrived); the seal with a vase in its nose; the green egg set—little tray, egg cup and salt shaker;

glass horses' heads bookends; blue-green glass ashtray. I know none of these are expensive, but they're sentimental value—and if they're retrievable, I'd like to get them. And—almost forgot, this *is* important—*you didn't send the electric cord for the waffle iron.* If the relatives got it, please send it to us, we can't use the waffle iron without it. Thanks.

■ ■ ■

To Howard A. Legge, a fan

October 29, 1944

Dear Mr. Legge:

Yes, of course, I believe *The Fountainhead.* You really shouldn't ask me such a question. Ask yourself whether *The Fountainhead* could have been written by anyone who didn't believe it.

Yes, I do make claim to an original idea. The idea of individualism is not new, but nobody has ever given the proper definition of the ethics of individualism. Where—in the whole history of moral philosophy—have you read the specific thesis of Roark's speech.

This is not by way of bragging, but just for the record. Since you understood and appreciated the code of *The Fountainhead,* I felt I wanted you to know that I am its originator. Thank you for saying that it is "the finest code of ethics the world has ever known." P.S. I believe you thought I am a man. I happen to be a woman. But it's quite all right, you may still write to me as "Dear Ayn."

■ ■ ■

To Leonard Read, founder and later president of the pro-capitalist Foundation for Economic Education, publishers of *The Freeman*

November 12, 1944

Dear Leonard Read:

Here is the copy of "Free Men Say!" which you gave me—with my notes all over it. I have marked with an E in red pencil the quotations which I consider excellent and which I think should be kept above all others. The next best I have marked "good." I have put brief explanations next to those I consider bad. A few I have not marked at all—they do neither good nor harm.

Now, to the criticism. "Free Men Say!" is the first of all the material you ever sent me that disappointed me pretty badly. Perhaps Gladys had the same feeling when she suggested that this should not be the second issue of *The Freeman*. I would go farther than that: I would say that if you issue this collection in its present form, you will kill *The Freeman* then and there. As I shall explain.

The announced purpose of *The Freeman* was serious, fearless, uncompromising education in the principles of freedom and individualism. Your foreword to "Free Men Say!" states that "Ideas move the world." And what do you then proceed to offer as ideas? Quotations from Harold Ickes and, *what is worse,* from Edgar Guest! You have some excellent quotations included—but instead of redeeming the collection, they make it worse. They are robbed of their power, earnestness and dignity by being presented on an equal footing with such pap as a poem about men "with flame of freedom in their souls and light of knowledge in their eyes." You have a few very bad quotations, contradictory to and downright destructive of your basic principles. But these few are not the worst flaw in the collection. The worst flaw is the preponderance of meaningless generalities which are neither good nor bad, but merely nothing at all. They give the collection an overall taste of sweetness, timidity, purposelessness and that tone of "benevolent bromides" which is the curse of our conservatives and which has cost the Republican Party three elections. It is precisely the same tone, method, intention and result.

And like all compromises of this nature, the collection not merely does not accomplish its purpose, but accomplishes the *exact opposite.* The net result in a neutral reader's mind would be: "Well, if this is the best that can be said for freedom and individualism, it ain't much!"

Since you are limited in the size of your booklet, your responsibility in the choice of quotations grows in inverse ratio to the number of pages used. Since you have little space, you can afford nothing but the best. Otherwise, you give a dreadful impression of the intellectual poverty of freedom's cause.

Just ask yourself what earthly purpose can be accomplished by spending money, effort and paper to tell men that "The ground of liberty must be gained by inches"? (What if Jefferson did say it? That was not all he said.) Standing by itself, such a sentence means nothing, says nothing, solves nothing. It is a generality, of no value unless the specific steps or inches are named. Anybody could subscribe to that sentence—and I mean anybody: Ickes, Roosevelt, Stalin or Hitler.

And *that* is the *first test* to which you must submit every quotation you choose: could a collectivist subscribe to it *legitimately*? That is, without contradicting his basic collectivist principles. If he can—your quotation is useless.

The second test is: does the quotation present a complete thought, by itself, out of context—and is that thought of value? If not—the quotation is useless. You have a great many quotes that are obviously parts of a general discussion, but of no particular strength by themselves. A good quotation must be a complete entity. It must be like a headline—sharp, clear, whole.

The third test: can the quotation be misinterpreted? If it can, it is worse than useless, it is dangerous. You have a great many quotations which were probably clarified in context. But by themselves, without amplification, they are open to a great many possible interpretations, most of them contradictory to your basic principles. You have many quotations whose meaning and intention are clear to me only because I know you personally and know what you were driving at. That is not proper. A quotation must be clear and unmistakable—by its own terms, through its own words—so that it retains its meaning no matter who said it or who is quoting it. I know that it is hard to find such passages from a long, serious book that depends on a long, closely reasoned argument. Still, only such passages can be of any value as quotations. Those that do not meet this requirement had better not be used.

Since the purpose of *The Freeman* is *education in principles*, you defeat your purpose by publishing anything that has no *intellectual* value, that does not contribute a forceful, uncompromising, *specific THOUGHT* on the subject of freedom. Mere ringing generalities, pretty sentences or emotional appeals are worse than useless. They support the general impression that freedom is a vague term without specific content—so that it is quite proper for Roosevelt, Browder and Stalin to pose as champions of freedom. *Unless every quotation you use ties freedom specifically to individualism* (and contributes some specific thought, reason or proof why this is so) *you achieve the opposite of your intention.*

You may ask: "But isn't it proper to stir up a general emotional response to the mere word 'freedom,' without specific content—and supply the content later?" And I would answer: No. That kind of stirring up is being done for you—by experts. That's what the New Deal is doing. You would only contribute to the general delusion that so long as we keep on yelling "Freedom" loudly enough, we are preserving it and no exercise of it in reality is necessary, since we do not even have to bother to understand what it means; so that it's quite all right to have ration cards, social security, forced labor and confiscation of property, so long as everybody shouts that this is a free country.

What is the purpose you wish to achieve by this booklet? *To give your readers the best thoughts men have expressed on freedom—the thoughts which they can use as ammunition in arguments on the subject.* If your quotations do not achieve this, you have failed. But most of what you have given your readers is not bullets—it's flowers. Hearts and flowers.

That is why I said that this booklet in its present form would kill the whole venture of *The Freeman*. If I did not know you personally, but had received the first issue of *The Freeman*, I would have subscribed with enthusiasm and interest; then, if I had received this collection, I would have said: "Oh well, it's just another one of those sweet Republican organizations, like the N.A.M." And I would not have bothered to read the following issues. You know what an ungodly amount of so-called "Conservative" pamphlets is being put out by hundreds of "conservative" organizations and how little good they do. Their fault is precisely the same as that of your collection—vagueness, generality, compromise—a feather duster where a meat-ax is necessary. You cannot afford to be placed in that category. Nor does it fit you as a person. Whatever *The Freeman* puts out must be *clear cut, specific* and *uncompromising*. Otherwise, you'll only help the other side—as all those conservative organizations are doing.

I hope you understand that when I say "you" in all the above criticism, I mean the Pamphleteers, not Leonard Read. I know that this is not your personal fault, since none of your own writing ever had the qualities to which I object here. I realize that this collection is a synthesis, a *collective* selection and, as such, bears the usual faults of any collective attempt. So I am trying, in this letter, to state the considerations and tests on which I think you can all agree and which can serve as a guiding standard in making your selections.

I must confess one thing: I feel a little indignant that your researchers simply passed up a book like *The God of the Machine*. All you have from it are only two quotations—not the best—picked from the end of the book. Obviously nobody has bothered to go through it. That gave me my usual, dangerous feeling of "what's the use?" It is a little discouraging to see those who attempt to find valuable thoughts on freedom pass up a treasure mine like this—and devote almost a whole page to Thomas Paine, who was not one of us, as the very quotations you chose demonstrate. This tends to shake my faith in what we were discussing here the other night— the fact that ideas live on their own and that those who need them will find them.

I also think that you should read Roark's speech from *The Foun-tainhead*—and *not* because it's my book or because I want more quotations from myself. But really there are much, much better quotes in it for your purpose than the ones included in the collection.

Now, a *MOST IMPORTANT* point: if you entitle your booklet "Free Men Say!" and state in your foreword that these are good ideas expressed by the *"lovers of liberty"* you simply *cannot* include Roosevelt, Ickes, Woodrow Wilson, Eugene V. Debs and *Leon Trotzky* (?!?) It is actually indecent. It does what your weaker organizations do—gives specific assistance to the other side—but does it openly, directly and deliberately. It whitewashes, sanctions and supports the enemy. It's inexcusable. NOW EVERYTHING ELSE I SAID MAY BE OPEN TO DEBATE, BUT THIS POINT IS NOT. If you quote any socialist or New Dealer as a champion of freedom—you have no case or cause left.

I would suggest that you should be very careful in your choice of authors—in view of your title and foreword. I do not know some of them at all. If they are not strictly of our side, if they are doubtful or in-between—throw them out, no matter what they said. No quotation is good enough to offset the harm done by including such names.

Now, a minor suggestion: I would include the titles of the books from which your quotations are taken, along with the author's name. It would induce your readers to read the complete works, if they liked the quotations—and that would help your purpose. (Provided, of course, that the quotes are from books on our side—another reason why they should be.) Personally, I am very much impressed with the quotations from William Graham Sumner and Max Hirsch, two authors I had not discovered for myself. Would you tell me the titles of the books from which you quoted? I would like to read more of these two.

And would you let me see the final copy of your selection before you print it? If I can help you to avoid dangerous mistakes, I would like to do it. The final decision, of course, is yours. But I would like to express my opinion—for whatever value you may find in it—when it is still not too late.

Exhaustedly yours,

P.S. And I'm the little girl who hates to write letters!

■   ■   ■

5

LETTERS TO ISABEL PATERSON

Friends and political allies for many years, Ayn Rand and Isabel Paterson were two of the champions of individualism of the 1940s. Paterson was a columnist for the *New York Herald-Tribune* and author of numerous books, most notably *The God of the Machine*. Rand and "Pat" saw each other on many occasions, often talking philosophy all night and often disagreeing. The contrasting approaches to ideas evident in their letters seem also to have characterized their conversations—Rand organized and logical; Paterson spontaneous and sometimes rambling. Rand later said of Paterson: "She had such switching metaphysics that it was frightening and you never could tell, not only from meeting to meeting, but within the same evening, when she would switch or why. At her best, she was enormously rational, with a very wide kind of abstract mind, could talk fascinatingly, make the best philosophical identifications and abstract connections. And generally was a marvelous mind. . . . At her worst, she would turn into a mystic." Their friendship ended in 1948, after Paterson's visit to the O'Connors in California, when, in Rand's words, Paterson insulted some of Rand's friends "in the most causeless, unnecessary way."

October 10, 1943

Dear Pat:

I got a special thrill out of your letter—all my life, reading the published correspondence of famous people, I have envied them because they received personal letters on important and abstract subjects, I mean from friends, not just professional correspondence. I thought nobody wrote that way any more—but you do—and now I have one of those letters myself. Also, I'm glad that here's one of your brilliant letters that's not wasted on some fool collectivist somewhere.

Darling, thank you immensely for everything you said. Particularly, for saying that I am your sister. Why did you add: "That is, if you also find it so"? I hope you don't have to doubt how I find it.

I know that I will now have to write *The Strike* [renamed *Atlas Shrugged*]—you'll push me into it. If I ever hesitate, I will just read page 2 of your letter again. Your quotation about Averroes is most interesting. And pertinent.* I am really beginning to think that the idea [of *The Strike*] is not fantastic at all, but probably more tragically real than I imagine. It seems to apply to many people, on different levels of ability or achievement—but when I think of people I have known, who have puzzled me because they seemed to kill precisely the best in them, I now see that that "strike" is the explanation, whether they consciously knew it or not. I find myself dropping everything and thinking about that story—which I shouldn't do right now. But by all the signs, I know I'm hooked—this is the beginning of my next one. That's how I usually start. So may God help me—also you and Frank.

I am sort of crossing my fingers when I say this, but things are still going awfully well for me, one thing after another. Bobbs-Merrill are most friendly and enthusiastic and I suddenly seem to be the fair-haired child there, even without Archie. They are laying out their ads right now, and ready to start. Incidentally, the money is to be spent between now and January 1—so the campaign will be good and thick—I hope. I have today's bestseller list here—and it's five mentions all right—and the fifth one is San Francisco. I wonder if perhaps you saw the list of next week, which would be nice, too.

Thank you with all my heart for the plug in your column. I was terribly touched when I saw that you thought of *The Fountainhead* and mentioned it last thing before finishing your column before going away. It was like a personal greeting—and I am very grateful.

Am I one of the "gifted novelists" you had in mind when you wrote that they threatened to use you in a novel? Because you'll certainly be in *The Strike*, though probably not in a recognizable form.

I met Dr. Virgil Jordan [head of the National Industrial Conference

---

* The quote read in part: "The happy few whom God has endowed with a philosophical mind should content themselves with a solitary possession of rational truth."

Board] Friday—and spent an hour talking politics with him. He has read your book and was most enthusiastic and admiring about it. Don't ask me, if so, what he is doing about it. I don't know. I still don't quite understand how these organizations function. He has not read my book yet—but he told me an interesting story about his son. You may remember that he sent my book to his son, who is in the Air Corps, and the son wrote a rave letter to Bobbs-Merrill about it, specifically about "magnificent individualists." So I took for granted that his son had always been on our side. But here is the story: the boy went to Dartmouth and emerged as a complete pink. This was his father's problem for years. Jordan says he tried everything—he spent hours and hours arguing with the boy—he gave him all the material they had in their organization—he tried *Zarathustra* on him, and Stirner's *The Ego and Its Own*—and nothing worked. And then my book turned the boy completely to our side—in two days. Jordan actually said it was "a miracle." His son wrote him a letter about it, and Jordan says it was like a revelation to the boy, like a "sudden explosion." I really think this is wonderful—the kind of effect I hoped to accomplish. By the way, Jordan himself hasn't read the book, in spite of this. But I can't hold it against him too much. Don't be angry at me if I say that I really liked him, he is very intelligent, and forthright, and there's nothing halfway or "compromising" about his political views. He seemed to think and talk as we do.

And today I met Tom Girdler. At his broadcast. The most flattering thing was the way he said: "OH!" when I was introduced to him. He has read my book—and spoke of it very highly—and asked me to have lunch with him week after next when he'll be back in New York. I liked him on sight—even before he praised the book. He rushed right to the airport after the broadcast, but the rest of us had lunch and Mr. Hill, his press agent, spoke to me in more detail. He said that Girdler showed him my letter and that Girdler "was very proud of it." (!) Then Hill asked me if I had seen Isabel Paterson lately. I told him you were away on your vacation. He has read your book, and so has Girdler. Hill said he thought it was one of the most important books ever written on our side and that it was "a book that will live." There you are.

By the way, about Herbert Hoover's admiration for you—Frank said that to match it I would have to win the admiration of Willkie. Which God forbid. But, seriously, I think that a lot of Hoover's sins can be forgiven him for that.

I haven't written a sentence on my present book—I'm still in a kind of stupor—but I have had to do a lot of things and running around for my novel, which is more important now and urgent, so I guess I can be excused. I think, though, that I will be better when all this is settled—and that I will really work.

I'm enclosing the "Wake up, America" debate. It ain't much—but let me know what you think of it. I was only glad and amused to see how Mr. Villard wiggled in order not to admit that he is a collectivist. Look at his opening sentence—and tell me what case he has left for himself after that. For once, it's their side that betrays their cause in the crucial point. Also, here he is, granting us theoretical correctness, that is, idealism, and pleading expediency. Oh, well, everything is screwy!

I can't force myself to answer a few lines to my fan mail—and here I am sending you a small manuscript. I hope you don't mind this complete report. I miss you a lot. And so does Frank.

Love from both of us,

Paterson wrote in response: "You still don't seem to know yourself that your idea is new. It is not Nietzsche or Max Stirner. . . . Their *supposed Ego was composed of whirling words—your concept of the Ego is an entity, a person, a living creature functioning in concrete reality."*

■　■　■

July 26, 1945

Dear Pat:

Thank you!

I have been afraid to write to you—but this time I want so much to thank you that I'm writing. I have received the two bestseller lists you sent me, and now I've received the third one. It means so much to me that I don't know what to say about it. It has knocked me out of equilibrium and made me slightly dizzy, for many reasons: not only the sale of the book itself, but the fact that you're watching it and that you wanted to send the lists to me. Of course I have been thinking all this time that you predicted the sale of the book and that "Isabel Paterson is always right." I wanted to gloat over it with you. I'm doing the gloating here in your honor anyway—but I wanted to tell you about it, so I'm writing.

I'm not sure that you won't give me hell for saying that I was afraid to write to you—and that you'll be offended by it. I can only say that of all the things I can do in relation to you, the one I *don't* want to do, above all else, is to offend you or to hurt you in any way whatever. I was at fault originally, that time when I didn't write to you for over a month. But when I tried to write and explain it, I made it worse. When I received your last letter, I wrote you six pages—and didn't send them. I thought anything I say will make it worse, again. Because, you see, I never thought that I wrote letters as a "favor" *for* a friend. I always thought that I wrote primarily for my own sake, because I wanted to talk to a friend and wanted to hear from the friend. Assuming at the same time, of course, that the friend did want to hear from me. But I never thought of it as being a matter of an "Ungenerous heart" on my part. So that if I suffer writing letters, I am a martyr for my own sake—not anyone else's, nor am I doing it only because the friend will get mad if I don't, nor am I saying I am tired as a reproach, that is, to show in effect: look, how much I am sacrificing for you. This is what you read into my last letter. [No copy was found.] It is not what I intended. So that gave me another good complex about letter writing—sheer terror of the mere attempt.

I know the reason why letters are so hard for me to write—and I will tell it to you, not as alibiing, but because it is a fact. Don't say in answer: "My good woman, if it's terror to you, you don't have to write to me." The point is that I *do* want to write to you—but that I cannot do it easily, lightly or casually. I must try to learn to do it better and easier than I do —but there is a valid reason for my complex. It's this: the first letters I ever wrote regularly were to my family in Russia, when I came here—and every letter was censored, so I had to be extremely careful of what I said, in order not to embarrass them. I always rewrote page after page, before I could mail a letter to them. I had to doubt and scrutinize every sentence for any possible misinterpretation. I have not been able to write any kind of letter spontaneously ever since.

I am very consciously aware of the fact that words on paper can be taken in very many different ways. So I am always trying to write letters as if I were walking on thin ice—so that what I say would be taken the way I said it. And, above all, it is letters to friends that I compose the most carefully—because that is when I want to be understood, and the things I write about are important. You said: "I assume that one speaks to a friend or writes a letter, spontaneously." I speak to a friend spontaneously—yes. But it is precisely to a friend that I am afraid of writing spontaneously. In conversation, a misunderstanding can be sensed and corrected at once. On paper—it's done. I had always gone over all my long letters to you, and edited them very carefully, and rewrote them. The sad part of it all is that my last letter to you was the first one I sent unedited and uncopied. And it was the one that did offend you. I am not saying this as a reproach to you. I can see your point and why you could take it as you did. It only made me realize more concretely my limitations as a letter-writer.

All I can say now is that I want to try and write to you. BECAUSE I WANT TO WRITE TO YOU. I hope you will also want to hear. But the effort is made for my sake, not as a bribe to you. I had hoped to be in New York much sooner and speak to you in person, rather than try to say anything on paper. But I undertook to do an extra screenplay for Hal Wallis, because he bought a book I wanted to adapt and bought it specially for my sake. This held me up longer than I thought it would take. I am free now —for six months, but I didn't want to go to New York in July. I am planning to come to New York in September, for at least a month.

I assume you're not completely off me—so I'll tell you briefly what I'm doing. I am getting along with the studios very well—almost too well. That is, they like my work—and I don't like it. I don't like the fact that what actually reaches the screen is just a distorted mess of what I had intended. Not so much because they rewrite it—no, it's more stupid than that. They okay a script as I did it—then the actors and director on the set adlib it out of all sense; then the producer cuts it in the cutting room in such a way that what is left doesn't make the sense intended. However, I expected all that, so I'm not whining—like the writers you referred to when you once said that you would feel no sympathy for anyone who suffers at the rate of $500 per week. I set myself two purposes when I signed the screen contract: a minimum and a maximum. The minimum would be just the money, the security and the freedom of all worry about financial returns in regard to my serious writing, my books. The maximum would be to gain a position in the studios when my pictures would be done *my* way. This last is not impossible. So far, at the end of my first year with Wallis, I have acquired a prestige with studio people which I didn't expect. It looks as if the people involved are beginning to think that when I say something I know what I'm talking about. I already have a position that none of the other writers here have—that is, more freedom about my scripts and more say about the results than is considered normal for a writer. So I might come to reach my maximum purpose.

I met Frederick Lonsdale, the English playwright, here. He admires *The Fountainhead* very much. He felt that I'm wasting my talent somewhat by working for the screen. I asked him: "Are you afraid that I'll go Hollywood?" He said: "Good God, no. If you stay here, it's Hollywood that will have to go you." I think he's right. At least that's what I'm working for. If I find it impossible, I'll finish the contract and quit the movies.

But for the present, I'm delighted to be out of the studios and on my own free time. I was unbelievably tired and beginning to be quite bored. I like screen work, but not too much of it. *Now*—I'm writing my nonfiction book *The Moral Basis of Individualism*. Pat, darling, I suppose you know what a difficult job it is! Much harder than I thought when I started it in New York. I reread what I had done then, and I was glad I had stopped. I knew then I wasn't ready for it—and I wasn't. The ideas were all right— but not the form and presentation. It has to be much, much more than merely a restatement of my theme in *The Fountainhead*. It has to start further back—with the first axioms of existence. It has to say everything I said in the novel—but it was so much easier for me to say it in fiction form, because I am primarily a fiction writer. That's my one real love in life. I have to retrain myself to a nonfiction viewpoint and tone, and do it on the hardest kind of theme I could have picked. But I'm doing it.

I am reading a long, detailed history of philosophy [by B. A. G. Fuller]. I'm reading Aristotle in person and a lot of other things. At times it makes my hair stand on end—to read the sort of thing those [non-Aristotelian] "sages of the ages" perpetrated. And I think of you all the time—of what you used to say about them. It's actually painful for me to read Plato, for instance. But I must do it. I don't care what the damn fools said—I want to know what made them say it. There is a frightening kind of rationality about the reasons for the mistakes they made, the purposes they wanted to achieve and the practical results that followed in history. When I'm in New York, I would like to talk to you about philosophers and help you to curse them.

Now, as to my personal life, I haven't much of it. Haven't the time nor the energy. I love living in the country, and I get furiously nervous every time I have to go out and meet somebody. I am becoming more anti-social than I was—and the reason is the same as yours, so I think you'll understand very well: I can't stand the sort of things people talk about. I've stopped reading the newspapers, beyond a general glance at the news. I can't stand the columnists and editorials: what they're doing in the world now is beyond any polite discussion and beyond the possibility of a legitimate disagreement between decent people. It's so monstrous that to read some fool discussing seriously something like the San Francisco conference is worse than a waste of time: it's like listening to a raving maniac, and a vicious one.

My happiest thoughts are, of course, about *The Fountainhead*. You know how I'd feel about the sale. It's gone much beyond what I expected. You remember I set myself 100,000 copies as the goal at which I'd be satisfied. It has sold 150,000 or more by now. I like to think that it might be a sign that there are many more people sick of collectivism than I suspected. I know there can be many explanations for that sale, but this factor is terribly important, if true. I haven't formed any set opinion of my own to explain the success of the book. I have just decided to wait and see and collect the evidence. For the present, I'm just terribly happy—and think only that there is a wider field for what I have to say than I thought I had.

I had started this as a short note to you—but there's so much that I'd like to talk to you about. I still don't know whether you want me to write in detail, and I feel a little presumptuous doing this. I just want to say one more thing: if you wonder how I feel about you, look at what I wrote in your copy of *The Fountainhead*. I meant it. I still do. I always will.

Love from both of us—Frank wants his included specifically,

■   ■   ■

August 4, 1945

Dear Pat:

Good God!

You must have forgotten me entirely. You do not seem to remember any more what I said, what I thought or why I thought it.

You spent pages arguing against things I have never said. Some of them, the exact opposite of what I said. I don't know what made you do it. I won't even try to explain it to myself.

To begin with the last and worst: you write: "For example, you assume that the order of events or inventions in *time* is somehow an order of value or merit. You have been annoyed, because I am not interested in movies and don't like the radio, when apparently you think I ought to because they are 'modern.' " I cannot argue on the basis of what I "apparently think." I speak on the basis of what I think. And I have told you what I think on this particular subject—at great length and in great detail. You may have forgotten. That is legitimate. But it is not legitimate to put words into my mouth which I never said, nor to ascribe to me reasons which are not my reasons. I have never defended anything on the grounds of its being "new" nor condemned anything on the grounds of its being "old." I do not even understand such a manner of thinking. If it can be called thinking.

Whatever else you have forgotten, you must surely remember that I am the person who's made a point of describing myself as "reactionary" when facing any so-called modern intellectual. That is the word that scares our good Republicans out of their wits—and that is the word I chose deliberately to apply to myself, with the explanation that if "modern" is what we have now, I am a reactionary who wants to go back to what we had before.

And *I* am the person to whom you find it necessary to write this: "In your philosophical assumptions you ignore the fact about this country— even when it was founded, it was actually less 'modern' than the contemporary fashion in thought. It was really a counter-revolution against the political ideas drawn from the scientific philosophy that begins with the Renaissance, etc."

My philosophical assumptions? When did they have anything to do with any questions of "oldness" or "newness"? Whose language are you speaking? Certainly not mine.

I have never defended the radio because it is "new." I have never even defended it as a means of communication, nor as a vehicle for the transmission of thought, nor as an "instrument of thought." I have defended it—and do—wholeheartedly, devotedly, enthusiastically—as a medium of the transmission of music. I have said that to you more than once. [The next fifteen typed lines in AR's copy are illegible.] The radio merely extends the audience of an orator. It has nothing to do with the audience of a writer. *WHO* has claimed that an "auditory gadget" is an advance upon the printed page? I haven't.

I do see a relation between the radio and a concert hall. It is a great convenience to be able to listen to a concert at home. It is a great technical advance when technical means can be found to achieve that. I say, a *technical* advance, not a musical one. The function of radio is not even to "change" music, nor to push it forward nor backward. Only to transmit it. And the transmission of music is the radio's only and proper function.

Do you mean to say that since radio can also be used by fools who'll try to substitute it for books, radio as such is evil and backward? If that is your argument, it is the same kind of argument as saying that an automobile is evil because bad drivers misuse it. If that is not your argument—what is your argument? And why argue that with me at all?

Neither have I ever defended the movies on the ground of their being "new." I have defended them on the ground of their being a superior dramatic medium—in relation to the stage, to the spoken drama. But I spent a whole evening in your country house discussing this one point—my views on the movies—and if all you cared to ascribe to me is the point of "newness," which I never uttered, I see no use in launching here into a detailed account of my ideas on the movies.

You write: "A thing is neither true nor false because it is old, or because it is new." Good God, Pat, are you really talking to me? Or do you have me confused with anyone else?

You write: "You have adopted the 'humanistic,' 'scientific,' theanthropic philosophy." I have not *adopted* any philosophy. I have created my own. I do not care to be tagged with anyone else's labels.

There may be many points in my philosophy which you may have grounds to question. If these grounds are rational, I shall always be glad to hear the questions raised and to discuss them and to acknowledge myself as wrong, if I am proved to be wrong, and to correct my stand accordingly. I see no point in discussing what some fools said in the past and why they said it and what error they made and where they went off the rails, if such a discussion is supposed to be a refutation of *my* philosophy.

You write: "The frightening kind of rationality you find in the philosophers is precisely your own kind." If 756 pages of a novel plus nights and nights and nights of discussion have not made clear to you what my kind of rationality is, a letter won't do it. The fault may be mine. It may be yours. I am past the point of caring to discover which. I simply won't make any more attempts to define what I mean by rationality.

But I will mention that the "frightening kind of rationality" I referred to in my letter—was the discovery I made while reading the philosophers that it is actually impossible for man to be irrational. Let him yelp against reason all he wants. Let him accept the premise that there is no such thing as reason at all. And all his subsequent ideas and actions will follow in perfect logical sequence from that premise. His actions will become irrational and insane—but in perfect agreement with his premise. It was not a discovery to me, it was more in the nature of an illustration and a substantiation.

Now, more of your points: as a denunciation of my kind of rationality and of the general weakness of the syllogism, you write: "Plato reports Socrates as saying that the community, the City, had a right to take his life, even unjustly, because the City was the same as his parents. There is the assumption first that parents actually have a right to take the life of their child for no cause and second that the collective is the same thing as a natural parent. Neither is true."

That's right, neither is true. But how are you going to prove that it isn't true? By rational argument? Or by the fiat of revelation? If this last, Plato can well say that *his* revelation tells him it's true—and that's that. In fact, that's just about what Plato did say. Or must we assume that there is no rational argument which could prove that parents have no right to the life of their child, and that the collective is not the same thing as natural parents? And if there is no such rational argument, we must accept something else? And if a rational argument is simply a statement that makes sense—must we assume something else when we find that we can't make sense?

Now, to the question of God—where your presentation of what you assume to be my position simply made me sick.

You state my assumption as: "If God exists, man is a slave," and you proceed to say: "Why? Your assumption there is actually that a creative mind necessarily makes a slave of any person less creative who also happens to exist. Does it? If that is so, you have no proper grievance against your reviewer who said that a world of Roarks was Fascism."

First, I do not wish to mention the name of Roark in any such connection. You could have made the same point using another illustration. I have always thought of you as a person of extremely delicate sensitivity, your fighting manner towards Republicans notwithstanding. I thought you had delicacy in important matters. I did not think you'd stoop to this. I, who love to argue, will not bother to argue or explain myself on this particular point. I'll let you guess what I mean, if you care to.

But I will discuss your point, omitting your choice of illustration. No, I do not think that a creative mind necessarily makes a slave of any person less creative who also happens to exist. A creative mind does not and cannot reach into another mind, whether more or less creative or otherwise. A creative mind does nothing to another mind—except offer it material to digest, which the other mind may digest or not, as it pleases. A creative mind is not omnipotent. Its greatness and beauty and nobility is precisely that it neither has nor seeks any power over any other mind. But I'm speaking of a human creative mind, am I not? That is all the word means to me, anyway, that is all I can understand.

But if you speak of God as a "creative mind," you imply something entirely different from the conception of a human mind. I do not know precisely what you or anyone ever really implies by the conception of God or God's mind. I gather only, by such definitions as are given, that God's mind is something which man's mind is not. Therefore, I see no possible, conceivable rational excuse for applying any conclusion whatever about God's mind to the sphere, nature and virtue of man's mind. I see no rationality in a statement such as: "Ah, you think that God's mind enslaves man? Therefore, you must think that man's mind enslaves men." But there, you see? I expect a *rational* excuse. That is probably the reason why I despise man's mind, despise man's creative faculty and write books that denounce creative men.

Can you interfere arbitrarily with what I am doing? Yes—physically. No—mentally. Can a brick kill me? Yes. Can a brick get into my mind and tell me what to think or do? No. Can an omnipotent being do that? Yes.

An omnipotent being, by definition, is a totalitarian dictator. Ah, but he won't use his power? Never mind. He *has* it.

You may be surprised to hear, however, that the above is not even my main argument against God at all.

My main argument is that the conception of God—or such as I have ever heard or read—denies every conception of the human mind. What is omnipotence? What is infinity? What is a being which is limitless—when the basic conception of existence in man's form of consciousness is the conception of an entity—which means a limit? An entity is that which other entities are not. What is an entity which is everything?

If there are answers translatable into human terms, I am always very interested in hearing them. If there aren't—I shall just have to recognize my limitations, one of which is the inability to understand anything at all, except in human terms.

The only important point in all this is why you found it necessary to take up with me the subject of God, at this time, by letter—when it is probably the most difficult subject of all, and we didn't succeed very well even when discussing it in person for hours. You told me once (oh, more than once!) that for the purposes of the book I am writing—my statement of man's proper morality—the question of God does not have to be discussed, that I do not need to go into the metaphysical questions of the origin of man and the universe, that my thesis will hold as based on man's nature—without any explanation of the origin of that nature. Then why fight me on that at this particular time? Or is it merely in the nature of a general discussion?

I ask this, because it seems to me that I gather the purpose of this particular discussion. You see, I am very careful in my choice of words. I do not put words into your mouth nor ascribe to you intentions you never had. I don't say this was your purpose, I say certain indications in your letter point to the possibility that it may have been your purpose. If it wasn't, correct me. The purpose I mean is that you believe that unless I accept God, I will have betrayed the cause of individualism, that the case for individualism rests on faith in God—and on nothing else. To the best of my rational understanding, the opposite is true. But you may be right—if you can prove it. But before you proceed to tell me how Descartes, Voltaire, the "humanists," the "scientists," etc. destroyed individualism, destroyed the dignity of man and prepared the way for the totalitarian state—explain to me how Thomas Aquinas, the greatest philosopher ever to accept and defend the conception of God, advocated the Inquisition and the burning of heretics for *the good of society*? When you have accounted for that, philosophically, you may proceed to batter those in whom you see some similarity with my thesis (though there really is none) all you wish.

Actually, if I can sum up my attitude on the question of God, it's this: from all I can gather, the definition of God is "That which the human mind cannot grasp." Being a rationalist, literal-minded and believing that it is a moral obligation to mean what you say, I take the persons who made the above definition at their word, I agree and obey them: I don't grasp it.

Incidentally, I know some very good arguments of my own in favor of the existence of God. But they're not the ones you mention and they're not the ones I've ever read advanced in any religion. They're not proofs, therefore I can't say I accept them. They are merely possibilities, like a hypothesis that could be tenable. But it wouldn't be an omnipotent God and it wouldn't be a limitless God. [AR never mentioned these arguments again.]

Now, to the personal. I have been at this letter for over four hours now. No, it's not a reproach. Just an observation. I dropped my writing and grabbed my typewriter. I am almost tempted to add: it serves you right, now go ahead and read all this.

You still tell me to have a good time. I still don't know how to go about it. My good time is only at my desk. Yes, I bought some stunning clothes—the best there is—Adrian's. I'm delighted with the way I look in them. It even surprised me. But I feel, a little wistfully, that there are really very few people for whose sake it's worth making the effort to look attractive. However, I'll wear the clothes in New York—and hope Leonard Read will be stunned—and hope you will be, too. That will be worth enjoying. I'm planning now to be in New York by September 10—or as near to it as the studio can arrange the transportation.

Did Linda write to you that Frank and I have adopted a son? Well, not exactly—he's twenty-one, so he can't be adopted. But he's now living with us—and we both consider him in the nature of a son. He was a pilot in the Pacific—out of the Army now, by reason of two airplane crack-ups and malaria. How did I find him? He hitchhiked across the continent from New York, because he had read *The Fountainhead*. I'll tell you more about him when I see you. It's a very curious thing to me—he's a replica of me, as I was at twenty-one, or as near a replica as one person can be of another. Frank says that he's a kind of reincarnation of me before the time.

Frank asks me to tell you that he's knee-deep in alfalfa irrigation—
and is perfectly willing to let the world go to hell. I'm not. I'll always hold
out for the exceptions.

Love from both of us,

*AR's paragraph about her "adopted" son refers to Thaddeus
Ashby, a young fan, who later admitted to AR that his whole "history" (including being a combat pilot) was fictitious.*

■ ■ ■

August 28, 1945

Dear Pat:

Yes, of course I'd like to "ride in triumph through Persepolis." If that's
your romantic streak, it's mine, too—I like and understand that kind of
romanticism. I'd be delighted to meet the man from DuPont, if he likes
and understands *The Fountainhead.* You didn't mention his name—is he
by any chance E. E. Lincoln, their chief economist? [Paterson's friend at
DuPont was Jasper Crane.] I believe I told you about Mr. Lincoln—he was
one of the men to whom my "nature's nobleman," John Gall, sent copies
of my book. He (Lincoln) made a trip to New York to meet me—and I
liked him very much, he seemed to be one of those who don't compromise.
In any event, I'd be very happy to be invited to Wilmington and see some
of those men. You may tell the Du Ponts that they and I have something
in common: I deal in explosives, too.

Thank you for your letter—it was delightful—sounded like your old
self. (And I don't mean just because of the compliments to me—though
the compliments did make me happy—I mean the general tone and mood.)

As things stand, I think I shall be in New York definitely on the 8th.
The studio cannot get the train reservation set until the day before, but they
told me that it's practically certain they'll get it. We'll start from here on
September 5th and arrive in New York on the morning of the 8th. Our
hotel reservations are at the Essex House. I'll telephone you in Ridgefield the
moment we arrive. I'm beginning to feel terribly excited—and can't concentrate on anything, I'm completely and most wonderfully demoralized.

What do you mean about not being sure whether I'm happy to see my
book rising on the bestseller lists? I'm so happy about it that I'm practically
unable to think of anything else or to concentrate on my new book. I catch
myself in semi-Peter-Keating moments of just sitting and staring at the

bestseller lists spread before me. Though it's not quite Peter Keating—I worked to get it there. I suppose Linda didn't write to tell you how you contributed to throwing me into a fit of hysteria once—when you sent to her the first list on which my book was reported by a New York store. When Linda gave me that list, I started screaming—literally and aloud, just plain screaming. Frank came running from upstairs, thinking I was hurt. Hal Wallis's secretary was in the house at the time—and he must have thought I was totally nuts. That was the first time in my life that I wanted to scream inarticulately from a kind of pure physical happiness. No, I guess I'm not glad about those lists—not much! I asked Linda to thank you for sending that list—it gave me one of my nicest moments that I'll always remember.

Why, yes, I used to be mad when you told me that the book would sell big—not mad at you, but at the whole rotten situation. That was in the first months when it looked as if the book had been most efficiently murdered—and none of our goddamn "conservatives" would lift a finger about it. The fact that the book was potentially a big seller just made the situation seem more horrible. But now I am glad—though with a touch of bitterness that the book made its own way, without their help. It's better as a tribute to the book itself—but the bitterness is for those people who'll profit by the fact that I broke two blockades for them, the book publishing one and the movie one, that I've done more for their free enterprise than the N.A.M. with their million-dollars-a-year budget—and those so and so's will now pat me on the back—yet where were they when the book needed them? But to hell with them. You were right, we can do it without their help. We'll have to save capitalism from the capitalists. You told me once that the time would come when I would be able to help *The God of the Machine.* I think I can now. I have a plan about it, which I want to discuss with you in person.

It's wonderful to think that I'll be talking to you in less than two weeks. I haven't attempted to answer your letter-before-last—it would take a whole philosophical article—so I'm bringing it with me (your letter) and would like to answer it and discuss it in person. Also, I'm most eager to tell you about one result of my philosophical reading—I think I have a definition to make about free will which will be as important in that field as my antialtruism was in ethics. No, it's not atheistic nor theistic, again I think it can fit either—but nobody seems to have thought of it. I'd like to check my idea against yours—see how it strikes you. And I am most interested to hear your explanation of the end of a cycle in Asia, which you only mentioned. You have certainly been right about so many general developments before that you shouldn't be surprised if you predicted it right again.

Love from both of us—and an enthusiastic "We'll be seeing you!"

■   ■   ■

There is a two-and-a-half-year gap until the correspondence resumes.

February 7, 1948

Dear Pat:

As I told you on the phone, I have been engaged in a wild orgy of weeding—not of devil's grass, but of adjectives. Or would you say it is the same thing? I have removed tons of them from the chapter [of *Atlas Shrugged*] I had left unfinished when I went East. I finished that chapter and have just now finished the next one. This is the first time I have come up for air.

I have had such a wonderful streak of writing that I did not dare interrupt it. I think my trip to New York caused it—and a great part of the credit is probably yours. It was your line about my book having to be written like a piece of sculpture that was extremely helpful to me. I can never learn anything unless I grasp the basic abstraction involved, and that was the line that made clear to me your objection to adjectives and repetitions. I don't think I will always agree with you on every particular application, but I think I do understand the principle.

Now I promised to tell you about my trip in the locomotive. I will not attempt to describe how it felt, except to say that it was the greatest experience of my life. I have seldom enjoyed anything concrete or in the present tense, I am always in the abstract or future. That locomotive ride was one of the very few times when I enjoyed the actual moment for its own sake.

There is one observation I made that may be philosophical. I have always been a little afraid of riding on trains, particularly now; not actually afraid, but just in the sense of thinking that some dreadful accident may happen at any moment. So I thought that I would be more afraid riding right in front in the engine. But I found that I was not afraid at all. It was the feeling of being in front and of knowing where I was going, instead of being dependent on some unknown power, that made the difference. All I felt was a wonderful sense of excitement and complete security, even a few times when I saw some headlights in the distance coming toward us which, I had read in stories, could have been trains coming on our own track (which, of course, they weren't).

Now if you want the specific details: When I entered the first engine in Grand Central, dressed in my slacks and railroad cap, and the old engineer saw me, he said, "Good God!" I asked him, "What's the matter? Weren't you told it would be a woman?" He said, "The hat!" I told him that that was given to me by the company, and he said it was more than they ever did for him. He was not offensive about it, but extremely nice and amused in a very friendly way. The most thrilling moment was when the engine started moving, and the ride through the underground tunnel out of Grand Central. Everything I thought of as heroic about man's technological achievements was there concretely for me to feel for the first time in my life.

At Harmon they changed the engines, and I got into my first diesel. Their efficiency was amazing. It took just a few minutes. Everybody seemed to know about me in advance, and they switched me around as quickly as they did the engines. The moment I got into the diesel, they took pictures of me leaning out of the cab window. The crew of the diesel had the same attitude as the one in the electric engine. I had been afraid that they might regard me as a nuisance, but they seemed to enjoy my presence as much as I did. They were patronizingly amused, very superior, and very glad to be asked any kind of questions. The company had sent a road foreman along to give me all the explanations. He took me through the diesel units behind the engine, and I saw everything—all the motors, the high voltage, the boiling oil, and every sort of gadget that I couldn't possibly understand, but the total effect was magnificent. The noise in the motor units is unbelievable. You can't speak at all—the man could only point at things silently. As to riding in the cab—it is much more comfortable than in the best compartment. There is less shaking, not too much noise, and the engine rides as if it were floating. It actually seems to glide; you don't feel the wheels under you at all. Every time the engine started, I tried to catch the moment of the start and couldn't; it starts as smoothly as that. Incidentally, the fireman gave me his chair, and it is an upholstered leather armchair, more comfortable than any in the best tycoon's office.

When I got out of the engine in Albany, the conductor was waiting for me and escorted me in person back to my car. Frank was waiting for me in the vestibule of the car, and the first thing he said was, "You're marvelous!" In the nineteen years of our marriage, this is the only time he has ever paid me a point-blank compliment like that. When I asked him why, he said, "You do such exciting things." After which we went into the dining car to have dinner. The steward came up to me to ask how I had liked riding in the engine. Apparently, the whole train crew knew about it. To make the day perfect, there was a young couple sitting at the other side of the dining table, and after a while the girl turned to me and said, "I have been urging my husband to gather courage to ask you, are you Ayn Rand?" It seems they recognized me and they were great admirers of *The Fountainhead.* So you can imagine what a wonderful dinner I had, except that I couldn't eat at all.

The next morning I had to get up at 6 o'clock and got into the engine again at Elkhart, Indiana. During the night they had had their first snow-storm. It was still dark when we started riding through the snow. There was a different crew and a new road foreman. These people had the best time with me. The following is strictly confidential, I don't want to get them in trouble: They put me into the engineer's seat and let me drive the engine myself. Believe it or not, I have now driven the Twentieth Century Limited. They let me start the engine from a small station and, of course, there were three men standing behind me watching every move, but still nobody touched a lever except me, and I started the train and accelerated it to 80 miles per hour. The men apologized that they couldn't give me a real ride, because they were ahead of schedule, so they couldn't go faster than 80 miles. Otherwise, they said, they could have shown me a speed of 120 miles per hour. I think 80 miles was nice enough, but actually I couldn't tell that we were going that fast. It was extremely smooth and the only sign of speed was that the signal lights seemed to be coming along every few seconds. The men were as anxious to show me everything as I was to see it. The road foreman broke the seal on a special gadget that registers the speed of the train, to show me how it worked. This was strictly against regulations. There was a diesel inspector who traveled most of the time in the motor units. He came up a few minutes later, saw the broken seal and remarked that it was broken. Whereupon the road foreman said with the most innocent look I have ever seen, "Yeah, something happened to it." Later, they took me down into the very front nose of the diesel, which is under the headlight. It is a kind of secret compartment, and they showed me how the headlight worked. That was something special which I needed to know for my story. The fireman complained that his job wasn't much; he had nothing to do on a trip except sit in his chair. I said that that would be an ideal job for a writer who could sit there and work out the plot of a story, and I asked why didn't he try to write a book. He said, "Why should

I? The Government would take it all in taxes." Now there is common sense from the alleged common man.

When we arrived in Chicago, we were met by a photographer from New York Central, who took our pictures right there in the terminal, with all the passengers staring at me. I have a wonderful photograph of me with the engineer, the fireman and the road foreman, standing in front of the nose of the engine. All I can say in conclusion is that I am completely ruined now as a train passenger. I was bored all the way out of Chicago, riding in a compartment. That's much too tame. I would love to travel across the whole continent in the engine.

Now a special message to Stewart Holbrook [author of *The Story of American Railroads*]: Please tell him for me that I will match what he calls a (deleted) diesel locomotive against any of his old coal burners. Never mind the glamor. There is nothing as glamorous as a brilliant achievement of the human mind and a diesel engine is certainly that. I was permitted to ring the bell and to blow the whistle, too. And if he boasts that he "waved to a few farm maidens seen along the way," I'd like to tell him about an old railroad man who was riding on the cowcatcher of a switch engine on a siding; when he looked up, as our train came along with me in the engineer's seat, the look on his face was something I have never seen on any human face before. It was like an exaggerated close-up in a movie farce. *There* was a man who was staring, stunned and stupefied. (I suppose it's better not to mention this last in your column—because it might really get my nice engineer into trouble.)

In Chicago, I had a marvelous time on my visit to the Inland Steel plant. That was a real steel mill, not at all like Mr. Kaiser's WPA project in Fontana. It's funny that I knew that the Fontana plant was a phony, even though I had never seen a real steel plant before. The General Manager of Inland Steel arranged a luncheon, at which I met all the top executives of the plant. These were not the financiers or the directors, but the real working executives of the mills—the chief metallurgist, the chief superintendent, etc. I was the only woman at the luncheon, so you know how I would love that. I think they were more amazed by me than I was by seeing steel being poured and by all the rest of the things they showed me which were truly magnificent. What amazed those men were my political views—the extent to which I am a "reactionary." They simply could not believe that there was any "intellectual" who intended to glorify them in a book. They seemed to be wearily resigned to getting nothing but smears from writers. They were all conservatives and in quite an intelligent way. The stories they told me about their problems with regulations and regimentations are simply hair-raising. Here is a sample: The ICC now controls the distribution of freight cars. They have threatened an embargo on freight cars for deliveries to steel plants, which, if put into effect, would stop the entire steel production of the country. The excuse given is that the steel companies do not empty freight cars fast enough. The real reason—the bureaucrats want freight cars for coal, to ship the coal to Europe. This is an example of stopping a country's production for the sake of looting—an example which nothing I invent in my book could equal.

Incidentally, I asked Linda to read one chapter of my book. By the time she got through, she had read four chapters at her own request, not mine. She said she would keep my theme confidential, but asked me whether I would allow her to tell people only that my novel is going to be the most controversial book of this century. Being a very modest author, I gave her this permission.

If you want details of my home life, as you said you liked, well, I found a lot of my flowers still in existence when I came back, and I was able to collect seeds, so that I will have a second generation of my own flowers next year. My bachelor buttons are still blooming, in spite of the frost. We have had wonderful weather, but it has been very cold for a few nights and one of our moats was frozen solid, which has never happened before. I suppose that is nothing much to boast about, in comparison with what is going on in the East right now. Aren't you all supposed to be having a terrible time with snowstorms?

And speaking of gardening reminds me to thank you for the very nice column you wrote about me on the Sunday we left New York. I didn't see that column until I got home and found the *Herald-Tribune* here. You asked how I managed to look elegant while gardening. The answer is, I don't. That is what I like about gardening—that one doesn't have to look elegant. In the summer, one of our family fights has been Frank bawling me out for trailing dirt all over the house.

When I try to talk of homey matters, all the politics I would like to talk about rush into my mind. I can't resist asking you what you think of the Gandhi assassination. Isn't that an almost crude piece of historical irony? Almost as if there were a higher intelligence in the universe, that indulged itself in a nice sardonic gesture. Here was a man who spent his life fighting to get the British out of India in the name of peace, brotherly love and nonviolence. He got what he asked for.

I think I had better finish now because I could go on like this for hours. I know you will not accept it as an excuse, but it is true that I am afraid of writing to you because I know that I won't be able to stop, and I can't do it casually. There is almost too much I would like to discuss. I miss you terribly, and I hope I will be back in New York when I finish my book.

Love from both of us,

■ ■ ■

February 14, 1948

Dear Pat:

This is what the principle of voluntary action will do to people. The moment you tell me that you will not be offended if I do not write often, I have an irresistible urge to write to you. I seem to feel easier about it if I know that you will not be angry at me the next time some difficult chapter of my novel prevents me from answering immediately. I was so glad when I saw, in my mail, an envelope with the letterhead of the Herald-Tribune Books and then when I saw your inimitable typing, that I realized how much I have missed your letters for all this long time. Incidentally, you are the only person I know who manages to have a handwriting on the typewriter. This is really the triumph of man over machine.

YES, by all means, mention my name in speaking to Mr. Shuster of Appleton-Century, and tell him anything you find of importance about our personal friendship and political closeness. I will be only too glad if this can help in any way to interest him in backing the *Think* magazine. I have never met him in person, but if you find that he is really as enthusiastic about my work as I was told he is, you might tell him that I would like to be one of the contributors to the magazine. There are a great many things I would like to say in articles for which there really is no suitable publication, and I have heard the same complaint from several good, intelligent, conservative writers. If, as Isaac Don Levine said, my name has value on a magazine cover, I will be more than happy to have it used as a possible attraction for the *Think* magazine.

If Mr. Shuster thinks that such a magazine is not "practical," you might tell him about the twelve publishers who rejected *The Fountainhead* as "not practical" or "noncommercial," and tell him how you predicted its commercial success with more assurance than I had about it and certainly more than Bobbs-Merrill had. This might help to convince him that you do know the practical side of writing and publishing.

For your information, or for any psychological clue that you may find in it, I will tell you exactly what I was told about Mr. S. by Mr. Purdee, their editor, who came to see me here in California about a year ago or more. He told me at the time that Mr. S. was not what he called a literary man. He said, "If you meet him, don't expect a real literary discussion of his reasons for liking *The Fountainhead*. He would probably not be able to tell you. All he said to us is that 'it is the kind of book I like.' " Of course, to me that was the kind of statement that would predispose me in Mr. S.'s favor. I asked the editor whether Mr. S. was an uncompromising man in his political convictions, because my new novel would be an extremely uncompromising story politically, in defense of industrialists and free enterprise. The editor said that if Mr. S. knew this he would give me another $100,000 for it. So you see, the man sounds awfully good. I hope he really is. I think it is an excellent idea for you to try to interest him in the magazine, I hope you will do it, and I hope you will succeed.

I knew that Luce had postponed his magazine. I had just received a letter from John Chamberlain [well-known conservative writer] about it, in which he asked me to keep the advance they had paid me for my article. Incidentally, is this the usual practice in such cases, and is it ethical to keep the advance? I feel rather embarrassed about it, since I had not yet finished the article, and it seems to be unearned money. I intend to put the article aside for the time being, but shall finish it anyway, when I can take some time off the novel without risking to interrupt a good streak of writing.

I was very sorry to hear about their postponing the magazine, because I quite agree with you that such a magazine is desperately needed, and I was looking forward to seeing it. But perhaps it is for the best. If you are able to get several of your boyfriends together to start such a magazine independently, without the kind of interference and what you called "wobbling" that they would have had on the Luce publication, perhaps this will amount to an intellectual event of the first importance.

As to your question about where are our "practical men" going when they die if there is no hell—I have to admit you've got me there. This argument in favor of hell is practically irrefutable.

Thank you for your compliments to my letter. I was sort of childishly happy about it, because I did not write that letter with any kind of literary intention, in fact, I thought it was too hurried, and I am delighted if you found it good. Yes, I have a carbon copy of it. If you find it suitable for your column, by all means use it, all or any part of it, except the things that might get somebody into trouble. I can see only three things in it which we should not use in print: The references to the railroad men breaking the rules for me, the reference to Mr. Kaiser's steel plant (he might sue both you and me for it) and the story about regulations told to me by the men at Inland Steel; if you want to use this story, then I think it would be better not to name Inland Steel as the source—I don't want some lousy bureaucrat to take it out on them. As for my riding in the locomotive, it does not have to be kept secret so long as we don't name the railroad and the train. I know that the incident of the old guy on the cowcatcher is the funniest thing that happened on the trip, but I don't want the company to make trouble for the engineer for putting me at the throttle. If you think it is worth the bother, perhaps you could ask Col. Henry about it. Since the engineer did not seem to hesitate about giving me his seat, and I was seen by quite a few people in the stations we passed, maybe it is just one of those rules that everybody winks at, and maybe it's quite all right to print the story without naming the train. You know better than I do what is permissible in a column and what is not, so I will leave it up to you. I don't mind your using it, in fact, I am always delighted and fluttered when I see myself in your column, but you can understand why I don't want to make trouble for those train crews when they were so nice to me.

No, I can't use that little incident in my novel, I don't have any lady novelists, nor any women driving diesel engines. Having a woman operating vice president is bad enough.

Thank you tremendously for the detailed statement of reasons why I should not use superfluous details in my novel. That was a beautiful exposition. The line describing a train as "almost as if the power of the engine streamed out behind in the form of the train like an airflow or wake," is magnificent. I think I understand the comparison, and I certainly agree with you. The only question now would be in the application of it to the specific terms of a novel. I am not sure that we will always agree on what constitutes an essential part of the engine and what constitutes lace curtains in the cab window. But I will be as strict as I can about it, to the best of my understanding.

I am not in the least surprised by your having a congressman among your admirers. All I can say is it's about time. I wish you had about 600 of them. You're only half-kidding when you ask whether you and I are setting a new fashion in females. I never thought of it in that way before, but I think it's absolutely true, we are. I can't judge that about myself, but I really and most seriously see it in you. I have the testimony of my two best boyfriends, Frank and Albert [Mannheimer], who speak admiringly of your feminine charm, and they do mean it, so there!

I have no new news about myself. It is the same as a week ago, with the exception of such an event as that I got a haircut—the first one since I came back from the East. This will give you a good homey idea of what

I looked like. I got the haircut only because I had to go to Hollywood to run the Italian movie of *We the Living*.* I have finally received a print of it for myself. The screening took a whole day off my work, and I am slightly sore about it, but I had to attend to that. We are still in the process of negotiating about that picture, and if the Italian company meets my conditions, I might let them release it in this country. The picture is quite good and the performance of the girl in the starring part is magnificent. But they did garble and distort the end of the story, so that it kind of lost fire. If I let them release it in this country, I will have to change the ending by means of new English dialogue and extra film footage. That will be quite a job, but if we reach an agreement, I will have a writer of my own choice do it for me; I cannot take time off my novel now for this work.

I am thinking very hard of something nonintellectual to tell you about us, but can't find anything. We are just too damn intellectual, and all I can think of is how much I love my new novel and how happy I am that it is going well at the moment. There really isn't any other thought in my brain right now.

Give my best regards to all your boyfriends. And love to you from both of us,

P.S. You have a wonderful line in your column of February 8—"Good fiction is private life or high imagination of adventures of the spirit set in suitable time, place and persons." "Adventures of the spirit" is what my own novels are to me. I would like to quote your line, with due credit, in my unfinished article about novels, if I can fit it in. May I? That whole passage in your column was swell, particularly the description of the kind of novels that foreign correspondents turn out.

■ ■ ■

February 28, 1948

Dear Pat:

In regard to the news about the movie of *The Fountainhead*, yes, it is true, they may go into production now. Confidentially, the fact is that they are now in the state of figuring out the budget, and they will decide within a week or so whether they can afford to produce the picture immediately. So far they have signed a director and a star for it. The director is King Vidor,

* An unauthorized version of *We the Living* was made in Italy in 1942, starring Rossano Brazzi and Alida Valli. After editing by AR and later by Leonard Peikoff, it was released with English subtitles in 1988.

who is very good. I don't know him personally, but he is said to be a conservative. The star is Gary Cooper, and I am delighted about that, because of all the stars, he is my choice for Roark. His physical appearance is exactly right—he looks like Frank.

Now as to your discussion of the conception of "need" in relation to my theory of individualism, I can't argue about it very much, because I did not understand your exposition. I see no connection between it and my theory.

You have always said that words should mean just exactly what they say, no more and no less. So when I said that "He needed nobody," I meant that he did not need anybody, and not that he was trying to prove that he could do without. And when I used the word "need," I did not mean "communication" with other people. I spent 400,000 words defining and illustrating just exactly what sort of need I meant.

I was stopped by your sentence, "The baby sees that the world is there already, on which it intends to exercise its rights." I cannot conceive of exercising any rights *on* another human being. One of the cardinal points of my theory is a basic differentiation between a man's relation to inanimate matter and to other men.

If somebody asked me "What in the world would you have done without Frank?" I would never answer, "Why in the world *should* I have done without him?" I would consider such an answer an evasion of the issue. The question, "What would you have done without him," does not imply that I *should have* done without him. The question says just exactly what it says. My answer would be: "I would have had a much harder and much more unhappy struggle."

Also, my tongue would not turn to say such a thing as "I got my rights" in relation to Frank. I had no right *on* Frank whatever. I had no claim on him of any kind except whatever he wanted to grant me. A grant is not a right. I have the right to get married—provided the man involved is willing. *My* consent to the marriage is my right—but *Frank's* consent is not *my* right. No right of mine constitutes an obligation on any man living. If I say that it was my specific right that Frank should marry me, it would amount to saying that he had to marry me. God help us both if we were on such a premise!

I strongly suspect that we are not discussing the same theory or the same problem. We could probably discuss it better in person, and it would probably take us from dinner to breakfast. When the time comes and if you are interested, I am willing.

No special news about myself. Frank and Albert have both read my last chapter this week, and their reaction was simply wonderful. Albert said it is the best chapter so far and I think so, too. As the story progresses, I am amazed by the extent to which it is possible to make business and economic matters dramatic and human in terms of fiction, not in terms of an economic treatise. I knew that that was to be my main problem in this novel, and I knew that it could be done, but I did not realize to what extent.

I am not too good at making predictions about the reception of my novel, but I will venture one: I think that the most disgusting opposition to it will come, not from Pinks, but from businessmen of the N.A.M. type. They'll say I am too extreme. I am unequivocally opposed to seeing their throats cut, and they will never forgive me for that.

I believe I told you the story told me by Henry Hazlitt about the lady financial expert who said in a radio broadcast, "Of course, I am for free enterprise—but not for *free* free enterprise." I think this is the classic statement of the century. I choose it as my nomination for the most monstrous words ever uttered, because it contains the whole rottenness of our age. Please give me a corner of the hell which you are preparing for "practical men"—I want to put there the people who are not for *free* free enterprise.

I think this will be enough—if I close on such an angry note, it will probably please you.

Love from both of us (without needs or rights—just voluntary love)

P.S. I let Frank read your letter and my answer. He is glowing over being the subject of a philosophical issue.

■ ■ ■

March 13, 1948

Dear Pat:

Thank you very, very much for telling me about Don Levine's attitude. It is not a matter of repeating personal remarks, since the remark was not personal, but philosophical. I think it was quite proper for you to tell me.

Yes, I intended to help him raise money for research for the articles I told you about. But I was not too certain, in my own mind, as to whether I should do it, because our so-called conservatives here in town are in a state of something like panic, and I felt a strong reluctance to undertake any action with them.

I am not too surprised to hear that Don Levine doesn't believe in principles. I had only one philosophical discussion with him in New York, about the general policy and future of his magazine. I believe I mentioned it to you at the time. It was then my impression that he was quite confused philosophically and that he did not think of politics in fundamental terms, as you and I do. But what impressed me in his favor was the fact that he conducted the argument honestly, that is, he did not evade issues and whenever I made a point clear to him, he agreed with it. But, I suppose, if a person does not understand the nature and function of principles, then no argument will take, and one can never convince him of anything since he starts from the premise that there can be no such thing as conviction.

I can't say that I even resent his attitude. If that is the extent of his thinking, he has to fight whatever he thinks is his battle in his own way. I can only say that that is not my way.

The strange part of it all is that what he approached me about in New York was that he felt his magazine needed a new policy in the sense that it had to present *abstract principles.* It was not I, but he who told me that merely exposing factual records of Communist plottings is not enough, and that his magazine also had to have a positive side, that is, a philosophical or intellectual one. I think I mentioned to you that he wanted me to do a regular column for him devoted to articles on the subject of individualism. I told him that the subject could not be treated that way. I thought then that he did not quite understand the proper approach to philosophical issues. But since the request was his own, and he had grasped the need for such a policy, I thought that he might be able to adopt the proper course for his magazine. What do you suppose prompted his request, if he doesn't believe in principles?

Of course, the alleged idea that one can be "practical" without principles stumps me completely. I, too, am simply unable to understand what it is that people think they mean when they say it.

The only explanation I see is the "malevolent universe" idea. This case interests me, in a sort of morbid way, because it does seem to bear out rather obviously what Albert and I had concluded on the subject. People nowadays think that the universe *is* malevolent, that reality is evil, that by the essential nature of the world, man is doomed to suffering and frustration; and therefore, if any fundamental principles could be discovered in objective reality, it would have to be the principles of evil. So these people prefer to avoid discovering such principles, and they think that to be practical one has to cheat reality in some way, that one can hope to survive only by fooling the laws of the universe (though how they expect to do that I can't imagine), since their natural fate should really be horror and destruction. Isn't that, in effect, what Levine believes, if he says that any tolerable periods of history were only a lucky accident? Would you say that that is the explanation?

Of course, his plan about splitting government up into numerous agencies that would oppose one another, is one of the goofiest things I have ever heard. I know I don't have to point this out to you, but there is just one particular example which I can't resist. The ICC ordered the railroads to adopt a certain policy and charge certain rates, during the war, and all the railroads had to obey—and right now the Department of Justice is suing the railroads over this same policy and rates as constituting an improper monopoly agreement or something. Is that Levine's idea of the solution to our troubles? I wish, if you ever felt like it, that you would throw this at him and ask him to answer it. But hell, I suppose I am wrong even in being curious about what he would answer. I still believe that a person should be crucially concerned about not preaching logical contradictions, but I have certainly had plenty of evidence that that does not seem to bother anybody the least bit. Well, the world shows the results of that, too.

If you want an example of the same sort of thing, Albert told me about an encounter he had with a group of writers who are supposedly conservatives, and who are trying, so they think, to fight the influence of Communists in the Screen Writers' Guild. They were discussing what action to take in a situation where they themselves had played right into the Communists' hands. Albert tried to point out what they should do by explaining to them the principles involved. They listened for a while rather impatiently, then one of them said, "Yes, yes, we all know about principles, that's all well and good, but now let's get down to fundamentals." (!) (I'm not sure you'll understand or believe that he meant, "let's talk business.")

I am not surprised that another congressman has discovered *The God of the Machine.* I think it is wonderful that he did. You yourself told me that the ideas of your book would take a long time to get to people—and if they are reaching a few people now, I am glad to think that there is some intelligence left in the world. But, oh God! how slow it is!

You know, it's strange, but I am getting pessimistic about the state of the world for the first time, after all these years. While the general trend of public opinion is going our way more obviously than ever before, and while there are a few indications of people doing some thinking in the right direction, I suddenly find myself wondering whether things are hopeless. By that I mean that I am not certain, as I was before, that we will see an intellectual renaissance on a large scale in our lifetime, or see the right ideas being applied in practice, in politics. I always thought that we would see it, but now I am doubting it. The reason is that the scale of horror in Europe has reached such a blatant state that I am beginning to think there can be no intellectual redemption for the whole present generation of people who permit this to go on. There is now no room to plead ignorance or confusion. If people still talk about "the middle of the road," they are much worse than cowards; they are truly and totally corrupt.

If you have the time and inclination, would you tell me what you think of this? You said (in your first letter of this week) that there are a lot of things you would like to talk about in regard to the present state of the world, but it's almost impossible to put it into a letter. If you can do it, I'd like to hear your ideas on it, because I do feel pretty sick about the situation. I think the Czechoslovakian and Finnish issues were the straw for this camel's back.

I can't think of anything cheerful at the moment, except for personal matters. My book is going well, the flowers and the grounds here are wonderful right now, this is the only beautiful time of the year in California. You said, "Love to all, wish I were there." Oh God, how I wish you were!

Love from both of us,

■ ■ ■

April 3, 1948

Dear Pat:

The stationery is just for dramatic effect—it will tell you the whole story before you read this letter. Yes, I am back at work at Warner Bros. writing the final screenplay of *The Fountainhead*. This has been another of those wonderful bolts out of the blue that have been descending on me in the last few years and that really make me think I may be God's child as you say. It all happened very suddenly. I had heard nothing from Warner Bros. since the original announcement that they intended to go into production, and I thought that there was some trouble about it. Then, on Monday, March 22, I got a call to come to the studio next day. On Tuesday morning, I had an interview with the producer and the director, and went to work on Wednesday morning. I am still slightly groggy in the most wonderful way—it's almost the same feeling I had when I sold the movie rights to them originally.

The thing that makes me so happy is that both Henry Blanke, the producer, and King Vidor, the director, are in complete agreement with me on the treatment of the picture. Their intention is to make the picture as close to the novel as possible and to preserve the theme and spirit of the story. I had been afraid of possible attempts to compromise, but they have given me no indication of any such intention.

As you know, one can never be certain of anything in Hollywood until the picture is finished, so there may be trouble or arguments or interferences later. All I can say is that there is no sign of it at present and that, for the moment, the situation is ideal. I think if they intended to distort the picture they would have kept me away from it; but since they called for me, I believe I can trust their intentions now. I must say that both Blanke and Vidor have discussed the book and the screenplay with me most intelligently.

You may be interested to know that Warner Bros. are actually sincere about the stand they have taken against Communism. They have actually cleaned house. When I worked here before, their list of writers was full of some of the worst Reds in Hollywood; now there is not one of them. There may be some minor Pinks, since they are everywhere among writers, but I don't see one name that I know to be an active Pink. And they have three other writers, in addition to me, who are known, open conservatives. I think this is wonderful, and it does give me confidence. You can imagine what sort of twisting and evading most of the other studios are doing here at present, in order to appease the public and yet not take a real stand against Communism. It is sickening to watch. But here is at least one studio that seems to be completely sincere about politics.

Your letter made me homesick when I read the sentence that you were writing it after having finished checking proofs. I wished I could be back on my job as one of your high-priced assistants in the composing room. I hope you will think of me next time you check the proofs. I really enjoyed doing that—and every time I notice some misprint in the Herald-Tribune Books, I think that I would have caught it and corrected it. This is not boasting, just wistfulness.

Yes, I agree with you completely that it is the "irrationalist" philosophy that leads to such a conception as a "malevolent universe." If it were possible to conceive man without his rational faculty (which is inconceivable), one would have to say that the universe is malevolent indeed.

Of course, I agree with you when you say that you cannot really form a concept of a malevolent universe. It *is* a contradiction in terms. My own basic definition of evil is that it is destruction, as you say; therefore, a malevolent universe could not exist. I think that any philosophical error, by definition, proceeds from or leads to some conception which is actually inconceivable. I am merely interested to know what sort of error leads people to some of the terrible notions they hold. As near as I can guess, without becoming a Beaver myself, I think those people believe that the universe may go on existing as inanimate matter, but that it is essentially malevolent to man—that man is a kind of misfit on this earth, who does not belong here and cannot survive because this world is improper for him and, therefore, dooms him to suffering and destruction. I know how many holes there are in such an idea. But, as you say, since they have discarded reason and logic, holes or contradictions do not bother them. They leap over it by saying that everything is a contradiction, that life is illogical, etc. I am thinking of the girl who made that sort of criticism of your book to John Chamberlain in his school class, you remember. I think I said at the time that that girl's attitude contained the root of all evil on earth.

Incidentally, have you noticed a new kind of philosophical party line —not Communist party, but the general argument of collectivists? I am now encountering it repeatedly in articles and book reviews. When the present-day collectivists find themselves smack up against the dead end of the final results of their own ideas, they try to wiggle out by saying that man's life and the universe are essentially a paradox, or else "a dynamic paradox"—and we're supposed to let it go at that and swallow any contradiction. Is such a thing as a "paradoxical universe" conceivable?

You have probably glanced through a copy of a book that has just come out called *Communism and the Conscience of the West* by Fulton J. Sheen. Bobbs-Merrill sent me a copy of it, and I have read it. I would like very much to hear your comment on it. I am sure you can guess why.

I quoted to Frank what you said about Don Levine's attitude toward conscription—that he is in favor of it because the Communists are against it. Frank said: "I suppose even Communists are against smallpox. Is he for it?"

I was happy and actually relieved to hear you say that you believe we will see a turn for the better in our own lifetime, since you had been more pessimistic about it than I. I do trust your judgment if you say that you see hopeful signs. You have been right about all the long-range trends which you predicted. It's true that I probably feel less optimistic now partly because of the attitude of the people who tell me that they are on my side. They usually turn out to be sickening. But what I can't stand above all are the so-called "middle-of-the-roaders." I don't think I have ever actually felt hatred. But I do feel something which is probably real hatred when I hear somebody say he believes in "the middle of the road," *now*, when he sees an ocean of blood in plain view at one side of the road of which he proposes to take the middle. Wasn't there some quotation from Dante to the effect that the lowest circle of hell is reserved for the people who, in times of moral crisis, remain neutral?

When and if you feel like telling me your explanation of current events, I would like very much to hear it. I have actually stopped reading the newspapers, except for looking at the headlines, because I can't stand to read all the details of what is going on and the ghastly evasions of those who are allegedly opposing Communism.

I hope you won't mind that I have had to interrupt my new novel for a while. I don't think that the job on *The Fountainhead* will take too long—and it is a thing which I have to see through to the end. Do you remember your prediction that the picture would give me the kind of "Hernani" controversy that I envied Victor Hugo for? From the way things look now, I think it will. Well, Isabel Paterson is always right.

If you say that I am a brave gal, I think I will need it in the months ahead, and I think I will win. Thank you for saying that, and I am very proud that you added, "besides *me*, of course." I mean this seriously. I am proud to be mentioned together with you in this respect—just as I was when I heard that Don Levine had coupled us together as "the dangerous people who have principles." Maybe we are much more dangerous than he suspects, if I understand what sort of danger he means. I hope I will prove it to him.

Love from both of us,

■   ■   ■

April 11, 1948

Dear Pat:

How can you expect any man, woman or beast not to be tortured by curiosity when you write such a thing as "Someday when I am up to form, I will explain to you that you are wonderful, in full detail." Nobody could resist impatience at such a promise, so please get up to form as soon as you can, because I must know why I am wonderful, in full detail.

My script of *The Fountainhead* and everything at Warner Bros. is going along beautifully. No disagreements, and the ideas which King Vidor has expressed to me about the way he intends to direct the picture are excellent. If I understand him correctly, he wants to keep it simple and stylized, that is, without cluttering it up with unnecessary "realistic" details, which has always been my idea of how it should be done. I can never be sure of a director's method until I see the first scenes he shoots, but what he says so far is exactly right.

If all goes well, I think my new novel and this picture will come out at about the same time—and then I think there *will be* an explosion of some sort. I'll hope for the best.

You were in excellent form in your exposition about the relation of man's mind to the universe. It is one of your best statements, and I wish you would use it in your column. If you don't have a carbon copy of it, I will copy it and send it to you. I read it to Frank, and he laughed with delight at the sentence, "But if people will not use their minds, I suppose then one may expect them to sit down and complain that this earth wasn't arranged for *them.*" I'm going to show it to Albert when I see him next.

I know that the idea of hiding behind a "paradox" is not new in philosophy, but I just noticed that it is being used repeatedly, as a kind of desperate last twist, by the pseudo-philosophical intellectuals in magazines. I read a review of a book by Jacques Maritain called, I believe, *Man and the Common Good* [*Person and the Common Good*], which gave detailed quotations, and it was all about a "dynamic paradox." The reviewer seemed to find this quite a satisfactory answer to the most preposterous bunch of contradictions I have ever seen in what purports to be a serious book.

Something awful seems to be happening to the Catholic thinkers. If I can untangle their stand at all, they seem to be turning quite deliberately toward Statism. What shocked me about Fulton J. Sheen's book is a blatant hatred for capitalism. It seems to underlie the whole tone of the book. To tell you the truth, it reminded me of the tone which struck me and which I hated in Soviet books on dialectics and economics, when I read them for the first time in college. I have not observed that particular tone in books since, and the sudden reminder left me pretty much aghast. Just to give you an example, here is what Sheen says on Page 50: "The only contribution that communism makes to capitalism is to shift booty and loot from one man's pockets to another, while leaving the lust of acquisition untouched. . . . Communism, from the economic point of view, is rotted capitalism, with the difference that in one case the people live off the largess of a capitalist, and in the other, off the largess of the bureaucrat." (Good God, Pat!) You have been angry at me before, for bothering you with disgusting quotations, but please don't be angry this time. I don't think that this book is important as such; but as an indication of the trend of these people, a thing like this quotation is significant and very dreadful.

However, I do think that they will not succeed in this direction and that they have missed the boat. You remember you said that the Catholics were up against a basic contradiction and that they would have to decide which way to choose. Apparently they have chosen the wrong way, and it is really too bad, particularly when the world is slowly being cured of the ideas of Statism. I do agree with you about that. I do think that the intellectual atmosphere has definitely turned in our direction. Intellectually, we have won already, because collectivism is done for. Since philosophical ideas precede men's application of them in practice, I suppose it is natural that we have to wait for the concrete results; but what is going on in the meantime is pretty revolting. I, too, have the definite impression that there is "a growing wish and readiness to hear some sense." People have not understood or accepted the right ideas yet, but they have discovered the need of right ideas, and that is quite a step forward. They know, at least, that collectivism and the "common good" ain't what they were cracked up to be.

I think you are probably right about Warner Bros. Warner Bros. are famous as having a genius for seeing public trends ahead of everybody else. I think that's all to the good. If more people learned to understand their real business interests correctly and to act accordingly, we would have a much better world. One of the ghastly things of our age is the fact that every social group has been causing its own suicide—such as big businessmen, for instance. Anyone who forms an accurate judgment of his proper, legitimate self-interest and acts upon it, instead of working like mad to cut his own throat, is quite an unusual and welcome phenomenon these days.

I was amused by your saying that "this letter is too long." Do you know that when I receive a letter from you, the first thing I do before opening it is to weigh it in my hand? The heavier it is, the better I like it. I know that that's no way to measure intellectual value, but in the case of your letters it is, because no ounce of it is ever wasted. So if you have the time, please make them as long as you can. It's always an event for us when there is a letter from Pat.

Love from both of us,

       ■ ■ ■

April 24, 1948

Dear Pat:

Your letter was certainly "heavy enough to sink a lifeboat." And what it did sink was the last shred of philosophical respect I had for the Catholic Church.

Your letter really stunned me, in a way. The position of the Catholic Church, as you describe it, is completely logical. It is precisely what I would deduce from their basic premises and it supports me in my hatred for those premises. But what I did not know was that the Church realized and consciously accepted the consequences of their premises as you described them. I knew the philosophical ideas of the Catholic Church in a general way, but I did not know their exact attitude on the application of their ideas in practice. I thought that since their ideas were contradictory, they would act in a contradictory manner, attempting to reconcile their ideas as best they could. I did not know that they had consciously chosen to follow the most evil line which could be deduced from their premises, that instead of choosing the best elements of their dilemma, they chose the worst and proceeded on that.

Do you know my first reaction to your letter? It was a horrible feeling of guilt that I had given those people any sort of respect or consideration at all. I felt almost as if I had been caught belonging to a front organization and associating with Communists without knowing it. May I ask you a rather naive question? The first question that occurred to me was: How could Pat respect them, knowing all this?

Here is what baffles me: If I understood you correctly, the attitude which you describe as the Church's attitude towards social systems seems to be an exact description of the worst kind of "expediency" as practiced by our present day "middle-of-the-roaders." You say their position is "the ideal political form may be impracticable at any given time or place. So the Church does not declare that any one form or another is necessarily best for all times and places, but can permit, accept, allow rather less than ideal forms as most workable for this or that given time and place." Isn't that a description of the policy of expediency? All the arguments which we make against the vulgar exponents of expediency apply to the above attitude, only a million times more so. If there are no standards, how does one decide what is workable for any given time or place? If there are no principles, how does one decide what is practicable? etc. I am not saying this to argue with you, as I know that you do not share this attitude. I am merely indicating the kind of questions that would arise in my mind. If it is inexcusable for some bewildered little businessman to advocate a policy of expediency in the hope of getting by with it for the moment—how much more dreadful it becomes when such a policy is advocated by thinkers who deal with fundamental philosophical principles.

But it is even worse than that, if I understood your exposition correctly. It would seem as if the Catholic Church is willing to tolerate any social system—*except* the only good and proper one, which is Capitalism. Did I gather this correctly? I understood you to mean that the Church can accept any other system consistently, because any other system is imperfect and does contain elements of evil and will require suffering and sacrifice; but the system which works to make men happy is the one which the Church cannot accept. To me, this seems to be a position of total evil. As you know, my fundamental definition of evil is the action of damning the good for being the good. (For example: A man who opposes the Capitalist system because he thinks that it is a bad system, is merely ignorant, not immoral. A man who opposes the Capitalist system *because* it is *good*, is truly evil.) The theme of my new novel—or one of the aspects of it—is a protest against the penalizing of ability for being ability. In other words, the penalizing of virtue for being virtue. *That* is the essential pattern of any sin or evil, and that is the attitude of the Church toward Capitalism, if I understood you correctly.

Of course, I know that they could not arrive at anything else or at anything except evil, starting from the premise of man's original sin. Of all human conceptions, the conception of original sin is *the* most vicious and destructive one, much more so than the philosophical crimes committed by Hegel. If I were to select only one idea as the most depraved ever conceived by man, that is the one I would pick. And your letter actually gives a better demonstration of the evils of that idea than I have ever put on paper so far. Apparently, the idea is not merely that "man is imperfect" (and I've always known that the idea was much worse than that). If man is only "imperfect," there is no reason why he should not try to perfect himself; and if he discovers the best social system possible to him, he should certainly adopt it. But when a school of thought rejects a social system which has been demonstrated in theory *and in practice* to be the best, then it can mean only that that school of thought holds man as essentially *depraved*, irremediably depraved as far as his earthly existence is concerned.

I know which paragraph you thought I would pick out particularly. It's the paragraph about the necessity of man sacrificing himself to God, isn't it? But actually that paragraph did not shock me as much as the description of the Church's attitude toward Capitalism. Sure, I know that they preach man's sacrifice to God, without any clear meaning ever having been defined about how or why man must do it. But I would like to defend God against them. The philosophical conception of God does not necessarily imply that man must be sacrificed to Him. It is, however, a strange thing that all religions, and all philosophical systems that attempted to describe man's relation to God, have always made of man a sacrificial animal. Why?

I do not know whether the fact that Christianity was the first system to establish the conception of a human being as a free, spiritual entity, is a beneficial achievement if, at the same time, Christianity introduced the conception of original sin. True, philosophically, the first is a great achievement. But, historically, if these two ideas were preached together—then, I think those who preached them were responsible for a monstrous crime. To declare that man is a free, moral, independent and *responsible* entity— and then to load him with the responsibility of some undefined sin which he did not commit, that is, to load him with guilt and evil about which he had no choice, is a monstrous thing in terms of morality. The conception of morality can apply only to the realm of free choice. That which is not open to a man's choice, cannot be either moral or immoral. To tell a man that he is free and at the same time evil, with no volition on his part, is unspeakable.

It seems to me (again if I understood your letter correctly) that the crime committed by the philosophers who subscribe to this doctrine is infinitely worse than anything done by Hegel or Marx—worse precisely because it is on a much higher plane and deals with much higher subjects. Marx seems nothing but a cheap hoodlum by comparison. If Marx denies the existence of the human spirit and says that man is a bunch of meat, he cannot injure any thinking or honest person, because it would take no more than five minutes of serious thought on this point to discard the whole of Marx right then and there, with no further damage done. But to teach man that he has a soul, and then to damn that soul by definition—well, I don't suppose I have to describe to you the logical, psychological and spiritual consequences of that. We see them all around us.

The doctrine of man's essential depravity did exist in Oriental philosophies. But it did not exist in Greece and Rome. If Christianity introduced it into Western thinking, together with the idea of an individual soul—was the net historical result beneficent, or monstrous?

The question puzzling me most right now is why you have been much more tolerant of Catholic thinkers than of lesser people whom you have damned for a weaker version of the same crime. You have always refused to tolerate (and rightly so) a businessman who refuses to recognize principles and preaches expediency. You have refused to tolerate any part of a "mixed economy" or any suggestion that we ought to have "some State control." Then why do you give a respectful philosophical consideration to a system which preaches these very same things, only in a much deeper, and therefore more vicious, form? I am asking this, not as a reproach to you and not in order to pick a fight with you, but most strictly as a question, just for information, because I do not really know what your attitude is on this issue.

To finish off with Mr. Gallagher—no, pardon me, Mr. Sheen, I did not read his book for the purpose of getting information. I read it by request.

Mr. Williams of Bobbs-Merrill sent it to me and asked for my opinion of it. I supposed that he wanted an endorsement from me which he could quote, if I happened to like the book. So I read it, because I would always be glad to have my name used to help sell any book of which I approve. In this case, of course, I didn't.

Yes, I would like very much to have the two gold dollars. Only, if you remember, you promised to let me pay for them. I don't want to accept them as a present, since I asked for them, and I don't think it's right to accept a present by one's own request. Frank has not decided how he'll wear his dollar, but I want to wear mine on a long, thin chain, like a medal. Or, borrowing your style of expression, if I were irreverent I would say that I want to wear my gold American dollar in the way others wear a cross. But please don't bother finding a chain for me. I will have to find one myself and try it for the kind of length I want.

It is a funny coincidence, but I didn't want to remind you about the gold dollars until I had sent you the California gold I had promised, that is, the oranges. I had just shipped them to you when I received your letter. You have probably received them by now. It took me so long because I asked our neighbor, who is a specialist and a Sunkist orange grower, to select and ship the proper kind of oranges. He had to wait until the right season for them. I hope you will find them good even though they are full of vitamins, as you said once before.

Love from both of us,

P.S. Because of the heavy discussion above, I forgot to tell you how enthusiastic I am about your column of April 11, in regard to Mr. Koestler and the ex-Communists. It is a brilliant column, actually a philosophical essay. Frank and Albert both read it and simply cheered. Also, I created a minor sensation at Warner Brothers' studio, at the writers' table in the restaurant, when I brought them this column. Koestler had been here a couple of weeks ago and gave a lecture, which was considered as a big intellectual event here. I did not go, of course, but the day after the lecture the whole writers' table was talking about it at luncheon. The general impression was that Mr. Koestler is "confused," that he does not know where he stands nor what he advocates. He said such things in his lecture as "Communism is not to the *Left*, it is only to the *East*," meaning that Stalin is bad, but Communism as an idea is all right. So I brought your column to the table the other day, and I wish you could have heard the general enthusiasm. One of the writers asked me for a copy of your column, so I hope you won't mind if I give it to him. He makes speeches here once in a while, and his main theme is that we should not forgive the "liberals" who played with Communism. He said he wants to use your arguments about the navigator and the witch doctor. I will close now, with the collective compliments of the whole writers' table to you for that column.

■   ■   ■

May 8, 1948

Dear Pat:

You say in your letter: "It almost seems as if nobody, dead or alive, ever did know or does know how Capitalism really works, except Me." Does it really seem to you that I have not been born yet? It seems to me that I was born as long as 43 years ago, and it almost seems that you had noticed the fact.

It was from my theory of ethics that you learned why the morality of altruism and sacrifice is evil and improper to man. Until I explained my theory to you, you believed—as you told me—that the morality of altruism was proper, but men were not good enough for it. I am very happy that you learned from me an idea of philosophical importance, just as I learned many important ideas from you. But what am I to think of your intellectual accuracy, if—in a discussion of the relation between Capitalism and the morality of sacrifice—you tell *me* that you are the only one who understands how Capitalism works?

You say (about the Catholic political philosophy): "So don't ask me *how* they come to do that; ask yourself." I never asked you once in my whole letter *how* the Catholics came to do that. I know how. The only questions in my letter were about your attitude, not theirs.

Yes, I remember your telling me that you could never be converted to Catholicism. I did not say or imply that I thought you were in agreement with the Catholics. I merely wondered, and still do, why you gave a *sympathetic* consideration to Catholic philosophy *as such*.

I asked you once why you did not endorse books favorable to Capitalism if they contained minor errors while the major part of their content was good. You told me that there is no such thing as a minor error in this issue, and I had to agree with you. That is why I was philosophically curious about your attitude toward the Catholic philosophy—since their error is not minor, but just about the biggest and most pernicious error one could preach.

You say that I paid no attention to what you really said, because you did not say that the Church knew consciously what it was preaching about

Capitalism. Here is exactly what you said: "In a queer subconscious way, it would almost seem that the Church knows what Capitalism really is better than the Capitalists, realizing that Capitalism does *not* operate by sacrifice!" My letter was based, not on this sentence, but on your next paragraph in which you described the Church's political philosophy: that an ideal political form is impossible to man because human nature is not perfect. That paragraph dealt with their philosophy, not their subconscious.

Furthermore, I question the meaning of the term *"subconscious ideas."* No one has given a clear definition or explanation of just what is the mental process whereby one holds an idea subconsciously. As near as I can understand the term, I think it means a state of mental fudging.

If it is pretty much inexcusable for plain, everyday people to relegate their convictions to some sort of semiconscious haze, it is completely inexcusable for philosophers. If the Catholic political philosophy contains all the elements which add up to opposing Capitalism because it makes man happy, but they have not consciously admitted to themselves that that is what it adds up to—it does not make them any the less guilty. Their philosophy still adds up to it.

Here is a paragraph of your letter which baffled me. You seem to reproach me for saying that I regret having given "those people" any sort of respect or consideration, and you say: "Who are 'those people'? Human beings? Man, in brief? Can you indict such a considerable number of the human race, including some of the greatest minds the human race has exhibited, without certain implications as to the human race itself?" Why, yes, I certainly can. It is possible that the entire human race, with the exception of me, might become collectivist—and I will then damn the whole bunch of them, without damning man as such. I do not form my conception of the nature of man by counting numbers. (By "those people" I meant Catholic thinkers *as such.*)

I am still more baffled by another paragraph of your letter: "There is an odd look about this sentence of yours: 'If I were to select one idea as the most depraved ever conceived by man, that (Original Sin) is the one I would pick.' You are sort of bringing Original Sin in by the back door while you throw it out of the front, or vice versa, I don't know which, with the 'depraved idea conceived by man.' " This is where I just sit and stare at the words. As near as I can guess at what you mean, it seems to me that you are speaking of morality in some sort of deterministic terms. Did you mean that if man can conceive a depraved idea, he must be *essentially* depraved? I have always understood morality to apply only to the actions open to man's choice. I have always thought that morality cannot be divorced from free will. Therefore, man's essential nature is his ability to conceive a good idea or a depraved one. The nature of a being endowed with free will is that he is capable of both good and evil and must make the choice. If he is essentially incapable of evil, then he is good automatically, by predetermination, good without any choice about it—and if so, then he is outside the realm of morality. A robot, capable only of "good" (?) actions, is neither good nor evil. The fact that man can conceive a depraved idea does not make man depraved by nature. It merely leaves him what he is—free. He cannot be guilty by potentiality. He becomes guilty *only* by the choices he makes—if and when he chooses evil. If the whole human race, except one, chooses evil—this cannot make the one guilty, too. A being of free will has to be judged by his own record. Man has no predetermined moral character—that would be a contradiction in terms. Every man creates his own moral character by the choices he makes.

The idea of Original Sin simply damns man for the fact of possessing free will. Apparently he was perfect before the fall, because he was a moral robot, and became evil by acquiring the faculty of moral choice. That depraved notion is simply the condemnation of free will as an evil.

I don't remember the letter which you sent me from Ridgefield about Original Sin. I'm sorry if I forgot it. I remember only one conversation of ours on the question of Original Sin. It was in your house in Ridgefield. I remember the gist of it very clearly. You explained to me that since every man is potentially capable of evil, this constitutes his Original Sin. I asked you why the same reasoning did not apply to man's good. Since every man is potentially capable of the highest virtues, why isn't he also given credit for an Original Virtue? The conversation ended on that. You did not answer. I believed that you were thinking it over, and I thought that you had accepted my argument as valid. We never discussed it since.

You say that the doctrine of Total Depravity is Lutheranism and predestinate damnation is Calvinism. You add that "you ought to get your creeds straight." Here is where I can accuse you of not reading my letter exactly. Here is what I said: "But when a school of thought rejects a social system which has been demonstrated in theory *and in practice* to be the best, then it can mean only that that school of thought holds man as essentially depraved, irremediably depraved, as far as his earthly existence is concerned." I did not say here that that is what the Catholics *say* they preach. I said that that is what their theory *means*. Whether they admit it or not, the meaning is still there. Also I made it a point to say, "as far as his earthly existence is concerned." This is where I did have my creeds quite straight. I know that the Catholics do not preach total depravity in the theological sense; they hold that man can be redeemed in the hereafter. But their social philosophy for man on earth makes him depraved in the terms of his earthly existence and for the duration of it. Which is all I am concerned with.

The political intention which I gather from the recent writings of Catholics is quite clear to me. And I am very good at catching that sort of intention—I was trained in it by experts, I have seen it in Soviet universities. The intention is this: Instead of realizing that it would be destroyed under any form of modern Statism, the Catholic Church sees in the return of Statism a chance to reestablish the union of Church and State. It hopes to have a form of Statism run by the Church—which simply means that it hopes for a return of the days of the Inquisition.

I forgot to mention a sentence of Frank's which, I think, covers my opposition to the Catholic philosophy much better than all my long discussions. We were discussing the subject once, and I was saying that it seems as if Catholics do not want man to be happy on earth. Frank said: "Oh, sure, they want you to pursue happiness—but never to catch it."

Now to conclude with a cleaner subject, by which I mean my new novel, you say that you don't think the human race has *consciously* penalized virtue for being virtue, but that they do penalize it. Well, here again I question the exact meaning of an "unconscious" attitude. I cannot speak with absolute certainty about the minds of other people, but I can say that by observing their actions I have concluded that they do penalize virtue *consciously.* If this subject interests you, I can give you the specific examples that made me conclude it.

Well, is this enough for one letter? Apart from philosophies, everything is going very well here. Frank was relieved to hear that the mice and rabbits had ruined the star magnolia which he had hurt by accident. He says he no longer feels like a rat about it. He is doing wonders with his flowers here, and our garden is really magnificent. Everything is still going perfectly at the studio, and I hope it will continue this way.

Love from both of us,

The Estate of Isabel Paterson has asked that the following excerpt from Paterson's reply of May 13, 1948, be reprinted: "No, my dear, I never did tell you that I 'believed that the morality of altruism was proper, but men were not good enough for it.' That is what numerous people have believed and do believe, but not what I ever believed. . . . I always thought that proposition was a manifest absurdity—it would be an absurdity for any kind of mo-

rality, a contradiction in terms—and how could it be a morality,
a rule of conduct for *human beings, if human beings were*
incapable *of practising it? As well say sawdust is a proper diet for*
human beings only they can't digest it. . . ."

■   ■   ■

May 17, 1948

Dear Pat:

I am so delighted about your coming here that I consider it conclusive proof of a totally benevolent universe, and I *almost* feel benevolence toward the Catholic philosophers.

I won't take time now to continue that discussion, but if you want to, we will do it in person. I am terribly sorry if I gave you too much trouble answering me point by point. I was delighted that your letter was so long, and it was extremely interesting, but I am sorry if the job of writing it tired you out. Maybe I shouldn't bother you with discussions of the ideas of other philosophers, but only discuss our own ideas.

Most certainly, you were the very first person to see how Capitalism *works* in specific application. That is your achievement, which I consider a historical achievement of the first importance. How on earth did you gather that I was denying you that accomplishment? I learned *from you* the historical and economic aspects of Capitalism, which I knew before only in a general way, in the way of general principles. What I take credit for is the definition of the ethical theory on which Capitalism has to be based. Since we were discussing the relation of Capitalism to ethics, that was the reason your statement astonished me.

I am glad you know that I would not invent or misrepresent what I said about your former ideas on morality. I did not imagine it. That was what I remembered from one of our conversations. However, if you tell me that you did not hold such ideas, I will take your word for it. I know that I do not always understand you clearly and that you do not like to explain things in detail, so it is very possible that I misunderstood you through my own fault or yours, or maybe both. I will not accuse you of a belief you did not hold, but I do remember the conversation that gave me that impression, though I must have been wrong.

Don't take the blame for the expression: "unconscious ideas." You did not use that expression in your letter, you merely said that the Catholic Church did not consciously know what it was preaching about Capitalism, so I took the liberty of describing it as "unconscious ideas." I think this is what it amounted to, but you did not use such a blatantly inaccurate expression—and I would not expect you to use it.

There is an awful lot of other things about your letter which I would like to discuss—and I mean *discuss*, not argue—because all these points interest me very much, and I am looking forward most eagerly to staying up with you all night, if you care to. Incidentally, the sunrises here are very beautiful, so I think we will have a good time.

Is it very unphilosophical of me that I don't want to discuss philosophy right now, but only think about your visit? We are both so excited about it that we are running around in circles. Yesterday I had my director, King Vidor, and his wife here for dinner and also our neighbors, Adrian and Janet Gaynor, and I was telling them at great length about your coming. They are all excited and waiting for you. Adrian and Janet have been hearing from me about you all these years, so now this is the big event of Chatsworth—the personal appearance of a star from New York.

I don't know whether you gathered on the phone yesterday what I tried to explain to you about the picture. I will have my script finished within a few weeks now, if all goes well, but there is a possibility that the studio may keep me on while they are actually shooting the picture, which I would love to do, of course. If they don't, I will be free as soon as I am finished with the script. But, in either case, I think it is wonderful that you should come here just when they are starting the picture, and I hope they will start it before you leave. That seems to be another sign of God's hand over the picture. I'll tell you in person how many things have happened to justify your prediction that the studio will not be able to ruin the story. You said that the idea of the story would protect itself—and so far it has done just that. If you can be here on the set with me when they take the first shot of the picture, I really think that it will be a wonderful philosophical omen. That is what would happen in a well-written novel—and I would love to see it happen in real life.

I have all sorts of plans on what we can do here in regard to the magazine. I'll tell you about it in person, and you can tell me what is the best practical way to go about it. There are many people here who are on our side and who are sincere about it, they have the enthusiasm and the money—but no way of doing anything constructive for the right cause. I think that it may be possible for us to get them behind the magazine.

Since you are Frank's guest, he will tell you himself about all the practical details of your trip. I will say only that it is getting to be very hot here, so you had better bring your lightest summer clothes, but you will need a warm coat or jacket for evening. I suppose you know that the California climate is always too hot in the daytime and too cold at night.

I am probably forgetting all the things I wanted to say, but I am actually too excited to think straight at the moment. I suppose you will never believe how much Frank and I love you, so there!

■ ■ ■

July 14, 1950

Dear Pat:

Thank you for your letter. I am glad that you told me about Henry Hazlitt's business plans for the new magazine. I did know about the project of the magazine, but I did not know the details.

I telephoned Hazlitt long distance when I received your letter, and spoke to him in person, pointing out to him all the principles and philosophical aspects which should be considered in this undertaking. I have not heard from him since and I don't know what his decisions will be.

I hope that this will be the kind of *Think* magazine we have been expecting for years, but I suppose that we won't know for sure until we see the first few issues.

Sincerely,

■ ■ ■

August 11, 1950

Dear Pat:

Thank you for your letter. If you see any way in which I can be of value to the new magazine and if you care to tell me about it, I would be glad to know it. I am very much interested in the magazine, but I wonder whether I can have any influence on it by long distance. I would hesitate to force my advice or suggestions on Henry Hazlitt and John Chamberlain, unless they care to discuss it with me, but if they care to, I would like to help them in any way I can.

Sincerely,

■ ■ ■

September 8, 1950

Dear Pat:

I will not come to New York this year, so I won't be able to meet the backers of the magazine.

However, I know a man here who is a representative of one of the backers and a member of the magazine's board of directors. His name is Herbert Cornuelle [an executive of the Hawaiian Pineapple Co.]. If you and John Chamberlain want me to discuss with him some particular matter about the magazine, I will be glad to do it. Cornuelle seems to be very clear in his philosophical ideas and I believe that he could be of practical help to the magazine. But will you please tell me only those facts which you feel are not confidential and on which you are willing to be quoted. I cannot in good faith approach a man with advice and refuse to reveal my source of information.

Sincerely,

■   ■   ■

October 6, 1950

Dear Pat:

I have seen Mr. Cornuelle recently and have discussed with him the matters pertaining to the new magazine, which you described in your letter. He is going to New York this month and will look into the situation.

He feels as strongly as you do that the magazine should be a businesslike, commercial proposition and I hope that he will be able to persuade the other people involved. He will also discuss with them the matter of their policy in regard to advertising.

I understand that the first issue of the magazine has come out, but I have not yet received my copy of it. I hope that it is good.

Sincerely,

■   ■   ■

6

THE FOUNTAINHEAD AND *ATLAS SHRUGGED* YEARS (1945–1959)

To T. A. Robertson, of King Features Syndicate

January 7, 1945

Dear Mr. Robertson:

Some error must have been made in the text of my wire to you. Your second wire (of January 2nd) reads: "By all means be completely feminist in doing piece for us"—whereas I said in my wire: "Am not a feminist and would be no good at doing article from woman's angle."

I would not be able to write a feminine piece on the home—such as what gadgets or devices or conveniences a housewife should expect in the home of tomorrow. That is not my specialty, I know nothing about it and care less, being the worst housekeeper on earth. What I suggested in my wire (but I am wondering now whether that wire got completely garbled) is that I do a piece on the theme of: why the Home of Tomorrow should be modern architecture. I intend to stress the human, psychological reasons, more than the purely architectural ones—so that the article would, I think, interest the laymen, both men and women. But of all writers on earth I'm the worst one to pick for an article aimed at women from the angle of women. I just *ain't* that kind of writer.

As to illustrations, there are three architects whose houses would fit my article: *foremost* and above all Frank Lloyd Wright; Ely Jacques Kahn, and Richard J. Neutra. I would suggest that you get in touch with them (or if you need only one, then get Wright), let them know what type of article I am doing and ask their permission to use photographs of their designs of *modern* homes.

King Features expressed no interest in AR's proposal.

■   ■   ■

To Pincus Berner, AR's attorney

February 3, 1945

Dear Pinkie:

Please tell your charming wife that she is indirectly responsible for a grand movie which you'll see within the year. Anne might remember that it was she who recommended that I read *The Crying Sisters*, the mystery novel by Mabel Seeley, several years ago. It has been one of my great favorites ever since. Well, Hal Wallis has just bought it—on my enthusiastic recommendation and insistence. He wanted me to do one more script for him, before I take my six months off. I didn't like the stories they had—but told him I'd stay for *The Crying Sisters,* so he bought it. I'm doing the script now—and I think it will make a wonderful movie. I hope you, Anne and Rose will go to see it when it opens in New York—it's sort of a Berner godchild.

Although AR completed a screenplay on June 13, the movie was not made.

■   ■   ■

To D. L. Chambers

Chambers wrote AR, telling her he had heard "confidentially" that Maeterlinck wrote Archduke Franz Josef of Austria that *The Fountainhead* is "one of the grand books of the year."

February 4, 1945

Dear Mr. Chambers:

Thank you for letting me know about Maurice Maeterlinck's opinion of *The Fountainhead*. I was very happy to hear it, and I am glad if it adds to the prestige of the Bobbs-Merrill list.

Thank you also for the copy of Mr. Robert S. Henry's letter which you sent me. I am interested in railroads for the purpose of my next novel in which the railroad business will be an important part of the background. I will not be able to start research work for this novel until I am on my own time, that is, the free six months of my picture contract—but I expect to be free to start it in the near future.

■　■　■

To Esther Stone, wife of AR's cousin Burton, part of the family with whom she stayed in Chicago upon her arrival from Russia in 1926

February 15, 1945

Dear Esther:

I am working now on an unusual assignment—the screenplay for a picture about the Atom Bomb. It is the most difficult writing job I have ever attempted. And it keeps me chained to my desk as usual.

Please give my regards and best wishes for the success of the store in Momence to Mr. and Mrs. Stone.

> *After much research, including interviews with Robert Oppenheimer and Gen. Leslie Groves, AR did a complete treatment and seventy pages of script for a movie tentatively titled "Top Secret." The project, however, was sold to another studio in 1946 but never produced.*

■　■　■

To O. W. Kracht, a fan

March 4, 1945

Dear Mr. Kracht:

Thank you for your interesting letter. I really don't think that an author should explain her book—a book must speak for itself. But since you were interested enough to write out your analysis in detail and to ask me how near you came to the truth, I feel I must answer you.

Your analysis comes close to the truth on some points and goes very far wrong on others. It is curious that the aspects you have covered correctly are legitimate deductions from the material of my book, they *are* contained in the book—but they are only secondary aspects of my theme, secondary consequences, and therefore they are correct only in the sense of a partial truth. The truth, but not the whole truth. You did not state the basic thesis of *The Fountainhead*. As I shall explain.

To take up your analysis point by point: I do not understand your comparison of *The Fountainhead* to Plato's *Republic*. I presume you meant it only in a general way, in regard to my method—and even then it's not correct. I hope you meant no comparison in philosophical content—since Plato's *Republic* is the exact opposite of everything I and *The Fountainhead* stand for. Plato's *Republic* is the archetype and granddaddy of all the collectivist schemes that have plagued mankind since; as Plato is the ancestor of all collectivist thinkers and the spiritual father of Ellsworth Toohey. If you must classify me in relation to the ancient philosophers, count me in with Aristotle, the father of logic.

No, my characters are *not* symbols. They are persons in whom certain human attributes are focused more sharply and consistently than in average human beings. They are personifications of spiritual forces, if you wish— four basic types of the human soul. But, above all, as characters in a story, they are *men*, persons, people. They are most definitely "meant to be human beings"—though *not* "parodies of other living men in the public limelight," not any actual public figures. Don't tell me that there are no such people in real life. If there aren't, it's God's fault, not mine. But, as a matter of fact, there are.

You are correct in assuming that the four men whose names head the four parts of the book are the four pillars of my theme. But your definition of them is not correct, because you seem to have looked at the theme only in its secondary aspects.

The thesis of *The Fountainhead* is the statement of a new—and proper—code of ethics. Altruism (*living for others*), which has always been mankind's moral ideal, is actually the most vicious principle ever stated, the source of all evil, the principle of slavery, dependence and degradation. The proper moral ideal is *independence*—spiritual independence—which means absolute egoism in the sense represented by Howard Roark.

If you want the key sentence to *The Fountainhead*—it's in Roark's speech. "I wished to come here and say that I am a man who does not exist for others. It had to be said. The world is perishing from an orgy of self-sacrificing." Everything that *The Fountainhead* is about is right there, in that sentence. All the rest of the book is a detailed illustration of the various aspects of this statement, a picture of how the abstract principles of egoism and altruism work out in people and in the events of concrete reality.

The general theme of *The Fountainhead* is the conflict between good and evil—in a new definition. More specifically, it is the conflict between Individualism and Collectivism. Not in politics, but in man's soul.

This, I think, is where you missed the point. Since all theories about "historical necessity" or "historical determinism" are so much tripe invented by the Tooheys of the world for the sole purpose of enslaving humanity—the field of politics is a secondary one, an effect, not a cause; a result, not a reason. Men make politics, not politics—men. Political events are determined by political theories—not by any sort of "economic necessity"—and political theories are determined by men's thinking. To understand Individualism and Collectivism in their political consequences, we must begin at the beginning—by understanding what these two principles actually mean in application to men, to men's minds, characters and behavior, how these two principles work, what are the roots, the reasons and the motives behind them, what kind of human spirit produces an individualist or a collectivist.

So, you see, *The Fountainhead* is a political book only in a secondary sense—only in the sense that politics *are* determined by the kind of moral philosophy men have accepted. Primarily, *The Fountainhead* is a book on ethics.

Now, to be more specific, the question of Individualism and Collectivism is a question of man's relation to other men. The relation of the *EGO* to society. Therefore, every character in my book, down to the most minor ones, represents one of the many possible aspects of that relation.

My four key men are the four basic forms of *the relation of the self to others*. Here is where your analysis shocked me: the antagonists of my story are *not* Wynand and Toohey, but *ROARK* and *TOOHEY*. They are the two poles of good and evil. Everybody else stands somewhere between them. Roark—the complete individualist. Toohey—the complete collectivist. Roark—the ideal. Toohey—the absolute evil.

Roark is the prime mover, the originator, the totally self-sufficient man, for whom other people do not exist in any *primary*, important sense. The man who lives *only* for himself. The man who lives by, for and through himself. The absolute egotist.

Toohey is *literally* the selfless man—the man without personal content or meaning—the parasite who can exist *only* through others, through his power over them—the complete, real and consistent altruist. The man who—knowing his own viciousness—wants a world built on viciousness.

Keating is the parasite who tries to fool himself by moral justifications in order to escape the realization of his own mediocrity—the unthinking cannon fodder of collectivism.

Wynand is a prime mover who has gone wrong by making one crucial mistake, the mistake made by so many great men—that of placing his goal within others, of seeking greatness in power over others (which is a form of spiritual collectivism). A man who should have been a Roark, Wynand destroyed himself by living his life as a secondhander. Wynand is the man who makes the Tooheys possible—since the Tooheys are impotent by themselves.

(Wynand is not the opposite of Toohey—*Roark is*. Wynand is not an individualist—he certainly did not live as one. He should have been one, but he wasn't. *That* is his unforgivable sin.)

If you start with the principle that independence is the keystone of human greatness, that the absolute individualist is the moral man, the perfect man, the great man—here is how my four key characters stand in relation to that principle:

Keating—who could not be great and didn't know it.

Toohey—who could not be and knew it.

Wynand—who could have been.

Roark—who could and was.

Now, to come back to your analysis: you have described Toohey and Keating fairly accurately. You're completely wrong on Wynand. Wynand is *not* the symbol of free enterprise—*Roark is*. (If you wish to call it a symbol.) Free enterprise was not made by those who catered to the masses, as Wynand did, but by the originators and innovators who went *against* the masses, against all public opinion, against all "trends" and "currents." Wynand—if you want to look at him in one of his lesser aspects, in the narrow, "journalistic" sense of contemporary events—represents the men who are destroying free enterprise today—the industrialists and capitalists who are digging their own graves and cutting their own throats by fostering, feeding, employing and supporting their own murderers. As witness any so-called conservative newspaper or any other business enterprise today.

You are frightfully wrong in your definition of Roark. He is *not* "the symbol of man's conscience." He is the symbol of *man*. He is man as god, the perfect human being, the absolute human ideal.

When you say that Roark "cannot possibly be a human being," you are using the word "human" as Toohey would use it—that is, to mean something weak, small, cowardly, uncertain and depraved. To mean a Peter Keating. That's just another form of our present-day corruption of thought and language. It implies the idea that vices are human, but virtues are not. I grant you that this is the way everybody uses the word "human" nowadays. The Tooheys of the world saw to the spreading of that habit. Its purpose is simple. It tells us in effect: "Don't try to have integrity, to be strong, brave, honest, intelligent, great—it isn't human. Be satisfied with your rottenness and your sweet little drooling weaknesses—*be small*—that's human."

Roark is the only one in the book who is completely human—man as he should be. Keating is subhuman. If Keating were the typical representative of humanity, we would never have risen out of the swamp and the cave. It was not the Keatings who got us out. Never mind about there being more Keatings than Roarks. It's the Roarks who count.

And—oh hell!—(excuse me, but *this* point does make me angry)—you're wrong when you speak of Roark "building the symbol of a dying era." What dying era? Individualism is *not* dying, but it will die if those who defend it do not stop talking about "dying eras." That's pure Ellsworth Toohey party line. True, at the moment, the world is headed toward the chaos, horror and depravity of collectivism—but the world does not have to go that way. There are no "waves of the future" and no "historical materialism." Any trend can be stopped. Any step can be retraced—if men understand where they're going. Collectivism cannot win. It can only destroy. Toohey did not gain control of the *Banner*—he merely destroyed the *Banner*. Toohey did not destroy Wynand—Wynand destroyed himself. Who won? Roark.

Free enterprise as a system may be wiped out for a while by fools, cowards and secondhanders—but its spirit (Individualism, which means Man's spirit) cannot be destroyed, it will go on and win in the end, even if it takes centuries, as it has always won in the past. Because individualism is the only thing that works or can work.

You have not understood my book at all if you really thought that I wrote some sort of dirge to a "dying era." But I take it you merely used that expression carelessly, since one hears it so often nowadays. *NO*, Roark did *not* build any kind of memorial to the grave of free enterprise. He built a monument to the spirit of Man, which is invincible and indestructible.

Didn't you understand how completely Toohey was defeated in the book? True, Toohey will go on—the Tooheys will always go on—but they can never win. What could possibly have led you to the conclusion that the Wynand Building was a symbol of the end of capitalism, which would mean a symbol of Toohey's victory? How could anyone read that into my book? Didn't you understand the last three pages?

Now as to Dominique, she is not the symbol of anything. She is merely the kind of woman who would be worthy of Roark. She is not "the symbol of woman's soul"—I wouldn't know what that means. When you say that she is "expected to share and understand, to partake, enjoy and forgive" all men—you forget that she is the most unbending and unforgiving character in the book, much more unforgiving than Roark.

Now that I've written you a whole treatise—(and here I thought that 754 pages on a subject were really enough)—will you answer a question for me? This baffles me a little. How—if you were interested in my book enough to give it thought and discussion—did you miss the three places where I present my whole thesis as clearly, specifically and completely as one would do in a nonfiction article? I mean: 1. The conversation of Roark and Wynand aboard the yacht. 2. Toohey's speech to Keating. 3. Roark's speech at his trial. Particularly this last. I see no reference in your analysis to the ideas presented in these passages; no reference to moral philosophy. Yet every character and event in the book is a direct, specific illustration of the statements made in these three passages. And I cannot quite understand how there can really be any question about the theme or meaning of *The Fountainhead* when Roark's speech is in the book. No other author ever wrote a summary of his theme within his book as explicitly as I did. Everything I said in this letter is in that speech. If you can answer this question, please do. I'd like to know.

As to my title—well, isn't it implicit in my theme? Man is the source of every achievement, of everything high, noble and great on earth. Man, not men. Man, not society. Man, not the collective. Man's *EGO* is the source, the dynamo, the prime mover—*THE FOUNTAINHEAD*.

■   ■   ■

To Ruth Alexander

March 18, 1945

Dear Ruth:

Congratulations on your syndicated column! I was delighted to hear that you got it—and I wish you a long, successful career as a columnist. I hope the Hearst papers here will be among the first to carry your column—but if they don't I'll count on you to save me copies of it, I want to be among your first constant readers.

As to your being a doctor at the bedside of a dying patient—well, a doctor does what he can, but *never* tells the patient that he's dying. Even a doctor knows that there's always the chance of a miracle—which is not really a miracle, but merely the first time that a certain patient recovered, when all others in similar circumstances did not. I think this particular patient will recover—he has achieved miracles before.

■ ■ ■

To Hal Wallis, movie producer

June 18, 1945

Dear Boss:

How could I ever forget? [The photograph you sent] will be an inspiration—and a threat. It's a wonderful picture. That's the way I like to see you look—hard and ruthless (except in relation to *my* scripts). Thank you immensely.

You might like to know what was the first thing I did on regaining my freedom: I went out and bought five dresses by Adrian and the complete works of Aristotle. This will give you an idea of the real nature of—

—your loyal wage slave,

■ ■ ■

To Alan Collins, her literary agent at Curtis Brown, Ltd.

Collins wrote AR of an offer to syndicate an illustrated synopsis of *The Fountainhead.* Newspaper serializations of bestsellers were common in the 1940s.

July 29, 1945

Dear Alan:

First, the matter of the King Features offer for a serialized strip of *The Fountainhead.* I like the idea, but I will accept it *only* on condition that the text and drawings will be submitted to me for approval before they go to press. In regard to the drawings, I will have the right to okay the artist's proposed visualization of my characters before the actual pictures are made. In regard to the text, I will have: first, the right to okay the general outline of what scenes or parts of the book the syndicate's writer wishes to dramatize; second, the right to edit all of the actual text used. No line of text is to appear in print without my approval. One specific point I want to be agreed upon in advance: Roark's courtroom speech is to be included in the text. I will shorten the speech for them myself, if they want it shortened. I insist on this because the opportunity to have this speech syndicated is the main appeal of their offer to me.

I do not know on what terms such strips are usually contracted for— so I hope King Features won't find this unreasonable. You may point out to them that my only interest in such a strip is the publicity it would give my book. Therefore it must be the *right* kind of publicity, a condensation true to the theme, style and spirit of the story. If the condensation makes the book appear garbled, weak, or pointless (through careless choice of incidents), it will do positive harm in discouraging prospective readers.

My contract with Bobbs-Merrill gives them the right to make deals for condensations—but states that all condensations must be submitted to me for my approval. May I count on you to make sure that this is observed? Bobbs-Merrill have broken that clause once before when they arranged for a condensation in *Omnibook* magazine and it appeared in print before I knew anything about it. They pleaded at the time that they forgot to send me the text. I don't intend to let this happen again. Since this offer came through you, perhaps it might be wise—to avoid future trouble—if you would warn King Features not to sign any deal with Bobbs-Merrill without my approval.

■ ■ ■

To PFC Gerald James, a fan

August 18, 1945

Dear Gerald James:

Thank you. I'm glad you thought *The Fountainhead* was "out of this world." That's what I intended it to be—in more ways than one.

To answer all your questions in proper order:

1. How was the book received by the public? Beautifully—for which I'm very grateful. It was made by the public—against the opposition of all the intellectual Tooheys. The book's been growing in sales for two years, through word-of-mouth publicity, until now it's high on all the bestseller lists.

2. Who is Frank O'Connor? Howard Roark, or as near to it as anyone I know. Incidentally, he's my husband.

3. Are my characters copies of people in real life? No. I'll let you in on a professional secret: Don't ever believe the stories about authors putting people into novels. That idea is a kind of joke on both authors and readers. All the readers believe that authors do it. All the authors know that it can't be done. What an author actually does is this: he observes real life, deduces the abstract principles behind certain actions or characters, and then creates his own characters out of the abstraction. The resemblance to real people is one of principle—not of literal, personal copying.

4. Have I embodied some of my own qualities in Dominique? Yes. Am I Dominique? No. As the enclosed picture of me will demonstrate. Sorry to disappoint you there, but I never thought I'd live to be a pinup girl, so I couldn't pass up such a chance—if that space on your wall is still blank.

5. Have I published any other novels? One other. My first novel was called *We the Living* and was published in 1936.

6. What type of house am I living in now? In a house which I own and which is extremely modern—made of steel, glass and concrete, mostly glass. So you see, I'm the kind of ballplayer who endorses only what she really smokes—and smokes only what she really endorses. And that goes for all the other ideas, principles and philosophy endorsed in *The Fountainhead*, besides architecture.

I'm glad you liked my book. We're even. I liked your letter.

■   ■   ■

To Alan Collins

August 20, 1945

Dear Alan:

Thank you for your letter and the samples of the King Features book strips.

I could do a swell job of condensing Roark's speech into 1,000 words—that's what I did for the screenplay version. But I can see by the samples that two days of a theoretical speech might be too much for this kind of condensation. So—if the syndicate editors feel they can give me two days, I'll be very happy. If they feel it's too much—I'll agree to just one day and five hundred words, in which I'll use just the quotes I consider most important and attention-getting.

I don't mind what you call the "terrific compression"—it amounts to just a long, illustrated synopsis. I think they can do a good job of it—if the writer keeps his narrative as hard and simple as possible and goes easy on the adjectives.

I'd like to make the same suggestion about the illustrations: keep it *SIMPLE.* My whole book is done by understatement—and I'd like the strip done the same way, if possible. It should be hard, simple, clear-cut, *stylized,* underdrawn—nothing but the bare essentials, as uncluttered as possible. Of the artists in the samples you sent me, I like Harold Foster best, if I have any choice in the matter—but perhaps they can find someone with a still harder and simpler style of drawing. [Illustrator Frank Godwin was chosen.]

If the deal goes through, I'd like to send them some specific suggestions for the artist about how the characters should look, and some advice to the writer about how to condense the story. Being an ex-synopsis writer myself, I know all the tricks of how these things are done. I hope the deal does go through—I'm curious to see the thing illustrated.

The Fountainhead *was King Features' first postwar serial. It began in the* Los Angeles Herald-Express *on December 24, 1945, ran for thirty episodes of 500 words each, and was published in two dozen other US and foreign newspapers.*

■   ■   ■

To Gerald Loeb

August 21, 1945

Dear Gerald:

I am getting to be a little more "competent" and human—I'm actually writing a letter. You have always been both—so thank you for your patience.

I have met your friend Jack Kapp—have seen him twice. I liked him a lot and was quite impressed. In fact, I think he's rather wonderful. Thank you for introducing me to him.

You want me to explain *Love Letters* to you. Well, first, I agree with your reaction to it—and you were completely correct. NO, don't go about reading reviews in order to see whether you're wrong. That's not the way to discover the truth. When will I cure you of that particular superstition? I sure would like to. The truth about *Love Letters*, as I see it, is this: it is essentially a very silly and meaningless story—by the mere fact that it revolves around so unnatural a thing as somebody's amnesia. No, it has no moral lesson to teach, nor any kind of lesson whatever. So, if you look at it from the standpoint of content—it has none. But it has one valuable point as a story—a dramatic situation involving a conflict. This permits the creation of suspense. If the basic premise—amnesia—doesn't interest you, then of course the rest of the story won't interest you. A basic premise in a story is always like an axiom—you take it or you don't. If you accept the premise, the rest will hold your interest. As for me, I accept the premise out of sheer curiosity—nothing more deep or important than that. That is, granting such a setup—let's see what can be made of it. My only interest in that picture was purely technical—how to create a good construction that would be dramatic and suspenseful, out of practically nothing. The novel on which the picture was based was a holy mess. Whatever story interest and unity it has, I had to invent. But we picked this particular novel because it had the elements of a possible situation. That is very rare in picture stories.

I think the picture will be successful—for that reason only: dramatic construction. As a technician, I like it. As a person or a writer, I don't like it at all. That is not my type of story. But you are extremely wrong if you expect pictures with a serious problem and an important content. I don't mean that such pictures are impossible to make. I think they could and should be made—and would be extremely successful. But at the moment I do not see anyone in Hollywood who wants to make them. They are making good pictures here, good entertainment, even some good taste. But serious moral lessons or problems? No. Not yet. Maybe *The Fountainhead* will be one—if they don't ruin it in production. The trouble here is that very few writers know how to make a picture with a serious lesson also an entertaining one. The few literary phonies who have tried it, have turned out such dull trash, that I do not blame the producers for turning away from all serious themes and concentrating on simple entertainment without morals. This last is really more honest and sensible. I think I have written to you once that the art of integrating propaganda, that is, an abstract theme, with a concrete story, is the hardest of all arts. I honestly don't know anyone who can do it at the moment—except myself. So don't expect serious content from the movies. Not for a while yet.

As for me personally, you know of course that I have no freedom over the material which I write for pictures. I can select stories within a certain limit—but I have to select out of the things they want to make—not the things *I'd* like to make or write. When I signed a movie contract, I set myself two goals: a minimum and a maximum. The minimum would be just the money, the freedom from any financial worries in regard to my own serious writing, and the attempt I always wanted to make—to find out for myself whether good pictures can be made. The maximum will be to reach a position where I will make the kind of pictures I want—my way. If I can't reach this maximum I will finish my contract and quit the movies. But I think that I have a good chance to reach it. Only I must be patient —the things I'd like to do are too new and different—it will take time to convince anyone here to let me do it. However, I seem to get along with Hal Wallis very well—he's a very able, intelligent man with a great deal of courage—and if I can have any influence on him, to take him away from the usual Hollywood influence which is a terrific pressure on every prominent man here—I might be able to see the day when he and I will make the kind of pictures you expect and would like.

As to *You Came Along*, it was originally a very cute story—not profound—but clever and appealing. The picture represents a compromise between Hal Wallis, the director John Farrow, the original author Robert Smith, and me. Like all compromises, it could only turn out as a second-best.

Well, does that answer your questions?

You asked whether your plot about a man "with death first, life later" would be a good story or whether it is a "standard." No, it is not a standard; I have never seen it used in just those terms before. Yes, I think it would make a very interesting story—and a serious one. But you'd have to write it first as a novel—if you hope to have the screen version preserve your theme and intention. If you try to sell it as a screen original—all the chances are that it will be "standardized" and your original intent will be lost.

■ ■ ■

To Fred Dickenson, art department at King Features Syndicate

November 20, 1945

Dear Mr. Dickenson:

Here are chapters 19–24. I have had to change the content of chapter 19 and the beginning of chapter 20, for the following reasons: in chapter 19 the first episode (Roark and Wynand talking) and the last episode (Roark meeting Dominique in the garden) were inessential to the progression of the story—and they took up space badly needed for the exposition of Roark's motives in agreeing to design Cortlandt. This scene between Roark and Keating is a crucial key spot of the story. It is here that we must lay the ground for his later acquittal. If we don't make Roark's motives and reasons clear at this point—nobody will understand his dynamiting of Cortlandt, and it will appear as an act of senseless brutality.

So I devoted chapter 19 to the Roark–Keating scene. This will change the choice of illustrations. I suggest the following pictures for it: a scene of Keating begging Toohey for help; a scene between Roark and Keating; a scene where Toohey laughs at the drawings brought by Keating.

I covered the matter of the completion of Wynand's house at the beginning of chapter 20, eliminating the episode of Wynand seeing the drawings of Cortlandt. This last was not essential—and we needed the space. This, I suppose, will change the first illustration of chapter 20—but we can have, instead, a good picture of Roark, Wynand and Dominique on the shore of the lake—or of Wynand and Dominique at the fireplace.

In chapter 24 I have stated briefly the issue behind the public fury against Roark. This had to be made clear and specific, otherwise the readers won't understand the trial nor Roark's speech.

In the rest of the chapters I have preserved your continuity and choice of incidents. Thank you for an excellent job of selection in what was probably the hardest part of the book to condense.

I am enclosing a copy of Roark's speech. It contains exactly 407 words (I've counted them). This is the best I can do—I was supposed originally to have 500 words for the purpose. If there's space in that installment above the 407 words, you may add the lines about the trial, which you mentioned in your last letter, and let me see it. The speech itself can't be cut any further and present any semblance of the book's theme. I'm sure I can help you to work the expositionary material about the trial into the preceding and following chapters, if necessary.

Do you have copies of the first chapters printed with drawings? I am most eager to see them.

■ ■ ■

To Ross Baker, sales manager of Bobbs-Merrill's trade book department

November 21, 1945

Dear Ross:

Here is the copy of the pamphlet about me and *The Fountainhead.*

It was a much harder job than I feared, and I've worked on it ever since I came back home. After many tries, I found that it was impossible to do it in the third person, as an article written about me by somebody else. It sounds less stuffy, more natural and with more life to it when coming straight from me. If the readers want to know something about me as a person, this will do it.

I suggest that you call the pamphlet "To the readers of *The Fountainhead*," and that you put an explanatory note at the beginning, something like: "We have received so many enquiries from readers about *The Fountainhead* and its author that we have asked Miss Rand to write a special answer."

I would like to have the "Thank you" and the signature reproduced from my handwriting at the end of the printed pamphlet, just as I have it in the copy. I think that would make a nice personal touch—unless you find it inadvisable. Also, if advisable, you might use my picture on the cover (same one as on the book's jacket)—I get a few requests for pictures, so that would cover both types of requests.

Since the article is in my name, I want to have it printed exactly as I wrote it. But if you have any objections to any part or some suggestions to make, please let me know and I'll try to adjust it, or send me the copy back, marked with your suggestions. Please do not set it up in print with changes without my approval. If you okay it as it is, please send me a proof of it before the final printing. I'd like a chance to go over it once more. And I'll return the proof to you promptly.

■ ■ ■

To Fred Dickenson

November 29, 1945

Dear Mr. Dickenson:

Well, here are your final chapters—with my compliments and thanks. You've done a swell job on an incredibly difficult undertaking—so pin a little medal on yourself from at least one grateful author.

The last chapters were very good—I've made no changes in the choice of incidents, only in some of the details. The courtroom chapter (28) is practically untouched, but I retyped it along with the rest, since you probably need the extra copies.

Would you do me a favor and watch one small detail for me? In Roark's speech (second page of chapter 28) there is an important sentence: "Civilization is the process of setting man free from men." In your copy it was typed as: "setting *men* free from *men*," which blasts the whole meaning of the sentence to pieces. That's a very natural typographical error that can easily occur. Would you make a note of it and check the proofs to be sure that the typesetter doesn't make the same error and that the sentence appears correctly? The first word must be "*man*" and the second "*men*." It's one of those small but crucial things where one letter can break an author's heart. I love that sentence.

Would you ask Mr. Godwin to use, for the last illustration, the last sentence of our copy? That is—just the figure of Roark against the sky. I would like so much to see it ended that way.

Thank you for the completed proofs of the first week, which I have just received. The drawings are fine—and I was very pleased with the looks of the whole thing as set up. Please do send me further proofs as they come out—I'm looking forward to seeing them with real pleasure.

■ ■ ■

To Michael O'Shaughnessy, a fan

To Michael O'Shaughnessy, a fan

November 30, 1945

Dear Mr. O'Shaughnessy:

No, I have not thought about a play from my book and I would not let anyone attempt such an undertaking. Neither the theme of *The Fountainhead* nor its story nor any important part of it could be presented within the limitations of a stage and of two-and-a-half hours. It is most positively *not* stage material. Are you a playwright? If you are, I am sorry to disappoint you. But I do appreciate your interest.

If *The Fountainhead* has helped you in your views on life and in your decisions—that is very important and I am very glad.

How it feels to have written it? Well, that is a question I couldn't answer. But as an approximation, look at the last paragraph on page 327.

> *The paragraph describes Roark looking at the just completed Enright House, his first major project. It reads in part: "The young photographer glanced at Roark's face—and thought of something that had puzzled him for a long time: he had always wondered why the sensations one felt in dreams were so much more intense than anything one could experience in waking reality . . . the quality of what he felt when he walked down a path through tangled green leaves in a dream, in an air full of expectation, of causeless, utter rapture. . . . He thought of that because he saw that extra quality for the first time in waking existence, he saw it in Roark's face lifted to the building."*

■ ■ ■

To W. M. Curtiss, a fan

November 30, 1945

Dear Mr. Curtiss:

I am glad that Mrs. Curtiss and you liked my book—and that you chose as the high spots the two passages which I consider most important: Toohey's speech and Roark's speech. These are, of course, the heart and essence of the whole novel.

No, I don't believe that an individualist must be a "queer sort of person"—but then, you see, I don't think that Roark is "queer." He is merely a perfect human being.

You say that someone could have Roark's philosophy and still be "normal," and you give Leonard Read as an example. Well, well, well, what makes you think that Leonard Read is a "normal individual"? I think he's much more than that. As you must have guessed, I am not very enthusiastic about such conceptions as "normal" or "average." If there is such a thing as an average man, who cares about him or why should anyone care? What I am interested in is the great and the exceptional.

But if you wonder how I look at Roark in relation to men as we see them around us—I'll say that any man who has an innate sense of independence and self-respect, and a spark of the creative mind, has that much of Roark in him. Any man can follow Roark's principles—if he has intelligence, integrity and courage. He may not have Roark's genius, but he can function in the same manner and live by the same morality—within the limits of his own ability. He *must* live by the same morality—the morality of individualism—if he wants to survive at all. The opposite principle—collectivism—has now brought its ultimate results, in practical demonstration. Look at the world around us. Men must turn to individualism or perish The choice is pretty eloquently obvious at the present moment.

■ ■ ■

To Gerald Loeb

November 30, 1945

Dear Gerald:

This is not an answer by return mail—but still, it's better than I did before, isn't it? I really intend to improve.

To answer your three questions: 1. I have not seen Mr. Blanke yet, have only spoken to him on the phone—and he did not comment on the Frank Lloyd Wright fee, except to say that he will have to discuss it with Mr. Warner. I shall see Mr. Blanke next week, so I hope to find out then more about this matter.

2. My impressions of Taliesin? It's magnificent. All of the FLW buildings are so much more beautiful in reality than any photograph can convey. I was truly thrilled to see it. We had a very interesting weekend there. My impressions are more complex than I could tell in a letter—so I'll tell you about it in person, when I see you.

3. No, I didn't see any more work on your house. I did not see much of their work, because, unfortunately, they had moved all their models and drawings to an exhibition in Milwaukee. I don't suppose they took your drawings there, but Mr. Wright did not show me through their drafting room—his secretary did, and it was practically bare.

We were unable to find any land we liked while in the East—it is really too difficult a thing to decide in a hurry. But, surprisingly, Mr. Wright agreed to design a house for us without the land—he calls it "a dream house." I was afraid that he would kill me for such a request, but he didn't. I told him in detail what kind of a house we needed, how much we wanted to spend, what kind of land we'd get—and he agreed to design it now for the future. Is it necessary to sign a contract or agreement with him about it? He said it wasn't necessary. Did you have any letter of agreement about your house? Or is it usually done merely by verbal agreement?

■ ■ ■

To Rose Wilder Lane, a pro-individualist writer and daughter of Laura Ingalls Wilder (author of *Little House on the Prairie*)

November 30, 1945

Dear Rose Wilder Lane:

Thank you for your note on *The Fountainhead* in the National Economic Council's Book Reviews. I was startled to see it, and I appreciate it very much.

I want to congratulate you on your review of the Bastiat books. It was a masterful job. I shall look forward with real pleasure and interest to future copies of this magazine. It is such a rare treat to read intelligent book reviewing for a change.

I am sorry that I did not have a chance to see you while I was in New York, but I hope that we shall meet some day in person, as we certainly must.

■ ■ ■

To Archibald Ogden

November 30, 1945

Archie darling:

This is just to show that I do write letters occasionally—and that I think of you, not occasionally, but always.

Seeing you again was one of the best memories I've brought back from my trip to New York—next to the memory of the Empire State Building. And maybe even as good as the Building—though in a different way. But while the sight of the Empire State will have to last me only for another year—the sight of you will have to do for *four* years, and I hate the idea.

You're going to cause me to become a split personality: on the one hand, I wish you the most sensational success with your job in England; on the other hand I hope they'll fire you in a month and send you back to us. But since I've said that I'll make almost every kind of exception for you, I'll be an altruist, for once, and wish you the first, since that is what you want. As an egoist, I'd prefer the second.

I hope you're still watching *The Fountainhead* on the bestseller lists and feel about it as I do. Bobbs-Merrill have kept their promise, they are running good ads for the book, and I'm pleased about it.

Wait till you see the King Features condensation of the book, with pictures. I've seen the first week's advance proofs—it's amusing and quite exciting. It will begin to appear in the newspapers on December 24—just like a Christmas present. Do you want me to send you a complete set of proofs when they're ready? I guess they'll have to go to you in England.

Drop me a line before you leave, so I won't feel too badly about it. All my best wishes, darling, for a safe trip, a good time and a great success.

■   ■   ■

To Ross Baker

December 2, 1945

Dear Ross:

When you write me a letter containing a sentence such as "and further paper has been ordered beyond the 90,000 planned for," you may be sure that I'll be a good girl and that everything's right with the world for me.

So look at the enclosed pamphlet. I've accepted all the cuts you made and have even made a few more for you. I see by the cuts that you didn't want the pamphlet to be more political than the book itself. You're right —though not for the reasons you mention in your letter. I've made some more cuts because some of the things you left in lost all punch out of the full context. So they're better out entirely.

On page 3—please give Roark's lines in full. It's my favorite passage in the book. Since I've made other cuts, this won't take too much space.

Page 4—the reader's statement must be given here, in order that my answer make sense. Are you afraid it sounds like adverse criticism? I'm not.

Page 6—"Not by the public as an organized *collective*"—that, you must let me say. First, in justice to our readers. Second, if I don't make the distinction clear, every pink punk will be justified in yelping: Look, the collective made you successful!

In regard to the facsimile of my signature—you're right.* Omit it.

You must have forgotten, since we spoke over the telephone, that you did not say you wanted 1,500 words. You said 2,500. You might remember that I gasped slightly and said: "That much?" And you said: "Well, we might cut it later." I don't mind having it shorter now—I even think it's better—but please don't think I got carried away by the sheer pleasure of talking about myself. It would have saved me a lot of work if I'd known that 1,500 words would do.

Please don't make other changes without letting me know. If this version is all right with you—please send me a proof of it before the final printing.

Thank you for the ad in *Publishers Weekly*. It's very good. When you run the big ad you mentioned in the *N. Y. Times*, please send me a copy, too. I mean, after the fact, if you don't have time to do it before. As a suggestion, do include something in that ad that would indicate something of the nature of the book and make it interesting or exciting; I do think it would help. I hope, when you get the space, that you will run some individual ads for the book. It's earned them, hasn't it?

I am, of course, extremely glad that you are now getting the paper for more books beyond the 90,000 copies. It is not too soon. I am counting on you to see, well in advance, that no breaks in the supply of books occur again. Los Angeles was completely out of books for three to four weeks —while the demand was growing. It was horrible. The shipments didn't arrive here until last week, November 23 to be exact. So you see why I was and am so concerned. Even though you've done your best to get the books out early in November, we still lost the month of November—due to the shipping time involved. *PLEASE* do not let this happen again. Please plan your printings enough in advance to allow for shipping and delivery.

In fairness to you I must say that I am very happy about the situation of the book now, when it's in print, and I am counting on you not to let me down. Thank you for the 90,000+, (and I hope many more +'s).

■   ■   ■

* Baker had pointed out that AR's personal autograph on copies she mailed to fans would mean much more to them than would a printed signature.

To Mimi Sutton, AR's niece, a daughter of Frank's sister, Agnes Papurt

December 2, 1945

Dear Mimi:

Thanks for your letter. I'm answering hurriedly, but not too late as usual. We had a nice trip back—though the Superchief did shake unmercifully. The weekend at Frank Lloyd Wright's house was extremely interesting—it would take an article to describe it—but Taliesin looks magnificent—I am more crazy about his architecture than ever—and he promised to design a house for us, even without our having bought the land; he'll design it in advance, for the future—and that made me very happy. We found our home here in perfect order and have just about settled back to rest after our vacation in New York. Frank feels and looks wonderful—and is delighted to be back with his chickens.

I hope you will be happy in whichever of the two jobs David decides to take. I wish him a great success and lots of happiness to both of you.

I'm glad that Doc [Mimi's sister Marna, a.k.a. "Docky"] approved of our plans for her—I hope she'll work very hard—and don't let her marry the first boy she sees—I strongly suspect that she's much better than that and she should not end up as a housewife before she's even started to live. Let me know when you're settled and all the details.

I presume the poetry which you said was "by my dear little sister" is by Connie [Mimi's other sister]. We howled, reading it. It's really not bad at all, you know, in fact some of it is quite good—but it was very funny to see her writing about "Time changes us all until only a fragment of the old is left"—at her great old age.

Tell the family to look for the illustrated condensation of *The Fountainhead* in the Hearst papers beginning December 24th. I think they'll get a kick out of it because the artist has done a wonderful job of making Roark look like Frank. I've seen the advance proofs, and everybody here gasps, seeing them, without any warning from us: "Why, it's Frank!" Don't tell them about it—let's see if they discover the resemblance themselves; I think it might be a funny surprise, particularly for Connie, if she's movie-struck and such.

Your Auntie,

■   ■   ■

To Ross Baker

December 5, 1945

Dear Ross:

NOW you're acting as I hoped my publishers would act.
    THANKS!

P.S. Of course I mean the ad from the New York daily *Times* which you
sent me.

■ ■ ■

To Henry Blanke, producer of *The Fountainhead* movie

December 6, 1945

Dear Henry:

This is in the nature of a postscript to the script of *The Fountainhead*. I
think I can do better by putting it on paper than by attempting it in
conversation.

    I can say in all sincerity that while I was working with you on the
script, you did not say one thing nor make one suggestion that were out of
the style and spirit of *The Fountainhead*. So I know that you understand
the book and I feel complete confidence in your judgment—so long as it
remains your own judgment. But now that I have been in Hollywood for
two years, I know what happens when a picture is being prepared for production. The pressure put upon the producer is truly inhuman—an awful
landslide of contradictory opinions from everywhere and everybody. It is
not a reproach to you nor lack of faith in you when I say that I know you
will be subjected to that pressure and you will have a hard time trying to
keep your own way clear. This letter is my attempt to stand by you in spirit
in a battle which is mine, too, but which I will not be present to share.
This letter is in the nature of ammunition that I'd like to give you. I'd like
you to refer to it when you find yourself in doubt and under fire.

    As a picture, *The Fountainhead* must be treated on its own particular
terms and in its own particular style. If treated so—it will be a tremendous
success. If not—it will be a terrible flop.

    The Fountainhead is a thing that belongs in a class of its own. I don't
say this boastfully, I don't mean that it's better or worse than the works of
other authors. I mean only that it's *different*—different from beginning to

end, in theme, conception, style, form and method. Therefore, the rules or approach used for the production of other stories will not work with it. Only its own style and method will.

The Fountainhead is constructed like a very delicate and complex mechanism: a cruder engine can withstand an awful lot of pounding; but one careless snap of an inept finger at this one will make it collapse into junk.

Specifically, *The Fountainhead* represents a form that has always been extremely successful in novels, on the stage and on the screen, but which has become very rare because it's the most difficult of all forms: Romantic Realism. The method of romantic realism is to make life more beautiful and interesting than it actually is, yet give it all the reality, and even a more convincing reality than that of our everyday existence. Life, not as it is, but as it could be and should be. *That* is what the public likes, wants and is starved for.

But this cannot be achieved without a very clear understanding of what it is, how it's done—and a very conscious policy in doing it. The general school of writing and movies nowadays aims at cheap journalistic realism —trying to represent life "just like the folks next door." Any touch of that approach would destroy *The Fountainhead*.

The characters of *The Fountainhead* are not average people. They are unusual people who do unusual things. To make them convincing one must keep them strictly consistent with their own peculiar natures. Then the audience will accept them. If they are weakened and diluted, they will become unreal, false—and silly. For example, people accept and admire Roark because he is presented consistently as a hard, ruthless idealist with a single passion for his work. People can understand his actions, because he is shown as that kind of a man. But let someone come along with an attempt to make Roark more "human," let him add some such scene as Roark kidding about architecture—and the whole of Roark's character will be blasted out of existence. Nobody will believe anything he does. Nobody will understand his other actions. He will have become unreal and ridiculous.

The whole of *The Fountainhead* is stylized to a heroic scale. It must be kept on that scale. One single "humanizing" touch will cost us the whole picture. Here is the best illustration of what I mean: if we had a homey little painting, say a still from Disney's *Snow White,* and if we painted in a handkerchief tied around Snow White's cheek, because she had a toothache—it would not destroy the picture, but only give it a cute touch of humor. Now if we painted such a handkerchief around the cheek of a

Raphael Madonna—would there be anything left of the canvas? Could we wonder why people snickered and refused to accept the painting as sacred, important or uplifting?

The surest way to kill *The Fountainhead* would be any attempt at any so-called "human" touch—by people who mean "vulgar and commonplace" when they say "human." Heroes don't have toothaches, don't act like the folks next door and don't use dialogue such as: "Gee, it's swell." If we want the audience to respond to a hero, we must give them a hero to respond to. And keep him a hero.

I stress this because I know that you will be subjected to a deluge of advice, suggestions, interference and criticism, all of it to the effect that "The characters aren't human—their dialogue is too literary—the whole thing is too intellectual—it won't play well—it's not a *regular* movie—etc." I know it, because I have gone through all of that before. *That* was precisely the kind of opposition I found when I submitted my book to publishers. Twelve publishers rejected it. They rejected it because they said it was *too intellectual to be popular.* I've heard everything you're going to hear now: too intellectual—too literary—not human—people don't talk that way—etc. Specifically, the publishing house of Little, Brown—which is considered *the* expert house of book salesmanship—rejected *The Fountainhead* telling me that it was "almost a work of genius," but their sales experts had decided *unanimously* that such a book could not and would not sell.

Look at the results.

The Fountainhead is now considered a phenomenon in publishing history. No other book has ever sold in quite this manner—by a steady, growing, voluntary word-of-mouth campaign. It has been made *precisely by popular appeal.* The success of other books was always due in large measure to big-scale publicity, organized pushing, book-club-wholesaling. My book is the only one that rose, unhelped, through sheer, genuine popular response.

What is the practical moral in this? The following: *The Fountainhead* represents something totally new; what it represents is wanted and liked by the public; but since it is so new, it frightens and bewilders all the so-called experts. They don't know what to make of it nor what it's all about. This is natural—since they became experts by dealing in books of quite a different kind, by acting on precedents and according to standards of quite a different kind. Whatever they learned, it was correct in regard to other books. It was totally wrong in regard to *The Fountainhead.*

Had I followed their advice, had I tried to compromise, to soften my book or conventionalize it a little—it wouldn't have sold two copies and it wouldn't have been worth two cents.

It is the unity of the book—the unity of theme, style, conception and execution—the unity and the complete, ruthless consistency that made the book successful. People are starved for something strong and definite. They're so sick of halfhearted evasions, generalities, compromises, standard patterns and feeble attempts to please everybody—which is all they get nowadays.

You do not have to wonder whether the public will like something as radically new as *The Fountainhead*. The history of the book is the answer in practical demonstration.

Book publishing is not different from pictures, in essential procedure. Both professions want to capture popular appeal—and both professions are full of timid, stale-minded people who don't know how to gauge popular appeal, except by referring to some trite precedent. My book was considered *too literary* by men who deal in literature. Now it will be considered too literary for the movies. It wasn't so in the first instance—and it isn't so in the second.

The truth of the matter is that in the present state of the entire literary and entertainment world, there is a wide gap between two camps which should be one, but aren't: the experts and the public. The experts—most of the writers, editors, publishers, producers, directors and critics—go by such worn, dated, and deplorable standards that they've lost all touch with the public. That is why we see constant occasions when books and movies are praised to the sky, then flop miserably—and books and movies which are panned or ignored, yet become sensationally successful and popular.

You have to admit to yourself the fact that you are faced with a choice in regard to *The Fountainhead*: either you attempt to please the usual taste of Hollywood experts—or you please the public. *You can't do both at once.* The first course means certain failure. The second—a success that will stun you, as the success of the novel has stunned Bobbs-Merrill. In the same way and for the same reasons.

You have to make this choice, fully and consciously. There can be no compromise on *The Fountainhead*. There is no possible way in which it could preserve its power and appeal—yet also please those who hate it precisely for its kind of power and appeal. There is no possible way to make it successful—while destroying the very elements responsible for its success.

Do not attempt to devise a different plot or a different climax. It can't be done. It took me seven years to work out this one—and I know. Don't waste your time and money. This story—to be what it is—has to be told in these particular events. If you change them—you won't get "something like *The Fountainhead*." You'll get *nothing like The Fountainhead*. You know that people receive a sense of exaltation from this book. And you know that from the sublime to the ridiculous is just one step.

Be careful of those who advise you to take that step. A story about spiritual and artistic integrity is a difficult, dangerous, delicate subject. Think of the endless pile of tripe that's been attempted on this theme—it's the favorite attempt of all the arty phonies; and no other subject ever comes out in quite such a dreadful, dripping, maudlin, embarrassing way. That theme is like a tight wire. I am one of the very few writers who have ever walked it successfully. I know the steps which were necessary to walk it —and for this particular wire, there are no others. If you try some substitute steps—well, you know what can happen on tight wires. This one hangs pretty high.

Do not attempt to "humanize" the characters—to make them more conventional or nearer to the average. Conventional people would not do the things nor go through the events of this story. If you make the people average—you'll make the events preposterous. None of it then could or would be believed.

Do not attempt to "humanize" the dialogue. When people suggest that to you they do not really mean "human"—they mean the phony, cheap, grotesque Hollywood version of what is supposed to be "human"—the would-be truck-driver manner of self-consciously illiterate talk- ing (which no real truck driver ever uses)—the shoulder-slapping he- mannishness—the pseudo-slang—the artificially inarticulate—the coyly bad grammar. The public has never accepted *that* as human. People eve- rywhere refer to that sort of thing as "Aw, that's just Hollywood." And they mean the worst of Hollywood.

Do not allow one touch of that in the picture. You'll lose your au- dience's respect.

It is not "inhuman" to talk with precision and to express a clear thought clearly. A serious theme cannot be presented in sloppy, illiterate dialogue. Characters presented as intelligent must talk intelligently. Char- acters presented as unusual must not talk in bromides. Heroes do not say "Gee whiz"—nor any equivalent of it.

Let me warn you that my kind of dialogue requires expert acting and superlative direction. But can you hope to make anything of *The Foun- tainhead* at all—unless you have expert acting and superlative direction? No, the usual Hollywood ham or glamor-girl could not possibly deliver my lines. But what is the alternative? To rewrite the dialogue to the level where the ham is at home—scale the whole thing down to him—and then expect the result to be *The Fountainhead*?

Do not attempt to make the story "less intellectual." If you remove the intellectual element—there is nothing left. The events as such—without the deeper significance and motivations—simply do not make sense and contain no drama at all. Only the most inept kind of Hollywoodians believe that a serious theme is bad entertainment. It is the *best* of all entertainment. People like to feel uplifted when they leave a theater.

Do not attempt to make this story more "movie." It *is* a movie—in the real and best sense of the word. Jazzing it up or "Hollywoodizing" it will not improve it, but simply wreck it. There's not enough of the conventional in the story to base a conventional movie on. The story is so completely unconventional that it will play holy hell with any attempt to straitjacket it down to the standard and the usual. The story itself will defeat the attempt—and the result will be laughed at.

You have a Stoddard Temple on your hands. Unless everyone whom you select to work with you and whom you allow a voice in the production shares the spirit of Roark—what you'll get will be a Home for Subnormal Children.

There is a simple, specific rule to follow in any issue that arises in the production of *The Fountainhead*. Whenever anything is suggested, just ask yourself: *is this the way it's usually done in pictures?* If it is, you can be certain that it's the wrong thing for *The Fountainhead*. Whenever anything is criticized because *it hasn't been done that way before,* you can be certain that it's the right thing.

Above all else, I want to warn you against the most pernicious kind of menace—the people who will give you advice such as: *"The Fountainhead* has its own admirers—but there are also those who don't like it. Now if we just compromise with them a little, give them some touches they like—we'll please everybody. We don't have to worry about the book's admirers—we've got them anyway. Now let's appease the dissenters and we'll get everybody."

May God save you from this—if ever the pressure becomes too hard and you feel tempted to give in! *This* is the worst of all possible courses to take—the most surely fatal. It never works that way. It works exactly the other way around. You don't please everybody—you lose everybody. It's what's known as "sitting between two chairs."

Those who don't like *The Fountainhead* will never like it—no matter what you do. But those who like it will get so sick at any touch of the trite, the "human" and the "Hollywood"—that you'll make enemies of them. You'll find yourself without any audience at all.

Do not underestimate the admirers of *The Fountainhead*. They're not just readers who liked a book. It's much more than that. It is becoming something like a cult. There are now 260,000 copies of the book in print. By publishers' estimates, each copy sold represents five readers who've read the book. This means that *The Fountainhead* has, at present, a personal following of 1,300,000 people. It will be much, much larger by the time the picture is made and released.

And this is the choice you have to make: if you produce a picture of *The Fountainhead* which is really *The Fountainhead*—these readers will constitute an audience you can count on in advance, an audience ready for you and violently enthusiastic; they will become 1,300,000 voluntary press agents for the picture, just as they did for the book. If you produce a Hollywood compromise these same people will become 1,300,000 enemies who will stay away from the picture and keep others away; the same spontaneous combustion that burst out in favor of the book, will turn into indignant fury against the picture. And whom would you please in this last case? To what audience would you appeal? Those who did not like the book will not like the movie, no matter what you do.

Do not give in to "Hollywood." Do not give in to the director. Do not give in to the stars. The greatest box-office name will not save this picture if, in order to get that name, you had to compromise and destroy the story. Do not accept anyone for any job on this picture, if his ideas are not your own and a compromise is required to find "a middle road."

You must believe the thesis of *The Fountainhead* in regard to its production. That thesis is not just fiction and it does not apply just to architects: *man must act on his own judgment.* You must produce *The Fountainhead* on your own independent, original, uninfluenced judgment. There is no other way to do anything well in any sphere of life—and certainly not in this case. If you compromise and then hope to make a success of *The Fountainhead* by acting in a way exactly opposed to the way it teaches—it is *The Fountainhead* itself that will defeat you. And that would be ironic and tragic.

You had the integrity and the courage to be first to discover *The Fountainhead* in Hollywood. Do not let others rob you now of that courage and of your own vision. Make the picture as *you* think it should be made. Preserve your own judgment—as strictly and honestly as you can.

I know this is not easy to do when hundreds of people start pulling at you from all directions. One is apt to lose sight of where one's own judgment ends and somebody else's influence begins. You have to fight as hard a battle as Roark did. And as I did. He won. I won. You will.

■   ■   ■

To Ross Baker

December 11, 1945

Dear Ross:

I am glad that the pamphlet is now in the shape you wanted. It was one of the hardest assignments I've ever had to do.

I am happy that you liked *Anthem*. Your comment   "I don't believe I ever was more delighted to see the word 'I' than when it showed up in *Anthem*"—was a very valuable one. If that was your reaction to the book, I did accomplish my purpose in it.

For how many copies have you ordered paper beyond the 90,000? You didn't mention it and I naturally would like to know

I am returning the enclosed Literary Guild ads. Thank you for sending them to me—I did want to see them. I have a copy of the black-and-white one; it's vulgar, but not too bad as an ad. The colored one, however, is so appallingly dreadful that I don't want to keep it. No wonder it did not sell the book for the Guild people.

Those to whom such an ad would appeal could never read or like *The Fountainhead*. I don't even think they could read—period. And there's no moron on earth who wouldn't see that the quotation from the daily *Herald-Tribune* (in the box) is an out-and-out panning. Why do the Guild people really do such things to an author and to themselves? Apart from the fact that it's a gratuitous insult to me—is it practical? How do they expect to sell a book that "changes people's lives" by calling it "A six-ring circus"?

When they have on their hands a book that's growing in sales through its serious, philosophical, inspirational aspect—what kind of sense is there in trying to palm it off as a cheap, lurid dime novel? Is that good business?

No, I am not writing this as any kind of reproach to you—since you had nothing to do with the composition of this ad, and you did me the courtesy of sending it to me when I asked for it. I am writing this only because there is an extremely valuable lesson for us in this ad. I'd like you to consider it when you plan your own ads and publicity for the book. I could have told you two years ago that such an ad would flop and that the Literary Guild would not get any response to it. I suspect that you would have then thought I'm just an author who wants to be "highbrow." So I'm glad the Literary Guild did use this ad and did flop with it. Now you have an objective, practical demonstration. I think Bobbs-Merrill can save money, by learning from an experiment on which the Literary Guild wasted its money.

When you hear talk, comment, raves, fan letters, all on a single theme—an ecstatic kind of admiration for the figure of Howard Roark—you're not going to sell the book as "the great story of an amazing woman." You aren't—because *it ain't*. Furthermore, there's been nothing but books about "amazing women" ever since Scarlett O'Hara—practically every book ad has tried to feature that idea—and the public is sick of it. If that's all a book has to offer—there's no attraction in it any more, it's been worn out. *BUT* you have a book about an *amazing man*—a strong, positive character—a hero who is really a *hero*—and *that*, after a decade of male mush, is such a surprise to the readers that it's one of the main reasons of the book's popular appeal. Yet the Guild's sales experts hide that—and feature a naked woman. What's the sense in it?

As a practical suggestion: I think you should have some ads that contain some copy about the book—not just old quotations; every book can muster a few favorable quotations, that's not much of a sales point any more; quotes can be used—but not as the chief attraction. I think the copy should tell the readers something of the real nature of the book—at least a hint, an indication or a come-on. If we want to attract new readers, why not feature that which got us 200,000 old ones? Why hide the actual sales power of the book from its potential buyers?

I see you're afraid of the word "individualism." I think you're wrong, but okay, you don't have to use it. Use an equivalent. Take a tip from the King Features Syndicate people. Did you notice their caption for the strip? "Based on the great, bestselling novel of a man who dared to pit his genius against the world." They did that—I had nothing to do with it—I never discussed the subject of a caption with them and never saw it until I received the proofs. *There* is what I consider good salesmanship. They knew it was a man's story—and they stressed its real theme in a dramatic way.

If you don't want to stress philosophy in ads—stress Roark. The effect will be the same, only in popular form. I suggest something like this:

"The story of a great man who stood alone against the world."

"Howard Roark did all the things you were taught to believe as evil. Read this book to find out why thousands of readers consider him the noblest character in modern fiction."

"Why do most men think they're Howard Roark—and most women wish it were true?"

Isn't this last one lurid enough (by implication) even for the taste of the Literary Guild people? Yet it's true—and the readers, seeing such a line in an ad, will stop, wonder and feel intrigued.

As for quotes, there are two which you haven't used—and they would be excellent, not by themselves, but with the above kind of copy.

"Roark is like the sun . . . to see anybody else afterward is impossible."   *Saturday Review of Literature*

"Howard Roark towers over any man in the United States . . . Howard Roark is the hero (a real *hero*, not just the 'central character') in the most original and daring book of fiction written in this country—*The Fountainhead* by Ayn Rand."   *New York Journal-American*

You told me that you thought of advertising the book as "a modern classic." You were right. Try it. A book expert in New York told me that the biggest fiction sellers of all times (and the surest recipe for a bestseller) have always been religious novels with a good story (*Ben-Hur*, *Quo Vadis?*, *The Robe*)—and that *The Fountainhead* is a *religious novel*. So it is—but not in the conventional sense of the word; it gives to modern readers the same thing which simpler people get from a Biblical story—a sense of faith, courage and moral uplift. Why not try handling and selling the book as that? The results might surprise you—as this book has surprised you many times.

All this is in the nature of suggestions—not reproaches. I don't want you to think that I don't appreciate the fact of your advertising the book as you promised. I do appreciate it and am pleased to see good-sized Bobbs-Merrill ads. I merely hope that the above analysis might help your copywriters to get some good punch lines into the ads.

■   ■   ■

To Barbara Brandt, editor of Popular Publications, Inc.

December 11, 1945

Dear Miss Brandt:

Complying with your request, in your letter of November 2nd, to name my favorite short story, I have been thinking it over and I find it hard to answer—because I read very few short stories and would hesitate to name any one as "The Best I've Read."

However, the *very best* I've ever read, my favorite thing in all world literature (and that includes all the heavy classics) is a novelette called *Calumet K* by Merwin-Webster. It was first published in the *Saturday Evening Post* in 1901—and I think it is still available in a booklet published by Macmillan in 1923 [published now by Second Renaissance Books].

Would that fit your purpose? You might consider running it, perhaps, in two installments. If you are planning a reprint magazine, I do not believe that you will find a better story anywhere. And if you wish to use it under my recommendation, I am certain that it will appeal to all the readers of *The Fountainhead.* It's that kind of thing.

If you decide to use it, let me know and I will be glad to write a short preface for it—without charge, of course.

■ ■ ■

To John L. B. Williams, editor, Bobbs-Merrill

February 4, 1946

Dear Mr. Williams:

Thank you most sincerely for the beautiful flowers you sent me for Christmas. I can not tell you how much I appreciated it. It made me feel that it was a greeting from you, from New York City and, in a way, from *The Fountainhead*—so it was just the kind of reminder that made me happy on Christmas day. This sounds involved and romantic, but you understand authors, and most authors are romantic, and I am extremely so.

With my best wishes for a very happy year,

■ ■ ■

To Leonard Read

February 13, 1946

Dear Leonard:

Thank you. I am glad that you liked *Anthem*. No, it has not been published in this country at all. At the time I wrote it, my publishers were Macmillan—and they would not publish it because they had gone violently pink.

Just a few days ago I received a request from a magazine that wants to use *Anthem*. (How or where they ever heard of it, I don't know.) It's the *Famous Fantastic Mysteries* magazine, published by Popular Publications, Inc., at 205 East 42nd Street, New York City. I have never heard of them before. Do you happen to know whether they are a "reactionary" outfit? I suspect they must be.

I don't want to issue *Anthem* as a regular book now, because it is only a novelette and not big enough to follow *The Fountainhead*. But when you asked, in your letter: "Why don't we get it published?"—did you mean as a pamphlet—specifically by The Pamphleteers? I think that might be a very good idea—if a fiction story fits in with The Pamphleteers' program. Perhaps you might even be able to arrange to sell it, as a pamphlet, in bookstores and, if so, might get quite a large sale on the strength of my following. Let me know what you think of this.

I don't know whether you can buy a copy of *Anthem* from England, but I shall order some more copies for myself and will present you with one.

Thank you for the new issue of Rose Wilder Lane's reviews. I have read *Science and the Planned State* [by John Baker]. It is excellent and should be recommended to everyone on our side.

I am working very hard on the screenplay about the atom bomb. I would appreciate it very much if you would get me any information they care to give from the industrial concerns who were connected with the bomb project, such as DuPont, Stone & Webster, Westinghouse, General Electric, Kellogg, Eastman Kodak and others. I do not need statistical data on costs, materials, labor, etc., nor technical details, nor anything that is confidential. What I need are *factual incidents,* concrete episodes or events that occurred during the work on the project and that would illustrate the methods of free enterprise—concrete incidents showing the ingenuity, efficiency, resourcefulness of American industrial concerns in solving unprecedented problems—any incidents typical of and symbolizing free enterprise. I should like to use real facts in my screenplay, rather than invented episodes.

Incidentally, I have read *Manifesto for the Atomic Age* by Virgil Jordan. All I can say to you by way of a literary review is: *run.* Run from the National Industrial Conference Board as fast as you can.

■ ■ ■

To Mimi Sutton

February 15, 1946

Dear Mimi:

Before you undertake to bring Docky to Boston, we must clarify the situation, since your letter is not in accordance with our discussion in New York.

You write that I will have to pay for extra things Docky might need, such as dental work. This implies that you expect us to assume full financial responsibility for Docky from now on. We did not undertake to do that.

You write that you will minimize expenses and send me a monthly expense account. This implies that you expect us to give you an open charge account against which you will draw whatever is necessary and we will foot the bills. We did not undertake to do that.

You intended to have Docky move in with you, regardless of anyone's help, at your own cost—and we offered only to help you with her expenses, for one year, to finish high school, to the extent of a definite amount each week, agreed upon in advance. You told us that $10 per week would cover her expenses amply—and that is what we undertook to give you, plus her transportation from Cleveland, and furniture for her room, this last on condition that you give us an estimate of the cost in advance and that this cost is reasonable.

This is what we discussed in New York and it is not what you ask for in your letter.

Since you find that you cannot contribute to Docky's support at all, I don't see how you can bring her to Boston. Once she is there, she will have to be somebody's responsibility. One cannot tell what her expenses may possibly be. There may be medical expenses, debts she may decide to contract, or any number of things. The *total* support of a person can never be predicted. We did not and cannot assume such a responsibility, which amounts to adopting a child. This was the risk and responsibility which *you* wanted to assume. If you cannot do it, you should not bring Docky to Boston.

There is another point in your letter which we don't understand. You want Docky to come to Boston now and have her live in a place where her room and board will cost $15 a week. What about her carfare to school and her lunches? That should be at least another $5 a week, probably more. Since you can't contribute that, how is she going to go to school while she lives at that boarding house? It can mean only one of two things: either she will just sit in Boston and wait until you have an apartment; or we will be expected to send another five or ten dollars a week; which would be twice (or more) what you gave us as the maximum needed.

In view of all this, there are only two alternatives. One is to wait until you are settled and can tell us what weekly amount will cover Docky's expenses—provided it is clearly understood that the responsibility for Docky's support above that amount and for any emergencies is *yours*. Then, if the amount is not too much over your original estimate, we may contribute it—on the clear understanding that this will be all you can expect from us and that there are to be no sudden wires for money; and that should anything happen to prevent Docky from going to school—then we shall stop sending the money, since this money is to be strictly in the nature of a scholarship, for the purpose of Docky's going to school and for no other purpose.

The other alternative is to have Docky go to school in Cleveland. I am writing to Agnes to ask what the cost will be of having Docky finish school right where she is, while she is her mother's responsibility, which is much more proper. This seems to be the more practical plan, since it should not be very expensive for her to go to school while living at home.

■ ■ ■

To Agnes Papurt, Frank O'Connor's sister

February 15, 1946

Dear Agnes:

While Frank and I were in New York, Mimi asked us to help Docky finish high school. She told us that she would have Docky move in with her, when she was settled, and would send her to school. We offered to help her with Docky's expenses for that purpose—to the extent of a certain sum each week, agreed upon in advance.

Now we have received a letter from Mimi which makes us dubious about the whole undertaking. Not only does she raise the weekly amount she had asked for, but she also expects us to assume full financial responsibility for any expenses Docky may need—which we cannot do.

So we wonder whether it would not be a better plan to have Docky finish high school in Cleveland, and we would like you to tell us what such an undertaking would cost.

I must confess that Mimi gave us quite a confused picture of the situation. Could you tell us what the situation really is? Is Docky living with you now and what is she doing? Does she have only one year to go to finish high school? When and why did she stop going to school?

If she stopped because you could not afford the expense, we would like to help you with it. If the idea is agreeable to you, would you let us know how much you would need per week to cover Docky's expenses while she goes to school? If the amount is reasonable, we would be glad to contribute it, provided we know the exact amount in advance and do not have to assume responsibility for unforeseen expenses.

I hope you won't consider this offer as a presumption. We thought that Mimi was acting with your consent, but now we realize that she probably has not discussed it with you at all. Please let us know what you think of this. We would like to help Docky finish her education, if we can.

■   ■   ■

To Leonard Read

February 28, 1946

Dear Leonard,

I have read the prospectus of your proposed organization very carefully. No, you have not given our case away. But you have not presented it completely. You have covered only one minor, secondary aspect of it. The partial presentation of a great issue, featuring a secondary aspect, will amount in practice to giving the issue away. Therefore I don't think that your organization will serve your purpose—if this prospectus represents its program.

The mistake is in the very name of the organization. You call it The Foundation for Economic Education. You state that economic education is to be your sole purpose. You imply that the cause of the world's troubles lies solely in people's ignorance of economics and that the way to cure the world is to teach it the proper economic knowledge. This is not true—therefore your program will not work. You cannot hope to effect a cure by starting with a wrong diagnosis.

The root of the whole modern disaster is philosophical and moral. People are not embracing collectivism because they have accepted bad economics. They are accepting bad economics because they have embraced collectivism. You cannot reverse cause and effect. And you cannot destroy the cause by fighting the effect. That is as futile as trying to eliminate the symptoms of a disease without attacking its germs.

Marxist (collectivist) economics have been blasted, refuted and discredited quite thoroughly. Capitalist (or individualist) economics have never been refuted. Yet people go right on accepting Marxism. If you look into the matter closely, you will see that most people know in a vague, uneasy way, that Marxist economics are screwy. Yet this does not stop them from advocating the same Marxist economics. Why?

The reason is that economics have the same place in relation to the whole of a society's life as economic problems have in the life of a single individual. A man does not exist merely in order to earn a living; he earns a living in order to exist. His economic activities are the means to an end; the kind of life he wants to lead, the kind of purpose he wants to achieve with the money he earns determines what work he chooses to do and whether he chooses to work at all. A man completely devoid of purpose (whether it be ambition, career, family or anything) stops functioning in the economic sense. That is when he turns into a bum in the gutter. Economic activity per se has never been anybody's end or motive power. And don't think that any kind of law of self-preservation would work here—that a man would want to produce merely in order to eat. He won't. For self-preservation to assert itself, there must be some reason for the self to wish to be preserved. Whatever a man has accepted, consciously or unconsciously, through routine or through choice as the purpose of his life—that will determine his economic activity.

And the same holds true of society and of men's convictions about the proper economics of society. That which society accepts as its purpose and ideal (or to be exact, that which men think society should accept as its purpose and ideal) determines the kind of economics men will advocate and attempt to practice; since economics are only the means to an end.

When the social goal chosen is by its very nature impossible and unworkable (such as collectivism), it is useless to point out to people that the means they've chosen to achieve it are unworkable. Such means go with such a goal; there are no others. You cannot make men abandon the means until you have persuaded them to abandon the goal.

Now the choice of a personal purpose or of a social ideal is a matter of philosophy and moral theory. *That* is why, if one wishes to cure a dying world, one has to start with moral and philosophical principles. Nothing less will do.

The moral and social ideal preached by everybody today (and by the conservatives louder than all) is the ideal of collectivism. Men are told that man exists only in order to serve others; that the "common good" is man's only proper aim in life and his sole justification for existence; that man is his brother's keeper; that everybody owes everybody a living; that everybody is responsible for everybody's welfare; and that the *poor* are the primary concern of society, its holy shrine, the god whom all must serve.

This is the moral premise accepted by most people today, of all classes, all stages of education and all political parties.

How are you going to sell capitalist economics to go with that? How are you going to get them to accept as moral, proper and desirable such conceptions as personal ambition, economic competition, the profit motive and private property?

It can't be done. Their moral ideal has defined these conceptions as evil and immoral. So modern men are consistent about it. Our "common-gooder conservatives" are not. It's one or the other.

Here is the dilemma in which the public finds itself when listening to our conservatives: the public is told, in net effect, that collectivism is a noble, desirable ideal, but collectivist economics are impractical. In order to have a practical economy, that of capitalism, we must resign ourselves to an immoral society, that of individualism. This amounts to saying: you have a choice, you can be moral or you can be practical, but you can't be both. Given such a choice, men will always choose the moral, because it is preposterous to expect them to choose that which, by the speaker's own assertion, is evil. Men may be mistaken about what they think is good (and how mistaken they've been! And what lying they indulge in to deceive themselves about it!), but they will not accept evil with full, conscious intent and by definition.

Nor will men accept the idea that a moral ideal is impossible, that it cannot be achieved in practice. (And they are right about that, too—it's a thoroughly *unnatural* proposition.) Therefore it is absolutely useless to tell them that Marxist economics are impractical, so long as you're also telling them in the same breath that Marxism is noble. They will merely say:

"Well, if that's the ideal, and it cannot be achieved through the economics of capitalism, to hell with the economics of capitalism! If Marxist economics do not work, we'll find *something* that works. We *must* find it. So we'll go on experimenting. At least Marxism tries in the right direction, while capitalism doesn't even *try* to achieve the collectivist ideal. Capitalist economics do not even *try* to offer us a solution." How often have you heard this last one?

Now the most futile and ludicrous of all stands to take on this question is the one attempted at present by most of our conservatives. It may be called the "mixed philosophy." It's a parallel to the theory of a "mixed economy," just as untenable, silly and disastrous. It's the idea that capitalism can be morally justified on a collectivist premise and defended on the grounds of the "common good." It goes like this: "Dear pinks, our objective, like yours, is the welfare of the poor, more general wealth, and a higher standard of living for everybody—so please let us capitalists function, because the capitalist system will achieve all these objectives for you. It is in fact the only system that can achieve them."

This last statement is true and has been proved and demonstrated in history, and yet it has not and will not win converts to the capitalist system. Because the above argument is self-contradictory. It is *not* the purpose of the capitalist system to cater to the welfare of the poor; it is not the purpose of a capitalist enterpriser to spread social benefits; an industrialist does not operate a factory for the purpose of providing jobs for his workers. *A capitalist system could not function on such a premise.*

The economic benefits which the whole society, including the poor, does receive from capitalism come about *strictly as secondary consequences*, (which is the only way any *social* result can come about), *not* as primary goals. The primary goal which makes the system work is the personal, private, individual profit motive. When that motive is declared to be immoral, the whole system becomes immoral, and the motor of the system stops dead.

It's useless to lie about the capitalist's real and proper motive. The awful smell of hypocrisy that accompanies such a "mixed philosophy" is so obvious and so strong that it has done more to destroy capitalism than any Marxist theory ever could. It has killed all respect for capitalism. It has, without any further analysis, simply at first glance and first whiff, made capitalism appear thoroughly and totally *phony*.

The effect is precisely the same as that produced by Willkie, Dewey and all the rest of the "me-too," "I'll-get-it-for-you-wholesale" Republicans. Do not underestimate the common sense of the "common man" and do not blame him for ignorance. He could not, perhaps, analyze what was wrong with Willkie or Dewey—but he knew they were phonies. He cannot untangle the philosophical contradiction of defending capitalism through the "common good"—but he knows it's a phony.

Is there anything more offensive and preposterous than to tell an unemployed worker that the millionaire who is throwing a champagne party on his yacht is doing so only for his, the worker's benefit, and for the common good of society? Can you really blame the worker if he then goes out and demands that the yacht be confiscated? Is it economic ignorance that makes him do so?

The more propaganda our conservatives spread for capitalist economics while at the same time preaching collectivism morally and philosophically, the more nails they'll drive into capitalism's coffin.

That is why I do not believe that an economic education alone is of any value. That is also why you will find it difficult to arouse people's interest in the subject. I believe you are conscious of this difficulty; your prospectus shows anxiety on the scope of "creating a greater desire for economic understanding." You will not be able to create it.

The great mistake here is in assuming that economics is a science which can be isolated from moral, philosophical and political principles, and considered as a subject in itself, without relation to them. *It can't be done.*

The best example of that is Von Mises' *Omnipotent Government.* That is precisely what he attempted to do, in a very objective, conscientious, scholarly way. And he failed dismally, even though his economic facts and conclusions were for the most part unimpeachable. He failed to present a convincing case because at the crucial points, where his economics came to touch upon moral issues (as all economics must), he went into thin air, into contradictions, into nonsense. He did prove, all right, that collectivist economics don't work. And he failed to convert a single collectivist.

The organization desperately needed at present is one for *EDUCATION IN INDIVIDUALISM,* in every aspect of it: philosophical, moral, political, economic—in *that* order. (*That* is the actual order in which men's thinking proceeds on these subjects.) As part of such a program, an education in sound economics would be essential and valuable. Without it, it is a wasted effort.

I suspect that you might have been misled by the fact that you have heard businessmen accept the most preposterous economic fallacies; and you concluded that once the fallacies are exposed, the trouble is cured. Do not be deceived by superficial symptoms; the trouble goes much deeper than that; the trouble is not in the nonsense they accept, *but in what makes them accept it.*

I have written all this at such great length because I consider an organization created by you as potentially of tremendous importance. I consider you the only man in my acquaintance who has the capacity to translate abstract ideas into practical action and to become a great executor of great principles. Therefore I would hate to see you fail in what could be a great undertaking, by attempting it on the wrong premise and in the wrong direction.

I am particularly worried by the fact that you intend to start on such a grand scale (a $3,000,000 budget). If you do not lay the proper foundation first, a three-million-dollar skyscraper will collapse on you more surely and more disastrously than a little bungalow. You will find yourself widely, publicly known and tagged as another ineffectual outfit like the N.A.M. or the Industrial Conference board; your name will become that of "another one of those conservatives," instead of a new, powerful figure that would attract national attention by representing a real cause, and gain a following through courage, integrity and an unanswerable case, which is what I want you to become. You will find yourself caught in the ruins and forced to go on by the responsibility of so expensive an organization. The end of such a process is—Virgil Jordan.

It would be so much better and so much more practical to start in a smaller way and grow by a natural process rather than a forced one. You do not have at present the men and the educational material to use on a $3,000,000 scale. It would be better to gather your specialists and train them first, rather than release on the nation a flood of unprepared, "mixed philosophy" propagandists.

This letter is my contribution to your cause. If it helps you to analyze the situation, that is the best help I can offer you. If you agree with my analysis, I can continue to help you in this way, in the matter of philosophical direction. I know you have plenty of economists to call on for your work, but no people capable of undertaking the philosophical-moral part of it. Your main problem is to find them. And I will help you long-distance, to the extent that I can.

I shall be most interested in your answer to this.

As to your proposed radio program, I don't think it's a good plan. Personally, in spite of my interest in the subject, I'm afraid I would not listen to such a program. I think it would bore me. Five men talking on the same subject from the same general viewpoint would be more monotonous than just one man making a connected speech. The fact that the five men disagree on details would only add confusion, dilute and diffuse the subject and make the whole of the broadcast inconclusive and probably pointless.

If you decide to use *Anthem* in *The Freeman*, let me know. I'd like to have you do it, only I'd want to edit the story a little first; it's old and there are some passages which I think are bad writing and which I'd like to straighten out.

■   ■   ■

To Polly Goodwin, of the *Chicago Tribune* Sunday book section

March 14, 1946

Dear Miss Goodwin,

I have just finished reading *My Father Who Is on Earth* [a biography of Frank Lloyd Wright by his son John Lloyd Wright]. I am extremely sorry to say that I cannot undertake to review it.

The book is terrible. Just a sample: a son describes a great marital tragedy of his father in the following sentence: "And thus a private mangle bangle became a public jingle jangle extravaganza bonanza" (p. 111). This is typical of the book's intellectual quality and literary taste.

I have too much respect and admiration for Frank Lloyd Wright to criticize his son publicly as he deserves to be criticized. Besides, I don't think it's proper to review a book just to pan it, and certainly not in a featured review. And there is not a single thing I could say with honesty in favor of the book.

I am mailing the book back to you special delivery, so that you may have time to arrange for another reviewer.

If my answer disappoints you, let me assure you that it is as great a disappointment to me. I had looked forward to doing the review.

■   ■   ■

To Hal Wallis

March 19, 1946

Dear Boss:

This is not a legal agreement, but only a moral one. Here are the conditions of work I need in order to do my honest best:

1. Time to think over an assignment before I take it—not to be rushed into one unexpectedly at a moment's notice.

2. A long, detailed story conference with you alone before I start a script—with you telling me as completely as possible your idea of and approach to the story.

3. No weekly deadlines while I am on a script—leaving it up to me to deliver a sequence as soon as it is finished (as we did on *Love Letters*), so that I may present a completed piece of work and *not* so many pages each Friday.

4. Story conferences with you alone after you have read a sequence.

5. No mass story conferences while I am doing the first script. After I have finished the first script, I can meet with as many other people as you wish, and this will not upset me or throw me off.

6. Time, after I have finished a script, to go over it once more for a final polishing. I have not had a chance to take a last look at any of the things I've done, and yet, in my own work that is the time when I get my best perspective of the piece as a whole and eliminate the rough spots. This means that I cannot be cut off one assignment and put on another overnight, and have to start a new story while polishing the old one. (This happened between *You Came Along* and *Crying Sisters*.) The reason for this request is that I am unable in these conditions to do justice to either story; and I start a new story under a handicap, because the first two weeks on a new assignment is the time when I most need a clear head and exclusive concentration.

7. If big changes (such as whole added scenes) are made during the shooting of my story, please tell me about it in advance, and give me a chance to tell you my opinion of the change. The decision as to whether you want the change will still be yours—I want only a hearing, so that I can present my reasons for objecting (if I do), and you can decide whether my reasons are valid. (I don't insist on this point—but boy! what it would do to my feeling of confidence and interest in my work and its results!)

8. If you consult me about a story before you buy it, and I say I can make a good screenplay out of it—the responsibility is mine, and I can

then do an honest job (and the chances are that you *will* like it). Please do not expect me to be able to do a good job on a story about which I was not consulted—and do not consider me difficult if I say I dislike such a story. Please believe me that each writer is limited to a certain kind of thing, and that he is unable to do anything and everything equally well.

9. Whenever you have something *important* to tell me (like last Saturday)—please tell me yourself, not through a third person.

10. If at any time you are displeased by my personal attitude, or feel that I am becoming unreasonable, difficult, temperamental or arrogant, please call me in at once and tell me so, in order not to let a misunderstanding grow out of what one word could have corrected.

If this meets with your approval, I think we will both be very happy and the results will show in my work.

■ ■ ■

To Anna Rothe, of *Current Biography*

March 21, 1946

Dear Miss Rothe:

Please excuse me for my delay in filling the biographical questionnaire which you sent me.

I cannot give you the names of my parents nor any details about my childhood, because my family may still be in Russia and it might be embarrassing for them. Please do not mention this fact, and do not include in your article anything about my Russian background, except what I state in the questionnaire.

I am enclosing an autobiographical pamphlet which my publishers have printed for the purpose of answering the questions of readers about me. Since this does not give any dates, I have listed the chronological order of events in my life—on the inside pages of your questionnaire. Please do not publish my private home address.

You may use the biographical material which I am sending you only on condition that you will send me the proofs of your article for my approval before publication, and that you will not give as references for your article any publications of a leftist nature. You can readily see my reasons for this request. I shall return the proofs to you promptly after I receive them.

■ ■ ■

To Mary Shannon, a longtime friend

March 23, 1946

Dear Mary:

No, we didn't know or suspect that you and Rollie were going to break up. And your letter was quite a shock to both of us.

You say you want to hear my reaction. Don't you know what my reaction would be? Nobody has a right to blame you nor to pass judgment on such an issue—except yourself. If you found, to the best of your honest and serious judgment, that you had to leave Rollie—then that was the right thing to do. And I know that you wouldn't have decided it lightly.

I am terribly sorry that it had to happen, and I feel sad for both you and Rollie, simply because I thought you were happy together. But if you weren't happy and knew you couldn't be—then it was better to end it now, rather than live your whole life as a pretense. Sacrifice never works, it only destroys both people involved. No marriage can be preserved as a matter of mere duty. Every person's first duty is to find his real and honest happiness.

That's my reaction—with the advice that no reaction, neither mine nor anybody else's, is of any importance in such a question. Nothing is important, except your own best judgment.

So, of course, we're still friends—if that's what you questioned by implication in your letter.

I didn't write you sooner, not knowing where you would be. I hope this will reach you in Seattle. And I certainly hope that I'll see you (and "the object of your affections" too) if you're anywhere near Los Angeles. Until then—let me know what you are doing. And I *will* answer. Damn it all, I *do* feel concerned about you.

I want you to be happy, darling—whatever you decide to be your happiness. I know it must be terribly hard for you now. I hope you'll get what you really want and the kind of life you want. I'll stand by you and with you—at least in my wishes for your future.

■　■　■

To Mimi Sutton

March 24, 1946

Dear Mimi:

I have not answered you sooner, because I was waiting to hear from Agnes. I wrote to her at the same time when I wrote to you last—but have not had an answer from her.

I simply do not understand your letter of February 18th—except that it reads as if you were bargaining with us. You write that you would be willing to "pay half the expense" should any costly emergency occur to Docky. Who is to pay the other half?

What we wanted you to understand now, in advance, firmly and clearly, is that we *do not commit ourselves* to pay "the other half," nor any part of it, nor any extra sum whatever for any purpose. We do not accept any sort of financial responsibility for Docky's future in an unknown amount, large or small. If there is any risk involved in bringing Docky to Boston, the risk will be exclusively yours, not ours, and what you do about it will be your problem, not ours. We wanted this to be understood, so that you would not feel we left you holding the bag, should such an emergency arise.

The situation is really very simple, and the decision to make is up to you, not up to us. We offer to give you the money for Docky's transportation to Boston and a certain *stated* amount for her support each week for a year, provided she goes to school. That is all. If you want to take the risk of extra expenses that she might incur, such as illness—it's your risk and your responsibility. If you don't want to take the risk—then call the whole plan off. It's up to you.

But what is *not* up to you is to count on us for extra money in the future, should an emergency arise. We don't want to mislead you with any unstated or half-stated implications. If you want to go ahead with the plan as we discussed it specifically—do so, but on condition that we are never to receive any sudden demands for extra money and that you are not to expect it.

To simplify matters, we will send you $50 a month, for Docky, on the first of each month—provided she is actually going to school. If she stops school for any reason, then we stop sending the money. The enclosed $125 is for Docky's transportation and expenses up to May 1st. The rest is for her clothes, if she needs things immediately. You may use this money for her clothes, since you are not buying any furniture for her. But in the future you are to expect nothing except the $50 a month.

If this is all right with you, you may bring her on to Boston. If not—please send the money back to us. It's no use holding up Docky's schooling while we bargain about it—and I have no time to bargain.

Best of luck to Docky,

∎ ∎ ∎

To Lorine Pruette

March 25, 1946

Dear Lorine Pruette:

Thank you for your letter. I was happy to hear from you—because you will always have a very special place in my life, and a very special affection. You were and are the only reviewer who gave *The Fountainhead* an intelligent consideration. Fifty years from now, I will still say "Thank you" to you for that.

I am happy that you are watching the success of *The Fountainhead*. You are one of the very few people who have a right to consider that success as a tribute to their own judgment.

I shall send a copy of the book to Mr. and Mrs. Westerling in Holland. It *is* strange and rather touching that they should have discovered the book in Europe and decided to ask for it.

> Gratefully yours—as before,
> Now and ever,

■ ■ ■

To Fred Dickenson

March 25, 1946

Dear Mr. Dickenson:

Could you send me another set of the proofs of our strip of *The Fountainhead*? I would like to give it to a friend of mine. If this involves any special bother, such as running off an extra set, please don't do it, I don't have to have it. But if you have a set which you can spare, I would appreciate it very much.

Also, could I have the original drawings of some of the pictures? There are a few which I liked particularly and would like to frame for the walls of my study. Again, I don't know whether this is an unconventional request that would upset your system, rules or records—and, if so, please ignore it. I ask it only if it is feasible without giving you too much trouble. If it is, I would like to have the originals of the following drawings:

> Picture No. 1 of release No. 1
> Picture No. 1 of release No. 6
> Picture No. 2 of release No. 7
> Picture No. 3 of release No. 7
> (This last one above all)

I enjoyed very much watching the strip run here, in the *Los Angeles Herald-Express.* On the first day they announced it with a headline across the bottom of their *front page.* (I don't suppose that is called a "headline.") I thought that was really swell of them. I enjoyed being "a newspaperwoman with a byline" for thirty days (courtesy of Fred Dickenson). I always wanted to be a newspaperwoman, anyway.

■ ■ ■

To Gerald Loeb

March 25, 1946

Dear Gerald:

Thank you for your correspondence with Warner Brothers re: Frank Lloyd Wright sets for *The Fountainhead,* and for your interest in this issue. I still do not know what the final decision on this will be. Mr. Blanke told me only that no decision could be made until a production date is set for the picture—and this has not been set as yet.

I'll keep in mind your gracious offer to use the model of your house in the film, and I hope Warner Brothers will decide to take advantage of it.

Thank you also for the interesting article on the stock market situation, which you sent me. I must say I am still a little bewildered on any matter pertaining to Wall Street and do not understand the actual process of its function. Someday I'd like you to explain it to me from the ground up, if you ever have the time.

■ ■ ■

To Franklin Brewer

March 25, 1946

Dear Franklin:

Your libretto of *Masterpiece* is delightful. I enjoyed reading it, and your lyrics are as good as I remembered them to be, or better. My congratulations.

I have checked on the situation with *Chantecler* and here is what I found out: the plays of Rostand are *not* in the public domain; the representative of the French Authors' Society, which handles them, is right here in

Hollywood, and I spoke to him; he told me that he doubts whether I could get the rights, because, unfortunately, *Chantecler* was made into an opera quite a long time ago (this shows, at least, that I had a good idea). The representative thought that the musical rights would be so involved that it might be impossible to clear them; however, he will inquire from France and will let me know exactly how it stands, in about two or three weeks.

I shall let you know as soon as I hear from him. Don't be too disappointed if this project proves to be impossible. It was only a tentative idea of mine—and even if I can get the rights, I am not sure that I'll be able to get the time to do the adaptation.

■ ■ ■

To Archibald Ogden

March 28, 1946

Archie darling:

I am enclosing a little love letter ["To the Readers of *The Fountainhead*"] to you. Bobbs-Merrill asked me to write this piece for the purpose of answering the questions of readers about me. They get a lot of questions. I wish you were there to answer them.

Thanks a lot for your letter. I was delighted to hear from you. If you still think of me across an ocean, I guess you'll always think of me. So I won't feel it's too one-sided, because I'll always think of you.

I'm glad you're watching *The Fountainhead* on the bestseller lists. Yes, it's still going strong. You may be proud to know how many countries have decided to follow the example set by you and publish *The Fountainhead*: nine of them, including the USA. Here's the list of foreign rights sold: England, Brazil, Argentina, Sweden, Switzerland-France, Switzerland-Germany, Holland, Denmark. There are more coming, other countries are negotiating for it. *You* had to risk your job to make one country publish it. Doesn't this make you feel global?

I have just obtained six extra months of freedom from my studio—for the purpose of working on my new novel, and I'm working on it now. Of course I will send you a copy of the manuscript for your personal opinion and advice. Nobody's literary opinion will ever mean as much to me as yours.

I was glad to hear that you're enjoying your job—and I'm not at all surprised that you're successful with it. I was afraid you would be. But do you mind if I remain a little skeptical about your account of England as "a very pleasant spot"? However, I hope it remains pleasant—for you.

You say you hope that "I will still consider you a brand worth snatching from the flames." Darling, I always will—and you're the only brand of this kind whom I give a damn about. But I'm growing older and wiser. I'm beginning to see that I cannot snatch you from it, and nobody can, except yourself. And I think you will do it someday.

■ ■ ■

To Vladimir Kondheim, her cousin

March 28, 1946

Dear Volodia:

You wrote to me that you have heard from Ludmilla, and you wanted to ask my advice about your situation, when I come to New York. I find that I will not be able to go to New York this spring (I might go later, in the fall, but I am not sure of it). So I want to try to give you my advice by mail—because I am worried about you and I think I understand what you wanted to ask me.

If you really want my advice, if you really think that I am intelligent and you attach importance to my opinion, here is my *most urgent* advice: You must forget everything and everybody, and ask yourself only *one* question: *what do you want for your own personal happiness?*

If you want to stay with Peter, you must stay with her. If you want to take Ludmilla back, you must take her back. Your personal, honest, sincere happiness is all that matters in such a situation. A decision like the one you're facing cannot be made in any other way—*only* on the ground of your sincere desire. If you consider anything else, the results will be disastrous, no matter what you do.

If my opinion ever meant anything to you at all, I don't know how to impress upon you strongly enough that *self-sacrifice never works.* Lying and dishonesty never work—and it is a great human tragedy that people think dishonesty can work "for a good motive." It can't and it doesn't, for any motive, good or bad—and, besides, self-sacrifice is *not* a good motive. It's the rottenest motive of all, and leads to the worst results for everybody concerned, for yourself and for the person to whom you sacrifice yourself.

You must not think of Ludmilla or of Peter, you must not think of how either one of them feels, you must not think of your past, you must not think of any duty you owe to anybody. In a situation like this, *you don't owe any duty to anyone but yourself.* You cannot help others at the price of a lie; to sacrifice your own happiness is to attempt to live a lie; no motive, selfish or unselfish, can change the fact that a dishonest action is dishonest; so, instead of helping others, it will only destroy them. You must think first, above all, and in complete honesty, of what *you* want.

If you don't do this, if you decide one way or another because you think it's your "duty" to the woman involved—you will cause a triple tragedy. If you are unhappy, you will make the woman you choose twice as unhappy. Those things cannot be hidden; no well-meaning hypocrisy will help. You will only succeed in ruining three lives.

If you are thinking of any "unselfish" motive, then, for God's sake, choose the woman you really want, for the sake of unselfishness, if nothing else. It's the only way to achieve any happiness for anyone concerned, if you're not thinking of yourself.

I believe that you do not want to go back to Ludmilla or to take her back. If so, then in the name of God, *don't do it!* It doesn't matter what your past life with her has been. It doesn't matter whether you have hurt her or she has hurt you or both. If you don't love her, it doesn't matter whether it's her fault or yours. Nothing on earth, *nothing*, can demand that you sacrifice to her what remains of your life.

You write: "you can advise me only when I have told you all the details of my previous life." You are making a great mistake right there. The details of your previous life *do not matter. Nothing* can justify self-sacrifice.

The proper and practical thing to do is only to help Ludmilla financially. Send her some food while she is in a helpless position in Germany. Then, as soon as it is possible, arrange for a divorce, if that is what you really want. After that, you may help her financially if she needs it and if you are able to do it. But *not* at the price of any self-sacrifice.

You are fifty years old. You have had a very hard life and much unhappiness. You have a right to be happy now, in the years that could be the best of your life. It's not only your right, it's *your duty* to be happy. If you think it would be noble to sacrifice these years—don't fool yourself. It wouldn't be noble. It would be vicious and monstrous.

I think you have been happy with Peter—and, if you have, you must remain with her. If you are not happy with Peter or with Ludmilla—then leave them both. The issue is really simple. Ask yourself what *you* want, answer it honestly—and if you act on that, whatever you do will be right.

If you don't act on that, but pull something self-sacrificing—whatever you do will be wrong.

That is my advice, Volodinka. If you ever valued my advice, now is the time I would like you to consider it most earnestly.

You may show this letter to Peter, if you want to.

Let me know what you decide.

Love,

■ ■ ■

To Anna Rothe

April 6, 1946

Dear Miss Rothe:

Thank you for sending me the biographical article about me. I have corrected it and am returning it fast, as you see. You may publish it only as I have corrected it.

The article surprised me a great deal. Since you sent it to me, I take for granted your good faith and courtesy. But I believe that you have not read it yourself before you mailed it to me. Have you seen what your writers perpetrated on page 7? Do you believe that I would let things like that be printed with my permission and cooperation? I dislike to think of the motive which prompted those who made these selections. If objectivity was the purpose in the selection of these quotations—then why was the review of the Sunday *Times* Books so conspicuously omitted, to name just one of several others?

There is no obligation upon *Current Biography* to publish any biography of me at all. But if they find that they want to do it and if they get requests for it, they are publishing it for people who are interested in reading about me. They have, therefore, no moral (or legal) right to use me and my life as a sounding board for smears.

I must insist that you use no quotations from reviewers at all about *The Fountainhead*—good or bad. A biography is a factual record; opinions have no place in it.

I think you owe me the courtesy of stating what the theme of *The Fountainhead* actually is—as I have marked it on your copy. Otherwise, the article gives the impression that it's a novel about architecture; it isn't.

Also, you should state the real history of the sale of the book—as I have marked it. It was *not* an immediate success. People such as those you quote did their damnedest to prevent it from being. I want the record to be kept straight.

If you find that the article is now too short, I suggest that you quote a few things from the printed letter I sent you. This will give your readers a truer picture of me than anything else can—and a true picture of me is, I presume, what they want.

For my protection, as well as yours, I would suggest that you send me the actual proofs of the article before you print it. I shall return them as promptly.

■   ■   ■

To Ethel Zeugner, a fan

April 11, 1946

Dear Mrs. Zeugner:

As to your question, the Stoddard Temple in my book was pure invention. I have never seen or heard of the unfinished temple in Chicago to which you refer. Nor have I read any mentions of it in the histories of modern architecture. If you have more information about it or the name of its architect, I would be curious to know about it, too.

■   ■   ■

To Leonard Read

April 16, 1946

Dear Leonard:

I am enclosing "The Scope of Economics and of Economic Education." I have read it very carefully and to tell you the truth I find it completely confusing: I cannot quite figure out its point or purpose. It either contains too much or not enough. If it's intended as a defense of capitalism, it's not enough. If it's intended as a prospectus for your educational program, it should not contain arguments, it sounds too much on the defensive; it should then contain nothing but statements.

The dictionary definition of economics, which you give on page 1, is clear and valid as it stands. So I don't see the point of the elaboration that follows. I fail to see the purpose of the argument that to economize means to use to best advantage, therefore economics concerns only free men. This is not a good argument and will not hold. By this very definition, collectivists will claim that the best choice men can make is to let a central planning board plan all their economic activities, using everyone to best advantage, eliminating waste, duplication, etc. In fact, this is just what the collectivists *do* claim; society as a single collective, they say, functions much more economically than a group of free, competing individuals; they call this last "economic chaos." Of course, we'll say that this isn't true, that collectivism doesn't accomplish any of its claims and that free enterprise is the only system that works to man's best advantage. Then it becomes, or remains, an argument about the merits of two economic systems. The above definition accomplishes nothing; it can be claimed by both systems as a starting point for argument.

Page 3 of the article contains the truly dangerous confusion. To refer to burglary as an economic, though misdirected, activity is really to rob definitions of all meaning. Burglary comes under the head of "crime." "Criminal activity" and "Economic activity" are two distinct conceptions. You may prove, and rightly, that the rulers of totalitarian economies engage in criminal activities; that their policies belong in the class of criminal violence. But you cannot say that a common burglar is engaged in economic activity. Yet this is what you do say, in a sentence such as: "Burglary may be an economic activity for a few successful and unpunished burglars." This is really talking Communist dialectics and adding to the present day idea that "all terms are relative."

Why do you say—paragraph 2, page 3—that Communism, etc. restrict the economic opportunity "for at least a part of the citizenry"? Which part of the citizenry is not restricted under Communism? Do you mean to imply that Commissars have freedom of enterprise?

If you tell me what this article is intended to accomplish and to whom it is directed, I may be more helpful with positive suggestions on how to rewrite it.

■ ■ ■

To Mimi Sutton

April 30, 1946

Dear Mimi:

I am enclosing the check for Docky, for the month of May.

You don't have to send me the rent receipts, but I will expect to get

Docky's report cards. I hope she has started going to school. I feel sure her reports will be good, since she was in the school for exceptional children in Cleveland. Tell her for me that ability is the only important thing in the world, and the most wonderful one, and the only real human virtue. (This is her old aunt speaking.)

Let me know how she's getting along.

■   ■   ■

To Leonard Read

May 18, 1946

Dear Leonard:

I am enclosing your correspondence with Pat [Isabel Paterson], which you asked me to return. I am glad you showed it to me. Thank you. It has solved a dilemma for me, even though it was a bad shock.

No, you were not too rough on Pat in your letter. I admire your letter, because of the clear and honest explanation you gave her. You were wrong in simply staying away from her for a long time, without explanation—but I have done the same thing in regard to her (for somewhat different reasons), yet you and I are not people who evade issues. The truth of the matter is that she forces her friends into such a position—and our fault, yours and mine, is in not having recognized this sooner.

Here is what shocked me in Pat's letter to you: Pat read *Anthem* in 1942, long before she read *The Fountainhead* (I was writing *The Fountainhead* then); it was, in fact, the first book of mine Pat had ever read. She told me then that she did not like it. She did not mention the reasons she gives you in her letter—she stated only that she did not like it, because she felt the characters weren't characterized enough, whatever that means. I did not argue with her nor question her any further, because I have never respected her literary judgment as I do her political one, so I let it go at that. She did not refer to the thesis of *Anthem*, and I did not discuss it.

Much later, after long abstract discussions with me and after she read *The Fountainhead* (do you know that she doesn't like *The Fountainhead*, either?), Pat understood and evaluated my theory of the proper ethics of individualism, and told me that it was "the greatest ethical discovery since Christianity." (These are her exact words.)

Now here is what's terrible: my whole theory of ethics is contained in *Anthem*. That was my first statement of it on paper. Everything I said in *The Fountainhead* is in *Anthem*, though in a briefer, less detailed form, but there explicitly, for all to see who are interested in ideas. And *that* is the book about which Pat tells you: "yes, I know all that; it is tedious to have to go over it."

Sure, she knows all that—*now*; she's learned it from me. But she did not know it at the time when she read *Anthem*. She was reading a book which presented what, by her own estimate, was a great new idea—and she found it uninteresting, because it had no new idea to offer.

Do you see what this means?

I have never approved of Pat's incredibly offensive manner toward people, you and me included, but I thought that it could be explained (if not justified) by her fierce intellectual honesty, her strict devotion to ideas and her constant suspicion that others do not take ideas as seriously as she does, and are not as scrupulous about intellectual matters as she is. Well? If she was capable of reading *Anthem* and missing its idea—what right has she to scream at you that you haven't read her book carefully enough or haven't given it enough thought? What right has she to scream at anyone?

Well, that's that.

Forgive me if I went into this at such length. I felt I had to tell you this. I didn't answer you sooner, because this was hard for me to face and to say. But I repeat that I am glad you sent me Pat's letter, because I'd rather face the truth, whatever it is, than be protected from disappointment.

I will keep this confidential, as you asked. Some day, when I see Pat in person, I would like to talk to her about this and say to her what I said in this letter—but I won't, unless you permit me to. If you'd rather I didn't, I won't. And I suppose there would be no point in discussing it with her, anyway.

Now to a more cheerful subject.

I have read your "I'd Push the Button" speech—and I cheered aloud as I read it. After my harsh criticisms of some of the articles you sent me, I am delighted to be able to say that this one is excellent, first-rate, and perfect. Not a single slip to "give away" our case. Clear thinking and beautiful presentation. And the last two sentences in it are magnificent. My congratulations to you.

As I've said to you before, I seldom find any major intellectual mistakes or any indications of basic collectivism in the things which you write yourself. Usually I find that I disagree with you only on lesser points or on the manner of presentation; your basic premises are sound. It is only when you allow someone else to compose something for you or with you that collectivism creeps in. Be careful of reformed collectivists. I am not sure that they are ever completely reformed.

■   ■   ■

To Waldo Coleman, a fan

May 18, 1946

Dear Mr. Coleman:

Thank you for your letter. I liked it. It read as if your suggestions for what you take to be factual inaccuracies in *The Fountainhead* were prompted by a sincere interest, not by any ill feeling—so I will answer you in detail.

1. You say that "the scale for quarry workers is $1.62½." So it is—now. You must have overlooked the fact that the quarry sequence in my book took place in 1928. I had a New York granite company check through back records to tell me the exact scale for that year, and the one I have is correct.

2. As to the business about the marble setters, I don't know whether unionization was that strict in Connecticut in 1928, but if it was, do you think that would have made any difference to the characters and the situation involved?

3. You say that a D.A. would have arrested Roark for a sex crime. Even if he knew about it, the D.A. could do nothing about it unless Dominique pressed charges. Would she?

4. You say that Roark would not be allowed to take an exam for a license—"You couldn't get away with that in Nevada." Well, I don't know about Nevada, but in the state of New York a man without a college degree is allowed to take an examination if he has worked in an architect's office for a certain number of years. In my story Roark had worked the exact number of years necessary.

As to your analysis of Dominique's psychology, you are wrong in explaining it as a reversion to what you call a "caveman type." It is not a reversion, it is the way any truly feminine woman feels about a truly masculine man. Think that one over.

You say you will be watching for my next book. I hope you will like it. I am working on it right now.

■   ■   ■

To Betty Andree, a fan

May 24, 1946

Dear Miss Andree:

Thank you for your letter.

I am glad that *The Fountainhead* helps you when you feel unhappy, but you should not feel that you are "a peculiar sort of failure" at the age of 18. If, as you say, you want to write, you cannot expect to be a success that early, you must be prepared to struggle towards the time when you will be ready to write. I feel a great sympathy for all young writers, and I wish you the best of luck.

■ ■ ■

To Winfield L. Holden, a fan

May 24, 1946

Dear Mr. Holden:

You told me not to thank you for your letter, but I do. I appreciate it very much.

No, I do not intend to write another book "like" *The Fountainhead*, but I am working on my next novel now, and I don't think you will find that it is a blasphemy against *The Fountainhead*.

As to your question on why I did not kill Ellsworth Toohey—the reason is that the kind of defeat he suffered was much worse than physical destruction.

■ ■ ■

To Airman First Class Victor Hugo, a fan

May 24, 1946

Dear Mr. Hugo:

No, I don't feel insulted that you say that you regard *The Fountainhead* "in the nature of a psychiatric treatment." It was intended as that—or rather as a philosophical treatment. Philosophy is the only basis on which psychiatry can rest.

If my book has helped you to gain confidence in yourself, that is one of the best reactions I could have from a reader.

■   ■   ■

To Allee Chatham, a fan

May 24, 1946

Dear Miss Chatham:

I was glad to hear that you consider me a desirable relative, but I am sorry to disappoint you, because Rand is only my pen name; so we are not related.

We can still be friends, however, and I am glad that you liked *Love Letters*.

■   ■   ■

To Cadet Thomas Gee, a fan

May 24, 1946

Dear Mr. Gee:

I am glad that you liked *The Fountainhead* and that you found it extremely logical.

No, it is not an "oversimplification." Be very careful of that word. It is the one used at present by all collectivists whose purpose is to make you think that all truth must be complicated beyond any human understanding and that, therefore, you should do nothing but take their orders.

■   ■   ■

To Daniel Goodman, editor of *Analysis*

May 24, 1946

Dear Mr. Goodman:

I appreciate your interest in my work, but I can not accept your suggestion that I become a contributor to *Analysis*. *Analysis* is a publication advocating the single tax theory, to which I am most emphatically opposed. A theory which advocates state ownership of land is pure collectivism, and it doesn't matter whether its advocates consider themselves individualists or not.

Without private property in land there can be no private property right at all, and without property rights no other kind of rights are possible.

■ ■ ■

To Mrs. Robert Reid, a fan

May 24, 1946

Dear Mrs. Reid:

Don't ever apologize for your brains, if you were able to understand and enjoy *The Fountainhead*. As you see, I do not apologize for saying this.

Do not be surprised if you have found intellectuals who do not like my book. They are the Ellsworth Tooheys of our present age.

■ ■ ■

To Armitage Watkins, of Ann Watkins, Inc., AR's literary agent

May 28, 1946

Dear Mr. Watkins:

Your letter of May 24th was certainly a bombshell to me. I am extremely indignant at the piracy of *We the Living* by the Italian producers, and at the use which they made of it. Thank you for finding this out for me. I shall now blast them with the kind of lawsuit which they deserve. I am amazed at the whole procedure, and can not understand how a picture company which is still in business could have done such a thing. How did they hope to get away with it?

■ ■ ■

To John C. Gall

May 28, 1946

Dear John:

I have always thought that if I ever had to be involved in a big lawsuit with political implications, I would choose you as my champion. Well, here is the case—and if you find that you can handle it for me, I would like very much to have you represent me.

I am enclosing copies of two confidential letters which I received from my agent yesterday, and which will tell you the whole case. *We the Living* is my first novel, and was published in Italy by Baldini and Castoldi in 1937. This is the first I have heard about its piracy for the screen by an Italian motion picture company.

As you see, it will probably be a big and difficult case. I gather from Mr. Downes' letter that the Italian producers, who were Fascists, are now connected with what is probably the "pink" elements in the Allied Commission. I suppose that such a case would have to be handled through American government departments, and that there will be difficulties or obstructions from the "reds" in government positions in Washington. I want, above all, to be able to rely on the political views of my attorney; so I hope very much that you can undertake this case.

I have not consulted anyone about this as yet, and do not quite know what such a case might involve and what I should do about it. It seems to me that I should sue not only for whatever royalties are due me, but also and primarily for the damage to my reputation as a writer, damage caused by the fact that a book of mine was produced as Fascist propaganda. *We the Living* is a story laid in Soviet Russia, and it is anti-Soviet but, above all, it is anti-dictatorship. Therefore, it is as much anti-Fascist as anti-Communist, and I resent, more than the financial piracy, the use of my material or the distortion of my message into a pro-Fascist picture.

It also seems to me that I should claim damages as an American citizen against the Italian producers' use of my property in war time for the purpose of enemy propaganda and for showing in enemy countries. On the purely financial side, I think I should sue not merely for whatever author's rights the two pictures have earned, but for the fact that the making and release of these pictures has spoiled the world market of my book or what is known as world motion picture rights, which are bought by American producers only if a property has never been used on the screen anywhere.

There may be other angles involved, and I would like you to tell me just what the proper legal approach to such a case must be, and on how many different counts I must sue these people. As you will see from Mr. Downes' letter, the financial amount involved will be tremendous, but the case will be very difficult politically, and I would like you to tell me if there are any precautions I must take against the probable opposition of the "reds" in Washington.

■　■　■

To Waldo Coleman

June 5, 1946

Dear Mr. Coleman:

Here is another letter to leave to your heirs, since you say that is what you intend to do with my first one.

Your confession about your personal problem made me feel that I have to lecture you a little bit. I am afraid that you have misunderstood the relationship of Roark and Dominique in a very improper way. You write as if you thought that the lesson to be derived from it is that a man should force himself on a woman, and that she would like him for that. But the fact is that Roark did not actually rape Dominique; she had asked for it, and he knew that she wanted it. A man who would force himself on a woman against her wishes would be committing a dreadful crime. What Dominique liked about Roark was the fact that he took the responsibility for their romance and for his own actions. Most men nowadays, like Peter Keating, expect to seduce a woman, or rather they let her seduce them and thus shift the responsibility to her. That is what a truly feminine woman would despise. The lesson in the Roark-Dominique romance is one of spiritual strength and self-confidence, not of physical violence.

In regard to the girl who sent you *The Fountainhead*, I would guess that sex was not the point she wanted you to see in the book; sex is only a minor aspect of a much wider theme—which is man's integrity—and that is probably what she wanted you to see.

Thank you for saying that the twelve editors who rejected *The Fountainhead* were "out of character in the publishing business." I got a kick out of hearing that.

■   ■   ■

To Alan Collins

June 24, 1946

Dear Alan:

Thank you for your letter of June 20th.

I would be delighted if Bobbs-Merrill considered *The Fountainhead* "too valuable a property to sell," as Ross Baker told you. My whole complaint against Bobbs-Merrill is the fact that I do not think they consider *The Fountainhead* valuable enough.

If their opinion of the book's value remains merely an opinion or a personal emotion, that is of no practical importance to me or to them. An opinion is important only when expressed in action. If Bobbs-Merrill want me to trust them, let them mean what they say: let them show *in action* that they consider *The Fountainhead* a valuable property.

If, in regard to advertising, publicity, uninterrupted supply of copies, printings ordered well in advance, etc., Bobbs-Merrill do as much for me as other publishers do for their top writers, I will have no reason to wish to leave them. If they do not, I will.

The truth of the matter is that Bobbs-Merrill want to keep what they consider a top property at the cost (to them) of an average novel. And they hope to keep me on their list on the terms of an average novelist. Well, it can't be done. Nobody can have his cake and eat it, too.

Since I have consented several times to amend our original contract in favor of Bobbs-Merrill, this is the time when I want them to amend it in my favor. I want you to include in our letter of agreement about the foreign rights, the following amendments: Paragraph 4 of our original contract is to be amended to the effect that the publishers shall have to obtain my consent about the date and time when a popular reprint edition of *The Fountainhead* is to be issued (if it is ever issued). (I want to make sure that Bobbs-Merrill do not issue it too soon, that is, not until the full-price sale of *The Fountainhead* is exhausted. They have believed it exhausted so often and so mistakenly in the past that I want to have this protection for the future.) In Paragraph 14 it is specified that the rights to *The Fountainhead* will revert to me if and when the publishers allow it to remain out of print for six months. I should like this changed to one month.

There is, also, another point in regard to the future which I am wondering about, and which perhaps should be rectified now. My contract contains no provision for what is to happen if Bobbs-Merrill ever go bankrupt. I think there should be an agreement to the effect that in such case all rights to *The Fountainhead*, as well as the plates and the remaining copies revert to me. (I believe that such provisions are now put into book contracts.) No, I do not expect Bobbs-Merrill to go bankrupt, but since the book apparently will have a very long sale, I would like to be protected against such a possibility in the distant future. I do not insist on this point, unless you think it is advisable. If you do, please include it in the above letter of agreement with them.

As to my next novel, I am progressing on it very well and hope to have it finished by Spring of 1947. But don't hold me to the date, since I can never tell for sure in advance.

■   ■   ■

To John William Rogers, book editor of the *Chicago Sun* book section

June 24, 1946

Dear Mr. Rogers:

Thank you for your letter of June 18th. I assume that it represents your honest opinion about my work—I appreciate it—and I can only regret that you are not the book editor of some other newspaper.

I cannot write for the *Chicago Sun.* If you want to know my reasons, look up the *Chicago Sun*'s review of *The Fountainhead.* A newspaper which considers a review of this kind as honest or competent, must be judged accordingly.

■   ■   ■

To James C. Ingebretsen, attorney and one of the "Pamphleteers," an activist group that published *Anthem* and other books and articles

June 24, 1946

Dear Mr. Ingebretsen:

I am enclosing your draft of a pamphlet for *Anthem.* I think it is excellent on the whole, and whoever wrote this is a good press agent. I have made a few minor corrections, which I have listed separately on the enclosed page. The numbers I have marked on the pamphlet correspond to the numbers of the paragraphs which I think should replace the passages I have crossed out.

To give you my reasons for these changes:

1. The sentence, "Can such things ever come to pass," on the cover of the pamphlet is a little bewildering as it stands. I have shown it to three people, and all had the impression that "such things" referred either to *Anthem*, to Ayn Rand or to *The Fountainhead*—since there is no indication that it refers to the content of *Anthem.* Therefore, I think it would be better to omit it entirely or to substitute the paragraph I have marked as #1.

2. "A novelette you will never forget!" is not too good, because it

rhymes, and because it has been said about books very often. My suggested paragraph #2 would make the definition of the story a little more interesting.

3. I have reworded the third paragraph on page 2 of the pamphlet in order to make it clearer that *Anthem* is a fiction story and not a nonfiction treatise.

I would suggest very strongly that you omit from page 3 the line, "Order copies now at the special low quantity rates." It sounds a little bit shocking and improper after your last paragraph on page 2. It has too much the tone of a special bargain sale. I don't think it is necessary, since your first paragraph on this page followed by the order blank conveys and implies the same thing more tactfully.

At the top of page 2, the line, "Too daring for 1937," is very good and intriguing, but the line following it, "Too incredible," weakens the effect by qualifying it. I suggest that you eliminate this last.

For a minor correction, it would be better if you did not say, "*Her* US publishers turned it down," because my publishers at the time was Macmillan, but people would suppose that the accusation is against Bobbs-Merrill; so it is best to have the line read merely, "US publishers turned it down."

I am very happy to have *Anthem* published by Pamphleteers, Inc., and I wish a great success to all of us.

■　■　■

To Ellis G. Bishop, advertising manager of Royal Typewriter Co.

July 3, 1946

Dear Mr. Bishop:

I am enclosing my endorsement of the Royal typewriter [see below].

This statement is what I really would like to say—but if you find that it is too long for your purposes, please let me know and I will try to say something briefer.

I am also enclosing a copy of the release which I have signed. As you will see, I have modified it a little, and I have added the provision that I want to see any copy in which my name is used in advance of publication. I hope this is acceptable to you.

I have no photograph of myself using my typewriter, but I shall be glad to pose for one if you wish to have one taken.

Thank you very much for the new machine which I have just purchased. I hate to use bromides, but "it is a thing of beauty and a joy forever" (but don't use THAT in print). I appreciate very much your courtesy in making it possible for me to get it.

Cordially yours,

The first big investment I ever made (big for me at the time) was in my Royal Portable Typewriter, seventeen years ago. It has stood by me ever since, without repairs, without a single breakdown under the terrible battering I have given it.

At a time when there is too much crying over "the poor consumers," here is one consumer who wishes to acknowledge a debt of gratitude to the productive genius of American free enterprise. Only in America could such a typewriter be made—and only in America could I write what I wrote on it.

■   ■   ■

To Ruth E. Meilandt, of the Pamphleteers

July 3, 1946

Dear Miss Meilandt:

Thank you for your letter of July 2nd. I am returning the proof of the cover of *Anthem* which you sent me.

I am sorry to say that I do not like the cover. I object to it for three reasons:

1. It is not well designed, because the actual focus of attention is the large blank space,

2. The title, *Anthem*, being in handwriting is hard to distinguish at a glance, and the kind of handwriting chosen makes it particularly illegible,

3. The words, Author of *The Fountainhead*, should be in much larger type, larger than the one used for my name, because it is actually *The Fountainhead* that will help us to sell this pamphlet.

I would strongly recommend that you have another design made for the cover. I had given Mr. Read my proposed suggestion of the way the cover should look, and he had told me that that would be the design used. I do think that plain, clearly cut print is always much more effective than printed handwriting.

If you are already committed to the cover you sent me and it can not be redesigned, then of the two possibilities, I prefer your suggestion with the title slanted across the page. It does look better than the first proof, but I would feel much happier if the cover were redesigned, omitting the handwriting.

■ ■ ■

To Sylvia Austin, a fan

July 9, 1946

Dear Mrs. Austin:

Thank you for your letter. I appreciate the honesty and seriousness of your inquiry—and particularly the last paragraph of your letter. It would take a whole philosophical volume to answer your questions properly, but I shall try to indicate a few brief answers.

You say that "Roark is like a portrait of Jesus." This statement can mean many different things. In a very general sense, if you mean that both Roark and Jesus are held as embodiments of the perfect man, of a moral ideal—then you are right, but there the comparison must end. The moral ideal represented by Roark is not the one represented by Jesus.

There is a great, basic contradiction in the teachings of Jesus. Jesus was one of the first great teachers to proclaim the basic principle of individualism—the inviolate sanctity of man's soul, and the salvation of one's soul as one's first concern and highest goal; this means one's ego and the integrity of one's ego. But when it came to the next question, a code of ethics to observe for the salvation of one's soul—(this means: what must one do in actual practice in order to save one's soul?)—Jesus (or perhaps His interpreters) gave men a code of altruism, that is, a code which told them that in order to save one's soul, one must love or help or *live for* others. This means, the subordination of one's soul (or ego) to the wishes, desires or needs of others, which means the subordination of one's soul to the souls of others.

This is a contradiction that cannot be resolved. This is why men have never succeeded in applying Christianity in practice, while they have preached it in theory for two thousand years. The reason of their failure was not men's natural depravity or hypocrisy, which is the superficial (and vicious) explanation usually given. The reason is that a contradiction cannot be made to work. That is why the history of Christianity has been a continuous civil war—both literally (between sects and nations), and spiritually (within each man's soul).

The solution? We have a choice. Either we accept the basic principle of Jesus—the preeminence of one's own soul—and define a new code of ethics consistent with it (a code of Individualism). Or we accept altruism and the basic principle which it implies—the conception of man as a sacrificial animal, whose purpose is service to others, to the herd (which is what you may see in Europe right now—and which is certainly not what Jesus intended).

You ask: "Do you think it would demean man to think that he was the child of the Creator of the earth, stars, etc.? Don't you think it would make his noble dreams and acts even more noble to think that he has a divine heritage?" To your first question I would answer: No, not necessarily. Perhaps a philosophical statement could be made defining God and man's relation to God in a way which would not be demeaning to man and to his life on earth. But I do not know of such a statement among the popular conceptions of God.

The second question contains a most grievous demeaning of man, right in the question. It implies that man, even at his best, even after he has reached the highest perfection possible to him, is not noble or not noble enough. It implies that he needs something superhuman in order to make him nobler. It implies that that which is noble in him is *divine*, not *human*; and that the merely human is ignoble. This is what neither Roark nor I would ever accept.

You say: "Jesus said we were to love one another, and to bear each other's burdens." "To bear each other's burdens"—is the purest statement of collectivism and altruism, the very thing to which Roark's whole philosophy said "NO."

As for "loving one another" (this means, I presume, indiscriminately), it is a precept which I do not understand. It has no actual meaning and no possible application in practice. Love is the recognition one grants to value or virtue. Since all men are not virtuous, to love them for their vices would be a monstrous conception and a vicious injustice. One can not love such men as Stalin or Hitler. One can not love both a man like Roark and a man like Toohey. If one says one does, it merely means that one does not love at all. To love the ideal and also those who betray it, is only to betray the ideal.

You say: "It would seem to me that Jesus loved people in a way that you would approve." No, I do not approve of what you describe as that way. You say that "Jesus loved the dream of goodness He saw in every man." I do not see a "dream of goodness" in every man, nor do I see any inborn evil or original sin in him. I see man as, above all, a creature of free will. This means that it is up to him, and to him alone, to decide whether he will be good or evil. Then one judges him on his own record, and one loves or hates him according to what he has deserved. I do not approve of loving anyone for a potentiality, particularly when his every action is a denial of that potentiality, is its exact opposite.

As to Roark, in relation to the kind of love for others which you describe, it is the whole point of Roark and of my philosophy that he was not concerned with other men. Yes, his goal was perfection, but not the perfection of the world or of others; only the perfection of that which lay within his power—of himself and his work. He did not set himself up as the power who should or could bring out the potential perfection in others. First, because he knew he could not do it; second, because he would not want to do it, if he could. Others did not interest him enough to become his concern. If he made it his goal to perfect them, it would mean that he had made them his concern, and he would then become the kind of second-hander whom he denounced most clearly and specifically.

Roark did better than to love men—he respected them. He granted to each of them the same right which he did not let them infringe in him— the right of an independent entity whose fate, life and perfection are in his own hands, not anyone else's and certainly not Roark's.

As to your sentence that Roark would want to serve that kind of God—that is the only sentence in your letter which was offensive to me. The word "Roark" and the word "serve" are opposites—the two antago-nists who will never meet and must not be connected. There is no such conception as "service" in Roark's consciousness nor in the kind of uni-verse to which he belongs and which he represents. Roark would not "serve" God nor anyone nor anything. He would never even use such a word in relation to himself. He would never think of "serving himself" or "serving his art." Roark is a man who does not *serve*—that is his whole meaning. Roark is *man as an end in himself.* That which is an end in itself does not serve anything. That which *serves* is the means to something which is the end.

■ ■ ■

To Alan Collins

July 19, 1946

Dear Alan:

Thank you for your letter of July 15th. It was such a pleasure to read an intelligent literary opinion from a literary agent. This is not a dirty crack, but merely a confession of what my experience along these lines has been. Just as Archie Ogden cured me of contempt for all editors, I think you will redeem the profession of agents in my eyes.

I agree with your first criticism of *Ideal*, but not with the second. It is true that after about the second scene of Act I, the audience will know what the pattern of the play is to be; but I don't think that this is necessarily a weakness. Up to that point, I expect to hold the audience through their wonder about *what* is to happen. After that point, I expect their interest to be held by the question of *how* it is to happen. Once they get wise to the idea of the play, they will then be interested in how the idea is worked out, and there will still be, to hold them, the question as to how the hell all this is going to come out.

As in everything I write, I have here two different levels of potential interest: the intelligent audience will be interested in watching the development of the philosophical theme; the less intelligent audience will be interested in the mere "stunt value" of the play, because it *is* a stunt.

Now, as to your second criticism, that the "characters aren't people at all, any more than they were in *The Fountainhead*—they are symbols," I am surprised at you. The characters are people, as they certainly were in *The Fountainhead*—unless I am very much mistaken on what you mean by "people." My characters are never symbols; they are merely men in sharper focus than the audience can see with unaided sight. What gives them the appearance of symbolism is not their characterization, but the circumstances through which they move and which bring out their wider significance, so that they become not merely specific men, but also representatives of all men of that kind. For instance, George S. Perkins in *Ideal* is a concrete characterization, and you would have taken him as such in any conventional story. It is the circumstances in which I place him that make him not merely George S. Perkins, but also a representative of all stuffy "family" men. The symbolism in my characters is something *added* to the characterization, not *substituted* for it.

So I am not worried about the reaction of the audience to my "symbolic" characters, any more than I was when publishers told me that the characters in *The Fountainhead* were not people. That is an old one to me. My characters never will be people in the usual sense of the word. That would bore me to death.

Of course, *Ideal* is strictly an experimental play. I have no way of being sure that a play of this kind will be a hit, but a Broadway producer once told me that the greatest amount of money on Broadway is lost on "surefire" plays that follow a tried pattern. So I'll take a chance on this play, just as I took one on *Night of January 16th*, which was also an experiment, though of a lower order. Everything I write will always be an experiment. I'm no good at following precedent.

■   ■   ■

To Ev Suffens

July 19, 1946

Dear Ev:

I was delighted to hear from you—and all my congratulations on your new business. As far as I can guess, I think you are the type who should do best on your own—your talents are really wasted on taking somebody else's orders.

You have my permission to do a television performance of *Night of January 16th*, and you may have it royalty free if you are to be the producer yourself (if it is a commercial production by somebody else, then I want to be paid, being capitalistic minded). You understand, of course, that I give you this permission for just the one performance, and it does not involve the sale of television rights to the people or the producer or the broadcasting company who will do it.

As to "What's with us"—we are having a wonderful time right now, because I am working on my next novel, and I am not due back at the studio until later in the Fall. I am doing quite well with the novel at the moment, and I strongly suspect that it will be the kind which you'll like. I miss New York terribly, but California is almost bearable for the present, since I am so busy. Believe it or not, I have learned to do a little gardening, and spend some of my time as a weed exterminator. This is not too far removed from my literary activity either. Frank is a complete gentleman farmer, and our estate has grown into a zoo of every kind of exotic bird you can imagine—even a man secretary, to whom I am dictating this.

I don't know whether I will be able to come to New York this Fall, but would like to if it is possible. In the meantime, why don't you write to me once in a while? As you see, I am answering promptly. As one of your early admirers, I would like to know how your progress is in the new business.

Oscar and Oswald send their very special regards, and the same from both of us to the three of you.

■ ■ ■

To John William Rogers

July 22, 1946

Dear Mr. Rogers:

Thank you for your letter of June 28th.

I had not seen any reviews of *The Fountainhead* except those that appeared at publication; so in fairness to you, I wrote to the *Times-Herald* of Dallas to obtain the review which you mentioned. I have read it with interest, and appreciate it very much.

I fully appreciate the sincerity of your attitude and of your offer, but it does not change the fact that I cannot write for the *Chicago Sun*. I most certainly "put my basis of cooperation on reviews which have appeared," as you say in your letter. I assume you meant and realized that much more than a literary issue is involved in this attitude on my part.

The review of my book in the *Chicago Sun* was not a literary review, neither in fact nor in motive. It was a sample of the usual "smear" technique practiced by collectivists against all those who advocate the philosophy of Individualism, as I do. The *Chicago Sun* is a newspaper whose policy preaches Collectivism. No, I do not say that you are necessarily a collectivist yourself. In fact, I strongly suspect that you are not. It is possible that you might make the Book Week of the *Chicago Sun* into an honest literary paper, if they permit you to. But even though I would like to cooperate with you personally, I cannot let my name appear as that of a contributor to the *Chicago Sun*, because this would amount to an endorsement of its policy and an acceptance of its inexcusable insult to my book. I do not cooperate or collaborate with Collectivism.

You say in your letter that you wished "to make a gracious gesture in my direction" and "hold out a hand in friendship." I accept your gesture in just that spirit as far as you are concerned. I suspected that this was so and that you were new on the staff of the *Chicago Sun*, from your first letter.

Of course, an offer from a newspaper to write an article is not a one-sided favor done to an author—but an exchange to the mutual advantage of both parties, like any proper exchange in a free capitalistic society (in which I believe). It would be to my advantage to have my name and article appear in a newspaper's literary supplement—and it would be to the newspaper's advantage to run an article by me, since there are readers interested in what I have to say. This is the only kind of proper and moral cooperation between men, cooperation that profits both sides. What would make it immoral in this particular case is the fact that I cannot accept the help of the *Chicago Sun* nor offer it mine.

■ ■ ■

To Rose Wilder Lane

July 24, 1946

Dear Rose Wilder Lane:

Thank you very much for your review of *Anthem*. I did not expect any reviews on this little booklet, and appreciate yours most sincerely.

Just between you and me, were you actually stuck on what kind of literary form *Anthem* represents—or was it just a very clever method you employed to arouse interest in the book? If you are really wondering about it, *Anthem* is a poem.

Mrs. Lane's review was published in the newsletter of The Economic Council, a pro-capitalist group.

■ ■ ■

To Sylvia Austin

July 29, 1946

Dear Mrs. Austin:

Your letter of July 15th astonished me.

The peculiar example you propound—about Roark and another man fighting over the same piece of land—reads as if you had never heard of such a thing as the institution of private property. Private property is based on the idea of *rights*, not *needs*. A man holds his property because it is *his*—regardless of how many parasites claim that they need it more than he does. Anybody who makes a claim upon others on the basis of his *need* is a parasite.

The answer to your dilemma is simply that the owner of the land in question will sell it to the highest bidder, and whichever man wants it most will get it. Each of the three men will be properly concerned *only* with his own interests, but the owner's interest will be decisive, by virtue of his right of ownership. This is how issues are settled among individualists, because individualists respect the *individual* rights of others, including property rights.

Roark's principles do not and cannot depend on any particular piece of land or material property, and certainly not on one belonging to somebody else. Since man is not an animal dependent on his background, but a creative being who adapts his background to his own wishes, no creative man is ever dependent on somebody else's property. He works to get his own, and he gets it through a voluntary exchange of sale and purchase. He doesn't kill others in order to get it. Only the altruist kills for gain, because he is a parasite by nature and definition. A man who lives *for* others lives *off* others, both spiritually and materially.

The preposterous situation which you describe could occur only in a society of altruists, where human rights are trampled for the sake of parasites' needs. (Incidentally, who decides whose need is greater than that of another? You?) Let's examine your example on your own terms. If both men were altruists, the silly deadlock could not be solved, because each would try to sacrifice himself to the other. If one accepted the sacrifice, it would mean that the evil one won and the virtuous one lost. (Self-sacrifice being your criterion of virtue.) If both men wanted to be virtuous, it would develop into an "Alphonse and Gaston" situation, with each assuring the other that the other's need is greater than his own. This would mean a contest of sores between two beggars, each claiming that the other one is scabbier than himself, on the theory that the more miserable one is, the more one deserves the reward at stake. This would go on until a humanitarian came along and killed both men "for their own good," then gave the property to the village idiot.

No, each man is *not* "his own criterion of what is right."

Reason is the criterion. A man deciding that something is right just because he says so, does not make it right. Morality is an objective standard, true for all men, if it is a rational morality that proves on rational grounds why certain actions are good and other actions are evil. Only on the basis of the morality of Individualism is each man free to decide what is right for himself, and *only* for himself—so long as his decision is not concerned *primarily* with others, and is not to be forced upon others. This leaves the altruist out.

You cannot claim that altruism is right merely because it is your own choice of what is right, and then believe that this makes it moral. Altruism is profoundly and totally immoral. Neither you nor any philosopher in history has ever been able to defend it on rational grounds.

In choosing it, you deny the first premise—that of man's rights, freedom and choice.

So you land in a vicious contradiction.

Each man is free to seek salvation in his own way *only so long as he leaves others alone*. Then he leaves them the same right. But if he decides that his salvation lies in forcing his own immoral ideas of what is right upon others (as altruists do) on the ground that *he* thinks it is good to do so—men will have no choice but to answer him in the same way, by force; by cracking his skull in self-protection. That is the vicious contradiction inherent in altruism.

You cannot take the premise of the morality of Individualism—each man's individual right of choice—and use it to justify its opposite, your decision to sacrifice other men to your own preference for the immoral collectivistic horror of altruism.

As to Father Damien [a Belgian priest who ran a leper colony in Hawaii in the nineteenth century], I do not say that he was necessarily and consciously motivated by power-lust. I do not know his motives, nor care. I merely say that his action was neither virtuous nor admirable.

It is an evil to sacrifice oneself for others, as it is to rule them. Both forms differ only superficially. Please notice that the humanitarians are among the loudest advocates of dictatorship.

You refuse to admit to yourself that Roark did not consider "help to his fellows" as a good motive or a good result, and that he had *CONTEMPT* for those whose aim in life was to help others. Didn't you understand that it was a *housing project* which he blew up to hell, where it belonged?

It is clear to me that you are trying to reconcile the conception represented by Roark with your own devotion to altruism. This cannot be done. The two are opposites. If you consider altruism noble in any form, you must accept the fact that you are Roark's enemy and belong with Ellsworth Toohey. Evading the issue will not alter the fact.

There is no obligation on you whatever (except intellectual honesty) to admire Roark, but apparently you do; apparently he has made you feel

uneasy about the kind of morality you have been taught before. You liked
Roark because you recognized the fact that he is a man of integrity; but
his integrity rests solely on the fact that he is the exact opposite of an
altruist. You must make up your mind which you prefer. You cannot have
both. Either you go with Roark or you go with Ellsworth Toohey.

If you attempt to ease your own conscience by telling yourself that
Roark would approve of the very things which he fought, you are not
harming me or Roark, but yourself. Intellectual evasion hurts those who
practice it, not those who have to hear it. If you like intellectual integrity,
this is the question that calls for it.

■   ■   ■

To Burt MacBride, senior editor at *Reader's Digest*

July 30, 1946

Dear Burt MacBride:

I am glad you liked *Anthem*, but I don't agree with you when you say that
it "cannot hope to influence many people." *It* hopes to do so and will.
Have you noticed what its big brother has done through the same method?

Now to your $64 question.

You write: "Answer me this one: Why in the name of all that's holy
do supposedly intelligent Americans espouse the Kremlin's cause, when
there's such damning evidence of Communism's completely vicious character as Kravchenko's book?"

That's a question right up my alley.

The answer is: because most people believe that Communism is a
moral ideal. They do not call it Communism; they call it altruism. But the
essence is the same; one is the logical consequence of the other.

Altruism preaches *self-sacrifice*; the idea that man must live for others
and place others above self. Most people, including our conservatives, have
now accepted this as their moral credo. But on such a basis a capitalistic
free-enterprise society cannot continue to exist.

Now, why do Americans espouse the Kremlin's cause in spite of books
like Victor Kravchenko's [*I Chose Freedom: The Personal and Political
Life of a Soviet Official*]? *Because it's books like Kravchenko's that make
them do it.* Kravchenko denounces Stalin—not Communism. Kravchenko
still believes in Communism and still preaches it as a noble ideal. So does
Barmine. So do all the current denouncers of Soviet Russia. That is why

their books have no effect—or rather, the only effect they do have is to make more converts for Communism.

Joe Zilch is much more logical than these authors. Here's what he tells himself while reading their books: "If it's moral to sacrifice yourself, why isn't it moral to sacrifice others for an ideal? What if Stalin *did* slaughter million? It's for the sake of humanity, of the poor, of the underdog—and everybody tells me that sacrifice is the first law of virtue. What if Stalin cheats and lies? It's for the sake of the cause. What if the Communists have achieved nothing but misery so far? Their ideal is so noble that it's not easy to achieve. It's men's selfishness that hampers them. Give them time—they'll achieve it. What if they've sacrificed a whole nation of 170 million? It's for the sake of the happiness of many more millions in the future generations. If it's good to sacrifice one man for the sake of ten others, why is it bad to sacrifice 170 million men for the sake of ten times that number of others in the future? What if Commissars live in luxury at the expense of terrorized slave labor? It's their reward for their efforts, since they're working for an unselfish cause, while the rich in our own country enjoy luxuries just for their own private selfish sake."

That's what Joe Zilch is thinking. And on the premise of an altruistic morality—Joe Zilch is right.

Once men have accepted the idea of self-sacrifice as good, they have accepted the idea of sacrificing others, too. *They have accepted the idea of man's immolation as proper*—just as they accepted it in the days of the ancient human sacrifices to Moloch. Then they are impervious to the spectacle or recital of any horrors. They read Kravchenko, they shrug and say: "So what? The noble cause is worth it."

Facts per se are meaningless, unless we draw conclusions from them and learn something. A mere recital of facts is useless. What is Kravchenko's book? A catalogue of facts about Soviet Russia. They are horrible facts—but the conclusion he draws from them and passes on to his reader is that Communism is good in principle. The reader will accept his facts, believe them to be true—and still remain a Communist sympathizer. The net result is only that the reader might dislike Soviet Russia, but will continue to advocate Communism for America, claiming that "our" brand of Communism will be different and better than the Russian brand; we'll get it wholesale.

Besides, Americans are not shocked any longer by descriptions of a whole country in abject poverty. They all scramble for material prosperity here, but most of them do it guiltily, because they have been taught that a desire for wealth is immoral. So their struggle for material advantages ceases to be an honest endeavor and becomes a dirty racket. Notice the unconscionable greed of pressure groups for gain at public expense. This is always the result when men accept the idea that the honest, proper, capitalistic method of working for private profit is evil. Men are then still faced by the fact that they must make a living, that is, make money, but since it's evil in any form, they feel that anything goes.

When man's best virtues—ambition, energy, ingenuity, independence, and the enjoyment of their rewards—are declared to be sins, he has no choice but to turn to depravity.

The free-enterpriser works for what he gets. The modern American collectivist grabs what he can get away with. And the dirtier he becomes in his methods, the guiltier he feels; so he despises all wealth in his heart and thinks longingly of Communism, to ease his own conscience. He ceases to believe that material prosperity is good or desirable. Not prosperity, but self-sacrifice is noble—the altruists tell him; not enjoyment, but suffering. So he begins to despise the United States, *precisely because it's prosperous,* and to admire Soviet Russia, precisely because it's a land of filth, disease, misery, starvation—and sacrifice. If sacrifice is redemption, he reasons, then surely a country that has been brought down to such an unspeakable state and bears it, must be a virtuous country.

That is why true and factual books about the horrors of Soviet Russia are and will continue to be ineffectual. That is why they will not cure Americans of sympathy for the Kremlin, nor check the trend toward collectivism in America. Facts alone won't do it. Only the proper philosophy derived from the facts, will. No, Joe Zilch is not stupid. He absorbs just exactly what he's being taught. He understands his teachers well—too well. It's his teachers who are committing a dreadful crime, and the responsibility for the present world tragedy is theirs, not his.

■ ■ ■

To Leonard Read

August 1, 1946

Dear Leonard:

Thank you for your letter of July 22nd. I see why I enjoy political discussions with you. I like your way of facing and answering criticism. You're always fair about it.

Now, to the political discussion of your letter. I fully sympathize with your anger at the conservatives who claim that they oppose compulsion except for their particular pet cause. That is their usual attitude, and the one most damaging to our side. Nothing can be done about it, except by attacking it at the source. The source is the fact that people have lost all conception of principles. The cure has to begin by reeducating them to an understanding of the nature of principles and of their application. This is one instance that shows that our battle has to be fought on philosophical grounds.

I liked your saying, in your letter, that you do not know what an intellectual is. There certainly aren't many samples of that species around us nowadays. An intellectual is a man who thinks. That leaves out most of our contemporaries by definition. The awful objects who parade as professional intellectuals at present are a bunch of worthless phonies who are mostly pink and might as well remain so. They would do us no good on our side.

What we need are real intellectuals, that is, thinkers. But we cannot "convert" thinkers or "regain their devotion." We need them to *convert us*—that is, to teach businessmen and conservatives the proper kind of philosophy.

Such thinkers still exist somewhere and we need them desperately. No, they are not "fainthearts," as you say in your letter. And they have not given up. They have been choked off, stopped, prevented from functioning publicly through the fault of our businessmen. You know that for the last fifteen years every legitimate avenue of expression—newspapers, magazines, book publishing houses—has been closed to them. All these so-called respectable publications, owned by conservatives, have been staffed with pinks who maintain a blockade against all real advocates of our side. Only the Hayeks and such other compromisers are allowed to get through, the kind who do more good to the communist cause than to ours. Now the real thinkers whom we need will be hard to find, because they have not been allowed to make a name for themselves, to come out in the open and be discovered. So it's our job to find them. And, believe me, *that* should be the most important job of your organization.

It's not fair to call them "fainthearts," when they lead such a desperate, lonely struggle, against our own side, and have no avenue to get into print—just as I did not have for many years. I broke through on my own, and I don't want that struggle to be as hard for other writers of Individualism as it was for me. Let's clear the way for them.

And whenever you have a chance to discuss the situation of intellectuals with any of your big business backers, you must drive relentlessly, at every opportunity, toward the goal of having them use their influence to clean up the Republican newspapers and magazines of their filthy load of pinks, and to hire the writers of our kind. That should be your purpose. That is the purpose for which I will fight by your side with everything I've got.

Your fighting "ghost,"

■ ■ ■

To Vladimir Kondheim

August 6, 1946

Dear Volodia:

I want to ask you to do me a very big favor. As you have probably heard, it is now permitted to send food packages to Russia. I am afraid to write to my family, but would like to send them a food package in the hope that they will then write to us, if they are now permitted to send letters to America.

Because I am so well known here for my political views, I am afraid that if I send them the packages from myself, it might prove embarrassing to them; so I would like you to do it for me. I have seen a Gimbels ad from a New York paper, which lists the type of parcel that Gimbels undertake to deliver to Russia. What I would like you to do is as follows: please order two parcels, listed as #126 at Gimbels. They are supposed to contain the following: 1½ pounds roast beef, 1½ pounds bacon, pound rice, pound roasted coffee, ½ pound cheese, ½ pound tea, ½ pound powdered milk, 2 tins sardines (3¼ ounces each), 2 tins powdered whole eggs (equivalent one dozen), 3 packages dehydrated soup, 2 bars of soap (5 ounces each bar).

I am enclosing a check for $20 to cover the expense. (Gimbels list the packages at $8.13 each) Have them send one package to my sister, Nora, and the other one to our cousin, Nina. I enclose their addresses on a separate page. If they have moved, I hope one or the other of the two packages will reach one of the two families, and they will probably communicate with each other. PLEASE PUT YOUR NAME AND ADDRESS ON THE PACKAGES, AS THAT OF THE SENDER, AND DO NOT MENTION MY NAME TO ANYONE ANYWHERE IN CONNECTION WITH THESE PACKAGES. I want them to come from you as the sender. Do not give my check to Gimbels, cash it yourself at your own bank.

If it is possible, ask Gimbels to send you back a receipt personally signed by the persons to whom the packages are sent. This is most important if it is possible. If there is any extra charge for such a service, please pay it. If Gimbels cannot get a personal receipt, but have to deliver the packages to the Russian postal authorities, send them anyway, and we'll hope that we'll get a personal letter from one of the girls or both.

I do not know the address of your family, but I suppose that you have already sent something to them. If you haven't, and would like to, let me know, and I will be glad to pay the cost of another package.

I am told that mail is now allowed to come through from Russia, but you can understand why I am afraid to write to them. If you have written to your family and heard any news, please let me know.

Please keep this confidential between just the two of us, and burn this letter after you are through with it. If you write to your family, DON'T REFER TO ME AT ALL EXCEPT to say (if you wish) that you have seen cousin Alice, and that she is well. Above all don't tell them anything about my success as a writer, don't refer to my writing career, don't mention where I live, and don't ever use the name Ayn Rand.

If you receive a letter from Nora or Nina in answer to the packages, please send it to me air mail registered. Don't answer them until you have heard from me. My hope is that if they write you, you will write to them, and I will send you a note from me to put in your letter, so that they will hear from me, but I won't have to give my name or address.

I think this would be the safest plan to communicate with them without causing them any embarrassment. But if for any reason you find that you cannot do it, let me know, and I will try to arrange something else.

Please write to me as soon as you can, and tell me what you hear from Gimbels about the situation and about the chances of the package being received. Ask them for any information that they can give you.

■ ■ ■

To Marie Strakhow, a longtime family friend from Russia and AR's first English teacher, who wrote her that AR's father had died in 1939 and her mother a year later

August 8, 1946

Dear "Missis":

Thank you for your letter. I have heard nothing from Europe for eight years, and the news you told me was a great shock to me. But I am very grateful that you got in touch with me and let me know.

You mentioned that you would tell me of a strange dream on the day of ZZ's death [Zinovy Zacharovitch, AR's father]. Would you write to me what it was?

I stopped writing to Europe when I stopped receiving letters from them, realizing that it was probably dangerous for them to correspond with people abroad. At present food parcels are being accepted here for delivery to all European countries. I have sent a parcel to Nora, and I hope that she will write to me if she gets it. I do not know whether I should write to them first myself or not. I have become very famous here as an author of pronounced political views. I think you can guess what those views are. Because of this fact, do you think that a letter from me would prove embarrassing or dangerous to them? I would appreciate very much your advice about this.

Also, if you have any information that you can safely give me in a letter on the names or addresses of people who might assist me in locating Natasha and Nora [AR's two sisters], I would be very grateful.

I do not know whether the mail going to and from you passes through American hands, or whether it is handled by representatives of other countries. Therefore, I hesitate to send you my books, as I do not want them to cause you any embarrassment. If, however, you tell me that the mail is handled only by American authorities, I will be glad to send you my books. They represent the strictly American philosophy of life.

I am very happy to know that you are now free. Would you like to come to America? I would like very much to see you and to ask you a great many things that cannot be covered by letter. I would like to have you here with me, as you are now my only link to the past. The financial part of your trip would not be a burden to me in any way. I am now quite rich, and I would be more than happy to pay for your passage to America, and to have you as my guest here. Do not consider it as any kind of an imposition on me, but rather as a favor that you would do me, if you say that you care to come. I remember the many favors which you have done us, and this may be my chance to reciprocate. I would like you to enjoy a rest in a free and decent country, and a chance to do the things you want to do.

I hope very much that you decide to come. If you do, you must apply for a visa to the American consul nearest you. I was told here that the Resident Representative of the Intergovernmental Refugee Committee (the Mr. Ross who first wrote to me about you) can accept your application for a visa and assist you with the necessary formalities, if there is no American consul in Salzburg. The application for a visa has to be made by you, but

I will send you an affidavit of support which you must submit to the consul with your application. The American government is now permitting refugees to come here under a quota, if they have an affidavit of support from an American citizen, which I am.

In the meantime I have sent you two food parcels, and hope that they contain things which you will find of use. I shall continue sending them; so please let me know what particular food products you like or need more than others, and I will try to send those.

As to news about myself, it is a long story which I would like to tell you in detail when I see you. In brief, I have had a very hard struggle for many years, but have finally achieved a great success. Three years ago I wrote a novel which became a sensational bestseller and which has made me famous. I now live in California, where I own a house and ranch of my own outside of Hollywood. I have a long term contract to write for pictures, at a huge Hollywood salary, besides my income from my books. I mention this so that you will see that financial considerations are no longer a problem for me.

Both my husband and I would like very much to see you, and perhaps we can help you to feel a little happier than you are at present. At least, we would like to try.

■   ■   ■

To Sylvia Austin

August 14, 1946

Dear Mrs. Austin:

I was glad to hear that you seem to be sincere and serious about intellectual arguments.

No, I didn't mean that to test the logic of an idea by questions is to be intellectually dishonest. You must really be careful not to confuse issues like that. The first sign of intellectual honesty is precisely to ask as many questions as one needs, until one has reached a complete logical understanding. I have written to you at such great length, because I respect the questioning mind.

Intellectual dishonesty comes, when one begins to muddle the premises of one's questions and to attempt to reconcile a blatant contradiction, a procedure which is best expressed by a question such as: "Why can't I have my cake and eat it, too?"

It is not dishonest if one is unable to see a point at first glance. It *is* dishonest when one is unwilling to see it. The person asking a question is the best judge of which is which, but the person hearing it will always be able to tell the difference.

As to the present political trend of government controls, I quite agree with you. It is vicious, immoral, collectivistic—and will achieve, if continued, neither freedom nor security, but only total destruction.

If my letters have helped you to clarify some important issues, I am very glad.

■   ■   ■

To John L. B. Williams

August 20, 1946

Dear Mr. Williams:

I have just learned—from a pamphlet entitled "The Thought Police" by John T. Flynn [author of *The Roosevelt Myth*] that a group of reds, headed by Rex Stout [detective novelist] are conducting a smear campaign against the new Sunday Literary Supplement of the *Chicago Tribune*. Specifically, they are urging writers to ask their publishers not to advertise in the *Chicago Tribune*.

I am writing to you to register my most emphatic protest against Rex Stout's disgusting group, against everything they stand for, and against the boycott which they recommend. I would like you to do me a favor and give me an opportunity to express my protest in action.

The decision on where to advertise is the privilege of Bobbs-Merrill. But when you next consider where to place ads for *The Fountainhead*, please keep my request in mind—and, other things being equal, please give first choice in your placement of ads for my book to the Sunday Literary Supplement of the *Chicago Tribune*.

I would consider this a great courtesy to me on the part of Bobbs-Merrill.

■   ■   ■

To John T. Flynn

August 20, 1946

Dear Mr. Flynn:

Thank you for sending me your pamphlet, "The Thought Police." My compliments to you for taking action against Rex Stout's group and their revolting campaign.

I am enclosing copies of the letters which I am sending to my publishers and to the Sunday Literary Supplement of the *Chicago Tribune*. Please let me know whether there is any further action I can take to help you in the battle against red control of literature.

I agree with you that the particular tactics used by Rex Stout in this case (the "organized" appeal and the cover-up by respectable names without their consent) were contemptible. But I must tell you—just for the record—that I do not agree with the principle on which you base your stand.

You claim, in effect, that no advertiser has the right to be concerned with or even to consider the editorial policy of a publication which he supports by his advertising; and that if he considers it, he becomes guilty of an improper "domination" over a free press. This is an example of the modern confusion about the concepts of rights, freedom and force. *Economic* power is *not* the same thing as *political* power—nor is its exercise a violation of the rights of others.

No advertiser, or any other man, has the right to suppress any publication by political action, that is, by passing a law, that is, by *force*. But he has an inalienable right to withhold his economic support from people or publications who advocate the exact opposite of his own convictions. Any other definition amounts to a claim that it is his duty to finance his own enemies.

The right of a free press is the right not to be prevented by force from acquiring the means to print whatever one wishes to print. It is *not* the right to demand that one's own opponents furnish these means; and their refusal to do so is *not* an act of "domination."

The rise of people like Rex Stout to a position of public influence from which they can choke all free literature, has been due precisely to the fact that advertisers acted on the principle you advocate—on the idea that it was their duty to finance the expression of opinion of any stray pink who came along. This has led to the spectacle of big business supporting, through advertising, the people who openly advocate the expropriation, destruction and looting of all business. The formerly respectable, conservative publications have been taken over bodily by pinks; conservative writers have been driven out, choked off, blacklisted—and the performance has been financed by conservatives! This is the result of industry acting on the principle that it owes support to its own murderers.

A man has a constitutional right to bear arms. But if a man has declared that he intends to murder you, it is *not* your duty to provide the knife and place it in his hands.

Rex Stout has a perfect right not to advertise in the *Chicago Tribune*. The *Chicago Tribune* has a perfect right to (and should) refuse to carry his advertising. And all those who oppose communism have the right to (and should) withdraw their advertising from communist publications.

No, this is *not* "domination" over editors. It is our inalienable right to choose whom we wish to patronize and support.

I believe that we should fight against Rex Stout and his group and everything they represent. But we must conduct the fight on clear-cut principles. We cannot start by accepting a purely collectivistic premise, the notion that economic power and political power are *identical*.

■ ■ ■

To Albert Mannheimer, a friend and the screenwriter of the original *Born Yesterday*

August 21, 1946

Dear Fuzzy:

Well, I guess you don't miss me, since I haven't heard from you (that's just a dirty crack—I wouldn't write letters from New York either). I am writing this for no particular reason, except that I do miss you; so it is just to say: "hello."

The first Sunday after you left, I had a rival, Walter, here. The second Sunday I had a wonderful time being entirely alone (also a dirty crack), but lately I have started holding long philosophical discussions with Frank, and I am not sure but that he may not enjoy them quite as much as I do —so he might wire you to please come back and rescue him from it.

Thank you for the nice note you sent me before you left. Your postscript about my book was a peculiar kind of encouragement to me—and you know that I seldom react to anybody's reactions to my writing. I must tell you that you did me a good turn by listening to my all-night synopsis of my novel. I found that I was very stimulated and clear-headed for the next few days, and solved a lot of the outline problems. It is almost completed now, although still not quite. I still have details to straighten out.

Have you seen Pat? As a reminder of the three messages I asked you to give her, that is, about my parents, about my troubles with Hal Wallis, and about the fact that I haven't written to her, because I don't know how to write to her. Besides that, give her my regards, but do so at your own risk. I don't know whether she will be glad to have them, or will throw something at your head.

Regards from Frank, and all my love, darling (keep most of it, but give a little from me to the Empire State Building).

■　■　■

To Rose Wilder Lane

The first paragraph refers to AR's "Textbook of Americanism," printed in May 1946, in *The Vigil*, a publication of the Motion Picture Alliance for the Preservation of American Ideals.

August 21, 1946

Dear Rose Wilder Lane:

In regard to my definition of rights, in the second installment of my "Textbook," I am inclined to agree with your suggested correction, that the sentence should read: "a right is exercised without permission" instead of "can be exercised." I think the general meaning is the same, but the sentence reads stronger your way.

I did not quite understand the basis of your definition of rights, which you mentioned briefly in your letter. I agree with you that rights are a natural human function, indispensable to man's survival, but I did not understand your argument to the effect that even though it is possible to kill one man, it is impossible to exterminate all of mankind. I don't quite see your point, but I see some danger in that argument, for two reasons: 1. If we maintain that the right of life is collectively inalienable, that is, that the race can't be destroyed—this is no defense or consolation for any particular man who is being murdered. 2. On such a basis a collectivist could claim that when he violates the rights of individuals, he is not violating human rights, since he can't enslave or destroy all of mankind. But as I say, I am not clear on the meaning in which you used the above argument.

My own definition of the existence of human rights rests on the fact of man's survival. Rights are intrinsic to the survival of a rational being, because the mind is man's only means of survival, and the mind is an attribute of the individual which cannot function under compulsion. If we accept as an axiom that man's survival is desirable, we have to recognize man's rights. The violation of these rights leads to the destruction of individuals, and, if continued, can and will destroy the whole human race—since such violation is based on a premise which makes man's survival impossible.

Now to your second question: "Do those almost with us do more harm than 100% enemies?" I don't think this can be answered with a flat "yes" or "no," because the "almost" is such a wide term and can cover so many different attitudes. I think each particular case has to be judged on his own performance, but there is one general rule to observe: those who are with us, but merely do not go far enough, yet do not serve the opposite cause in any way, are the ones who do us some good and who are worth educating. Those who agree with us in some respects, yet preach contradictory ideas at the same time, are definitely more harmful than the 100% enemies. The standard of judgment here has to be the man's attitude toward basic principles. If he shares our basic principles, but goes off on lesser details in the application of these principles, he is worth educating and having as an ally. If his "almost" consists of sharing some of the basic principles of collectivism, then we ought to run from him faster than from an out-and-out Communist.

As an example of the kind of "almost" I would tolerate, I'd name Ludwig von Mises. His book, *Omnipotent Government*, had some bad flaws, in that he attempted to divorce economics from morality, which is impossible; but with the exception of his last chapter, which simply didn't make sense, his book was good, and did not betray our cause. The flaws in his argument merely weakened his own effectiveness, but did not help the other side.

As an example of our most pernicious enemy, I would name Hayek. That one is real poison. Yes, I think he does more harm than Stuart Chase. I think Wendell Willkie did more to destroy the Republican Party than did Roosevelt. I think Willkie and Eric Johnston have done more for the cause of Communism than Earl Browder and *The Daily Worker*. Observe the Communist Party technique, which asks their most effective propagandists to be what is known as "tactical nonmembers." That is, they must not be Communists, but pose as "middle-of-the-roaders" in the eyes of the public. The Communists know that such propagandists are much more deadly to the cause of Capitalism in that "middle-of-the-road" pretense.

Personally, I feel sick whenever I come up against a compromising conservative. But my attitude is this: if the man compromises because of ignorance, I consider him worth enlightening. If he compromises because of moral cowardice (which is the reason in most cases), I don't want to talk to him, I don't want him on my side, and I don't think he is worth converting.

P.S. I had just finished this letter to you, when, strangely enough, I received an appalling answer to the question you asked me—a final proof that our "almost" friends *are* our worst enemies. It was the worst shock in all my experience with political reading. I received the *Economic Council Letter* of August 15th. (Incidentally, I subscribed to that Letter mainly in order to get your book reviews.) And I read that Merwin K. Hart, a defender of freedom and Americanism, is advocating *a death penalty for a political offense.*

I am actually too numb at the moment to know what to say. I don't have to explain to you that once such a principle is accepted, it would mean the literal, physical end of Americans; nor to ask you to guess who would be the first people executed under such a law; nor to remind you that the crucial steps on the road to dictatorship, the laws giving government totalitarian powers, were initiated by Republicans—such as the draft bill, or the attempt to pass a national serfdom act for compulsory labor.

I know that you know all that. What I wonder is: is it in your spiritual power to discuss this with Hart? If you can, if you have arguments that would reach him—please do it. I confess I'm helpless in such an instance. It's too monstrous.

■ ■ ■

To the "Patter" editor, *Reader's Digest*

In September 1946, *Reader's Digest* quoted from *The Fountainhead*: "She was only a shell containing the opinions of her friends."

August 27, 1946

Dear Patter Editor:

Thanks for quoting me in your "Picturesque Speech and Patter" department in your September issue. I am always glad to see myself in the *Reader's Digest*.

I also read page 63; so don't you owe me five bucks, or is it twenty-five now?

■　■　■

To Leonard Read

August 29, 1946

Dear Leonard:

As an advance warning, for God's sake DON'T recommend *Animal Farm*. You have probably heard about it—it's a little booklet that has just come out and is being whooped up as a lesson against Communism, which it is not. I have read it. It made me sick. It is a book against Stalin, *not* against Communism. In fact, it is the mushiest and most maudlin preachment of Communism (I suppose the author would call it Socialism, but there is no difference), that I have seen in a long time. The moral of the book is not: "Communism is evil," but: "Stalin's Communism is just as evil as Capitalism." Don't let's help to preach *that* idea.

■　■　■

To Barbara Stanwyck, actress and friend

August 29, 1946

Dear Miss Stanwyck:

I should like very much to talk to you about the next story which I am to write for Hal Wallis. I want to discuss it with you before I undertake the assignment, because I think the story would interest you. I had a slight disagreement with Mr. Wallis about the kind of part you would care to play; so I should like to get your ideas on it firsthand.

Would you have lunch with me next Wednesday, September 4th? I should be delighted to have you come to my house (I live in the valley close to your former ranch), but if the distance is too great and it is inconvenient for you, I will be glad to meet you in Beverly Hills, if you prefer.

I have no phone in my house, so would you drop me a line, and let me know whether we can meet, whether the date is convenient for you or you prefer to make it another time. I have tried to reach you by telephone, but I was given the wrong number.

■　■　■

To Robert S. Henry, assistant to the president of the Association of American Railroads and author of many books about railroads

August 29, 1946

Dear Colonel Henry:

You may remember that at our meeting in New York, almost a year ago, you graciously said that you would assist me in getting factual information for my new novel which deals with railroads. I am now ready to take advantage of it.

I have completed the outline of my novel, and am about to start the actual writing, but I have a number of questions which I would like to discuss with a railroad man. Could you give me an introduction to someone in Los Angeles who would be willing to be bothered for information? I am interested mainly in the problems of the management of a large railroad system, so I would like to speak to an executive familiar with these problems. I would prefer to speak to a man who shares our political views, since my novel will be a most violent defense of free industry, private industrialists and private railroads.

I have read with great interest and pleasure your two books, *This Fascinating Railroad Business* and *Trains*. Are there any particular books dealing specifically with the problems of railroad management which you would advise me to read? Also, can you tell me where I can obtain some copies of the railroad magazines put out for employees, such as the *Santa Fe* magazine? I understand that those are not available to laymen, and I would like to see a few numbers, just to get an idea of their tone and nature.

■   ■   ■

To Burt MacBride

August 30, 1946

Dear Burt MacBride:

Thank you for your interesting letter. I still don't agree with you on what you consider the proper way of fighting Communism, but I don't want to engage you in another long argument.

However, since you say that my explanation has given you "a new slant on the subject," I must warn you against a grave mistake, as I don't want to be responsible for a mistake of this nature. You propose to claim that there is no such thing as Communism. Actually, what exists in Russia *is* Communism—it is the only way in which Communism can ever work in practice—it is the only way in which it will *always* work, no matter who attempts it or where—and it is completely consistent with the basic philosophical promises of Communism, though not with the superficial slogans of the Communists. If you claim that Russia is not a Communistic state but a perversion of Communism, you will merely reaffirm to people that Communism is a noble ideal, but Russia has betrayed it.

You say: "The countless persons who are trying to overthrow our system aren't idealists or moralists at all." I didn't say they were. They are the *product* of the wrong kind of idealists and moralists. And it is the wrong kind of idealism and morality—or rather, perverted and corrupted remnants of a moral sense—that make people tolerate the contemptible gangsters who are trying to overthrow our system. If it weren't for the morality of altruism, nobody would tolerate those people and their attempts for one minute. And until the morality of altruism is blasted out of people's minds, nothing will save us from Communism in one form or another.

No, I don't think that the job of exposing the fallacy of altruism would be difficult or would take long. No honest, competent or intelligent person has ever lived by the principles of altruism. None has ever believed it. It is not a matter of teaching them something new, but a matter of giving statement and voice to what the best of mankind has always believed, but never found words for. You would be surprised how quickly it can be done, and what the results would be. Again, I refer you to the spontaneous public response to *The Fountainhead.*

No, it is not as late as you think. It is merely early—in the age of the rebirth of Individualism.

■ ■ ■

To George Peck, a conservative columnist

August 30, 1946

Dear Mr. Peck:

Thank you for your letter and the copies of your column, which you sent me.

I have read your columns with great interest. I like particularly the column of July 21st, entitled "Remove that Appendix." I was glad to see that you advocate the repeal of the Wagner Act instead of advocating new laws to shackle labor, as so many of our conservatives are doing.

I cannot resist pointing out to you that you really must not say things such as the statement you made in your column of July 9th, to the effect that love of God and love of country are more important than freedom. Nothing is more important than freedom. Without it, neither love of God nor of country, nor even life itself, are possible.

No, I did not think—after reading your bulletin on the Speer testimony [Albert Speer, Hitler's architect]—that you were a Communist sympathizer. What I thought was that some Communist stooge on your staff had put one over on you in the matter of that headlining of Speer's envy of Russia. If there had been such a stooge, that is precisely what he would have done. That one touch would have meant a lot to his party.

Of course, I know that all you said was that Speer envied Russia, because Russia was "forced to improvise." But by the context of the rest of his testimony, it is made clear that improvisation in this case meant freedom from bureaucratic controls, since he complained that the bureaucrats did not permit the German industrialists to improvise. Therefore, it implied that Russia was free of such controls. And this is an implication which you should not have left unchallenged, and which you should not help to spread.

For the life of me, I can't imagine where Speer saw any improvisation in Russia. Who does he think did the improvising? The Commissars or the GPU? If your intention was to quote Speer verbatim, then you should have covered this particular point by some editorial explanation from yourself, and not left the implication that you, the editor, agreed with Speer's view of Russia.

You say that you "don't wish to get into a controversy as to whether or not Mr. Hitler was the greatest exponent of totalitarianism the world has ever known." There can be no controversy on this point—because there can be no conceivable standard by which anyone could claim that Hitler was worse than Stalin, or vice versa. There can be no degrees of evil between two dictators representing exactly the same principle.

I don't think that the word "rules" substituted for the word "controls" will be a proper change to express the idea you have in mind in regard to the relation of government to industry. If you believe, as you say, that government must act as an umpire, then remember that the umpire does not make up the rules himself, and he certainly does not make them up arbitrarily as the game goes along. It is not rules that govern a free society. It is principles, which is quite a different thing. Principles are objective and not set arbitrarily by a government or a majority. A free society is governed by objective laws based on objective moral principles.

■   ■   ■

To Lorine Pruette

September 3, 1946

Dear Lorine Pruette:

You are the only reviewer I know to whom I am happy to send a book of mine.

It is a novelette which I wrote in 1937, but this is its first publication in America. I want you to read it, because it has the same relation to *The Fountainhead* as the preliminary sketches which artists draw for their future big canvases. I wrote it while working on *The Fountainhead*—it has the same theme, spirit and intention, although in quite a different form.

If you should care to review it for the book section of the New York *Times*, it would make me very happy. I have asked the publishers not to send out any review copies to any publication, but only to individual persons in the literary field whose judgment and integrity we can respect. If you find that you care to do it, please ask the book editor of the *Times* to let you write the review. You are the only one on the *Times* to whom we are sending a copy of *Anthem*.

If you do not wish to write a review, I would still like very much to know your opinion of this book, and if you will write to me about it, I will not use it for publication (whether it is good or bad), unless you permit me to.

If you knew how profoundly I despise the literary opinion of today, you would accept this as the only tribute I can pay to you.

Gratefully, still and always,

■   ■   ■

To Jay Chidsey, a fan

September 5, 1946

Dear Mr. Chidsey:

I note with particular interest your saying that you are just going to college, and that you are going with the ideals of my book in mind. You will need them. In most modern colleges, there are many people who will make a concerted attack on your mind with the Toohey philosophy, in more insidious forms than you can possibly imagine. I would like you to be prepared against that. The battle will be tough, but if you will remember the ideas which you liked in Roark's speech and in Toohey's speech, you will win. If it becomes too tough and the Tooheys get you confused beyond endurance, write to me again.

If you intend to be a writer, I can give you encouragement in one particular respect, because it is a hopeful sign: you have picked as your example of good writing what is one of the two best passages of writing in *The Fountainhead*—the opening of Part 4. The other passage is Wynand's walk through the streets

■　■　■

To Henry Blanke

September 5, 1946

Dear Henry:

The enclosed [copy of *Anthem*] is a personal present to you, rather than a submission of a story for pictures, but you might be one of the few who would like it as a picture possibility.

It is, in a way, an ancestor of *The Fountainhead*. I wrote it in 1937, when I was working on *The Fountainhead*, and it has the same theme, though in an entirely different form and on a much smaller scale. This is its first publication in America.

So I thought you might be interested in it, and I wanted you to have it, to put on your bookshelf next to its child.

With best regards.

■　■　■

To Hal Wallis

September 5, 1946

Dear Boss:

Here is my novelette [*Anthem*], a review of which I have shown to you.

Don't let the foreword frighten you. It is a story, not a political treatise. I would like you to read it for your own pleasure.

I don't suppose you will be interested in this for pictures, but I want you to see it, so that you won't accuse me of disloyalty if someone else decides to buy it.

■   ■   ■

To Cecil B. DeMille

September 5, 1946

Dear Mr. DeMille:

You complained once that I make my books too long for you to read. Well, here is a short one—and if you really like my writing, I hope you will read this yourself, not in synopsis form.

This is my contribution to the cause of freedom—and perhaps it could also be yours. I would like you to consider most earnestly the possibility of making it into a picture.

There are few producers in Hollywood who would have the courage and imagination for this, but I think you would. I see it as a picture on the grand scale, as a dramatic fantasy, on the order of the magnificent spectacles which you made in the silent days. It would be completely different from any picture made now. It would be an artistic and dramatic event of world significance, and I don't have to point out to you what the political importance of it would be.

Of course, if you are interested, I would have to expand the story into greater detail, and give it a more complex plot; perhaps, add a modern story to it, running parallel, showing our present-day trends and their ultimate counterparts in the story of the future—using the method you used in *The Ten Commandments*. But, first, I would like to know whether such an idea and theme would appeal to you.

You have asked my opinion on what we could do to save America from collectivism. This is my answer. Since we have a tremendous medium such as the screen at our command—we should use it, if we want to serve our cause and our country. We should use it openly, dramatically, full blast. Organizations, speeches or editorials are almost futile, when compared to the power of the screen in presenting ideas and reaching the conscience of people.

This is my way of fighting our battle. I hope it might be yours. I think you and I are destined to make a picture together someday, and I would like it to be *Anthem.*

In March 1947, AR received a letter from DeMille's assistant, expressing DeMille's praise for Anthem *and suggesting she contact Agnes de Mille about producing a ballet based on the story.*

■ ■ ■

To Walt Disney

September 5, 1946

Dear Mr. Disney:

I am sending you an advance copy of my novelette, *Anthem*, which is being published in America for the first time. I would like you to read it, because I think its theme would appeal to you.

If you like it, I would ask you to consider making it into a picture. I know that it would be a complete departure from the conventional Hollywood film, and that is why I thought it worthwhile to call it to your personal attention. You might see it as I do, because you have never been afraid to venture into new fields and to do the different and the unusual.

If this story can be translated to the screen, I would like to see it done in stylized drawings, rather than with living actors. If you like the idea, I don't have to point out to you how important a picture with such a theme would be at the present moment.

■ ■ ■

To Barbara Stanwyck

September 7, 1946

Dear Barbara:

Now that I have a better idea of the kind of story and characterization you like, it occurred to me that I should show you *Red Pawn*, a synopsis of which is attached.

This is an original by me, the first story I ever sold. Paramount owns it, but has never produced it.

I would like you to read it, keeping in mind that if it were to be made now, I would suggest changing the locale and having the story take place in an unnamed dictatorship, rather than in Soviet Russia. It would give the story deeper significance.

I called this story to Mr. Wallis's attention, when I first started to work for him. He read it and liked it, but hesitated for a long time over the question of the locale, saying that he did not like to have a story in an unnamed background. I don't agree with him on that. He did admit that the story has the same dramatic pattern and the same basic situation as *Casablanca* (I wrote it long before that), but he could not quite make up his mind to do it, so I let it go and have not discussed it with him since.

As far as I am concerned, since Paramount owns the story, I would not get any kind of extra payment for it—so this is not an attempt to sell you an original of mine for any reason except that I love this story. I think it is still the best film story I ever wrote, and I would rather work on it than on anything I know.

The starring role is an acting part of the kind which a writer can succeed in devising very rarely; I know it, because I've tried since. She is the only woman in the story—and a kind of advance echo of Dominique. After seeing *Martha Ivers*, I can't think of anyone who could do it as you could.

Since you said that what you were anxious to find was a love story, a story about positive characters, and a story that had a quality of prestige—I could not help sending you this one. It is all three.

If you like it, I think we can persuade Mr. Wallis to make it; and I would be one of the happiest authors in Hollywood. But if you don't, I shall do my best with *Be Still, My Love*, as we discussed it.

I will telephone you Monday morning to learn your reaction before I make an appointment to see Mr. Wallis. If the time is not convenient to you, would you leave a message as to what time I may reach you, and I will call then.

Stanwyck replied by telegram that she and her manager had decided that Red Pawn *was not "the right kind of story" for her to do.*

■ ■ ■

To Leonard Read

September 9, 1946

Dear Leonard:

I was delighted to see your mimeographed copy of my "Textbook of Americanism." I hope your staff and trustees will study it carefully, as I know that it will be valuable to them in helping them to avoid giving our case away.

Your introduction is excellent. You picked out the most important point—my definition of what constitutes the violation of a right. This definition is original with me. As far as I know from my reading, it has never been made before. And I think it is extremely important, because it is clear, concrete, specific and objective.

Good luck to you on this, and I hope it helps you in philosophical arguments with your associates.

You really should not leave your ghost floating up in the air (even though ghosts are supposed to do just that). You owe me an answer to two long letters.

■ ■ ■

To Henry Blanke

September 9, 1946

Dear Henry:

I am sending you the enclosed clipping from *Life*, in case you have not seen it. I suspect that *Life* has received a great many letters of this kind, and of course I hear this from everywhere myself.

What concerns us in this is the fact that the public has made up its mind to connect Howard Roark with Frank Lloyd Wright. Therefore, if we have Mr. Wright design our buildings, it will be a wonderful boost for the picture and will create a great deal of satisfied comment. If we do not, there is bound to be disappointment, reproaches and criticism. I think people want to see Mr. Wright connected with *The Fountainhead*, and will not accept a substitute.

If you have not changed your mind about this since I saw you last, and do intend to have Mr. Wright design the buildings for the picture, I just wanted to remind you that it is most advisable to have him start on it as soon as possible. He is 76 years old, and since he wants to do it and you want him, it will be such a shame if we miss our chance through some tragic accident of fate that might happen at any moment.

Since you will make the picture eventually, it is better to have the designs in your files for the future, and not lose out by waiting. I would urge most earnestly that you do it at the earliest time you find convenient.

■ ■ ■

To Leonard Read

September 12, 1946

Dear Leonard:

I offered you my services, without charge, to protect your publications from internal treachery.

You chose not to take advantage of the offer. And you have published a booklet [*Roofs or Ceilings?*] which is, without exception, the most pernicious thing ever issued by an avowedly conservative organization.

I presume that you do not know what your booklet actually advocates. So I had better tell you: it advocates the nationalization of private homes.

When you come to Los Angeles, I will be glad to discuss this with you, if you want me to.

I cannot attempt to do it in a letter.

If you feel that you owe me an explanation, I would like to hear it.

P.S. I have shown a few passages out of your booklet (no, not page 10) to my secretary. Without any advance comment by me, his comment was: "Jesus Christ!"

■ ■ ■

To William Mullendore

September 20, 1946

Dear Bill Mullendore:

If you were writing a treatise on the various ways in which a young man can make a living in civilized society, you would not end up by saying: "And then there is always the possibility of robbing a bank."

If you decided to mention such a possibility, you would write of it in the manner of a dire warning, stating how evil it is and why one must not attempt it.

If such were your intention, you would not describe in great detail the method of cracking a safe, and then conclude, as your sole comment, with: "It would be a lot of bother for a young man. It would take him so long!"

Yet this is precisely what the authors of *Roofs or Ceilings?* have done in their discussion of the socialization of private homes, in the chapter entitled "The Method of Public Rationing," pp. 16–17. What objection have they raised against it? None, except that it would take an OPA board "too long to decide." (!)

Where, in that whole unspeakable passage, is there one word of condemnation against the idea of seizing private homes? Nowhere. The authors have most carefully refrained from expressing any disapproval of it in principle. What is more, they have skillfully *suggested* approval.

They say that "rationing by a public agency is unlikely to be accepted on a thorough-going basis."

Do they say that it *should not* be accepted? Why, no. Do they say people would be right in not accepting it? No. Just that it's unlikely.

They say that: "it is utterly impracticable from a political viewpoint to order an American family owning its home either to take in a strange family (for free choice would defeat the purpose of rationing) or to move out."

Only from a *political* viewpoint? From what viewpoint would it be practicable?

If you were discussing wholesale slaughter, you would not choose the word "impracticable" as your sole objection against it.

When the general public hears it said that some proposal is "politically impracticable" and "unlikely to be accepted"—*with no other condemnation added*—the public gets the impression that the proposal is desirable, in fact noble and idealistic, but people are too stupid or backward or selfish to accept it. Which is precisely the impression conveyed in the passage on pp. 16–17.

No, the authors have not said it out loud. Yes, it's only an implication. But an implication of this kind is worth a lot to the Communist Party.

When one presents a proposal of unspeakable horror, and then condemns it with some weak little rebuke—the condemnation amounts to a whitewash. A logical reader will then think: "Well, if *this* is the worst that can be said against it, the proposal is not so bad."

Now let us examine another point (the two are connected).

Do you really think that calling the free pricing system a "rationing" system is merely confusing and innocuous?

The word "rationing" does not mean "distributing." The two are not synonymous. "Rationing" has a specific meaning of its own. It means: to distribute in a certain particular manner—by the decision of an absolute authority, with the recipients having no choice whatever about what they receive; it also means that all the recipients involved have an equal claim to that which is being rationed, and are entitled to an equal share.

That is the precise meaning of the word "rationing"; *that* is the sense in which it has always been used. And it has been used—quite properly— only in application to two main instances, both involving absolute authority: in military life (the rationing of soldiers), and in stock farm parlance (the rationing of animals).

In the mind of the American people, the word "rationing" is infamous—and quite properly so. It is the word and the badge of slavery. Americans will not accept rationing as a permanent way of life (they should not have accepted it temporarily, either). Any proposal that involves rationing will be defeated by that word alone, as the bureaucrats are now finding out. Americans do have that much sense left.

But what if that word could be made respectable? Would it or would it not be of inestimable help to those who want to bring us to a total and permanent system of rationing?

Remember how such words as "democracy," "isolationism," "reactionary," etc. were put over, and what use was made of them, and for what purpose. They, too, merely created a slight confusion—at first.

If the trick pulled by the authors were merely innocent stupidity, wouldn't such a confusion of terms still be inexcusable? Particularly on the part of an organization that professes as its goal *a sound education in economics* and the clearing up of the popular *confusion* about economics?

Can an organization educate people to understand the nature of principles, if it permits a statement such as this: "War experience has led many people to think of rationing as equivalent to OPA forms, coupons and orders. But this is a superficial view."

I submit that this is a statement of plain intellectual depravity. It has the effrontery to call a judgment by principles "a superficial view." *Certainly* rationing *is* equivalent to OPA forms, coupons, and orders—in principle and by definition. Rationing *IS coercion,* that is, *orders,* and nothing else whatever. The *essential* distinction of a free market, as against any other kind of system, lies in the absence of coercion and in the method of exchange by voluntary choice.

Can an educational organization call the above distinction "a superficial view" and still retain the moral right to try to educate people in clear thinking?

After that, it is shocking to read, on the card inserted into the booklet, that: "The Foundation for Economic Education is devoted to explaining the distinctions between free private enterprise and coercive systems; between voluntary and involuntary action." (!)

The trick perpetrated by the authors of the booklet is neither innocent, nor innocuous, nor accidental.

If we accept the idea that a free pricing system is a form of rationing, the *unavoidable* logical implications and consequences are as follows: if a free pricing system is a form of *rationing*, then every person living under it has an equal claim upon and title to all the goods produced. (To *ration* means to *share*; a free pricing system is not based on the idea of *sharing* anything; a rationing system *is*.) But anyone can see that under a free pricing system everybody *is not* getting an equal share of everything. Therefore, *this form* of rationing is not working well or fairly. Why isn't it? Because the rationing is done by private persons in their own selfish interest. What is the solution? *Another form* of rationing—which would be run by disinterested public servants for the common good of all.

Once the people's mind has reached *this* stage of confusion, the rest is easy. The collectivists have won, because their basic premise has been accepted. There is no real issue left. Subsequent arguments will always be won by the collectivists—(as all modern arguments are, on any issue, and for the same reason)—because the collectivists will be consistent with the premise accepted by both parties, which the defenders of free enterprise will not: these last will become self-contradictory, self-defeating, hypocritical and helpless.

Instead of an issue between two absolute opposites, such as freedom or slavery (free exchange or rationing), the argument will be counterfeited into a squabble over "forms," "two versions of the same thing," "a mere difference of 'opinion' or 'interpretation,' " etc. Instead of a difference in *principles*, it will become merely a difference of *methods*. Instead of a difference *in kind*, it will become merely a difference *of degree*.

And here is the payoff: when the groundwork is ready, a collectivist says to the average American: "Don't fool yourself, brother. You've always lived under a system of rationing and always will. The only choice you have is this: Do you want to be rationed by selfish, greedy capitalists for their own private profit—or would you rather be rationed by a public authority who will have no motive except your own good and the general welfare?"

If the average American then chooses this last, will you blame him? Will you call him illogical?

The above sequence of reasoning is *implicit* in the definition of a free-market system as a system of rationing. Any reader who is able to make logical deductions from the premises he reads and to trace the ultimate consequences of an argument by its beginning, will see it without any trouble. But the authors did not leave it just for somebody like me to deduce. They made sure not to have it missed; they indicated the whole progression—step by step. It's all there. We don't have to infer anything. They've blueprinted it.

Page 9 "Everything that is not as abundant as air or sunlight must, in a sense, be rationed. That is, whenever people want more of something than can be had for the asking, whether bread, theater tickets, blankets, or hair-cuts, there must be some way of determining how it shall be distributed among those who want it."

This is the first piece of intellectual counterfeiting. This is where they make readers start by swallowing a collectivist premise. The above is not a definition of Capitalism—not in *any* "sense."

Nothing produced under Capitalism can be had "for the asking"; it can be had only *for a price;* which is quite a different principle. Capitalism does not presume that everything *wanted* by people is to be *distributed* among all those who want it; nor that *want* constitutes a *claim*; nor that the total of goods produced is intended for the total of the population as by right and on equal shares.

If five yachts are produced, under Capitalism, the principle of the system *does not* imply that we must then find "some way of determining how they shall be distributed" among 130,000,000 people who undoubtedly want them. Under Capitalism, a man produces *for himself* and exchanges his product with whomever he wishes for whatever he wishes. If he has produced only ten pairs of shoes for ten customers, the fact that there are 2,000,000,000 barefoot men on earth is no concern of his. And the 2,000,000,000 barefoot men have *no claim* whatever—theoretical, practical or moral—upon him or his customers. The paragraph I quoted is a definition of pure Collectivism.

Page 9 (further down) "The advantages of rationing by higher rents are clear from our example . . ."

This time, the "in a sense" has been omitted. What, at first, could have been taken by a careless reader as merely a sloppy figure of speech, has now become an unqualified, matter-of-fact definition.

From this point on, there are no such words as "free market," "free exchange" or "free pricing" in the booklet. It's "rationing by higher rents" throughout. Do you think that's accidental?

Note the particular tag chosen: "rationing *by higher rents.*" No demagogue could have hit upon a catch-phrase more damning to Capitalism, one that would sound more unjust, obnoxious and offensive to the average man, particularly to the poor, one more certain to arouse resentment. Accidental, too? Innocently chosen by authors intent on championing a free system of rentals?

Page 14 "Rental property is now rationed by various forms of chance and favoritism." This refers to present rentals under price ceilings. The text that follows performs another piece of counterfeiting: apartments are not *rented* by harassed, hogtied landlords—but are "rationed by favoritism." Implication: a landlord has no right to choose the tenants of his own property, if there are more than one applicant.

Page 16—the payoff: "The defects in our present method of rationing by landlords are obvious and weighty. They are to be expected under private, personal rationing, which is, of course, why OPA assumed the task of rationing meats, fats, canned goods, and sugar during the war instead of letting grocers ration them."

Dear Bill Mullendore, there is no excuse and no possible forgiveness for this paragraph. And there is no possible way to misunderstand it.

I never thought I'd live to see the day when Leonard Read would endorse a vindication of the OPA (and with an "of course" included) as against "private, personal" grocers.

The chapter that follows the above quotation is the passage on pp. 16–17, which I have discussed. This passage speaks about ordering people out of their own homes and forcing tenants into private houses. Is this procedure identified by the proper, specific name which exists for it? Do the authors call it *socialization*? Why, no. It's not socialization—it's only "*rationing* by the OPA" (!) Is this another accidental bit of innocent confusion?

This chapter is the core of the booklet and of the authors' argument, the purpose of the whole contemptible performance. The rest is pure guff and space-filling.

No, this booklet alone will not convert people to the cause of property socialization. It's not direct propaganda—collectivists never work through direct propaganda. It's groundwork-laying. To the extent to which this booklet has any influence, is taken seriously or makes any point at all—to that extent it will prepare the ground (the necessary intellectual confusion) upon which the demand for socialization can be planted, when the right time comes. The booklet itself is just a little drop in the bucket. All the successes of collectivist propaganda and of various collectivist proposals have been achieved through just such little drops, carefully planted in systematic progression.

No, this booklet does not advocate socialization of property in so many words. But neither did Willkie advocate the election of Roosevelt in so many words. Yet that is what Willkie achieved.

As to the lip-service plea for removing rent ceilings and returning to a system of free pricing—it is mere window dressing, weak, ineffectual, inconclusive and unconvincing. What reasons do they offer in support of free pricing? Not one word about the inalienable right of landlords and property owners. Not one word about the inalienable right of tenants to pay whatever they wish to pay. Not one word about any kind of principles. Just *expediency* (will get more housing space)—and *humanitarian* (*sic*—the word is used on p. 16) concern for those who can find no houses.

The net result is the impression that free pricing won't work very well, anyway; that it's a temporary makeshift, a regrettable compromise with the selfish homeowners; that it's an evil—but a lesser one than other evils (see last sentence of booklet).

I have given you this detailed analysis in order to make *the basic premise* of this booklet unmistakably clear to you. Actually, however, it is clear without the details, because the authors have stated it explicitly at the beginning of the booklet and at the end.

Their basic premise is that everything belongs to everybody—and that the arguing among various factions is only about methods of dividing it up.

NOW I SUBMIT THAT IN A CIVILIZED SOCIETY ONE DOES NOT INCLUDE THE SOCIALIZATION OF PRIVATE HOMES AMONG THE SOCIAL "POSSIBILITIES"—AND ONE DOES NOT DISCUSS IT IN THAT TONE OF CALM, ACADEMIC DETACHMENT, AS IF IT WERE A COURSE AS PROPER TO CONSIDER AS ANY OTHER.

I submit that a Foundation which is dedicated to the defense of individual rights and which has permitted such a discussion to be issued under its imprint, has forfeited all moral right to continue to exist.

On page 22, the authors state, as their conclusion: "We should like to emphasize as strongly as we can that our objectives are the same as yours: *the most equitable possible distribution of the available supply of housing* and *the speediest possible resumption of new construction.*"

I submit that it is not *my* objective to distribute other people's property; and that private homes *are not* an "available supply of housing" to a nation, no matter how large the number of the homeless nor how great their need.

(Private homes are discussed throughout the booklet as if they were to be considered "an available supply." Well, they are "available" to the people and to those authors only in the sense in which a man's wallet is *available* to a pickpocket.)

Since the above "objectives" are those of the Foundation for Economic Education, by explicit statement—I can permit myself no further cooperation of any kind with that Foundation.

Now I shall ask you an ethical question. I have not referred to the disgraceful performance on page 10. Without any of my analysis, the last paragraph on that page proves that the authors are Collectivists. The Editor's Note proves that the publishers know it. (The lack of dignity and integrity in the hypocrisy of that Editor's Note is appalling. But that's not my main point.) If the publishers classify their own authors as "those who put equality above justice and liberty," this means—in plain language— an admission that they are publishing the work of Collectivists.

Here is my question: At a time when good, competent conservative writers are being blacklisted and starved by the pink clique that controls so many commercial magazines—why did Leonard Read hire two reds, with money entrusted to him by conservatives anxious to preserve Capitalism?

I think it is a question that should be asked of him, and I think it is proper that you—as a trustee of the Foundation—should ask it.

■   ■   ■

To Alan Collins

September 23, 1946

Dear Alan:

I am not the kind of person who falls for tags (particularly those of Communist origin), nor who helps smear campaigns. I didn't think you were, either.

What exactly do you mean by the word "reactionary"?

By whom have Flynn and Lyons been labeled as "reactionaries"? For what specific actions? Was it not for their uncompromising stand against Communism?

You are actually advising me to remove from our leadership the effective men who are dangerous to the Communist cause and turn our leadership over to some naive, befuddled "liberal" who is open to leftist influence and won't know how to conduct the fight.

Have you ever heard of a battle won by appeasement?

You are advising me—in order to be "practical," I suppose—to adopt the policy which has worked with such eminent success for Willkie and Dewey. I am extremely shocked, and don't know what to think of your attitude.

As far as I am concerned, the only thing I have against Flynn and Lyons is that they are not "reactionary" enough.

If *"reactionary"* means *anticollectivist*, I am the most complete *"reactionary"* living—and proud of it!

P.S. Have you ever read a book called *The Fountainhead*?

■ ■ ■

To Ben Stolberg, organizer of the American Writers Association, a group of anti-Communist writers

September 26, 1946

Dear Ben Stolberg:

As you know, I am a member of the American Writers Association. You can imagine how strongly I feel about *that* battle.

I want to give you a bit of information I received—which might be meaningless, or might be a sign of something we should investigate.

I got a letter from a very prominent literary agent in New York. I am acquainted with him personally, and he claims to be a Republican. He writes that he saw my name among those who joined the American Writers Association—and he assures me that New York agents and publishers are solidly on our side. But, he says, they have all agreed "in informal talks," that we're not going about it in the right way. They think that we should remove from our leadership the people "who have for many years been labeled rabid reactionaries," and we should "have the fronting done" by people "who have long been known on the liberal side although never allied with the extreme political left." He names a couple of names, as examples of what he means by both. I don't quote the names, because I don't want to help spread stuff of this kind. He concludes by saying: "I am writing this letter to you absolutely on my own. It is just a thought for what it's worth."

What do you make of this?

I am inclined to think that the "I am writing absolutely on my own" indicates the exact opposite. Is there some sort of sneaky movement among New York publishers and agents (of all people!) to sabotage us?

I think this letter could mean one of two things: either it is just the usual kind of Republican timidity, that is, those people really want us to win, but are fool enough to think that we should do it by appeasement, by playing up to the "liberals," by saying "me, too" to the Communists— just as they thought that the Willkie-Dewey method was the practical one to win an election. If that is the case, we can safely ignore the nasty nonsense.

Or it can mean that there is a secret campaign afoot, a few Communist spark plugs planted around to use literary agents and publishers—most of whom are befuddled cowards—as stooges for their own purpose. Namely: the agents and publishers undoubtedly do want us to win, so the Communist plants are busy giving them the following advice on how to win: just re-move from our leadership all the effective men who are dangerous to the Communist cause ("because they are reactionaries") and turn the leadership over to some naive, befuddled "liberal" who is open to leftist influence and won't know how to conduct the fight.

The purpose of such a campaign would be to spread dissension within the American Writers Association, even before it is formed—to spread doubts and timidity among the "middle-of-the-roaders" (if we have any) —to use these doubters as a pressure group that would try to make us adopt a policy of appeasement, and would try to turn our leadership over to appeasers and compromisers; either to some ineffectual person open to influence—or to an actual fellow traveller. In other words, to take the As-sociation over just as so many "liberal" organizations were taken over.

I am usually good at smelling out the party line—and it seems to me that that is what's going on.

But you know much more than I do about the specific cliques, persons, methods and intrigues of the pink intellectual underworld in New York. So I thought I should tell you about this, and ask you to look into it.

I would like to find out whether the letter I received is just an isolated example of personal timidity—or whether other letters of this nature are being sent to our membership as part of a general whispering campaign. If it is this last, we should expose it at once, before it gets going and achieves any results.

The person who wrote me started his letter with: "All this is strictly confidential." I do not consider myself bound to keep a matter of this kind confidential and thus become an accessory to what may be a Communist campaign. If it's just his own blundering, I won't mention his name. But if you find that this *is* an organized campaign and you need the information, I will give you his name.

Of course, as far as I personally am concerned, if the Association ever adopted such a policy as disavowing the "reactionaries" and featuring the "liberals," I would resign at once. But I don't think we're likely to fall that low.

Please let me know whether there is anything I can do out here to help you fight the battle. Are those of you who started the Association carrying the whole financial burden? Should I offer a contribution? What method of financing our expenses are you planning to have?

Stolberg responded that he agreed the agent was trying to disrupt the group.

■ ■ ■

To Lorine Pruette

September 26, 1946

Dear Lorine:

Thank you very much for your answer. I am happy to know that you do want to review *Anthem*, and whatever you say about it, I know that it will be an honest review. The publication date of *Anthem* is October 21st.

I was glad to hear about the young people who are reading and discussing *The Fountainhead*. If, as you say, I am going to be a classic, you were the first one who said so to the world.

■ ■ ■

To Rose Wilder Lane

October 9, 1946

Dear Rose Wilder Lane:

Thank you with all my heart—and in more ways than just literary—for the two mentions you gave me in your September issue. The thing that meant a great deal to me was the fact that you told me privately that you liked my pieces in *The Vigil*—and then you also said it in print. I consider that an action of great professional integrity. You see, I am slightly embittered on this point. I have known several persons who paid me high compliments in private correspondence and conversations, but carefully avoided doing so in print. It is an attitude I was never able to understand, so your action made me feel better about people in general.

You asked my opinion of your review of Hazlitt's *Economics in One Lesson.* Your review is excellent, and I agree with all of it (except one small point). I think you have been eminently fair in giving him credit for the virtues of his book—and there are many. But you picked quite properly on its basic weakness. I think this is another case such as that of Ludwig von Mises. Hazlitt tried to divorce economics from ethics. He presented a strictly economic argument, telling how things work out, and carefully omitting to state why the way they work out is proper—that is, what principles should properly guide men's actions in the economic field. He did not say that we should sacrifice minority groups for the sake of the whole, but that was certainly the implication of his book, which is certainly a collectivist implication.

This is an example of why I maintain that no book on economics can have real value or importance if economics are divorced from morality. When one attempts to do it, one merely spreads the implications and premises of the collectivist morality and defeats one's case for the more thoughtful readers.

I wish you had blasted one particular passage in the book, which made me more angry than all the other flaws, and really spoiled the book for me. That was the passage where Hazlitt states that a virtuous, responsible man of wealth should donate to charity and should refrain from buying luxuries, because these take productive resources away from the manufacture of necessities for the poor (p. 192). That was really a crucial betrayal of our case. It is not true as economics, and it is wrong as morality. It is pure, explicit collectivism.

I take exception only to one paragraph in your review, on the second page, which refers to "love thy neighbor as thyself." First, I have never agreed with that slogan. It is just as impossible and improper as the idea of loving your neighbor *above* yourself. (What we owe our neighbors is respect, *not* love.) Second, your sentence, "human beings survive on this planet only by working together in that mutual effort," is an unfortunate one. I know what you intended to say, but this particular sentence could be taken as a statement of collectivism. It is true that if men want to live together, they cannot do it by robbing one another; but it is not true, as a general statement, that human beings can survive only by working together. The best among humanity can survive alone, and actually do so; in fact, they make it possible for the less competent ones to survive.

Also, I would object to the statement that one's own welfare "depends upon the welfare of *all* other persons." (The italics are mine.) It depends upon one's own efforts and upon dealing with others justly (that is, according to the proper moral principles). But that is all. My welfare does *not* depend on whether the Cambodians have or haven't got any milk. I think you probably agree with me on this—but you see where your sentence, taken as a general statement, could be interpreted in the Henry Wallace kind of way.

I was delighted to see you take the position that you are an "extremist" and proud of it. So am I. At least, there are two of us.

And this leads me to something which is actually tragic. I have had a crushing disappointment, and I think you are the only one who will understand how I feel about it. By this time you have probably read *Roofs or Ceilings?*—the second booklet issued by Leonard Read's organization. I think you will agree with me that that booklet is the most dreadful thing ever put out by a conservative organization. Nothing done by poor Mr. Peck or any of our other befuddled conservatives, can equal this thing. I never expected that from Leonard Read. He was really my one last hope of a conservative who would act on the proper principles, and take some positive practical action for our cause; and it is awfully hard to see a last hope go.

Here again is a case of our "almost" friends, and in this case no excuses or forgiveness are possible. The mistake is too terrible and the principles betrayed are too important. I wish you would tell me, if you can, what is the matter with Leonard. What happened to him in New York?

I am enclosing a copy of a letter I wrote to Mr. Mullendore about this *Roofs or Ceilings?* He agreed with me. Please keep this letter confidential between us—I do not want to embarrass Mr. Mullendore in any way, since this letter was intended for him and since he said that he would take action upon it. But I wanted you to see my reasons for the burning indignation I feel against that booklet and against a conservative organization that would issue it.

■　■　■

To Albert Mannheimer

AR uses the term "rationalist" here to mean an advocate of reason. In later writings she used the term in its technical, philosophical sense, meaning an advocate of the view (which she opposed) that knowledge is derived from mental content divorced from perception of physical reality. See her title essay in *For the New Intellectual.*

October 10, 1946

Albert darling:

I hope that you have remained a good rationalist—because if you have, you won't feel too badly about any of it. I've read some of the New York reviews [of your Broadway play, *The Bees and the Flowers*], and my feeling is: to hell with the bastards!

I know that it's hard to take, but I also know that it's not as hard as it might seem to lesser people. Since you're not one of the lesser people, I hope you have discovered already that it's not too damn important. And it shouldn't hurt you too much.

The only important thing is what you think of it yourself. If, according to your own best judgment, the critics were wrong (and I think they were)—then you should feel angry and disgusted, but nothing more than that. If you think that they were justified to any extent, if the play was not produced as you wanted or did not satisfy you when you saw it acted— then look at it as an experiment, as experience, and make *your own* conclusions about what was right or wrong. But make conclusions yourself, as you saw it—*not* because of what critics or anybody else has said.

Personally, I say it's a good play and I will say so no matter who disagrees. But you saw it acted—and you must not take my opinion, any more than anyone else's. Judge it for yourself.

If you are not sure of your own estimate of the production, then let it go honestly at that—that you're not sure, and that you'll decide in the future. But don't take the word of others.

There is only one thing which can be tragic and terribly wrong for you—and that is, if you were satisfied with the play and the production, to let yourself doubt your own judgment because of the opinions of others. That is the only permanent and fatal damage that the occasion can cause you—and it will be caused by yourself, not by anyone else. I hope you do understand and believe *rationally* that there is no escape from your own judgment, and no substitute for it, that it's the final, crucial one, the only one that counts.

Whatever you do, *don't doubt yourself because of others.* That's the only thing I want to impress upon you, as strongly as I can. Don't let secondhandedness make you suffer unnecessarily. If you don't let that happen, the rest is not too important. Of course, it's unpleasant—but that's all. It's just a *practical* disappointment for you—not a spiritual or artistic one. It means that you won't make as much money as you could have made, and that you won't get, for the moment, the prestige which you have a legitimate right to want. But what of that? You don't need money, and you have plenty of time ahead to get the prestige. It is only one of those chances which any writer has to take and be prepared for, before he starts his career. If you don't let it get *inside you*—it won't matter very much. I can tell you that from firsthand experience. I know.

I gathered from the reviews that you had a very successful opening night and that the audience roared with laughter. (I noticed how the bastards had to mention it, yet tried to cover themselves.) So I don't know what the fate of your play is now. If it is financially possible to keep it open and give a chance to word-of-mouth—I hope your producer will do it. If he can beat that dirty little gang of "Broadway intellectuals"—I wish he would.

If you don't feel like writing letters, don't, until later. If you can— I'd like to hear from you, at least a few words. I miss you, and I wish I could be with you right now.

All my love, darling—(and also, which is more important, all my philosophy—if you'll use it)

■　■　■

To Richard Neutra, the well-known architect who designed the San Fernando Valley house purchased by the O'Connors in 1944

October 11, 1946

Dear Mr. Neutra:

Thank you very much for the copy of the speech by the Federal Housing Administrator, which you sent me. I was very interested and amused to see it. Considering the man's position, it was certainly funny to see him talking about *The Fountainhead.* I wonder what he thought of the dynamiting of the Federal Housing Project.

■　■　■

To Rose Wilder Lane

October 25, 1946

Dear Rose Wilder Lane:

By all means, you are free to tell anyone you wish that you have received a copy of my letter to Mr. Mullendore—and free even to quote it in your review, if you wish, in your own name or in mine, as you prefer.

The reason I asked you to keep the letter confidential was only in regard to your publication. I didn't want to have any accusations against Leonard Read quoted in print until he had seen it. But now he has seen it, and I am extremely indignant about his attitude, as I learn it from your letter. When Mr. Mullendore came back from New York, he sent me a note stating that he had shown my letter to Leonard Read, and that Leonard agreed that his booklet was a mistake, but he did not agree with me that it was as fatal and crucial as I considered it to be. Now, the disgusting and inexcusable thing is their writing to you that you and I accuse them of being Communists, "making no attempt to substantiate such a charge." (Incidentally, I didn't accuse them of being Communists. I accused them of publishing a Communist booklet, which it is.)

I think I had better tell you the whole story of what makes me so indignant against Read personally. Since he had always told me that he considered me one of the best and most strict authorities on the proper philosophy of our side, and since he admired my ability to see when our cause had been given away by implication, I offered him before he started the Foundation to serve as an unofficial editor for all his publications—without pay, of course. He was to send me everything he intended to publish, in manuscript, and I was to mark every passage that betrayed our cause in any way, and then give him my detailed reasons for considering it objectionable. In this way I was to protect him from publishing anything improper, and at the same time educate him and his associates to a better understanding of our proper philosophical line. This was agreed between us, and both he and I referred to me as the Foundation's "ghost."

The last time he was here, he told me he was sorry that he had not sent me the manuscript of his first book, as he had not had time to do it, but all future publications would come to me first. And the next thing I know I receive the printed copy of *Roofs or Ceilings?* with a rather offensive letter from Leonard, offensive in that it had a kidding tone in which he told me that he had had trouble with his authors, but that all passages betraying our cause had been eliminated. There was, of course, no reference to our agreement.

That is why I did not want to send him a long detailed analysis of the booklet, but I did write it for Mr. Mullendore. I saw no point in forcing my opinion on Read after the booklet was published, since he had chosen not to ask my opinion, for his own protection, as we had agreed. In view of this and in view of the fact that he has seen my letter to Mullendore, which is more than an article in itself, I can say nothing except that his attitude is dishonest, unfair and disgusting if he or Watts write to you that I am making charges "without attempting to substantiate them."

I would suggest, of course, that you keep Mr. Mullendore's name out of it (if you quote the letter in print), because he has behaved very honorably, and he does agree with us, but you may quote me against the booklet in any way you see fit.

■   ■   ■

To Lorine Pruette

October 28, 1946

Dear Lorine:

I was very startled and sorry to hear that the *Times* had given *Anthem* to another reviewer. If it was my publishers who sent a copy of *Anthem* to the *Times*, they did so in spite of a specific agreement with me to the contrary, and I shall have to inquire as to how or why this happened.

Thank you for the nice things you said about *Anthem*—I wanted to know your opinion. No, I don't agree with you that the end is not as good as the beginning—I think the end is much the best of the book. The last two chapters are the actual anthem. But I am glad that you liked the rest of it.

As to my next book, I think I will put it in my contract that you are to review it, if you are willing to, by that time. At least, I intend to try, as I still don't want any other reviewers for my writing, and I won't change my mind until and unless you tell me to. I think the next book will interest you. It is a very serious undertaking, and it will be in the nature of a bombshell.

■   ■   ■

To Kelsey Guilfoil, of the *Chicago Tribune's Magazine of Books*

October 30, 1946

Dear Mr. Guilfoil:

Yes, I would like very much to do some book reviews for you. But my interest in reviewing is of a special kind, so I had better explain it to you in advance.

You ask, must I like a book in order to review it? No, not necessarily. But "like" was the briefest way to state it in a wire. To be exact, what I should say is that I would be glad to review a book if I find that it would be interesting for me to review it. This means: if the book has some aspect which I consider important, so that something serious or important can be said about it. I may then praise or condemn the book, or both in part, as the case may be.

Now the fact that a book is by Mr. Marquand does not necessarily mean that I will find it important as far as my particular intellectual interests are concerned. The book will, of course, have professional or trade importance, but that is quite a different matter.

My writing commitments are so heavy and my working schedule so crowded that I cannot undertake to do reviews just for the sake of reviewing. What I should like to do—and I'd like it very much, indeed—is write a report, occasionally, on some book which arouses my own interest enough to make me eager to express my views of it in print.

As examples: I would have liked to review *Animal Farm*—though I consider it a very bad book; but it has great historical significance—as an eloquent and frightening revelation of the mind of a modern socialist. (I mean, the author. The book is not anti-Communist, you know. It's merely anti-Stalin, but *pro-Communist*. This should have been said in reviews, but wasn't.)

I would have liked to review *Mr. Adam* [by Pat Frank]. It is not a literary work—but its antibureaucratic satire deserves attention, both on its own merit and as a healthy symptom in our literary world, after all these years of maudlin glorification of bureaucrats.

I would have liked to review Hazlitt's *Economics in One Lesson*. It's a magnificent job of theoretical exposition—though I don't agree with everything in it.

Now there you have samples of my approach to books and reviewing. If that fits your purpose—I'm at your service.

I know that I will be difficult about it, because there are very few modern books that interest me at all. If you do not consider it too much bother and are willing to send me books for consideration—with no hard feelings involved if I keep rejecting them until I find the right one—then let's try it.

As a general suggestion: what interests me is *Individualism*. Any presentation or aspect of it: ethical, philosophical, political, fiction or non-fiction. If there are any books coming that advocate the principles of Individualism—send me those. They don't have to be books by prominent names. I suspect that they are more likely to be found among the work of new and unknown authors. Also, do allow me some margin of time—considering my geographical distance from you.

Please do *not* send me any books of morbid psychology studies (so many of which are being published nowadays), such as stories about the insane, drunkards, perverts, etc. I don't think they are worth writing, publishing, reviewing or reading.

Let me know within what limits of length you want a review to be. Also, there is one condition which I attach to anything I write: it must be published exactly as written, without cuts or changes. If you find you want to make some change for some special reason, then you must obtain my consent to it, or, if we can't agree, not run the review at all. If this is agreeable to you in principle, please allow time for such communications. I mention this only in case such occasion arises—I don't really suppose it will.

The printed letter about me, which I am enclosing, is for the purpose of getting acquainted. It will give you some idea of what I'm like, which might interest you, if we are to work together. I hope we are.

There is no record of AR doing book reviews for the Chicago Tribune.

■   ■   ■

To Lee Lyles, assistant to the president of the Atchison, Topeka and Santa Fe Railway system

October 31, 1946

Dear Mr. Lyles:

Thank you very much for the most interesting collection of material which you sent me. I am glad to have a copy of the book on the Santa Fe— presented to me by the Santa Fe itself.

I enjoyed meeting you, and appreciate the time you gave me, including the personal visit to "The Mighty 6000." You have given me a great deal of precisely the kind of information I needed.

You might recall that you offered to let me have a copy of your speech, which you showed me. Unless you prefer not to give out any copies, I should like to have one.

■ ■ ■

To Leonebel Jacobs, an artist who painted portraits of AR and her husband

November 2, 1946

Dear Leonebel Jacobs:

I would like to thank you—in a way which I can't quite express—for your letter and the things you said about me. I was awed by your reaction to me, and it made me very happy. My first impression of you was that you saw in people much more than you would ever tell them—and if this is what you saw in me, I am truly grateful.

I am delighted with the little print of my picture. I did want to see it again, and it cheers me up when I look at it. I have shown it to my friends, Adrian and Janet Gaynor, and you would have been pleased by the compliments they expressed about your work.

If this is only an experimental print, I am most eager, of course, to get the one which you will consider good.

I hope very much that you will come to California again, as I don't want to lose you. I am sorry that we will not be able to come to New York this year, but I hope to next year.

■ ■ ■

To Robert Bremer, a fan

November 2, 1946

Dear Robert Bremer:

If we continue corresponding—and I hope we will—you must make allowance for one peculiarity of mine: I have certain periods when I am working on my writing day and night, and cannot answer any letters. This is an understanding which I have with all my friends, so that if it should happen that you don't hear from me for a long time, do not take it as neglect or indifference. I will answer as soon as I can.

You have asked me so many questions and some of them are so important, that it would take an article to answer you properly. I can only do it briefly this time.

First, let's start with what probably interests you most (and properly so)—yourself. I am very much impressed by what I can gather about you from your letters. I think I am impressed in the right way—so stop worrying about my opinion of you. I think I know exactly how you feel, but take my word for it—you don't have to be afraid.

I am startled by the fact that you are 16, and I can tell you right now that you have an unusual intelligence. The passages you selected as your favorite from *The Fountainhead* are the most important ones in it. What impressed me particularly is that you selected Roark's conversations with Wynand. Those passages are the least obvious ones, and the most important ones philosophically. If you were able to pick them, and if that is what interests you—you have my compliments. You have passed the test brilliantly.

You asked me if I have any suggestions to give you about the choice of a career. That, as you probably know, is something that no other person can suggest to you. I can only tell you this: don't expect any outside circumstance or observation to give you a desire for a particular career. That desire comes from your own convictions about life, its purpose, what you want to do with it, and in what form you want to express it. When you say, "I want something that can mean to me what your writing means to you"—it seems to imply that you hope to find it just by looking around and waiting to have your interest aroused. You will never find it that way. What you should do is ask yourself what do you consider the most important thing in life, and why? When you have thought that out carefully, the work that you want to do will suggest itself, and also the desire to do it. But you certainly don't have to hurry. When you say, "Why is it taking me so long to find it?" you are really a little too impatient. I think I understand your impatience, and it is natural that you should feel it, but at the age of 16 your choice of a career for life does not really have to be set. There are no rules about this—some men make a choice earlier, some much later, and any age is proper for any particular person. If you have not made your choice, it merely means that you are not quite clear enough about your basic convictions. Since you seem to have an unusual mind, it might take you longer than it would another, simpler person. So I suggest that you think about it, but do not worry too much.

I doubt whether you should be an actor, but I can't say this with certainty, since I do not really know you. I say it only as a suggestion, for the following reason: if your interests are mainly intellectual, you would not be happy in a profession which is not essentially an intellectual one. Of course, good acting takes intelligence, like any kind of good work, but that is quite another matter. Acting is an interpretative profession, and I suspect that what you are really after is a creative one.

You mention that you wrote some poems, which you would like me to see. Do send them on if you want me to read them. I am wondering why you said that they are morbid. If you like *The Fountainhead*, I wouldn't suppose that you are essentially a morbid person, because it is probably the most "un-morbid" book ever written.

In connection with that I was a little startled by the questions you asked me. You ask, "Do you ever think about death? Do you look forward to it, merely accept it or don't think about it at all?" I wonder why that question occurred to you, and above all why you ask, "Do you look forward to it?" Do you imagine that I would? To answer you properly, I would have to write a treatise, so I will say only this: I don't think about it at all—although I have definite philosophical reasons why one should not think about it. I have given it that much thought, and no more. I think it is the essence of human life that death should be no part of it, and by definition it isn't. When you die, you stop living. I am concerned only with the living. *The Fountainhead* is an affirmation of life here, now, on this earth. I think so much of this life that I am not interested in what comes after, if anything. But tell me why you asked this.

You ask, "Exactly why don't you believe in God?" Because I have found no rational argument in support of such a belief.

You ask, "Is Dominique any less human than Roark? In what way?" Dominique potentially is not less human than Roark, but in the period covered by the book, she functioned on an extremely wrong premise, on a very mistaken idea about life. Roark is the genuine human being, because he exemplifies a man who has reached perfection. He found the philosophy proper to man, and he acted upon it. You asked a very intelligent question when you said, "Why didn't Dominique do any serious writing after she married Roark?" It is my own conclusion that she probably did or would—and I was interested to see that you thought of that, too. But that would not be part of the story. Her story was the search for the proper philosophy. When she found it at the end, we can infer that she then lived accordingly, which would include a serious endeavor of her own.

You ask me about my next novel. I can't tell you very much about it, because it is very difficult for me to discuss unfinished work. I can only tell you that its theme will be Individualism, but from a different angle than *The Fountainhead*. I think you will like it.

As to *We the Living*, it is out of print, and you can obtain a copy only from a public library or by advertising for a used copy.

Does this answer your questions for one letter?

I want to add that your last letter to me is a magnificent piece of writing. You don't have to "go naked and eat bread crusts and water" in order to write as I do. I think you will.

Yes, I am very much interested in you now. If you say you want a Henry Cameron—that is what I wanted at your age. I never found him. I would like very much to see whether I can really be a Cameron in relation to you. But it is much too early to think of that now. It would take years to see whether I am the right person for that purpose or whether you are the right pupil.

Now tell me more about yourself, and why you should be morbid at the age of sixteen.

■ ■ ■

To Robert Bremer

November 3, 1946

Dear Robert Bremer:

After I mailed my letter to you, I glanced over your letters again (you see, I do take you seriously), and I noticed that you are a little sensitive about being sixteen—and that I had referred to your age repeatedly in my letter. So this is just a postscript to tell you not to take it as any kind of disparagement. Quite the contrary. I don't hold your age against you in any way, I hold it in your favor. I don't think that your views are "less sincere or less stable," because you are young. I think it is remarkable that you have reached such views and are interested in such subjects so early. So I don't intend to write to you as to a child, but as to a person who is my equal in intellectual interests, if not in experience.

■ ■ ■

To Jerome Mayer, theatrical producer, who in 1937 contracted with AR to produce a stage version of *We the Living*

November 3, 1946

Dear Jerry:

No, I don't agree with you about *Ideal*. The play *is* about the people's attitude toward the movie star—*not* about the movie star. She has to be only a symbol. The theme is the relation of men to the ideal, and the various things for which they betray it—the theme is not the inner life of a great artist. If the theme were to be this last, an entirely different play would have to be written, with an entirely different plot. The pattern of visiting one fan after another would not fit at all; it would become totally irrelevant. A great artist's problems are not her fans.

I hope you find a play which you like—I'd be sorry to see you leave the theater. I know plays are harder to find than ever now, but I'd say keep on trying, maybe there are some better playwrights coming up among unknowns—I know that the ones available now are awful. As to your question about Hal Wallis—he has no playreaders (just one story editor), and no assistant producers, because he produces only three pictures a year, himself, without subsidiary production units. If you're interested in that, you would have to get in with a major studio. But are you really interested? I always thought that the stage was your real love.

■　■　■

To Rose Wilder Lane

November 3, 1946

Dear Rose Wilder Lane:

Here is the philosophical letter I owe you.

1. About "Love thy neighbor as thyself." You are right that one of the troubles here lies in the word "love." It's certainly the wrong word, with no exact meaning in this particular slogan. That is the first reason why the slogan should be dropped. Any inexact statement of what purports to be a principle, creates nothing but harm.

But whatever meaning we attempt to attach to this slogan—it still remains a tenet of collectivism. If "love" here means self-preservation, as you say, or the protection of one's interests—well, it still means that you must preserve and protect others *as much as* yourself. Since your chief activity of self-preservation on earth is work to obtain food, the slogan means that you must work for others just as much as for yourself. If so— collectivism is the proper social system for men. (A slogan or precept should be applied and observed literally, concretely, consistently, in every instance which it covers—or not at all.)

Actually, you not only must not preserve and protect others as yourself—you *could not* do it, if you attempted to. Each man's fate is essentially his own. Any help you can give him is strictly of a secondary nature. Example: any poor relative. Have you ever succeeded in helping a person who did not want to help himself?

Now when you say "my interests require that I do not jeopardize (and that if and when necessary, I protect) my neighbor's"—this is quite another matter, and not at all within the meaning or intention of that slogan. "Not to jeopardize" is not the same thing as "actively to preserve." What you owe yourself is to work for your living; what you owe your neighbor is not to interfere with his work. This is not loving (or preserving) "as much as yourself." Every moral duty you owe to yourself requires a positive action; everything you *owe* your neighbor is negative—to abstain from action that would infringe his rights.

It's that element of *owing*, of a moral duty, which is crucial here. If you *owe* your protection to your neighbor—then it is a claim which he can and must present against you, should you fail in your duty. And who would define the debt and the failure? You or he?

"If and when necessary" is an extremely dangerous statement—again, because inexact. Here you have the base of the New Deal pattern of declaring one emergency after another. If you *must* help your neighbor in an emergency, then a man who is starving by reason of his own errors, shiftlessness or laziness is certainly in a state of emergency, he *needs* your help, so he would be justified in demanding it.

Now I say, you *owe* nothing to your neighbor. If you *want* to help him—that is another matter. Then the determining factor is *your desire— not* his need. It is then a favor to him—*not* his rightful due.

Now, *must* you always want to help him? Is it morally desirable that you should? No. Here is where the real issue comes in: you may (morally) wish to help him *only when such help does not involve the sacrifice of your own interests.* Example: you may loan money to a friend in need, if you really like him and can spare the money; but if you give him money which you need yourself for a major purpose of your own—I say you are positively *immoral.* More specifically: if your friend needs money for food, and you pass up buying a new dress and give him the money—that is all right. But that is *not* a sacrifice, because you actually wanted him to have food more than you wanted a new dress. But if that money was required to finance your education, or career, or wedding, or even if you wanted that dress for a date with your sweetheart—then you would be immoral if you gave that money away. You cannot place the interests of another man *above* yours, nor on an *equal* basis with yours. Yours must come first. (Always remembering that *his* come first for him.) That's the only way men can live together at all. Any conflict of interests must be solved by mutual voluntary agreement. Actually, there can be no *essential* conflict of interests among men, if none demands or expects that which is not his, if each man recognizes that none of the others exists for *his* sake and that he can *demand* nothing from them on the ground of his need.

Take your own example—about rushing to put out the fire in a neighbor's house. You may (and would) certainly do that—*if your own house is not on fire at the same time.* But if it is? Whose house would you and *should* you save first? Of course your own, and properly so. Therefore, you cannot "love him as you love yourself."

Now of course I don't believe that there is *any* "natural" or instinctive human action. (I won't try to state my reasons here—that would have to be a treatise on the nature of man.) Human actions proceed from intellectual premises, accepted consciously as convictions or on faith, as axioms. So I don't think that you run to save your neighbor's house by reason of a natural impulse. You do so by reason of the premises you have accepted about human relations in general—and one of them is benevolence toward other men, which is *natural* in the sense that there are good rational grounds for it—unless the particular man has forfeited this benevolence. Would you always rush to save that house? I am sure that if it were the house of, say, Henry Wallace—I would not rush to save it.

And this leads me to my main point about human relations: man being a creature of free will, any blanket commandment about what one should feel toward him is completely improper. Feeling proceeds from judgment based on a code of values. Man must be judged by his own record and actions—which may be anything. You love or hate him accordingly. A blanket command to love is collectivism. Love (or any feeling toward another person) is and can only be individual, with an individual object, for the individual reasons of each particular case.

Personal note: Love is such a tremendous thing that it makes me twist with anger (almost "instinctively," only I know that it isn't an instinct) whenever I hear it said that I must love my neighbors or men in general. Love is such a great, magnificent exception which one grants only to such great qualities (to me, love is what I feel for Howard Roark) that it makes me sick to think I am expected to feel it for Hitler, Stalin or the village idiot. Yet, they're men, aren't they? No, I'll never agree to love men, collectively, indiscriminately, just for being men. I love Roark too much.

Incidentally, you say that you "don't exactly love" yourself. I know this will sound strange, but I *do* love myself. Though I grant you it's a somewhat different kind of feeling than the one I feel for other people whom I love.

2. Now, next point. You ask, "Isn't there a vital distinction between cooperation and collectivism?" There is—and how! And it lies precisely in *not* having to love your neighbor as yourself. When you deal with men on a basis that involves no self-sacrifice—when you make contracts, or agreements, or hire people, or take a job, *only* as your personal interests may require—only then can you have true cooperation. *Collectivism* requires self-sacrifice, the subordination of one's interests to those of others.

You are right, of course, when you say that collectivism disintegrates human cooperation and comes to "dog-eat-dog." Only free, independent men can cooperate and feel benevolence toward one another. But they can do it *only* because (and only so long as) they know that cooperation will involve no pain or injury to them—that is, no demand for self-sacrifice.

But cooperation cannot be placed first, in the sense of saying that we *must* cooperate with others—if by cooperation you mean acting in a common enterprise. There are instances when we wish to act together with others—and instances when we prefer to act alone. Here again, how would you apply it concretely, if you preached cooperation as a general rule of conduct, as a conscious policy to be adopted by every man? If the community in which I live needs me and wants me to be a night watchman for them, and I want to be a writer—do I have to cooperate?

Cooperation is not and cannot be a conscious, deliberate consideration, or a rule of conduct, or a set policy. It's a consequence—call it a natural result, if you wish—of voluntary association among men, each acting in his own interest. The overall result of each pursuing his own interest will be a society of peaceful, harmonious cooperation—such as a capitalist society. But it's not done through any "will to cooperate"—only through pursuing one's own interests, while respecting the same right in those with whom we deal.

Of course, Individualism doesn't mean isolation, aloofness or escaping to a desert island. In fact, only true Individualists are fit to associate with other men. But they do it *only* on the basis of the recognition of each man's essential independence: each man lives *primarily for, by and through himself,* and recognizes the same right in others; all relations among men are secondary; men are legally and morally free to associate together or not, on any particular occasion, as their personal interests dictate. *There* is the pattern of a free, moral society, of human cooperation, and of benevolence among men.

3. Now, about self-sufficiency. It is true that if I were born alone, in pre-civilization days, I would not have radios or typewriters. But all the wonderful things around me now, which are the products of civilization, *are not mine* and are not available to me—unless I produce, by my own effort, some material equivalent which I can exchange for the radios, type-writers or any other object I may want. If I don't produce it, I can't have it. Neither morally nor in fact—I have no right to demand it and nobody is going to produce any material objects for me.

Each man actually produces only that which he produces—and no more. Yet we do see that the total material wealth of mankind grows greater, as civilization advances, and the average material wealth grows greater. Why is that? The personal qualities or abilities of men in general are not improving, not growing greater—and in some periods, like now, they are actually deteriorating. Then where does that extra wealth and pro duction come from?

There is only one great debt that men owe to others—and it's not a material one (though its results are material). The only real benefit we receive from others is the benefit of the accumulated thinking of the men who preceded us, or of our own contemporaries who have superior intel ligence. If I were born alone on a desert island, I could work as hard as I do now, with the same ability—and I would not achieve a material return equivalent to the one I get now. It is the accumulated thought, knowledge and discoveries of the past that make my efforts produce more (materially) than if I were starting alone from scratch and had to spend my life inventing the wheel (if I were even able to invent it). The fact that billions of human beings are working at something and producing something around me does not actually add to my material welfare. What they produce, they keep for themselves—or, to be exact, they keep its material equivalent, in the proc-ess of exchange. The something extra I get from men, the thing that raises the material efficiency of my own efforts is not the anonymous hordes of the "common man." It's the thinking, the ingenuity of the exceptional men who discovered and showed me better ways of doing things, which I would not have discovered by myself. The great advantages of an exchange society—of a division of labor and specialization—were made possible only by these thinkers and discoverers. Now the degree to which I profit from this accumulated intelligence depends upon my own intelligence, upon my ability to understand great thinking, to grasp it and to apply it. If my ability is great—then to carry it forward. If my ability is of the lowest order—then I still get a benefit from the intelligence around me, only in this case almost totally undeserved, completely "extra."

No, the food in my cupboard and the typewriter I use do not come from the "less competent men," who feed me while I write. They don't feed me. I've paid them for it. It is only themselves that they feed. If I were alone, I'd grow my own food—and I would grow more than they would, if they were left alone. But what I haven't paid—and can't pay— is the man who invented the telephone or the typewriter. The material comfort which I now have and couldn't have if left on my own—comes from him.

A good mechanic may earn his own living by his own honest effort. But a great part of the material return which his effort brings him is due to the engineering genius who designed the engine or the scientist who discovered the necessary knowledge—achievements which the mechanic could neither equal nor grasp. Now suppose the genius and the mechanic are each born alone in the jungle, separately, starting from scratch. The genius will discover fire. The mechanic will perish. It is in this sense that the best brains of mankind carry the rest. The geniuses do not need the mechanics in order to survive. The mechanics do need the geniuses. (There is no harm in this relationship, no literal parasitism—so long as men are left free to work as they will or can. The genius exchanges his material product with the lesser man in a fair and proper exchange. The only point is that the exchange is equal materially—but not spiritually. The lesser man gives the genius *only* a material product; the genius gives him a material product—plus the knowledge of a discovery that adds to his, the lesser man's, effort. The genius *could have* produced what the lesser man gives him; the lesser man could not have produced what the genius gives him. This is quite all right—and the genius is not robbed in this process—so long as he is left free to function. But his part in this process must be recognized and acknowledged for what it is.)

But, you'll say, what about the lesser jobs? Aren't mechanics neces- sary in our industrial civilization or our mass production? And I will answer that without the mechanics, no mass production would be necessary. The geniuses would satisfy their own needs through a different form of pro- duction on a smaller scale and would receive for it materially as much as they do now (if not more).

I believe you are extremely wrong when you say: "I think that you have only to decide not to buy a can of salmon, or fail by your efforts to obtain money to buy it, and the welfare of every one of them will be adversely affected." Here, I think, you have unwittingly accepted a collec- tivist view of economics. The canners of salmon do not actually produce a can intended for me—and I do not let them down if I fail to buy it. A capitalist exchange economy—in essence and principle, though not in form—is an economy of independent, self-sustaining production. The salmon canner produces *for himself*—in the same sense as if he were operating a self-sustaining farm. If I am there to offer him something he wants, he gives me a can of salmon in exchange. If I'm not—he doesn't make that extra can, but spends his labor on something else.

This applies to any production for a free market. Any producer produces only as much as he can exchange profitably (or as near as he can gauge the market). This means: only as much as he can convert into products for his own use. If men fail to provide him with a market, if they have nothing to give him in exchange—he doesn't continue producing for them; his effort goes into another endeavor. So whatever he owns is the result of his own production—though it may have gone through many stages of exchange—a material equivalent of the material wealth he has produced.

Would we all get more if all men on earth were free to work productively? In proportion to the actual count of added noses—no. But to the extent to which there would be chained geniuses released to function—ah, yes!

No man produces any extra material value for another man—except the man of superior intelligence and to the degree of that intelligence. Most men just carry their own weight. Some do not even do that. And some give an inestimable extra benefit—free—to all mankind: the thinkers, the new discoverers. (Free—because whatever material return they get, it is never an equivalent of what they give.) *They* can exist and survive anywhere, by their own effort—except in a collectivist society, under compulsion; in that case, they are first to perish. And that is the chief reason why a collectivist society perishes, why it cannot prosper, produce or even exist for long.

You ask, what happens to my supply of food if all the stevedores stop working? Why, nothing whatever—in a free society. I will have to pay a little more for stevedoring—and ten men will rush to take each vacated job. (It's only in a controlled society—like now—that we are at the mercy of anyone and everyone.) What if nobody wants to do stevedoring? Then I—and the rest of society—adjust our productive labor accordingly. The decision of the stevedores (or of any other group or man) affects us only superficially and temporarily—not essentially. And that, precisely, is the essence and advantage of a free economy—that nobody depends on anybody. Any man is free to change his mind about his work—and the rest are free to count him out and adjust their own production accordingly, without any material loss to themselves (or, at worst, only with a temporary loss).

I know that I am profoundly indebted to Aristotle, to Thomas Edison, to Henry Ford. But to the Malayans and Cambodians?—hell, no!

(Do you know what I've written to you here? It's the theme of my next novel. This is only a brief, partial statement—the subject is extremely complex. If I haven't stated it clearly enough—you'll see me do better when I present it completely in the novel.)

(This is the kind of letter-writer I am—either silence for months, or a whole treatise. You'll wish I hadn't become regular in my correspondence. So I'd better stop now.)

Now to answer your last letter, which I received yesterday. Yes, of course you may quote me from *The Vigil*, any time you wish.

I think you have undoubtedly analyzed Leonard Read correctly—and that makes me feel very sad. But it's true. I was surprised to hear that he has repeatedly ignored your advice and offers of help (though in view of the general course his activities have taken, I shouldn't be surprised). But he has always spoken to me about you with the greatest enthusiasm and respect, and he quotes you very often. I suppose, as you say, he just doesn't understand the nature of application of principles—and he may not even know when he has contradicted your advice or mine. Or does he know? Anyway, I shall not attempt to help him or "enlighten" him any more.

It was interesting for me to read that you find it difficult to understand people. So do I, and always have. Only I don't believe they understand one another, either. Look at the world right now, or listen to any conversation. It's all meaningless gibberish and double talk. I don't think that "to understand" means to them the same thing as it does to us. What their equivalent for it is, I can't imagine. Somebody once told me that the most cruel thing one can do to people, is ask them: "What do you mean?"

Report from a faithful reader: Have bought *Mr. Adam* on your recommendation—and enjoyed it immensely. Have sent for *Labor Unions—or Freedom?*, but haven't read it yet. Have subscribed to *Plain Talk.*

With my exhausted, "philosophical" regards,

■   ■   ■

To Richard DeMille, movie producer and son of Cecil B. DeMille

November 27, 1946

Dear Mr. DeMille:

Thank you for your letter about *Anthem*. It was very interesting to me, more so than if it were a business letter about picture rights, precisely because it was an unsolicited personal letter. I am glad that you liked *Anthem* enough to want to write me about it.

I don't really think that you knew, while reading the book, how "it would turn out" after the escape of the protagonists. Are you sure that you know it now? Read Chapter XI again.

I don't quite understand why you refer to my use of the word EGO as a "symbol." I did not use it as a symbol, I used it in its exact, literal meaning. I did not mean a symbol of the self—but specifically and actually Man's Self.

You say that there are those to whom the word EGO is "too strong —even, immoral." Why, of course, there are. Against whom do you suppose the book was written?

I wonder why you wanted to warn me about that. I presume it means that you have not read *The Fountainhead.* If you haven't, I think you should read it—particularly since you describe yourself as "a person with an anthropocentric attitude" (it's a good word all right—I like it, too).

Just to show you that I appreciate your letter, I will tell you that I am making an exception for you—it is my policy never to ask anyone to read my book. I shall be interested to hear from you again after you have read it.

■　■　■

To Retah Wodlinger, a fan

November 29, 1946

Dear Miss Wodlinger:

I appreciate most sincerely your interest in *The Fountainhead* and your concern about its fate on the screen. It is going to be filmed by Warner Brothers some time in the future—and I have reason to believe that it will be a good picture.

But should it turn out to be otherwise, don't let it disappoint you. A book cannot be "ruined" through a film or "through the interpretations of some of its readers," as you say. Nothing can ruin a book. It is a completed entity. Misinterpretations are merely the misfortune of those who make them.

■　■　■

To James Schuler, a fan

November 29, 1946

Dear Mr. Schuler:

Howard Roark's hair was what you would call "unkempt." That's even
stated in the book.

Now please tell me why on earth you wanted to know that. I am very
curious.

■ ■ ■

To Mimi Sutton

December 2, 1946

Dear Mimi:

Here is the check for Docky for December.

Give Docky our congratulations on her school grades. I'm very happy
that she is doing so well.

Thank you for the snapshot of Docky which you sent us. She is very
pretty—she looks quite a bit like Agnes and like yourself. Yes, we would
like to have her picture in a bathing suit, which you mentioned.

We were glad to hear that you are all right and that everything is fine
now. I was amused and pleased by your description of Connie. I knew on
my single encounter with her that she would grow up to be something
special. She had a lot of spirit even at the age of six.

No, the strikes in the studios haven't bothered my work, because I
work at home. But they are certainly making a lot of trouble for pictures
in general.

We won't be able to come East this year, but hope to do it sometime
next fall.

■ ■ ■

To Rose Wilder Lane

December 1946

Dear Rose Wilder Lane:

Thank you for your very interesting letters. You are right when you say
that the difficulty in discussion is the fact that "no two persons think on

precisely identical assumptions." That is why I intend to write a book someday, stating my case from my basic premises on.

So I won't attempt a treatise, this time, but will just answer briefly the points which you raise.

First, to begin with your last letter (of December 6th) in regard to my latest piece in *The Vigil*. You say that my piece "seems to assume that persons are members of a super-individual social entity exerting coercion on its members." I don't know what could possibly have given you any indication of such an assumption. What particular statement or statements gave you this impression?

I am a little shocked by your question: "Am I to understand that you mean to state as a principle: A person should act for his own advantage as opposed to that of other persons?" I have stated explicitly in that particular piece, and in all the others, my principle: A person should act for his own advantage as independent of that of other persons.

Man's interests, or advantages, are neither opposed nor united to the interests and advantages of other men; they are independent. As a secondary consequence, a man's pursuit of his own personal advantage often does benefit other men—such as a man's scientific, artistic or industrial work does benefit society—but it is only a secondary consequence, it is not always so and does not have to be so. An artist, who is not recognized by society, should and must, morally (I'll define that word for you in a moment) continue to pursue his work, if that is what he wants to do, whether it is of any advantage to others around him or not. He must, of course, provide his own means to support himself—he cannot demand support from others, if they don't care to buy his works. But he must do what he wishes with himself, his life and his money—whether he is doing any "good" to others or not. (Once more, just to be exact: He must not use physical violence against others; that is the only moral restriction on him.)

When you say that "it is not a question of being sacrificed . . . it is a question of individual decision and individual action"—I do not quite know what you mean. In reality, we can see instances of both: men being sacrificed by other men, through brute force (as in any concentration camp or political slaughter) and men sacrificing themselves, of their own volition, because they think it is proper to do so. This last makes the first possible. I am not sure which is the more vicious of the two. It is the idea that self-sacrifice is proper and moral which permits men to sacrifice and butcher others also. My principle is: No sacrifice (self or others) is proper or even necessary.

As to your example about eight persons on a raft, with one man having water, and should he hoard it or share it?—well, the answer can tell him what to do, in such a case, no precept or philosophy ever devised. The decision would have to be his—and whatever he decides will be right.

But this example has no validity whatever for formulating rules about proper human conduct, nor any application to human life—because it reverses the actual realistic conditions of human life on earth. Man's proper independence rests primarily on the fact that man is equipped to provide for his own survival (through his work, directed by his mind) and that his survival does not depend upon any one other man holding the only available supply of food (or water) which he needs. Man does not live on a raft with one bottle of water. He lives on earth, which gives him infinite resources —and it is up to him to get them. His proper conduct and morality must be based on this fact.

Now, if we did, in effect, exist in a position like that of your men on the raft (that is, if we were dependent upon the will of other men), then nothing would be possible to us, except to exterminate one another. Just carry your example a step further: Let us assume that the eight men divide the water, on the basis of brotherhood, for a while. But if they are not rescued in time and the water supply grows smaller and smaller—what are they to do? All perish equally and at the same time? Or start killing one another off, in the hope of survival? This is unavoidable if we assume that men's means of survival (food, water and every material product men need) are a fixed, static quantity on earth, which must be shared. That is the Collectivists' view of men and production—and they do achieve nothing but mutual extermination. Man's actual existence is on earth, not on a bare raft, and he must produce his own wealth, not wait for a voluntary handout (sharing) from another man, nor attempt to loot that other man's property.

Now, to your letter of November 22 and its many interesting philosophical points.

You say that you do not know the meaning of "moral" or "morality." My definition is: Morality is a code of behavior proper to a human being. On what is it to be based? On man's nature, which is that of a rational being, on earth (in space and time, as you say). Why is it necessary? Because man is a being endowed with free will. This means that his actions are not automatic; that he has to function through choice. The necessity of making a choice presupposes a standard of values as a guide; a standard of values is a code of right and wrong, good and evil. Good and evil for whom? Man—his nature, essence, survival and happiness on earth.

The conception of "morality" is applicable only to issues in which choice is involved. That is why I am a little bewildered by your sentence: "If it is moral that man be self-controlling and responsible, then it is moral that water seek its own level." Aren't you confusing a few different things here? That man is self-controlling and responsible is neither moral nor immoral; that is an actual fact of nature—just like water seeking its own level. But for man to recognize that he is self-controlling and responsible, and to act accordingly—that is moral. It is possible for him not to recognize it; is possible for him to try to act as if he were a robot by nature—that is what most of mankind is doing right now. But it is impossible for him to succeed or survive in the role of robot.

In this sense, the moral is the practical. In this sense, it is based on the reality and conditions of man's existence here, now, on earth. Morality (the proper, rational kind) is as absolute and objective and real as the laws of nature. But the crucial difference is that water seeks its own level and can do nothing else. Man can do a great many things, his field of choice is immense; some of his possible actions are beneficial to him—if they are in accordance with the basic principles of his nature as man; some lead to his self-destruction—if they are opposed to his nature. It is up to him to discern and define which is which. The statement of such definitions, of the rules of proper human behavior, is a code of morality.

Every moral precept amounts, in effect, to: This is what you should do because it is good and proper for a man to do so but you have the possibility, the choice, to do otherwise.

I'm sorry if I confused you by using the expression "neither morally nor in fact." I grant you that perhaps this was not clear—so the above will help to clarify it. When I said that others will not produce for a man, I meant: they neither should (by moral commandment) nor will (in actual practice).

As to the word "spiritually," I use it to denote all that which pertains to man's consciousness, most particularly to his thinking (which is the base and essence of his consciousness). I do not know (nor care too greatly) whether man's consciousness is a special spiritual element, different from the material, much as the religious conception of a soul—or whether it is only a function and manifestation of his physical body. I am concerned only with how this consciousness works, here, on earth, what it can do, what it should do, how it should live. Whether material or nonmaterial, a man's consciousness (his spirit) is the essence of man and of his life, and it is (as you have often stated) a prime source of energy—spiritual (thinking) and physical energy, both.

I am in complete agreement with you that anything we say about man and his life is valid only if we keep it in terms of this earth, of the physical world, of space and time. (Did I understand you correctly in this?) Man's consciousness is a fact of this world, too, of course.

I regret I have even less sympathy or interest than you have in anything relating to the mystical, to the "other-dimensional," the irrational or "super-rational." (I don't believe there are any such things or realms.) I am an atheist. Therefore, I cannot follow you at all in your definition of why the existence of a finite world presupposes that it was created by God. It doesn't.

I do have a quarrel to pick with you (and a serious one) on your statement that "neither logic nor demonstration can prove this assumption (the existence of man and the world); therefore it is an act of faith." Now this is truly a dangerously careless statement. What do you take logic and demonstration to be? Logic is the art of reasoning correctly about observed facts—but not of creating the facts. Logic cannot start in a vacuum. Logic presupposes something about which one reasons. Logic presupposes existence. And what on earth do you think demonstration is? If the existence of our senses is not demonstration—then what is? The existence of man and the world does not need logic or demonstration—it is an axiom. It is self-evident. What we learn about ourselves and this world does require logic and demonstration. But not the fact of existence itself. To attempt to prove that fact is a contradiction in terms.

Now "an act of faith" is belief without evidence. That is the most vicious action of which men are capable; it is the real root of all their sins, crimes and misery. But if you say that to assume we exist is "an act of faith"—then you can have no argument and can make no valid objection to anything anyone may claim as his particular act of faith. Hitler did believe that he was mystically appointed to be a world leader. If any "act of faith" is proper—then all acts of faith are proper.

Do you know that my personal crusade in life (in the philosophical sense) is not merely to fight collectivism, nor to fight altruism? These are only consequences, effects, not causes. I am out after the real cause, the real root of evil on earth—the irrational.

■ ■ ■

To John L. B. Williams

January 8, 1947

Dear Mr. Williams:

Thank you very, very much for the beautiful Christmas flowers.

I had a wonderful Christmas this year, and your present contributed to the things that made me happy. Some of the chrysanthemums, which were truly magnificent, are still alive and fresh. I think of you every time I look at them.

■ ■ ■

To DeWitt Emery

January 20, 1947

Dear DeWitt:

Thank you for your letter. I was glad to hear from you again—and will be waiting for you to write more fully, as you promised.

This is just to correct a minor point. Leonard Read is not correct if he told you that I had "raised hell with him for putting out a pamphlet on such a trivial subject." I didn't raise hell about the subject—and it's certainly not a trivial one. I raised hell with him for publishing that whole pamphlet (*Roofs or Ceilings?*)—because it advocates collectivism in its premises and implications; because it hints that the nationalization of private homes might be the proper solution for the housing shortage; and because there is no excuse for anyone in his right mind to call the free-market, free-enterprise system a "system of rationing." (!)

I am glad to see that you're fighting to teach people to state their ideas in proper, clear and exact language. This is certainly needed badly among conservatives. I think their sloppiness with words and slogans (and, therefore, with ideas) is the root of all their troubles.

■ ■ ■

To Vladimir Kondheim

January 20, 1947

Dear Volodia:

It was completely impossible for me to help you with the purchase of a house. I suppose that you do not realize what the income tax situation is. My taxes are so high that I am not able to lend to anyone a sum as large as the one you needed.

I presume you have not heard anything about the packages sent to Europe. I don't think that you should ask Gimbel's to inquire—because I am afraid that it might prove embarrassing to our relatives. So let us wait and not do anything further for the time being.

I hope that you are doing well and that your practice is growing satisfactorily. I am sorry that we could not come to New York this year, and I don't know when we'll be able to, but I hope to come when and if my work permits it.

Thank you for your Christmas greeting, and please give my thanks to Peter for the present she sent me—the "Fountainhead" soap. (!) That certainly surprised me, and I would like to know who is putting out that soap. Would you ask Peter to find out the address of the manufacturer, from the store where she bought it, and to let me know?

■ ■ ■

To Richard Mealand

January 20, 1947

Dear Dick:

My congratulations on the completion of your novel [*Let Me Do the Talking*]. I was most impressed to hear that you had finished it already. That was really fast, so you must have worked very hard. To me, the finishing of a novel is about the most important event that can happen in life—so if you feel as I do, you must want (and deserve) more congratulations than on any other holiday.

I am, of course, very eager and curious to read your novel. Do you have any extra carbon copy of the manuscript that you'd care to send me? If you have, I'd love to see it—but if not, I'll wait patiently for its official appearance in book form.

I have just finished a script for Hal Wallis (*House of Mist*) and am back on my own time once more (with a great sense of relief, as usual). I am now going to do the actual writing of my next novel—I did all the research and the complete outline of it in my last six months of freedom. I hope to have the novel completed this year.

Warners will probably make *The Fountainhead* this year—though no official date has been set for it as yet. *Love Letters* was voted one of the ten most popular pictures of 1946 in a Gallup-*Photoplay* poll, which pleased Wallis very much, and pleased me, too, mainly for his sake.

I don't want to rush you about reading *Anthem*—I know that reading is the hardest of all jobs for a writer, I hardly have time to read anything myself. I want, of course, to hear your reaction after you have read it—but this is not a hint, only for whenever you have the time.

I wish you speed and success with the new novel you are planning—but, first, my most sincere wishes for the greatest success to *Let Me Do the Talking*. I can't think of any novelist about whose success and happiness I feel as strongly as I do about yours.

■   ■   ■

To Alden Cornell, a fan

January 27, 1947

Dear Mr. Cornell:

I am glad that you liked *The Fountainhead*.

I do not quite know what you mean when you say that "genius is always impossible." If genius were impossible, mankind would not have survived.

Yes, I am opposed to everything represented by the New Deal. But you are wrong when you wonder whether this had been the inspiration of my book. A book like *The Fountainhead* cannot be inspired by hatred, nor by the things which one opposes. It had to be inspired by the things which I believe.

■   ■   ■

To John C. Gall

■   ■   ■

January 29, 1947

Dear John:

I have another problem which I would like you to handle for me, if you find that you can help me in this matter.

An old friend of mine, a White Russian woman who left Russia at the beginning of the revolution (in 1918), is now in Austria, in the position of a Displaced Person refugee. She lives near Salzburg and got in touch with me through the American Resident Representative of the Intergovernmental Committee on Refugees in Salzburg.

I would like very much to bring her to the United States, and would, of course, assume responsibility for her support. But I was informed that there are as yet no provisions for the admission of immigrants to this country, that only close relatives of citizens are admitted at present, and that she would have to wait until some new rules of admission are made.

In the meantime, she is in an extremely precarious position as a Displaced Person, because her permit to remain in Austria will expire on March 31, 1947. I am very worried about her fate, because if she should be turned over to the Russians out there or forcibly deported to Russia, it would mean certain death, since she is a White Russian. I am worried also because there does not seem to be any clear legality about the whole situation in Austria—and I am afraid that the arbitrary decision of some local authority might take her out of the protection of the American authorities and turn her over to the Russians.

If you find that this is a matter which you can handle as an attorney, here is what I would like to ask you to do:

1. Obtain a visa for her to be admitted to the United States—if there is a way to obtain it in an individual case, without waiting for a general ruling. (I suppose this would have to be obtained from the State Department.) I would provide the necessary affidavit of support for her.

If this is impossible, then:

2. Establish a personal contact with some influential person in the Army, for the purpose of enlisting the help of some important American Army official in or near Salzburg, so that he would take my friend under his personal protection and see that she is not left at the mercy of Austrian or Russian authorities.

In either case, we must be careful to deal only with conservatives in the State Department (if there are any) and in the Army—because I do not want to attract the attention of any Reds, here or in Austria. My interest in her would be dangerous for my friend as far as the Reds are concerned.

If you find that you can help me with this, I will send you her name, address and all the particulars. If you cannot handle this, perhaps you can tell me whether there is anything I can undertake to assist her.

■   ■   ■

To J. J. P. Oud, a Dutch architect

January 29, 1947

Dear Mr. Oud:

Thank you for your letter. I was interested to hear from you and pleased by your request for a copy of *The Fountainhead.*

Yes, of course, I know who you are and that you had a great deal to do with the birth of functional architecture. When I was doing research for my novel, I read many accounts of your work in the histories of modern architecture, and I have seen pictures of your very interesting buildings.

Under separate cover, I am sending you a copy of *The Fountainhead.* I shall consider it a privilege if you will accept it as a present from me, and I shall be interested to hear your reaction, after you have read it.

■   ■   ■

To Marna Papurt Wolfe, AR's niece

January 31, 1947

Dear Docky:

I have just received a letter from Mimi, telling me that she is leaving for Washington and sending you back to Cleveland. She did not say anything about what your plans are, how far you have progressed in school or how long you have to go before you graduate.

Will you write me yourself and tell me in detail how things stand with you? As you probably know, I had agreed to send Mimi the money for you to go to school for one year, and Mimi had assured me that one year was all the time you needed. That year will expire in March, so the next check will be the last one. I don't know whether Mimi has just left you up in the air, and I don't know what it was that she intended for your future. I had made it very clear to her that I would send the money only for one year.

So will you write to me and tell me how long you still have to go before you graduate from high school; and what are your plans?

I had asked you to write to me, so that we could get acquainted, but you haven't done it. I suspect that you are afraid of me and that that is Mimi's fault. So don't be afraid, and just tell me directly how things stand with you, what are your plans and what you would like to do. Tell me something about yourself. I would like very much to help you, if I can, but I can't help you if I don't know what you really are or what you are doing.

And I can't help you by just sending money on indefinitely. That is very wrong, both for you and for me. I hope that Mimi has not made you into the kind of girl who expects that. And I am very angry at Mimi, if she led you to believe that I am the kind of person who'd agree to be used in that manner. There is a great difference between helping a friend and just being used. Mimi has put us both in the second position. And I had wanted very much to be your friend. I still do. Now let me hear from you.

■ ■ ■

To Marie Strakhow

March 12, 1947

Dear "Missis":

Forgive me for the delay, but here it is at last. I am enclosing an affidavit of support for your use in applying for a visa to come to the United States.

Of course, I am very eager to have you come here and to see you again. I am sorry if my silence made you doubt my interest or made you think that I had changed my mind. I was busy getting information on what could be done here to help you get a visa quicker. What made it difficult for me and took such a long time is the fact that nobody could give me any definite information here, in Los Angeles, and such information as I got was vague and contradictory. So I finally had to appeal to my attorney in Washington, and all my correspondence with him took time.

I am enclosing a copy of his letter to me, which contains information on what steps you must now take in order to apply for your visa.

Please let me know whether the American Consul finds my affidavit satisfactory. If he needs any additional information on or documents about my financial standing, let me know and I will send it.

I am glad that you received the CARE packages which I sent you. I hoped they would help you while you are waiting for the visa. I will continue sending them.

Please don't worry about your being a financial burden to me when you come here. I don't quite know how to assure you that I can afford the expense of your trip, and that I will be truly happy to have you here as my guest. As you will see by my affidavit, a guest will not be a burden for me financially, so I would like you to forget that part of the matter entirely. Should you wish to work, when you come here, I think you will be able to find many opportunities to use your wide experience and knowledge of languages. The situation here is entirely different from that in Europe, and you don't have to worry about finding yourself helpless or "useless" here.

No, I have not heard from my sisters in reply to the food parcels I sent them. I have made no further inquiries, because I don't want my literary name to cause them any embarrassment.

I hesitate to write much about myself to you, since I don't know the conditions of the mail service, so I will rather wait until I see you here in person, and I hope it will be soon. Please let me know what answer you get to your visa application.

■   ■   ■

To John L. B. Williams

March 21, 1947

Dear Mr. Williams:

My belated, but most sincere thanks for the two page ad of *The Fountainhead* which you sent me, both for the proofs and the final copy.

I must say quite simply that I was delighted to see it. It came in the nature of a rather stunning surprise. It is excellent advertising. I appreciate it most sincerely, and I would be very happy to think that it does represent Bobbs-Merrill's present and future attitude toward my work.

You ask "how goes the new novel?" My delay in acknowledging your nice courtesy and such an important matter as this ad, is my best proof of how well the new novel is going. I am working on it full blast, day and night, which is my usual way of working. This is the first day when I could permit myself to stop, after finishing a sequence. I'm sure you will forgive my silence, since this was its reason.

The new novel is going wonderfully. No, it's not "marching toward a triumphant conclusion," as you say, since I have only been on the actual writing for the last two months—but it's certainly marching triumphantly. I love it. It is turning out in a way that even surprises me.

■   ■   ■

To Linda Lynneberg, a friend

April 17, 1947

Dear Linda,

Now, about your definition of Individualism. No, I don't think it's good, in fact, it's extremely dangerous. You say: "Individualism—personal responsibility to act in accordance with known moral and natural laws so as to promote human creative activity." Do you realize that such a definition could be accepted in and used by Soviet Russia? It could. As it stands, it would fit them.

The most dangerous thing in the world is a definition which is not specific, not objective, but open to the arbitrary interpretation of anyone who wishes to use it. Now you are absolutely right when you say that communication requires precise use of words. In order to be a definition, a statement must be objective, that is, have only one possible, undeniable, meaning, a concrete meaning. But now look at the holes left open in your definition, and at the pitfalls involved:

1. What do you mean by "personal responsibility?" Responsibility *to whom*? I would take it to mean, to oneself. The Church would say, to God. The Communists would say, to the Collective.

2. "—in accordance with *known* moral and natural laws." *Known to whom?* It is the whole problem and tragedy of mankind that no incontrovertible moral code has ever been defined. (That is what I will attempt to do when I write my nonfiction book.) Men do not even agree on their interpretation of natural laws, let alone the much more difficult moral laws. You are right in your intention, if I understand it correctly, that the proper code of Individualism has to be based on moral and natural laws. But a basic definition cannot be based on a code which has not yet been defined. As you have it, the Communists can very well claim that they are living up to your definition: they do claim that Marxism represents the absolute truth about natural and moral laws and that they slaughter people only because these people refuse to bear the responsibility assigned to them by the Commissars as their share of "promoting human creative activity."

Now even if we all had a rational moral code and we all agreed on it, we would have no moral right to *force* it upon an individual who refused to accept it or did not believe in it or could not understand it. We would, of course, have the right to defend ourselves against any immoral action that he might commit against us—but we could not tie our definition of individualism to our code and say that only those who accept it come under the conception of individualism. It would amount to saying that only those who think as we do are individualists.

But the point to which I would object most violently in your definition, the point which is the most profoundly philosophical and the most dangerous error, is this: you set *a purpose* for men's rights and existence. You say that Individualism is a means to "promote human creative activity." This makes the conception of Individualism (and, by implication, of Man) a means to an end. It amounts to the same thing as the error made by the Individualist philosophers of the XIX century when they defended a free economy on the ground that it achieved "the common good" or "the public good." Taken literally, your definition means that the conception of Individualism applies only to those who promote human creative activity and only so long as they do so. It means that a man who has no ability or no desire to be creatively active, an invalid for instance, must remain outside the province of Individualism and any rights it implies, since he does not fulfill its conditions. It also means that the conception of Individualism is dependent upon and subordinated to whatever definition one makes of what constitutes "human creative activity" and what are the best means to promote it. Now here is where the Collectivists would grab your definition, and how! They claim that human creative activity is social and collective, they claim they have a *natural* (scientific) case to prove it, and they claim that only a collectivist society will "release" the individual to be creative. That, in fact, is their oldest claim, one of the loudest points of their Party Line.

Now the essence of Individualism is that *nobody*, neither you nor I nor Marx, can tell a man what he must live *for*, nor subordinate his rights to a goal set by us. Individualism is not *for* ANY purpose, not "to promote" anything, not anything whatever, right or wrong or indifferent. It's true that Individualism leads to the development of human creative activity (and is the only code that does), to human happiness, to human prosperity and to every desirable thing men can wish for. But these are consequences, not goals; secondary results, not purposes set in advance. These cannot be made part of a definition of Individualism.

Also, didn't it strike you as significant that you made a definition of Individualism that included the word "responsibility," but not the word "freedom"? Do you remember when Henry Wallace defined his conception of human rights by saying that we should have duties instead of rights and responsibilities instead of privileges, or some such thing? I am afraid that you are on the same track.

Now, what do I suggest? Why, the definition I give in my articles in *The Vigil.* "Individualism holds that man has inalienable rights which cannot be taken away from him by any other man, nor by any number, group or collective of other men. Therefore, each man exists by his own right and for his own sake, not for the sake of the group."

This is all you need for a political definition of Individualism. The moral definition of it is implied in this statement also, but would need elaboration. This statement leaves to man all his freedom—but it precludes "license" or crime, because a man who bases his actions on this definition or invokes it as a sanction for his actions has to recognize the same rights of others as he claims for himself. If he claims the right to exist for his own sake (which *is* his right in nature and morality), basing his claim on his nature as man, he cannot then sacrifice others to himself, or demand that they exist to serve him, or use violence against them. If he does this last, he has forfeited his own right—but it is he who has done so, not society. I cover all these points more fully in the articles (and they are subtle, difficult points). Read the articles carefully. I'm sure you won't have any trouble elaborating on them (they are very brief for the subjects I cover) and I think you will find them helpful for the purpose you have in mind.

For a practical definition, if men merely agree that no man or number of men have the right to *initiate* the use of force against any human being (and that includes the forcible seizure of his property), that they have no such right for any purpose whatsoever, at any time whatsoever—that would be all we need, that would achieve a perfect Utopia on earth, that would include all the moral code we need.

I hope this will be helpful to you. I could write volumes on the subject (and intend to some day), but I can't do it in a letter. As it is, this is just a hasty statement, without revisions. You see what I'm like: I let personal news or matters go by, but just ask me a philosophical question and I can't resist a long answer, even when I'm rushed.

Incidentally, you don't have to concede that you were "a considerable pain when I was your guest," as you put it. You weren't. I was only sorry that you were so unhappy when you were here—and I'm glad that you feel better now. Your letters seem to show it. Some day, I'll ask you to concede that you're intelligent, as you seem to resent my thinking that you are. You seem to take it as an overestimation of you on my part, and therefore almost as an imposition. But it isn't. You *are* intelligent, and some day I will give you my definition of what I mean by intelligence. Albert and I have been sort of working on this subject—that is, the definition of the nature of human intelligence—and we have some most startling ideas and discoveries on the subject.

Frank asks me to thank you for "the best secondhand book of the month." He got a big kick out of it. He hasn't read it yet, but intends to. I can't make him read a book—or even speak to me at length—he has become such an active landowner that he is out of the house most of the time. He is now going into growing flowers professionally, as a business, and I think it's going to go very well. Our place has become wonderful. It's painted and furnished, at last, the garden is fixed, and it's simply unbelievably beautiful. Even I am impressed. It's becoming a kind of showplace, thanks to what Frank has done. One girl who came to visit us said that she didn't believe anybody could live like that. I wish you could see it as it is now.

I am on Chapter VII of the new novel—and that's my whole universe at present. I love it and am very happy with the way it's moving.

■ ■ ■

To Marie Strakhow

May 3, 1947

Dear "Missis,"

I was delighted to hear that you may be able to start on your journey here in July. We are looking forward eagerly to seeing you.

I am enclosing the documents which you requested, in support of my affidavit. They are: a statement from the Bank of America about my bank account, a letter from my literary agent about my motion picture contract, a copy of my Income Tax Return for 1946, photostatic copies of my checks in payment of the Income Tax, and a photostatic copy of the paid tax receipt for 1946 on the property which I own jointly with my husband. I am enclosing two copies each of the above documents.

Of course I shall be glad to pay for your trip. I am writing about it to Mr. David Ross of the Intergovernmental Committee on Refugees, so that he may start to make arrangements for your departure as soon as possible. I am enclosing a copy of my letter to him.

Mr. Gall, my attorney, has written to the American Consul in Salzburg and has sent him a copy of my affidavit. I am enclosing a copy of the reply which Mr. Gall received from the American Consul General in Vienna. I suppose that this was written before the Consul in Salzburg received your formal application for a visa.

Our very best wishes to you, and hope that we may be able to see you soon.

■   ■   ■

To John C. Gall

May 28, 1947

Dear John,

As we discussed in our telephone conversation, I phoned Superfilm in New York and obtained their permission to run the two Italian pictures of *We the Living*. [It was a two-part film of the novel.] I am enclosing a copy of the wire I received from them, authorizing the screening.

I have now seen the two pictures. I had an Italian interpreter present, who translated for me the general action of every scene and the key lines of dialogue. But it was impossible for her to translate literally every single line. So I was able to form only a general opinion of the two pictures.

The cast, direction and production are excellent. The adaptation follows my novel closely—until the last part of the second picture, at which point some changes have been made.

My impression of the political nature of the pictures, as far as I could judge, is as follows: the story has not been distorted into Fascist propaganda in any major way, but it does contain some lines of dialogue stuck in without relation to the story, which are most objectionable and most offensive to me. The interpreter caught one blatantly Fascist, anti-Semitic line —and I do not know how many other lines there may be, which she did not get.

If we find it advisable to negotiate with Superfilm and to settle with Scalera Films out of court, I will have to demand, before anything else is discussed, a complete literal transcript of the pictures' dialogue. I will want to have it made here, by people of my own choice, and the cost of the job will have to be borne by Superfilm or by Scalera. I have inquired at the studios here and was told that such a transcript would cost between $1,200 and $1,500. If we agree to an American release of these pictures, I will have to have the absolute and final right to cut out of the pictures any lines or scenes which I find objectionable, and to approve the final versions before they are released.

However, before we undertake negotiations with Superfilm, I should like to have your advice on the following problems even if the Fascist touches in the pictures consist of only a few lines, what decision must I make about the fact that the pictures were released and played all over Europe, without my permission, and that such lines appeared in a story bearing my name? (The screen credits mention the names of the adaptors, but also display my name very prominently, as the author of the novel, and even include a shot of the book itself, of its Italian edition.)

The objectionable lines could be easily cut out for the American release of the pictures, but it is the fact that they have been released in Europe that worries me, because it does constitute damage to my professional and political reputation. I am not sure that we would ever be able to collect for damages from Scalera Films, if we sue them. But on the other hand, if we settle out of court and permit the release of these pictures in America, it may be construed as my approving and condoning the use of such lines in previous releases.

This, incidentally, could serve as material for the Reds to smear me and brand me as pro-Fascist. I do not care about any Red smears, so long as some action of mine does not give them justification. Smears which are plain lies never work and cannot hurt anybody; but I do not want to give the Reds a factual basis for smearing me.

Is there any way or legal form or procedure which would permit me to allow the release of these pictures in America and clear me completely of any connection whatever, even an indirect or implied one, with the former releases of these pictures? Would a formal, written apology, or a damage payment from Scalera Films made specifically for this particular aspect of the situation, accomplish this purpose?

If this can be accomplished, I believe that I would like to have these pictures released in America, subject, of course, to my final opinion of the complete dialogue transcript—I cannot commit myself to this until I have checked the transcript. But the pictures are extremely well done, a great many scenes are magnificent—and I should like to see an anti-Soviet picture released in this country.

Now in regard to the immigration visa of Mrs. Marie von Strachow, I have not heard from her yet on whether her application has been granted or rejected. I believe that the definition of displaced persons to which the letter refers, applies only to people who had been imprisoned in a Nazi concentration camp, which Mrs. von Strachow was not. Can anything be done in Washington to help her get a visa? If a letter from me to the American Consul in Salzburg would help, please send me the text of how such a letter should be worded.

■ ■ ■

To John C. Gall

July 12, 1947

Dear John:

I have some interesting information, which if true, would tend to make me rather lenient toward Scalera Brothers. I met Alida Valli, who played the lead in the Italian picture of *We the Living*, and who is now in Hollywood under contract to David O. Selznick. She told me that the picture was released in Italy, played for two months with great success—and then the Italian newspapers began objecting to it and saying that it was anti-Fascist propaganda (which, of course, it is essentially). The Italian Government demanded to see the picture, and Miss Valli believes that Mussolini himself saw it. After which the picture was banned and Scalera Brothers had to withdraw it from circulation.

If this is true, I think it is wonderful. It would make the greatest kind of publicity story in this country, not just publicity for my book, but an important proof to demonstrate concretely the similarity of Soviet Russia and Fascism, which even Mussolini recognized, though some of the fools in this country refuse to. This makes me more interested in having the picture released here. It also indicates that if there were any pro-Fascist touches in the film's dialogue, they were minor and can be easily eliminated. Miss Valli told me that she has Italian clippings to prove all this and she has promised to send me translations of them.

Please let me know what you think of the situation.

■ ■ ■

To George C. Frank, assistant to the president of the Erie Railroad Co.

July 31, 1947

Dear Mr. Frank:

I was happy to hear that you liked *Anthem*, and I am glad that you used a quotation from it in your magazine. If you will look over your lists of those who receive the *Erie Railroad* magazine, you will find my name among them. I have been receiving it for some time, and you may be interested to know that my new novel, which I am writing now, will have railroads as its background. This new novel will glorify the American industrialists, and I hope it will do for businessmen what my novel *The Fountainhead* did for modern architects.

■   ■   ■

To Jerome Mayer

July 31, 1947

Dear Jerry:

Please forgive me for my delay in reading the script of *Now I Lay Me Down to Sleep* and for my silence about it. I have been in such a mad rush that it was impossible for me to write a coherent letter of criticism, but I have not forgotten and this is the first chance I have had to write.

I am sorry that I had to send the script back to you without comment. No, it is not because I disliked it. I have read the play with real interest. I think it is very well done. I enjoyed many of the scenes, and the dialogue is excellent. But as you know, I am most firmly opposed to plays or books which do not have a strong plot. So it is impossible for me to venture an opinion on whether this play would succeed on the stage or not. There have been plotless plays which have succeeded, therefore I must suppose there is an audience for them, but I am unable to judge what is responsible for a play's success in such a case. I am afraid that *Now I Lay Me Down to Sleep* is the kind of play which is better in reading than in acting.

You asked whether I knew of anyone who would be interested in backing a stage play. I am sorry that I don't, as I do not know many people in the theater now.

■   ■   ■

To Richard Mealand

July 31, 1947

Dear Dick:

I am looking forward most eagerly to reading *Let Me Do the Talking*. John Mock had a synopsis of it and paid you very high compliments about it.

But I did not want to read the synopsis—as an ex-reader, I don't believe in them—so I am waiting to buy and read the book itself when it comes out. If you had such a thought, please don't send me a copy of it, I don't believe that authors should give copies away. I believe in buying books, because I firmly believe in the profit motive for authors as well as everyone else.

The theme of your new novel, as you mentioned it in your letter, sounds very interesting indeed. I hope it is progressing to your satisfaction.

As for me, I am simply in love with my new novel. It is much better than I thought it would be, and writing it is difficult, but wonderful. I do not know yet when I will have it finished. I hope to get an extension of my free time from Hal Wallis in order to finish it, as I have no desire to go back to screen work now.

In your comment of *Anthem* you said it should have been a poem. Well, that is exactly what it is. When I see you, I would like to have a little political argument in regard to your statement that individualism can be good or bad according to "whether the reaction it starts is directed toward health or destruction of the mass in which it operates."

Individualism, which means a way of life based on inalienable individual rights, cannot be anything except good. Any other way whatever is destruction. But a statement such as yours is a statement of collectivism, because it implies that the "health of the mass" is the standard by which the rights of the individual are to be gauged. Actually, individualism is the only principle which benefits both the individual and the rest of society— but it is *not* the "social good" that is the standard and justification, it is the right of the individual to live his own life for his own sake—which means, neither sacrificing others to himself nor sacrificing himself to others.

■　■　■

To Archibald Ogden

July 31, 1947

Archie, darling:

I had a strange little experience the other day. I have been receiving the *New York Times Book Review* for months and letting the copies accumulate without having time to read them. Recently I started to clean them out, and I was just about to throw out the copy of May 4 without looking at it, when I saw "Sundry Reflections on British Books and British Weather" by Archibald G. Ogden. I started to read it, and I got a real emotional jolt when I saw suddenly a mention of "Ayn Rand's *The Fountainhead*." Thank you, darling. Not only for the publicity, but for the fact that you are still thinking of it, and when you mention an American book, that is the one you mention. I sat over your article for a long time and felt desperately homesick for you. I miss you terribly, even though I don't write letters. Incidentally, your article and your style of writing are excellent, but I would expect that.

I am hoping selfishly that Twentieth Century-Fox will not renew your option and that you will come back to America. Doesn't your option come up some time this fall? I have been waiting hopefully to hear that you are on your way back. If they do pick up the option, then I wish you would talk yourself out of it anyway. Haven't you had enough, both of Europe and of the movies by now?

Thank you for your letter about *Anthem*. I am happy that you liked it. I have not answered you sooner, because I had to start a political fight with you about some of the things you said, but I really meant it when I told you once that you could do no wrong as far as I am concerned, so I am simply unable to fight with you. Let me answer just very briefly—that much I can't resist. You say "The ultimate political extension of individual freedom is anarchy. . . . Unfortunately anarchy presupposes a world of individualists who believe in the right of others to individual freedom as strongly as in their own right." But the proper purpose of government in a free, capitalistic society is precisely to protect individual rights—so that we don't have to wait for the whole of humanity to become perfect before we can have a free, decent and moral society. I am enclosing one installment of a series of articles which I have been writing here. It is the exact answer to your statement.

You say that editors did not reject *Anthem* in 1937 for political reasons. At that time, Ann Watkins submitted it to three publishers. I do not know (but suspect) the reasons why two of them rejected it; but I know the reason given by Macmillan who were my publishers then. They said that *I did not understand socialism*. I think you are probably in a position to see right now how well I understood it.

Yes, it was Cassells who published *Anthem* in England. I have not kept track of the number of copies they sold. I don't think the sale was very large, but it kept selling slowly for over ten years until they went out of stock during the war. They told me they intended to reissue it when they get the paper, so I suppose they still have a market for it. Perhaps they have reissued it already. Let me know if they have—my agents don't keep track of that very well.

Under separate cover, I am sending you a new translation of our child—the Swiss–German edition. I have not yet received any of the other translations, but I have thirteen contracts for it, so our family is growing.

You say in your letter "I shall always be grateful to you for writing that one." You will understand if I say I was happy to hear that, but I had to laugh about it. No matter how good a writer I may be, I'll never be able to tell you the nature of my gratitude to you. Between us, that word has to remain a one-way term. They say that people forget gratitude very easily, but as I grow older I find that every bromide about human beings is exactly reversed in my case. My gratitude to you is not fading, it is growing stronger. You have become a kind of private legend in my mind and nothing can change it. Time only makes it more so.

Now this brings me to a special request. I want a photograph of you (autographed). If you have one, would you send it to me? Do you know why such sudden sentimentality? Because I am deep in work on my new novel and I want to have your picture on the wall looking at me as I write.

Every time I write a passage that I am pleased with, I feel a bitter little emotion in thinking that you will not be the editor of this novel. There are so many things in it that you would like, and very many that you would be the only one to understand and appreciate completely, and many questions on which you would be the only one who could give me advice. Of course, I will send you the book anyway, and I hope you remember that you said you would be my private editor for it, but I wish you could be the official one as well.

The book is coming along wonderfully. I have 247 typed pages ready. I can't tell yet how long it will be or how long it will take me to finish it, but it is moving well, and I love it, and it is much better than I expected it to be.

I may have to be interrupted to go back to the studio this fall for the next installment of my contract, but I don't want to go back and I shall try to negotiate an extension from Hal Wallis to finish the novel first.

Would you write to me, when you can? I really need your presence, at least symbolically, while I am writing what is going to be another *The Fountainhead* or better.

∎ ∎ ∎

To Ev Suffens

August 1, 1947

Dear Ev:

I have been receiving copies of your television magazine and am most impressed. You have a good idea there and it is quite characteristic of you to be the first with the first television magazine. Am I right in thinking it is the first in the field?

I was glad to hear that you found that you are doing better on your own than by holding a job with someone else. As you say, I have always been "an on-your-owner of the first water" (I love that expression of yours), so I approve most thoroughly and wish you the greatest success.

Anytime I write a letter, the news about me is always the same which is that I am working. Right now, however, it is extra-special—because I am working on my new novel. I have quite a big piece of it finished, though not nearly half, and I am crazy about it. I know that you, for one, will like it. It is my strongest tribute to date, to the "on-your-owner." If you never saw fireworks, you'll see them when this one comes out. But as usual with writers, I can't tell as yet when that will be, as I don't know how long it will take me to finish it. All I know so far is that it is coming out much better than I expected.

■　■　■

To J. J. P. Oud

August 4, 1947

Dear Mr. Oud:

Thank you for your wonderful letter. I am very happy that you liked *The Fountainhead*. A reaction such as yours means a great deal to me.

When I was writing the book, I intended it to be, among other things, a tribute to the leaders of modern architecture, and it has made me very happy that the great names among modern architects have accepted it as that. I am proud to add your name to my list. Of course, the Classicists, the eclectics, and some of the mediocrities of the architectural profession have hated *The Fountainhead* and attacked it in every way they could, which was to be expected and did not do them much good.

I am particularly proud that you said "I am more than astonished to see how deeply you penetrated into the essence of architecture and architects: especially in the sense of modern architecture." Frank Lloyd Wright said almost exactly the same thing. I suppose I was able to do it because I love and admire your profession.

No, of course I could not describe Roark's buildings in detail. To devise the complete, specific plan and appearance of one of his buildings, I would have had to be an architectural genius myself. I would not attempt that and no writer should ever do it.

I was interested to hear the story of your encounter with a pastor about your design for a modern church.* My compliments to you for the stand you took. If I had known of this story when I was writing my book, I would have probably asked your permission to use it.

You asked me to tell you what you could send me in return from Holland. There is something which I would like to have very much—I would like a photograph of the building which you consider your best, autographed to me. If you can send it, it would make me very happy.

■ ■ ■

To Marie Strakhow

August 22, 1947

Dear "Missis":

I was terribly sorry to hear that your visa had been refused and that you have to wait longer. I have asked my attorney to see whether we could do anything in Washington to help you obtain a visa sooner, but he wrote to me that we can do nothing at present and have to wait until Congress passes legislation to enlarge the admission quota.

I had stopped sending you the CARE packages because I thought that you would be able to come here by now, but I placed an order with them as soon as I heard that you could not come. On July 25 I sent you three CARE packages of three different kinds: food, wool and blanket. I hope it will not take them too long to reach you. I will continue sending you a food package every month and I hope that it will help you and that you will not be too uncomfortable while waiting for your visa. I will also cable you some money to the Julius Meinl store, whose application blank you

* Oud's story was of a pastor unable to accept the lack of "embroidery" in Oud's design for his church. Oud asked the pastor if he were willing to die for his faith. The pastor said he was, and Oud replied he was willing to die for his design, whereupon the pastor told Oud to build the church the way he designed it.

sent me, and I hope this will help you until the CARE packages start to arrive.

I have tried to send you some cigarettes as you requested, but was told at the post office here that we are not permitted to send cigarettes to Europe.

I was very happy to hear that you obtained a copy of *The Fountainhead* and that you liked it. Thank you for the nice things you said about it. Now that you have read it, you can probably see that I hesitated about sending it to you because of Mr. Toohey.

I think it might be helpful if the American lady who gave you the book would find out for me the name of some person in the American Consulate in Salzburg or in the American Embassy in Vienna who has read *The Fountainhead* and likes it as much as she does. I could then write to that person, telling him of my interest in you and asking him to assist you in any way that may be possible. I think my literary name would be of help with a person who liked the book, but could be a handicap with someone who is opposed to it.

■   ■   ■

To Ben Stolberg

August 22, 1947

Dear Ben:

Could you tell me whether there is an organization or person who could help me to protect a White Russian friend of mine in Europe? This friend, an elderly woman, is a Displaced Person in the American occupied zone of Austria. I have sent her an affidavit and all the necessary documents to apply for a visa to come to America, but there is no quota at present for friends, only for relatives of American citizens.

In view of the extremely precarious political situation in Austria, I am very worried about her fate in case of a Communist revolution out there. The position of a White Russian in Europe is extremely dangerous, and I am sure you understand why I am worried about her.

Is there anyone who could help her to obtain an American visa or help her to remain under American protection, should there be a change of government in Austria? I would appreciate it very much if you could let me know what one can do in such a situation.

How is the American Writers Association doing? I understand that we have beaten the Cain Plan.* My congratulations to all of you for that.

■ ■ ■

To Carleton B. Tibbetts, CEO of the Los Angeles Steel Casting Co.

September 12, 1947

Dear Mr. Tibbetts:

Thank you very much for your courtesy in inquiring from General Mark Clark about the situation of my friend in Austria. I was sorry to hear that the situation is hopeless, but I appreciate very much your help in inquiring about it.

May I take this occasion to thank you for the most interesting time I had in visiting your plant and for your courtesy in answering all my questions. I think you will like my version of a steel man when you will meet him in my novel.

■ ■ ■

To Richard Mealand

September 22, 1947

Dear Dick:

I have just finished reading *Let Me Do the Talking*. My compliments to you. It is very clever, amusing and well done. I must say that I started by disliking your hero intensely, but by the time I finished the book you had succeeded in making me like him—and I consider that a literary achievement, because I feel very little affection for the general species of literary agents.

As a personal (not literary) opinion, I think you were really too kind to the profession. I can't resist asking you the most conventional question —*WHO* is the prototype of Mr. Gabriel in real life? If there is an agent who actually originates ideas to build up the careers of his clients, I'd like to know it. Don't tell me that Gabriel is just an author's daydream of an agent—I am afraid I know he is.

* The Cain Plan was a proposal by left-wing writers to outlaw contracts between individuals and studios or producers. The plan was not adopted.

If I send you my copy of the book, would you autograph it for me?*

The idea you mentioned for your next novel sounds extremely interesting. I hope you won't be too kind to the spiritualists. They are essentially, philosophically vicious. I see possibilities for the most bitter satire, and I hope your good nature doesn't prevent you from making mincemeat out of those people, as they deserve.

I have not yet "come up out of my next book." It's an extremely complex job, so I am not moving as fast as I would like to, but I am delighted with what I have done so far. If I can make arrangements with Hal Wallis to give me enough time off for it, I may come to New York next spring. I feel that I need it, both for research purposes and for personal satisfaction, because I am beginning to miss New York unbearably again.

■ ■ ■

To J. J. P. Oud

September 22, 1947

Dear Mr. Oud:

Thank you for your letter and for the autographed pictures of your buildings which I have just received. They have made me very happy, and if you have enjoyed *The Fountainhead*, we are now even.

I admire your buildings very much. I think the Houses in Hook of Holland are one of the best examples of workers' housing architecture. But I agree with you, that your Shell building is a step forward. I did not read the article you mentioned in *Architectural Record*, but I read your answer to them, which you sent me, with great interest. I can see that they criticized you precisely for the best things about the Shell building—for the fact that it is beautiful. In the booklet which you sent me, I admire your detail, the design of the brick work on what I believe is a rear entrance, and the design of the column in the photograph of the gallery.

I suppose you know that your battle with the alleged modernists who object to ornament, is the battle of an abstraction against minds who, like animals, can understand nothing but the concrete and are unable to grasp the principle involved. Your abstract principle is the same both in the Shell

---

* The copy he sent her was autographed: "To Ayn—and I'm sure that if you hadn't stimulated me, I never would have attempted this."

building and in the workers' houses, but the mentality of Collectivists cannot understand that. They are anxious to stop at specific forms and consider them general rules, so that they may then steal them and copy them. They do not understand (or don't want to understand) that the only rules possible in any art are abstract principles, whose specific translation into a concrete form has to be created by the artist and has to be new each time, in each particular case. You can see why they would not like that. They are able to do nothing except to copy the ready-made forms of others.

My compliments to you for your battle and my best wishes that you win it, as, of course, you will.

■ ■ ■

To Ben Stolberg

September 27, 1947

Dear Ben:

Thank you for your very nice letter. I will be glad to be nominated on the slate for the Board of the American Writers Association. It is a cause about which I feel very strongly. But would you ask them to send me a copy of the constitution and bylaws which I have never seen? If I do undertake to be a member of the Board, I would want to be active, and I would like to know the specific stand and program of the organization, apart from our fight against the Cain Plan.

Thank you for your praise of the "Screen Guide for Americans." I was very happy to hear your reaction—yours is one of the few opinions which I value on political matters. Under separate cover I am sending you twenty copies of the "Screen Guide," together with envelopes which were made for the purpose of mailing them. It will be wonderful if you can distribute them wherever you feel they might do good. Let me know if you need more copies and I will be delighted to send them.

Thank you also for the letter in regard to the International Rescue and Relief Committee. I shall try to approach them here through their Hollywood chapter.

The "Screen Guide for Americans" was written by AR and published by the Motion Picture Alliance for the Preservation of Amer-

ican Ideals. It presented "A List of the More Common Devices Used to Turn Nonpolitical Pictures into Carriers of Political Propaganda." The "Guide" was published in the November 1947 issue of Plain Talk, *a conservative political magazine.*

■ ■ ■

To Fulton Oursler, Sr., senior editor at *Reader's Digest*

October 2, 1947

Dear Mr. Oursler:

Rupert Hughes told me that you wanted to have a copy of the "Screen Guide for Americans" which I wrote for the Motion Picture Alliance for the Preservation of American Ideals. You will find a copy enclosed.

I was happy to hear of your interest. We would like to give this "Guide" the widest circulation possible and bring it to the attention of all those who stand for Americanism. We believe that the country needs it, because the public has been uneasily aware of Red propaganda in films for a long time, but nobody had defined or explained what Americans must object to and why.

■ ■ ■

To Fred Gillies, general manager at Inland Steel

December 13, 1947

Dear Mr. Gillies:

Thank you for the courtesy you extended me and for my most interesting visit to Inland Steel.

It was an extremely valuable experience for me, both as information and inspiration. You may be surprised—pleasantly, I hope—when you see how I will melt the experience and what sort of an alloy will come out of it on paper.

Please give my personal regards to the men at our luncheon. I shall prove to them that there is at least one writer who will pay tribute to industrialists, the tribute which they deserve and which is long overdue.

■ ■ ■

To Henry Doherty, of the New York Central Railroad press bureau

December 13, 1947

Dear Mr. Doherty:

Thank you ever so much for the pictures which you sent me and for the Report of the Railway Mission in Mexico. If you use the pictures in your employees' magazine, would you send me a copy of it?

I will not attempt to tell you how much I enjoyed my ride in the engine cab. I expected it to be thrilling, but it was better than anything I imagined. The cap which you gave me is now a priceless souvenir, and I am wearing it in the disgusting California sunshine, feeling very homesick for New York.

■ ■ ■

To Raymond F. Blosser, manager of the New York Central Railroad press bureau

December 13, 1947

Dear Mr. Blosser:

Thank you ever so much for the pictures which you sent me. They are wonderful. The one of me with the engine crew is going to be my favorite photo ever taken.

Mr. Doherty sent me the pictures of me in the cab of the diesel taken at Harmon, which were excellent too.

Thank you for our very interesting trip to Little Falls, and please give my best regards to Mr. Wright. As for my ride in the engine, it was the greatest experience I ever had.

■ ■ ■

To Clarence Dugan, manager of public relations at New York Central Railroad

December 13, 1947

Dear Mr. Dugan:

Thank you for your courtesy in giving me the appointments which were the most interesting part of my visit to New York—and particularly for the ride in the cab of the Twentieth Century.

That ride was a magnificent experience. I will not attempt to tell you how much I enjoyed it. But I must report that your engine crews are a wonderful bunch of men. They were extremely nice to me—and it was such a rare pleasure, these days, to see efficient men in action.

Please give my regards to Mr. Borntrager. Now that I am safely 3,000 miles away, I can say that he is one of the most interesting men I have ever met, and I would like you to repeat this to him. The information he gave me was of great value for my particular purpose.

I am very grateful to New York Central—and I shall let my novel say it for me.

■ ■ ■

To Mr. and Mrs. John C. Gall

December 13, 1947

Dear Mr. and Mrs. Gall:

Thank you for the lovely day we spent at your house. I am still thinking, with a kind of wistful envy, of your beautiful estate and looking forward to the time when we will be able to settle in the East, too.

The peacocks we promised are reserved for you—but Frank is afraid to send them now, because the change of weather would be too abrupt for them, and they would not be able to survive the sudden transition to a cold climate. We will send them in the spring. So as soon as it gets warmer, you may expect to hear them screaming on your doorstep.

■ ■ ■

To Rose Wilder Lane

December 13, 1947

Dear Rose Wilder Lane:

I was very happy that I had a chance to meet you at last, after all these years. I am looking forward already to my next visit East. I hope to do it within a year when I finish my novel. I am back at work on it now, and I hope to make it my most startling contribution to our cause. I am looking forward, with a real curiosity and anticipation, to the kind of discussion we will have after it is finished.

■ ■ ■

To Hal Wallis

January 24, 1948

Dear Boss:

Thank you ever so much for the beautiful bag you gave me for Christmas. I was happy and flattered to see that you chose one which is exactly of the style I like and even with the personal touch of my initials.

I had hoped that I would see you and thank you in person—but should I bring that up? So I have to do it by letter, but nonetheless most sincerely—

P.S. I Where is that $10 which I didn't want to win?

P.P.S. II Or should I also give you an extension of a year and wait until after Christmas 1948? I am sure I will still collect it then.

P.P.P.S. III I hope I won't.

■   ■   ■

To Jack Moen, a fan

February 6, 1948

Dear Mr. Moen:

Thank you for your letter. I am grateful for your reaction to *The Fountainhead*, and I was startled by your saying that your other favorite in literature was Hugo's *Les Miserables*.

It happens that Victor Hugo is my favorite writer in all world literature, not for the content of his ideas, but for his literary method, and he is the only writer who had some influence on my style of writing. Of all the letters about *The Fountainhead* that I received, yours was the first one that mentioned Victor Hugo—and that is the only comparison of which I can feel proud, so I do believe that if you liked *The Fountainhead*, you probably liked it for the right reasons.

■   ■   ■

To Jack Warner

February 14, 1948

Dear Mr. Warner:

I am writing to ask you whether you would be interested in seeing an Italian motion picture made from my novel *We the Living*.

This picture was "pirated" in Italy during the war and made without my consent or knowledge. Its producers are now negotiating with me for the rights to release the picture in America and to settle the matter out of court. They have sent me a print of the film. I do not know as yet whether I will be able to reach a settlement with them.

The story is laid in Soviet Russia and is a very dramatic denunciation of Communism. I admire the sincerity of the stand you have taken against Communism, and so I thought that you might be interested in seeing this picture for several possible reasons: If you like the story, you may want to buy the rights to make an American version of it; or you might be interested in some possible arrangement to release this picture through Warner Bros.; or you might be interested simply in seeing a sample of an anti-Soviet picture. Or, since you own the screen rights to *The Fountainhead*, you might like to see how another novel of mine has come out on the screen.

If you would like to see it, I can send the film to you to be screened at your convenience. The picture is quite long; it was released in two parts and runs for four hours. The dialogue is in Italian, but I have a transcript of it translated into English. As far as production is concerned, the picture is well done, and its star is Valli, who gives a great performance.

■   ■   ■

To DeWitt Emery

February 14, 1948

Dear DeWitt:

Thank you for the comic-strip booklet, "The Man from Mars," which you sent me. Since you ask for the frank opinions of your readers, I would like to give you a detailed review of it.

The basic fault of the strip is that it is simply political propaganda, which has not been *dramatized* at all. The politics are in almost every speech, and they are merely tacked on to the pictures. The characters *talk* about politics, they don't *act*. All that happens in the strip—as far as the story is concerned—is that a man from Mars arrives on Earth, takes an automobile ride and hears a lot of talk about politics from an Earthman. He does not get involved in any action that would illustrate the state of things which the Earthman describes.

This is an extremely bad mistake which inexperienced writers who attempt to deal in propaganda usually make, and it is the reason why they fail. The artist who did the drawings for you is very good, but your writer is no dramatist and that is the crucial flaw in the whole scheme. As the strip stands now, it falls between two intentions: since its political ideas are presented only in speeches and not in the action of a story, the drawings are entirely wasted and irrelevant in relation to the message. The speeches are merely editorials which might as well be printed as an editorial. If your purpose is to convey political ideas in dramatic form, then it is the *story* that must illustrate and dramatize the points you wish to make. It is not a matter of just placing speeches into pictures.

I can best make myself clear by giving you a brief example of what I mean by *dramatization*. Taking the same material as you have in this strip, your story should have had some such pattern as: The man from Mars arrives on Earth. He sees a beautiful girl and falls in love with her, but doesn't know how to approach her. He sells his airplane to an Earthman for a thousand dollars and sets out in pursuit of the girl. He has to buy himself an automobile; he has to buy suitable clothes; he has to stop at hotels, travel on trains, etc. At every point, he clashes with the state of our economy on Earth and finds that his thousand dollars will not buy him anything. He is promised an automobile, but cannot get it because there is a strike in the automobile factory. He gets into a train wreck because the railroads cannot get proper equipment, etc. All this is built around the suspense of his anxiety to catch up with the girl, and his being frustrated at every step. Thus you make your political points in specific story terms that the reader would understand. You bring home to him what it actually means to have money but no goods to purchase with it when one needs them most.

This is just a very crude example and I don't mean to say that this is the story you should use, but I am citing it only as an illustration of how to present any abstract idea, political or economic, in fiction form. A comic strip is fiction, it is a variation of stage or movie technique, and therefore, to be successful, it has to be dramatized; it has to hold the reader *primarily* as a story. Otherwise, it is a complete waste.

As your strip stands now, I do not know what audience it is intended to reach. It is certainly too political, and therefore would be dull, for school children. It is too childish, and therefore would be unconvincing, for adults.

Now as to the content of your strip, there are several points to which I would object most vehemently: (1) I cannot say that the idea of a man from Mars coming to Earth is good. It is such an obvious and old one. It's too trite.

(2) The social and economic system on Mars is presented so vaguely that it is bewildering and suggests some very bad implications. In the first two pictures, where you have men voting and a man holding a veto, etc., you suggest some sort of economic regimentation, yet later we are told that the system on Mars is a good one and much superior to the system on Earth. But what you have on Mars is certainly not free enterprise—so what did you intend to suggest? Such a title as "Head Man" implies a dictator, so if your setup on Mars means anything at all, it vaguely suggests Fascism—and, God forbid, that is not what you want to preach.

(3) The sequence where your Earthman is given a treatment on Mars to cure him of his wrong thinking is, philosophically, most vicious. I believe that your author intended it only as a joke about "loose screws" and probably thought it was very funny to talk about such things as screws, short circuits and burnt-out tubes in a man's brain, but do you realize the real implications of this sequence? It is nothing less than the Marxist, materialistic, deterministic idea that a man's thinking is conditioned by physical factors, that his body will make him think right or wrong according to its condition, and that there is no such thing as an intellectual process. Look up Point 8 of my "Screen Guide for Americans," for the details of my reasons why this issue is a Marxist one. The speech in one of your pictures, "The Head Man has ordered us to tighten some of the loose screws in this guy's thinking machine!" is nothing less than the ghastliest Communist or Fascist idea—the idea that a leader can order a man's thinking to be straightened out and, of all things, by means of a physical operation. Just think of all the implications and connotations of such a speech. What I see in it are the German gas chambers, the German experiments on living human beings, and the Soviet concentration camps for people whose thinking is wrong according to the Soviet Head Man.

Believe me, I am a good propagandist as you know, and I know how propaganda works. Your readers may not be able to analyze all this in words, but they will get all the implications which I described, and *that* is certainly not what you want to preach.

(4) I object to your use of the words "sharing" and "dividing" when you speak of wages or incomes. In one of your pictures, the Martian Head

Man says, "We finally found out that the more we produce, the easier it is to share the rewards and the more everybody gets." In your last picture, the Earthman says, "Now let's get to work because the more goods we can produce, the more we have to divide in exchange for our dollars." Since you argued so well with Leonard Read about the proper use of the terms "freedom of opportunity" or "equality of opportunity," you understand the importance of using exact terms in politics, and I am surprised that you let this one get past you. Whenever we speak of incomes as "sharing" or "dividing," we merely drive in the collectivist idea of the national income being there for the purpose of being shared. I know that you use these words figuratively, but you can see what they mean literally. I think it will be a great step forward when conservatives overhaul their vocabulary most carefully and discard from it, once and for all, all the words smuggled into it by collectivists. National wealth is not there to be shared. An employer does not *share* the income of his factory with his workers. That income is *his*. He pays the workers what he has agreed to pay for their services through voluntary negotiations, and the basis of the agreement is the law of supply and demand. He *does not* pay on the basis of the income of his factory. This last is the vicious idea which was being advocated, as you will remember, a couple of years ago by labor unions who demanded wage raises according to manufacturers' incomes. The writer of your comic strip has added his two cents worth to this idea. It is true that an employer can pay more only if he produces more; but that is not *sharing*.

I think you will see from the above that an undertaking such as your comic strip will not only fail, but will be actually detrimental to your own cause—UNLESS your writer is both a trained dramatist and a clear, consistent thinker on politics, a man whose thinking has no loose screws or contradictions. I do not know how to impress upon you strongly enough that it is particularly in fiction, more than in any other form of writing, that the confusion of a man's thinking comes across most disastrously. So there is only one practical suggestion which I have to offer you, and I would like to urge it most strongly: Get yourself a real writer, if you intend to continue with this comic strip. It breaks my heart to think of the money and the effort which you are putting into this undertaking and which will be wasted, if not worse, unless your writer knows what he is doing.

■   ■   ■

To Raymond B. Young, Jr., a fan

March 6, 1948

Dear Mr. Young:

Thank you for your letter. I am glad that you liked *The Fountainhead*, and if you are an individualist, I would like to think that you understood its thesis.

If you are an individualist, I can well believe that you are having a terrible struggle. I think I know how terrible it can be, and I also know that it is much too early to become embittered or discouraged.

If I understand you correctly, I think I do know the kind of intellectual loneliness you speak about, and I can appreciate your desire to meet another individualist. As you see, I cannot arrange to meet you at present, since I live in California, but I will be glad to do it on my next visit East, if I find that we are really in agreement philosophically. If you would care to send me one of your books, the one you consider most representative of your convictions, I will be glad to read it, and it will give me some idea of your philosophy.

■ ■ ■

To Marna Papurt Wolfe

March 20, 1948

Dear Docky:

Please forgive me for taking so long to answer your letter. I have been working so hard on my novel ever since I came back that I could not do anything else.

Thank you for your nice letter. You really write very well, so I hope you will write again and not share the sin of all the O'Connors who are even worse than I am about correspondence.

I was very interested to read about your first stage experience. Mimi wrote to me about it too and said that you were very good. If you find by now that you enjoy the work, I wish you a lot of success with it.

I am sending some clothes for you and Mimi, and I am mailing them to Mimi's address because I am not sure that you are in New York at present. The blue suit, which I am sending, is for you. I hope you will like it since you seem to like the same kind of tailored clothes that I wear. It's probably much too large for you, but I think it will be becoming when you have it taken in.

I won't attempt to tell you about my ride in the engine now. I'll tell you all about it when I see you in person. It was a wonderful experience.

What was it that you wanted me to tell you about Oscar and Oswald? They are two lion cubs (stuffed), and they are supposed to represent the bad sides of Frank's character. Whenever he pulls a bad joke, he blames it on Oswald; and whenever he loses his temper, it's supposed to be Oscar growling. That's how it all started, but now they have become very real members of our household in the same kind of way as Charlie McCarthy. They have specific characters of their own. You will have to see and hear them to believe any of this.

Now as to the address of the place that has the creoles, it was a German pastry shop on the east side of Lexington, a few doors before you come to the corner of Eighty-sixth Street, coming from downtown. I don't remember the name of the place; I think it was something like Bauers. I don't know if it is still there. If you find it, and they still have the creoles, please buy a pound of them for me too and send them to us along with a bill. I would love to have them, but I want to say in advance that I don't want them as a present because they are quite expensive.

Please let me know what you are doing and how you are getting along. I will try to answer you more promptly next time.

Love from your Aunt and Uncle.

■   ■   ■

To Sam Rapport, editor at Appleton-Century-Crofts publishers

March 20, 1948

Dear Sam:

I am looking forward to seeing you again when I come to New York. I am glad that Katie remembers me, because the performance of *Medea*, including her part of it, was one of the highlights of my trip east. I feel flattered if she says that my presence in the audience influenced her work, because what I remember most is the wonderful air of classical dignity which she conveyed on the stage.

Thank you for your kind words about *The Fountainhead*. Please tell Archie that I feel like a woman scorned because he has not written to me. But I am so bad about correspondence myself that I cannot be too angry at him.

■   ■   ■

To Mimi Sutton

March 20, 1948

Dear Mimi:

The suede dress is for you and the blue suit is for Docky. I am also sending a blouse which I bought and never wore because it is too feminine for me. I thought it would go with the suit for Docky; but since it is so feminine, maybe it would be better for you, so I will let you two decide it. The blue skirt, which I am sending, is a very good hand-knitted one, but it is too short for me now. If you find that it is too short for either of you, maybe it will fit Connie. I am sending the blue bag, gloves and hat which I used to wear with the suit. The hat is quite old, but maybe Docky can use it by having it reblocked.

Frank is sending a bunch of ties. He does not remember which tie it was that David liked. If it is not among the ones he is sending, would you describe what it looked like, and if it is not one of my particular pets, we'll send it on.

My long silence has been due to uninterrupted work on my novel. It's going very well, but it's very difficult, and I am working hard. I have done nothing else since returning to Hollywood, and I have no news about myself, except 150,000 words on paper which, I think, will be news when they are published.

You said in your letter that I have been your "conscience" and that you carry on conversations with me in your own mind. That is something you really must tell me more about. Do let me know what it is that I am saying.

Love to you, David and Docky from your old Aunt and Uncle.

■   ■   ■

To John L. B. Williams

March 20, 1948

Dear Mr. Williams:

Thank you ever so much for *I Saw Poland Betrayed* [by Arthur Lane] and *Communism and the Conscience of the West* [by Bishop Fulton J. Sheen] which you sent me.

I have read *Communism and the Conscience of the West*, since you asked me to tell you my opinion of it. I am sorry to say that I disagree with it quite emphatically. If you want to know my reasons, I will mention just one out of many: Monsignor Sheen is opposed to unrestricted, laissez-faire capitalism, claiming that it leads to monopolies. He does not prove or illustrate his point, but merely states it as a flat assertion; yet it is not true, neither theoretically nor historically. This point is so crucially important that I wish he had either stated his grounds for the assertion or refrained from making it. As you know, I am a supporter of free, complete, unrestricted, unlimited, laissez-faire capitalism.

I am glad that you sent me this book, because it interested me very much. I am interested in every philosophical viewpoint on this subject, even though I do find that most of them are sadly in error.

My novel is gathering speed as it goes along. I was moving like a heavy freight at the beginning, but I am a good passenger train now and hope to become an express pretty soon. Would it please you to know that I have about 150,000 words done? I hope it won't frighten you, but the novel will be much longer than that. Not as long as *The Fountainhead*, however (I hope). [*Atlas Shrugged* is more than 50 percent longer than *The Fountainhead*.]

■　■　■

To Lawrence G. Frank, consul general of the American legation in Vienna

March 27, 1948

My dear Mr. Frank:

Under date of March 25, 1947, my attorneys, Gall and Lane, of Washington, D.C., transmitted to you my affidavit of support on behalf of Marie Strachow, of Lager, Neumarkt bei Salzburg, Austria, in order that Mrs. Strachow might be granted a visa for admission to the United States. You acknowledged receipt of this document and correspondence by letter to Messrs. Gall and Lane under date of April 17, 1947.

I understand that your office is now considering the application of Mrs. Marie Strachow for a visa, and I, therefore, write further to express my anxiety on her behalf and to urge that her application be given every favorable consideration.

I am extremely anxious to bring my dear friend, Marie Strachow, to this country, and that everything possible be done to insure her admission. I understand that the nature and sincerity of my interest in her is one of the matters which will have to be considered in arriving at a decision respecting the issuance of her visa, since she is only a friend of mine and not a relative. This is to assure you that my feeling and concern for her are much more than a casual friendship and that I consider her as a member of my family.

I had always hoped to bring my parents to America some day, when I had made good. But my parents have died since I left Russia, and I have no way of finding any other relatives of mine, or even of learning whether any of them are still alive. Mrs. Strachow was my mother's closest friend and my first teacher of English. She is now the only tie to my childhood and family left to me. So you will understand my eagerness to see her and to take care of her in her old age, as I had hoped to take care of my mother.

I am well able to provide for Mrs. Strachow's support financially, and I am in a position to assure you that she will not become a public charge in this country.

I shall be profoundly grateful if you find it possible to grant my request.

■ ■ ■

To John L. B. Williams

March 27, 1948

Dear Mr. Williams:

Just as I wrote to you that my new novel was gaining the speed of an express, the express has had to be shunted on to a siding, temporarily, because the main track had to be cleared for another powerful special by the name of *The Fountainhead*. Which is another way of saying that I have just gone back to Warner Bros. to write the final screenplay for the picture. The picture is now definitely in production. If all goes well, the studio intends to start the actual shooting in a few months.

I am sure that the news will please you. I trust that Bobbs-Merrill will not sell any reprint rights until long after the picture is released—because if the picture is as good as it promises to be at present, it may put your original edition of *The Fountainhead* back on the bestseller lists. I have reason to hope that it will.

■ ■ ■

To Raymond B. Young, Jr.

April 17, 1948

Dear Mr. Young:

Thank you for the copy of your book, which you sent me.

I have read it and I find that your philosophical ideas are fundamentally opposed to mine. You seem to be a Platonist, you quote from Plato repeatedly, and on page 34 of your book, you say: "The prophetic genius of Plato affirms itself in all his opinions (his important errors are few and he corrected them later in his life)."

As a matter of fact, Plato is the source, root and spiritual father of Collectivism. Every collectivist philosophy is based on Plato. In Soviet universities, the courses given on Communist ideology begin (quite rightly) with Plato. Have you read Plato's *Republic*? If there is any one thinker who has caused the greatest intellectual harm to mankind, with the most disastrous practical consequences, it is Plato (with Hegel next).

Since you are interested in philosophy, you have probably heard the statement that every philosopher (and every man) is essentially either a Platonist or an Aristotelian. This is one of the truest statements ever made. Plato and Aristotle *do* represent the basic division of mankind. Aristotle is the father of Individualism and of logic, the first and greatest rationalist. I am an Aristotelian.

I would suggest that you study this question thoroughly, if you have not done so. I can give you a helpful hint of what to look for: the crucial difference between Plato and Aristotle lies in their respective Theories of Knowledge and in their views on the nature of reality. *That* is the root. Their ethics, politics, etc., are the consequences.

I cannot undertake to discuss philosophical problems in correspondence, and I do not believe that I can be of much intellectual help to you, until you have studied this question by yourself and made your own choice.

■   ■   ■

To DeWitt Emery

April 17, 1948

Dear DeWitt:

I am glad that you agree with my analysis of your comic book. If you continue with it, I shall certainly be glad to have you send it to me before publication and to help you with it in any way I can.

Thanks for your nice compliment to my "Manifesto of Individualism." I don't think it would be advisable to use the "Manifesto" now, it's not complete enough for the subject which it covers. If you remember, it was written just as an outline for our proposed intellectual organization at the time. If I were to issue a booklet on this theme now, I would like to make a much more thorough job of it, and I cannot undertake to do it at this moment.

If you would like to use some material of mine, I wonder whether the "Screen Guide for Americans" would serve your purpose. I think you could reprint it as a pamphlet of your Economic Foundation and send it out to your members. I would have to ask the consent of the Motion Picture Alliance, but I am sure they would be glad to let you do it. Since we did not copyright the booklet, we would be glad to have it reprinted and distributed by anyone who agrees with us.

I believe it should interest your members, because the ideas it contains are of much wider application than merely to the movies. Also, I think the fight for Americanism in the movies is a very important one and affects, not just Hollywood, but the whole country. There has been so much publicity and so much nonsense on this issue that a clear cut stand on it would be extremely important.

I believe that it is up to the American public to bring about the production of movies preaching Americanism. The Reds are screaming their heads off, putting up a disgusting kind of smear and pressure campaign in order to intimidate Hollywood producers and stop them from making anti Communist movies. You may have heard about the campaign the Reds are now conducting against the picture, *The Iron Curtain*. Our side, which is the majority of the country, is indignant against Red influences in pictures, but has done nothing about it.

Ideas cannot be forced or outlawed by legislation. It is preposterous to expect some sort of law to stop the Red influence in Hollywood. It can be stopped only by the public. The producers have the right to make any kind of movies they wish. And the public has the right to patronize these movies or not. That is the only way in which any issue can be settled in a free enterprise society. Therefore, it is up to the public to know clearly what they want or do not want to see in pictures—and then to act accordingly.

That is why I think that the "Screen Guide for Americans" would be a valuable booklet for you, if you want to reprint it and get behind a campaign for American movies. Your members, the small businessmen, represent the real bulk of the moviegoing public—and the class which has been most consistently insulted on the screen. If they decided to take a stand on this issue and make themselves heard—believe me, Hollywood would take notice and your organization would be accomplishing a real patriotic service.

As for me, I am busy writing what will be, I hope, the first truly pro-

American picture ever produced. You may have read in the papers that Warner Bros. are now going to put *The Fountainhead* into production— and I am back at the studio writing the final screenplay. It is coming along wonderfully. One can never be sure of anything in Hollywood until a picture is finished, but, so far, every indication is that the picture will be produced properly and uncompromisingly. Warner Bros. are one of the few studios that have taken a clear-cut and honest stand against Communism. If all goes well, as I hope, you will see a real "Manifesto of Individualism" on the American screen. I don't have to tell you how much the country needs it at present.

■   ■   ■

To Joanne Rondeau, a fan

May 22, 1948

Dear Miss Rondeau:

You asked me to explain the meaning of my sentence in *The Fountainhead*: "To say 'I love you' one must know first how to say the 'I.' "

The meaning of that sentence is contained in the whole of *The Fountainhead*. And it is stated right in the speech on page 400 from which you took that sentence. The meaning of the "I" is an independent, self-sufficient entity that *does not* exist for the sake of any other person.

A person who exists only for the sake of his loved one is not an independent entity, but a spiritual parasite. The love of a parasite is worth nothing.

The usual (and very vicious) nonsense preached on the subject of love claims that love is self-sacrifice. A man's *self* is his spirit. If one sacrifices his spirit, who or what is left to feel the love? True love is profoundly *selfish*, in the noblest meaning of the word—it is an expression of one's *self*, of one's highest values. When a person is in love, he seeks his own happiness—and *not* his sacrifice to the loved one. And the loved one would be a monster if she wanted or expected sacrifice.

Any person who wants to live *for* others—for one sweetheart or for the whole of mankind—is a selfless nonentity. An independent "I" is a person who exists for his own sake. Such a person does not make any vicious pretense of self-sacrifice and does not demand it from the person he loves. Which is the only way to be in love and the only form of a self-respecting relationship between two people.

■   ■   ■

To Mimi Sutton

May 23, 1948

Dear Mimi:

We were glad to hear from you as we were beginning to wonder what had happened to our nieces. And as I see, something pretty drastic has happened to one of them. I don't know what to think of Docky's marriage. Of course, as you say, it is strictly her own business, and if that is what she wanted, I hope she will be very happy. My regret is that she is rushing into motherhood too soon, but again that is her own decision. I do think that to be a mother at twenty is much too soon, but my attitude on motherhood is just about like yours. I think your statement about it in your letter was very sensible indeed.*

Frank and I are a little startled that Docky did not even let us know. I had a letter from her at the end of December, and since she was already married then, isn't it strange that she did not want to mention it? Did she keep it secret from all of us because she felt certain that we would disapprove? Well, I cannot attempt to guess her reason, so I can only wish that it will work out for the best.

■   ■   ■

To Henry Blanke

June 26, 1948

Dear Mr. Blanke:

This is to confirm our understanding, as agreed upon on Monday, June 21, 1948.

After I have completed the writing of my screenplay of *The Fountainhead*, identified as Final Script, I shall remain available at the studio,

---

* Sutton had written to AR that she couldn't think of any good reason to have a baby, and she rejected the notion that one achieves immortality through reproducing oneself.

in my office, during the whole period of the shooting of the picture, for the purpose of doing any changes, rewriting or revisions of the above script, if such should become necessary. I shall do this work without payment, salary or any financial compensation whatsoever. I shall do it for the purpose of preserving the unity of style and conception of the above script.

In return, it is understood and agreed that any and all changes in or additions to the dialogue of the above script will be worded and written by me.

While I remain on call at the studio, I shall be free to do writing work of my own, for my own benefit, but I shall be available at your request whenever you should need me.

I shall not visit the set during the shooting of the picture, except by your specific permission or request.

Thanking you for the pleasure I had in working with you—and wishing our picture the success it deserves.

■ ■ ■

To John L. B. Williams

June 26, 1948

Dear John:

I have just finished my work at Warner Bros. on the screenplay of *The Fountainhead* and am now going back to work on my new novel. The screenplay is wonderful, at least I think so and so does everybody else. The studio seems very happy about it, and all the indications are that the picture will be as great as we all expected it to be.

The starting date of the actual shooting has been set for July 8.

As things look now, this is *the* big picture of the movie industry— and one of my New York literary friends predicts that it may put *The Fountainhead* back on the bestseller lists.

Here's luck to Warner Bros., Bobbs-Merrill and myself,

■ ■ ■

To Henri Glarner, husband of AR's Russian cousin Vera, then living in France

June 26, 1948

Dear Henri:

How are conditions in France now and do you find it possible to obtain food? What kind of work are you doing now? Is Vera employed in her specialty as a doctor? How is Lisette? I am curious about having a niece whom I have never met. There are so many things I would like to know to catch up with the events of twenty-two years.

At the time when I wrote to Vera last, I was not able to transfer money to a bank in Switzerland—as the banks here would not undertake to do it. I tried to obtain some photographic paper for you, as Vera had asked, but I could not get it here—not even through the picture studios— as there was a great shortage of it at the time. I did not have any warm clothes to send Vera, but when the CARE packages came out with parcels of woolens, I sent her some, hoping she could make use of them for clothing. I hope she has received them. Please tell me whether you still need the CARE packages, and I will be glad to send them. If the situation in France is anything like it was in Russia at the time I left, I know that people lead a half-starved existence, even if they are working. So I would like to help, if possible.

I was very shocked to hear that Vera's parents had died and that her young sister, Nina, had disappeared. I appreciate your hesitation over the telephone in telling me this. You may probably know that Nina was my best girlfriend all through our childhood and college days. Would you tell me what it was that Vera has heard from Russia? Is there any hope of Nina being found or was she lost in the siege?

I have a great favor to ask of you. If Vera is in correspondence with her sister, would you ask her to inquire about the fate of my two sisters? I have heard through an old friend in Europe that both my parents have died, but I was not able to learn anything about my sisters. If Vera is able to inquire (if questions in letters are permitted, without embarrassing her sister) I would be very grateful if she would ask her sister about my family. And I would also like to know any news she has about any of our relatives and friends. But please warn her not to mention my name or anything about me, if and when she writes to Russia. I am quite famous here for my political views, so any connection with me may be dangerous or embarrassing to our relatives. If Vera has any news about my sisters, I would like to know it, even if the news is bad. But if the news is uncertain and her sister does not know for sure what happened, then I would rather not know it.*

You may write to me in French. I understand it perfectly, but I find it difficult to speak, having had no occasion to speak French all these years.

---

* AR eventually learned that her sister Natasha had died and much later discovered that her younger sister, Nora, survived the war.

Please excuse my halting attempts at it over the telephone. I understood every word you said, but I could not think in French fast enough to answer you. Please thank your sister-in-law for her efficient translation.

■ ■ ■

To Ely Jacques Kahn, the architect for whom AR worked while doing research for *The Fountainhead*

June 26, 1948

Dear Mr. Kahn:

I was delighted to hear that you and Mrs. Kahn are coming to California, and I am looking forward eagerly to seeing you.

It is strangely and nicely appropriate that you will be here when Warner Bros. will be shooting the motion picture of *The Fountainhead*. You may have read in the papers that the picture is going into actual production at last. I have just finished writing the screenplay, and if all goes well, I think it will be a great picture. I hope I will have a chance to take you on the set and show you the shooting of a scene.

■ ■ ■

To Archibald Ogden

June 26, 1948

Dear Archie:

This is to tell you in person that our child—*The Fountainhead*—is going on the screen at last. You have probably read about it in the papers, but I thought I should tell you myself. I have just finished writing the final screenplay for Warner Bros., and it has been completed in a blaze of glory. Everyone is very happy about it, both the studio and myself. If all goes well, as it has so far, the picture will be great.

The actual shooting is scheduled to start on July 8th. The director is King Vidor, one of the best in the business. The star is Gary Cooper who, as you may remember, has always been my ideal for the part. Dominique is to be played by Patricia Neal, a new young actress from the stage. I will know about the rest of the cast in a few days. Wynand will probably be Raymond Massey, but that is not completely official yet.

Do you remember that you promised me a letter? But I said I would forgive you anything, and I shall always be running after you, if you want me to. (I ought to say that with a smile, but I don't know how to convey a smile on paper.) Do let me hear from you, and if you want the details about our child's screen incarnation, I will keep you informed. It's going to be very exciting.

P.S. Would you please give me your home address and phone number, if you have one. I can see no better way to spend my Hollywood income than by indulging myself in the luxury of an occasional long-distance call to you.

■ ■ ■

To Gerald Loeb

July 3, 1948

Dear Gerald:

Thank you for your letter of June 29. Yes, Mr. Blanke showed me the copy of Frank Lloyd Wright's letter, which you sent him. I have tried to fight for Mr. Wright in every way I could, but as you know, the decision was not up to me. I do not know all the details of what has happened, but I am very sorry that this is the way it has turned out.

If it is not confidential, would you send me a copy of what Frank Lloyd Wright wrote to you about me? As things look now, Mr. Wright is wrong in being afraid for me or thinking I will be "treated quite badly" by the studio. So far the exact opposite has been true. Everything has gone very well at the studio, and I have every assurance that my script will be produced exactly as written. I have no authority over the casting or the sets, but my script and my ideas will be preserved. If the picture comes out as well as I think it will, it will be a demonstration of the power of an idea and of the fact that one can deal with people on honest, rational terms if one sticks to these terms oneself.

■ ■ ■

To Marie Strakhow

July 10, 1948

Dear "Missis":

I am sorry that your departure is still being delayed and that you are having such a difficult time. I hope that things will be settled as quickly as possible, and I am waiting impatiently for your arrival.

I am enclosing receipts for two food parcels which I have sent you. I have ordered them from a company here who specializes in it, and I was told that this is the quickest way to get the parcels to you. The parcel called "Cheer" contains most of the foodstuffs which you wanted. It is to be delivered to you in two weeks from the date of the order, so I hope that you will receive it in about another week. The parcel called "KA-12" contains mainly chocolate and sugar. It goes through a different route and will take a little longer in reaching you. The Kaven Travel Service which handles these parcels has an office in Hamburg, and if you don't get them in time, you may inquire there, referring to the numbers on the receipts. I hope this will help you.

I was not able to send you any penicillin. We are not allowed to send it, and the only way to get it, I am told, would be for an American doctor in Germany to order it for you from America. If you know a doctor who can do it, I will be glad to pay for the penicillin here, but he would have to tell you what procedure to follow to arrange it.

If you are not able to send me a wire when you leave, then please write me airmail as soon as you know the date of your departure and the name of the ship. I suppose that the Tolstoy Foundation in New York will arrange to meet you on your arrival, but I will also ask some personal friends of mine to meet you and to help you with all the arrangements for going on to California.

■   ■   ■

To Archibald Ogden

July 10, 1948

Archie darling,

Thanks for your letter. It's always an event for me when I hear from you, so maybe I should exploit you more often.

The Fountainhead goes into production Monday, July 12. In fact, the company is leaving today to go on location. The first scenes shot will be the quarry. They are going to shoot it in a local quarry near Fresno. I have seen pictures of the place, and it is quite impressive. Funny, isn't it? I remember the time when that quarry was nothing but my imagination and now it is going to be made into a physical reality. I do feel somewhat in the position of a god, since something which I made out of spirit is now going to be translated into matter. However, I am not omnipotent, unfortunately—so I have no way of knowing whether the translation will be what it should be. It's out of my hands now, and I can only hope for the best. So far, I have reason to think that it will be good. If I am a god in this case, then you are a holy ghost or my first prophet. Anyway, if you are religious, pray for our child in the next two months.

It's true that Barbara Stanwyck has left Warner Bros. because they did not give her the part of Dominique. The story which you referred to is true—it *was* Barbara Stanwyck who discovered *The Fountainhead* for Warner Bros. and made them buy it. If you remember, they bought it before the book became famous. Like all the other studios, Warner Bros. had a synopsis of the book, and they were not interested in it until Barbara Stanwyck persuaded the producer, Henry Blanke, to read the book itself. She really was entitled to get the part of Dominique, and I fought for her in every way I could, but the decision was not up to me. I am terribly sorry about this.

Is there really a possibility of your coming to Hollywood soon? I can't tell you how much I wish you would. If you have any way of arranging it, please try to do it. No, don't wait for a preview. Come now, while the picture is shooting. If there is anyone who should be present for at least one scene, it is you.

You asked how different my final screenplay is from the original version which I wrote in 1944. It's quite different in many respects. In the original version, both the producer and I wanted to follow the book too closely and include everything, which could not really be done successfully. The main change we made in the final version was to eliminate the whole episode of the Stoddard trial. Two trials within the space of a screenplay were too much. Also, I introduced Wynand at the beginning of the picture, rather than have him appear late in the action as he does in the book. I had not read my first version of the screenplay for a couple of years, and when I went back to work on it, I discovered a very interesting thing which I did not know before: The scenes which I took verbatim from the book were not as dramatic in the screenplay as they were in the book, because their dramatic value depended on the context. The same scenes, without all the rest of the complicated structure, lost their power. It showed me that my writing was much more integrated than I suspected. To achieve the equivalent of the effect my scenes had in the book, I had to rewrite them for the screen. When you see the picture (if the script is not tampered with, and I don't think it will be) you will find that the total effect of the story is the same as that of the book. But I have learned that an equivalent cannot be achieved by a literal copy.

I got a great kick out of hearing you say in your letter: "Maybe the great strike is on already and no one has told me about it." Well, of course it's on. That's just what's happening to the world. The only difference between reality and my story is that I make it a conscious, organized action, while in real life the intelligence of the world has now stopped functioning simply because conditions make it impossible for intelligence to function. All collectivist systems of society, by their own stated theory and in fact, are conspiracies against intelligence. They are an attempt to have the competent work in the service of and under the orders of the incompetent. This is impossible in the mere statement of it—and look at it in practice.

You say: "I like to think that the state of the world has something to do with the complete dearth of good fiction coming out today." Why, of course, it has everything to do with it. Good fiction cannot be written without a very firm, very specific basis of philosophical principles, most particularly moral principles. A man without a philosophy of life, with a mass of woozy contradictions in his thinking, cannot write a good story. There are not going to be any good writers until men have learned to think again.

You are quite right when you say that you feel your capacities are not being fully utilized in your movie job. No, it's not "a possibly immodest feeling," as you say. If you don't want to be immodest, let me do it for you. I have always felt that your talent is being wasted in the movies. It's quite all right to work in the movies for awhile, but it's not a permanent, full-time profession, certainly not for you or for me. That's why I am still thinking, wistfully, of the Ogden House. Do you remember that? Maybe it will remain only my dream, but maybe not. Anyway, I hope to God that you'll go back to publishing sooner or later.

Thanks for what you said about my "reflected glory." If there's anyone on whom I would like my glory to reflect, it's you. But it's not a reflection, darling, in this case. The glory is entirely your own. You have earned it.

Now here is a reminder—where's the picture you promised me? I am back at the writing of my new novel, and I would like to have your picture for the purpose I explained to you before. Please be immodest enough to believe that I want it for inspiration—and please send it, if you have one.

■ ■ ■

To Gerald Loeb

August 14, 1948

Dear Gerald:

The movie is going along wonderfully. I have visited the set several times and seen some of the key scenes being shot. My impression so far is that it is better than my best hopes. If all continues as well, it will be a great picture.

I cannot say that I like the models of the buildings, but as you know, I had no part in the choice of the designer.

You asked me about obtaining a 16 mm print of the finished picture for you. I am afraid that I would not be able to help you with that, because from what I hear, all the studios have a strict policy of never giving prints of pictures to anyone. I understand that even stars and directors cannot obtain them. Only Jack Warner himself could help you in this matter.

You write: "Tell me how to make $525,000 after taxes." That's a nice question to hear from a big financial tycoon like you. I can't resist saying that I could tell you how to make it. It's very simple: Bring back the system of free enterprise.

■　■　■

To Mimi Sutton

August 21, 1948

Dear Mimi:

I was very interested to hear that Connie intends to be a writer. Tell her for me that if she really wants to be one, nothing on earth can or will stop her. When she is ready for it, let her write me about her career and her plans. It's one profession in which I can help her and will be delighted to help. If she is serious about it, I can teach her many shortcuts, save her a lot of time and teach her a lot of things a young writer usually takes years to discover.

Thank you for the nice things you said about me and *The Fountainhead*. To tell you the truth, I really didn't know how you felt about my book. Give my thanks to the people in the bookstore who told you that *The Fountainhead* will always be current fiction. I appreciate that very much.

To answer all your literary questions: I am halfway through the writing of my next book now. Its theme will be to glorify the American industrialist, and the background is mainly railroads and the steel industry. I can't tell you much about the story, except to say that I think it will be better than *The Fountainhead*. I have not selected a title for it as yet, and I cannot say exactly when it will be published because it is impossible for me to predict when I will finish writing it. I hope to have it ready for publication in 1949.

Frank and I have been rushed like mad, alternating between the studio and our ranch. Frank has had to neglect his flowers and chickens a little, but he is enjoying it tremendously, and it is all very exciting at the moment.

■ ■ ■

To Mimi Sutton

September 12, 1948

Dear Mimi:

I was sorry to read your request that we loan you money. We are not able to do it—and I had hoped that I could be friends with my nieces without the constant threat of having to assume a financial responsibility for them.

I thought I had explained it before, but I will say it again and then I will leave it up to you: If you feel affection for us and want to maintain friendly relations, then it must be on the understanding that there will be no requests for money. I do like you, and on our last meeting in Washington, I had the impression that you were becoming the kind of person of whom I approve—but if you understand my philosophy, as you say you do, you must understand that I do not believe that friendship means an obligation to turn oneself into an object for the use of one's friends.

There is a great deal that I could explain to you about this, but I don't think it is necessary, and you can probably understand it by yourself. So I shall only say that if you want us to remain friends without any financial matters involved, I will be happy to remain your friend. If not, then not. I cannot deal with people on any other terms.

■ ■ ■

To Marie Strakhow

September 12, 1948

Dear "Missis,"

This is just a hurried note to send you the International Mail Coupons which you asked for. I am enclosing 20 coupons of 9 cents each. These are the only ones which the post office had here, and I hope they are the ones you needed.

I have written to the Tolstoy Foundation asking them to expedite your arrival, if it is possible, and I am trying to do everything I can here to help you obtain your visa.

I shall be glad to send you a statement to the effect that I will give you employment in my home. As a matter of fact, you could be a great help to me if you took over my housekeeping duties, for which I have no time; that is, to take over the management of the house, the servants and all domestic supervision. As soon as I find out the proper form to write this statement, I will send it to you.

■ ■ ■

To Leonebel Jacobs

September 19, 1948

Dear Leonebel:

Many thanks from both of us for the wonderful cheese which you sent us. It is a real treat, one of the nicest I have ever tasted—and we are eating it with grateful thoughts of you.

I have been madly rushed on my picture, so I have not had many guests in the house, but the few who have been here and have seen Frank's portrait were most impressed by it and expressed the nicest compliments to you. I feel happy every time I look at it. I am sorry that my own face gave you so much trouble when you were here.

■ ■ ■

To Ross Baker

October 2, 1948

Dear Ross:

I am glad to know that you are not considering a popular reprint [i.e., paperback edition] of *The Fountainhead* in connection with the picture. I believe that the release of the picture will give a great boost to the sales of our full-priced edition.

I saw a rough cut of the picture this week. If some unforeseen disaster does not happen in the cutting, which I do not expect, the picture will be excellent. The predictions in the studio are that they expect it to be sensational.

I am now back at work on my new novel. My work on the movie was a bad interruption for me, but it was worth it, and the new book is now picking up speed again.

■   ■   ■

To Mia May, silent-screen star

AR had seen Mia May films in Russia in the mid-1920s. In the diary AR kept of movies she attended, she underlined Mia May's name, indicating she was a particular favorite. Mia May was the wife of renowned Austrian movie director Joe May, also one of AR's favorites.

October 11, 1948

Dear Mrs. May,

I find it very difficult to tell you how grateful I am for the pictures you sent me. I have no way to explain how much they mean to me. It is my youth brought back—or, rather, a reward for the very difficult years of my youth, when the name "Mia May" and the things you represented were the symbol of the only beauty and relief I had while being imprisoned in hell. You will always remain a symbol of beauty to me.

I have had a very hard struggle to reach the things I wanted. That I should meet you in person, when I have finally broken my way into pictures, is like a special reward to me, something very personal and precious—because the kind of pictures I want to make are in the style and spirit of the pictures you made. It is a spirit which does not exist in the world any longer—and part of my battle is to bring it back.

I would like very much to see you again and to thank you in person.

With all my admiration,

■   ■   ■

To King Vidor, director of *The Fountainhead* movie

October 11, 1948

Dear King,

Thank you most sincerely for your nice letter and your present. It was such a beautiful gesture on your part that I have to offer you my admiration for it in return.

I, too, am very sorry that things happened as they did, but you made me feel that all of us are big enough to preserve the wonderful unity we had when we began our work on the picture. I am happy to think that if the picture is the kind of success I hope it will be, we will all celebrate it together.

Henry [Blanke] told me that you are out of town, and he has just left for New York. I shall not open the champagne until both of you are back. I would like the three of us to drink it together to the success of our picture.

During shooting of the movie, AR had fought Vidor over his desire to change Roark's courtroom speech. The speech was shot as AR wrote it, but one line was later cut.

■   ■   ■

To Leonebel Jacobs

October 17, 1948

Dear Leonebel:

I am taking out insurance on Frank's portrait, and the insurance company has asked me to ask you to write them a letter stating that you did the portrait, and the price which we paid for it.

The portrait is probably the best of my material treasures. It makes me happy every time I look at it. Thank you for it once more.

■   ■   ■

To John C. Gall

October 30, 1948

Dear John:

I have just received word that my friend, Mrs. Marie Strachow has obtained her visa and is on her way to the United States. She is due to arrive in New York tomorrow, Sunday the 31st.

I am extremely happy that she was able to get on the first boat of displaced persons coming here. Please accept my most sincere gratitude for your help in this matter.

■   ■   ■

To Robert Spencer Carr, a science fiction author

November 14, 1948

Dear Mr. Carr:

I was deeply touched by your letter and your present to me of your novel [*The Room Beyond*]. I appreciated it as one of the nicest gestures that one writer can do for another. I have read your book very slowly and carefully. Now I find myself profoundly puzzled. I assume that you want to hear my serious reaction, so I will state it, even though I am not certain whether you care to discuss philosophy.

From a literary aspect, *The Room Beyond* has a great deal of merit. Your style and your entire approach to writing are so superior to the vulgarly journalistic method of the majority of modern writers that it was a pleasure to read your book—up to a certain point. Up to the point where your philosophy took over.

Your theme and your philosophical ideas leave me stumped. I cannot understand why you liked *The Fountainhead* and how you could have chosen me as any kind of inspiration. The philosophy which you preach is the exact opposite of mine. Your heroine is supposed to represent the ideal of selflessness and altruism. The theme of *The Fountainhead* is a denunciation of altruism and self-sacrificing as the greatest evil conceivable. My philosophy is based on the idea that man is *not* a sacrificial animal, that it is man's moral right and duty to exist for the sake of his own happiness. The character of Cristina in your book is the symbol of that which I consider as the total evil. In my book, her spiritual counterpart is Ellsworth Toohey.

The thought has even occurred to me that your intention in sending me your book was malice or sarcasm. But on rereading your letter, I concluded that it was not. Therefore, I am truly bewildered. Either you have no respect for me at all and assumed that I did not mean what I preached. Or you had no respect for your own ideas and so were able to like your own opposite—*The Fountainhead*. Or else, you simply have no respect for philosophy, ideas and convictions of any kind whatsoever. But there is too much talent in your book—so I hesitate to believe that you are one of those superficial persons who dismisses the most profound issues of philosophy with some such meaningless thing as "the blending of opposites" and with some such assertion as that faith is above reason and the most monstrously irrational contradictions are to be ignored by means of some mystical emotion.

If you do not care to discuss these ideas philosophically, in rational terms, but wish to take refuge in mysticism—then, of course, this discussion is futile. I do not argue or deal with mysticism. I have no mystical instincts, intuitions or revelations of any kind—therefore, there is nothing you can communicate to me in those terms. But since you have approached me, I will answer you in the only terms I speak or respect—the terms of reason.

I want to point out to you that your own novel, the very story which you present, refutes and denounces the thesis of altruism which you set out to preach. Your talent as a novelist asserted itself in opposition to your weakness as a thinker. There are many examples of that in literature— where the honesty of a writer works to destroy his own mistaken abstractions. Tolstoy is a classic example of it. I believe that this is inherent in the medium of fiction. One can state any number of vague, undefined, contradictory abstractions in a nonfiction work. But a fiction story has to be told in terms of concrete reality. An impossible thesis cannot be translated into concrete action to illustrate it. When one attempts it, the story defeats the thesis. A reader will accept the author's events and characters just as the author presents them, but *not* the interpretation which the author tries to force upon them. Now here is what I see in your story: the character of Cristina, just as she stands—and you have drawn her extremely well— is a vicious monster. I am judging her by her own actions and words—not by Daniel's judgment of them—and I see the dreadful cruelty of the woman. She showed kindness only to the mindless and the miserable. The moment Daniel or any of the other characters brought up some issue more serious, more crucial and much more profound than an infected colon— Cristina met them with the most cruel weapon of all: sarcasm. That is the weapon of Ellsworth Toohey.

I was appalled when I read Cristina's first meeting with Daniel Bryce. The way you present the sincerity of his love for her is magnificent and completely convincing. Here was a sensitive boy of thirteen, and here was a catastrophe in his life, upon which his entire future depended; Cristina did nothing but laugh at him (laugh casually!) in the coldest, most heartless manner every time the earnestness of his feeling reached her. I could not imagine that an author had shown Cristina's cruelty accidentally and was not aware of it. I thought you were doing a beautiful, subtle job of denunciation. But you weren't. At the end I found that you did intend her as an ideal.

After that first meeting, the whole of Daniel's life is a dreadful tragedy. It is not I who say so arbitrarily; it is you who have shown it, most convincingly. Daniel was robbed of all joy, of all ambition, of pride, self-respect and peace of mind. He went through life doing a kind of continuous, desperate penance for some nameless guilt which he had never committed. Daniel comes across very convincingly as a very sympathetic character, a man of courage, strength, intelligence—yet he is put on a torture rack for no reason whatever. If Daniel is the best, the healthiest human being among the characters in your story, then in his person Cristina has destroyed the best and most vital aspects of human life. The cruelty with which, understanding his tragedy, she keeps deserting him and then laughing casually as if nothing had happened when she meets him ten years later, is truly one of the most sadistic things I have ever read in literature. Her spiritual counterpart, my Ellsworth Toohey, has never done anything to match her cruelty. I think Ellsworth would have hesitated; her behavior would have been too much, even for him.

And what about the other characters in your story, all those men who loved Cristina and were influenced by her? All of them were left in a state of bitter, hopeless, frustrated longing. She helped Freeman Rabb and Leo Lasta physically, when they were sick children—then left them mangled and crippled spiritually, when they grew up. They—and also Dr. Hand—became men in whom the joy of living had been killed.

And *this* is another paradox of the mystical-altruistic viewpoint: while you stress, in theory, the superiority of the spirit over the flesh—you show, in practice, that Cristina helps people to cure the suffering of the flesh and gives them a horrible suffering of the spirit, instead. She heals the flesh and mangles the spirit. Is that what you wanted to say? I am sure you didn't, but that is what your story says and shows.

On the other hand, the character of Wendra destroys your philosophy in another manner. You have tried very hard to make her unsympathetic—and yet she is the most vital person in your story. Did you notice that she is the only one who does some good for Daniel? You tell us that she had nothing but a selfish motive in mind. Quite true. And I say that only when one has a selfish motive in mind, can one be of any service to others. Your story proves my point. It is Wendra who saves Daniel's life when he is beaten up. It is Wendra who offers to give him her estate, in order not to let him live as her dependent—a truly noble offer which no altruist would ever make. The sole passion of an altruist is to see everybody dependent upon him. (Cristina loved only the crippled and helpless, that is, the dependent; she lost interest in them the moment they were cured and free.) It is Wendra who meets Daniel when he returns from the war, lost and lonely. Everything that Wendra does for Daniel is a joy and a comfort in terms of this earth. Everything that Cristina does is just another torture.

Now you may say that that is precisely your point, that one must live on earth in perpetual suffering—in order to be happy in some undefined fourth dimension after death. If that is your thesis, you should admit it openly to yourself and to your readers. You should state that you are an advocate of torture and death. Only on this earth? But self-deception aside, this earth is all that any of us know or care about or have a right to discuss.

It is not an accident that you had to make Cristina a supernatural being. Again, the honesty of your talent as a novelist asserted itself and made you do it. You could not have made her an actual human being of flesh and blood. An actual human being acting on the altruist premise is Ellsworth Toohey. Altruism is impossible to man—impossible by the whole nature of the universe. Altruism is death and destruction.

Throughout your novel you ran a race between yourself as a novelist and yourself as a mystic. The novelist won up to a certain point—and then the mystic destroyed the achievement. (That, too, is in the nature of reality.) The device which you chose for the structure of your novel—the prologue in which you promised the reader that your hero had a tremendous secret to disclose at the end of the story—was an excellent device and it kept up the reader's interest. But surely you realize that a device of this kind amounts to a promissory note which the author gives to his readers. Its effectiveness lies in the readers' trust that the author will live up to his promise and will disclose something of tremendous importance. When your disclosure finally came, your story collapsed. This reader experienced an angry sense of disappointment—the feeling of having been cheated. It was a fraud on two counts: First, philosophically—the idea you intended Daniel to disclose was nothing more than an assertion about life after death, presented in the vaguest terms, adding nothing that had not been said before, lacking all element of philosophical importance or freshness. Second, literarily—the fact that Daniel neither made his speech nor leaped from the balcony, but went back into the dining room as a vapid old man and nothing happened except some bromidic toasts—was a dismal anticlimax. It was a dull thud. After such a build up, you had no artistic right to do this to your readers. And yet, on your premise, there was nothing else you could do. No story can reach a climax or a proper conclusion if it is built on a false principle—just exactly as a man cannot do it in real life.

Your "Coda" is an open confession that you knew you had not done right by your readers. It was an attempt to justify your position, to give the readers something of importance—but you had no arguments to offer.

The thing that struck me as the most revealing sentence in your book, as a kind of personal cry and as a clue to your own tragedy, is the question on Page 424—"Why else do men go on searching after they have lost their hope of finding anything, were it not from this secret ache where something indescribably precious has somehow slipped away, and must be re-captured?" I think I can answer you. The indescribably precious thing which men have lost is this earth. All men have it at first, in their childhood, perhaps before they learn to speak, before contact with others corrupts their minds. A child starts with the idea that this is a wonderful world in which he will be happy and that he has a moral right to be happy. The monstrous conceptions of turning himself into a sacrificial animal and of happiness being guilt never occur to him. Then, later, every idea he absorbs from the adults leads to a damnation of himself and of this earth. Yet, since he *is* a human being, he cannot accept completely the inhumanity which is taught to him. He retains a faint memory of the paradise which he has given up and lost. I am one of the very few people who have never lost it. *This*— I think—is what you drew strength from in *The Fountainhead*. And, if so, I am very happy that you did.

I shall be interested to hear your answer, if you care to write me. I am unable to decide whether this letter will cause you to become my worst enemy or my best friend. I am curious—philosophically.

May I ask you to regard my letter as personal? It is intended for you as an author—but not for your publishers nor for quotation.

■ ■ ■

To John Chamberlain, a conservative writer

November 27, 1948

Dear John Chamberlain:

Thank you most sincerely for the last paragraph of your article, "The Businessman in Fiction," in the November issue of *Fortune*. It was wonderful of you and I am deeply grateful. I am going to live up to it, too. Mr. Tinker won't be disappointed. My new novel, in effect, has to blast away the accumulated smears of a century. It will.

From a political and literary viewpoint, I must thank you for the whole article, of course. It is excellent. I read it with great pleasure and also with furious anger at the sordid parade of pink brains that you presented so expertly. It was really a ghastly procession to see all at once. Reading it, I wished somebody would wipe the whole rotten bunch off the face of the earth. So it was the more startling and thrilling for me to find myself named as the antidote and the avenger.

I was struck particularly by one observation of yours: "Indeed, the latter-day novelists are not only antibusiness; they are also antifecundity and antilife." You have hit the heart of the whole issue. *That*, precisely, is the basic theme of my new novel—that those who are antibusiness are antilife.

I wonder whether you still intend to write the article about *The Fountainhead* which we discussed in New York, or whether you have given up the idea? The reason for my asking is that *The Fountainhead* has been produced as a movie, to be released early next year, so the book will be timely news again. If you still want to do the article, I thought that that would be a good time for it. My experience with the movie has been perhaps even more miraculous than with the book. I wrote the screenplay myself, preserving my theme and philosophy intact. For the first time in Hollywood history, the script was shot verbatim, word for word as written. I had no legal control over the production, yet the picture was made as faithfully as if I controlled it. This in Hollywood—where they ruin and distort every story they buy, particularly every serious story, and where they are scared of the faintest suggestion of a controversial subject. The first picture ever shot here verbatim will be—not some weak, compromising, middle-of-the-road script—but the most uncompromising, most extreme and "dangerous" screenplay they ever had. I think this is an illustration of the power of an honest idea to reach people and to accomplish things which no amount of force or collective pressure could accomplish.

The studio heads may still lose their courage and ruin the picture in the cutting, but it does not appear likely now. If the picture is released as is, it will be the atom bomb of the movie industry. Then, I think, somebody should tell the public the story and the meaning behind it—and I wish it were you.

■　■　■

To Raymond P. Blosser

December 19, 1948

Dear Mr. Blosser:

Would you do a favor for a faithful fan of the New York Central and send me one of your railroad calendars for the coming year? The one you gave me last year has served as an inspiration, hanging here on the wall of my office while I write my railroad novel, and I will miss it next month, so I would love to have a new one.

I am back at work on my railroad story now and hope to finish it some time in 1949. I have just completed the sequence which involves a ride in the cab of an engine—and I am glad to say that when you read it in print, you will find I have done justice to your courtesy in letting me ride in that engine a year ago.

■　■　■

To Mrs. M. Beyleiter, a fan

December 28, 1948

Dear Mrs. Beyleiter:

If you want to write a novel of your own about architects in your country, you are free to do it and do not need my permission—provided that the content of your book comes entirely from your own imagination and is not taken in any way from my novel. Any writer is free to handle the subject of architecture in his own way. But if you want to use the story of my book and paraphrase it into a book of your own, or use my title, *The Fountainhead*, or use any part of my novel—then my answer is: No, I do not permit it. It is a request which nobody should make and which no author can permit. It is the same as if you asked me to use parts of my child to make a child of your own. No parent would permit it and that is not how children are made. If you want to write a book, it must come entirely from your own observation and imagination. You cannot use parts of somebody else's work.

■　■　■

To Ethel Harris, a fan

December 28, 1948

Dear Miss Harris:

Do not doubt the existence of integrity such as Roark's. It exists in every person who chooses to make it exist.

■　■　■

To Constance Woodward, a fan

December 28, 1948

Dear Miss Woodward:

You ask if I'm a Roark or if I wrote *The Fountainhead* in "the spirit of mockery." Nobody could write that book in the spirit of mockery.

You ask me why I wrote the book and if I expect readers to be "brave enough" to believe it. I wrote that book for the same reason that Roark built his buildings. How people would react to it was not my primary concern. If they are not brave enough, it is their tough luck, not mine. I have found, however, that a great many of them were brave enough for it.

■ ■ ■

To Vera Glarner

In a copy of a letter from Vera's sister Tania, AR learned of the deaths during the war of many family members, including Natasha, AR's sister, and Nina, her cousin and closest childhood friend.

December 28, 1948

Dear Vera:

Thank you very much for your letter and for the photograph of Tania's letter which you sent me. It was a terrible experience for me to read her letter, but I was prepared for it by what Henri had told me, and I am glad that I could see the letter for myself.

Henri has explained to me why you prefer not to write to Tania. If you should ever have a chance to write to her or to inquire in any way, I would be very grateful if you would try to learn something about the fate of my little sister, without mentioning my name. But, of course, I will leave it entirely up to you to decide when and if you think it is safe to do it.

I was very glad to meet Henri, and I hope that perhaps someday you may come on a visit to America yourself. I found Henri very interesting—but I suppose he has told you that we had political arguments and we did not agree philosophically on many things. I hope I have not frightened him—I suspect that as a charming Frenchman, he does not approve of a woman who stays up until 3 in the morning arguing about the nature of the universe.

I wonder whether he has explained to you why I did not send you a copy of my book. I did not want you to buy it, because you may not like it. I asked him to ask you to get it from a library. Then if you like it, I will be happy to send you an autographed copy of it. I do not feel offended if someone does not like my book, but since it means a great deal to me, I do not give a copy of it except to those who like it. The reason which made me think that you may not care for it was Henri's attitude. He read the first 60 pages of it and began to criticize it and to object to its philosophy without waiting to find out what that philosophy was. In such a case, I would prefer that a person would not read it at all.

I tried to gather from Henri what your tastes and philosophy are now, but I could not form too clear an idea of it. I remember you as a person of very delicate poetic taste, and it interests me very much to learn what sort of books or art works you like now. I suspect that you will not like my kind of writing. You probably remember me as a very violent person. I have remained the same, only more so.

I was happy to see a very small photograph of you which Henri showed me. You do not seem to have aged or changed much, and you look just as I remember you. Lisette is a very pretty girl, judging by the photographs which Henri showed me, and she has definitely the look of your family. I would love to have a picture of her in the coat I sent her. I was worried about that coat because it was my idea to get it a size larger than necessary, just in case.

■   ■   ■

To Leonebel Jacobs

January 8, 1949

Dear Leonebel:

Thank you immensely for the photographs of Frank's portrait. We were both thrilled to see how beautiful it looks in the black-and-white print. I am so happy with this portrait that I am terribly tempted to put it on the book jacket of my next novel as a portrait of its hero. All my heroes will always be reflections of Frank, anyway.

A rendition of the painting did appear in some newspaper advertisements for Atlas Shrugged.

■   ■   ■

To Alan Collins

January 8, 1949

Dear Alan:

We had a preview of *The Fountainhead* day before yesterday, on January 6. Jack Warner, Henry Blanke and all the executives who were present said it was the most sensational preview they ever attended. The picture was given the hardest test—it was previewed in an industrial district which they consider lowbrow. It went over so brilliantly that Jack Warner decided they needed no further previews, and the final negative is being printed right now. Warner did not make a single change or cut.

The picture runs for an hour and 56 minutes, and the audience sat on the edge of their seats every minute of it—including Roark's speech. The speech will go through as I wrote it. When I suggested that I could make certain cuts in it, if they wanted me to, Warner would not allow me to cut a single line. The studio is in an uproar, and Henry Blanke is simply stunned, just as I am. It was a real triumph.

Right after the preview, Jack Warner told me that he would buy my next novel right then and there, and I said that if he did as well with it, I would be happy to sell it. This is not a commitment, of course, but it will give you some idea of how we all felt. Blanke has done wonders with the editing of the picture, and I am completely satisfied with it.

■　■　■

To John L. B. Williams

January 8, 1949

Dear John:

We had a preview of the movie of *The Fountainhead* day before yesterday, January 6. According to all the studio executives present, including Jack Warner and Henry Blanke, it was the most sensational preview they had ever attended.

I think Bobbs-Merrill may be glad to know that the first or title frame of the film is a photograph of the book itself, with a closeup of the jacket. If you can arrange to have copies of the book in the bookstore windows at the time when the picture is playing at the local theaters, I think we will be headed back for the bestseller list.

■ ■ ■

To Vladimir Kondheim and his wife, Peter (now named "Elo")

January 8, 1949

Dear Volodia and Peter:

Our congratulations and best wishes on your happy event. We were startled to hear the news, since you did not warn us about it at all, but I am delighted that you have solved your difficulties—and we wish you many years of happiness.

I cannot quite get used to Peter's new name, but I will when we see you again. I don't know yet when we will be able to come to New York, but I am looking forward to it and hope to congratulate you in person.

■ ■ ■

To Raymond P. Blosser

January 9, 1949

Dear Mr. Blosser:

Thank you very much for the calendars. They cheer me up every time I look at them.

No, I have no complaint about having been interrupted to write the screen version of *The Fountainhead*. But I thought that New York Central might complain that a year has passed, and I have not produced my railroad novel yet. I did not want you to think that you had wasted all the diesel units of the Twentieth-Century on a lazy author. However, I am sure you won't think it was wasted when you see the result, even though it does take me a long time.

I would be delighted to take you up, gratefully, on your offer to "turn loose" one of your operating people on my script to check it for technical accuracy. I am not ready for that yet, but when I finish the novel I will come to New York with it and then I will have to have it checked by real railroad men.

■ ■ ■

To Robert Spencer Carr

January 23, 1949

Dear Mr. Carr:

Thank you for your letter. It has answered my philosophical curiosity. I appreciate your taking the time and effort to do it in detail.

I did not think it was possible that anyone would write to me the following paragraph: "In the formal study of ethics (a course for which no attractive woman has ever enrolled), months and years of cruel discipline are required to drill into the average young man's mushy little monkey-mind this basic principle: That an ethical act, to be ethical at all, must be performed with total disregard of the personal profit, loss, praise or blame attached to it."

That paragraph states exactly the rotten corruption in all the systems of ethics which I am fighting—yet you present it to me as if you intended it to be news, or explanation, or expected me to agree, or—no, I cannot try to guess your intention. In *The Fountainhead*, I have presented a new system of ethics, the basic principle of which is that an ethical act, in order to be ethical at all, must be performed with the most profound regard for one's personal interest, that one's personal profit must be its sole motive and purpose—and that any other act is totally immoral.

The vicious nonsense which you quote from "formal ethics" (?) simply means that man has *no personal interest* in ethical behavior, that his *personal* interests are outside the realm of ethics, but that he must perform some allegedly ethical acts for some unknown reason which has nothing to do with himself. Sure, *that's* your formal ethics. And that's why they haven't worked after centuries of professors mouthing them at mankind. And that's why men prefer any kind of sin to this sort of ethics. Brother, have you come to the wrong person! I'm the little girl who has set out (and succeeded) to prove that ethics must be based on *man's self-interest* and can be based on nothing else.

You say that Howard Roark is an example of "not caring a damn either way what the hell happens to *him*." This means that you have concluded that Howard Roark did not care about his actions or their results—that he did not care a damn either way whether he happened to design a modern building or a classical monstrosity—that he refused to design bad buildings out of some sort of selfless devotion to some sort of woozy "truth," but his real feeling would have permitted him to design them with pleasure—that his real interest lay in a Peter Keating kind of career, but he sacrificed himself—that when he fought for the kind of buildings he liked, it really meant nothing to him, he had no personal interest in his work, he derived no joy from it and no personal profit—he did not care in what way he used his creative energy, nor in what way he spent his time —he did not care about anything at all—he was just a disinterested amoeba, totally indifferent to life, to reality, to thoughts, emotions and actions. If that is what you got out of *The Fountainhead*, the loss is yours, not mine.

If one approaches writing or thinking with such terms as: "selfish altruist," then your statements are not surprising. You write: "I'm curious as to how and why your scorching letter, no matter how indignantly intended, turned out to be an altruistic act." There is no mystery about it at all—just look up the word "altruistic" in the dictionary. "Altruistic" does not mean "kind" or "valuable to others"—which is the way you use the word. "Altruism" means placing others above self—and placing the interests of others above your own. If you keep this in mind, you will, perhaps, feel a little ashamed of such a paragraph as: "These are the real, the selfish altruists, of whom you are one. Evidence? *The Fountainhead*, a book that has benefited hundreds of thousands of readers, and harmed only a few humbugs who deserved to be exposed."

Do you call the fact that my book benefited readers "altruistic"? Do you mean that they derived from it greater benefits than I did, spiritual or material? Do you mean that their benefit was achieved at the expense of mine or at the price of some sort of self-sacrifice by me? Do you mean that I wrote it for their sake, not mine? Do you mean that I wrote it for the purpose of benefiting them, with no personal interest involved in the matter? Or do you mean that in order to be selfish, I had to expect my book to *harm* people—but since it didn't, this makes me an altruist?

Whom and what are you answering when you tell me: "It is not true that any act which benefits another human being is *per se* a sickly, hypocritical fraud"? Who said it was? What *The Fountainhead* said is that *only an act of true selfishness motivated by and intended for one's own benefit can be of any benefit or value to others—and only as a secondary consequence.* But any act motivated by "the good of others" is a vicious act. "The good of others" as one's aim or motive is a vicious motive. The sole and inevitable result of such acts or motives is to destroy both the do-gooder and his victims. Any attempt to act for the "good of others" is a piece of vicious impertinence.

So if my letter or my book benefited you or anyone, it is not paradoxical, and it can surprise nobody except the moralists of the "disinterested" school. My book is of value to people, because my purpose in writing it was my own philosophical interest for my own pleasure. I did not attempt to do good to my readers. I did not attempt to render any sort of service to mankind. I did not consider it my duty to be of value to anyone. I did not think of anyone, only of my subject. I am happy if readers found benefit in my book, but that benefit was not my purpose.

As you see, I expect principles to have specific meanings, applicable to concrete reality and serving as a guide to one's actions. Therefore, such a statement as dividing people into "truth-loving persons" and "hypocrites" for purposes of philosophical explanation is totally meaningless to me. What truth? What love? What constitutes loving truth? History is full of people who believed what they taught—yet caused the most unspeakable disasters. Robespierre believed completely in his right to guillotine his opponents. Hitler believed in some mystical visions that had appointed him to be the ruler of mankind. Are these the "truth lovers"? Is one's own blindness a guarantee of one's virtue? Do you use emotion ("love") as a standard for a philosophical definition?

These are terms in which I do not deal, nor do I deal with such statements as: "stretching a generality that last fatal notch to 100 percent that invalidates any generality." What is that? A Sunday supplement version of Hegel?

I made the accusation that Cristina was the counterpart of Ellsworth Toohey. Your answer is: "Only an initiate can tell the two species apart." An initiate into what? (The question is rhetorical. I know the answer.) So you say you're not a mystic? In the realm of rationalism, there is no such term as "an initiate." It takes no "initiation" to explain anything in rational terms: it takes simple words and common sense. If you wrote a book, in which your readers cannot tell whether your heroine is a saint or a monster without some sort of "initiation" into something, previously to and apart from the content of your book—can you then complain about being "misunderstood"? If you wrote a book in the Tibetan language (which, I think, you did), then offered it to English-speaking readers, and then sighed at people's lack of understanding, saying nobly that you "forgive" them—do you know the proper English answer to *that*?

After innumerable passages (in your book) in which you state that Cristina had achieved "total selflessness," that she "desired nothing for herself," that her eyes lighted up with interest only when she thought that Dan was sick, so that she could "help him"—you attempt to tell me that she had something in common with Roark—because she, too, had consecrated herself to her work, such work consisting—*here, on earth*—of washing other people's infected colons.

I suppose I should point out to you that the thesis of *The Fountainhead* is *not*: Do whatever you wish, so long as you believe it. The thesis is: Do whatever you wish, so long as you are independent of other men. This thesis rests, for its justification, on man's nature—you may discover why and how if you care to study Roark's speech, all the steps of the argument are included there. This thesis cannot be stretched to include those who wish to have its benefits without its base—those who wish to spend their lives in the unnatural perversion of serving others, yet try to claim all the rights pertaining to independence, at the same time.

I shall now have to quote from Roark's speech: "The first right on earth is the right of the ego. Man's first duty is to himself. His moral law is never to place his prime goal within the persons of others. His moral obligation is to do what he wishes, provided his wish does not depend *primarily* upon other men. This includes the whole sphere of his creative faculty, his thinking, his work. But it does not include the sphere of the gangster, the altruist or the dictator."

The intent of this paragraph was to close the door to all the Cristinas who might attempt to climb on the Roark bandwagon with no better ticket than the alleged happiness they claim to find in self-immolation. Nothing doing, sister!

You say of Cristina: "Of course, her motives were selfish; she was seeking full selfhood." If you attach any meaning to words, if you made the above clear in your novel, but I missed it—then you should have told me what her "full selfhood" specifically consisted of. In your book, she achieved something which you called happiness somewhere after death. All that she did in life and on earth was to take care of sick children. What, specifically, was the connection between her "selfhood" and the sick children? What, specifically, gave her happiness? Why did she have to nurse the children in order to achieve happiness? If her happiness did not consist of the good of the children, what did it consist of? And where? And how?

You say that you can't understand why I blame Cristina for ruining every life she touched. Perhaps I took your book and your character more seriously than you intended them to be taken. (I did not know, for instance, that you intended your book as a piece of "science fiction.") I took Cristina to represent an ideal—that is, your version of a human ideal. I did not gather that all the men in your book wanted to sleep with her. I gathered that their longing for her was the spiritual longing for an ideal which they could not reach and which left them dissatisfied with everything else thereafter, so that they never found happiness in any form with any other woman after they had known Cristina. If this was not your intention, then I am wrong, but then your book has no philosophical meaning at all. If Cristina *was* intended as an ideal, then she does ruin every life she touches, because she is an unattainable ideal. She arouses in men a longing for something which they cannot reach or achieve, which they cannot make part of their actions and their daily lives. This, of course, *is* the nature of altruism, and I gave you credit for presenting it correctly. Anyone who would hold altruism (*living for others*) as an ideal, would be condemned to a state of miserable frustration, fear, guilt and inferiority—because the only way to be a complete altruist is to offer yourself as a meal to the first tribe of cannibals you can find. Anything less than that is way short of the ideal, and leaves one in the position of a weak, imperfect, unhappy sinner.

Why do I blame Cristina for Dan's unhappiness? Because she was a woman who professed to live for others, because she spent her life relieving suffering, the physical suffering of children—yet ignored the much greater suffering of Dan and of all the other men who wanted her, a suffering which she herself had caused. I gathered that they wanted her spiritually— they wanted her companionship, her understanding and the love which she had allegedly shown them and then withdrawn. If she was concerned with relieving the suffering of others, then it was her duty to give them what they wanted. And if, as you say, what they wanted was to sleep with her —then, as an altruist, it was her duty to do that, too.

No, Dominique or I do not have to say "Yes" to every man, because Dominique and I are not altruists. We do not consider the suffering or the desires of others as our responsibility or concern. But an altruist would have to say "Yes" to any and every desire of any and every man—and this is just another minor example of the vicious nonsense which is altruism.

You ask: "How do you treat admirers who interrupt you in the midst of your very important work and importune you with pastimes for which you have neither the time nor the inclination?" Well, for one thing, I do not make them carry my basket. I do not *use* them.

You ask: "If you know any kindlier way of turning down a man than gentle laughter, let's hear it." The answer is: *respect*. Take the man seriously and tell him the truth. There can be no such thing as *gentle* laughter when one laughs at someone's pain or disappointment.

Do you really want to know why your readers liked Wendra? You say that she was "a bad, vain, worldly woman trying futilely to *buy* love and happiness." You forgot a very important point: she did not try to buy love, she actually *loved*. She loved one man all her life. Any person capable of doing that is neither bad nor vain. The capacity for a love of this kind comes from a very deep, very noble and very *selfish* quality of the spirit.

Some of your readers would not, perhaps, be able to explain it to you or give you their reasons, but they all know it. They know that Wendra knew more about love than Cristina ever could. Cristina, who—as you said repeatedly in your book—*loved everybody*, actually loved nobody at all, not even herself.

I strongly suspect that the real difference between you and me is that I did take your book more seriously than you intended. When you write a story in which the heroine vanishes through a shimmering film of air into the fourth dimension, and then returns, walking on a light ray—when you are then accused of being a mystic and answer that you are not, because you once got a letter from Einstein who does not write to mystics—I cannot take it in any way except as humor.

■ ■ ■

To Charles Sternberg, International Rescue and Relief Organization

January 29, 1949

Dear Mr. Sternberg:

I am glad to say that Mrs. Strachow has arrived already and is now in the United States. But I appreciate very much your keeping track of this case and of my request for your assistance.

If this comes within the province of your organization's activities, I would like to mention to you the cases of two displaced persons in Europe who are in bad need of food packages and assistance. Mrs. Strachow told me about them. Their names and addresses are:

> Mrs. Julia Dietrichs
> Neumarkt near Salzburg
> former camp
> US Zone Austria
> and
> Mrs. Tatiana Weber
> 21a Detmold
> Friedrich str. 22
> British Zone Germany

They have no friends abroad who can help them. I am not able to assist them myself, but if your organization does do relief work of this kind, I would appreciate it very much if you would call their cases to the attention of your representative in Europe.

■ ■ ■

To Vera Glarner

February 12, 1949

Dear Vera:

Thank you for your letter. I am terribly sorry if I have revived for you all the tragic memories of the past. I will not ask you about it again, unless you have some news about our families or relatives. If or when you have, please let me know. I, too, do not know the married name of my little sister. I suppose, if we can ever inquire about her, it would have to be through Tania, who would know her name.

I will be very interested to know your opinion of my novel, when you have had a chance to read it. I have not read many French books since coming to America. I have not read much of the work of Colette, so I cannot express a real opinion, but the few of her stories which I have read, I found to be very charming and intelligently written.

Thank you for saying that you feel as if we have found each other again. I feel so, too, and I think you will find me a better correspondent than I used to be in my youth.

■ ■ ■

To Robert Spencer Carr

February 12, 1949

Dear Mr. Carr:

Thank you for your letter of February 2—and my congratulations. To recognize one's own mistake in an argument and to admit it, is a rare act of honesty and one of the cardinal virtues (Rand Ethics). I sincerely respect you for it.

I do not say this because you have agreed with me. You have not agreed with my philosophy. But if you recognize that the philosophy of Roark and that of Cristina are opposites, it is all that I can ask you to recognize. Which one you consider right and which one you choose to believe is up to your own judgment. But if this question interests you and if you realize its importance, the fact of knowing that these two philosophies are opposites places you three-quarters of the way out of what you call "the misty limbo of the damned." I suspected that in some inconceivable way you thought that you could combine both these philosophies. If you realize that you can't, that you have to make your choice, that it's one or the other—you will be able to clarify all your philosophical problems, if you care to clarify them.

Thank you for your nice offer to send me some "material tokens" from your travels, if I collect any. But please don't do it. Being a "materialist," I don't collect anything except ideas. So, instead, I will take you up on a hint contained in your letter of December 8. You said: "Is it your fault if I cut my throat because I arrive in Hollywood next week and you refuse to see me?" I suspect that this was a hint, because I don't think one makes a crack of this kind unless one has some formed or semi-formed intention. So, if I am right, I'll say that if you come to Hollywood, you will not have to cut your throat, at least not for the above reason. If your travels should take you to the West Coast, I would be glad to meet you in person, and then we can fight further, if you care to. If my letters have really been of value to you and of any help in clarifying serious problems, then I will be glad to discuss philosophical issues with you in person, which, as you said, is much easier than doing it by mail.

■　■　■

To Henry Blanke

February 26, 1949

Dear Henry:

This is to remind you of our discussion about *The Isle of Lost Ships* and to present my views on it for your consideration.

I believe that *The Isle of Lost Ships*, which is owned by Warner Brothers, is one of the best screen stories of all time, and I want to urge you most enthusiastically to make a new, modern version of it.

This story has a *real* and extremely dramatic central conflict—the kind of idea that contains all the elements of a real plot. Such ideas are very rare, the best of writers do not hit upon them often, and this is one that any writer who understands plot construction, as I do, would give his eye-teeth to have invented.

A real dramatic plot is the one surefire element for a great popular success, in a novel, a stage play or a picture—most particularly in a picture. Few stories have a real plot; most of them have to be faked dramatically and, therefore, their success is a gamble; real plot ideas are the rarest and hardest of all to devise. When one does find such an idea, then it is priceless beyond calculation—artistically and financially—because its success is *certain.*

If you remember my advance predictions about the success of *The Fountainhead,* if you remember that I never had the slightest doubt or fear about its "intellectual" quality being "too much" for an audience, you may, I hope, be convinced now that I do know the secret of a picture's success. Of course, a writer is not the only one responsible for a success on the screen. A picture has to have a good production, direction and cast. But these elements have a high degree of perfection in Hollywood—and most certainly in *your* pictures. These elements are a constant. It is your writers who let you down. And they do, because most of them have no idea of what constitutes a real plot structure.

Yet *plot* is the one absolute *must* in a story. Characterization, dialogue, mood and all the rest are only secondary "gravy." They help and they have value *only* when based on a good plot. Without it they are worthless. The plot of a movie is its motor. It is not an accident that people call pictures "vehicles" for stars. A vehicle has to move. A plotless story is like an expensive car with a wonderful body design, luxurious seats, upholstery, headlights (production, direction, cast)—and no motor under its hood. That is why it gets nowhere.

I think I was probably the least surprised person at our preview of *The Fountainhead*—the least surprised by the wonderful reaction of the audience and the fact that they behaved as if we held them on strings. We did. They simply reacted as I intended them to react; it was in the script—and God bless you for the magnificent way in which you carried it out! I am not boasting or taking sole credit. I only want to convince you (if you are not fully convinced, although I hope you are) that I knew, foresaw and planned that audience reaction in advance—and my only fear was of any tampering with the script, which would have destroyed it. I did not write that script by guesswork or "inspiration." I gave the cast a chance to hold the audience bridled—by conscious, deliberate, calculated intention. The secret of it was *plot structure.* I am not an "artist"—I am an engineer.

Can you imagine what would happen to an automobile factory, if its motor designers had to guess whether a motor would run or not? If they had to find it out only *after* a car was made? Yet that is precisely the way in which most writers approach script writing in Hollywood. They have no plot sense—and a writer without a plot sense is like a blind cameraman. I am not the only writer in Hollywood who does know plot—but I am one of the very, very few.

Well, this is a long introduction in order to tell you what an exceptional plot value you have in *The Isle of Lost Ships*. If this story is given your kind of beautiful production—I will go on record, here, on paper, to predict that it will be a multimillion dollar hit.

This story has the same elements of appeal as *The Fountainhead*. No, not literally the same in specific surface detail, but the same in general principle—and that's what counts. It is not "realistic" (the audiences are sick of sordid realism), it belongs to my school and style of writing—romanticism. It is not a story of trite, homey, "everyday" people and events (and are audiences sick of *that*!)—it is a story of strong, unusual characters in unusual, exciting events and in a real, dramatic conflict. Its sex angle is, in spirit, exactly the Roark-Dominique romance—sex through antagonism, the love story of a society girl and a convict. Of all forms of romance, this is the most powerful one and the surefire one. This form is difficult to write—that is why we don't see it often on the screen nowadays. But the audiences are starved for it. People are sick of the lukewarm, sentimental, "mushy" treatment of most love stories on the screen. That is why they now laugh at love scenes. Observe that they did not laugh at our "rape" scene. The time is right for a real, strong *sex* story. But few stories have the elements needed for it. *The Isle of Lost Ships* has them all. As a sex story, it's tops.

I saw the silent version of *The Isle of Lost Ships* (with Milton Sills and Anna Q. Nielsen) when I was a child in Europe, and I have never been able to forget it. It was a tremendous hit and I remember the delighted excitement with which everybody talked about it. A good story is timeless. It cannot be dated. Its essential appeal will always remain the same. One merely has to modernize the surface details, such as the dialogue. A good story is like a beautiful body. A beautiful body is beautiful to any audience in any day, age or century; the only thing that changes is the fashion in clothing. *The Isle of Lost Ships* needs a writer to modernize its clothing, which is its treatment, technical details and dialogue. The body is there.

Needless to say, I am most eager to be that writer. This is the kind of story I love and can do well. I will not be available for screen work for about a year, not until I finish the novel which I am now writing. But if you decide to make this story and if we can agree on its treatment and on other conditions, as I think we can, I would be delighted to undertake the job when I am free.

As a warning and for the record (and not just in order to cinch the job for myself), I must say that I cannot guarantee any of the predictions I make here about the success of this story—if you entrust it to a writer who is not a plot specialist. I dread to think what he would do to it. In fact, I would predict a disastrous flop, almost for certain. It is the lesser, the medium kind of story that can survive a bad script treatment. A good story cannot.

But if this story is made as I see it, as a great romantic drama, I will guarantee another audience reaction such as we had in Huntington Park. I am so sure of it that I would back my judgment even in material terms, if the studio wanted me to—I would take a percentage of the picture in place of any payment for the script. I don't mean to say that I want or would ask a percentage—I merely mean that if the studio wanted me to, I would do this as proof of how sure I am of what I am saying.

With all my love and gratitude to you for the past—and with great hopes for the future,

There is no record of Blanke's response. The movie has not been remade.

■   ■   ■

To Marjorie Hiss, a longtime friend

March 5, 1949

Dear Marjorie:

I don't have to tell you how much I sympathize with you. I am appalled by Philip's behavior, but I fully believe him capable of doing the things you write. With the kind of ideas he held, it was unavoidable that he would become worse and worse with the years.

I know how badly you feel now. I wish I could be with you and talk to you, because I think I could help you to overcome some of it. There are so many things I'd like to say that it's impossible to do it in a letter. I'd like to convince you that you must not torture yourself by regretting the past. You must not feel that you have wasted your life, because that is never true. Every person develops and learns as he grows, so it is foolish to reproach yourself for not having had eighteen years ago the knowledge which you have now. You have done the best you could, according to your judgment of that time. You have given Philip every possible chance. You had no way of knowing in advance that Philip would never change. No man's character is set for life. Philip could have changed if he had cared to change his ideas. Since he didn't, you must not let him ruin the rest of your life through regrets over the past.

It is never too late to start on a new road, and it is certainly not too late for you. If there's one thing I have learned by personal experience and by observing the people around me, it's that a person's life actually starts from about 35 on; I mean, the best and the most active part of one's life. Up to that time one merely learns and accumulates experience. I wish I could beat out of your head the idea that a woman is interesting, attractive and happy only in the bobby-soxer's age. It is one of those vicious bromides that people believe only because everybody repeats it without any reason. I think it's a remnant of savagery, as so many popular ideas are, and it comes from the times when women were married off at the age of 12 and were old at the age of 30.

It is not true, as you say, that you have no experience or ability to earn a living. You've always had the ability, and experience is something one acquires. You cannot expect to start at the top in any profession, but if you want to learn it, with your ability it should not take you long, and you will find that the years behind you are not wasted. I have always thought that you should have a career, not just for financial security, but because you are too active a person to be happy without it. I think you should choose a career now, regardless of whether you get a proper financial settlement from Philip or not, and it is most certainly not too late. We have talked about this before, and I don't know whether you are in a mood to discuss it right now—but if you want me to, I'll be glad to try and discuss it in letters.

Now to a practical question of the moment: You say that Philip is paying you nothing at present. Do you need money until the question is settled? If you do, I will be happy to return a favor which I have never forgotten. Not happy that you are in trouble, but happy that I would have a chance to repay you. I will always think that I can never quite repay the two friends who stood by me in my worst time—you and Albert.

You ask what I think about hiring a ghostwriter to write a book for you. I would advise you against it most emphatically. I don't know of any novel that was ever written successfully by a ghostwriter. A novel is not a matter of writing down real events as they happened, no matter how exciting they were in real life. It takes something else entirely. A writer capable of doing it would not be a ghostwriter. The only successful ghostwriting jobs are nonfiction books such as biographies of celebrities. Ghostwritten fiction seldom finds publication, or is published by some obscure house and gets nowhere. Besides, ghostwriters charge quite a considerable amount for their services in advance, much more than their work will ever bring in print.

■   ■   ■

To Edna Lonigan of the American Writers Association

AR had been subpoenaed to testify before the House Un-American Activities Committee. Her testimony as a "friendly witness" about Communist influence in Hollywood was reprinted in *The Objectivist Forum* (August 1987).

March 26, 1949

Dear Miss Lonigan:

Thank you for your letter of March 16.

Yes, I certainly think that we should make an issue of the case of Jim McGuinness, provided we make it an issue of all the Friendly Witnesses who appeared at the Hollywood hearings in Washington and have had to suffer for it since. I have not been in touch with all of them, but from what I hear, some of them have taken a terrible beating.

I would suggest that we prepare a factual report on the present standing of all the Friendly Witnesses. It could be quite brief: merely list their income and their work for two years preceding the Washington hearings and for the year since. Of course, there is a depression in Hollywood at the moment, so that everyone's income has probably suffered in the past year, but that can be covered by citing a few comparative cases of people in the same income brackets, and showing the difference between the losses suffered by other, nonpolitical people in Hollywood (the losses caused purely by curtailment of Hollywood production) and the losses suffered by the Friendly Witnesses.

Incidentally, I cannot claim that I have been a victim (except for some unsuccessful intrigues against me), although I am one of the Friendly Witnesses, because I am writing my new novel now and have not been available for picture work. Therefore, my suggestion is not motivated by the desire to have someone defend me personally. I think that the fate suffered by some of the other witnesses, who were in a less favorable professional position, is outrageous—the worst part of it being that our side has not risen to their defense. If we do not defend the people who take the risk of standing openly on our side, we shall defeat our cause completely, and we shall deserve to be defeated.

The plan I would like to propose to our Board is as follows: have the survey made by one of our members in Hollywood; have the survey mimeographed, with a few brief, eloquent comments on its significance, and send it to the newspapers, to all the columnists and commentators who are on our side, to all the patriotic, anti-Communist organizations in the country—with the request that they all take action, that they voice their protest in print and that their members write letters of protest to Hollywood. Would it work? Oh, boy!

The dirty things going on in Hollywood are not caused by the sympathy of the majority of the producers with the Reds—but only by the fact that the Reds are an active pressure group, while our side is inactive, so that it becomes safe to sacrifice the conservatives. Let a real, loud, concerted protest be made just once—and Hollywood will be safe for conservatives for a long, long time. This will be much more effective than any Washington hearing.

■ ■ ■

To Vladimir and Peter Kondheim

March 26, 1949

Dear Volodia and Peter:

I am not able to lend you the money which you request, and I am sorry to have to say that this time your request has hurt me.

You have asked me for a similar loan before. I explained to you at that time that I am not in a position to dispose of large sums of money. You then asked me whether I was offended by the request, and I told you then that I wasn't, because I assumed that you did not understand my financial situation. Now, however, I do feel offended, because I did explain it to you. Now I find that you think it proper to plan your future counting on me and my income as part of your plans. I do not think it is proper.

It is not right to tell me that this loan would not be a risk. If it were not a risk, you could obtain the money from a bank or loan company. Since you cannot obtain it through commercial channels, then you know that the money is to be risked. After I have explained the tax situation to you, you should have paused to figure out what amount of money I have to earn and how long I have to work for it in order to make $6,500.

I have always been willing to help friends, if it is possible to me, when they are in an emergency. When, however, it is not a question of pressing need and involves the request for a major sacrifice on my part, then I have to say that I resent the attitude which makes such a request possible.

■　■　■

To Edna Lonigan

April 10, 1949

Dear Miss Lonigan:

I would be glad to write a pamphlet for our Association at some future date, but I cannot undertake to do it at present, because I am working on my new novel and it is such a difficult job that I find it impossible to take my mind off it for any other task of serious writing. Doing a whole pamphlet would amount to writing a book.

I spoke to Morrie Ryskind [coauthor, *Of Thee I Sing*] and asked his opinion about our taking action in defense of the Friendly Witnesses. He agreed with me and said that he approved of our taking such action. He has suffered personally from the political boycott and, therefore, hesitated to suggest action in his own defense, but he does think that we should do it.

Rupert Hughes sent me a copy of the statement on the "Cultural Conference" which you sent him, and I am forwarding it to Morrie. I must say that I do not approve of this statement.

I do not "support the right" of *Soviet delegates* "to meet in free America and discuss any issue." To pretend that a man acting at the point of a gun is exercising any "rights" is to corrupt the whole concept of rights and to lend support to the gun-holders.

I do not "understand the tragic dilemma of the Iron Curtain delegates," and I do not "pity these men." I despise them. The men I pity are the ones who preferred to go to a Soviet concentration camp rather than make careers under a totalitarian government and go crawling on their bellies all over the world, glorifying their own slavery and their masters.

I do not "heartily endorse the attitude of the State Department" and

I most emphatically denounce and despise the idea of any "cultural rapprochement between the American and Russian peoples." I do not wish to seek rapprochement with a people while it is enslaved and to make deals with a slave "culture." No kind of "rapprochement" or "culture" is possible while the Soviet government remains in existence. To make friends with slaves, while they remain slaves, is to support the regime of their masters. Instead of talking about "rapprochement," the decent and self-respecting people of all free countries should impose the most rigid cultural blockade and boycott against all totalitarian countries—and thus declare that they do not accept as "culture" any product of a reign of brute force, and that they do not deal on "cultural" terms with bloody mass-slaughterers.

I will not make a public repudiation of our statement at present, since the issue of that Conference is dead, but I would like you to place this letter on the record of our Association, so that I will have proof that I have officially denied the above sentiments. I take pride in my reputation for being totally, completely and uncompromisingly opposed to Communism and to anyone who makes terms with it.

■　■　■

To Alan Collins

April 16, 1949

Dear Alan:

I am very happy that you liked the picture [*The Fountainhead*], and I am delighted that your favorite scene was the courtroom speech.

I don't agree with you about the importance of reviews for this picture and about your saying that it is not a picture for the neighborhood theaters. I expect a great many, and perhaps most, of the reviews to be bad, because the intellectual Pinks will not like this picture—and these reviews will not make any difference whatever. As to the box office, I think that the picture will do very well both in the big cities and in the neighborhood theaters. But if there is any difference, I will stick my neck out, just for the fun of it and for the record, and predict that this picture will be more successful at the neighborhood theaters than in the big ones.

P.S. Was my friend, Archie Ogden, at the showing of the picture? If he was, please tell him that I would like to hear from him.

■　■　■

To Archibald Ogden

April 23, 1949

Archie darling:

It was wonderful to hear your voice on the telephone. You said that it made you want to write to me again, but you didn't, so far—and I'm doing it, as usual.

Thanks for your letter. You were the only man in the world, except Frank, whose opinion was very important to me, so yours was the letter I was waiting for impatiently. It was wonderful that you recognized my style of writing in the picture. That's why you're the editor for me, and the only one, and will always remain that—because you are the only person who really understands my style and method of writing. I am glad that you saw all the problems involved in the adaptation and knew my reasons for the changes which I had to make, without changing the theme and essence of the story. It was a question of finding dramatic equivalents which would tell the same story as in the book, without sticking literally to every specific detail.

As I told you on the phone, we considered the possibility of having the judge at the trial comment on the question of "criminal intent," but we were told by the lawyers we consulted that this would have been legally incorrect.

Nothing could make me happier than to hear you say that you are "more than ever eager to see the new Ayn Rand." I love that expression. It's more deeply true than just as a term in the publishing business. Ayn Rand, new or old, *is* her novels, and doesn't want to be anything else. Well, the new Ayn Rand is growing wonderfully, and I am extremely happy with her. For a long time, Frank refused to agree with me that it is bigger in scope and scale than *The Fountainhead*—and he is the first person who hears every sequence as I write it. I read it to him from my longhand before I have it typed. Well, not long ago, he was so impressed with a sequence I read that he was literally shaking and he gave in and said it was bigger than *The Fountainhead*. By the way, he is a severe critic, and getting a compliment from him is like pulling a tooth. Wait till you see the book. The chapters you have read have been rewritten and very much improved, and they are nothing anyway, compared to what follows. When I come to New York, I'll bring everything written so far. No, I won't have it finished yet, but I am approaching the end of Part I, which is the longer of the two.

At present, the manuscript is 3½ inches thick and weighs 5¼ pounds—I have just measured it this minute. Don't let it frighten you.

You ask: "If I should return to publishing in the fall, is there a possibility of your ever returning to me?" You know that only the restraint of a legal obligation—or your joining some publisher who's impossible for me, such as Simon & Schuster—would prevent me from returning to you. If this is an asset to your reputation among publishers, please use it as such. You know what my commitment is in regard to the new novel. Bobbs-Merrill have the right of first submission on it, and I intend to play fair with them, but I am not at all sure that they will have the courage to offer me as much as I am objectively entitled to, and I will not sell the book for less than that. But please don't join a house that has a lot of Pinks on its staff—because that would be asking for disaster for yourself and me, if I followed you. Also, I'd hate to go to any publisher who rejected *The Fountainhead*—but this point is open to discussion.

You know, of course, that I would love to see you return to publishing. I can't attempt to give you advice about it, particularly from the financial angle involved, but I do know that you should return to publishing sooner or later, because you are being wasted in the movies. I grant you that most publishers aren't much nowadays either, but that is precisely why you are needed in the profession. I think it is a question of your finding a position where you would really have a chance to do things your way, to publish the kind of books *you* like and to show the secondhanders in the business what a real editorial genius is. And I mean it, darling.

P.S. Where is that photograph of you? I wanted it on my wall while I'm writing the new novel—and it looks like the whole novel will be finished before I get it.

■ ■ ■

To DeWitt Emery

April 30, 1949

I was surprised, DeWitt,

very much surprised, to read an article in which William Green [president of the American Federation of Labor] stated the fundamental American principle of inalienable rights, and *you* called it "a weak technicality." (Your editorial in the March issue of *Pulling Together*.)

When businessmen were the victims of New Deal legislation, they talked about principles, and the New Dealers said that principles were mere technicalities. When labor is being choked in its turn by legislation, we get the fantastic spectacle of William Green defending rights and DeWitt Emery talking about "starving babies."

The issue is really very simple: do we or do we not accept principles as a rule of conduct in public affairs? If we do, we have to state clearly what these principles are and act upon them. If we don't, then we must admit that we are acting in the manner of criminals, on the so-called "expediency" of the moment—and take the consequences. The consequences are that this sort of expediency is not very expedient: it leads to nothing but self-destruction.

The principle involved in your editorial is: has a man the right to dispose of his own labor—or does his labor belong to the government? If man is the owner of his labor—then nobody can force him to work, nobody, nowhere, at no time, for no reason whatsoever. If the government has the right to dispose of a man's labor and compel him to work against his will—then the government owns men, their lives and their property. There's no "middle of the road" here. It's one or the other. Either a right is inalienable—or it doesn't exist.

If you do not accept a worker's right to his own work—you have no way to defend the employer's right to his business, the farmer's right to his land, my right to my own home, your right to the shirt on your back, or any man's right to exist. All these rights rest on the same principle. Drop the principle and the rights vanish along with it. If your principle is that the government may—when it deems necessary, for a "good cause," for the sake of starving babies, for instance—violate a man's rights, then there is no reason why anybody should respect any rights whatever. Then any pressure gang who happens to control the government at the moment may grab anything it pleases, for any cause it chooses to call "good." Certainly, the property of the rich, of the industrialists and the capitalists, should then be seized first—because that's the most direct and immediate way to relieve the starvation of any babies that might be around (to relieve it for five minutes, after which everybody starves). The "starving babies" will always be with us. That's always been their function in politics—to justify the looting and the enslavement of others. Do you call what is happening in Europe "a weak technicality"? It is happening as a result of the appeal, in one form or another, to feed starving babies at the expense of man's rights.

The quotation from William Green in your editorial is unanswerable —and you have not answered it. Every word he says is true. If a man is compelled to work against his will for one minute or one second, for any cause, reason or purpose whatsoever—*that* is involuntary servitude. The purpose for which he is compelled to serve, is totally irrelevant. The concept of *slavery* does not say that it is slavery only when practiced for a bad purpose, but freedom when practiced for the sake of starving babies. Slavery is slavery, and its purpose does not change its nature.

You have not answered Green in the paragraphs that follow his quotation in your editorial. You used sarcasm—unconvincing sarcasm, which is not an answer. You did not refute his argument—you evaded it. You said that since workers are "doing their regular work at their regular rate of pay," this means that they are not in the position of slaves. But the sole issue is: do they or do they not want to work? And if they do not, have they the right to stop or has the State the right to force them? And if they are forced to work at the point of a gun—would it matter if they were given a million dollars an hour as overtime? A man forced to work against his will is a slave, and no bribe or reward will change that. You might argue, if you wish, that you consider slavery proper in certain circumstances. But it's no use trying to pretend that what you're advocating is not slavery.

In the next paragraph you said that the public has the right to protect itself if and when labor union bosses are able to shut off food, fuel and everything else for everyone in the country. You did not, however, add what you stated in your letter to me: that it was Roosevelt and Truman who built union labor up to the point where it has that sort of power over the nation. It is the Wagner Act and all the rest of the New Deal legislation that brought about the possibility of babies starving at the will of labor union bosses. The solution, therefore, is to repeal that labor legislation—and not to give the government more power over the babies, the milk and the workers.

Instead of fighting for the Taft-Hartley Law, the businessmen and the defenders of free enterprise should have fought to repeal the Wagner Act. They should remove the cause of an evil rather than perpetrate another evil—of the same kind—in the hope of counteracting the first. The villain in the picture is not labor, but the Bureaucrat—government regulations which, by *forcing* men to join unions, gave labor bosses the power to stop our whole economy. And what is the Taft-Hartley Law? An attempt to give more power to that same Bureaucrat. If the Wagner Act tied the employers, the Taft-Hartley Law ties the workers. Both groups lose and the only winner, as usual, is the Bureaucrat.

I have heard it said by the preachers of "expediency" on the Capitalist side that the repeal of the Wagner Act would be the most desirable objective, but since such repeal is impossible, the next best thing is the Taft-Hartley Law. It is not true that the repeal of the Wagner Act is impossible. There are union leaders and great numbers of rank-and-file workers who hate the Wagner Act as much as the employers do, because, actually, it is not to the workers' benefit, either. If the employers had the courage to stand on a principle, they could repeal the Wagner Act. I have not seen any major attempt to repeal it. I have not seen anybody making the attempt and failing. All I've seen is attempts to pass more regulations, of one sort or another. But no evil ever has or can be corrected by another evil. The proof? Look around you. Are we moving closer and closer to national bankruptcy and Statism—or are we not?

Never mind the fact that William Green contradicts his own quotation in his other actions and in his support of the Wagner Act. His betraying of a principle does not justify our doing so. His actions or policies do not alter the truth of the things he said in his quotation. These things are true—no matter who says them. I showed your editorial to Frank and his remark was: "Well, Bill Green has the right shoe on the left foot."

Now the last three paragraphs of your editorial—where you say that the income tax law is, in fact, a slave-labor law—are excellent. You are absolutely correct in saying it, and nobody could refute you on it. But what have you done? Since the first part of your editorial makes fun of Green's premise, the result is that it also makes fun of your own statement about the income tax, thus achieving the opposite of your intention. Instead of a proper attack on the income tax, your last three paragraphs are, by implication, a defense of it. You, in effect, say that it would be preposterous to consider the income tax as a slave-labor law, since it is preposterous to consider the Taft-Hartley a slave-labor law. This is a good example, within the space of one short editorial, of what happens when you depart from principles and attempt to make any sort of an argument. You merely defeat yourself.

Now to other questions. What on earth do you mean when you say that my reference to my new book sounds ominous and that you expect to be both surprised and angry? I thought you knew what I thought about businessmen. In my new book, I glorify the real kind of productive, free-enterprise businessman in a way he has never been glorified before. I present him as the most heroic type of human being, more so, in a way, than Howard Roark. *But* I make mincemeat out of the kind of businessman who calls himself a "middle-of-the roader" and talks about a "mixed economy"—the kind that runs to government for assistance, subsidies, legislation and regulation.

I will be glad to show you the manuscript of my new novel, when I finish it, because I will be naturally very interested in your reaction. But I don't think it will be suitable as a film vehicle for Bing Crosby. It's not a homey type of story. Its characters are not average businessmen, but heroic ones. I wish you would tell me more about what you have in mind for a Bing Crosby picture on business. I might be able to write a screen original for you, after I finish my novel, if I agree with the ideas you want to present.

■ ■ ■

To DeWitt Emery

May 8, 1949

Thank you, DeWitt,

for your interesting letter. This is like old times again—here we are in a political argument.

I don't want to lecture too much, but I can't let an argument of mine "fall flat on its face." Here is where I am going to make it fall on yours.

What do you mean here?* A group, as such, has no *rights*. Rights belong only to individuals. By joining any group or organization, an individual can neither acquire extra rights, nor *lose the ones he possessed*. According to the collectivist principle, "society" has extra rights which its individual members do not have; for instance, a man may not murder his neighbors, but may do so if he becomes a member of a social "majority." The opposite of this is just as ridiculous. You cannot maintain that a worker loses his rights when he joins a labor union.

The Wagner Act gave labor unions the sort of collectivistic "rights" which no group may possess. It forced men to join unions against their will. You cannot correct this by giving the government power to regulate union activities. That would be only a further step of the same injustice. First, men are forced into unions; then, as union members, they are forced to work against their will. Is this the free-enterprise system?

The root of the evil is the government's interference into economics.

---

* Emery contended that AR's argument fails because, if individuals have rights, so do labor unions.

To correct the evil, you must remove the root—not add more of the same evil. The basic principle is that the government has no right to regulate the relations between employers and employees. These have to be conducted on a strictly voluntary basis. Nobody should be compelled to join a union, nor to bargain with a union, nor to remain at work if his union calls a strike.

What I object to is the government's "right to curb a union"—or to curb anyone's economic activities.* I object to the collectivist principle of the government's right to bring *force* and *compulsion* into economics. "Labor unions can do no wrong" has nothing whatever to do with this issue. No group or person can "do wrong" in a free economy—because none can use force against others. Others are free to deal with such group or not, as they please; then objective economic conditions decide every issue. Without political regulations, no group has the power to stop or threaten the economy of the whole country.

I most emphatically object to an idea such as the government's right to act in protection "of public health and safety" with no further definition of those terms. What constitutes "public safety"? According to the American Constitution, the duties of the government in respect to public safety are clearly defined and specified. These duties are police protection and military protection—defense against violence from criminals inside the country and against violence from foreign aggressors. But if we begin to believe that the government may take any action it pleases whenever it decides that "the public safety" is threatened, if economic matters begin to be treated as "threats to public safety"—then I will remind you that this is the sole slogan through which all the horrors of history have ever been perpetrated. The guillotine during the French Revolution was being used by a "Committee of Public Safety." The liquidation of political suspects in Russia is done on the ground that their ideas may be a threat to "Public Safety."

Since it is government regulations which have brought about a condition where a strike can endanger a whole country, then it is these regulations which have to be removed. But what you are advocating is that the government, after having created a threat to public safety, be given more power in the name of that same public safety.

---

* Emery stated that the Taft-Hartley Act merely prevents unions from pursuing their selfish aims when those aims conflict with public health and safety. If AR opposes this goal of Taft-Hartley, he wrote, then she must believe that unions can do no wrong.

Where did you get the idea that the principle of "checks and balances" is a sort of universal principle which applies to everything and everybody?* It is a principle which applies *only* to the structure of the government, and its purpose is to limit the government's power. It most certainly does not apply to individual rights. Individual *rights* are an absolute, not to be "balanced" or limited by anybody. (And don't answer me that an individual's right to murder, for instance, is limited. Such a right never existed in the first place.) It certainly is not the government nor society that "*sets up* rights for an individual or group." These rights are not "set up" (nor "rigged up" nor "framed up"). They are inherent in the nature of man. Man is endowed with them by the fact of his birth. He does not receive them from society. The sole purpose and justification of government is to *protect* these rights. Government (according to the American principle) is the watchman of these rights—not the owner and giver.

Now a question: Why did you omit, from your answer to me, all reference to the Wagner Act? Can one properly discuss the evils which the Taft-Hartley Act purports to correct, without considering the cause of the evils?

I'd love to hear from you on this, but if the discussion is becoming too lengthy for letters, I'll be glad to continue it in person this summer.

■ ■ ■

To Ruth Alexander

May 21, 1949

Dear Ruth:

If you are serious about wanting to write, I think you could be successful with it. If you want my advice, I would say that the secret of writing fiction is the ability of extreme mental concentration. If you want to put the effort into it, you can do it.

We enjoyed seeing you here and are looking forward to seeing you in the East this summer. The picture of *The Fountainhead* will open in New York on July 2. The studio is considering having a big premiere here in Hollywood on the same date. If they do, I will stay here for the premiere and will come to New York shortly afterward, which will be sometime in July.

■ ■ ■

* Emery wrote that government must maintain a system of checks and balances, to prevent the rights it establishes from being abused.

To Leonebel Jacobs

May 22, 1949

Dear Leonebel,

I have learned, from an authentic source, that the movie department of *Life* magazine is against the picture of *The Fountainhead*.

Since you told me that Henry Luce is an admirer of my novel and that he truly understands it, I would like you to ask him to see the picture for himself before its release. Then, if he does not like the picture, it is certainly his right to let his magazine attack it in any way he pleases. But if he does like it, then I would like to see him do justice to it.

The picture is more faithful to the novel than any other adaptation of a novel that Hollywood has ever produced. Therefore, I think it would be somewhat tragic, if Mr. Luce's own magazines attack it—*if* the novel did mean a great deal to him. In view of the fact that the picture is totally unprecedented and different from all other movies, every man has to judge it for himself.

I would like you to make very clear to Mr. Luce that this is not a hint for favorable reviews or an attempt to have you influence his judgment. It is only a request that he give the picture a hearing and judge for himself. I'll rest on the evidence. If he does not like the picture—fair enough.

I expect a violent public controversy about the picture, and I am prepared to take care of its enemies. But this is the time when I would like the friends of *The Fountainhead* to stand by it.

If you know Mr. Luce well enough to speak to him about this, I would appreciate it very earnestly indeed. But if you feel for any reason that it would not be right for you to do it, then please don't. You may tell him that the request comes from me and show him this letter, if you wish.

■　■　■

To Connie Papurt, AR's niece, a daughter of Frank's sister, Agnes Papurt

May 22, 1949

Dear Connie:

You are very young, so I don't know whether you realize the seriousness of your action in writing to me for money. Since I don't know you at all, I am going to put you to a test.

If you really want to *borrow* $25 from me, I will take a chance on finding out what kind of person you are. You want to borrow the money until your graduation. I will do better than that. I will make it easier for you to repay the debt, but on condition that you understand and accept it as a strict and serious business deal. Before you borrow it, I want you to think it over very carefully.

Here are my conditions: If I send you the $25, I will give you a year to repay it. I will give you six months after your graduation to get settled in a job. Then, you will start repaying the money in installments: you will send me $5 on January 15, 1950, and $4 on the 15th of every month after that; the last installment will be on June 15, 1950—and that will repay the total.

Are you willing to do it?

Here is what I want you to think over: Once you get a job, there will always be many things which you will need and on which you might prefer to spend your money, rather than repay a debt. I want you to decide now, in advance, as an honest and responsible person, whether you will be willing and able to repay this money, no matter what happens, as an obligation above and ahead of any other expense.

I want you to understand right now that I will not accept any excuse —except a serious illness. If you become ill, then I will give you an extension of time—*but for no other reason*. If, when the debt becomes due, you tell me that you can't pay me because you needed a new pair of shoes or a new coat or you gave the money to somebody in the family who needed it more than I do—then I will consider you as an embezzler. No, I won't send a policeman after you, but I will write you off as a rotten person and I will never speak or write to you again.

Now I will tell you why I am so serious and severe about this. I despise irresponsible people. I don't want to deal with them or help them in any way. An irresponsible person is a person who makes vague promises, then breaks his word, blames it on circumstances and expects other people to forgive it. A responsible person does not make a promise without thinking of all the consequences and being prepared to meet them.

You want $25 for the purpose of buying a dress; you tell me that you will get a job and be able to repay me. That's fine and I am willing to help you, if that is *exactly* what you mean. But if what you mean is: give me the money now and I will repay it if I don't change my mind about it— then the deal is off. If I keep my part of the deal, you must keep yours, just exactly as agreed, *no matter what happens*.

I was very badly disappointed in Mimi and Marna [Docky]. When I first met Mimi, she asked me to give her money for the purpose of taking an art course. I gave her the money, but she did not take the art course. I supported Marna for a year—for the purpose of helping her to finish high school. She did not finish high school. I will take a chance on you, because I don't want to blame you for the actions of your sisters. But I want you to show me that you are a better kind of person.

I will tell you the reasons for the conditions I make: I think that the person who asks and expects other people to give him money, instead of earning it, is the most rotten person on earth. I would like to teach you, if I can, very early in life, the idea of a self-respecting, self-supporting, responsible, *capitalistic* person. If you borrow money *and repay it*, it is the best training in responsibility that you can ever have.

I want you to drop—if you have it in your mind—the idea that you are *entitled* to take money or support from me, just because we happen to be relatives. I want you to understand very clearly, right now, when you are young, that no honest person believes that he is obliged to support his relatives. I don't believe it and will not do it. I cannot like you or want to help you without reason, just because you need the help. That is not a good reason. But you can earn my liking, my interest and my help by showing me that you are a good person.

Now think this over and let me know whether you want to borrow the money on my conditions and whether you give me your word of honor to observe the conditions. If you do, I will send you the money. If you don't understand me, if you think that I am a hard, cruel, rich old woman and you don't approve of my ideas—well, you don't have to approve, but then you must not ask me for help.

I will wait to hear from you, and if I find out that you are my kind of person, then I hope that this will be the beginning of a real friendship between us, which would please me very much.

Your aunt,

■　■　■

To Connie Papurt

June 4, 1949

Dear Connie:

I must tell you that I was very impressed with the intelligent attitude of your letter. If you really understood, all by yourself, that my long lecture to you was a sign of real interest on my part, much more so than if I had sent you a check with some hypocritical gush note, and if you understood that my letter was intended to treat you as an equal—then you have the kind of mind that can achieve anything you choose to achieve in life. Just stick to that kind of thinking and you will be surprised how far it will take you. Don't let anybody discourage you or tell you that intelligence doesn't pay or that success in life has to be achieved through dishonesty or through sheer blind luck. That is not true. Real success is never accidental and real happiness cannot be found except by the honest use of your intelligence.

When you have the time, let me know something about yourself and your future plans. This is not an obligation; you don't have to do it, but if you feel like it, I would like to know more about you. Mimi told me that at one time you wanted to be a writer. Is that still your interest? If so, we have a great interest in common.

I don't know whether you remember me at all, but I remember you as a perfectly adorable kid who sat on my lap and criticized my shoes and haircut. Let me see what you have turned out to be.

Frank and I will come to New York in July for the opening of the movie of *The Fountainhead*. We don't know our exact plans as yet, but we may be able to drive East instead of coming by train. If we do, we will stop in Cleveland and then will have a chance to meet.

Your aunt,

■ ■ ■

To Leonebel Jacobs

On June 1, Henry R. Luce (editor in chief of Time Inc.) wrote to Jacobs that he was "greatly impressed" by *The Fountainhead*, wanted to see the movie version, and would contact the appropriate *Life* editor.

June 4, 1949

Dear Leonebel:

Thank you for your letter and for the letter from Mr. Luce which you sent me. I appreciate this most profoundly. What Mr. Luce decides to do about it is up to his own conscience—but you have done a heroic effort for *The Fountainhead*, so I know that you are one friend of the book who stood by it, and I am deeply grateful.

No, we wouldn't think of descending upon you and "camping" in your studio. We thought of making the exchange only in case you were coming to California. But since you're not, we won't encumber you with a couple of refugees from Hollywood.

■   ■   ■

To DeWitt Emery

June 10, 1949

Thank you, DeWitt,

for your letter of May 25. I waited to answer you until I got your new editorial in the May issue of *Pulling Together,* which I received yesterday.

Your letter made it clear to me that we were not really talking about the same thing in our argument. Our crucial disagreement, I think, is in our understanding of the word "rights." It is the most fundamental principle of the American philosophy of life that human rights are *inalienable.* These rights are inherent in man's nature and are not a gift from the Government. The idea of "rights" being granted to men by their Government is strictly European. A "right" granted by the Government is not a right, but a permission. This is exactly why no European country ever had any real freedom.

When you say that Government "sets up rights and privileges," you are using the word "rights" in its colloquial, but not in its exact sense. It is true that colloquially people do speak of the Government granting somebody the right to do something, but this is a most dangerous misuse of the word—and I think it is very important that the fighters for free enterprise correct the public in this misuse. Now the word "privilege," which you use in the above sentence, is absolutely correct in this context. What the Government grants to groups of people, in such legislation as the Wagner Act or the Taft-Hartley Act is *special privileges*—and that, you will agree, is an un-American form of legislation. In the American philosophy, all men are equal before the law, and no man or group may be granted special privileges by law. This is really the heart of the whole issue and of our disagreement.

I still do not understand how you came to accept the idea that "a Government of checks and balances" means checks and balances placed on the citizens, instead of on the Government. You have taken it to mean that the rights of citizens or private groups must be balanced against one another and curbed or destroyed when necessary. What I can't understand is how you have ignored the fact that the method of "checks and balances" in the American Constitution applies *strictly, exclusively* to the *power* of the Government—and to nothing else. Surely you know that this method was established for the sole purpose of limiting the Government's power and making it impossible for the Government to become a dictatorship. This method applied *solely* to balancing the power of one branch of the Government against another; it was never intended to mean that the Government may distribute special privileges to private groups and balance group against group. If you want to apply that principle to the rights or activities of citizens—particularly to economic activity—you must realize that such a method can have only one result: the *limiting* of the productive activity of the man or group involved. Which, of course, is what these regulations do accomplish in practice. But do you approve of it and do you really care to advocate the growth of such a policy?

I must say, however, that I admire your conscientiousness. I think it was an act of intellectual honesty on your part that you decided to write another editorial if you felt that some point of the issue needed clarification. Very few people in public life are as conscientious nowadays, so I do appreciate your attitude.

■ ■ ■

To Lyon Van & Storage Company

June 23, 1949

Gentlemen:

Please give 31 cans of the film which is stored in my name (Lot #HF 493) to Mr. Walter Wanger for temporary withdrawal for a period of about five days. Please give him the complete film *with the exception* of the can marked *"FILM CUTS."*

■ ■ ■

To Ginger Rogers, actress, whose mother, Lela, was a conservative activist

June 25, 1949

Dear Miss Rogers:

Thank you for your nice wire. I am sorry that you could not come to the opening of *The Fountainhead* as I had wanted to meet you for a long time.

I am leaving for New York tomorrow for the eastern opening of the picture, but when I come back I will start nagging your mother to arrange a chance for us to meet.

■ ■ ■

To Julius Birge of Bobbs-Merrill

August 27, 1949

Dear Mr. Birge:

Thank you very much for the copy of [David] Muzzey's *A History of Our Country* which you sent me. I believe it is just the kind of book we needed.

■ ■ ■

To Ruth Alexander

August 27, 1949

Dear Ruth:

I am sorry that I did not have a chance to see you again, but I want to thank you once more for your reaction to *The Fountainhead* and for the wonderful column you wrote about it. It might please you to know that my friends, Janet Gaynor and Adrian, were so delighted with your column about the picture that they ordered several copies of it and are showing it to all their friends. You are the first and only one of the conservatives I know who has come out publicly in support of the picture, and I shall never be able to tell you how profoundly I appreciate it.

■ ■ ■

To Cecil B. DeMille

After screening *The Fountainhead* movie, DeMille wrote to AR: "Need I tell you that I liked the philosophy of [*The Fountainhead*]. Gary Cooper's final speech at the trial was a summing up of what we are fighting for in the world today."

August 27, 1949

Dear Mr. DeMille:

I have just returned from New York and found your letter waiting here for me. I was happy to learn that you had seen *The Fountainhead*. Thank you with all my heart for your letter. Your opinion will always mean a great deal to me, as it did in the days when I first met you.

   The Fountainhead is doing extremely well at the box office, particularly at the neighborhood houses, according to such information as I was able to obtain so far. Every report I have had tells me that the audiences everywhere break into applause at the end of Roark's speech. This makes me very happy, not only personally, but because it is an indication that the political sympathy of the country at large is with us.

■ ■ ■

To Faith Hersey, a longtime friend

September 3, 1949

Dear Faith:

Yes, I did want to see you without Isabel Paterson. I still feel guilty about that incident, and I had hoped that I would make up for it this time. It may please you to know that Isabel Paterson and I are not friends any longer. I did not see her at all on this trip. I am very slow and reluctant to condemn people, so it took me all these years to realize that she had a bad streak of malice. If you remember, at the time of that incident with you, she came in and started telling me such tragic things about herself that I felt I had to console her, and I neglected you as a result. I thought that it was an emergency. I have learned since, from her subsequent behavior, that it was a deliberate action on her part, an attempt to force me away from all my friends. Well, it didn't work, but I hope that you will forgive me for that incident.

■ ■ ■

To Leonebel Jacobs

September 3, 1949

Dear Leonebel:

Thank you for the lovely letter you sent us just as we were leaving New York. I think that your good wishes worked, because we had a wonderful trip back, with no flat tires and no trouble of any kind. It was better than I had hoped and gave me more than I expected to find for my new novel.

Now that we are safely back home, I want to thank you once more for your wonderful attitude toward us and for the party which you gave for us. You are one of the very few people whom I consider a real friend of *The Fountainhead*. I cannot consider those who are not friends of my book as real friends of mine no matter what feelings they may profess to have toward me. Which means that I know very few people whom I like, and you are one of them.

I am sorry that Mr. Luce let us down, but I will always be grateful to you for your attempt in regard to him. Strange things went on in the Luce offices after you left. A reporter from *Time* magazine came to interview me and was very favorable to *The Fountainhead*—then I was notified that the interview would not be published. *Life* magazine called my publishers for a photograph of me for their "*Life* Congratulates Department"—then informed them that the photograph would not be used. You can guess what was going on behind the scenes. There appears to be a civil war going on between two factions in that office. It looks like the fight between good and evil and, so far, it is the evil side which Mr. Luce has allowed to win. Well, as I firmly believe, the victim of it will be himself, not you or I.

I was very intrigued by the sentence in your letter about Frank's portrait being a combination of three persons. Would you tell me more exactly what you meant? I have always regarded it as a portrait of two persons, but who is the third?

■　■　■

To Archibald Ogden

September 10, 1949

Archie darling,

Thank you for your letter. I didn't quite believe that I would really get it, at least not so soon, but you did give me a pleasant surprise for once. I can never read or answer a letter of yours without emotion, because it means such a great deal to me—and this, I realize, is my great handicap in regard to you. You don't want me to take you quite so seriously. All right, don't protest—this is my turn to bait you a little.

Thank you for what you said about my "new baby." I was delighted to hear that you find your mind returning to it in the midst of the other things you are reading. I hope that your mind will continue to do so, I hope that you will be really impatient to see the rest of it—and I will do my damndest not to let you down.

Now, if you want to continue that fight about the author-publisher relationship, okay, I'll continue. Our whole disagreement, I think, lies in the concept of "trust." You seem to believe that it is moral to trust someone, and you feel that a lack of trust is improper, immoral, and somehow insulting. I, as a rationalist, consider any form of blind faith or trust immoral.

I would not want anyone to trust me blindly, in the sense of accepting my good intentions as a guarantee of a good performance from me in the future. Intentions are not a guarantee of anything, because human judgment is not automatic and infallible. The complete honesty of my intention and desire to write a good book is not an automatic guarantee that the book will be good. The quality of the book will depend on the kind of judgment I exercise in writing it. And any act of human judgment is a new, fresh act each time. A man's past performance is only an indication of the likelihood that his future performance will have the same quality; an indication, but not a guarantee.

The same applies to a publisher. A publisher's honest intention to do his best with a book for the purpose of mutual profit to himself and the author is no guarantee of what he will do. It may be his best according to his judgment—but the great question mark is: what will be his judgment? Publishing, just like writing, is not an automatic performance. Every book is a new, special problem of its own kind. What may be right for one book may be disastrously wrong for another. (And this is most crucially true of books such as mine, which go contrary to all the established rules and precedents.) Therefore, an author has the right to know in advance what judgment the publisher has passed upon his book, and into what specific action the publisher intends to translate his judgment in practice. An experienced publisher is able to tell, after he has read a manuscript, what he considers the best plan to put it on the market. An author has the right to know this plan, before he decides whether he wants to sell his book to this particular publisher or not.

Publishers do not treat all the books on their list equally, even though "mutual profit" is their aim in regard to every book. They decide, for instance, that an advertising appropriation of $1,000 is all they can afford to risk in the case of one book, but they risk $10,000 in the case of another. You know how frequently and how disastrously publishers have been wrong in a guess of this kind. Yet an author's lifework and livelihood depend upon this guess and upon a series of such guesses. Why, then, do you expect him to rest blindly on the fallible judgment of another man? Do you believe that the economic fate of a book is not a vital concern to the author? And if it is a vital concern, do you believe that he has no right to form his own judgment about it and to act accordingly?

I believe that every man is responsible for every aspect of his life, most particularly for his livelihood. Therefore, it is his *moral duty* to act upon his own judgment. If he does not use judgment but trusts others blindly to do their best for him, he is a secondhander. When an author decides to sell his book to a publisher, he must have his own idea about what terms he wishes to sell it on, what terms he considers wise, fair and practical. The publisher is free to reject his terms and the author is free to decide whether he is then willing to accept the terms which the publisher offers him, on the basis of how nearly these terms match his own. Such is the pattern of any business transaction. But to expect a finished product on one side of the deal and nothing but good intentions on the other—is the relationship of a paternalistic "benevolent" dictator to an incompetent ward.

You say that your idea of the proper contract between a publisher and his authors is a contract "implying that I trust them to do their job and they trust me to do mine." To apply this principle to both parties involved, you would have to undertake to publish an author's book sight unseen. If you do not think that the author has the right to know in advance how the publisher intends to do *his* job, then the publisher has no right to know in advance the kind of job the author has done; then the publisher must agree to spend large sums of money and take great risks, in the case of a successful author, without ever reading the author's new book. He must then take the content and quality of the book *on trust*. Would you do that? No? Then, in all justice, you should not expect blind trust from an author, either. Either both parties act blindly, with their mutual past performances as the basis of their trust—or both parties submit a specific job to the judgment of the other and know what they will get before they make the deal. But you cannot expect a full-grown, groomed, pedigreed Persian in exchange for a cat in the bag.

Personally, I would not want a publisher to accept a book of mine without reading it, even if he were willing to do so. This, really, is the basic quarrel between us: I would consider blind trust insulting; I do not want trust, I want rational judgment. You, in this case, consider rational judgment insulting. Do you know that the essence of our argument is actually the issue of reason versus faith? I really don't think that we will reach an agreement unless we discuss that whole deeper issue. Do you care to? I am willing.

Be that as it may, I was delighted to hear that seeing me influences you toward the desire to return to publishing. I know that it is a difficult decision for you to make at present, but I will hold the wish for my influence to win. I can't resist adding a lighter touch to your problem: You say that it is difficult for you to decide because you're broke. Well, since you're broke on the high salary of the movies, you might as well be broke on the low salary of a publishing house; at least, you would be broke and happy.

■ ■ ■

To Pincus Berner

September 10, 1949

Dear Pinkie:

Our trip back was wonderful, but I'll save all the descriptions of it for my novel. I must say, however, that if you ever want to see the most beautiful part of the country, go to Colorado. Frank and I fell in love with it. The next time you boast about the beautiful bay you discovered in Massachusetts, we will tell you about the valley we discovered in Colorado.

■ ■ ■

To DeWitt Emery

September 17, 1949

Dear DeWitt:

I am glad that you liked the movie of *The Fountainhead*. I can see your point in feeling that Gary Cooper's performance should have been stronger. Personally, I feel satisfied with his performance because, even though the real Roark of the book should have been stronger, there is no actor in Hollywood who could have come closer to being the right type for it than Gary Cooper. I would rather see the part underplayed than overdone by some phony-looking ham.

■ ■ ■

To William B. Duce, a tax attorney with the law firm of Rainey and Blum

October 1, 1949

Dear Mr. Duce:

In answer to your letter of September 13, here is the detailed account of my trip to New York in the year 1947.

The main purpose of my trip was certain research which I needed for my new novel. There were also a number of literary business matters which I had to handle in New York. Since I was subpoenaed to Washington [by the House Un-American Activities Committee], I attended to all these matters in New York at the same time rather than take the time and expense of another trip East, as I would have had to do by spring of 1948.

My new novel, which I hope to complete next year, deals with heavy industry, mainly with railroads and steel. The research I needed in New York was firsthand information and background material on eastern railroads. The appointments I had in this connection were as follows:

Inspection tour of Grand Central Terminal, particularly the underground track systems, under the guidance of F. W. Bingman of N.Y. Central;

Trip to Little Falls, N.Y., for the opening of the Little Falls Project (construction of new rail curve) with the executives of the N.Y. Central Railroad—and interview with A. H. Wright, then vice president in charge of operations;

Interviews with C. R. Dugan, manager, public relations, N.Y. Central, Raymond F. Blosser, manager, press bureau, Henry Doherty of press bureau;

Showing of special educational films produced by N.Y. Central on the subjects of: railroad engines, track, signals, freight yards;

Interview with K. A. Borntrager, Manager, Freight Transportation, N.Y. Central.

On my way from New York to Chicago, I obtained permission to ride in the cab of the train's engine—an electric engine from New York to Harmon, then a diesel engine from Harmon to Albany. This gave me a view of the engine ride at night—then the following morning I rode in the engine by daylight, from Elkhart, Indiana, to Chicago. The N.Y. Central sent a road foreman of engines to accompany me in the cab, to answer my questions and to take me through the motor units of the diesel while in motion.

I stopped in Chicago for an inspection tour through the mills of Inland

Steel at Indiana Harbor, where I had a luncheon interview with Mr. Fred Gillies, then general manager, and with the head operating executives of the mills.

The other literary matters to which I attended in New York were:

Conferences with Archibald G. Ogden about the first draft of the first six chapters of my new novel which I brought for him to read. Mr. Ogden was my editor on *The Fountainhead*, when he was editor at Bobbs-Merrill.

Conferences with my publishers, Bobbs-Merrill, about the sales of *The Fountainhead* and about my new novel.

Conferences with Alan C. Collins, of Curtis Brown, Ltd., my literary agent, about the above matters and all my current literary business.

Conferences with Ann Watkins, my former literary agent, who handles the rights to my earlier works.

Interviews with Sam Rapport of Appleton-Century, and Denver Lindley of Holt's—both in connection with their interest in my next novel, in case I should decide to change to another publisher.

Two interviews with John Chamberlain of *Life* magazine: (1) for an article on *The Fountainhead* which he was then writing, but has not yet published; (2) about an article on "Purpose and the Novel" which he commissioned me to write for a new Luce magazine then being planned.

Interview with Burt MacBride of *Reader's Digest*, in regard to an article which he wanted me to write for the *Digest*.

Interview with Kathleen Bourne of *Cosmopolitan* magazine in regard to the serial rights of my new novel and to a special story which she wanted me to write for them.

Interviews with Isaac Don Levine of *Plain Talk* magazine in regard to articles and the possibility of my writing a column for them.

Interviews with executives of Superfilm Distributing Corporation (representing Italian film producers) in regard to the Italian movie of my novel *We the Living* which was pirated by Scalera Films during the war—and a showing of the movie in their offices.

Interviews with John C. Gall, my attorney, in regard to the above matter.

Meeting of the American Writers Association Board of Directors, of which I am a member.

These were the main business matters covered in New York. There were other, lesser ones, since my chief professional interests are in the literary-publication field rather than in the movie field, and there are a great number of New York contacts which I have to keep up.

My husband accompanied me on the trip, because he acts as my editorial and research adviser on all my literary works. Since I was not born in this country, I need his assistance in all matters of authenticity of background and style of expression pertaining to the American scene.

■ ■ ■

To Ross Baker

October 29, 1949

Dear Ross:

Thank you for your letter of October 19 and for the copies of the mailing piece on *The Fountainhead*. I was delighted to see it.

I have just received today a letter from the Indianapolis office with this same ad for *The Fountainhead* printed on the envelope. I must tell you that it gave me a thrill. I love original stunts in advertising, and I was glad to see that Bobbs-Merrill went for such an unorthodox idea.

■ ■ ■

To James P. Birch, manager of the Corn Exchange Bank Trust Co. in Manhattan

October 29, 1949

Dear Mr. Birch:

I am considering the purchase of a piece of property in Westchester County, and I wondered whether the Corn Exchange Bank has a service which could help me in this matter.

I would need the advice of some person experienced in real estate values who could appraise the particular property I have in mind, who could tell me if it is a good investment and negotiate the purchase with the owner, including the matter of bargaining for the proper price. If you have such a service, what would be your charge for it?

I am unable to come east in the immediate future so that if I decide to buy this property, it would have to be done on some expert advice. My interest is primarily from the angle of an investment—not with the aim of making a large profit on it, but with the aim of preserving the exchange value of the money I would pay for it. In other words, I would like to find property which I could sell in the future for an approximate equivalent, in purchasing power, of the money I would pay for it now. What I have in mind is to protect myself against a possible devaluation of the dollar. Could you tell me your opinion as to whether such a devaluation is likely to come in the next few years? I have read reports in the newspapers which seem to indicate that possibility.

■   ■   ■

To William Mullendore

November 25, 1949

Dear Bill Mullendore;

Thank you very much for your letter and for the nice things you said about my speech on Money (from *Atlas Shrugged*). I was very happy to know that you liked it.

I appreciate the two suggestions you gave me. I cannot include them in this particular speech because, as you probably realize, it is not a speech about improper monetary policies nor even about the free-enterprise system, but only about the essential, *moral* concept of money and the principle of trade which it represents. The purpose of this particular speech is to answer people's personal attitude towards money, which is usually based on that very vicious quotation from the Bible. Much later in my novel I will have a very long speech by the hero in which I will summarize the entire philosophy of the story and cover all the important details of the free-enterprise system. That is where I may be able to use your suggestions, if you permit me to. I like particularly the idea of describing the various monetary devices practiced by government as "counterfeiting." That is eloquent and correct.

■   ■   ■

To Suren Pilafian, an architect

November 25, 1949

Dear Mr. Pilafian:

It is with deep regret that I must tell you, in answer to your nice invitation, that I will be unable to come to Detroit this winter to address the Detroit Chapter of the American Institute of Architects. I am now working on a new novel, which I must complete by the Fall of 1950 and this makes it impossible for me to undertake any other assignment until that time.

I would like you to know that I appreciate most profoundly your invitation and your saying that I had contributed substantially to the welfare of the architectural profession. If I have, I feel very happy and proud of it—since you probably know, from my novel, the deep respect and admiration which I feel for architects.

■ ■ ■

To Montserrat Casanovas, a fan

December 2, 1949

Dear Miss Casanovas:

I understand from your letter that you are an admirer of my novels—and, therefore, I am completely bewildered by your asking me whether the character of Toohey in *The Fountainhead* is a portrait of myself. I cannot imagine what gave you such an idea. Would you please write to me and tell me what made you ask it and what you meant. I am truly curious.

The character who represents my own philosophy in *The Fountainhead* is Howard Roark. Toohey represents my definition of complete and total evil.

■ ■ ■

To Nathan Blumenthal, who later changed his name to Nathaniel Branden and was AR's associate until 1968

December 2, 1949

Dear Mr. Blumenthal:

Thank you for your letter of October 31. I am enclosing a copy of the printed letter which you requested.

Apart from the works which you mention, I have written only a few political articles and some screenplays. I cannot tell you the publication date of my next novel, because I am working on it right now and cannot tell exactly when I will have it finished.

P.S. Are you the gentleman who wrote me from Canada sometime ago asking what political system I believed in? If you are, I hope you have learned by now that I believe in complete, uncontrolled, unregulated, laissez-faire, private-property, profit-motive, free-enterprise Capitalism.

■ ■ ■

To Henry Blanke

January 6, 1950

Dear Henry:

Thank you very much for the CARE package which you sent to Europe as a Christmas gift in my name. It was a nice thing to do and I appreciate it deeply.

I have just received a letter of thanks for the package from a French mother who enclosed snapshots of her four children and told me how much they enjoyed the gift. It was very touching, as she did not complain, but it was obvious that they needed the food very badly.

■ ■ ■

To Nathan Blumenthal

January 13, 1950

Dear Mr. Blumenthal:

You asked me a great many philosophical questions and offered as a reason for me to answer you the fact that you have a high regard for my "intelligence and personal integrity." That would be part of a valid reason. The other part is the question of whether your interest in philosophical ideas is serious and sincere. It is hard for me to judge from your letter, but I will take the chance and answer you.

(1) You ask what right had Kira in *We the Living* to object to Leo being permitted to die, since [prior to the Communist revolution, members of the lower classes died because of the "indifference" of the upper classes]. Do you understand the difference between some starving man whom you did not help—and—a man whom *you* tied hand and foot and left to starve? The issue in *We the Living* is not the *indifference* of any classes, upper or lower. The issue is this: Before the revolution, people were not forbidden to earn their living and doctors were not forbidden to practice. After the revolution, the State forbade all human beings to take care of themselves. It forbade men to control the means of their own livelihood. It prevented Leo from being able to feed himself.

Nobody *owes* anybody any help, material or otherwise. Nobody is responsible for another human being, but nobody has the right to chain him. That is the issue between Capitalism and Socialism. As far as Russia is concerned, the Czarist regime was a rotten form of absolutism which was falling apart and Russia was moving slowly in the direction of Capitalism and freedom. The Communists threw it back in the form of slavery and savagery infinitely more vicious than any known in recorded history.

(2) You quote Kira's statement that "she can imagine no worse injustice than justice for all," and ask whether this is a belief to which I subscribe. It is a bad sentence when taken out of its context.

(3) [Blumenthal asks about the practicality vs. the morality of capitalism.] Capitalism is the *only* such system *possible* or *conceivable*—and I will challenge anyone to indicate even a shadow of a doubt to the contrary, provided the question is discussed by rational beings, meaning: by people who consider no argument valid except a rationally demonstrable argument. What other sort of system [besides a practical one] is worth discussing? If you have read my printed letter, a copy of which you requested, you know what I think of people who make a distinction between the theoretical and the practical. Of what use is a theory which cannot be applied to practice? And how can we deal with practice if we have no theoretical principles to guide our actions? By what standard do you estimate something as desirable or good, if that thing is not within the realm of the humanly possible?

(4) This little question of yours would take a heavy philosophical volume to answer, so I can only indicate a brief answer. You ask, how do I reconcile my atheism with my belief in free will. Most philosophers, in effect, have offered us the choice between a universe consisting of God, or a universe consisting of blind matter. Where is man in the picture? They have figured out everything, except that they forgot the existence of man. Man is a being endowed with consciousness—an attribute which matter does not possess. His *consciousness* is the free, nonmaterial element in him. But this attribute is in no way proof of the existence of a super-being, God, who is pure consciousness without matter. You say that each philosophy excludes the other? Well, observe that both kinds of philosophy—the religious or the mechanistic—find it necessary to deny the validity or the existence of logic, somewhere in their argument, in order to get away with the fancy structures which they then proceed to build.

(5) You ask what I think of a man such as Romain Rolland [described by Blumenthal as an advocate of both individualism and socialism]. Why confine the question to Romain Rolland? Any man who does that is a fool, whether his name is Romain Rolland or Joe Doakes. The definition of a fool is: a man who fails to make rational connections. What do *you* think of a person who wants to have his cake and eat it, too?

A good novelist or dramatist is not necessarily a good thinker. Just take a look at the political ideas of Tolstoy, or Dostoyevsky, or Mark Twain, or Bernard Shaw.

Romain Rolland was certainly not an individualist in his thinking—if by thinking, we mean the content of his ideas and *not* his alleged or professed intentions. Rolland certainly did a lot of emotionalizing about the individual—but what, actually, were his ideas? In *Jean Christophe* he has his hero coming to some sort of altruism or "duty to mankind" or "service to society" attitude. Well, the Communists proclaim that their *intention* is to make men free and prosperous; but if you see that the actual application of their ideas leads to (and *can only lead to*) concentration camps and mass starvation, would you still accept them as champions of freedom and prosperity, just because they say so?

When you say that Rolland observed "the breakdown of the capitalistic system"—you really show complete ignorance of the Capitalistic system. What breakdown? No European country ever had a real Capitalistic system. What they had, during the XIX century and up to World War I, was a precarious kind of mixture: their old bureaucratic systems of controlled economy plus Capitalistic elements of free production and free trade, borrowed from America. So long as and to the extent to which this last predominated, the European countries were achieving progress, prosperity and decency. But the collectivist-statist trend was rising and accelerating, particularly since the middle of the XIX century. The "breakdown" which Rolland saw was *not* the breakdown of Capitalism. It was the breakdown of Europe *abandoning* Capitalism—to return to statism, to a controlled economy. Just exactly as the present breakdown of America is not the failure of Capitalism, but the result of men abandoning the principles of Capitalism and introducing socialistic controls. If you see a man taking larger and larger doses of poison and then collapsing—will you blame it on the failure of his natural physical constitution?

When you say that Rolland was a fighter against "imperialistic capitalism"—you show the same kind of ignorance. "Imperialistic capitalism" is a contradiction in terms. There's no such thing and never was. It's a foolish tag taken from Marx. You really should have discovered, by now, that *every* economic tenet propounded by Marx was a fallacy—and has been exposed as such many, many times. *Capitalism* is the one system that leads to *peace*, not to war.

But now let *me* ask *you* a question: Do you really know what Capitalism is? It is my impression that you don't and that you have read nothing on the subject except of Marxist or Leftist origin. And this is the reason why I did not answer the letter you wrote to me from Canada. That letter showed such an appalling ignorance of Capitalism that I questioned your sincerity. I thought that a man who was sincerely interested in economic and political questions would have studied something besides Marxism before he attempted to argue on the subject. I am still puzzled by it, but I am taking a chance on answering you this time.

There are many questions I could answer about Capitalism, because the complete case for Capitalism has never been stated. But I cannot attempt to teach it to you from scratch. I think you should acquire the rudimentary knowledge of it by yourself. As a start, I would suggest that you read two books which are the best ones written so far on the subject of Capitalism: *The God of the Machine* by Isabel Paterson, published by Putnam's in 1943 (this might be out of print, so you would have to get it from some large library), and *Economics in One Lesson* by Henry Hazlitt (this is still available and, I believe, has even been issued in a 25¢ reprint edition, so you should have no trouble in obtaining it). These two books will give you a good, basic knowledge of just what Capitalism is and how it works.

Now if your interest in ideas is sincere and you really think that I am the person who can help you (if you are not prompted merely by a desire to correspond with some writer), I will suggest that you write to me, telling me something about yourself, that is, who you are and what is your profession—and, if you wish to ask more questions, give me your telephone number. If I find it possible, I will call you and we can make an appointment to meet. I believe that I might be able to help you in conversation—but I cannot undertake to write many letters of this length, and the questions which interest you cannot be answered briefly or casually.

■   ■   ■

To Ira Levin, author of *A Kiss Before Dying* (1953) and other novels and plays

Levin wrote to AR: "Like the very young man who stood beside Howard Roark and looked down on Monadnock Valley, I need say nothing but—thank you."

February 3, 1950

Dear Mr. Levin:

In answer to your letter: Thank *you*.

■   ■   ■

To Kenny Kato, son of friends and a fellow stamp collector

February 3, 1950

Dear Kenny:

Thank you for your letter. I was glad to hear from you and to know that you haven't forgotten us. I was very impressed to hear that you are doing well in school and have been elected Treasurer of your class. I always thought that you would be an efficient young man.

I will be glad to save foreign stamps for you. I haven't many at the moment, but I am enclosing some Norwegian stamps which you might use.

I hope that when you move to Burbank you will come to see us with your parents. I would like to see how you have grown in these years.

■ ■ ■

To Marna Papurt Wolfe

February 21, 1950

Dear Docky:

Our congratulations and best wishes to you on the birth of your little daughter.

I was very sorry to learn from Fabian, when he telephoned us while he was here, that the baby has a difficult heart condition. But I hope that the doctors will be able to help her and that an operation may be done to adjust the condition. I know that it is a hard problem for you, but I hope that you will have the brave attitude which Fabian had about it and that the baby will be alright. Needless to say you have all our sympathy and best wishes for her health. Love from both of us.

■ ■ ■

To Jasper E. Crane, vice president of E. I. DuPont Co.

February 21, 1950

Dear Mr. Crane:

On my visit to New York in 1947, you asked me my opinion of the magazine *Plain Talk* and whether it was a magazine worthy of support. I endorsed it at that time. If my endorsement had some part in influencing your decision to support *Plain Talk*, I feel now that it is my duty to withdraw that endorsement and to call your attention to a very shocking article which appears in the February issue of the magazine. It is entitled "Compulsory Voting?" by Leopold Schwarzschild.

If you have read this article, you probably realize that it is a piece of purely Statist propaganda. If our side advocates such a thing as compulsory voting, then there is no way for us to defend free enterprise or to object to the growth of government controls and regulations. A proposal to introduce compulsory voting is worse than mere looting of material property. Such a proposal establishes the principle that the government has the right to use compulsion against the human mind and to force an expression of political opinion from men who do not choose to express it. If an idea of this sort is proposed in some leftist publication, it will not do one-tenth the damage which it does in a publication allegedly devoted to the fight against Collectivism. If an average reader, who is trying to make up his mind, finds an article of this sort in a leftist magazine, he merely takes it for granted. But when he finds it in an anticollectivist magazine, he is forced to draw the conclusion that even the enemies of Collectivism accept the principle of compulsion and of State control—and in this manner *Plain Talk* contributes to the conversion of more people to Statism.

Mr. Schwarzschild's article states that it is the Republicans who are abstaining from voting and he ascribes it to their indifference. He ignores the fact that Republicans are abstaining from voting because they will not vote for the "me-too," new-dealish, socialistic platform offered by the Republican Party, particularly in the last presidential election. A refusal to vote represents a definite expression of political opinion—a rejection of the candidates and the programs offered. Half, and perhaps more, of the population of this country *is* opposed to the New Deal, *does* believe in free enterprise and represents the people to whom we should give voice and leadership, if we are to save free enterprise. Yet these are the people whom Mr. Schwarzschild betrays and seeks to push into endorsing socialism, at the point of a gun.

I was shocked to see that instead of its promised ideological campaign for freedom, *Plain Talk* has come out with an article such as "Compulsory Voting?" I do not know who Mr. Schwarzschild is, but I notice that he is listed on the cover as an associate editor. If this is a sample of his philosophical and political views, then it is my opinion that *Plain Talk* is not merely useless, but will be positively and disastrously dangerous to our side.

If you are still a supporter of *Plain Talk*, then I urge you to use your influence to see that this kind of intellectual trend is stopped in the pages of the magazine—or to withdraw your support. Since you had asked my opinion before, I feel it my duty to tell you that a need for a magazine of ideas on our side is more urgent and crucial than ever, but that *Plain Talk* and its editors are not and will not be able to answer that need.

Collectivism is winning mainly through the confusion of the public mind. We have to clarify that confusion. We need a magazine intelligently and uncompromisingly devoted to the philosophy of freedom, but such a magazine cannot be run by men so confused as to advocate compulsory voting. Therefore, I urge you to lend your support, if you find it possible, to the creation of a new magazine for our side, one which would be strictly a magazine of ideas. I believe that John Chamberlain and Henry Hazlitt have had such a project in mind for a long time, and perhaps you will find it possible to join forces with them. If a new magazine is not possible, then I would say that our side would be better off without any magazine at all and without any voice, rather than be misrepresented by a voice preaching Statism.

■   ■   ■

To Vera Koski, a fan

February 21, 1950

Dear Miss Koski:

You ask: "Aren't some of the character traits and ideals of Howard Roark taken from Frank Lloyd Wright's life?" No. There is no similarity between Roark and Mr. Wright as far as personal life, character and basic philosophy are concerned. The only parallel which may be drawn between them is purely architectural—that is, in regard to their stand on modern architecture.

■   ■   ■

To Alan Collins

April 7, 1950

Dear Alan:

I would like to ask you to do me a personal favor. I have just heard from Archie Ogden that he has become editor of Appleton-Century—and, of course, you can imagine how delighted I was to hear that he is back in the publishing business. He told me that he is to start working in about two weeks, but he did not know the exact date. Would you find out from some nice spy at Appleton what day Archie will start there, and then would you send him some flowers in my name. I would like the flowers to be there in his office on his first day. I will leave the choice and cost up to your judgment, but I want the flowers to be as beautiful as one can make them for a man's office without becoming ostentatious. Would you please enclose a card just saying, "Ayn Rand," and then please send me the bill.

I hope that this is not an imposition on you and I will appreciate it very much if you can do it. You know how much the event means to me.

■ ■ ■

To Alan Collins

April 14, 1950

Dear Alan:

Thank you very much for undertaking to send the flowers to Archie. If you think roses will be best, then let's make it two dozen of the reddest and most dramatic ones you can find. I am very grateful that you will do this for me, as I find that ordering flowers by wire is not very satisfactory.

In regard to your letter of April 6, I must say that I am puzzled by Appleton's offer for my next novel. If you will look up your letter to me of February 1, 1946, you will see what offer they made at that time. It was $125,000, to be split into a $100,000 advance and $25,000 guaranteed advertising, or $75,000 advance and $50,000 advertising.

Why are they now offering me less than half of their former offer? Have general prices changed so much in the publishing business? If so, what are the largest advances and advertising guarantees which have been made within the last year and to what authors?

I suspect that Appleton have decided that they can use my desire to work with Archie, for the purpose of getting me at less than my market value. If so, I would like you to correct them in their calculations. Of course, I do not want to commit myself to any actual business deal until the novel is finished. Then I will have to give first chance to Bobbs-Merrill. If Bobbs-Merrill and I do not agree on terms then I would rather go to Appleton in order to work with Archie—but only if Appleton consider my new novel as a major property and act accordingly. If, for any reason, they feel in doubt about the novel and do not want to go all out for it, then they are not the publishers for me. I will judge their attitude, not by personal assurances, but by the material terms of the offer they make. If they offer me less than the top market price which we can reasonably expect, then I will not consider them, because I cannot sacrifice the practical fate of the book to my personal pleasure of working with Archie.

I think that Appleton may derive a practical advantage from the fact of having Archie as editor in the following manner: whereas, their former offer was above the market, as a special inducement for me to choose them above any other publisher—now they don't have to offer me more than the market, since I have a very strong reason to prefer them to any other house; therefore, they can have me, if I leave Bobbs-Merrill, for my market price or perhaps even a little less. But they cannot offer me way less than what I have a right to expect. Please make it clear to them that their commercial estimate of my next book and their literary estimate have to match, and that I will not go with any publisher on second-rate terms.

■   ■   ■

To Mary Moffitt, wife of writer Jack Moffitt

April 14, 1950

Dear Mary:

Here are the recipes for the Beef Stroganoff and the salad dressing. I hope you won't find them too difficult.

We enjoyed very much seeing you both, and I hope it will not be too long before we can have another stimulating evening of political discussion.

■   ■   ■

To Jasper E. Crane

April 24, 1950

Dear Mr. Crane:

Thank you for your letter of April 7. I was glad to hear that you agree with me about the article "Compulsory Voting?" and I hope that you will be able to prevent the further publication of articles of this nature in *Plain Talk*.

I am greatly disturbed by the news which I heard from Mr. Luhnow and Mr. Cornuelle of the Volker Charities Fund, whom I met recently. They told me that they had been working with you for some time on plans to publish a new magazine devoted to the ideas of freedom—and that you have chosen Mr. Levine to be its sole editor, with Henry Hazlitt and John Chamberlain acting merely as columnists for the magazine. I am so disturbed by this prospect that I feel I must offer for your consideration the reasons why I think that this would be nothing short of disastrous.

Mr. Levine is not the editor for a philosophical-intellectual type of magazine. The realm of abstract ideas and political principles is not Mr. Levine's specialty or interest. He is a very able journalist and is very good on the factual kind of articles or journalistic exposés. His past work and career have been devoted exclusively to that field. He has demonstrated no interest in or understanding for the field of pure ideology. Yet ideology is what we most desperately need at present and the magazine we need is a magazine of *ideas*, not of journalistic reporting.

Mr. Levine's type of reporting can be of great value only when and if it serves as a concrete illustration for an intellectual campaign aimed at the rebirth of free enterprise. But taken by itself, mere factual reporting is futile at present. The value of facts lies in their proper appraisal and interpretation. The mere description of Communist horrors will not make people turn against Communism. The horrors are quite generally known by now, yet they do not arouse people to fight for free enterprise—because people have been saturated with the idea that the horrors are necessary, that the end justifies the means, that the Capitalistic system is just as bad, that Statist controls are proper, practical and unavoidable, and that nothing better is possible in the world anyway. We have to give people the ideas which will make them reject Collectivism root and branch. This is the basic, central, crucial part of the battle against Communism—and this is precisely the part on which Mr. Levine has failed dismally.

I am not sure whether you agree with me on the kind of magazine which is needed. I am convinced that it must be a magazine devoted primarily to ideas and, above all, a magazine that does *not* write down to the populace. This does not mean that it has to be a stuffy, academic sort of publication. It must be, on our side, what *The Nation* or *The New Republic* were at one time on the leftist side. It must be a magazine for intellectuals, for writers, teachers, professors and all those who in turn spread those ideas down to the masses. That is the way in which the influence of *The Nation* was built. Incidentally, the general mass of readers *would*, at present, support a serious magazine of our side. I know and have demonstrated in my own career that the so-called average reader has a much higher intellectual taste and a better mind than our intellectuals give him credit for. He can and will appreciate ideas, but he will not go for any kind of self-conscious popularization. Therefore, a serious, dignified magazine would appeal both to the intellectual and to the general readers, but a "popularized" magazine will appeal to neither.

Mr. Levine's approach, I am afraid, is strictly that of popularization.

The difference between a journalist and an ideologist is like the difference between a mechanic and an engineer. One deals with concrete appliances, the other with general abstract principles. Both may have high ability in their particular fields. But just as you would not put an expert mechanic in the job of chief engineer to run a factory—so you would not put a journalist to run an ideological magazine. If you attempt it, the results would be equally disastrous in both cases.

I say "disastrous" for the following reasons: The magazine would fail and its failure would have much wider consequences than just its own fate. Of any one national event of recent years, the Willkie campaign has had the most disastrous consequences for our side, because the public at that time had high hopes and a high enthusiasm for a rebirth of free enterprise. The miserable performance by Mr. Willkie killed these hopes, killed the enthusiasm and did more than anything done by New Dealers to create a mood of discouraged apathy among the supporters of free enterprise. The impression it made on them was, in effect: If this is the best fight that can be put on for our side, then the battle is not worth fighting. Precisely the same thing will happen in the case of the proposed magazine.

■   ■   ■

To Alan Collins

May 10, 1950

Dear Alan:

Thank you very much for sending the roses to Archie. I am very grateful for your courtesy—it made me very happy when I heard from him that he had received them. But where is the bill for this transaction? Please send it on to me. Don't you know that authors shouldn't be trusted for money for so long?

■   ■   ■

To Rebecca Weidman, mother of Barbara Weidman, later Nathaniel Branden's first wife

June 30, 1950

Dear Mrs. Weidman:

Thank you for your nice letter. I, too, was very sorry that I could not meet you in person while you were in California, but I hope that we will have a chance to meet in the future.

If, as Barbara tells me, you liked my novel, I must tell you in return that I am very much impressed with your work—namely, Barbara. She is one of the nicest and most intelligent young girls I have ever met. What impresses me particularly is her eager and serious interest in ideas, which is rare enough among people, and particularly among women. Yet, this is the only quality that I really like about people, so you will understand my interest in Barbara and Nathan. They are both remarkable children who will have a very hard time among the present-day intellectuals, because the modern trend is to penalize intelligence and ability. I will be very happy if I can help Barbara and Nathan with advice and moral support.

I feel a great sympathy for Barbara because she reminds me of myself at her age, and I know what sort of subtle injustice an intellectual girl has to suffer while she grows up. If I can help her against being hurt, I certainly will.

■ ■ ■

To Arthur Pierson, a friend and writer

July 14, 1950

Dear Arthur:

Thank you for your letter and the outline of the Horatio Alger idea which you sent me. I was very interested to read it.

If you want my suggestions, I must mention just one important point to consider at this preliminary stage. While the general idea of glorifying Horatio Alger would be very good indeed, I think that a dangerous issue will arise when you develop a specific story, and it will be very important to keep two different aspects of the situation clearly differentiated. One aspect pertains to industrial technology, the other to politics. You have indicated the first one in your outline, but not the second. The first is the fact that technological progress offers men *more* opportunities for advancement, and not *less*, as the leftists claim when they whine that "there are no frontiers left." Industrial progress makes opportunities grow, *but only so long as a society remains free.* And this is where we come up against the second or political aspect. In our present age, men have much less chance to rise and make a success than they had in Horatio Alger's time. Their opportunities are being killed year by year—*not* because of our industrial development, but because of our growing Statism and controls over industry.

If you ignore the above point and write a story merely from the technological angle, a story laid in modern times, then your picture will tell people, in effect, that we are just as free to advance as we always were, that private enterprise and initiative have as much chance as ever, and that individual talent still has unlimited opportunities. This would be an untrue and undesirable idea to give the public, because it would whitewash the present controls and blind people to the real nature of a controlled economy. The truth is that the essence, purpose and result of any controlled economy is the destruction of individual talent and individual opportunity, that is, the destruction of the self-made man. I have heard any number of prominent self-made industrialists say that they would be unable to make a success if they were starting today.

Therefore, if you wrote a picture on the theme of Horatio Alger, you would have to make it a protest against the controlled economy. Your story would have to show that while our technological advances give us greater opportunities than ever, the economic controls imposed upon us are killing these opportunities—and that while individual talent and self-reliance are still the only qualities through which a man or a nation can survive and prosper, these are the qualities now in danger of being destroyed.

If General Motors would allow you to make an uncompromising picture with this sort of message, then I think you would have a great film of tremendous patriotic importance. But if you find that they don't want to say that much, then I think it would be better not to attempt the theme—because a halfway treatment of this theme would be extremely harmful; it would be, not merely futile for the cause of free enterprise, but it would actually achieve the opposite of its purpose and would help the enemies of free enterprise, as any timid or compromising presentation of any theme always does. I hope that they will let you carry out this Horatio Alger idea fully. If they do, I think it could be a very important picture.

■   ■   ■

To Faith Hersey

Hersey wrote that she "cried with joy" when she saw AR's name on the screen during the opening credits of *The Fountainhead* movie.

July 21, 1950

Dear Faith:

Thank you for what you said about your reaction to the opening titles of *The Fountainhead* movie. No, it was not silly of you. It was wonderful. Only a real friend would have felt that.

I can't disagree entirely with your opinion of the picture itself. I can't say that I consider all of the casting or direction as ideal. But as Warner Brothers allowed me the miracle of having my script shot verbatim, without any distortion of my theme or dialogue, I am willing to accept the smaller imperfections and I am happy about the picture. However, I can't blame you if you felt that it could have been better.

No, I won't come to New York this summer, because I am deep in work on my new novel and I plan not to come back East until I finish it. I can't tell yet how long it will take me but I hope I will finish it sometime next year. It is going to be as long as *The Fountainhead* or longer, but I must say that I am extremely happy with it. The few friends to whom I have shown what I have written so far, all say that it is much better than *The Fountainhead*, and I think so too.

Thank you very much for the clippings of the kitten, and of the hat named after *The Fountainhead*. I am sure that the title of that hat is not accidental, and it amused me a great deal. This is what I would call a real philosophical fame.

No, I don't think that I can make up with Isabel Paterson. I would speak to her if I met her again, but I could never be friends with her anymore.

■   ■   ■

To Tony Barrett, actor. He had starred in *The Freedom Story*, a weekly radio broadcast by Spiritual Mobilization, a group which had adapted *Anthem*.

August 25, 1950

Dear Mr. Barrett:

Thank you for your wonderful performance in *Anthem*. I feel that I want you to know that this was the first time I have ever heard my own words read by an actor in a manner which made me proud to hear them.

This morning, I played a recording of the broadcast for my secretary, who had worked with me on all the various versions of the script. In the middle of the playing, she suddenly interrupted to say: "Who is Equality? He is great!" I thought that you should hear this, too.

If you remember, I said to you that you would have to supply the emotional element which the script could not provide in view of its brevity. I did not expect to hear it provided as perfectly as you have done—and for this I am very grateful.

■   ■   ■

To Barbara Weidman

September 1, 1950

Dear Barbara:

First, thank you for your wire. It reached us early in the morning and you might be glad to know that I felt an immense relief. I find that I was very worried about both you and Nathan, only he kept me worried for a longer time.

I'll tell you frankly that your letters are delightful. You have an unusual ability for suggesting the whole picture and atmosphere around you and it is very interesting to read. I am pleased to see how calm and rational you are—particularly in comparison to Nathan. I'm glad you have no [important] problems, and that I don't have to lecture you on why one should not scream in arguments, as I lectured Nathan. If you've quarreled "with only three or four acquaintances" that's an unusual example of stoical self-discipline.

I'm waiting with great interest to hear what will happen in your philosophical encounter with Wiffie [Wilfred Schwartz, friend of Barbara Weidman]. I hope you have told him by this time that he is probably a victim of the division between mind and matter. If your theory about him is correct, I would like very much to know what effect it had on him. Anyway, give him my regards and tell him that from your accounts about him I think he is a person worth saving. My congratulations to you on your first convert. If your sister-in-law has begun to call you with questions about the Capitalist economy—then the circle is complete. You are repeating what I did with you and Nathan—and this is wonderful. Just continue and let the light spread further.

We both miss you very much. If you're unhappy in Winnipeg and impatient to get back, we are just as impatient to have you back. I do miss your reading the chapters of my novel. As I told you, it did inspire and stimulate me instead of detracting me from my work. I am still struggling with Chapter 19.

With our best regards to your parents and love to you from both of us.

P.S. By the way, John Galt is the heroic in man.

■ ■ ■

To Nathan Blumenthal

September 1, 1950

Dear Nathan:

How can I cure you of screaming at collectivists in political arguments when I am still suffering from the same ailment myself? However, since all your symptoms seem to be exactly the ones I have gone through at your age, I will try to give you a little long distance therapy and I hope it will help until you come back.

You have all my sympathy. I know just exactly how you feel and in one respect you are justified. The temptation to scream is irresistible because that is what those people deserve. But the important consideration is not your opponents, but yourself. It is bad to scream at them, not because it hurts them, they ought to be hurt, but because it hurts you. Anger is a form of recognition. It amounts to admitting that those people are important to you and that they have the power to hurt you. Actually, they haven't.

You get angry when your opponents begin to be dishonest. Your anger comes from two reasons; anger at yourself for having been fooled, for having accepted them as honest, and your fear of the evil represented by any human being acting irrationally—which is *the* one essential evil. As, I think, we have discussed before, intellectual dishonesty is Steven Mallory's "drooling beast." You're right in hating the irrational, but you are wrong in assuming that the irrational can hurt you. By definition, it can't. It is powerless. You are wrong in assuming—as I do myself in those explosions of anger—that the irrationality or dishonesty of any one particular person is of any danger or importance to you or to the ideas you represent. I know that my anger always comes from the realization that I thought I was speaking to a rational person and suddenly find myself cheated, so that I am angry both at my mistaken judgment and their betrayal of their standing as human beings. But if you repeat this to yourself very firmly before you enter an argument, you will find that the anger will disappear. As a practical rule, I find that the thing which works best in such cases is contempt. When you feel your anger rising, ask yourself as fast as you can: Do those people and their ideas really matter to me? This one works miracles for me when I have time to practice it. Try it next time and see whether it helps you.

Frank and I laughed over your letters in sympathy and affection for you. I am proud of your violence, but don't let it go too far and don't let it hurt you. And don't construe this as encouragement. The first step is to feel a conviction strongly enough to want to scream about it, but a still better step is to feel it so strongly that no screams are necessary. If you feel like Steven Mallory now, it's good, but a still better step is to feel like Roark. You understand very well why he would not scream at anybody.

I was amused to hear that it is the words "selfish exploitation" that blew you up. Can you tell me why? I suspect that this is the influence of my new novel. Is it because you see Hank Rearden when you hear those words? I know that's the reason of my own anger at this sort of attitude.

I am watching with interest your reports on your sister, Florence. It will certainly be a philosophical achievement if you are able to convert her. You say that you feel she knows you are right, yet she chooses to be illogical and irrational about it. I can give you a clue to the nature of such an attitude. I have found that whenever a person chooses consciously to be irrational, it is only because he or she expects the rational person involved to fill the lack and to assume an unfair burden. She expects the rational person to grant her something, to which rationally she is not entitled. This is an issue of what I call the moral sanction. The simplest example of it is the kind of irresponsible parasite who never seems able to find a job or stand on his own feet, but is always supported by friends or relatives; yet if and when he is left alone, he is suddenly able to take care of himself. In other words, he indulges in irrational irresponsibility, only so long as he has the rational conviction that his friends and relatives will take care of him. Now, the same applies in any spiritual or intellectual issue, only it is then much subtler and much more complex. As a rough example: If Florence is not interested in political issues but wants to keep your respect and affection, without the effort of adjusting her ideas so that she would deserve respect and affection—she can do it only so long as you give her any evidence that she might be able to accomplish it. So long as you continue to argue, to be hurt by her ideas, or to be concerned about them, you are giving her proof that she holds the place she wants in your mind. This is where you must refuse her your moral sanction. You must make it clear that you will not discuss nor be concerned with anything irrational, that you will not grant any irrationalist the right to the intellectual respect implied in any discussion. If my diagnosis is correct, I think this will bring her to reason.

I am afraid to give you advice about your struggles with your novel, because that might confuse you. Literary advice is bad, sight unseen. But in a general way I can tell you that your struggle *is* natural, but that you seem to be in danger of overdoing it. I think I mentioned to you that a writer has to grow with his own work and that by the time you finish your first novel you will have learned so much that you will need to rewrite most of its first chapters. It is natural that each time you do a rewrite you learn more and you find more things to correct, but if you don't stop yourself in this process, you might spend the whole time needed to write your novel in just rewriting its first chapter. There is a balance needed here which nobody can tell you but yourself. You have to get your first chapter into some form that satisfies you, that says what you want to say, and then force yourself very quickly to go on. Don't expect to make the first chapter perfect. You won't be able to do that until the whole novel is done.

Now, as to the personal element, it might please you to know that you have discouraged me about the joys of motherhood. When we kept receiving your very amusing postcards from the road, I thought that I should really adopt you—but I changed my mind when the postcards stopped abruptly and I realized that motherhood involves worry and looking through the newspapers for reports of accidents to students from California. In other words, yes, we were both worried about you and that is something I have not done about anybody for a long time, so you may gloat, if you wish. We were very relieved when we got your first letter from Canada. I see that the worry was justified to some extent since you did have car trouble, but I am glad that it all came out alright.

Yes, we miss you very much and if you want to call me at 3:05 a.m. when you return, I will be quite agreeable to launching into Hume or any other subject you might choose.

I hope that your parents will drive back with you. I am still very interested to meet them—but I hope that you have not given them the impression that my influence has turned their son into what you call a homicidal maniac.

I am working hard on the novel, but I am still on Chapter 19. The work on *Anthem* took some of my time, but the *Anthem* script came out very well and I am very happy with it. It will be broadcast here this Sunday, day after tomorrow, but it is broadcast from recordings so that it is not released on the same day on all the various stations of the chain. I was unable to find out when it will be played on the stations nearest to you. However, I have a complete recording of it, so that if you don't hear it on the radio, I will play it, when you come back.

This letter has taken an hour away from a big scene between Dagny and Francisco, so is this enough of a sacrifice on my part?

■ ■ ■

To Marjorie Hiss

September 25, 1950

Dear Marjorie:

I am very sorry that I was not able to see you this time. I have had a very difficult time, as I am just approaching the end of Part 1 of my novel and had to attend to training a new servant, which disorganized me and the household completely. I am just coming back to normal, though I have not finished my Part 1 as yet.

Thank you very much for the Chinese lanterns which you sent us. We were startled by them as they are really magnificent. Since Frank had mentioned to you that he wanted to buy some, would you be angry at me if I ask you to let me pay for them? I hope that you did not intend them as a present, because I think it would be wrong at a time when you are furnishing a house, and your courtesy in getting them is enough of a present. Would you let me do it now and not give me any gift until you have finished your house and I have finished my novel; then we can celebrate together, but I would feel guilty about accepting presents in the middle of the stream.

■ ■ ■

To Peter (or "Elo") Kondheim

October 6, 1950

Dear Peter:

It is not a question of forgiveness or resentment on my part against you. The difference between us came apparently from a fundamental difference in philosophy. I am glad to know, and I believe you, that you did not intend to hurt my feelings. But this does not change the fact that the ideas which led to your actions are the ones of which I disapprove very highly and which are the opposite of my ideas. I form my opinion of people according to their actions and their convictions—and, therefore, if their convictions are the opposite of mine I cannot feel about them as I did before I discovered it.

However, ideas are always open to discussion. If you feel that this is not a fundamental difference between us, but only a misunderstanding, I will be glad to discuss it with you when I come to New York and I will be glad to straighten it out. It is difficult to discuss it by letter because it involves some very wide issues. For instance, I am unable to like people for their faults, as you say you do. I like them for their virtues. I have always liked you for the good qualities which I saw in you, such as your intelligence and your courage. If I see a quality which I consider a major defect, I cannot forget it, I have to include it in my estimate of a person. But if I find in the future that this difference between us can be eliminated, I will be happy to return to my original estimate of you. It is not that I resent you now, it is simply that I disagree, and my feeling towards people proceeds from my ideas.

I do think, if I judge by your letter, that we will be able to straighten it out eventually. I do not know yet when I will come to New York, but it does not mean that I will be your enemy until that time. We will merely let the issue rest until then, and in the meantime I will wish you happiness and success in your new home and your work.

■ ■ ■

To Stanley Greben, a fan

October 15, 1950.

Dear Mr. Greben:

You wrote that *The Fountainhead* made a powerful impression on you and that you are unable to explain the reason why it did so. Your entire letter appears to be a quest for that explanation. I found your letter very interesting, because the explanation you are seeking is so obviously contained within your own words. Therefore, I want to point out to you a fundamental error in your approach to life, as revealed by your letter.

You have listed all the things (e.g., experience, background, education) which you consider as possible sources of a novel and you have omitted the most important one, the only source from which any novel or any action can come, the source which determines experience, feelings, etc., which determines all the irrelevant things you name: the *mind*. You make no reference in your letter, explicitly or implicitly, to reason, thinking, ideas, logic, as if these did not exist. If you are confused and troubled, as I gather from your letter, then *this* is the source of your troubles.

You seem to be an irrationalist, a young man who has accepted as an axiom the vicious and preposterous premise which underlies modern education: the premise of determinism. You seem to believe that the human mind does not exist, that man has no capacity to think, that he is a helpless, "conditioned" robot, and that his ideas are merely the by-product of his experiences, feelings, background, breakfast food, etc., the by-product of anything and everything except logic. You have accepted the premise that a man's ideas are the effect, not the cause, of the events of his life. The exact opposite is true. A man's ideas are the *cause* which determines every aspect of his life and character.

Your letter gave me the impression that *The Fountainhead* was your first contact with the world of rationalism, of the possibility of whose existence you had no concept. You sounded to me like a man stunned by the discovery that man is a rational being. You sounded like a jungle savage at his first sight of New York skyscrapers—and I intend this comparison, not as an insult to you, but literally—because modern determinism, the view of man as a non-thinking, conditioned brute, *is* a return to the mental state of the jungle. If the men, the emotions and the whole approach to life presented in *The Fountainhead* appealed to you, it is because you recognized suddenly, for the first time, a picture of existence proper to a human being.

You say you feel that there is in *The Fountainhead* "some power, some force which I must recognize." That power is Reason. *The Fountainhead* impressed you as it did, because it presents a philosophy of life which contains no logical contradictions. Since reason is our only means of perceiving reality, a rational thesis will have an irresistible power for any person who has the capacity to think, or for any part of a person's mind which he is willing to exercise. The modern determinists spend their lives evading the responsibility of thought. But to the extent to which a man is rational, to that extent *The Fountainhead* will impress him. My diagnosis of you is that you probably have a better mind than you have allowed yourself to realize, and that you have chained your own mind by accepting the irrationalism which was probably taught to you in college.

Now to answer your questions: I did not write *The Fountainhead* on the basis of my experiences or feelings or any of the things you listed. I wrote it on the basis of my thinking. I arrived at my ideas by means of logic and by the process of rational consideration, not by means of whatever accidental experiences I might have had in my life. I am not a product of my "environmental history"—and if my letter can be of any value to you, the best advice I can give you is never to regard yourself as a product of your environment. That is not the key to me, to you, or to any human being. It is not a key to anything, it is merely an alibi for weaklings.

You ask from what authority my ideas and characters arise. If you were a rationalist, you would never ask such a question of the author of a book like *The Fountainhead*. I write upon no authority but my own—and I spent a whole book telling you that no man can do anything of value upon any authority but his own, which means: the authority of his own mind.

If you were a rationalist, you would not ask me if I write tongue in cheek, laughing at "credulous readers." This is a good example on which to give you a lesson in rationalism. Your question is futile by its own terms. If I wrote my novel sincerely, then I would have to answer you that I was sincere. And if it were possible for me to have written *The Fountainhead* as a hypocrite, then I would still have to answer your question by assuring you of my sincerity. If it were possible for me to be willing to lie to the whole world on such a scale as *The Fountainhead*, wouldn't I then lie also in a private letter to one reader?

A rationalist would know that a book such as *The Fountainhead* was not and could not have been written by a hypocrite. The book presents a philosophy which is irrefutable in terms of reason. How would it be possible for me to write it "with tongue in cheek" and to laugh at "credulous readers"? It would amount to considering people credulous because they accept reason. If so, then what is it that I would have to hold as my true belief? That reason is not valid and that real wisdom lies in insanity? Does this sound possible for the author of *The Fountainhead*?

Yes, of course, I am sincere about my philosophy, much more so than you imagine possible, I not only believe what I write, I actually practice it, I live by the principles which I preach and they have worked for me exactly as they have worked for Roark. But if you are to learn the principles of rationalism, you should not ask me to tell you this, you should prove it to yourself by analyzing *The Fountainhead*. This can be done only on the premise that logic is a valid means of judgment. If you believe that logic is not valid, then nothing is, but then no such concepts as sincerity, ideas, morality, judgment, language or human existence are possible.

I cannot attempt to discuss in detail the many other fallacies which I found in your letter. I can only point them out briefly. You say that you recognize "the limitations" of the novel to characterize man and his emotions. There are no such limitations. If you learn to attach real meaning to the words you use, you will see this for yourself.

You mention that the characters in my book are heroic, even though in their actual lives they engage in nonheroic, everyday activities. This is another gaping hole in your thinking. Of course, these chores and activities exist. What of it? There is nothing evil nor degrading about them, but neither do they constitute the significance of human life. It is what you do with your life after eating, sleeping and eliminating that counts. These activities are the means, not the meaning, of human existence. They do not interfere in any way with the heroic qualities of a man—and one does not include them in a novel, not by reason of any "limitations," but because the proper purpose of a novel is to present that which is significant, not to catalog indiscriminately every move and moment of a person's life. I would suggest that you clarify your ideas about literature. I think that you are suffering from a bad case of literary "Naturalism." And, again, it comes back to the issue of rationalism. If man is a conditioned animal, then his food and his bathroom activities are of equal importance with his creative work, except that nothing can then be of any importance whatever. If man is a rational being, then it is his mind and his chosen purpose which determine his standard of value and tell him why the time he spends at his work is significant and the time he spends in the bathroom is not.

Whatever confusion there may be in your thinking, it all stems from the same source and I suggest that you review your entire philosophy of life, starting with the premise of rationalism. The "mysterious" power which impressed you in *The Fountainhead* is not mysterious at all and its entire secret is contained in the word *Reason*. It is a power which is available to you—and if the kind of life presented in *The Fountainhead* appeals to you, you can have it in reality, you can live it, but you can do so only on the basis of complete, total, uncompromising rationalism. I cannot attempt here to lecture you on the Theory of Knowledge. I can only suggest that you go back to Aristotle and start from there. I suggest that you do it now, because I have no words strong enough to tell you how much you will regret it as you grow older, if you permit yourself to proceed on the theory of "conditioning" and irrationalism. I can only tell you that every form of human misery, suffering, ugliness, evil, failure and frustration stems from that one source—from the inexcusable tragedy of a living being who rejects his essential nature and his only means of survival, which is his mind.

■   ■   ■

To Henry Hazlitt, a pro-capitalist economist and writer

December 25, 1950

Dear Harry,

Here is the detailed story of what I told you in our telephone conversation.

The movie of *Born Yesterday*, produced by Columbia [and released in 1951], was adapted from a play by Garson Kanin, who is known as a Pink. The play was actually and mainly a nonpolitical farce, but Kanin stuck into the plot some political touches of crude collectivist propaganda. This, as you know, is the usual technique of the Left, in regard to plays and movies. Few works openly preaching collectivism have ever succeeded with the public. The technique is to introduce the propaganda into otherwise innocent stories and make the public swallow the poison in small doses—which mount up to a thorough job of indoctrination, if that is all the public hears whenever politics are mentioned on the screen.

The disastrous and tragic part of this situation in Hollywood is that the Pinks have succeeded, *not* because the movie producers are Leftist, but because the producers are as ignorant and confused politically as the rest of the country—and the so-called conservatives have done nothing to enlighten them. The conservatives in Hollywood, with very few exceptions, have been just as muddled and inconsistent as they are everywhere. They have put up no *ideological* battle in the studios. They have confined themselves mainly to denouncing *persons*, not ideas—and, as a consequence, the Pinks have won by default. Collectivist propaganda is permitted to go on the screen, simply because few people have the courage and intelligence to fight against it.

By the usual Hollywood practice, a play such as *Born Yesterday* would have been given to a Leftist writer to adapt for the screen (the Leftists always see to that and the studios don't care), and all the political poison which it contained would have been preserved in the movie, to be shown to millions of people the world over and to do an infinitely greater amount of damage on a wider scale than any Broadway hit could do. But in this case, Columbia Studio, unaware of and unconcerned with the political issues involved, gave the adaptation job to Albert Mannheimer, for purely literary reasons, because they considered him an excellent comedy writer. And so it happened (which is almost unprecedented in Hollywood) that a big "property" slanted to the Left, such as *Born Yesterday*, was given for screen adaptation not to a Leftist nor even to a middle-of-the-roader, but to a real conservative like Mannheimer.

If you read the studio's statement, which I am enclosing, you will see the nature of the political problem involved in this adaptation and what Mannheimer has done with it. (This statement was sent by Columbia Studio to their New York office for the purpose of answering one critic who attacked the movie as "Marxist," not on the ground of the movie itself, but on the ground of the play and of Kanin's political record. This statement was written for the studio by Mannheimer.)

It is most unusual for a Hollywood studio to support so clear-cut a political statement in defense of Free Enterprise. This will give you some idea of what a Herculean job of political teaching Mannheimer had to undertake while working on this script. The heads of Columbia were not Leftist, but they were truly "babes in the woods" politically and they did not know a Pink line of dialogue when they heard one. The director of the picture, George Cukor, was a close friend of Garson Kanin; he kept in constant touch with Kanin; there were also other influences at work, which I can only suspect. They fought to keep in the movie every collectivist line of the play. Mannheimer was, at first, alone to fight against them. He had nothing to fight with, except ideological persuasion—and he had to convince producers who were indifferent to politics, annoyed by the issue, and, normally, would probably have preferred to give in (with the "Who cares about a few lines?" attitude) to the director—particularly in the case of George Cukor, who is one of the big Hollywood names.

The movie of *Born Yesterday* is not as good politically as I could wish it to be. That is, Mannheimer had made the pro-Free Enterprise aspect much clearer and more explicit in his script than they finally shot for the screen. Some of his political speeches were cut out by the director. Some of Kanin's vague touches of Pinkness remained on the screen, in spite of Mannheimer's protests; but these touches now are merely innocuous.

Mannheimer could not, of course, win on every point. But he won the two major victories which were politically crucial: the elimination of the "Free Enterprise Amendment" and of the "You've got all the oil and all the lumber and steel and coal—" speech. (I've marked them on the enclosed statement.) To keep millions of screengoers from hearing it preached to them that a law which "guarantees no interference with free enterprise" is Fascism—represents, to my mind, an enormously valuable service to the cause of Free Enterprise, and it is more than most conservatives have so far been able to achieve in Hollywood.

To the credit of Columbia Studio, it must be said that they are finally beginning to understand the issue and that this battle seems to have had an extremely good effect on them. But they are literally like children learning to walk and making their first stumbling steps. *This* is why I think it tremendously important that they get ideological encouragement and support from the conservative press.

If they hear the conservatives noting the elimination of Kanin's collectivist ideas from the movie, they will begin to believe the full importance of political ideas, of what they should permit on the screen and how careful they should be about it. If nobody notices or gives them credit for the changes they made, it will throw them right back into the attitude of "Who cares about ideas?"—which is where the Pinks want to keep them.

Whenever a Hollywood writer or studio puts out something favorable to collectivism, the whole Leftist press cheers them for it. So it would be tragic if, when a studio tries to respect Free Enterprise, the fact is denounced or ignored.

I do not know whether it is true that Westbrook Pegler intends to attack this movie or whether it is only a rumor, nor from what aspect he wants to attack it. If he wants to denounce Garson Kanin's politics or the Hollywood practice of buying any stories at all from Pinks—he would be fully right and I would certainly agree with him. But I hope that if he discusses the content of the movie, he will note the changes made and evaluate the political message of the movie accordingly. I hope that he will not lump it together with the play, on the ground that the general story is the same. The general story is nonpolitical. The issue lies in those crucial little touches and slants. If he cares to look up and compare the texts of the play and the movie, he will see the full difference, better than I can present it here in outline.

If you find that you agree with me and if such an occasion arises, I would appreciate it very much if you would point out to Pegler the exact nature of the changes made in the movie, as explained in the enclosed studio statement, or show him that statement, if you wish. But please consider my letter confidential—because I am not connected with Columbia Studio. I know the inside story of the battle only from Albert Mannheimer and this behind-the-scenes battle should not be made public. It would be most unfortunate if any publicity came out praising Mannheimer at the expense of the Columbia producers, just as they are beginning to adopt his political viewpoint and are now coming to him for political guidance. You may, of course, tell Pegler, if you wish, that it was I who called your attention to this picture.

■ ■ ■

To Alan Collins

December 30, 1950

Dear Alan,

The lapse in my correspondence was due to the great event that on the night of December 22, at 3 a.m. to be exact, I finished Part I of my new novel. I am sure that at this point you will say: "Oh hell, only Part I!" But I will wait for my vindication until you read the completed novel, and then you will believe me what a job this was and that I have not taken too long for the kind of work it represents. Part I is 1,382 pages long (I'll let you figure out how many average-length novels this is). [In the final novel, this part itself was divided into Part I and Part II.] Part I represents about two-thirds to three-quarters of the whole novel in length, therefore Part II will not take me too long. [In those days, the novel had only two parts.]

I would like very much to have you take over certain properties, as I have not been too happy about the manner in which they were handled by the Ann Watkins office. The most important one of them is my first novel, *We the Living*. It was published here by Macmillan in 1936, but the American publishing rights have reverted to me. There is now a great demand for this novel. I keep getting letters about it constantly, and Bobbs-Merrill have been after me for several years to let them issue a new American edition of it. I have refused, because I don't want to have it issued as a follow-up to *The Fountainhead*, since, being an earlier novel, it would be an anticlimax at present. But I want it to be reissued shortly after my new novel is published, and I would like to make arrangements for it at the time I sign the contract for the new novel, whether it will be with Bobbs-Merrill or another publisher. Therefore it will be much better if both novels are handled by you.

We the Living *was reissued by Random House in 1959.*

■ ■ ■

To Joseph G. Butts, Jr., of the law firm of Gall and Lane

January 5, 1951

Dear Mr. Butts:

If Mr. Gall believes that we should sue Scalera in the Italian courts in regard to the exhibition of *We the Living* in Spain, the arrangement will be agreeable to me in principle, as outlined in your letter, but I would like to know a few details about it.

Would this suit be a separate matter which must be handled apart from our war claim? If so, will the outcome affect our basic claim in any way?

I assume that under the peace treaty the State Department is to handle only that part of the case which pertains to Scalera's actions during the war. Is the exhibition of the picture in Spain considered as a new and separate infringement? If so, should we not include in this suit all the exhibitions of the picture since the end of the war? If you remember, the picture was reissued in Italy a few years ago during the last Italian election, and I suspect that it has also been released in other European countries. I wonder whether it would be possible for the Italian attorney to obtain information on all the exhibitions of the picture since the war and include them all in our suit against Scalera.

Have you any way of judging, at least approximately, how much we would be able to collect from Scalera for the exhibition of the picture in Spain? I suppose that we could get a rough idea by finding out what is the average gross of an Italian picture in Spain, and what percentage do the Italian courts allow an author in such cases, if there have been any precedents to go by.

Ten years later, AR was awarded 14,000,000 lire (then $22,778) in an out-of-court settlement of her suit.

■ ■ ■

To Henry Hazlitt

February 26, 1951

Dear Harry:

I do envy you for the fact that your novel [*The Great Idea*, later retitled *Time Will Run Back*] is finished and is about to come out. Archie Ogden was here and told me a little about it. It sounded extremely interesting, and I am looking forward to reading it. All my best wishes to you for the success you deserve.

I have not been able to read every issue of *The Freeman* from cover to cover as I would have liked to, but I have followed your political editorials "The Fortnight." I have no criticism to offer in that respect, only my best compliments and my wish that you keep it up.

Of the articles which I liked very much, I'll mention "Council for the Minority" by Robert Morris, "Lord Keynes and Say's Law" by Ludwig von Mises, "For President: Mickey Cohen" by Morrie Ryskind, "Plan for Counter-action" by Rodney Gilbert—particularly this last.

But I must, regretfully, object to two articles which I have read, both of them in the December 25th issue. I was shocked by "The Teamsters Drove Off" by Jonathan Mitchell. This article proclaims the one fatal fallacy of the Republican Party which, I thought, we all agreed to consider as fatal, namely, the creed of compromise. I think that *The Freeman* should do everything possible to oppose and denounce the Republican methods of "middle-of-the-road-ism" and "me-too-ism." *The Freeman*'s credo, in its first issue, stated this very clearly and strongly. Therefore, I hope that you will not be tolerant of the advocates of compromise and will not give voice to ideas such as Mr. Mitchell's.

But the above article is nothing compared to the truly outrageous piece entitled "Mid-century Survey" by William A. Orton. I am baffled by this piece—and by its appearance in the pages of *The Freeman*. In another publication, this piece would have to be taken as advocating ideas which coincide with some of the cardinal points of the Communist party line. This is inconceivable for *The Freeman*—but if these points are not what Mr. Orton is preaching, then what *is he* preaching?

1. Mr. Orton advocates One World—or, as he calls it, "planetary community." What is a "planetary community"? Community with whom? On what terms?

2. Mr. Orton asks us to drop "exaggerated fear and exaggerated hostility." Fear of whom and hostility towards what? Mr. Orton never mentions the words "Soviet Russia" or "Communism"—yet as far as I know the only fear and hostility which Americans now feel are towards Soviet Russia and Communism. Are these fears and hostilities exaggerated—or are they insufficient, considering the nature of our danger?

3. Mr. Orton writes: "We should all prefer to scrap the guns and share the butter (especially in America, where we have more butter than we know what to do with)." Good God, Harry, is this the statement of a defender of free enterprise? When we are on the brink of economic ruin brought about by policies such as the Marshall Plan and other orgies of giving things away—do we have more butter than we know what to do with, and does our salvation lie in some more sharing?

4. After two pages of apocryphal warnings about the possibility of the total extinction of mankind, Mr. Orton comes out with what he calls "some categorical observations" on the methods to save ourselves, as follows:

"The reporting of events from 'enemy' societies has in our time been grotesquely biased." (!) Is *this* the great threat to mankind and the first problem of our time? Does our trouble lie in our "*biased*" reporting about Soviet Russia? If Mr. Orton did not mean Soviet Russia, what other "enemy society" did he have in mind?

5. Mr. Orton objects to our "excessive secrecy" and wants to share our "intellectual, technical and even medical advances" with the "world-community." If this does not mean giving the atom bomb away to Soviet Russia—what does it mean?

6. Mr. Orton wants us to get "increasingly liberated from the current exigencies of power politics." *Whose* power politics? Since Mr. Orton states, in his last paragraph, that we can do all these things "without waiting for every other party to act first," one must take it to mean that he finds America guilty of power politics. Is the thing going on in Korea power politics on the part of America? Is Mr. Orton accusing America of *imperialism*?

I am unable to see in what manner Mr. Orton's message differs from the things advocated by the Communist party line. If this was not his intention, if he had some other message in mind and I missed it, would you tell me please what it was and where to find it in that article? The question that disturbs me most is, of course, why you allowed this article to be published. If you care to, would you tell me why? I hate to criticize *The Freeman*, but since you asked me to let you know whenever I found anything politically improper in *The Freeman*, I felt that I had to tell you my reaction to this article and to tell you that I found it more than improper.

Hazlitt answered that he hadn't seen the two articles prior to publication but agreed with AR's analysis.

■ ■ ■

To Raymond F. Blosser

February 26, 1951

Dear Mr. Blosser:

Thank you very much for your nice Christmas Greeting. But has the New York Central forgotten me this year in regard to the calendar? If I am not too late in reminding you, I would like very much to have your calendar for 1951. The 1950 is still on my wall, waiting to be replaced.

No, my railroad novel is not finished yet, but I have about 1,400 typewritten pages of it done and hope to finish it this year. It's going to be very long, but worth it. With best regards.

■ ■ ■

To Don Helgeson, a college student

February 26, 1951

Dear Mr. Helgeson:

I am glad that you liked *The Fountainhead* and that you have selected it as the subject of your term paper. But I am sorry that you seem to wish to narrow my novel down to an aspect which would be insignificant and incorrect.

In regard to the points you mention, I must tell you that *The Fountainhead* is actually *not* a novel about architecture—or rather, architecture is merely the background I use for a theme which applies to all human activities and professions. You may be justified in seeing some parallel between Howard Roark and Frank Lloyd Wright only in a strictly architectural sense, that is, in the fact that both are great fighters for modern architecture. But if you have read Mr. Wright's books you must know that there is no resemblance whatever between Roark's personal character and the character of Mr. Wright, between the events of their lives, and between their fundamental philosophies of life. You may see a resemblance between Henry Cameron and Louis Sullivan in the general aspect of a great professional tragedy. The other comparisons which you mention do not have even that general aspect in common.

You are, of course, free to approach *The Fountainhead* from any angle you wish, but since you have asked my opinion of your approach, I must say that I find it regrettable. I think that you are reversing the process of serious study. If we want to learn anything from life, we must observe the specific people and events around us and draw some wider principles and abstractions from our observations. But what you are doing is taking wide fundamental principles and reducing them to the narrow, the specific, and the accidental. You are reducing fiction to journalism—and these are two entirely different fields of endeavor. May I suggest that you reverse your approach?

■ ■ ■

To Y. Ashihara, a Japanese architect

February 26, 1951

Dear Mr. Ashihara:

Thank you for your very interesting letter. I am glad that you liked the motion picture of *The Fountainhead*, and I appreciate profoundly that you wrote to me about it. I am particularly glad that it was the philosophy of the picture that interested you and that it has made you want to read my novel. It supports my belief that philosophical ideas hold true for all people everywhere and that there will always be men who will respond to a philosophical truth in every country on earth.

You say that the picture conveyed to you the impression that I place too much emphasis on the ability of an individual. I cannot possibly emphasize it too strongly. The ability of an individual is the only thing that counts and the only source of all great achievements, in architecture and in every other profession. You refer to the techniques and materials provided by science. Where does science come from, if not from the ability of individuals? The higher the scientific development of mankind, the more ability is required from individuals in order to use the achievements of science. An incompetent man cannot use the products of scientific genius. Collectives of men have never achieved anything. There is no such thing as a collective anyway—it is only a number of men. Each man has to be judged by his own ability, and his ability is the only thing that matters. A hundred morons do not constitute a genius. The fundamental tenet of my philosophy is that individual ability is the fountainhead of all achievement, of all good, of all greatness in human life, and the only means of man's survival.

I think that you will be able to understand my philosophy more fully after you have read my novel. I will be very interested to hear from you about it.

Thank you very much for the pictures of your building which you sent me. I was very impressed with your work and I think that it is an excellent example of modern architecture.

■   ■   ■

To Pincus Berner

October 12, 1951

Dear Pinkie:

I have not written you sooner because this is the first chance I have had to write a letter in the midst of the mad rush that we have gone through. Our furniture has finally moved out of here yesterday, and we shall follow it by car. We will start on Wednesday the 17th and will arrive in New York on Tuesday the 23rd or early the next morning. We intend to arrive ahead of the furniture and we will be there to receive it. Should anything happen to delay us on the road I will wire you and then I will take advantage of your offer to receive the furniture in our name and to pay for it.

P.S. I still don't quite believe it that I am coming to New York—and I feel wonderful!

AR and her husband moved back to Manhattan permanently on October 17.

■ ■ ■

To J. H. Gipson, president of Caxton Publishers

December 23, 1952

Dear Mr. Gipson:

Thank you for the advertising material on *Anthem* which you sent me. I am enclosing copies of it, which I have revised and retyped, and am also returning your original copies, so that you may see what particular changes I have made.

I have attempted to follow the form of the original material, but to stress the positive theme of Individualism, rather than the negative aspect of an expose of the Collectivist State. This last might give readers the impression that *Anthem* is merely another sordid story on the order of Orwell's *1984* (which, incidentally, was written many years after *Anthem* had been published in England).

I have rewritten the copy about the story because I felt that it was both too detailed and too confused, and that it suggested the tone of a non-fiction political treatise. I can't say that I blame the young man who wrote it, however—it was a terribly difficult job to do, even for me.

You will note that I have included in this copy a brief mention of the publishing history of *Anthem*. I consider it most essential that we do not mislead the public and do not give the impression that *Anthem* is a *new* novel by me, written later than *The Fountainhead*. It is essential that all our publicity mention the fact that this is a new edition, not a new work.

As a small publicity suggestion, I would not feature the description "tender and terrific" out of the context of Ruth Alexander's review. It is good and impressive in the review, but not right when given without quotes (*Anthem* is anything but tender).

Under separate cover, I am returning the sketch of the jacket design. It is excellent and I like it very much for its dignified simplicity. The only suggestion I would make here is that the color yellow tends to give the lettering a faded, "yellowed" look. A pale green or blue-green would be infinitely better. Yellow and black is a bad combination, it suggests life-lessness.

■ ■ ■

To William Mullendore

April 1, 1953

Dear Bill Mullendore:

I have just received a letter from Louis Dehmlow, telling me about the strike against the Southern California Edison Company and sending me copies of two of your ads (of March 11th and March 17th). I had seen no reference to this strike in the New York newspapers.

I want to express my deepest admiration for the stand you have taken. What impressed me most was the tone of unapologetic and uncompromising *moral* assurance in your ads, the tone of a *moral* issue, which, as a rule, is the quality most disastrously missing from the public utterances of modern businessmen. As you know, it is my fundamental conviction that the battle for free enterprise cannot be won unless we fight it in *moral terms*—so you will understand what I felt when I saw your manner of fighting. I must say that the last paragraph of your letter to the Company employees is the greatest statement by an American businessman I have ever read.

With my deepest respect, admiration and wish for your victory,

In the paragraph to which AR refers, Mullendore wrote that his company's stand against compulsory unionization is "a stand

taken by men who will, I assure you, never give in to these men in the face of these threats, and now speaking for myself only, I will further assure you that I will resign my position as President of this Company before I will give my consent [to the union's demands]." Los Angeles Times, *March 17, 1953.*

∎ ∎ ∎

To Gilles Rioux

February 15, 1954

Dear Mr. Rioux:

Please excuse this letter, if it is written to the wrong person. I have heard about you in a rather unusual manner from an anonymous admirer of yours, who would not give me his name. He told me that you are a man who is practicing my philosophy of life, that you are a student of architecture with an uncompromising integrity and devotion to your convictions, that you refuse to work for architects whose standards you despise and that you are working, instead, as a miner, to save money to get your architectural degree. This description is startlingly close to the hero of my novel, *The Fountainhead*. But your admirer told me that you refuse to read *The Fountainhead*, because too many people have advised you to read it.

I have no way of knowing whether the above description of you is true, but I am writing this letter on the assumption that it is. If you are an individualist, yet have decided that *The Fountainhead* could not possibly be your type of book, because too many people like it—it means that you have concluded that your values can neither exist nor succeed in the world, that the good has no chance, that only the worthless can be popular or can make itself heard, that only evil can win. A conclusion of this kind amounts to surrendering the world to your enemies and will be dangerous to your own ideals: it will tend to disarm you in your battle. Nobody can fight for that which he believes to be impossible.

I could not help you with your career and I don't think you are looking for help, but I would like to get acquainted with your ideas and I think that I could be of philosophical value to you. The reason of my interest is that your admirer was very convincing in presenting you as a Howard Roark and I don't want to see any potential Roark lose his battle, if I can help it.

If your admirer was wrong and has misled me, please excuse this letter and ignore it. If he was right, read *The Fountainhead*, then let me hear from you. You will see why I wanted you to read it.

Rioux responded that he read the book after receiving AR's letter, and he invited AR to contact him in New York.

There is a lengthy gap in AR's letter writing until the completion of Atlas Shrugged.

■ ■ ■

To Barbara Stanwyck

October 5, 1957

Dear Barbara:

Thank you for your letter. As you see, I don't forget, even if Warner Brothers do. I will be very interested to hear your reaction to *Atlas Shrugged*. Would you write to me, at the above address, when you have read it? Before I make any decision in regard to the movie rights of this novel, I would like to know whether you feel about Dagny Taggart as you did about Dominique Francon.

On October 7, Stanwyck replied that in reading Atlas Shrugged, *she "lost a week's sleep" which answers "how much I enjoyed [the book]." She thanked AR for remembering her and for considering her for the part of Dagny Taggart (the novel's heroine), but she said that Hollywood would want someone "young, beautiful, and all the rest that goes with it."*

■ ■ ■

To Steve Werner, a fan

November 23, 1957

Dear Mr. Werner:

Since you want to meet me, I must tell you that I am both the easiest and the hardest person to meet, depending on your own attitude. My time *is* for sale, but the price I demand is not money, as you suggested. I assume that you made this odd suggestion in an attempt to apply what I define in

Atlas Shrugged as "the trader principle" and to offer me a value in ex-change for a value. If this was your intention, you are on the right track, but in the wrong manner. So I will give you a helpful hint: in any trade, the currency must be appropriate to that which is being traded. If I were a professional teacher, your offer of money for my time would be appropriate. But since I am not, ask yourself what motive could make me wish to talk to you. There *is* such a motive and there *is* a currency you can offer me in exchange for a philosophical discussion: your sincere, serious and *rational* interest in ideas. If this is your motive, I will not be difficult to meet. If it isn't, I will—or, should we meet, it won't do you any good whatever.

P.S. I noticed the words "good luck" which you wrote on the envelope of your letter. I have a better expression for what I think these words were intended to signify, so I will wish it to you here: "good premises."

■　■　■

To R. M. Lynch, Standard Slag Co.

December 14, 1957

Dear Mr. Lynch:

Thank you for your letter. I am glad that you liked *Atlas Shrugged*. I am particularly happy when businessmen understand me—because, like John Galt, I feel that *they* are the great victims for whom I am fighting.

　　If I should visit Youngstown, I will certainly take advantage of your kind invitation—only you'll have to teach me the art of trout fishing, which I've never done, but would love to learn.

■　■　■

To Frederica McManus, a fan

December 14, 1957

Dear Mrs. McManus:

Thank you for your very attractive letter. Or, to be exact, "attractive" ap-plies to the personality that your letter seems to communicate.

　　I am glad that you liked *Atlas Shrugged*. You say that it frightened you. It was meant to. But—forewarned is forearmed. We are still free to stop the collectivist-altruist trend that is destroying the world. My purpose was not merely to portray the horror of altruism, but to show the kind of life and character men have the capacity to achieve on the proper, _rational_ morality. My purpose is not just to defeat Wesley Mouch, but to make John Galt possible.

You say that you cannot find anyone willing to listen to you. I know that a hopeless, cynical passivity is people's prevalent attitude today, as a result of our moral vacuum. But, for the same reason, there are people who are desperately eager to hear; they are those who have not given up. I suggest that you look for them. To whatever degree you succeed in making yourself heard, large or small—it is of such voices that the changes of world trends are made.

Wishing you "best premises"—

■   ■   ■

To Jackie Reading, a fan

August 31, 1959

Dear Miss Reading:

I can point out certain things to you on the basis of your letter. The first thing that a writer needs is _to think_, not to feel. Your letter shows that you are much more concerned with emotions than with thought. Yet language is the tool of reason. If you do not know fully and clearly _what_ it is that you want to say, you will have no way of knowing whether you have said it or not, and neither will your readers.

What makes you think that reality is "crude, harsh or ugly"? That is certainly not the reality I write about. But if some parts of reality—some people—_are_ crude, harsh and ugly, why write about them? Unless you have some specific idea to present or some moral lesson to illustrate, what is the point of writing—or reading—about crudeness and ugliness? They are not values in themselves, to be recorded and contemplated. The mere fact that something is real does not automatically make it a proper subject for literature. There is a difference between the job of a fiction writer and the job of a newspaper reporter.

You ask: "Will you tell me how to get started?" The first thing that a young writer must do is to give himself a very firm, very clear answer to three questions, which nobody can answer for him: "_Why_ do I want to be a writer? _What_ do I want to write about? _What_ do I want to say?" At eighteen, your answers to these questions will not be as full and specific as they will be at twenty-eight or forty-eight. Nevertheless, if you answer them as clearly as you can, in the context of your present knowledge, it will give you the right start and the means to expand your knowledge.

You say that you have tried to write about your own experiences. Experiences, as such, will not teach you anything. It is what you *think* about your experiences, what conclusions you draw from them, what estimates you place on them, that will be of value to you. A writer is not a dictaphone who records whatever an experience chooses to imprint upon him. A writer is a conscious being who does the choosing—and a conscious being has reasons for his choices.

You say: "But mostly, will you tell me if you believe in what I write? I need your help—I feel like Howard Roark going to Henry Cameron." Did Howard Roark go to Henry Cameron for *help*? Did he *need* Cameron's *belief* in his ability as an architect? I am sure that you did not intend to offend me, yet observe how offensive that statement of yours is to me. It shows that you have not understood Roark at all, that you have missed the essence of his character, that you did not give him enough thought to prevent you from writing to me, his author, a statement that represents the exact opposite of his principles. It is Peter Keating who needed Toohey's belief in his ability. Roark did not need anyone's belief. If you consider this, you will understand why, after a statement of that kind, your enthusiasm for *The Fountainhead* lost all meaning for me. Whatever it was that you were enthusiastic about, it was not what I had written.

I suggest that you read Richard Halley's statements in Chapter II, Part III of *Atlas Shrugged.** He is my spokesman. He speaks about music, but the same principles apply to all art and, most particularly, to literature.

If this helps you to understand the importance of thinking, it will be the best and only help I can give you. But nobody can control or direct another person's mind. It is up to you—and you alone.

■　■　■

---

* Richard Halley's statements are reprinted in *For the New Intellectual* under the heading "The Nature of an Artist."

To Gary Kline, a fan

September 14, 1959

Dear Mr. Kline:

Since you want to be a writer and, at sixteen, are able to express yourself as clearly, simply and rationally as you do, I must congratulate you and tell you that you have already acquired some of the most important premises needed by a writer. I am also impressed with the fact that you identified the right things to praise in my style of writing—and that you know how to think in terms of essentials.

If you maintain the mental attitude evidenced in your letter, you will go very far—and I am happy to wish you a great future.

■ ■ ■

To R. J. Sumners, of the Muskegon Manufacturers Association

November 17, 1959

Dear Mr. Sumners:

Thank you for your letter. It gives me great pleasure to accept your invitation to the luncheon on December 2nd. The nature of your attitude toward *Atlas Shrugged* is quite sufficient as an introduction and makes me want to meet you in person.

I mean not merely the fact that you liked *Atlas Shrugged*, which I do appreciate profoundly, but the fact that you approach it from the right intellectual aspect, judging by the copy of your letter to the members of your organization. I was glad to see that you stressed the issue of reason and rationality and that you selected the most forceful, uncompromising passages to quote in *moral* defense of businessmen. I am sure you realize that I regard businessmen as the greatest victims of the altruist code of morality and that I am eager to help provide them with intellectual ammunition in their fight against collectivism.

■ ■ ■

7

LETTERS TO A PHILOSOPHER

At the time of the following correspondence, John Hospers taught philosophy at Brooklyn College and at the University of California, Los Angeles. Much interested in Objectivism at that time, Hospers appeared on radio shows with Ayn Rand and devoted considerable attention to her ideas in his popular ethics textbook *Human Conduct*.

As a condition of reprinting the excerpts from his letters quoted by Ayn Rand, Professor Hospers has asked that the following statement by him be included. It is included without comment.

> The letters were interstices between oral conversations; they were written only when Ayn and I were at different geographical locations and could not meet in person. Almost all of the significant material in our communications with each other was in oral, not written, form. The letters may thus give a distorted view of the content of our conversations.
>
> You rightly have a great interest in reproducing everything that Ayn said; and you have no particular interest in whatever it was that I said, either to initiate a discussion or to respond to her. The result is that my thoughts just don't appear in these pages—not that you wanted them to, of course. But sometimes I thought that Ayn had not correctly apprehended a point I had made, and her summary of what I said sometimes did not reproduce what I really did say. Whether what I said was mistaken or not is beside the point here; I was often more interested in clarifying a point than in presenting it for acceptance. I am afraid the reader who read what Ayn wrote to me, and not what I wrote to her, would gather that I was a bloody fool. I daresay that in some ways I was, yet not so much as one would get the impression of from the letters. The trouble is, from her letters one gets *only one side of a dialogue*. And that isn't quite fair, is it?

April 17, 1960

Dear Professor Hospers:

Thank you for your very interesting letter and for the clippings you sent me [reporting on AR's talk "Faith and Force: Destroyers of the Modern World" at Brooklyn College].

I am enclosing the copies of my four radio broadcasts, which I promised to send you, and a pamphlet on the history of capitalism [*Notes on the History of American Free Enterprise* by AR], which I think will be of interest to you.

Let me start by saying that I was extremely pleased to meet you and to know that you are interested in discussions of this kind. I am glad that you are reading *Atlas Shrugged*. For my part, I am reading your *An Introduction to Philosophical Analysis*. I believe that this will give us both a firmer base for future discussions.

I was pleased that you heard my last radio broadcast, but I am puzzled by your comments on it. I assume, however, that part of the difficulty is the absence of a full context. So I will not attempt to give you a full answer by mail—I would much prefer to do that in person. For the time being, I will mention only a few points.

1. In objecting to my description of modern classrooms, you say that you have not yet seen the beatnik poets admired in any English course. Have you seen James Joyce being admired in English courses? What literary standards taught in what courses have permitted the modern literati to hail the beatniks as a serious and significant literary movement?

2. I did not caricature Kant. Nobody can do that. He did it himself.

3. You write: "sometimes they (the teachers) *seem* to be concerned with minor or trivial points, especially when they employ technical language, as they must do to make progress in their particular field of knowledge." You imply that this is what I would oppose. Far from it: I hold that no point is minor or trivial, in any field of knowledge—I hold that philosophers, above all, must be as meticulously precise as it is possible to be, and I am in favor of the most rigorous "hairsplitting," where necessary—I hold that philosophy should be more precise than the strictest legal document, because much more is at stake—and I am in favor of the most technical language, to achieve such precision. *But*: I hold that minor or trivial points cannot be studied ahead of their major or basic antecedents—I hold that precision in the discussion of consequences is worthless, if it starts in midstream and leaves in a state of undefined, unidentified fogginess those matters which are known to be the causes of such

consequences—and I hold that technical language is subject to the same rule as layman language, or slang, or anything that is to be defined as language, namely: that it must refer to reality and must denote something specific; if it does not, it is not language, but inarticulate sounds. (If, at this point, you are tempted to reply that "reality" is a "slippery" term, I will say that *this* is an instance of what I mean by the necessity of beginning any discussion by discussing fundamentals.)

4. This is the point (page 2 of your letter) which puzzles me most. You object to my classification of logical positivists as "witch doctors"— and, instead of arguments, you resort to the method of calling me an ' 'outsider" and implying my total philosophical ignorance. I assume that you did not intend to be insulting or offensive—and the reason for my assumption is the total context of my personal impression of you, of your letter and of your professional reputation. So I am acting on that assumption—and if I am wrong in assuming it, please correct me.

When I characterize or summarize any theory, I expect to be able to demonstrate the validity of my estimate to anyone in the field who cares to challenge it. Or, in colloquial terms: when I talk, I know what I'm talking about. Have I given you grounds to accuse me of ignorance or of rash judgments? If so, please name these grounds. The fact that I reach conclusions opposite to the generally accepted trend, is not one of them.

If you do not agree with me, please grill me on logical positivism— and if you prove me to be wrong, I will be glad to correct my views. But such proof will require agreement on the fundamentals of epistemology and on those very "criteria of verification" which, you claim, the logical positivists are studying and which, I claim, they are destroying.

If you care to discuss it, we would have to start with a discussion of Kant—since logical positivism is his epistemological descendant. I am sure you gathered from my speech at Brooklyn College that it is Kant that I am challenging, at his very root and base. I do not believe that modern philosophy can be discussed without reaching an understanding on Kant. Modern philosophy may and does depart from him on many issues, but it is his epistemological premises that have been accepted without challenge or proof. If you want to understand my philosophical position in a historical context, this is just a brief clue.

5. Now I come to the point which is the most important one for our mutual understanding. You recommend that I read *Ethical Theory* by Richard Brandt and your own forthcoming book *Human Conduct*. I will be very interested to read *your* book, in order to gain an understanding of your ideas. But what did you have in mind when you recommended the book

by Mr. Brandt? You state that it "examines thoroughly virtually every theory of ethics ever propounded, together with detailed evaluations thereof." I am sure that you understood me to say in my speech at Brooklyn College and in our discussion afterwards that I have defined a new theory of ethics, which is opposed to every existing one. Are you, therefore, implying that I made such a statement without any knowledge of past ethical theories? If so, what gave you grounds for it?

6. I trust that you did not conclude that "egoism" is the sum total of my ethical theory. I suppose that you probably know by now that it represents a much more radical departure from any historically accepted approach to morality. I mention this only because of the following passage on page 3 of your letter:

> In philosophy, an ethical egoist is one who says: "I am the only person who counts. I should pursue MY OWN interests exclusively. If I could save a thousand starving people by lifting my little finger, I should not take the trouble, provided that their welfare does not affect mine." I am sure you are committed to no such thing: if you were, there would be no point in your caring about the fate of Western civilization, or coming to Brooklyn College without a fee to address us. Thus, I conclude that your ethics belongs not under the general category of "egoism" (except sometimes as to means) but is universalistic—it is concerned with *all* human beings, but is distinguished from "altruism" if altruism means considering others exclusively at the expense of oneself.

In *whose* philosophy? I assume you mean that this is a classification widely accepted in philosophy today. Well, I don't accept it, because this sort of classification is what I would describe as *superficial*. My reasons are as follows:

a) This classification assumes *hedonism* as its basic premise, that is: happiness as the standard of the good—then divides ethical theories according to the recipients of the happiness: oneself, others or all. But hedonism is not a valid ethical premise; "happiness" is not an irreducible primary; it is the result, effect and consequence of a complex chain of causes. To say: "The good is that which will make me happy or that which will serve my interests," does not indicate *what* will make me happy or *what* will serve my interests. Hedonism, of course, assumes that the standard is emotional, subjective and arbitrary: anything that makes you *feel* happy is the good. But a *feeling* is not a standard of anything.

b) This classification assumes a clash of interests among men as a basic primary, without defining what *is* to anyone's interest, and yet—

c) it simultaneously presumes to dictate the specific *content* of one's self-interest, by decreeing that if I were to take the trouble to save others by lifting my little finger, I would thereby place myself outside the category of "egoism" and into the category of "universalism." By what standard?

Observe the illustrations you offer: if by caring about the fate of Western Civilization or by coming to speak at Brooklyn College without fee, I am no longer pursuing my own interests exclusively—what would my own exclusive interests consist of? Living in the Dark Ages? Surrendering the society I live in to irrationality and communism?

Now, as to your remarks about capitalism:

1. You say that you speak on politics from general observation and not as a philosopher. This is a point of difference between us: I never think or speak of anything except as a philosopher.

2. By now, you probably know the exact nature and reasons of my views on capitalism. So I will not attempt to argue with the allegations capitalists are vicious, exploiting, and warmongering that you make against it—I will say only that I do not agree with you.

3. I would like to ask you a question, which no critic of capitalism has ever answered: if capitalists are as evil as you say they are, what magic faculty endows a politician with virtue? If men who deal with others by means of voluntary trade are selfish monsters—how does the possession of a gun, with the right to *force* others, transform a man into a selfless public servant?

4. I will not state this point as an arbitrary assertion, but only as a question: doesn't your attitude toward capitalism support the thesis of my last radio broadcast? If you who, to my knowledge, are one of the most rational minds in modern philosophy, do not choose to identify the nature and the actual working of capitalism, but reject it, offering no argument or theory except: "greed"— isn't that an illustration of the fact that the morality of altruism has made it impossible for philosophers to evaluate capitalism? I do not want to be right, in *this* particular instance—and I hope that you will correct me.

As I said at the start, I would like to continue this discussion in person. May I invite you to my house on the evening of Friday, April 22 or Saturday, April 23? Would you telephone me and let me know whether either date is convenient for you?

Until then, please accept the length of this letter as the best proof I can offer you of my serious interest.

■   ■   ■

August 29, 1960

Dear John:

Thank you for your letter of August 12 and for the two postcards you sent me from the road. I was happy to hear from you and to know that your hometown has not swallowed you altogether. To tell you the truth, I miss you very much and I am looking forward to continuing our philosophical discussions by mail, in spite of my difficulty with letter writing.

I read your paper on "Art and Emotion" with great interest. It is always a pleasure to read the clarity and precision of the manner in which you analyze specific issues—the orderly rationality of the way your mind works, or of what I call your "psychological epistemology." I will not attempt to evaluate your theory of art on so brief a presentation. Am I correct in gathering that you suggest that a clue to the emotional meaning of art may be found in a parallel between the physical form of an art work and man's physical states? If so, then man's mental process in responding to an artwork would be purely perceptual and associational, rather than conceptual and logical. (The equation of horizontal lines with security, in the example you give, is associational.) If this is true, then how would your theory apply to literature?

I will not attempt to argue against your theory, since I am not sure that I understand it correctly. When you have time, please read my third radio talk ("The Esthetic Vacuum of Our Age"). It presents (also much too briefly) the essence of my theory of art, and will serve as my answer, if we disagree.

In any case, your theory is more sensible in its approach than the kind of mystic nonsense people proclaim nowadays. And I hope that by the time you receive this letter, you will have delivered your speech with great success.

Now to the issue of your book on ethics. Does your contract give your publishers the right to omit any section with which they don't agree? Or does the problem lie in the fact that they may not do their best for your book, if you don't reach an agreement with them? (If I remember correctly, you told me it was this last.) In either case, the issue is too serious to settle hastily, and they cannot demand that you work on revisions while travelling. Unless some crucial deadline is involved, I would suggest that you delay the publication date until you have had time to return to Los Angeles and to do any revisions you might decide on, under proper working conditions. Surely your publishers will not object to such a delay, since it is they who changed their mind after approving the manuscript.

As to the revisions you are considering, do your publishers want you to *compromise*, or merely to include some "good pro-religious arguments"? It is not the same thing. In fact, it is always advisable to present the best, not the worst, arguments of one's opponent, in order to blast him thoroughly: it is more convincing to annihilate his intercontinental missiles rather than merely to destroy his old pocket pistols. But which do your publishers actually want: a strong case for both sides with the "best man" winning—or an indecisive, inconclusive case, with neither side winning? This last would be a *compromise* and it would amount to an argument *slanted in favor of religion*, because it would imply that nobody can refute the religionists' case. Surely you wouldn't and couldn't want to do *that*?

A *"compromise"* does not mean a "fair presentation of both sides." When one side is right and the other is wrong, a compromise necessarily means the distortion and suppression of the evidence, in favor of the side that is wrong. Any compromise between truth and falsehood can be only falsehood—as you yourself demonstrated brilliantly in the example you cited: if one tries to "compromise" on "2 plus 2 is 4," it does not really matter whether one agrees to make it 4.5 or 5 or 10—if it is not *4*, then truth and reason have lost, falsehood and irrationality have won.

You say that you consider rewriting that section in the form of a dialogue, "giving the better of the argument to one side." You may be able to do it, but I want to warn you about the basic danger involved: if your publishers want a compromise, that is, *an inconclusive case*, they will see through your "slanting" and they will object; if you make the slanting so subtle and mild that they accept it, it will be of no value to the students whom you want to enlighten; in fact, it will harm them. A weak case is worse than no case at all; a half-truth is worse than a lie: it sanctions the lie.

Since I have not read your book as a whole, I cannot express a firm opinion on what you should do, but can only offer a tentative suggestion. As far as I can judge, I see two possible courses of action:

(1) Present the best, strongest, most authentic arguments tying morality to religion that you can find, in the words of their actual advocates (from Augustine on up)—and then, as answer and antidote, include in your book a presentation of *my* ethics. This would allow you to maintain the position of an impartial, critical observer and let *me* be the antagonist of religious doctrines, which I am known to be anyway. (Yes, of course, this would be to my own personal interest—but, as I've said in *Atlas Shrugged*, the personal interests of men do *not* clash, when men pursue rational goals. I am not suggesting this because of *my* interest, but because I do not know of

any other ethical theory or any other arguments that can defeat religious ethics fully and totally.) I know that you would need time to consider my ethics further, as you said, but your publishers ought to grant you that time. As for me, I would be delighted to help you with the presentation of my theory (the evaluation, of course, has to be your own).

If that would be too lengthy a job of rewriting, then my alternative suggestion is:

(2) Omit that entire section. It would be regrettable, but silence is always preferable to compromise. Silence, in these circumstances, is not a betrayal of one's convictions; a compromise is.

The difficulty in your case seems to be the attempt to deal with so explosive and controversial a subject as criticism of religion, in the form of a side issue in a book devoted to the wider theme of ethical history. Controversial subjects can be difficult or dangerous only when treated indirectly and incompletely. It would be much easier and safer to write a whole book openly criticizing religious ethics, presenting a complete case; publishers would be less afraid of it. Therefore, if you do not find a way to present a case for your actual viewpoint in your current book, I would rather see you omit the entire issue than see you compromise or fight a martyr's battle. I am opposed to martyrdom as well as to compromise: neither is ever necessary. Integrity does not require martyrdom; but it does forbid compromise.

In conclusion, let me mention how much I like you for saying that you "do not want to pull a Dr. Stadler on this issue."

Speaking of *Atlas Shrugged*, I was amused (benevolently) to hear that you chose Ouray as your favorite spot in Colorado. That is the little town I had picked for Galt's Gulch. To be exact, I marked it on a map as the right location, long before I saw it. Then, when I went to Colorado for research purposes and discovered Ouray, I fell in love with it. It is the most beautifully dramatic spot in the whole state, and it's even surrounded by a ring of mountains (though Galt's Valley would be somewhat larger).

I will be glad to answer any questions you may have about my philosophy. And I was delighted to hear that you found my philosophy helpful during your visit with your family.

Frank asks me to thank you for your comments on his painting (the cityscape), on your last visit here, which I told him. The perceptiveness and sensitivity of your reaction impressed and pleased him very much—so I thank you doubly, for both of us.

I am sending my three novels (the hard-cover editions) to your California address, and also a copy of the magazine *Vital Speeches of the Day* which contains the speech I delivered at Brooklyn College. I hope they reach you by the time you come back. I don't expect you to read my "complete works" all at once, so take your time. I will, of course, be very interested to hear your reaction when and as you read them.

I hope that you have enjoyed your whole trip. If you encounter any remnant of Aristotle's ghost in Athens, please give him my love.

■   ■   ■

November 27, 1960

Dear John:

Thank you for your letters and for the reports on Nathan's lectures [on the "Basic Principles of Objectivism"]. Both Nathan and I are very much interested indeed in hearing your reactions to the lectures. Please do continue sending them, if your time permits it. I deeply appreciate your interest. Whether we agree on specific points or not, your analysis is very valuable in helping to establish a fuller understanding between us.

To answer first your letter of November 2: you object to our statement (in the lecture brochure) that "Philosophy has been reduced to a linguistic game divorced from any application to practical reality." No, we did not mean only the "linguistic analysis" school of philosophy. We meant *all* the leading schools of today. There may always be individual exceptions in any majority trend—but, today, they are not heard from forcefully enough to counteract the trend. I shall be glad to discuss this with you in detail when you return to New York, with specific philosophical texts for evidence, as you suggest. For the moment, let me mention only two general points.

A. The dominant doctrine of today's philosophy is *epistemological agnosticism.* In application to practical reality, this doctrine is either futile or disastrously destructive, that is: either a man has to ignore it altogether and struggle as best he can, without any philosophical guidance—or, if he accepts it, he has to stop dead, paralyzed by uncertainty, and be taken over by the first thug or dictator who chooses to make loud, arbitrary assertions, while he, the victim, can refute nothing and answer nothing, possessing no intellectual weapons but the lethal: "Who am I to know? How can I be certain of anything?" Man *has to* act in reality, *he has* to have knowledge in order to act—and whenever philosophy collapses into epistemological agnosticism, it is defaulting on and betraying its primary function.

B. Observe that today's philosophical journals are devoted almost exclusively to out-of-context discussions of epistemological minutiae, and that the subject of *politics* has all but disappeared from their pages. And this in an age when politics is the crucial issue, when about one-third of the world's population has been enslaved by the bloodiest political system in history, which is advancing to take over the rest of the globe. Politics has always been and, logically, has to be a branch of philosophy. Where are the voices of philosophers at a time when they are needed most?

You say that you know modern philosophers personally and that "Each and every one of them that I know of is vitally interested in problems of practical reality." If I understand you correctly, you mean that they are interested *as men*, as individual citizens. This may be true, but what I am talking about is their work *as philosophers*, their *professional* and public —not their personal and private—interest.

In regard to Ziff's paper on God: it represents, in a condensed form, everything that is wrong with modern philosophy. I agree *enthusiastically* with your argument on why the idea of God as "self-caused" is self-contradictory. I hope you remember that passage of your letter: it is brilliant. What I found most important in your argument is not merely the specific content, but the *method*, the epistemological approach, best exemplified by your sentence: "the notion of cause is applicable only in a temporal context, and only in that context has the term been defined; it is unmeaning apart from this context." Now *this*, in essence, represents *my* epistemology or, to be exact, my method of dealing with concepts. It is the method I consider proper to a philosopher. (As a small aside: I would subscribe to everything in the above sentence, except the word "notion"; I take it that you meant "concept." But this is not directly relevant to the point I am now discussing.)

The epistemological method you used in that entire passage illustrates what you and I have in common philosophically and why I find great pleasure in talking to you. But I have two questions to ask you. A. I observe that you do not use this method exclusively, as your constant approach to all thinking and all problems. Don't you think that it should be one's constant and exclusive method? B. Do you think that the main tenets of modern philosophy could withstand the test, if you examined them by this epistemological method, with the same rigorous precision, with the same observance of the full context, the genetic roots and the exact definition of every concept involved?

Let me anticipate an objection which, I think, you might make. You might tell me: "But that method *is* the one advocated by linguistic analysis." And I would answer you: I believe that this method is *your* version of linguistic analysis, but it is not the version of Professor Lean, nor of Ziff, nor of that philosophical school as a whole. I would say that this method rests on basic premises antithetical to *their* basic premises, as I understand them. But a full demonstration of this will have to wait until our future detailed discussion.

Now to the question of Freud. You say: "I do not see that the psychological theory of Freud is involved one way or the other in the subjects we have discussed together." I would say: since the subjects we have discussed are philosophical, a discussion of them must necessarily precede any discussion of any particular science, such as psychology. I assume that you will agree that philosophy is the basic science which provides the frame of reference and the epistemological criteria by means of which one then approaches the task of judging or evaluating the theories of individual thinkers in particular sciences. Without a commonly understood philosophical base, any discussion of particular sciences would be futile, because we would have no means to understand each other. It is in this sense that I agree with you that the subject of Freud did not have to be raised in our discussions at this time—and I regret that Professor Lean raised it. The psychological theory of Freud is not involved in a discussion of philosophy; but philosophy *has to* be involved in any discussion of the psychological theories of Freud.

Since you discuss Freud in your comments on Nathan's lectures, he will answer you in detail on this subject; you may take it as my answer, too, since he and I are in complete agreement on it. For my part, I will answer only the particular or personal points of your letter.

You write a brief summary of what you consider to be the essence of Freud's theory (with which summary I do not agree), and then you write: "I really cannot see WHY you were so concerned to deny all this; surely it makes no difference to your theory one way or the other." My answer is: I am concerned to deny *any* theory which I regard as *false*. As to the second part of your sentence, surely, as a philosopher, you understand the difference between *my* theory of how a human consciousness acquires knowledge and draws conclusions about the facts confronting it—and any theory which asserts that at a certain stage of development every human consciousness *has to* (is predestined by nature) draw certain specific conclusions.

You write: "As long as we accept the statement that there ARE causes for human behavior, why need one be so alarmed that Freud has discovered what some of these causes are?" John, *who* is the "one" in this sentence, you or I? By the context, I assume that you were referring to me, and, therefore, I will say that you are here guilty of psychological "projection" (to use a Freudian term): I was not *"alarmed"* by this discussion; *you* were. I did not jump to my feet and shout insults instead of arguments; *you* did.

I disregarded it, because I did not want to let Professor Lean cause any trouble, confusion or unnecessary difficulties in our relationship—particularly when it was our last evening together and you were going away for almost a year. To be fully frank, he had caused trouble already: by arriving three hours earlier than expected and by deflecting the conversation away from the subjects which *you* and I wanted to discuss. You may take this as a compliment to you (I intend it as such): I resented his early arrival then, and still do now. It was he, not I, who brought up the subject of Freud, which I do not regard as of primary importance.

I had promised you not to be offended by any inadvertent occurrence, so I did not consider myself offended by you that evening, and I do not consider myself offended by that line in your letter: I consider both as issues to be clarified between us. Let me request the following: you know me well enough by now to know that I do not enter any discussion lightly, that I do not discuss subjects of which I am ignorant, that I have reasons for any judgment I form, and that my judgments will seldom coincide with the generally accepted ones; therefore, in the future, please do not resort to assertions about my ignorance in place of an answer to my arguments, if we happen to disagree. An assertion of that kind is merely offensive and cannot prove your point to anyone, least of all to me.

Now to come back to Freud. Apart from those personal elements, I take issue with your sentence on purely epistemological grounds: "As long as we accept the statement that there ARE causes for human behavior, why need one be so alarmed that Freud has discovered what some of these causes are?" If I accept the statement that there are causes for physical phenomena, need I or need I not object if someone claimed that the cause of measles is God's retribution for man's Original Sin, or that the cause of a volcano's eruption is the anger of a subterranean demon, or that the cause of a solar eclipse is the sun's frustrated emotion of love for the planet Venus? Freud did not discover any actual *causes* of human behavior (if by "causes" we mean basic motives, *not* psychological mechanics); the epistemological methods by which he allegedly "proved" his theory were so fantastic, so crudely irrational that they have been denounced in print repeatedly by philosophers and scientists.

That Freud observed and/or discovered many facts about the operation or the *mechanics* of a human consciousness, such as repression or conversion or other neurotic devices which a human consciousness has the capacity to employ, is a different issue; these are not *causes*, but functional potentialities. If I were the first scientist who discovered some of the things that man can do with his vocal chords, this would be valuable, but it would not entitle me to declare what songs all men would sing at a certain time nor why they would want to sing them. And if I made such a declaration, its validity would have to be judged by the proofs I offered, *not* by my achievements in the science of the physiology of vocal chords. If Freud discovered that men have the capacity to practice repression, this does not entitle him to declare that what they repress is the desire to sleep with their mothers or fathers.

As to the issue of determinism, the fact that human behavior does have causes is not sufficient to equate my view of it with Freud's; the crucial issue here is: is the *ultimate* cause of man's behavior within *his* control—or is he ultimately moved and motivated by forces outside his control? Or: is man free to draw his own conclusions about reality by the work of his mind—or is he predestined, *predetermined* to form certain conclusions at certain times, with no power of choice on his part? (I trust that you do not confuse *my* theory of free will with the traditional theory of the mystics who equate the "free" with the causeless or the insane, in the sense of a spontaneously generated whim.)

You say: "I am absolutely certain that there is a very great deal of truth in what Freud says." Are we talking about Freud, the theoretician, or Freud, the clinical observer? I would agree with you (in part) on the second, but not on the first.

You say: "I don't see how anything that Freud says conflicts with anything that you want to defend." John, I cannot believe that you mean it. If I took that sentence literally, I could not take it seriously. "Anything that Freud says?" Freud, the theoretician? Freud's view of man—and mine?

I agree with you that we should not discuss Freud at present. Please suspend this issue until we are ready for it—but suspend it as a disagreement to be resolved later. Please do not equate my views with those of my opposites.

Now, to another subject. No, I did not see the ad of "businessmen for Kennedy," which you mention. You are right when you say that "It's true that money has to be spent over a long period in order to get more money in the end, but that this does not constitute any reason why the *government* should do it." I would like to offer further objections to their argument as you present it in your letter: not *every* long-term investment of money is necessarily and automatically profitable or self-liquidating; that depends on the investor's economic judgment; bad judgment leads to a total loss, to bankruptcy or "money poured down the drain." When, however, the investor is the government, then the results are *necessarily* disastrous for the economy, for the following reasons:

A. There is no way, standard or criterion by which to judge the economic value and future of an investment, outside of the free-market mechanism of supply and demand (see Ludwig von Mises for the details of why *economic calculation* is impossible to a socialistic government). B. Assume in some specific case that the government has invested money in some long-term project which may actually have future economic value; the fact that it was a forced, premature investment which was not yet economically justified (that is: not yet profitable for private investors), which the economy could not yet afford, has disastrous repercussions on the whole economy and causes unpredictable, incalculably harmful consequences. The best example of that is the government-subsidized construction of the so-called first transcontinental railroad in the United States (the Union Pacific and the Central Pacific). A railroad, as such, is an economic value; but the premature construction of a railroad which private capital could not yet find profitable caused economic evils (the plight of the farmers, the Granger movement, etc.) which are still multiplying to this day.

To illustrate my point in a simple manner: suppose that you are an industrialist and that you want to market an invention which will bring you a fortune in ten years; if your calculations are sound, that would be a good investment, and you would be justified in saving your money for it and in living modestly for ten years. But suppose you decide to market an invention which will bring you a fortune in a hundred years and for which the savings of your lifetime are not sufficient. Would that be a good investment? Would you become prosperous by spending your life on the level of semi-starvation and by draining the resources of all those who may lend you money? Would that be wise or economically sound? By what standard could you be certain—even if your entire generation died in misery, pouring all resources into your project—that the invention would still be needed or valuable to your children or grandchildren who, by that time, would be perishing for lack of shoes, clothes and adequate shelter?

These are merely the economic or "practical" consequences of government "investment." The moral meaning and consequences are obvious: by what right does the government take the money of some individuals for the future benefit of other individuals? By what right does it *force* privations on an individual, against his own choice and judgment, for the future benefit of himself or others, actual or hypothetical? That which is *in fact* beneficial to an economy (that is: to the individuals who comprise an economy) is done by men voluntarily (as the history of capitalism demonstrates); that which cannot be *proved* to be beneficial does not become so at the point of a gun.

I believe this covers the questions in your letter of November 2. Now let me tell you some of the local news. By way of explanation and apology for my delayed answer, I will mention that your letter reached me at the same time as the galleys of my new book [*For the New Intellectual*] on which I had to work under a deadline. After that, I had to prepare and make two speeches within one week: one speech at Yale, the other at Hunter College. I enjoyed both occasions, but they involved a period of terrible rush and pressure.

In the meantime, I received a letter from Professor Lean, and my first chance to hold the discussion I had promised him was last Wednesday (November 23). The guests present were Professor Lean, his friend Miss Lutzky, Nathan and Leonard [Peikoff]. It was a very disappointing evening. We talked from about 8:30 p.m. to 4 a.m.—and I cannot actually say *what* we talked about. The conversation kept skipping all over the place, ranging from such subjects as Freud and the "analytic-synthetic" issue to Professor Lean challenging me to define the word "*which*." (No, this is not a "parody.") You know what happened to the conversation last time. The same happened this time—only more so.

As a more cheerful note: Your name was mentioned constantly during the evening, in the context of what you would or would not agree with, by both sides in the discussion (that is, Professor Lean as one side, Nathan, Leonard and I as the other). We even brought out your book and read passages aloud. So, at one point, Professor Lean said the following, indicating all of us Objectivists: "John Hospers, who seems to be beloved around here, would agree that . . ." I do not recall what his specific point was; but I remember this preface verbatim. I am repeating it to you in the spirit of a friendly "I-told-you-so," if you still think that Nathan or Leonard were ever antagonistic to you.

This letter is so long now that I will send it to you in order not to delay my answer further. I will take up your comments on Nathan's lectures in a separate letter, which will follow soon.

I hope that you will be able to hear all the lectures, but if your time does not permit it, I would particularly like you to hear Lectures 7 and 8, which deal with psychological subjects, namely Self-esteem and "Social Metaphysics." If you remember, we discussed these subjects briefly last spring, but the lectures give a much better and fuller presentation than I could give in a brief discussion. Needless to say, I would be very interested to hear your comments.

Thank you for the copy of *The Meaning of Life* by Baier. I have not read it yet, but will write to you when I finish it.

■   ■   ■

January 3, 1961

Dear John:

I shall now answer your letter of November 12, and your comments on Nathan's lectures 1, 2 and 3. I shall take them in order.

Lecture 1.

I was very happy to hear that you liked this lecture and that you agreed with most of it. As to the points which you criticize:

1. *"Injustice" to Plato.* Nathan classified the antireason trend of the nineteenth century as Platonism, after he had defined the specific sense in which "every man and every philosopher is either a Platonist or an Aristotelian," (this observation is not ours, but we agree with it). That classification is based on the fundamental metaphysical-epistemological conflict among philosophers. It is not an "oversimplification"—it is a wide abstraction. If one were to say that Marx is the direct consequence of Plato, *that* would be an oversimplification; but to say that Marx, Hegel, Kant and others belong to the philosophical camp whose earliest and most famous exponent was Plato, is an abstract summation in a context that deals *only* with the fundamentals they all have in common.

I disagree with your statement that Plato's views come close to the truth "after the metaphorical and allegorical elements are taken out." The same statement can be applied to any religion; most religions can be interpreted as containing a great deal of truth, if one decides to treat their doctrines as metaphors and allegories; but this would be a *translation* or an *interpretation*, and one could not equate it with the original doctrines. Would you treat Plato's world of Forms as a metaphor? Would you regard his epistemology (with abstractions as innate memories, with the ultimate mystic illumination that surpasses reason) as an allegory? If you did, what would be left of Plato, except broad generalities that would apply to *any* philosopher?

I do not know what you mean when you say that Plato is "the arch-objectivist among all philosophers." Don't you think that you should *stipulate* the definition you give to the word "objectivist," since you use it in some sense other than the one we have been using?

I do not understand the meaning or relevance of such an attribute as "a philosophically pregnant philosopher," which you explain as "has the germ of more fruitful ideas." I would assume that the criterion of what is "fruitful" in philosophy is: truth. But that does not seem to apply. You say that Plato is "more philosophically pregnant" than Aristotle. Does this mean the following: since Aristotle gave birth to a great many truths, which require no further seeking, he is no longer pregnant—while Plato is still bulging with falsehoods, therefore he left something for us to discover and give birth to? If this is not what the attribute means, what *does* it mean?

(Oh sure, I know damn well what it means in the language and context of modern philosophy, but I don't speak that language and I don't want to be accused of misinterpreting the modern truth seekers—so you tell me.)

2. The slogan "It will work if you *want* it to work" was used in a metaphysical, not a psychological, context. That slogan does not say: "*You* will make things work if *you* take the appropriate actions." It says: "*Things* will work as your desire commands *them* to work, regardless of their actual nature." That slogan means (*literally*, and in most frequent usage) that one's desire can affect the metaphysical nature of facts and of inanimate objects, as, for instance: "A perpetual motion machine will work if you *want* it to work." The example you cite is inexact: it is not an instance to which that slogan is applicable. If two sides in a battle are about equal materially, it is true that victory is likely to go to the side that *wants* to win the most; but it is not the *desire* as such that will win, it is the fact that the desire will inspire the men to a better performance, to countless *actions* which will lead to victory. Even in psychological terms, a desire can be only an incentive to acquire the knowledge and to perform the actions necessary to achieve the desired. There are many people who desire, wish or long to be a movie star, but do not take any actions and never become one. Whether a man actually desires to achieve a certain goal or not, the fact remains that it is not his emotional state, not his desire as such, that can achieve that goal.

3. The example of the geologist and the stone.* You say: "I don't call that subjectivism at all, but just plain cheating." Yes, of course, it is cheating. But *cheating* is not an irreducible primary; the question here is: what kind of metaphysical premise (held explicitly or *implicitly*) would allow a man to cheat in this manner? In order to hope to get away with it and continue enjoying the role of a scientist, that geologist had to forget the

---

* The example: a dishonest geologist moves the only stone that would invalidate his pet theory were the stone found in its original position.

absolutism of reality, at least for that moment and in that issue, and had to believe that reality could be altered by his wish or his evasion, that a fact would cease to exist if he refused to perceive it.

You say: "Who are these subjectivists, anyway? Many people are subjectivists about values, but I don't know any philosopher who is a subjectivist about physical reality." I would maintain that most philosophers *are* subjectivists (though they disclaim that title) and I will be glad to give you my reasons in detail, when we discuss it in person. For the present, I will answer only your specific point about "value subjectivists." Are values *unrelated to physical reality*? Do values belong to some separate realm, some other "dimension," of existence? Should man choose and pursue his values without any consideration of physical reality, that is: *apart from* or *against* his knowledge of physical reality? Is ethics independent of metaphysics, that is: should man form a conclusion on what he evaluates as good or evil, and act on the basis of this conclusion, *regardless* of the nature of the universe in which he lives and acts?

Since no values can be pursued or achieved (or even conceived of) except in terms of and in relation to physical reality, since man exists *in* physical reality and cannot step outside of it, any man or philosopher who chooses to be a "subjectivist about *values*" simply means that he proposes to act *against* the objective facts of reality (he proposes to choose *goals* which contradict his knowledge of reality, and to achieve them by means which contradict his knowledge of reality). And since no man would hold such an intention in full, literal, conscious terms, the only way to be a subjectivist about values is to evade knowledge of reality (when convenient) and to believe that reality is not a firm, *objective* absolute, but an indeterminate flux amenable to one's subjective *wishes*. (And the only way to believe *that*, is to assert that one's consciousness is not valid and that one can never be certain of what the facts of reality *are*.)

You say: "Even Bishop Berkeley, the arch-subjectivist of all time, agreed that there REALLY IS a table here; he just gave a different (and incorrect) analysis of what it MEANS to say that there is." I will answer: A. If the meaning of what Bishop Berkeley said constitutes agreement that there *really is* a table here, and he is thus to be regarded as an advocate of objectivity—then a new word with a new definition has to be stipulated for the meaning of what Aristotle said and of what I say. B. By what means would Bishop Berkeley (or anyone else) give an analysis (correct or incorrect) of "what it means to say that there *is*"? To "*analyze*" means: to resolve a complex into its constituent parts. Into *what* does one resolve the concept of "*existence*"? By what means does one *analyze* a primary—and what is the status of the propositions one uses while one is in the process of analyzing the concept *"is"*? (Do you remember the logical fallacy which I call "the fallacy of the stolen concept"? You agreed with me, when we discussed it.)

4. You ask: "Now why this diatribe against logical positivism as a new form of mysticism?"—and then you list three points which you regard as the main contentions of this group. 1. Logical positivists, to my knowledge, would never accept such a proposition as "There is an objective reality"; neither would they commit themselves to saying that there isn't; they get out of it by classifying the proposition as *"meaningless"* (along with all issues of ontology). 2. Logical positivists reject the concept of "mind" in the sense you (or I) use it. (Neurath [Otto Neurath, a member of the Vienna Circle of Logical Positivists] suggested that the word "mind" should be placed on an "index of prohibited words," along with such words as "entity, essence, matter, reality, thing.") 3. It is in their concept of what constitutes "verifiability," in their basic premise and approach (which is implicit in their specific, individual theories) that logical positivists become most mystical. You say: "One must be careful not to condemn it (the Verifiability Principle), en masse in all its forms"—because there have been many different formulations of it. Your statement implies that the Verifiability Principle is sound in essence, qua *principle*, and that it is only with its various formulations that one can legitimately quarrel. But what I challenge, oppose and condemn is the *essence* of that principle and of the method it proposes, in all and any of its variations. (I do not believe that "propositions" have to be "verified"; I believe that they have to be *"validated"*—it is a night-and-day difference.)

You say: "So when I hear people condemn 'logical positivism' as if it were ONE doctrine, without separating out SPECIFICALLY the various views that may fall under this head, I just sigh and conclude that they don't know what they're talking about."

John, isn't it time to drop this sort of remark, if you do not intend to be offensive? I do not wish to have to remind you of it in every letter. *Please stop asserting our ignorance of any subject on which you happen to disagree with us.* I do not care to argue in such terms nor by such means nor on such level.

To answer your remark on a *philosophical* level, I will say that there are over three hundred sects of Christianity, all of which interpret the Bible differently and all of which claim to be the only *true* version of Christianity. Since I reject the basic premises of the Bible and of Christianity as untenable, I do not consider it incumbent upon me to discuss or refute (or even to study) the particular interpretation of every one of the three-hundred-some sects. And if I were to discuss the issue with a philosophically-minded Christian, it is the *basic* premises that I would discuss.

Lecture 2.

First of all, I am glad that you agree with us on many points. It is inevitable, I suppose, that you and I should spend more time discussing disagreements than following up agreements, at least at this early stage.

On sensing colors. You say: "I would distinguish between the DIRECT report of the senses and CONSTRUCTS based on the senses." I would not accept such a term as "constructs" in this context. Our knowledge of ultraviolet and of radioactivity is *"conceptual,"* not "constructural." Would you call our knowledge of the existence of *air* a "construct"? It is certainly not a direct sense-experience; primitive people had no such knowledge. *DO YOU ACTUALLY USE THE WORD "CONSTRUCT" AS A SYN-ONYM OF "CONCEPT"?* If not, would you tell me *your* definition of the difference between them?

Perceiving incorrectly vs. perceiving inadequately. You cite the example of hallucinations as "perceiving incorrectly." But hallucinations are not *perceptions* at all; they are caused, not by an action of the senses, but by a malfunction of the brain.

If, as some theorists claim, man's emotions come from a separate faculty of his consciousness, which is independent of reason, against which reason, by innate necessity, is powerless at times—then man's life has to be *exactly* as it is presented in that example; then man's emotional faculty works by throwing fits of "emotional epilepsy" once in a while, and man lives in a state of temporary sanity alternating with periods of insanity at unpredictable moments. *Either* man's emotions are the *effects* of his cognitive faculty *or* they are not. There is no middle ground. Whether man can or cannot control his emotions is a different question, which can't be answered until one has answered the first question: what is the source or *cause* of emotions?

You say: "I can agree with everything you say about reason and YET insist on the very real and profound insights into human psychology that were made by Freud. Freud exposed better than anyone else the conscious *and unconscious* tactics of rationalization, repression, evasion that the human psyche is capable of." You know, of course, that here you change the subject under discussion. The "conscious *and unconscious* tactics of rationalization, repression, evasion" are issues that pertain to the mechanics, to the actions of a human psyche. The existence of such actions does not tell us their source or cause. *What* determines *which* "tactics" a human consciousness will use? Is it the innate mechanism, by and of itself? Is it man's "emotional faculty" as such? Is it man's cognitive faculty, that is: his mind? Which actions of a human psyche are causes and which are effects?

It is not the existence of such actions that was discussed in the lecture, but the source of emotions. Therefore, if Freud is here relevant at all, it is Freud's theory of the source of emotions that has to be compared to ours. Well, Freud's theory holds that man has certain "innate emotions" ("strivings")—or that man's psychological mechanism *has to* (is predetermined by nature to) generate certain emotions in response to certain existential situations, such as an Oedipus-complex response toward his parents, at a certain age. Since emotions represent value-judgments, innate or innately predetermined emotions mean: *innate* or *innately predetermined value judgments*. Now compare Freud's theory with ours.

You say: "One may conceive of the development of the human being as a kind of RISE TOWARD RATIONALITY. But in this upward struggle there are many things pulling him down—*especially* these very evasions and repressions and complexes that Freud exposed in such detail. Isn't the proper thing to do to RECOGNIZE these things, so that thereby one may conquer them? Surely this is better than inveighing against Freud, thereby pretending that these mechanisms don't exist in human nature."

What are the "things pulling him down"? Are these "things" innate? Are the "evasions and repressions and complexes" innate? Is man's consciousness predetermined to start evading, repressing and acquiring complexes *before* it rises toward rationality? If so, what form of cognition does it employ on this pre-rational level? Or are all these "things" created apart from any cognitive process? And how does one "conquer" them without knowing their relationship to whatever faculty is going to do the conquering?

Now I will ask you to look at the last two sentences of the above quotation from your letter. I regret that I have to remind you of logic, by the following example: If some faith healer were attempting to cure rabies by exorcising the demons which, he claimed, had been inhabiting the patient's body from birth, and if Pasteur objected to it, would an admirer of that faith healer be logically justified in declaring: "If you inveigh against him, you are pretending that rabies don't exist"?

John, this is a good instance on which to illustrate Freud's theory. The level of your argument in these two sentences is so far distant from the strict logic, the precision, the perceptiveness, the rationality you are capable of and have demonstrated on other subjects, that it indicates that some enormous complexity of emotions takes precedence over your judgment when you deal with the subject of Freud. I think that both Freud and I would agree on that. But here would be the difference: Freud *would believe* that you cannot help it; I *don't*.

I do not know what subconscious emotion made you say: "I tend to think that your group is a bit too 'voluntaristic' " and to ascribe to us some sort of "get hold of yourself, buddy" approach. I do know that it was not caused by an *objective* fact, viz., by the content of the lecture. If you heard a lecture on *anatomy* in a medical school, you would not conclude that the lecturer believed that all diseases can be cured by will power, just because he did not discuss diseases or their cures; you would know that pathology is not part of a lecture on anatomy, but is a separate subject, and that no doctor would discuss pathology *before* he had established what is the *healthy* state of a human body.

I do not know how to read the meaning of your criticism in that particular paragraph, except in one of two ways: either you believe that a philosophical view of man's consciousness in its healthy state must not be presented or discussed without a discussion of psychopathology, and that the two subjects are inseparable; or you believe that psychopathology is *the norm*, that it represents man's state at birth—as Freud believed.

I do not know what other premise would make you expect a discussion of pathology in a lecture on the nature and source of man's emotions. My impression is further heightened by the following peculiar remark: after setting up the straw man of "get hold of yourself, buddy," as your idea of our approach, you say: "This certainly helps, especially with superficial mental disturbances, but with the really deep-seated cases, such appeals are as ineffective as water is to dissolve a stone." Surely, you did not think that that lecture was intended as psychological "group therapy"—or that it was addressed to a group of the "mentally disturbed," whose derangements make them impervious to ideas.

The fact that most people, particularly today, *are* neurotic in various degrees does not change the fact that lectures, speeches, articles or books can be addressed *only* to whatever degree of rationality people are able or willing to exercise. And if any listeners or readers grasp the right philosophy, but find themselves emotionally unable to apply it, it is up to them to decide whether they need a course of psychotherapy.

You say: "I think your aim is the same as Freud's—to help people to behave in a rational manner. You do it by appealing directly to reason,

Freud does it by helping people who are incapable of it to BECOME capable of it, and thus living by your philosophy. You should not regard him as an enemy."

If you mean that I, as a philosopher, appeal directly to reason, then this is true—but it is also true of any philosopher and it does not imply that I, or any philosopher, deny the need of psychotherapy for neurotics and propose to cure them solely by means of philosophy. Do you actually equate psychotherapy with Freud? Do you mean that to oppose Freud is to oppose psychotherapy?

Neurosis is a disease, and has to be treated as such; it is the subject matter of a special science and is *not* the basic and central concern of philosophy. Which school of psychology any given philosopher will judge to be valid, depends on his epistemological criteria and on *his* view of the nature of man's consciousness. In forming his view, he has to take cognizance of the existence of neurosis, just as a doctor has to take cognizance of diseases in forming his view of the nature of man's body. And just as a rational doctor does not take disease as the innate and the normal, neither does a rational philosopher. As to me, you know why I would not think that any modernized version of the Original Sin theory can help people to become rational and to live by my philosophy(!).

Now I should like to offer for your consideration a hypothesis I have formed about a certain epistemological error which you seem to be making. I do not claim this as knowledge, only as a hypothesis, and I would like you to tell me whether I am mistaken.

You say: "I can't imagine why your group is so opposed to Freud. How do you suppose that psychiatry achieves its good effects on patients? THROUGH REASON, THROUGH UNDERSTANDING. The patient understands his own repressed mechanism, and through understanding he becomes a more rational human being." You might remember a similar instance which we once discussed: your statement that it is wrong to claim that Heraclitus denied the existence of entities, since "change" presupposes that which changes. In both these instances, the two thinkers involved, Freud and Heraclitus, are guilty of what I call "the fallacy of the stolen concept," which consists of using or counting upon the very concept one is attempting to invalidate or to deny. Whenever I can demonstrate that a theory is based on this fallacy, I consider it sufficient proof of such theory's invalidity.

Well, it occurred to me that you seem to regard this fallacy in the exactly opposite way, namely: that you take it as proof of a theory's *validity* and use it in defense, not in criticism, of a given thinker. For instance, you say, in effect, that since "change" presupposes that which changes, it would be irrational to claim the existence of "change" while denying the existence of "entities," therefore Heraclitus *could not have meant* what he said. And thus you whitewash him, in effect, by ascribing your own rationality to *him*. This implies the premise that reason is an absolute for all theorists, that no one could preach contradictions by conscious, deliberate intent or that no one could be guilty of evasion.

It struck me that you use, *in defense* of Freud, *the very argument* which I have always used *against* him (and against other schools of psychology who are guilty of the same kind of error), namely: that while he reduces reason to the role of a feeble "mediator" between violent, conflicting forces, he counts on the power of *reason* to cure a patient's neurosis. You take this as proof of Freud's championship of reason; I take it as proof of a basic contradiction in Freud's theory.

My hypothesis, then, is that you use a thinker's errors in his defense, or you use his contradictions as proof of his consistency, on a premise which amounts, in effect, to: "He couldn't have been as irrational as *that!*" Such a premise would be an epistemological "sanction of the victim": it would mean that you transfer the power of your own rationality to an irrational theorist and give him a credit he does not deserve, at your own expense. "The fallacy of the stolen concept," which you seem to take for granted as self-evidently simple, can be detected only by the most disciplined minds, because it requires an enormous, abstract range of integration. You, who possess that unusual capacity, toss it away, giving yourself no credit for it; when you encounter irrationality, you hand your own virtue over to the enemies of reason and place the blame upon your own mind, believing that you have failed to understand them, that nobody could be as irrational as they appear to be. Well, take their own words for it: they *are*.

I will be very anxious to hear whether I am right or wrong in this hypothesis, whether such is or is not your epistemological policy, your method of approach to more than one or two thinkers.

In case I am right, I will offer just two preliminary suggestions, which I would like you to consider, one philosophical, the other psychological. 1. In any process of thought, *contradictions* are our only evidence and proof of error. Whether in one's own thinking or in considering the theories of others, it is only by reaching or finding a contradiction that we can know that the reasoning was faulty and proceed to check our own premises or condemn the theories involved, as the case might be. What would be left of logic if we began to take contradictions as proofs of rationality and proceeded to twist concepts, language, theories and our own minds, struggling to ascribe a rational meaning to the irrational? 2. As a psychological suggestion, I would venture the following: do not be afraid of discovering how evil some people are. They do not rule the world and the only power they have is your own, when and if you transfer it to them. Which is more frightening: to be a giant among vicious dwarfs or to struggle to shrink and deform one's own stature down to the size of a dwarf, while inflating the dwarfs into monstrous giants by the transfusion of one's own virtue and power?

Now to your last comment on this lecture, your paraphrase of Pascal: "The head has its reasons which the heart does not know." It is a very intriguing statement, and very witty as an epigram to throw at those who agree with Pascal. But did you mean it literally, that is: do you accept reason vs. emotions as a dichotomy? I grant that such conflicts can and do exist, but not that they *have to* exist. In a man of fully rational, fully *integrated* convictions, emotions follow the judgments of reason as an unforced, automatic response. (That is the way they work in *my* consciousness; I am not saying this as a boast; I know what makes it possible—and I know also that the same harmony can be achieved by any human being, if he wants it, but it cannot be achieved easily or overnight.) May I paraphrase your epigram to state my exact view?—thus: "The head has its reasons which the heart must learn to know."

Lecture 3.

Your comments on this lecture are based on modern philosophy, as if modern philosophy (in all or any of its variants) were a primary absolute or an incontrovertibly proved body of knowledge. But we oppose and reject modern philosophy and, most particularly, its basic premises and its epistemological methods. Therefore, I could argue with you about basic premises—but it would be futile to argue about statements *derived from* premises which I reject.

I hope that you and I will discuss modern philosophy *from scratch*, from the basic premises on up, when you return to New York. I won't attempt to do it by mail. So I will comment only on your specific points, for the purpose of indicating where our basic disagreements lie.

You say: "How is 'A is A' a means of proving other propositions? (Can it be used to show whether this is red or blue?)" *Who* decided that *that* is the *use* of logic? Do you differentiate between a specific piece of knowledge and that which makes *all* knowledge possible? Or between particular sciences and philosophy? Or between the content of knowledge and the *method* by which knowledge is acquired? No, "A is A" will not tell you whether this *is* red or blue. It will "merely" tell you that it *is*. It will bring you to the stage where you will be able to grasp that *"this"* exists and that *"this"* has attributes and that you can differentiate between what *is* red and what *is* blue, and that you may not claim that *"this"* is red *and* blue at the same time and in the same *respect*. It will tell you why you may not claim that dictatorship is freedom, or that looting is production, or that self-sacrifice is happiness.

(Incidentally, "two plus two makes four" will not tell you whether I have four apples, four cows or four battleships.)

You say that "A is A" *does not* "provide a validation for any particular arguments," but "All A is B, all B is C, therefore all A is C," *does*. I will answer by telling you a story I heard years ago. Two men were arguing about which is more useful to men, the sun or the moon, and the argument was decided in favor of the moon, because, they declared, the moon shines at night, when it's dark—while the sun shines in the daytime, when it's light anyway.

What, if not "A is A," gives any validity to "All A is B, all B is C, therefore all A is C"? What is the latter but one of the concrete applications or derivatives of "A is A"? And if anyone claims that something *other than* "the Aristotelian laws of thought" was needed to *validate* that principle, he is using the same type of reasoning as the man in the sun-moon controversy.

I have mentioned to you that we challenge and reject the proposition that truth is a matter of propositions—or that knowledge is acquired by proving or disproving single sentences. We call that approach "context-dropping."

You say: "Sentences about physical things are based upon other sentences having to do with our PERCEPTIONS, and these in turn are based on other sentences having to do with IMMEDIATE EXPERIENCES (sometimes called sensations) in which the integration performed by the mind on the material of the senses has not yet been accomplished." By what means do we acquire *"sentences"*(!) when we are on the *pre-perceptual* level of development, when our consciousness is in a subanimal state? By what means do we acquire *"sentences"* when we are on the *perceptual* level, when our consciousness is in a state equal to an animal's? All sentences deal with *concepts* and originate on the *conceptual* level of development. How does a mind get to that level? Not by means of *"sentences."* Knowledge does *not* begin with and is *not* based on *"sentences."* Any school of epistemology that takes language as the given, and sentences as irreducible primaries is merely bypassing the real problem and cannot even be regarded as an epistemological theory.

You say that you do not know what we mean by "Existence exists." You have forgotten that you asked me that very question here, in New York, at one of our early meetings, and that I took a long time answering you exhaustively, after which you said that it was clear to you. I am sorry (and slightly discouraged) if you have forgotten, but I will not repeat it all over again. I will mention only what I do *not* mean. I do not mean what *you* mean, when you give the example that "grass is green, but greenness isn't green." *I do not regard existence as an attribute.*

You object to my definition "Truth is the recognition of reality," and you say: "No—for truth may not be recognized. . . . There are truths even when nobody knows them and nobody recognizes them. Many things are true about the world which nobody yet knows." Aren't you confusing "*truth*" with "*facts*"? "Truth" is a concept that refers to *epistemology*, not to metaphysics; to *consciousness*, not to existence or reality. "*Facts*" cannot be "true" or "false"; facts *are* ("existence exists"). "*Facts*" are the standard of truth or falsehood; it is by means of "*facts*" that we determine whether an idea of ours is true or false. "Truth" is the attribute of an *idea* in somebody's consciousness (the relationship of that idea to the facts of reality) and it cannot exist *apart* from a consciousness. You say: "There are truths even when nobody knows them and nobody recognizes them." No, there are "*facts*" even when nobody knows them and nobody recognizes them; these "*facts*" are *potentially* the *material* of truths; the recognition of these "facts" by some human consciousness constitutes "truths." You say: "Many things are true about the world which nobody yet knows." Isn't this a colloquial, verbal foreshortening, which is inexact? To be exact philosophically, one would have to say: "Many *facts* exist in the world, which nobody yet knows, and when somebody discovers them, he will be able to form many *true* ideas which nobody can form at present."

In regard to: the Law of Causality. Yes, of course, my formulation of it ("A thing cannot act in contradiction to its nature") is mine; it is not the usual: "everything that happens has a cause." Compare the two and decide which is the more fundamental.

You say: "But the truth of the statement, in your formulation, is guaranteed by the meaning attached to the word 'NATURE.' " You bet your life it is! But what shocked me was the fact that you seem to attach no meaning to the concept of "a thing's *nature*," even though it was specified most clearly in the lecture and in *Atlas Shrugged*. A thing's nature is that which it *is metaphysically*; a thing's nature is its *identity*, that which cannot be changed by miracle nor by any wish, whim or will, God's or man's. *This* is the meaning of "A is A"—and you have told me firmly that you accepted it. How, then, could you cite, as an example in *this* context, such a thing as a man's *"temper-tantrum"* and ask whether he "acted contrary to his nature"? On top of which, you assume that *we* would answer that this is "part of his nature." (!!!)

I will answer: This is what happens to logic (and language) without *ontology*.

No, I will not struggle to clarify this issue any further. We have given you enough evidence not to misunderstand us in *this* kind of way. If you care to understand us, and to untangle the contradictions of your argument, I will give you two leads: consider the *metaphysical* difference between the natural and the man-made; consider the role of the Law of Identity in the *scientific* quest for causal connections. If you do *not* care to understand us, no added discussion by me will help.

In regard to: the mystics' arguments about God. You say that we "have not answered what the proponents of the argument have wanted to say." We never answer what people *want* to say; we answer what they *do* say. You claim that mystics construe "the universe" to mean the *Physical* universe and that they demand a nonphysical cause for it, namely God. Well, here is where "Existence exists" comes in again: whatever it is that they mean by nonphysical, whether it is God, ectoplasm or simply X, either X exists or it does not exist; and if X exists, it is part of the universe; and if the mystics don't mean "the universe," it is up to them not to corrupt language and not to play on equivocations; if they mean that "God is the creator of *matter*," then that is what they should say (which would make their case still less tenable and would confuse fewer people).

In regard to: time as a measure of motion. You ask: "What of clocks which measure time? Are they a measure of a measure of motion?" Clocks do *not* measure time. Clocks are a mechanism that produces a certain kind of motion (a uniform motion, of unvarying speed, gauged in a certain manner to the motion of the sun); by taking the clock's motion as the unit or standard of measurement, *we* measure time. (Or: we measure all motion by relating it to the motion of the sun.)

In regard to: people's desire for the causeless. You say: "I don't think people ever want or expect anything to be CAUSELESS . . . they only want certain things to occur as a result of a DIFFERENT cause than the one we know is required to cause it." This is a psychological interpretation, open to debate. Philosophically, I don't equate reality with nonreality, or the existent with the nonexistent. If someone wants the impossible, as, for instance, a miracle, or wealth falling on him from heaven by miracle, I do not identify this as a desire for a "different cause"; I identify it as a desire for the *causeless*, which, in terms of reality, it is. Now, speaking psychologically, one could say that evaders of this kind want things to occur from a "different cause"; but that "different cause" is: their own wish; they desire their desire to be a sufficient cause for anything, to be omnipotent —"somehow."

You ask: "And who ever wanted to see the front and the back of something at the same time?" Anyone who ever claimed that man's mind is "limited." Anyone who doubts the validity of concepts (and calls them "constructs"), because they are "inferential," that is: not immediate, direct and automatic, like percepts.

In regard to: *mystics*. You ask what is our definition of the term "mystic." Our definition is: "Anyone who claims some nonsensory, non-rational, nondefinable means of knowledge." This includes the three groups you listed: those who doubt the validity of the senses (by means of what faculty do they doubt it?)—those who claim to have a sixth sense (*what* is that sixth sense?)—those who claim that something is true because they *feel* it (are feelings a tool of *cognition*?). There are many others.

You say: "As the term 'mystic' had traditionally been used, a mystic is a person who believes that God is unknowable because no attribution can be made of God—since He is outside all concepts, etc." Aren't you here describing one very narrow variant of mysticism, namely: so-called "negative theology"? By that definition, consider a person who believes in a God possessing all the conventional attributes (including a long beard); would you say that such a person is *not* a mystic?

Now, I will answer your letter of November 12th (which you sent together with your comments on Lecture 3).

You say that many issues were "*oversimplified*" in the lecture, and you ascribe it to the necessities of a "popular lecture." As I mentioned at the start of this letter (in regard to the issue of Plato and Marx), you do not seem to use the term "oversimplification" in the same sense that I would use it, therefore I am not sure of what you mean. I take "oversimplification" to mean: a brief summary which omits essentials and thus distorts the issue. In this meaning, nothing in any of the lectures is "*oversimplified*"; neither Nathan nor I ever talk or write "down" to a "popular" audience; we gauge the *knowledge* of our potential audience and decide how much explaining is necessary, but we do not distort issues to fit people's ignorance. I suspect that what you mean by "oversimplification" is a matter of how much detail is given to any particular issue. In this respect, our standard of judgment is: the *precision* of the abstractions by means of which we present the *essentials* of an issue. (And, as a corollary: if challenged to expand these abstractions into full detail, could we support our statements? Well, we can and do.)

You say that those present at the lecture seemed to accept what they heard without thinking. I am sure that this is true of many people there, and at anyone's lectures anywhere in the world. But what I resent profoundly is your implication that this is what Nathan and I want or seek. You write: "I would hate to have anybody accept ANY views, including my own, just on my authority or without giving them due thought; I always prefer intelligent disagreement to undigested agreement." John, have you dropped context to the extent of forgetting to *whom* you are writing this? To the first person who has made *thinking* the base of morality; to the only person in the modern world who is fighting for the absolutism of reason and thought, and against *any* (I repeat: *ANY*) form of subjectivity, of faith or of surrender to intellectual authority.

You are touching here upon what I regard as the most vicious, false and destructive dichotomy with which modern philosophy has infected modern men: dogmatism vs. skepticism—the idea that certainty implies mystical authoritarianism and that the sole alternative is an attitude of chronic uncertainty, which claims nothing but tentative "probabilities" and tolerates anything. (Or: the idea which equates mysticism with certainty— and reason with Richard Nixon, that is: with an apologetic, mealy-mouthed readiness to *compromise*.) Observe what is blanked out and swept out of existence by the mere setting up of this dichotomy: *rational certainty* and *rational knowledge*.

Does one's choice consist of "intelligent disagreement" or "undigested agreement"? "Undigested agreement" does not interest or concern me (you would be surprised how I treat any person in whom I detect "undigested agreement"; you would probably accuse me of "intolerance"). Through all the years that I spent formulating my philosophical system, I was looking desperately for "intelligent agreement" or at least for "intelligent *disagreement*." I found neither (I am here omitting my personal students). Today, I am *not* looking for "intelligent disagreement" any longer, and certainly not from children or amateurs (I realize too well that it would be a contradiction in terms). If a professional philosopher disagreed, I would always be interested to know his reasons; but what I *am* looking for is "*intelligent agreement*." That is what any thinker looks for, when and if he knows that he has discovered and stated something which is new.

To quote you further: "I do think that the rather dogmatic and brief presentation, the oversimplification of some points, and the sort of 'I'm right and everyone else is wrong' manner of the presentation, tends to

MAKE slavish dogmatists out of the audience." In other words: since some people in the audience are unthinking, evading, cowardly "social metaphysicians" who are looking for somebody else's certainty and are seeking some bandwagon to join, we (Nathan and I) must *not* admit or project the fact that we *are* certain of what we say? We must, instead, assume the manner which substitutes "it seems to me" for "it *is*"—the manner which implies: "It seems to me that I may be right, but I would not claim that everyone else is wrong"? Is *this* what you really expect of us? Haven't you read *Atlas Shrugged* and what I think of the "it seems to me" school of thought?

And if you think that our certainty will intimidate the poor little "social metaphysicians," what do you think our uncertainty would do to them? Would it make them think independently? You've handled enough students to know full well that it wouldn't. It would merely permit them to play the cynical, irresponsible, hooligan act that is so fashionable among today's youth: it would permit them to make loud, brash, arbitrary assertions of disagreement, while evading and ignoring everything they heard us say. Just as John Galt would not help Mr. Thompson pretend that he, Galt, had not made his radio speech, so *I* will not help anyone pretend that *Atlas Shrugged* has not been written (and neither will Nathan nor any other Objectivist). There are enough people in the world who are busy pretending it; they may continue to do so, but *not* with *my* sanction or help.

You write: "And I keep wondering: is the aim of the lectures catechetical or is it to provoke intelligent comment?" Neither. Has no alternative actually occurred to you? The aim of the lectures was best expressed by George Washington: "to raise a standard to which the wise and honest can repair." That is: to present what we know to be true, as clearly and rationally as we can, and to leave the rest to the intelligence and the honesty of any listener or reader. I have told you here in New York (and the lecture brochure states it explicitly) that "these lectures are not given to convert antagonists." And they most certainly are not given "to provoke intelligent comment," if, by that phrase in this context, you meant "to provoke, stimulate or encourage people to disagree with us."

Observe that we *are* tolerant, but *only* of honesty, *not* of evasion. We grant that most people cannot grasp an entire philosophical system from one novel; so we offer a course of lectures to help them grasp it; and we intend to give many lectures and to write many, many books to help them grasp it, to offer further and further details, elaborations and extensions. But we do *not* grant that my novel, or any lecture, or any future book, has said *nothing*. Therefore, we offer these lectures *only* to those who have understood enough of *Atlas Shrugged* to agree with its essentials. That some people are attracted, not by any understanding, but by some blind emotions, is *their* problem, not ours; they are sailing under false colors and it will come out sooner or later. We cannot let them prevent us from addressing those who *do* seek to understand. And those who seek to understand, do *not* disagree until they have understood; so if anything is unclear to them, the question period is available and they may ask questions which we are willing to answer; but there is a difference between a question period and a debate.

You write: "There was no discussion after the lecture—the group simply disbanded and each person went his separate way. I wonder whether this was Mr. Branden's intention." Nathan has no intention about it, one way or the other. He has neither forbidden nor invited them to hold discussions. That is up to the local group; I hear that some groups hold discussions after a lecture, others do not. The only thing that Nathan *has* made clear is that no one, including the business representative, is to assume the role of official spokesman for or authority on Objectivism; that is, they may all express their own views or opinions, but they may not speak for us.

I know that part of your attitude on this issue comes from a certain confusion which you might tend to have about your own policy in a university classroom and our policy in these lectures. A teacher in a university has to be concerned, to some extent, with the "psycho-epistemology" of his students, with the development of their minds, with the inculcation of independent thinking; but even then, only to some extent and not at the expense of the subject being taught. But *we* are not and do not regard ourselves as *teachers*; we are not part of a wider program of education, we have nothing resembling exams, we address ourselves to adults and have to leave up to them the full responsibility for learning something from the course. The difference is the same as that between a textbook and a book; people can and do learn from both, but the authors' methods and approaches are different.

I have watched you in your seminar and at the Esthetics convention here; on neither occasion did you project any tentativeness or uncertainty; you projected that you were very sure of what you were saying and that you were *right*. Particularly during the concluding passages of your paper on art, you were speaking with such intensity, self-confidence and righteous contempt for the views you were opposing that all of us wanted to cheer, and we admired you precisely for these qualities. So I do not think that you are actually an advocate of modern "non-commitment."

But I know also that some part of your attack on *our* certainty and self-confidence comes from modern philosophy, from its epistemological agnosticism. I know that this is a conflict within you. I hope that this letter will help you to consider it and to reach some solution. You know that I don't get hurt easily. Of all our many disagreements, this last issue *has* hurt me; it implied your tolerance of and concern for any weakling's needs, ideas and interests, as against *mine*; it implied that *they* must be considered, because they *have not* developed their minds, but *I* can claim no consideration, because I *have*. I *felt* (and knew) that I was being penalized, not for a flaw, but for a virtue—a very steady, patient virtue that has had to endure a great deal for a great many years, without receiving any acknowledgment or any justice. Don't add to that kind of burden.

■ ■ ■

March 5, 1961

Dear John:

I have given a great deal of thought to your note about the issue of "Roark and happiness," which I answered in my letter of December 28, and to your answer to me (your letter of January 4, 1961). I am unable to reconcile your note and your letter with each other, with our past conversations, with the fact that you have read *The Fountainhead* and *Atlas Shrugged*, or with any epistemological principles known to me.

I believe you, when you say, in your letter of January 4: "I don't want to play any games at all, but only to pursue important ideas. I want to pursue the ideas so badly that I am willing to endure abuse if need be in order to forward the course of the ideas." If I understand your meaning correctly, I admire you for this attitude; I consider it the most important of all moral premises. And I am answering your letter in full detail, because I believe you. But here is the tragic position in which we find ourselves: I am the last person on earth who would ever make anyone endure abuse as the price for the pursuit of ideas. If you regard my letter (of December 28) as abusive, I, on my part, regard your note on "Roark and happiness" as the most shocking, painful and insulting response I have ever received to any of my books (painful, because I did and do value your intellectual response). It is, therefore, obvious that an enormous epistemological difference exists between us and that our lines of communication do not work at all. If so, I cannot solve the problem alone: you will have to help me.

I believe that when you answered my letter, you had forgotten the actual content of your note on "Roark and happiness." So I am enclosing a photostat of it (for the sake of full accuracy) as well as a photostat of page 1 of your letter of January 4. Please check your note with my letter of December 28 and yours of January 4, then tell me how to reconcile the three.

I shall list the questions that bewilder me and I shall ask you to explain them to me specifically, in objectively clear terms.

1. Re: first sentence of paragraph 2 of your letter. You write that you were *asking* me, not telling me (and later you refer to your note on "Roark and happiness" as a "letter of inquiry" intended to ask me certain questions). How am I to reconcile that with the fact that your note does not contain a single sentence in the form of a question (nor a single question mark)?

2. Re: second sentence of paragraph 2 of your letter. If you were interested in "the limits of egoism" as I conceive them—my views on egoism are defined, discussed, presented and illustrated in *The Fountainhead* and *Atlas Shrugged. Egoism* is the basic theme of both novels—and in both I state explicitly what I consider evil in the idea of "serving others," and why. How am I to reconcile that with paragraphs 1 and 6 of your note?

3. Re: fourth and fifth sentences of paragraph 2 of your letter. If you were *merely* making the observation that "people who are always worrying about their own internal states are unhappy people," what does this have to do with Roark? How am I to read that intention into paragraphs 1 and 6 of your note?

4. Re: third sentence of paragraph 2 of your letter. The *traditional* concepts of an "egoist" are represented in *The Fountainhead* by Peter Keating and Ellsworth Toohey. (Keating is the unthinking, parasitical, "range-of-the-moment" secondhander—Toohey is the "Machiavellian schemer" or power-luster.) The relation of these two types to Roark is made amply clear. The theme of *The Fountainhead* is: to demonstrate in what fundamental sense and manner Roark is an *egoist*, while Keating and Toohey are actually *selfless*—and why *the traditional concepts of egoism are destroying the world.* I have stated explicitly (both in *The Fountainhead* and in *Atlas Shrugged*) that a man's *self* is his consciousness and that the center and motor of his consciousness is his *mind.* I have discussed, illustrated and proved this point from every relevant aspect known to me. How am I to reconcile that with paragraph 6 of your note, particularly with the words: "some center of their lives, which is NOT THEMSELVES"? Since you rejected, without stating your reasons, the total of my view of what *is* man's self—how could I tell what meaning you were assigning to the words "self" and "selfish" in your note? This leads me to a very important epistemological issue, in the next point—

5. *Re: paragraphs 1 and 3 of your letter.* You express astonishment and/or indignation at what you regard as my distortion of your views. My answer to that is contained in the paragraph above. Since, in your note, you rejected all of my *definitions* of the concepts under discussion (such as "self," "selfish," "happiness," "personal reward"), I had to infer *your* definitions from the content of your note. By *my* understanding of the meaning of the concepts involved, Roark and a social worker are diametrical opposites who can never be equated morally or psychologically, not in any manner whatsoever. Since you *did* equate them, it could be done only in the way you did it, i.e., by taking "concern with one's inner problems and conflicts" as *the definition of an "egoist"*; it is the only meaning given to the term in your note. And further: the reasoning, statements and propositions by which you equate Roark with a social worker apply to Stalin as well and as fully; if that reasoning is *sufficient* for regarding a social worker as (a) happy or (b) in any way a worthy human being, it is sufficient for regarding Stalin in the same manner.

Please reread your note and see whether it can be intelligible without the implicit definition which you now repudiate.

This is an example of my conflict with modern philosophy: I am incapable of switching the definitions of my concepts to fit each separate occasion and of letting them mean one thing when I use them, but another when Bertrand Russell uses them, and a third when you use them. I am incapable of reading a paper such as your note, by the method of dropping or forgetting *all* definitions and then, without reference or commitment to *any* definition, using wide, fundamental concepts, such as "egoist," in some special, narrow sense, while simultaneously regarding this usage as "nondefinitional." What is more, I do not believe that anybody can do it—and I know that the sole result of such an attempt is the sort of breakdown of communication in which you and I are now entangled.

6. *Re: last paragraph of your note.* Please tell me what I am to think of the following sentence: "Now whether one calls such people egoists I don't much care—certainly they are not egoists in any traditional sense." But I *do* care, and I have written four books with over 1,000,000 words to prove *why* one should care and what disasters are now destroying the world as a result of the general confusion over the meaning of "egoism." Yet you write the above sentence to *me*—and you want me to regard modern

epistemology as a discipline aimed at achieving linguistic precision. Please tell me how to reconcile these two facts.

7. Re: first and second sentences of paragraph 3 of your letter. Please *do* go through my whole letter—please read it as carefully as I am reading yours—please check every paragraph against your note, then answer every paragraph in which you find a distortion—and prove to me, in *objective* terms, that I am guilty of context-dropping, if you can. I have never been guilty of it, and I do not take such accusations lightly. You seem to imply that your accusation is clear and that I will let it go at that. It is not and I will not. I do not allow my statements to be dismissed, ignored and brushed aside in this manner.

I answered your note by keeping in mind its entire content, every single sentence and every single implication, on the one hand—and the total content of my two novels on the other. Please match this; please bear in mind the total context of the issues discussed in your note—then accuse me of context-dropping, if you find that you can. Do you remember the slogan: "When you say that, smile"? Well, my slogan is: "When you accuse me, *prove it.*"

8. Re: paragraph 4 of your letter. Please tell me how to reconcile this with paragraph 1, page 2 of *my* letter to you. Didn't you know that I was referring to the morality presented in *Atlas Shrugged* and to Galt's speech? Did I or did I not make clear in Galt's speech what I mean by "life" as the standard of morality?

9. On page 2 of your letter (which I did not photostat, but hope you remember) you quote Russell as saying: "If you try to live the life of a pig, your suppressed potentialities will make you miserable." I can fully agree with this sentence, if you take it to mean that man has a certain nature and must live up to it. But if you believe that, how am I to reconcile it with your defense of altruists? I have demonstrated, both in *The Fountainhead* and in *Atlas Shrugged*, that altruists (all those who find "great happiness in serving the interests of others") are destroyers of and traitors to *man's nature*, and, therefore, why I regard them as subhuman (or, I might say, as lower than pigs). If you do not agree with my view of man's nature, yet do not attempt to refute my arguments, but proceed to assert their exact opposite, what alternative have I but to conclude that you are ignoring my views and my arguments?

10. On page 2 of your letter, you say: ". . . if a person deliberately *pursues* happiness all his life he is not likely to achieve it. Roark was not pursuing happiness, he was pursuing perfection in his chosen work." Here

I *literally* do not know what you mean. Since happiness is an emotional *response to something* (and, therefore, an effect, not a cause), how can one *pursue happiness* except by pursuing that which will make one happy? In Roark's case, perfection in his chosen work is what made him happy (this is not the way I would formulate it, but I will accept your formulation for this context). *Now please tell me concretely and specifically what it is that Roark would do if he were "pursuing happiness," as you understand it?* (This is, perhaps, the most important question in my present letter. I suspect that it holds a clue to our epistemological differences. So please do not answer it abstractly or in generalities; please answer it concretely, specifically and literally.)

You write: "It is always important to distinguish happiness as a *motive* from happiness as a *result.*" I differentiate "happiness as a *standard* of value" from "happiness as a *purpose.*" But I do not know what an "*incidental*" or unsought-for happiness would be, psychologically, epistemologically or existentially. You write: "Roark was happy, but he didn't spend his life trying to be happy. Surely you agree with this? Or if you don't, I would appreciate hearing your reasons." I neither agree nor disagree. I *literally* do not understand what you mean. I would say: Roark was happy because he spent his life achieving the things (the values) that would make him happy, or: enacting the causes of which his happiness would be the result. And—I would add—he succeeded, because his values were rational; happiness cannot be achieved by indulging random whims or by pursuing irrational values (values which might be right for a pig, but not for a man). Therefore, I would say that Roark's goal in life was the achievement of his own happiness. But you seem to think in some totally different terms. So please tell me *concretely and specifically* what you have in mind when you project a person who "spends his life trying to be happy." Surely you do not mean a whim-worshipper or whim-pursuer?

11. You write: "The question I wanted to ask you in the previous note is this: Roark had tremendous ability at architecture, and was (incidentally) happy in pursuing it. Now here is a person, let's say, who has no ability at architecture but has great ability at something else, say medical research into tropical diseases, which often has to be performed in uncomfortable and disease-ridden tropical conditions. What would you say about this activity? What would you say about this activity if its prime motivation is to alleviate the sufferings of others? Would you condemn it on that account?"

I will refer you to Roark's speech, specifically to: page 737, paragraph 2—page 738, paragraphs 2,3,4,5,6,7,9—page 740, paragraphs 2,3,6—page

741, paragraphs 1,2,3. I will also refer you to Galt's speech: page 1021, paragraph 1 (last part of this paragraph)—page 1031, paragraphs 2,3,4,5,6. I assume that you know that these two speeches are the summations of what is demonstrated and illustrated by *all* the events of both novels.

Now as to the first part of your paragraph: surely you do not mean that a man is born with an innate ability for a specific profession, as specific as "medical research into tropical diseases"? If this were true, it would necessarily mean the possession of innate ideas. The choice of a profession is not *innate*: it is determined by a man's premises, by the interests he acquires and develops. (His brain capacity or the potential degree of his intelligence is probably innate, but not the specific use to which his intelligence will be put.) Now, if a man's premises lead him to choose medical research as his career, and if he has to work in uncomfortable disease-ridden tropical conditions, I would regard it as virtuous and heroic (but no more virtuous or heroic than the work of an industrialist in a luxurious office). My standard of moral judgment is a man's devotion to his career, to the creative, productive activity of his mind—not the degree of physical danger and of comfort or discomfort incidental to the pursuit of his career. (For instance, I would not regard a mountain-climbing explorer or a deep-sea diver as morally superior to a philosopher or a mathematician.) But if a man's *prime motivation* for such activity is "to alleviate the sufferings of others"—I would certainly condemn it as irrational and evil. If suffering is undesirable, what can justify the desire to alleviate the suffering of others at the price of one's own suffering? What can such a desire mean, logically and psychologically, but an enormous lack of self-esteem? (We are not discussing here the desire to save a person one loves, but the dedication to the service of others as a primary, lifelong goal.)

12. I observe that *in your note, paragraph 1*, you list *"students"* first among the recipients of "altruistic" service—and I wonder whether you regard your own profession as altruistic by its very nature. If you do, I want to state that this is a grave error. *Teaching* is one of the most crucial, responsible and important professions—since it consists of communicating *knowledge* and guiding the *intellectual* development of men. The *objective purpose* of teaching is the spread and communication of the right ideas, of intellectual values, which means: the creation of a culture. Students are the immediate and direct beneficiaries of a teacher's work, but they are *not* his goal, and the benefits they gain from him are *not* the purpose of his life. In an exchange society, in any trade of goods or services, there are direct beneficiaries, but *they* are not the motivation of the traders. For instance, a doctor's patients are the beneficiaries of his work, but his goal is *not* to save their specific lives; his goal is the conquest of disease. In the same way, your students are your beneficiaries, but your purpose (as a rational teacher) is the spread of knowledge. Please reread Roark's courtroom speech if this point is not clear to you.

The relationship between one's work and the beneficiaries of one's work is illustrated in *The Fountainhead* by the respective attitudes of Roark and of Keating toward their clients. *Roark* did not want his clients to suffer in the houses he built, he wanted them to benefit from his work, but their benefit, welfare, needs or desires were *not* his primary motive. It is *Keating* who placed the welfare of his clients first and regarded himself as their servant in the only way it can be done: by sacrificing his judgment and his values to their wishes.

Now observe the dangerous "package deal" and contradiction in your list of the beneficiaries of altruism (paragraph 1 of your note): "students, clients, the underprivileged, victims of disease and disaster." Students and clients are *not* objects of charity—the underprivileged and the victims of disease (in this context) and disaster *are*. What is the principle of differentiation? Whether the "benefactor" is engaged in trade or in charity, whether he has a *selfish*, personal goal and *reward* or not, whether he serves a legitimate, rational need of a default, a lack, a flaw. It is the issue of "zero-worship" in Galt's speech, which, I believe, you understand.

I do not know how you regard your own role as a teacher, but I would say this: if you regard yourself as an intellectual guide, like Hugh Akston, it is certainly proper, moral and "*selfish*" in my definition of the word; in such case, your prime concern is the *truth* of what you teach, *not* the happiness of your students. If you regard yourself as a selfless servant of your students' interests, it is a moral insult to them and to yourself, which can have many subtle and disastrous psychological consequences for both.

13. You write: "If someone is good only at safecracking, I would not recommend safecracking as a career on that account. I was only trying to generalize your example of Roark. Was it his ability at architecture, plus his actualization of that ability, that counts as a value? or is it more than this (as it would surely seem to be, since not just ANY ability, or the actualization of it, counts as a value)?"

By my understanding of this question, the whole of *The Fountainhead* and of *Atlas Shrugged* would have to be restated to answer it. If these books are not clear enough, what should I add to make my answer clear? I will refer you to Galt's speech, specifically to the passage from: page 1018, paragraph 6 to page 1021, paragraph 1 (inclusive). This is a detailed statement of what counts as a value in Roark, in Galt, or in any virtuous man. If this is not enough, you will have to tell me what issue or aspect is omitted; you will also have to tell me whether this is sufficient to differentiate between Roark and Galt, on one hand—and a dictator, a safe-cracker, an altruist and a social worker, on the other.

The last question, on page 3 of your letter, is: "How much like Roark must someone be in order to be worthy of admiration, and in what respects?" My answer is: *Exactly* like Roark, in all the basic *moral* principles involved—as different from Roark as one pleases, in all the concrete, specific applications which basic principles allow and which are innumerable: in the choice of profession, in degree of ability, in degree of success (which is not fully up to the individual alone), etc. And if you want me to state briefly how one achieves a moral stature equal to Roark's, I will answer: by a total, absolute, unreserved, unbreached, unbreachable commitment to *rationality* (as defined in Galt's speech), that is: to the fullest use of one's reason at all times and in all issues, to the fullest perception of reality within one's power and to the constant expansion of that power. (Which means: by *never* allowing one's mind to go out of focus in one's waking hours—or: by *never* acting, speaking or making decisions while one's mind is unfocused.) All of Roark's virtues are the consequences of this one basic virtue.

14. You write: "You see, I agree with you that 'feeling' is no criterion; just because someone FEELS so-and-so about something, doesn't make it a value. Agreed. But why do you try to make an enemy of me by saddling me with a view which I reject with all my head and heart? Surely you are aware that I do not, and have never, accepted this nonsense about 'feeling justifies all.' If I had accepted it, I would surely have said so in my comments on Branden's lectures dealing with this subject. Yet here I most enthusiastically agreed with him. Why then do you still think I accept it?"

This is precisely one of the contradictions that bewilder me, and it is I who should ask you to explain it, not the other way around. Yes, I did think that you were opposed to the idea of "feeling as criterion"—but how am I to reconcile this with the last paragraph of your note, in which you state that a "consuming passion" is more important than the choice of the object of that passion?

15. In both *Atlas Shrugged* and *The Fountainhead*—but particularly in *The Fountainhead* (in the history of Katie Halsey)—I have presented my views on the social worker, including the reasons for my views. How am I to reconcile this with the fact that it is specifically the *social worker* whom you insist on equating with Roark (both morally and psychologically) throughout your *note*? (See paragraphs 5 & 6 of your note.)

If you do not agree with my views, please state your specific objections. If my views are not clear to you, please formulate the questions that puzzle you. I am unable to translate assertions into questions.

16. You write: "What I did *not* expect was to have my views distorted out of all recognition and then be plied with insults into the bargain. For I am sure that you do *not* want to play that kind of game with me. I *can* play such games, and have acquired some experience at it in dealing with certain of my colleagues."

I have *never* played such "games"—an Objectivist epistemology (which demands precise definitions) would make it impossible for me and would give me no motive to do it—and I was not doing it in my letter to you. That letter represented my full, actual and honest understanding of your note. But since you say that you *can* and *do* play such games—how can you be certain that you were not doing it in that note to me?

I am not asserting that you were doing it intentionally; I am merely raising it as a psychological question and possibility. I am certain of nothing in regard to your epistemology, at present. But I do know that in situations of this kind, there is only one way to demonstrate objectively the sincerity of your devotion to the pursuit of ideas and truth: by answering all my questions, and all of the points I made in my letter of December 28, as conscientiously as I answered yours—and by proving your accusations or withdrawing them.

I know that I did make an effort to understand you, and I did make an effort to make my position clear (as witness the length and precision of my letters to you)—and now it is *your* turn to make an effort and to explain your note fully.

■   ■   ■

March 15, 1961

Dear John:

This is a hurried note in answer to your letter of March 7. I want to answer you before I vanish into the job of preparing a talk I am to give at the Ford Hall Forum in Boston, on March 26th.

I am glad that you liked my paper on "Objectivist Ethics" and am looking forward to your detailed comment, when and as your time permits. But this paper does *not* interfere with your writing an article on my ethics, if you still wish to do it. I had no immediate plans to publish my paper (and, to my knowledge, the Wisconsin Symposium did not plan to publish their proceedings, but merely to mimeograph them for the students of the

University of Wisconsin). If you wish to write that article, I will be glad to withhold my paper from publication, until *after* your article has appeared, and you are welcome to quote any passage from this paper that you may find of value. As I told you last summer, I will be glad to help you with your article, and would appreciate it very much if you would let me check it for accuracy of the summary of my views.

I would much prefer to see Objectivism presented to the philosophical profession by you, rather than by myself—for the obvious reason that a presentation by you would lend it more objectivity in the eyes of the readers. This does not mean, of course, that I expect you to endorse Objectivism nor to announce yourself as agreeing with it; what I would find extremely important and valuable would be an objective, precise, impartial presentation of my ideas—and as to the comments on them, that would be entirely up to you.

I was delighted, for the same reasons, to hear that you are considering the idea of presenting an outline of Objectivism to the organization of professors of philosophy in Southern California. Please do so, with my "blessing" and enthusiastic support. I would ask you only that you let me check the summary for accuracy—it is our differences on epistemology that would disturb me in this connection, since I have never presented my epistemological theory to you in full, consecutive, organized detail.

I would be happy to see you do it, for personal reasons as well: I believe that if you undertook a systematic presentation of Objectivism, it would help to clarify an enormous amount of confusion between us.

Thank you for your comments on Nathan's Lectures 12–14. Yes, of course, both he and I are very much interested in receiving all of your comments on the lectures. I will not attempt to answer your questions on economics right now (I still have a backlog of your questions I have not yet answered)—but I *will* answer all of them, as time permits.

You have probably received the copy of *For the New Intellectual*, which I sent you. Needless to say, I am very interested to hear your reaction—and I am looking forward to the publication of your book on ethics.

■   ■   ■

March 31, 1961

Dear John:

Just a brief note to thank you for your wonderful letter (of March 18).

The passage in *For the New Intellectual* which is specifically and personally dedicated to *you* is paragraph 2, page 60 [addressed to "the best among the present intellectuals"].

No, it is not pretentious at all, if you felt that my style of writing is close to your own. Coming from a writer, it is a great compliment and I appreciate it profoundly. I cannot say that I have felt this closeness stylistically (perhaps because I have read only your highly technical writing)— but what I did feel very strongly, almost from the first pages of your *An Introduction to Philosophical Analysis* was an *epistemological* closeness between your way of handling ideas and mine. Or, rather, I would say "psycho-epistemological," now that you understand what I mean by that term. I mean, not the *contents* of most of the ideas you present in that book (with which I don't agree), but the way your mind works, the method it uses to present ideas.

I say this in spite of our recent epistemological differences—and I am looking forward to the time when we will resolve them. At the risk of sounding presumptuous, I will say: at your best, you are so good that nothing less should ever satisfy you.

Affectionately and hopefully,

■   ■   ■

April 29, 1961

Dear John:

Thank you for your letter of April 1. I am answering it on the train, returning to New York from Indianapolis, where I spoke at a dinner of a journalist society (and also spoke at Purdue University).

I am glad to answer any and all questions you might ask about the Objectivist ethics—and I hope that my answers will make the subject clearer.

To answer first the questions in your letter: You ask the reason of my opposition to social workers. The basic principle involved (which applies to all similar cases and problems) is as follows: it is morally evil to choose, as one's full-time profession, any activity which is not supported by *trading*, but consists of *almsgiving*. Remember that man has to support his life by his own productive effort; living in a society of men does not change this fact and does not relieve him of his responsibility—it merely offers him the advantages of specialization and trade. Therefore, when a man is *paid* for his work (in a free economy), it means that he has produced a value (either goods or services) which another producer needed and has chosen to buy; it means that he has contributed to the productive effort of those he deals with and has *earned* the equivalent of his contribution; the specific beneficiaries in this case are producers: himself and those who paid him. But in the case of a social worker, two forms of *parasitism* are involved: the social worker (*qua* social worker) offers her services without payment to those who have failed to provide for their own needs. Who, then, provides for the needs, for the actual survival, of both the social worker and of those she serves? *The producers.*

Thus, to choose social work as a profession is to choose to be a *professional parasite*. This is the reason why social work and any other kind of charitable activity cannot be equated with or placed in the category of *productive activities* or professions. Charity is a social luxury, dependent upon and made possible by the work of the producers; as such, it is morally inferior to productive work. At best, charity is a marginal issue, as far as ethics is concerned; charity may be morally proper (in cases where no self-sacrifice is involved), but merely proper or permissible, *not* required and not to be regarded as a major virtue. Today, however, when it is regarded as a virtue by the altruist ethics, social work is monstrously evil—because it assumes a cloak of virtue (of "noncommercial selflessness") at the spiritual and material expense of those who provide the means to support it: the producers are damned for being "selfishly commercial" while *their* money (which means: *their* effort) is keeping all those "selfless" ones alive.

The claim that social workers are productive, because they allegedly rehabilitate human beings is not relevant here: doctors, psychologists and teachers also rehabilitate and help human beings. In fact, every rational profession contributes to the welfare of human beings. The special status of social workers consists of the fact that their profession is charitable and noncommercial, that their goal or motive is *not* the earning of their own living. The best illustration of this distinction can be seen in the case of doctors: according to the altruist ethics, a doctor is given moral credit only when he relieves human suffering without payment; doctors of unusual skill who charge high prices for their services are usually condemned for being "commercial." The Objectivist ethics evaluates this in the exactly opposite manner: I regard a doctor as virtuous if he develops his ability so highly that he earns and deserves large payments (provided, of course, that he actually earns it by ability, *not* by "social-metaphysical" fashion, provided he is a Roark of medicine, not a Keating). And I regard a doctor as immoral if he devotes most of his time to working without payment, if his *primary* goal is selfless, unrewarded service to his patients. (Charity can be proper only as a marginal activity, as an exception.)

You ask whether I would be opposed to the "unofficial rule" of European psychoanalysts to treat one patient free for every ten paying patients. Yes, indeed, I am *most profoundly opposed* to it—on the ground that *need* as such is *not a claim* and that *no human being owes any free services to another.* I would not object if an individual psychoanalyst treated *ten* patients free, provided he chose to do it on the ground of the specific values he saw in them, *not* on the sole ground of their need. But I would oppose, as immoral, his doing it as a *duty*—and I would certainly oppose as immoral any "unofficial rule" which demands this duty of a whole profession: such a rule can be based on nothing but the *altruist* morality.

You ask whether my opposition to social workers would change if it were proved that they make the streets of New York safer. My answer is: no, it would not. If this were the case, I would advocate a stronger and more severe police department. (Actually, social workers *have not* helped to eliminate crime or juvenile delinquency; the evidence indicates that they have helped to increase it.) But this question is somewhat irrelevant here, because it involves an enormously controversial issue: the source, cause and prevention of crime. And what we are discussing here is the question of *charity*, not the question of police work.

Now I should like to mention a *psychological* aspect of the motivation of a social worker, which I regard as the most profoundly *immoral* aspect of the whole issue: a person who chooses social work as a full-time profession chooses to devote her life to that which I define as "zero-worship": to human flaws, lacks, failures, miseries, vices and evils, to the morally, spiritually, intellectually or psychologically *inferior*—to those who lack *value*, with the *lack of value* as the claim and the incentive. If a person were actually motivated by a love of values and a desire to relieve human suffering, she would not begin in the slums and with the subnormal: she would look at what our present society does to the talented, the unusual, the mentally superior children, in schools, in colleges and in their subsequent careers; she would go out to fight *for them* and to help *them*, before they perish psychologically in loneliness and bewilderment.

There are two passages in my novels that refer to this particular issue. One is in *The Fountainhead*: from last paragraph, page 409, to first paragraph (incl.), page 411. Please note paragraph 2, p. 410—and paragraph 1, p. 411. (Observe that Catherine is concerned with Jackie's "creative frustration," but not with Roark's—and remember that, according to the altruist morality, it is proper to destroy Roark's achievement for Jackie's sake.)

The other passage is in *Atlas Shrugged*, paragraphs 2 and 3, page 906. You say that you are "trying to distinguish clearly between two views:

(1) that we should never make sacrifices for other people, and (2) that the *law* should never compel us to do so." These are not two different issues, but two aspects of the same issue. I uphold *both*, as stated above. All political systems and theories are based on and derived from some *ethical* theory; the laws of a society reflect its dominant moral code. If it were true that men were morally obliged to sacrifice for others sometimes, yet failed to do so, a law compelling them to do it would be passed sooner or later, because no moral opposition to such a law could or would be valid.

Now, as to the first view—"that we should never make sacrifices for other people"—the crucial point here is the *precise meaning* of the concept of *"sacrifice."* A sacrifice is the surrender of a greater value for the sake of a lesser one. "To sacrifice for other people" does not mean: "to spend one's effort for a goal which benefits oneself as well as others"—*but*: "to spend one's effort for a goal which benefits *others* at the cost of one's own interests, desires and goals."

Now consider the issue of love, benevolence, good will and friendship among men. Surely it is clear to you that love and friendship are personal, selfish values to a man, that he derives a personal, selfish pleasure and benefit from them; a "selfless," disinterested, charity-motivated love or friendship would be an insult to its object. (I refer you to pp. 32–33 of my paper on "The Objectivist Ethics.") Therefore, concern and desire for the welfare of one's loved person or of one's friends is a rational part of one's personal, selfish values. Surely, it would be absurd to claim that if a husband who is passionately in love with his wife spends a fortune to cure her of a dangerous illness, he is doing it as a "sacrifice" for *her* sake and that it makes no difference to *him*, personally and selfishly, whether she lives or dies.

Any action which a man undertakes for the benefit of his loved ones or his friends is *not a sacrifice*, if, in the total context of his values and of the choices open to him, it achieves the goal he *personally* (and rationally) wanted to achieve. The standard by which he should choose in any given case is: What is most important or of greatest value to *me*? For instance; in the above example, his wife's survival is of greater value to the husband than anything else that his money can buy, and therefore, his action is *not* a sacrifice. But suppose he were asked to let his wife die in order to spend that money on saving ten other women, none of whom meant anything to him—*that* would be a sacrifice. And *here* is where the difference between Objectivism and altruism can be seen most clearly: if "sacrifice" is the moral principle of action, then the husband *should* sacrifice his wife for the sake of ten other women. It's ten to one. What distinguishes the wife from the ten others? Nothing but *her value* to the husband who has to make the choice—nothing but the fact that *his* happiness requires her survival. Now, the Objectivist ethics would tell this husband: your highest moral purpose is the achievement of your own happiness, your money is yours, use it to save your wife, *that* is your moral right and your *rational, moral* choice.

Would *you*, John Hospers, qua moralist, be prepared to tell that husband the opposite?

You cite the example of the occasion when you spent two full nights typing a student's thesis, and you ask me why I approved of your action; you add: "and yet, believe me, it *was* a sacrifice, and my classes suffered somewhat, and so did I (I was sleepy for days)."

The effort required to achieve any goal is *not* a sacrifice, if one desires that goal; the effort is the means to an end—and it becomes a sacrifice only when the means requires the destruction of values which are higher than the end to be achieved. Consider the full context of your example: you liked that student (I assume), you wanted him to get his degree, you saw that he was the victim of an injustice and you chose to do an unusually generous thing to help him. The discomfort you suffered could be called a "sacrifice" only if your sleep were of greater value to you in this instance than the boy's future. Now suppose that it were; suppose that you were recovering from some illness, at the time, and that lack of sleep could cause a dangerous relapse, yet you risked it; in such case, your action would have been a *sacrifice*. Or suppose your classes suffered, not "somewhat," but considerably; *that* would have been a *sacrifice*.

I admired your action because it was *generous*. Generosity is not a sacrifice—it is a gift or favor greater than the friend involved could, in reason, expect. But if your action had been motivated by *altruistic duty*, I would not have admired it nor approved.

Furthermore, if your action had, in fact, been a moral *duty*, the student would have had a *right* to it; he would have had the right to demand it of you, to condemn you morally if you refused to do it, and to owe you no appreciation, no gratitude if you did do it. *Duty*, on the part of one man, implies a *claim* on the part of the other; thus (according to altruism) *you* owed your services to the student, but *he* owes you nothing thereafter—he has merely collected his rightful due. Wouldn't a moral situation or a human relationship of this sort turn your stomach? It turns mine. And yet this would be pure altruism consistently applied. (Observe that this is the exact way it is applied in politics, on a grand scale: men are taxed to support the needy, yet the needy owe them nothing in return, not even gratitude or respect—nothing but insults, denunciations and further demands.)

Now to the specific question you ask me in regard to your own career. First of all, since the chairmanship of the philosophy department is offered in recognition of merit, my congratulations to you—and to those who have the good judgment to recognize your merit. But whether you should accept the offer, is another question. Since you say emphatically that you "do not *want* this kind of job" and that it would "interfere most disastrously" with the work you want to do, particularly with your writing—I would say that this is a fully sufficient reason for rejecting the offer. (I assume that the above represents your exact estimate of the situation, according to the best of your knowledge.) *Morally*, the only thing to consider is your own career and your own future. *You do not owe any duty to others,* neither to the university, nor to the students, nor to education, nor to philosophy as such—no duty, as apart from or against your own rational interests. If administrative work does not interest you and does not contribute to or advance your own professional position, there is no reason why you should do it; if you were to benefit others, but not yourself, it would be *wrong*. (Incidentally, it is *psychologically impossible* to do a good job, if one's motivation is predominantly altruistic.) However, if this position can benefit your *own* career, then you should consider it, but *only* from this aspect. [Hospers answered that he had not been offered nor was he interested in the chairmanship.]

Now, to answer the questions which you list in your comments on Lectures 9–11.

1. You write: "Suppose that, at a considerable cost of time and effort, I have a chance to save a human life"—and ask whether I would say that you should do it. I will say that an ethical problem cannot be stated in this manner, or rather, that it can be stated in this manner *only* in the context of the *altruist ethics*. I will say that the question of saving a human life can arise only in an emergency; in some physical disaster, like a fire or a shipwreck, and then it has to be answered on the basis of one's hierarchy of values: if the person to be saved is a stranger and the risk (the danger to your own life) is great, don't do it; if the risk is small, do it. This last is all that I would allow in the name of the abstract value of a human life as such. I do value human life, but remember that only individual lives exist and, therefore, one cannot, in the name of the value of human life, advocate the sacrifice of one life to another.

Now, if the person to be saved is not a stranger, then the risk one should be willing to take is greater in exact proportion to the greatness of that person's value to oneself; if it is the man or woman one loves, then one can be willing to give one's own life to save him or her—for the selfish reason that life without the loved person would be unendurable. But this is *not* a duty. The guiding principle here is still one's own rational self-interest: the judgment of the value involved in relation to one's own life and happiness.

Now, conversely, suppose a man is able to swim and could save his drowning wife, but becomes panicky, gives in to an unjustified fear and lets her drown, then spends his life in loneliness and misery—I would not call him *selfish* and I would condemn him morally, on the ground of his treason to his own values, that is: his failure to fight for the preservation of a value crucial to his own happiness. (Remember that values are that which one acts to gain and/or keep, and that one's own happiness has to be achieved by one's own effort. Since one's own happiness is the moral purpose of one's life, the man who fails to achieve it through his own default, through his failure to fight for it, is morally guilty.)

Now, coming back to the exact form of your question, it is the issue of "time and effort" that I challenge. If the question of saving a life involves a long period of time, then it is not an emergency that you have in mind, but a rule of normal existence. If so, if we are formulating a rule of moral conduct, then the words "a considerable cost of time and effort" are a blank check that could mean your entire lifespan—and my answer is: *no*. It would be pure altruistic cannibalism to say that you should devote a major part or the total of *your* life and effort to saving the life of a stranger.

The guiding principle in cases of this kind is still your own self-interest and your own hierarchy of values: the time and effort you give should be proportionate to the value of the person in relation to your own happiness.

If another person's life is endangered as a result of *your* action, if it is *your* fault, then it is *your* responsibility and you have to do everything possible to save it. But—and this is *the* basic principle—another person's life, as such, is *not* your responsibility and, therefore, you cannot sacrifice your own goals, values, ambition and happiness to save any life that might be in need of saving. As a rule of moral conduct, the idea of altruistic responsibility is self-contradictory: why save a life, when neither the savior nor the saved has the right to live (since both would be morally obliged to spend their lives looking for further lives to save)?

It is important to differentiate between the rules of conduct in an emergency situation and the rules of conduct in the normal conditions of existence. This, of course, does not mean a double standard of morality: the basic principles and standards remain the same, but their application to either case requires precise definitions. The main difference between an emergency situation and normal existence is as follows: an emergency situation is an unchosen, unexpected event that threatens or negates normal conditions and is limited in time, as, for example: a physical disaster, an illness, a war. The goal of man's actions, in an emergency situation, is to combat the threat and restore normal conditions, as, for example; to reach land, in a shipwreck—to regain health, in an illness—to win peace, in a war, etc. An emergency situation is a condition which makes human survival impossible and, therefore, has to be fought and corrected. By "normal conditions" I mean "metaphysically normal," "normal in the nature of things." (It is metaphysically normal and possible for man to travel; since man is not omnipotent, it is metaphysically possible for a traveller to be caught in a shipwreck; but if this last were the rule, not the exception, then man would have to abstain from travelling by sea.)

In normal conditions, man has to *choose* his goals, project them in time, pursue them and achieve them. He cannot do it if his goals are at the mercy of and must be sacrificed to any misfortune happening to others. He *cannot* live his life by the guidance of rules applicable only to temporary situations and to conditions under which human survival is impossible. For instance, a man who values human life and is caught in a shipwreck, should help to save his fellow passengers (though not at the expense of his own life). But this does not mean that once they all reach land, he should choose to devote his effort to saving his fellow passengers from poverty, ignorance, neurosis or whatever other troubles they might have. Nor does it mean that he should spend his life sailing the seven seas in search of shipwreck victims to save. Or, to give a simpler example: if you hear that the man in the next apartment is sick and starving, you might bring him food (*if* you can afford it) or you might raise a fund among the neighbors to help him out; but this does *not* mean that you must support him from then on, nor that you must spend your life looking for starving men to help.

If your goal in life is the achievement of your own happiness (if you are an Objectivist), this does not mean that human life is of no value to you, that you are indifferent to all men and that you have no reason to help others in emergencies such as the ones described above. But it *does* mean that you do not subordinate your life to the welfare of others, that you do not consider helping others as the goal of your existence, that the relief of emergencies is not your primary purpose, and that any help you give is an exception, *not* the rule, goal or norm of your life.

Poverty, ignorance and other problems of that kind are *not* emergency situations: they are conditions which man must overcome by his own effort, since wealth or knowledge is not granted to him automatically by God or by nature, but must be achieved by *him*. One's sole obligation, in this respect, is to maintain a social system that leaves men free to achieve. But the principle that one should help men in an emergency cannot be extended to regard all human suffering or misfortune as an emergency and to spend one's life on relieving it.

Every code of morality is based on and derived from a metaphysics, that is: from a certain view of the nature of the universe in which man has to live and act. Observe that the altruist morality *is* based on a "malevolent universe" premise, on the view that man's life is, by nature, a calamity, that emergencies, disasters, scourges, catastrophies, are the *norm* of his existence. Are they? Observe also that the advocates of altruism always offer "lifeboat" situations as examples from which to derive the rules of moral conduct ("What should you do if you are caught with another man in a lifeboat that can carry only one?" etc.) The fact is that men do *not* live in lifeboats—and that a lifeboat is not the place on which to base one's metaphysics.

2. You ask whether you should, at a considerable cost of time and effort, help to improve the condition of a human being who *could* improve his own condition—and you assume that I would say: "Don't do it." Of course, that *is* what I would say, and more: it would be immoral to do it, it would constitute a sanction of the man's evil, of his parasitism.

3. You ask the same question as above, but in regard to helping a human being who is *unable* to improve his condition without help. My answer here is most emphatically: *"No, don't do it."* My reasons are the same as in my answer to question 1. It is moral cannibalism to demand that you spend your life or a major part of it on helping someone else to develop. As in the case of charity, it might be proper to help such a person only in a *marginal* manner, that is: if and when you can afford the time and the money—but *not* at the cost of "considerable time and effort."

You have a curious passage in your question 3: "But the high evaluation you place upon individualism—which surely includes each person developing his own character to the best of his ability—would lead me to believe you would say 'Do it; you will thereby be providing him with a *chance*—with the necessary *wherewithal* without which he could not develop himself.' "

I certainly include "each person developing his own character to the best of *his ability*." I hope the italics make my answer clear: to the best of *his* ability—but *not* by means of the ability of others and the sacrifice of others. Surely I have made it clear in *Atlas Shrugged* that it is monstrously evil to penalize virtue for being virtue. If individualism is a virtue, then it is a monstrous injustice to claim that a man who *has* achieved it, has no right to enjoy it (or to enjoy his own life), but must devote himself to helping those who have *not* achieved it. Why are *they* entitled to it? By reason of their failure to achieve it? *This* is a pure case of Roark versus Jackie. Roark does not demand that Jackie live to help or serve him. Jackie cannot demand that Roark live to help or serve *her*. (The mere thought of this last is obscene.)

(The following is written *after* our telephone conversation of Sunday, April 16th.)

4. The next question on your list is the one we discussed over the telephone, namely: should you sacrifice a position you want, for the sake of a rival whom you regard as better qualified for it? I hope this point is now clear to you. I will summarize it, as a reminder: "the granting of the deserved" requires only that *you* grant men the deserved in *your* actions and in the choices open to you; it does *not* require that you assume the responsibility of providing a man with the reward he deserves, if or when others have failed to do so in a case where the choice was not yours. More specifically: if you know that you are not qualified for a position you want, you should not seek it until you are ready for it; if you *are* qualified, then you should accept it, regardless of what rival you might consider better qualified. (Comparisons of this kind, involving one's ability or intelligence or competence, are too vague and nonobjective to be anything more than a guess about an undefined *potential*—in cases where *both* men are qualified for the job.)

5. Now, the extremely important issue of "Traditional Egoism." You write: "Traditionally, egoism has meant acting for one's self-interest only, and ignoring the interests of everyone else." Then you describe the "traditional egoist" and ask me in what sense I call myself an egoist. Observe that the description you give (the traditional view of egoism) is a description of "Attila": it assumes that one judges one's self-interest by the narrowest range of the immediate moment, without any context, without any concern for past or future, for standards, principles, means or ends, without any *reasons* behind one's choices, actions or decisions; it assumes that *whim* is the only standard of value and criterion of self-interest, and that an "egoist" is one who acts on his whims. *This* is the assumption which I challenge.

An egoist is a man who acts for his own self-interest. This does not yet tell us what his self-interest *is*. On what ground is it then assumed that an egoist does or must judge his self-interest by the arbitrary whim of the moment? On what ground is it assumed that his interests are antagonistic to or incompatible with the interests of others? On what ground is it assumed that human relationships have no *personal* value to a man and that an egoist has to be indifferent to all other human beings? On what ground is "Attila" supposed to represent the archetype of egoism—and why is "Attila's" view of self-interest taken as *the* view and the essence of self-interest?

As you see, the "traditional" concept of egoism is a "loaded," ground-less, unwarranted, unjustifiable package-deal: purporting to define only the basic motivation of a man (self-interest), it then proceeds to prescribe the specific concretes allegedly representing man's self-interest—and thus sub-stitutes the concrete values of "Attila" for the abstraction "self-interest."

I certainly maintain that an egoist *is* a man who acts for his own self-interest and that man *should* act for his own self-interest. But the concept of "self-interest" identifies only one's motivation, *not* the nature of the values that one should choose. The issue, therefore, is: *what* is the nature of man's self-interest? Since arbitrary desires, wishes or whims are *not* a valid standard of value or criterion of self-interest—an egoist has to have a *rational* standard of value and a *rational* code of morality in order to be able *in fact* to *achieve* his self-interest.

The "traditional" concept of egoism assumes that an egoist's standard is: "My self-interest consists of doing whatever happens to please me." A drunkard, a drug addict, a hot-rod car driver are men who act on that standard; they could hardly be regarded as exponents of self-interest. A self-destroying, whim-worshipping neurotic is not a representative of the *ego*; in actual fact, he has neither self nor interests—and it is certainly not self-interest that he pursues or achieves. The "traditional" view of egoism (with whim as its standard) can thus be proved to be a contradiction in terms.

Man's ego is his mind; the most crucial aspect of egoism is the sov-ereignty of one's own rational judgment and the right to live by its guid-ance. Yet *this* is the aspect which the "traditional" view of egoism ignores and negates: it regards as "egoistic" nothing but the momentary physical satisfactions of a brute. For instance, it regards a man's concern with social or political issues as "unselfish." It is absurd to claim that the kind of society in which he lives has no bearing on a man's self-interest; it makes a crucial difference to him whether he lives in a free country or in a total-itarian dictatorship. But the "traditional" concept of egoism does not allow him so wide a view of self-interest.

It is obvious that that "traditional" concept is a remnant and derivative of the "Witch Doctor" philosophy: it regards "Attila" as *practical* and, simultaneously, intends to bridle him, as well as all men, by means of *guilt*.

First, it claims that "self-interest" consists of nothing but brute evil—then, it damns *all* forms of self-interest as evil.

The most disastrous error (or fraud) in the history of ethics is the moral diagnosis of criminal actions: traditional moralists claim that the evil of a robber or a murderer consists of the fact that he acted for his own "self-interest." *I* claim that his evil lies in his choice of values, in what he chose to regard as his self-interest.

You can easily see the consequences of that difference: if "self-interest" is the element that makes crime evil, then robbery, torture, murder, mass slaughter are *not* evil when committed in the interest of others—and *this* precisely is the moral concept by means of which all the horrors of modern dictatorships are accepted, condoned, excused and justified today.

The "traditional" view of egoism does not and cannot differentiate between a producer and a looter: both are men acting for and on their respective views of *self-interest*. This is another symptom and remnant of the "Witch Doctor" philosophy: a Witch Doctor does not allow into his view of the universe the possibility of the existence of a producer.

The "traditional" view of egoism assumes that the standard of value by which one judges the worth of an action is not a principle, not a specific premise, not a defined concept of the "good," not any *objective* consideration, but only the *beneficiary* of an action. It assumes that the beneficiary is an ethical primary and a standard of moral value: if an action, regardless of its nature, is intended to serve your own benefit—you are an egoist (and, traditionally, evil); if an action, regardless of its nature, is intended to serve the benefit of others—you are an altruist (and, traditionally, good). This leads to all the vicious contradictions that I discuss in Galt's speech

So long as ethics remained the province of mysticism and subjectivism, so long as ethics was ultimately based on whim (God's whim, society's or one's own), so long as moral values were not objectively, rationally justified or justifiable—human *desires* had to be taken as irreducible primaries, and the basic moral issue had to be: whose desires?—yours or your neighbors'? (See pp. 30–31 of my paper on "The Objectivist Ethics," the passage dealing with the issue of ethical hedonism.) It is the irrationality, the primitiveness and the superficiality of that traditional approach that I challenge.

The task of ethics is to tell men how to live. Since neither self-interest (nor happiness nor survival) can be achieved by random motions or arbitrary whims, it is the task of ethics to define the principles by which man is to judge and choose his values, interests, goals and actions. (Only a mystic's, a Witch Doctor's, view of ethics could hold that man can live and act by the guidance of his desires or of arbitrarily chosen values, that is: values divorced from or opposed to the facts of reality with which he has to deal.) Therefore, the first question in ethics is: What *are* values and why does man need them? The answer to that will tell us what values man should choose and why.

You know the base and validation of the Objectivist Ethics; you know why man's right to exist for his own sake is not an arbitrary, "selfish" choice, but a metaphysical necessity derived not merely from man's nature, but from the *nature of life*, that is: of all living organisms—and why the specific moral code required for man's existence is necessitated by his nature as a living organism whose basic means of survival is reason.

Therefore, a man's self-interest is not to be determined by his arbitrary wishes or whims, but by the principles of an objective moral code. Man must pursue his own self-interest, but *only* by the guidance of, by reason of and within the framework of such a code. The moral rights and claims derived from that code are based on his nature as a rational being; they cannot be extended to include their opposite; an irrational claim invalidates itself by negating the base of man's moral claims or rights (by falling into the fallacy of the "stolen concept"). The right to exist and to pursue his own happiness does not give man the right to act irrationally or to pursue contradictory, self-destructive, self-defeating goals. Rationality demands that man choose his goals in the full, *integrated* context of all the relevant knowledge available to him; it forbids contradictions, evasions, blank-outs, whim-worship or context-dropping.

A rational man has to recognize that reason permits no arbitrary, subjective beliefs or values—and that the value he attaches to his own life and his *objective* right to it are based on the nature of life in general and of *human* life in particular; therefore, if he values his own life, he has to recognize the right of all other human beings to value their own lives in the same way, for the same reasons and *on the same terms*. If he holds the support of his own life by his own effort and the achievement of his own happiness as his primary goal, he has to grant the same right to others; if he does not grant it, he is guilty of a contradiction and cannot claim any rational validity for his own right. If he recognizes that living among other men (in a free society) is to his self-interest, he cannot be blindly indifferent to other men or "refuse to lift a finger to save a human life." It is his self-esteem and his self-interest that are the root of his benevolence toward others. (But if men enslaved him to serve their needs in a collectivist society, that root would disappear and it is then that he would feel indifference or hatred or contempt for others.) If he pursues his *rational* self-interest, he does not set his values and goals on the spur and range of the moment; therefore, he knows that it is *not* to his self-interest, it is neither moral nor practical, to rob, cheat, defraud or murder others—and he knows also that he must not seek the *unearned*, that is: seek to obtain any value produced by or belonging to others, without their voluntary consent and without trading them a value in return. If he claims the right to independence, he cannot live as a parasite on the productive work of others (trade is not dependence—charity and robbery are). He chooses and pursues only those goals which can be achieved by his own effort; he does not need others or depend on others in any fundamental issue of his life. And, above all, he preserves the independent sovereignty of his own judgment as his only guide.

This, in briefest essence, is the Objectivist view of egoism. This is the sense in which Roark, Galt and I *are* pure egoists.

To sum up the foregoing: there are *two* questions in ethics, which the traditional moralists lump together into an undifferentiated package-deal— a. What are values?—b. Who should be the beneficiary of values? Since all values have to be gained and/or kept by men's actions, any breach between actor and beneficiary *necessitates* injustice: the sacrifice of some men to others, of the actors or producers to the beneficiaries. Nothing could ever justify or validate such a breach. Therefore, the Objectivist ethics holds that the actor must always be the beneficiary of the action—that man must act for his own self-interest—but that this right is derived from the nature of values and the nature of man, and, therefore, is applicable *only* in the context of a rational, objectively demonstrated and validated code of moral values, which determines man's rational self-interest.

6. You write: "Your insisting (rightly, I believe) that Mr. A, B and C have the same rights that you do, would seem to lead naturally to the Golden Rule . . . and to the Kantian categorical imperative. . . ."

My answer is that I base men's equal rights on a much deeper premise and issue than either of these two rules—and, therefore, these two rules are irrelevant to my ethics. I do not regard them as necessarily antagonistic to my ethics, but as irrelevant and unimportant by reason of their ambiguity and superficiality.

You state the best criticism of these two rules when you say that they are *"content-less."* With this, I agree emphatically. They tell us nothing about moral values nor what values men should choose nor what a man should wish for himself and others.

At best, these two rules are popular generalizations illustrating one aspect or consequence of the principle of *objectivity* or *justice*. I would agree with these two rules (on the popular level) only if they were translated to mean: "Do not wish, seek or advocate contradictions"—and then only if they were regarded as derivatives or consequences of deeper, antecedent moral premises, *not* as fundamental principles or definitions of moral action.

If, however, these two rules are advocated as ethical primaries—then I am emphatically opposed to them. In their literal wording, both rules advocate ethical subjectivism, with one's *wish* as the standard of moral value; both declare, in effect, that one may do anything one wishes, provided one is willing to universalize one's wish.

In paragraphs 2 and 3, page 2 of your comments, you provide a full and unanswerable refutation of the Golden Rule and the Kantian imperative, when you give examples of how two opposite, arbitrary policies (of an altruistic and "egoistic" nature) could be pursued in strict compliance with either of those rules. Once you demonstrate it, it is sufficient ground to invalidate both rules as guiding principles of action.

When you ask why or how I would attack the altruistic policy in your example, yet would defend the "egoistic" one—your error is the assumption that I would base my argument on the Golden Rule or the Kantian imperative. I would maintain (though not exactly in this formulation) that "I do not want or expect others to help me when I am in trouble or need, and I do not consider it incumbent on me to help them when they are in trouble or need," on the ground of the fact that this is *objectively* the right policy for men to live by—and *not* on the ground of the fact that this is what I *want* to do and am willing to let others do. This is an instance of why I say that the Golden Rule and the Kantian imperative are irrelevant to my ethics. No part of my ethics and no argument of mine are or would ever be based on or validated by either of these two rules.

7. I am glad that you agree with me on the issue of justice vs. mercy. It is an enormously important principle that embraces all of one's relationships with men: private, personal, public, social and political. But you say that you are not clear on what I would regard as the deserved, in specific cases. My answer is: the basic principle that should guide one's judgment in issues of justice is the law of causality: one should never attempt to evade or to break the connection between cause and effect—one should never attempt to deprive a man of the consequences of his actions, good or evil. (One should not deprive a man of the values or benefits *his* actions have caused, such as expropriating a man's wealth for somebody else's benefit; and one should not deflect the disaster which *his* actions have caused, such as giving relief checks to a lazy, irresponsible loafer.) What specific form of reward or punishment is deserved in specific cases depends on the full context of the case. In personal relationships, the rewards de-

served by virtue range from an approving smile to falling in love; the punishments range from a polite reproach or protest (when the action involved is an error of knowledge) to a complete break (when the action is *proved* to be a willful, conscious, deliberate immorality).

But you ask me what is the punishment deserved by criminal actions. This is a technical, *legal* issue, which has to be answered by the philosophy of law. The law has to be guided by moral principles, but their application to specific cases is a special field of study. I can only indicate in a general way what principles should be the base of legal justice in determining punishments. The law should: a. correct the consequences of the crime in regard to the victim, whenever possible (such as recovering stolen property and returning it to the owner); b. impose restraints on the criminal, such as a jail sentence, *not* in order to reform him, but in order to make *him* bear the painful consequences of his action (or their equivalent) which he inflicted on his victims; c. make the punishment proportionate to the crime *in the full context of all the legally punishable crimes.*

This last point, I believe, is the question you are specifically interested in, when you write: "I find it difficult to say whether a man who has committed, e.g. armed robbery, deserves one year in jail, five years, ten years, or psychiatric therapy to keep him from repeating his offense." The principle of justice on which the answer has to be based is contextual: the severity of the punishment must match the gravity of the crime, in the full context of the penal code. The punishment for pickpocketing cannot be the same as for murder; the punishment for murder cannot be the same as for manslaughter, etc. It is an enormously complex issue, in which one must integrate the whole scale of legally defined crimes and mitigating circumstances, on the one hand—with a proportionately scaled series of punishments, on the other. Thus the punishment deserved by armed robbery would depend on its place in the scale which begins with the lightest misdemeanor and ends with murder.

What punishment is deserved by the two extremes of the scale *is* open to disagreement and discussion—but the principle by which a specific argument has to be guided is *retribution*, not *reform*. The issue of attempting to "reform" criminals is an entirely separate issue and a highly dubious one, even in the case of juvenile delinquents. At best, it might be a carefully limited adjunct of the penal code (and I doubt even that), *not* its primary, determining factor. When I say "retribution," I mean the point above, namely: the imposition of painful consequences proportionate to the injury caused by the criminal act. The purpose of the law is *not* to prevent a future offense, but to punish the one actually committed. If there were a proved, demonstrated, scientific, objectively certain way of preventing future crimes (which does not exist), it would not justify the idea that the law should prevent future offenses and let the present one go unpunished. It would still be necessary to punish the actual crime.

Therefore, "psychiatric therapy" does not belong—on principle—among the alternatives that you list. And more: it is an enormously dangerous suggestion. A. Psychiatry is far from the stage of an *exact science*; in our present state of knowledge, it is not even a science—it is only in that preliminary, material-gathering stage from which a science will come. B. The law, which has the power to impose its decisions *by force*, cannot be guided by unproved, uncertain, controversial hypotheses or guesses—and the criminal cannot be treated as a guinea pig (I am saying this *in defense* of the criminal's rights). C. Since the *prevention* of crime is a *psychological* issue, since it involves a man's *mind* (his premises, values, choices, decisions), it would be monstrously evil to place a man's mind into the power of the law, to let the law prescribe and *force upon him* any course of treatment involving or affecting his mind. If *"the prevention of crime"* were accepted as the province and purpose of the law, it would permit and necessitate the most unspeakable atrocities: not merely psychological "brainwashing," but physical mutilations as well, such as electric shock therapy, prefrontal lobotomies and anything else that neurologists might discover. No moral premise—except total altruistic collectivism—could ever justify that sort of horror.

Observe that it is I, the unforgiving egoist, who am more considerate of the criminals (of their *rights*) than the alleged humanitarians who advocate psychiatric treatments out of an alleged compassion for criminals. A penal code has to treat men as adult, responsible human beings; it can deal only with their actions and with such motives as can be objectively demonstrated (such as intent vs. accident); it cannot assume jurisdiction over men's minds, brains, souls, values and moral premises—it cannot assume the *right* to change these by forcible means.

(If a man is *proved* to be legally irresponsible, that is, *insane*, it is a different issue: the law then has the right to commit him to an insane asylum—since, being incapable of reasoning, he is unable to claim the rights of a rational man. But even then, the law does not have the arbitrary power to impose treatment on him, particularly not treatment that might result in physical damage or injury. And, even in cases of insanity, the issue of proving it is enormously complex, controversial and dangerous, since no fully demonstrated, scientific knowledge is yet available on what can be taken as proof.)

8. You ask whether I would agree with the distinction you make between "intrinsic good" and "instrumental good." I do not object to the concepts *as you define them*, but I would not use them, for the following reasons: A. The term "intrinsic" is extremely dangerous to use in ethics. It can be taken to mean "good of and by itself," regardless of context, standard, source, recipient and recipient's knowledge. For instance, if one decided that "security" is an *"intrinsic"* good, one would be justified in attempting to establish it by any and all means, on the ground that it would necessarily be good for all men—which is precisely the reasoning by which collectivists justify their policies. B. Values which are ends to be achieved by a certain process of action and which, therefore, could be called "intrinsic" in that context—become means to further and wider ends and thus become "instrumental" in a wider context. For instance, the process of writing is an "instrumental" good in relation to creating a book, which is an "intrinsic" good in this context; but creating a book is an "instrumental" good in relation to achieving a literary career, which is an "intrinsic good" in this context; and achieving a literary career is an "instrumental" good in relation to achieving one's happiness and supporting one's life. Since I regard all values as *contextual* and *hierarchical*, I would ultimately regard only *one* good as "intrinsic," in your sense of the term, namely: *life* (with happiness as its corollary—as defined in my paper on "The Objectivist Ethics," *particularly* in paragraph 3, page 28).

Frankly, I suspect that the distinction between "intrinsic" good and "instrumental" good belongs to a traditional view of (or approach to) ethics which is totally different from mine. But since I do not know the full context, place, and *purpose* of this distinction in *your* approach to ethics, I am open to further discussion and clarification.

You ask: "What is the relation between saying that man's life is the standard of value and that *one's own* life should be the thing one strives to promote?" The answer is stated explicitly on page 21 of my paper on "The Objectivist Ethics" (paragraphs 2, 3 and 4). I will add that by the nature of the standard involved, it is *only* one's own life that one can or *should* "promote."

You ask what I would say to someone who said: "Since the standard is man's life—not just your or my or my family's life—why then should we not strive to improve man's life in general, even if in doing so I do not improve my own, or even extinguish my own life completely?"

I would remind the questioner of the difference between an *abstraction* and a *collective noun*. ("*Man*" is an abstraction, "mankind" is a collective noun.) The standard "man's life" does not mean "just your or my or my family's life." It means: that which is proper to the life of man *qua* man —that which is proper to the life of every individual man qua individual man. "My life" cannot be "*the standard* of my life." A "*standard*" is an abstract principle of action, which tells me how I should live my life. And *the standard "man's life"* tells me why and how *my* life should be *my purpose.*

Since the standard "man's life" is derived from the nature of *values,* from the fact that only life makes values possible (that is: only the nature of a living organism, only the requirements of an organism's life make the existence of values possible)—to choose any value, other than one's own life, as the ultimate purpose of one's actions is to be guilty of a contradiction and of the fallacy of the "stolen concept." Do you remember the answer you gave to a student in your seminar, with which I agreed most enthusiastically? You said that one cannot ask: "*Why* should I be rational?"—because by accepting a "why" one has already accepted reason, because "why" is a concept belonging to rationality. Well, on the same grounds, by the same logic, one cannot ask: "Why should I choose my own life as my ultimate *value?*"—because one has already accepted it by accepting the concept "*value*," because the concept "value" has no other source, base, meaning or possibility of existing.

You write: "I especially appreciated your saying that my *Newsweek* letter was as important to you positively as the *Newsweek* review was negatively." I did not say: "*as* important," I said: "*more* important." I do not attach any importance to negatives: evil is *impotent.* It is not an issue of how many people will see your letter vs. how many people will see the review. Your letter proves the existence of a man of intelligence and integrity; the review proves the existence of a fool and a knave. The first is important, the second is not. (Or, to use *your* terms: the existence of the first is an "intrinsic" good—while the existence of the second is not even an "instrumental" evil.) When evil wins in the world, it is only by the default of the good. That is why one man of reason and moral stature is more important, actually and potentially, "intrinsically" and "instrumentally," than a million fools.

The above is my way of saying: *Thank you.*

And thank you also for the copy of *Human Conduct,* which I received a few days ago. It is very attractive in appearance—and very promising in content. I have barely had time to glance at a few passages, at random, but it was an enormous pleasure to see the clarity and precision of your style, the *epistemological* virtue that I admired in your previous work. I am looking forward eagerly to reading it. I did, of course, look up all the references to "Ayn Rand"—and I was delighted to see them; it gave me the feeling of a bond between us—and an almost "proprietary" interest in the book. I will conclude with one more "thank you," for those references—and my best wishes for the enormous success of your book.

P.S. If you find that you want to quote any passage from this letter in a discussion of Objectivism, you are certainly welcome to do so.

■　■　■

8

THE LATER YEARS
(1960–1981)

To Jennifer Sachs, a fan

May 27, 1960

Dear Miss Sachs:

I appreciate your interest in the philosophy of *Atlas Shrugged*, and your perceptive understanding of its application to modern problems.

You are right in your interpretation of Dr. Stadler's fate, but not of Eddie Willers's. Eddie Willers is not necessarily destined to die; in a free society, he will live happily and productively; in a collectivist society he will be the first to perish. He does not have the ability to create a new society of his own, but he is much too able and too honest ever to adjust himself to collectivism.

You are mistaken when you say: "It is for the Eddies and Dr. Stadlers that we must right the wrong and again teach man to be 'his own keeper.' " I am not quite certain of what you meant, but this sentence sounds like some form of altruism. If by "righting the wrong," you meant the acceptance of the right philosophy and the creation of a proper society, then one must do it for oneself and for those who are one's highest values—which means, in effect, for the John Galts, *not* the Eddies nor the Stadlers. The Eddies and all *rational* men will also profit in a proper society—but that is a secondary consequence, not one's primary goal.

■ ■ ■

To Stephen Sipos, a fan

June 1, 1960

Dear Mr. Sipos:

I must compliment you particularly on two points: your realization that both Communism and Catholicism are enemies of the independent mind— and your realization that a doctor should choose his profession for the sake of his own creative, scientific effort, *not* for the sake of service to others.

■   ■   ■

To Sen. Barry Goldwater

On May 11, Senator Goldwater wrote to AR: "I am particularly proud of the fact that you were the one to [defend my conservative position on Mike Wallace's show], because I have enjoyed very few books in my life as much as I have yours, *Atlas Shrugged*."

June 4, 1960

Dear Senator Goldwater:

Thank you for the autographed copy of *The Conscience of a Conservative*, which you sent me, and for your letter of May 11. Please accept this answer as my method of expressing my deepest appreciation.

I regard you as the only hope of the anticollectivist side on today's political scene, and I have defended your position at every opportunity. Therefore, I am profoundly disturbed by some dangerous contradictions in your stand, as expressed in *The Conscience of a Conservative*. I do not know the reason nor the extent of your intellectual commitment to these contradictions and, therefore, I am submitting the following for your consideration.

The opening sentence of your book is: "This book is not written with the idea of adding to or improving on the Conservative philosophy." But there is no such thing as a *"Conservative"* philosophy. It is the lack of a philosophy that has brought the American conservatives to helplessness, vacillation and successive defeats.

You indicate that by "Conservatism" you mean the political principles of the Founding Fathers, which created this country. That is true: that *is* what the term "Conservative" means in America today. The principles which created this country were embodied and expressed in the political-

economic system of *"Free Enterprise"* or *"Capitalism."* But it is dangerously misleading to call these principles "ancient and tested truths." They
were new, untested and unprecedented; the great achievement of the Founding Fathers was the fact that they created a political system *fundamentally*
different from any that had ever existed before in the whole of human
history—a system based on the concept of man's inalienable individual
rights. (Philosophically, the Founding Fathers were influenced by Aristotle,
via John Locke. But their own views were never extended into a full system
of philosophy.)

I assume, therefore, that by "Conservative" you mean: a defender of
Capitalism. That is the meaning of all the *basic* policies you advocate in
your book; that is the meaning of the term "Conservative" in the mind of
the American public: "Conservative" stands for *Capitalism*—as against
"Liberal," which stands for *Collectivism.* The conflict of today's world is
between these two political systems. Everybody knows it—but our Conservative leaders lack the courage to say it, which is the reason why they
are losing the Cold War internationally and every political battle domesti-
cally, even though the overwhelming majority of the American people are,
potentially, on their side. Since nobody would accuse *you* of lacking courage, I regard you as the man who might bring the American Conservatives
back to life, by means of a clear-cut, unequivocal stand. I don't have to
tell you that if the American Conservatives do *not* stand for Capitalism,
they're done for.

The major contradiction in your book is between Chapter I and the
rest of the book's content. More specifically, it is between the fight for
Capitalism and the issue of religion. There can be no more disastrous
error—morally, philosophically and politically—than to assert that the ultimate justification of Capitalism *rests on faith.* To assert this is to announce
that there is no *rational* justification for Capitalism, no rational arguments
to support the principles which created this country—and that reason is on
the side of the enemy.

The Communists claim that they are the champions of reason and
science. If the Conservatives concede that claim and retreat into the realm
of religion, it will be an act of intellectual abdication, the kind of intellectual
surrender that the Communists' irrational ideology could never have won
on its own merits.

The conflict between Capitalism and Communism is a *philosophical*
and *moral* conflict, which must be *fought and won* in men's minds, in the
realm of ideas; without that victory, no victory in the political realm is
possible. But one cannot win men's minds by telling them not to think;

one cannot win an intellectual battle by renouncing the intellect; one cannot convince anybody by appealing to faith.

Capitalism is perishing by default. The historical cause of its destruction is the failure of its philosophical advocates to present a full, consistent case and to offer a *moral* justification for their stand. Yet reason is on the side of Capitalism; an irrefutable *rational* case can be, and must be, offered by its defenders. The philosophical default of the Conservatives will become final, if Capitalism—the one and only *rational* way of life—is reduced to the status of a mystic doctrine.

I am not suggesting that you should take a stand *against* religion. I am saying that Capitalism and religion are two separate issues, which should not be united into one "package deal" or one common cause. This does not mean that religious persons cannot crusade for Capitalism; but it does mean that nonreligious persons, like myself, cannot crusade for religion.

According to the Constitutional principle of the separation of Church and State, religion is a private matter; it should not be brought into public issues or into the province of government, and it should not be made a part of political movements. Consider the implications of the attempt to tie Conservatism to religion: if such an attempt succeeded, it would make religion an *integral* part of our *political* system, in direct contradiction to the Constitution. The next question to arise would be: *which* religion? Religions have lived in peace with one another and with nonreligious thinkers only since the XIX century, since the American establishment of the principle separating Church and State. Some of them, notably the Catholic Church, have never renounced their dream of regaining control of the State's power of compulsion. Is this a goal that the advocates of Capitalism can support, assist or sanction? If this goal were to succeed, what would become of religious minorities? Or of those who hold no religion?

When I spoke to you briefly here, in New York, on May 17th, you mentioned your desire to unite all Conservatives in a common cause. I share your desire and I regard it as the most crucially important goal in politics. But it cannot be accomplished without a philosophical base, that is: without a set of *rational* principles, which all those who join can accept with full understanding and conviction. It cannot be accomplished on the basis of *"faith."* A secular political movement does not exclude religious people. A religious political movement *does* exclude nonreligious people, such as myself and those who agree with me.

As a man, you are free to hold any religious or nonreligious view you choose; but as a political leader, you must leave the same freedom to your followers. To make religion the basis of your stand is to slap the faces and reject the support of those whom a Conservative leader most needs: the independent thinkers, those who are fighting Collectivism by intellectual means and on the intellectual front.

Among the so-called Conservative intellectuals, I am perhaps the only one who has acquired a large *popular* following, and the only one who is gaining converts. I deal constantly with young people of college age—and I wish I could communicate to you the kind of apathy, indifference and contempt they exhibit whenever they hear any argument based on *"faith."* They are starved for a voice of reason. They are sick of collectivism and eager to fight for freedom. I cannot count how often—and how desperately—they ask me whether there is *anyone* in politics who holds a rational position. Your name is the only one I give them. I hope that you won't let them down. They have been disappointed too often by the ineffectuality of the Conservative leadership—by such incidents as the letter from the "Committee For Freedom For All Peoples," sent out at the time of Khrushchev's visit to the United States. You may recall that it was a letter signed by five senators and congressmen. (I was relieved to see that *your* name was not among them.) That letter suggested prayer (the holding of religious services) as a form of protest against Khrushchev—and this was the *only* advice for practical action that it contained.

Frankly, I suspect that Chapter I of your book, which stresses the issue of religion, was not written by you, but by your ghostwriter—because it contains contradictions that do not fit the precision and forthrightness of your usual style. On page 12, there is the statement: "The economic and spiritual aspects of man's nature are inextricably intertwined." *This is true*—but it is denied just one page earlier. On pages 10–11, there is the statement: "The Conservative believes that man is, in part, an economic, an animal creature; but that he is also a spiritual creature with spiritual needs and spiritual desires. What is more, these needs and desires reflect the *superior* side of man's nature, and thus take precedence over his economic wants."

If the economic and spiritual aspects of man's nature are "inextricably intertwined," neither can be *"superior"* to the other. Such a term as "superiority" does not apply in this context.

I do not know which aspects of my philosophy, as presented in *Atlas Shrugged*, you agree with. But you could not have enjoyed or admired my book at all, if you were diametrically opposed to its main thesis, which is: that man's material, industrial production, like all his other achievements, is the result and the expression of his noblest spiritual qualities: of his *mind*, his independent thinking, his creative genius—and that the false, mystic doctrine which splits man in two and regards his spiritual interests as opposed and *superior* to his material interests, is *the* basic cause of the destruction of Capitalism.

If the *economic* part of man's life is to be regarded as an *"animal"* function, then there is no reason to admire or respect the industrialists; there is no reason why their achievements should not be placed under the control of those *"superior"* creatures who are devoted to selflessly "spiritual," social goals and whose superiority consists of their contempt for vulgar "materialistic" pursuits.

Surely you know that the whole Collectivist case rests on such arguments. Surely you have heard the American businessmen reviled as "vulgar materialists," and America damned as a "materialistic" country. Surely you cannot wish to sanction, support and help spread that sort of ideas.

On page 10, your book states: "It is Socialism that subordinates all other considerations to man's material well-being." This is untenable and disastrous for the following reasons:

a. It implies that Socialism can and *will* provide man with material well-being.
b. It implies that the poor, the workers and all those who struggle for a living, *ought to* take the Socialist side—because Capitalism has nothing to offer them but "pie in the sky."
c. Socialism is not winning converts by "materialistic" promises or considerations; it is winning precisely on *"spiritual"* grounds. It is considered to be "idealistic"; it promises what men regard as a *moral* way of life: equal sharing of wealth, altruistic self-sacrifice to the needs of others, automatic help to the afflicted, universal "love," etc. The *material* poverty and the miserable standard of living in all Socialist countries are thoroughly well-known to everybody; this does not cause anybody to reject the Socialist side. The magnificent material prosperity of Capitalism is equally well-known; this does not gain any friends for Capitalism. The appeal of Collectivism is not "materialistic." And no authentic *spiritual and moral* justification of Capitalism can ever be offered on the mystic-altruist-collectivist premise of damning "material" pursuits and "material greed."

On page 88 of your book, in discussing the threat of a nuclear war, you state: "The American people are being told that, however valuable their freedom may be, it is even more important to live." Thereafter, you take the position that freedom is more important than life. This is a concession to the enemy, an acceptance of his basic premise and of another false alternative that he wants us to accept. The Communists are spending an enormous amount of money and effort to convince us that our choice is: freedom or life. This is a premise that we must never grant them. It is true that no man of self-esteem would buy his life at the price of his freedom; but it is also true that *life is impossible without freedom.* A slave may gain a short-range span of brute physical survival, which can and will be cut off at any moment by the arbitrary whim of his master. When men fight a war for freedom, they are fighting for their lives.

If men surrendered to Communism they would not gain safety for their lives: millions of them would be exterminated through purges, terror and starvation. Nobody could foretell who would survive: no matter how craven some people might be willing to be, this would not guarantee their safety; a dictatorship slaughters at random; survival would be a matter of blind chance; some would survive, others would not. Now if men "risked" a nuclear war, the same would be true: some would survive, others would not. But the difference is this: the risk of one's life with a fighting chance to win—or the risk of one's life in the role of a helpless, defenseless object of extermination.

This is the alternative that should be presented to the American people: not "freedom *or* life," but "freedom *and* life, or slavery and death."

In the nineteen-thirties, the Conservatives accepted, with disastrous results, the Collectivist premise that men's choice is: "*security* or freedom," and proceeded to advocate the choice of freedom, thus granting that Collectivism could give men security. If, today, they accept another one: "*life* or freedom," thus granting that life would be safe under a dictatorship, the results will be equally disastrous. On such premises, what is the purpose, meaning, or value of freedom—if freedom is nonessential either to security or to life?

I cited these issues in detail in order to illustrate the nature of the main contradictions that undercut the power of your book. There are many lesser ones. They clash with the major portions of your book and with the policies you are advocating. The major portions of your book have strength, clarity, forthrightness and courage—particularly the truly magnificent last chapter, "The Soviet Menace." (I cheered aloud at almost every paragraph of that last chapter.) The clashing element creeps in mainly in the brief allusions to abstract, philosophical questions; it is an element which I can best describe as something mawkish and foggy. Forgive me for the use of such words—but I find it difficult to believe that a man who has the understanding of principles and the moral integrity to advocate the idea of paragraph 2, page 101 of *The Conscience of a Conservative* ("When the Soviets challenged our rights in West Berlin, we handed them a victory by the mere act of sitting down at the conference table. By agreeing to negotiate on that subject, we agreed that our rights in Berlin were 'negotiable,' something they never were before. . . . Our answer to Khrushchev's ultimatum should have been that the status of West Berlin . . . is not a matter that we are prepared to discuss with the Soviet Union. That would have been the end of the Berlin 'crisis.' ")—I find it difficult to believe that that same man would advocate the tenet that material production belongs to man's lower, animal nature, without realizing what *principle* he is establishing and what monstrous moral consequences that principle implies.

Please believe that I am not reproaching or criticizing you for employing a ghostwriter. I know too well that writing is a full-time job, which cannot be combined with the responsibilities of a political office. But I *am* criticizing your ghostwriter for proving himself unworthy of his assignment.

This leads me to the subject of the *National Review*. I am profoundly opposed to it—*not* because it is a religious magazine, but because it *pretends that it is not.* There are religious magazines which one can respect, even while disagreeing with their views. But the fact that the *National Review* poses as a secular political magazine, while following a strictly religious "party line," can have but one purpose: to slip religious goals by stealth on those who would not accept them openly, to "bore from within," to tie Conservatism to religion, and thus *to take over* the American Conservatives. This attempt comes from a pressure group wider than the *National Review*, but the *National Review* is one of its manifestations.

When a political movement lacks a firm, consistent set of principles, it can be taken over by any minority that knows what it wants. In the nineteen-thirties, the Liberals were thus taken over by the Communists. According, I believe, to the FBI, two percent of the membership was sufficient to turn a Liberal organization into a Communist front. In any group of men, those who formulate basic principles will direct those who don't, and will determine the practical policy of the group. I am convinced that what the Communists did to the Liberals, the professional religionists are now attempting to do to the Conservatives.

The attempt to use religion as a *moral justification* of Conservatism began after World War II. Observe the growing apathy, lifelessness, ineffectuality and general feebleness of the so-called Conservative side, ever since.

You are, at present, a rising exception in the Republican ranks. I do not believe that that pressure group could succeed in making you its tool. But a *philosophical* pressure group is very hard to detect, particularly at first. That is why I want to warn you against them now, and help you to identify the nature of their influence.

I am not certain that you understood my relationship to the *National Review*, when I spoke to you here. I thought that you knew the facts, but perhaps you do not. In brief, they printed a review of *Atlas Shrugged* by Whittaker Chambers, which I have not read, on principle; those who have read it, told me that this former Communist spy claimed that my book advocates dictatorship. Thereafter, the *National Review* printed two articles about me (which I did read), one of them allegedly friendly, both of them misrepresenting my position in a manner I have not seen outside *The Daily Worker* or *The Nation*. What was significant was their second article: *it denounced me for advocating capitalism.*

I do not believe that you share the ideology of those people—and I deeply regret the fact that your stand is undermined and undercut by what I believe to be the philosophical ineptitude of a ghostwriter. If it is in my power, I would like to help you avoid the kind of side issues that can lead only to a political dead end. That is why I urge you to give these questions your earnest consideration. You are the first man of courage, stature and integrity to appear on the political scene in many years; you may be the last.

Since you told me, when I met you for the first time, that you had found the ideas of *Atlas Shrugged* helpful in your campaign of 1958, I am enclosing three political pamphlets (*Textbook of Americanism* and *Notes on the History of American Free Enterprise*, written by me, and *The Moral Antagonism of Capitalism and Socialism*, by Barbara Branden, an associate of mine), which we use for our students. I hope that you will find these pamphlets helpful, as a pattern of the method by which one can present Capitalism to a popular audience, using nothing but the Declaration of Independence as one's moral and philosophical base.

This letter will give you a chance to consider at your leisure the issues I wanted to discuss with you when I asked for an appointment to see you. If you are able to give me that appointment, I shall be glad to make a trip to Washington any time at your convenience.

In his June 10 response, Senator Goldwater contended that there is a "conservative philosophy" and that he is an advocate of both faith and "natural laws."

■   ■   ■

To Terry Lung, a fan

June 28, 1960

Dear Miss Lung:

Thank you for the photograph which you sent me. It is excellent—and, since you are devoted to your work, you may be pleased to know that it was the photograph that has earned my answer to your two letters.

What impressed me most, in that photograph, is the spirit which you caught in the young girl's face. But I do not know whether that young girl is yourself or not. If you have a copy of your second letter, you will see that you have not stated it. I do not know whether "the purity of Self," to which you referred, meant your own face or whether you meant it as a photographer who had found the right model to project her theme. I congratulate you in either case—if that photograph represents your idea of what you value in a human face and a human expression.

But I must tell you frankly that I do not understand your letters, particularly the first. They gave me no clue to your specific ideas, convictions or motives. If you have read *Atlas Shrugged*, you must know that I hold reason (not feeling) as man's highest faculty and as the only means of communication among men. (Feelings are the products of man's conscious or subconscious value judgments, and cannot be communicated directly; they can be communicated *only* via *rational* perception.) Your manner of writing is so confused that I do not know which of my books you have read. You state that you read my "first and second books"; my first and second books were *We the Living* and *Anthem*, but I doubt that that is what you meant.

I must object, most severely, to the following paragraph of your first letter: [Miss Lung writes that if her meaning isn't clear, she is justified, since her means of expression is a camera, not words.] I will answer that *you* write your letters, not I—and that the responsibility of making your meaning clear is yours, not mine. I have no way of knowing the content of your consciousness, if you do not make the effort to express it *objectively*. There can never be a "good reason" for intellectual carelessness.

I deeply appreciate your offer to photograph me, but I cannot accept it until I meet you and am able to understand you better. When you come to New York, please telephone me and we will make an appointment to meet.

If you find it difficult to express yourself in words, I will help you as much as I can—provided that you do not consider verbal confusion a virtue and *do* realize the importance of correcting it.

■ ■ ■

To Laura Janson, a fan

June 28, 1960

Dear Miss Janson:

You seem to be baffled by the response of students who say: "This philosophy is too idealistic, not practical enough." Don't let it discourage you. When you hear that (I hear it very often), you have actually won—and the rest is a matter of time. The moral code of altruism won its present victories, because people have been saying for years: "It's idealistic, but not practical." If you study cultural history, you will find that men are unable to oppose effectively any doctrine that they have recognized as "idealistic," which means: as morally *right*. They may try to oppose it short-range, in any given moment or issue, but they are spiritually disarmed in their long-range stand. This is precisely the manner in which capitalism was defeated by altruism—as I have shown you in *Atlas Shrugged*. So long as men like Rearden were regarded as merely *"practical,"* but men like James Taggart and Wesley Mouch as "idealistic," the Taggarts and Mouches had to win. Freedom and capitalism are perishing for lack of a *moral* base. But once men begin to realize that morality is on the side of capitalism, it will not take them long to see how dreadfully *impractical* (and immoral) collectivism really is.

Remember that the morality presented in *Atlas Shrugged* is new, unprecedented and radically opposed to all the traditional versions of morality. You cannot expect it to be accepted by everyone at once. Philosophical innovations take time. But what the collectivists-altruists needed centuries to accomplish, we will accomplish in a matter of years—because *reality* is on our side.

You ask, what is wrong with the students who seem passive and broken in spirit. The answer is: the kind of philosophy which is taught to them today and which dominates our culture. Again, I refer you to *Atlas Shrugged* for the essence of modern philosophy, which is: that man's mind is impotent, that thought is useless, that man is helpless. The students who accept these ideas will necessarily be broken in spirit.

This leads me to your question on: what can you do? Since the cause of today's collapse lies in philosophy, it is in philosophy that the battle for an intellectual Renaissance has to start. Before men can reach the stage of practical action, they have to learn the *right ideas*. The first step of any new movement is the spread of the new ideas. Therefore, you and those of your friends who agree with you, should train yourselves to become *competent advocates* of the philosophy you want to uphold—and then preach that philosophy by every means available to you, from private discussions with your acquaintances, to letters to the editors of newspapers and magazines, to the writing of articles, essays and books (this last if your choice of profession permits it). There is no other way for any philosophical movement to spread and grow—and it is much too early for a formally organized movement.

Observe that I have underscored the words "competent advocates." You cannot convert others to your ideas, if you have no consistent, logical arguments and proofs to offer. If you agree with my philosophy, you will need a great deal of thought, study and reading to understand it fully and to organize it in your own mind into an integrated set of principles; you will need it to guide your own life and to convince those who are willing to think, among the people you meet.

■ ■ ■

To Martin Larson, a "humanist" writer

July 15, 1960

Dear Dr. Larson:

Thank you for your letter of July 1 and for the copy of your revised article on my ethics [an apparently unpublished article for *The Free Humanist* magazine]. I deeply appreciate the fact that you have revised the article and that your corrections were reasonable and fair. Whether we agree philosophically or not, I thank you for your consideration and your courtesy.

In regard to the general questions discussed in your letter, you say that you are puzzled by my answer to the question of whether I am a conservative. In my letter of June 21, I said the following: "I am certainly *not* a conservative, if you meant the definition given to that term by publications such as *National Review*." I gather that you are not aware of the manner in which such publications (and professional religionists in general) are now trying to subvert that term: they are clamoring that a "conservative" is a defender of religious traditions (of "revealed truths"), not of capitalism, that his basic primary is "the preservation of continuity with the past," etc. In other words, according to them, a "conservative" is a champion of the "status quo," which, today, happens to be capitalism; in 1800, he would have been a champion of absolute monarchy, in 1500—of feudalism. By that sort of definition, I most certainly am not a "conservative."

In present-day usage, a "conservative" is an advocate of capitalism— but people use "capitalism" as a rubber word that can be stretched to mean anything, including the messiest types of "mixed economy," such as the one we have today. Therefore, I prefer not to describe my position by any of the loose, journalistic terms which can mean all things to all men. I am an advocate of "laissez-faire" capitalism. If, as you say, you take this to mean a "reactionary," then I am a reactionary.

Now to answer the numbered points of your letter:

1. *Humanism.* I agree, in a very general way, with the paragraph you marked on the cover of the July issue of *The Free Humanist*, the paragraph that begins with the words: "The Humanist philosophy declares that the cosmos is devoid of immanent, conscious purpose. . . ." But this paragraph is specific only in regard to a *negative*: the rejection of the supernatural. In regard to the *positive*, it is so generalized that I disagree with it, as a matter of epistemological principle: I consider it dangerously misleading ever to use value-terms, such as the "good" or the "higher development," in a declaration of one's stand, without stating by what standard of value one determines what is the "good" or the "high."

The consequences of vagueness on this point become apparent right on the reverse side of the same cover. Under the heading "The Aims of the Society," you have marked paragraph 2, which reads: "To develop a secular, ethical philosophy, based upon need, responsibility and the *unselfish advantage of human beings*"; (the underscoring is yours.) I do not know what the Humanists mean by those terms, but surely you know that both *The Fountainhead* and *Atlas Shrugged* are devoted to proving why the concept of "need" is vicious when applied to ethics, why the concept of "unselfishness" is vicious in any context, and why men should live by a morality of *rational selfishness*.

2. *Ethical Relativism.* No, I did not conclude from your article that you believed in Ethical Relativism; I merely objected to the passage which seemed to ascribe that belief to me—and I appreciate the fact that you have corrected it.

3. *Socialist Sympathy.* You say that you do not understand how I concluded that you were ascribing sympathy with socialism to me—and why I thought that you join with men who believe that Russia is a noble

experiment. In regard to the first, I concluded it on the ground of the passage in your article which alleged that I would deny that I am "conservative or reactionary." As there is no middle ground between freedom and compulsion, so there is no middle ground between capitalism and socialism; a "mixed economy" is merely a process of destruction, it is merely capitalism being gradually undermined and corrupted by socialistic regulations; therefore, anyone who does not advocate full capitalism, is, to that extent, prosocialist.

In regard to the second part of your statement (sympathy with Russia), I was referring to the Humanist movement as a whole. I know that there are many different groups with many divergent views who are loosely united by the general designation of "Humanism." (As far as I am able to gather, the only common bond among them is a negative: the rejection of the supernatural.) These groups include such men as Corliss Lamont. I do not ascribe their views to *you*, but I hold that such groups are *not* proper allies for those who wish to champion reason and freedom.

Under the same point 3 of your letter, you say that I should have stated my views on labor unions in full detail in Galt's speech. I hope that you did not say it seriously. Galt's speech deals only with *basic* issues: it presents, in the briefest form possible, the essentials of a full philosophical system, from metaphysics to epistemology to ethics to politics. It states explicitly that no man has the right to *initiate* the use of physical force against other men, and that all social relationships must be based on every participant's free, voluntary, uncoerced choice. This applies to *all* actions of *all* men, to *all* organizations of *all* men, to workers as well as employers, to labor unions as well as to corporations, associations, fraternal orders or ladies' clubs. And the only proper function of a government is to protect men from physical force, which means: to use force *only* as *retaliation* against those who *initiate* its use.

Now what would a detailed treatise on labor unions do in such a speech? I would no more dream of including it than I would dream of including a detailed treatise on business corporations, traffic laws, concert programs or dinner menus. Do you consider labor unions a metaphysical primary? I don't.

4. *Metaphysical Belief.* You say: "You call yourself an Atheist; I do not prefer that appellation, for I consider it negativist, and I prefer something which is positive."

I do not call myself an "Atheist" as an identification of my metaphysical position; I call myself an "*Objectivist*." But I do use the term "Atheist" in the appropriate context, such as, for instance, in answer to the queries of religionists or of those who spread verbal confusion by claiming that "a belief in natural laws is a belief in God," etc.

I agree with you when you say that the center of one's concern should be "Man." But as I stated in my first letter, it is a difference of life or death whether one takes the concept of "Man" to mean *the individual* or *the collective*. If the Humanists leave this issue open and admit advocates of both meanings into their camp, they are guilty of so enormous a contradiction that their declared intellectual stand becomes meaningless.

If men wish to unite for the purpose of upholding reason, the fundamental principle on which they must agree before they can validly declare themselves to be champions of reason, is: *the noninitiation of physical force*. No advocate of reason can claim the right to establish *his* version of a good society, if such society includes the initiation of force against dissenters in *any* issue. No advocate of the free mind can claim the right to force the minds of others. If the Humanists wish to be champions of reason, they should consider the following: just as they would not admit mystics into their camp, since no rational discussion is possible with men who substitute supernatural revelations for rational evidence—so they cannot admit advocates of force into their camp, because no rational discussion or agreement is possible with men who substitute guns for rational persuasion.

5. *Secular vs. Religious Tyranny.* You made it clear that your *intention* is to oppose both kinds of tyranny. But since you do not accept the fundamental principle stated above: the noninitiation of physical force among men, it means that in some issues you hold some considerations as superior to the freedom of man's mind. If so, then, no matter how good your intentions, your social ideas will lead to tyranny sooner or later—because you will never find a moral principle to justify the right of some men to initiate force against others. "A little bit of force" is like "a little bit of cancer." Observe the political history of the world in the last hundred years.

6. *My statement of ethics in* We the Living. By what incredible stretch of the imagination do you take my statement that "Every honest man lives for himself" to mean that "Every honest man is an ethical relativist or subjectivist"?(!) "Relativism" and "subjectivism" mean a *metaphysical* doctrine that denies the concept of an *objective* reality—a reality which exists independently of a perceiving consciousness and/or which is knowable to such consciousness. A "relativist" or a "subjectivist," therefore, acts without reference to or in *defiance of* the facts of reality. If a man lives for himself, and not for others, does it mean that he lives by the guidance of subjective whims? Is it to his selfish interest to defy or to fake reality? Do you equate *"personal"* with *"nonobjective"*? "To live for oneself"

means that the goal of one's actions is one's own benefit; it does not mean that one's own benefit is to be achieved in defiance of reality by means of subjectivist delusions.

7. *The role of government and society.* You state that "some laws are necessary, not only to prevent crimes of violence and embezzlement, but in other fields of human interrelationships." Your questions indicate that you mean something wider than the laws which formalize contractual relationships: you mean laws which *compel* men into certain relationships. I will answer you only: by what right?

Social issues cannot be discussed or judged in terms of random concretes; they can be discussed only in terms of principles. My fundamental social principle is that no man may demand or expect anything from other men, except by their voluntary, uncoerced agreement, which means: by contract. Therefore, men are free to make any contracts they choose, provided such contracts do not involve the initiation of physical force against anybody. And there is no principle by which some men could ever justify *their* right to impose by force on an individual man *their* idea of what contract he may or may not make.

You write: "You say you don't believe in the Wagner Act, the Right-to-Work laws, etc. Well, do you believe that there should be no copyright laws? That there should be no laws of any kind concerning the relationships of men and women, marriage, children, etc.?" Observe the confusion in the listing of these examples: the issue is *not* that all these examples involve human relationships. The issue is: which of these examples involve the initiation of force by the government?

The Wagner Act, the Right-to-Work laws and all similar legislation grant to the government the right to *dictate the terms* of a man's employment, the right to *prescribe* the kind of contract that men may or may not make, which means: the right to initiate force against men who have reached a voluntary agreement.

What is involved in the copyright laws? The government does not compel an author to copyright his work; he is free to publish it without copyright or to give it away to any and all comers. But if an author wants to publish his work only on condition that his readers do not make any unauthorized commercial use of it, then the government protects his right to his own property, in the form of a copyright. A copyright (or a patent) is merely a public contract, between an individual and the rest of society —a contract stating the condition on which the owner is willing to offer his product to others. Observe that the copyright law does not prescribe the terms, conditions or minimum royalties on which an author *must* sell his work; it merely forbids the use of the work without the author's *consent*, leaving the author free to consent to anything he chooses. The copyright law is not directed against the *owner* of a work, but against those who would attempt to seize his property without his consent.

As to marriage, children, etc., marriage *is* a contractual relationship and should be treated as such. The government may *formalize* the terms of what is to be regarded as a marriage contract, but it may *not* forbid people to live together on other terms, it may *not* compel people to marry or to stay single or to breed children or not to breed them, whatever the case may be.

In these examples, the government does not forbid alternatives, and the choice is up to the individual. But in labor legislation, the government assumes the right to dictate the conditions of employment, leaving men no choice and no alternatives; this means that men have no right to earn a living, no right to offer or accept employment, except on the government's terms. And you do not call *that* socialistic?

You ask: "Do you think there should be no laws dealing with tenant-landlord relationships?" Same answer: no laws except the laws of contract and the laws against fraud.

You write: "I believe that it is wrong for employers to use thugs or conspiratorial pressure to prevent a worker who wants to organize for his economic improvement from ever having a job again." Yes, of course, it is *demonstrably* wrong to use thugs. But one cannot equate the use of thugs with "conspiratorial pressure." One involves physical violence, the other is a peaceful policy decision. What is "conspiratorial pressure"? In this context, it is merely the right of employers to agree on a certain policy, to organize for what *they* believe to be their economic interests. Why do you grant that right to workers, but not to employers? (I hope that you do not unite "economic power" and "political power" into a single, meaningless package-deal labelled: "*power*." The power of production is not the same thing as the power of coercion by physical force.)

Incidentally, I do not believe that many employers would engage in such "conspiracies" nor that it would work for long, but this is not the issue. If *all* employers engaged in it openly *all* of the time, it would still be their inalienable right. Nobody has the right to tell them how to run *their own business*—and they do not *owe* employment to anybody. In a free society, competition corrects those employers (or workers) who adopt foolish or irrational policies. But the bad judgment of any specific employers (or workers) does not grant the rest of us the right to correct their judgment by force. We may disapprove of blacklists (or of the "Closed

Shop"); we have no right to forbid them by law. We are free not to deal with those of whom we disapprove.

I have explained this in detail in order to demonstrate the impropriety of your accusation, when you state that I "set (my) face against individualism and personal responsibility in the union movement and in society." If my denial of anyone's right to initiate force against others constitutes "opposition to individualism," and my insistence on every man's freedom of choice constitutes "opposition to personal responsibility"—then *what constitutes collectivism and irresponsible tyranny?*

You cite the example of an inventor who lost the right to his invention because he had signed an agreement that all his works would belong to his employers—and you ask me whether I would call it fair. Of course, it *is* fair. Nobody forced him to sign such an agreement; if he signed it—because, by his own judgment, it served his own interests, because he needed the job—he had no right to abrogate it unilaterally. (If he did not know what he was signing, his error cannot be used as an excuse for imposing controls on other inventors.) Such contracts are frequent in research institutions or in Hollywood scenario departments, or in any profession where a man is hired to exercise his creative inventiveness. Otherwise, what would prevent an employee from spending all his salaried time and thinking effort on inventions which he never delivers to his employer, but uses independently on his own? Creative thinking is an activity which is hard to divide between public day work and private night work. What is the solution? An inventor or a scenario writer should not engage in private scientific research or private writing while employed by an industrial concern or a movie studio; unless his contract permits it by agreement with his employer, if his contract forbids it, he should wait until he can quit his job and work on his own time.

If this is not fair, by what standard would we determine "fairness"? What would be "fair"? The use of force by the government? The principle that the government is the owner both of the inventor's mind and of the employer's mind?

You preface your remarks on this issue by asking: "Do you think that inventors should be protected in the ownership of the product of their genius?" Observe the contradiction in *your* principles: it is *precisely* because an inventor *is* the owner of his product that the government has no right to tell him on what terms he may or may not dispose of it. Ownership is the right of use and disposal. If the government were to dictate the conditions under which an inventor may or may not dispose of his products, what contracts he may or may not sign, it could do so *only* on the principle that *the government is the owner of the products,* that the inventor is mentally incompetent to judge his own best interests and needs a guardian to make his decisions for him. Is this your idea of "protection" for men of genius?

As to your statement that "laissez-faire" capitalism is the cause of depressions—this is an issue of economic fact and is simply untrue. The cause of depressions is government interference into economics. For proof, I refer you to such books as *Capitalism the Creator* by Carl Snyder, *Economics in One Lesson* by Henry Hazlitt, *How Can Europe Survive* by Hans Sennholz, and the works of the great economist Ludwig von Mises.

In your concluding paragraphs, you state that you believe "in law, in the minimum necessary for the regulation of human interrelationships" and that you think I do also. I hold no beliefs which I am unable to define *objectively* and *specifically*—and I will never hold as a belief, on any subject, such a loophole definition as "the minimum necessary." Necessary—to whom? By what standard? Who determines what constitutes a "mini-mum"?

I have stated the *specific* principle of law which I advocate—and I advocate no other. Please do not ascribe to me the opposite of my statements. I do not know what principle *you* advocate. I know only that a formulation such as "the minimum necessary" can be claimed by any social theorist in defense of any system, from a timid, middle-of-the-road Republican platform writer to a communist or any totalitarian statist: after all, even a dictator can claim that he imposes only "the minimum necessary" controls—necessary, that is, to *his* purpose.

I shall preface my next statement by the following reminder: you are free to hold any convictions you choose; but you have no moral right to ascribe them to *me* and to assume my agreement by means of ignoring everything known to you about *my* convictions. I am referring to your paragraph before last. You have no moral right to say to *me*, in the form of a blanket, arbitrary, unsupported assertion, that we must "find something" to establish "the best possible society," with the suggestion that that "best society" should be based on the very evil I am dedicated to fighting.

I shall leave that paragraph of yours without an answer. I shall say only that I do not consider any form of the idea it contains—the idea that human ability is a threat to the less able, or that men of ability are to be held down or restricted or controlled or chained or enslaved for the sake of the incompetents—I do not consider any such idea as *morally debatable*. I will not help anyone to pretend that *Atlas Shrugged* has never been written.

It is obvious that there is a *basic* disagreement between us. If you wish to discuss it further, it will have to be discussed in terms of principles, not of random, unevaluated concretes. The meaning of concretes cannot be judged as evaluated except by reference to a principle as a standard of value judgment.

■   ■   ■

To Donald S. Maffry, president of Maffry Frozen Foods

August 23, 1960

Dear Mr. Maffry:

I am glad that you find my philosophy helpful, since I consider business-men as the greatest victims of the present philosophical trend (particularly of the altruist morality)—and it is businessmen that I specially wanted to reach.

Please accept my sincere gratitude for distributing copies of my books and for helping their "rate of sale in the Kansas City area," as you say. This is one of the traits I admire in American businessmen: the translation of convictions into actions.

If I come to Kansas City some day, I would be pleased to meet you in person.

■   ■   ■

To R. A. Williams, a fan

August 29, 1960

Dear Mr. Williams:

Thank you for your letter of August 10. I will tell you frankly that yours is one of the few letters that I liked very much.

I am glad that *Atlas Shrugged* and *The Fountainhead* have helped you philosophically. I hope that you will understand and accept my philosophy fully, and—if I understand you correctly—that you will never give up the values you had once held.

You ask me about the meaning of the dialogue on page 702 of *Atlas Shrugged*:

" 'We never had to take any of it seriously, did we?' she whispered.
" 'No, we never had to.' "

Let me begin by saying that this is perhaps *the* most important point in the whole book, because it is the condensed emotional summation, the keynote or leitmotif, of the view of life presented in *Atlas Shrugged.*

What Dagny expresses here is the conviction that joy, exaltation, beauty, greatness, heroism, all the supreme, uplifting values of man's existence on earth, are the meaning of life—*not* the pain or ugliness he may encounter—that one must live for the sake of such exalted moments as one may be able to achieve or experience, *not* for the sake of suffering—that happiness matters, but suffering does not—that no matter how much pain one may have to endure, it is never to be taken seriously, that is: never to be taken as the essence and meaning of life—that the essence of life is the achievement of joy, *not* the escape from pain. The issue she refers to is the basic philosophical issue which John Galt later names explicitly in his speech: that the most fundamental division among men is between those who are pro-man, pro-mind, pro-life—and those who are anti-man, anti-mind, anti-life.

It is the difference between those who think that man's life is important and that happiness is possible—and those who think that man's life, by its very nature, is a hopeless, senseless tragedy and that man is a depraved creature doomed to despair and defeat. It is the difference between those whose basic motive is the desire to achieve values, to experience joy—and those whose basic motive is the desire to escape from pain, to experience a momentary relief from their chronic anxiety and guilt.

It is a matter of one's fundamental, overall attitude toward life—not of any one specific event. So you see that your interpretation was too specific and too narrow; besides, the Looters' World had never meant anything to Dagny and she had realized its "sham and hypocrisy" long before. What she felt, in that particular moment, was the confirmation of her conviction that an *ideal* man and an ideal form of existence *are* possible.

■　■　■

To Selma H. Levenberg, of the Ford Hall Forum

October 23, 1960

Dear Miss Levenberg:

Thank you for your letter of October 10. I am pleased to accept March 26, 1961, as the date of my appearance on the Ford Hall Forum.

The topic I should like to discuss is: "The Intellectual Bankruptcy of Our Age" (an analysis of the basic premises, the development and the present state of Western culture, and of the need for a new type of intellectual leadership). This would be based on a forthcoming book of mine,

For the New Intellectual: The Philosophy of Ayn Rand, to be published in the spring of 1961.

Since I am not a professional lecturer, I do not have a selection of speeches on hand. However, if you have some specific topic in mind, I may be able to prepare it for the occasion. I hesitate to offer you the lecture on "Faith and Force, the Destroyers of the Modern World," which I delivered at Yale University (also at Columbia University and Brooklyn College), because it has been widely reprinted.

The Ford Hall Forum is a nonpartisan assembly in Boston, presenting nationally distinguished speakers from a variety of fields. AR gave nineteen talks there between 1961 and 1981, regularly attended by overflow audiences of her admirers. On April 10, 1977, the Forum held a luncheon in her honor.

■ ■ ■

To Louis P. Smith, treasurer of the Ford Hall Forum

March 31, 1961

Dear Mr. Smith:

Thank you for your letter of March 27 and the enclosed check.

I am happy to tell you that I was very impressed with the Ford Hall Forum, the style and efficiency of its operation and its remarkably *intellectual* atmosphere, which is very rare these days. Please convey my sincere appreciation to Judge Lurie [Rueben L. Lurie, president and moderator of the Forum] for the brilliant manner in which he conducted the meeting.

My appearance before the Forum was a memorable and most enjoyable occasion, both for me and for my young friends.

I shall be delighted to appear again next year.

■ ■ ■

To George Boardman, a fan

May 19, 1961

Dear Dr. Boardman:

I appreciate your interest in my philosophy. But I object most emphatically to your use of the name "John Galt" or of a title such as "J. Galt

Associates" or of any names, characters or events from my novel *Atlas Shrugged*.

The abstract, philosophical ideas expressed in a novel may be used by all those who agree with them. The specific, literary, fiction elements of my novel are my personal, private property and are not to be used by anyone but me.

If you associate yourselves publicly with the characters of my novel, it means and implies that you act as *my* philosophical representatives. It is an intellectual blank check which I never have or will grant to anyone.

You state: "If you feel that such an action might imply a sanction which would be incompatible to you, we will drop the idea without further discussion." *Any* use of my fiction characters does imply a sanction which is most incompatible to me. I appreciate your statement and I shall take you at your word: I shall expect to receive from you the assurance that you have discontinued the use of the title "J. Galt Associates" and any other attempt, direct or indirect, to use the characters or any fiction elements of my novel.

■ ■ ■

To Robert Fuoss, executive editor at the *Saturday Evening Post*

August 4, 1961

Dear Mr. Fuoss:

The writing of this letter is a most painful experience; however the facts set forth below will demonstrate why I feel it is necessary to write you directly concerning an article that Mr. John Kobler is preparing for future publication in the *Saturday Evening Post*.

Several months ago Mr. Kobler telephoned me and requested an interview for the article which he explained was to deal with me and the growing public influence of my philosophy, or the Objectivist movement. He assured me that the article would be objective, factual and reportorial, after I pointed out that I had no desire to cooperate in an undertaking which might result in a personal attack on me or a misrepresentation of my philosophy. He further agreed, as a condition for my cooperation, that he would submit to me all passages in the article dealing with my philosophy and would correct any inaccuracies. I in turn agreed that he need not show me passages dealing with his personal views or opinions.

Subsequently I met Mr. Kobler for the first time on June 13, 1961, at a lecture given by Mr. Nathaniel Branden, who is a psychologist and head of Nathaniel Branden Lectures (NBL), an organization that gives lecture courses on my philosophy in New York, Philadelphia and other major cities. After the lecture Mr. Branden, myself and others conferred with Mr. Kobler and set up the procedure under which we would cooperate with him.

Mr. Kobler agreed without reservation to all of the following:

1. that his article would be objective, factual and reportorial;
2. that the article would be serious, particularly in his treatment of my philosophy;
3. that all passages of his article dealing with my philosophy, quotations from my works and/or summaries of my ideas, and all statements attributed to me and placed in quotes would be shown to me, including their relevant context, and that he would accept such corrections as I found necessary to assure accuracy;
4. that he would show me on the same conditions, all passages dealing with facts and factual information about me;
5. that he would show to Mr. Branden, for the same purpose and on the same conditions all passages of the article dealing with his ideas, quotations from his lectures, statements attributed to him and facts and factual information about him and NBL;
6. that if he used quotations from reviews of my books, he would balance a quotation from an unfavorable review with another from a favorable one;
7. that he need not show us such passages of his article dealing with his own personal opinions or comments on factual material, since he had assured us he was capable of separating opinions from facts.

Based on the foregoing understanding and agreement, and based on the standing and reputation of the *Saturday Evening Post*, Mr. Kobler was granted lengthy interviews by me at my home on June 14, June 15 and June 22. During this period he also interviewed Mr. Branden and his wife at their office.

Last week, Mr. Kobler telephoned me, stated that he had finished his article and made an appointment to see me on Tuesday, August 1, at my home.

During the entire course of the meeting on that date, which lasted from 1:30 P.M. until 7:30 A.M. of the morning of August 2, my husband was present and can substantiate all that follows.

Mr. Kobler, at first, made the corrections that I suggested, however as we progressed he became antagonistic, offensive, belligerent and finally abusive. Several times he got up to leave, and when no attempt was made to stop him, he remained and continued in this vein.

The cause of our difficulty was gradually apparent. Mr. Kobler had no concept of my philosophy, had not read all of my books nor did he seem interested in my exposition of the central points of my concepts.

As we went further into his article it developed that the personal references to me were of a nature that clearly indicated that he had no objective purpose in writing the article but rather was more interested in smearing my reputation and person. Several of the references I believe to be clearly libelous.

As the meeting progressed Mr. Kobler became most offensive, and only by exercise of great restraint could my husband and I continue. It was quite clear that Mr. Kobler wished us to order him to leave so that he could feel free of his agreement with us.

Despite the lengthy time devoted to our meeting, I never did see all of the so-called "factual or philosophical material" that his article contained.

Earlier that morning Mr. Kobler met with Mr. and Mrs. Branden and they have authorized me to state that their experience with him was similar and that some of the passages he showed them were false, misleading and libelous and clearly indicated that Mr. Kobler had violated his agreement with them as well.

As of the date of this writing we have neither seen nor heard from Mr. Kobler nor do we wish to have any further dealings with him.

One other person whom I know Mr. Kobler interviewed in connection with this article was my agent, Alan C. Collins, of Curtis Brown, Ltd. Mr. Collins tells me that Mr. Kobler stated to him that the original idea of writing an article about me was Mr. Kobler's and did not originate with another member of the *Saturday Evening Post*'s editorial staff. Perhaps this fact sheds further light on Mr. Kobler's approach to his subject matter.

In view of the above, it seems quite clear that both Mr. Branden and myself have been imposed upon and it would seem to us that a magazine of the standing and reputation of the *Saturday Evening Post* would not want to lend itself to the publication of an article that contains material which was obtained under such conditions and further, which by the innuendos that Mr. Kobler has injected, appears to both Mr. Branden and myself to be libelous.

I shall be most happy to answer any and all questions you may have, dealing with this most unfortunate incident.

Fuoss answered on August 9, saying that "we find the article to be a fair report on you and your philosophy." In its November 11, 1961, issue, the Saturday Evening Post *published an article entitled "The Curious Cult of Ayn Rand." There is no record of a lawsuit.*

■　■　■

To Bennett Cerf, founder and president of Random House, publishers of *Atlas Shrugged*

August 28, 1961

Dear Bennett:

Thank you for your letter of August 25, about the issue of the *Saturday Evening Post* article. I think you know why the attitude you expressed means a great deal to me and why I appreciate it profoundly.

I hope that you will succeed.

Love,

Cerf responded: "Your reputation grows every day, and your thousands of admirers know perfectly well who are your friends and who are your enemies. . . . I am very proud to be your publisher!"

■　■　■

To Mickey Spillane, detective novelist. Spillane, in his early works, was a favorite author of AR. She wrote that he "gives me the feeling of hearing a military band in a public park" (*The Romantic Manifesto*, p. 43).

October 2, 1961

Dear Mickey:

Thank you for your letter. I was delighted to hear from you—and if I am so late in answering, it is because New American Library did not forward your letter to me until recently. Please take note of my home address [36 E. 36th Street]. (An easy way to remember it would be: "the perfect 36.")

I wish I could have brought you in with me that night, after our meeting, because you might have been pleasantly shocked, as I was: when I entered my apartment, six young people (my students and close friends) were there, with my husband, waiting for me—and had been waiting for several hours—to hear what Mickey Spillane is like in person. The news that I was going to meet you had spread through our own grapevine—and there they were. All of them are enthusiastic admirers of yours—all of them (including me) had been disappointed too often, when meeting famous people—and so it was an enormous pleasure for all of us that I could give them a report on you (on any publicly reportable issues) which, for once, confirmed and raised, rather than lowered, our enthusiasm. You are the only modern writer with whom I can and do share the loyalty of my best readers—and I am proud of this.

Thank you for your compliments about the movie of *The Fountainhead*. I am glad you saw it. But I hope that you will read the book itself. It says much more than a movie can cover.

I am waiting eagerly to see you again. As you say, "Time ran out on us the other evening." But is there any reason why time should run us, rather than the other way around? I hope that you can arrange to be in New York a little longer on your next trip, so that we can continue our discussion.

Miss Tower's office tells me that you and I will appear together on the Mike Wallace show on October 11th. I am certainly looking forward to *that*! If it's drama they want, they'll get it.

Love,

■　■　■

To Uzi Hadari, a fan

October 28, 1961

Dear Mr. Hadari:

You ask whether the originators of the "Original Sin" idea and of other anti-man doctrines were fully and consciously aware of their ultimate purpose. No, that would be impossible, for the reasons you state: it would have required too great an intellectual development, incompatible with such doctrines. The originators of those doctrines, as well as their modern advocates, were and are *mystics*, which means that their ideas are dictated to them by their *emotions*, their wishes or fears, *not* by reason. This permits them to evade the meaning and purpose of the unidentified premises that produce their emotions. They do not have or seek a full philosophical understanding: when a man's basic premise is hatred for life and reason, the logic of this premise will do the rest.

You ask: "Why did destructive notions grow up 'naturally'—why didn't healthy, 'normal' theories accompany mankind from its start?" The answer is: Because man's consciousness is not *automatic*, because man does not acquire knowledge automatically and infallibly, because every step in the discovery of knowledge has to be gained by man's *choice*. To learn what is *true*, what is *right*, requires a long process of intellectual struggle and achievement. But no effort is required to promulgate mystical falsehoods. Mysticism did not grow up "naturally," it grew up *by default*—in the absence of rational knowledge.

This does not mean that every man accepts rational knowledge automatically, once it is discovered. But speaking historically, those who choose to remain irrational are impotent against the men armed with rational knowledge—in any society where men are left free. Culturally, mysticism has never won in a free contest with reason—which is why mystics resort to force to maintain their power over men, whenever they get the chance.

I suggest that you read the title essay of my latest book, *For the New Intellectual*, which deals with the intellectual history of Western civilization. You will find it relevant to your questions.

■   ■   ■

To Martin Lean, philosophy professor at Brooklyn College

November 30, 1961

Dear Martin:

Thank you for your note and your invitation to the meeting of the Conference on Methods in Philosophy and the Sciences, on this past Sunday.

I very much wanted to come, and I am sorry that I had to miss it. The wedding reception of two young friends of mine is the event (which may be considered philosophical) that I had to attend that Sunday.

My "estimate" of the *Saturday Evening Post* article cannot be stated in a letter—there is a law against sending obscenity through the mail, yet no other type of language would do it justice.

As soon as the present rush of getting *The Objectivist Newsletter* to the printers is over, I shall keep our date to discuss the Objectivist epistemology. It's my turn now, and I'm looking forward to it. Thank you again for your presentation of Wittgenstein. Even though our last discussion ended so indecisively, I believe that we will be able to start resolving our mutual misunderstandings *after* both sides have been presented.

■ ■ ■

To Ida Macken, a fan

December 10, 1961

Dear Miss Macken:

In your letter of November 1, you ask me: "Would you mind if I dedicated my book to you?" I would not permit or accept such a dedication, because it would imply a sanction which I cannot give to a person I do not know. I should also point out that I do not undertake to read unpublished manuscripts.

I appreciate your interest in my novels, but I must point out to you that the things you say in your letter are in direct contradiction to my philosophy. [Miss Macken writes that she and her friends refer to AR as a god, whom they would follow blindly.]

My philosophy advocates *reason*, not faith; it requires men to *think*— to accept nothing without a full, rational, firsthand understanding and conviction—to claim nothing without factual evidence and logical proof. A *blind follower* is precisely what my philosophy condemns and what I reject. Objectivism is not a mystic cult.

Since you are very young, I suggest that you study philosophy more carefully.

■ ■ ■

To Joy Miller, of AP Newsfeatures

January 12, 1962

Dear Miss Miller:

I have been waiting to thank you in person for the wonderful Cat Book which you sent me. My husband and I were delighted with it. I appreciate enormously both your choice and your intention.

I hope that I will see you in the not-too-distant future, and that I will have a chance to see the pictures of *my* cat.

■ ■ ■

To James S. Hunt, Florida real-estate developer

In a fan letter, Hunt asked AR for a personal meeting, explaining that he didn't (although he could) read books.

January 26, 1962

Dear Mr. Hunt:

Your letter of January 9 just crossed my desk. Inasmuch as I do not patronize resort hotels (I can, however), I am unable to accept your gracious invitation.

I would travel farther than Florida to meet someone who really wanted to meet my mind. But my mind is available on any drugstore or newsstand counter, at prices ranging from 50¢ to 95¢. The 95¢ economy size is the best buy. It took me thirteen years to write it, so I could not possibly give you its equivalent in a week or two. Considering what that week or two would cost you, I—as an admirer of Free Enterprise and of businessmen —would not want to cause you to make such a poor investment.

■　■　■

To John Brierley, a fan

February 3, 1962

Dear Mr. Brierley:

I appreciate your interest in *Atlas Shrugged* and in my philosophy. But I am puzzled by certain contradictory elements in your letter.

On the one hand, your interest in philosophy and your desire for knowledge sound genuine and sincere. And this is the reason why I am answering your letter. But on the other hand, you seem to be much too concerned with other people.

I do not understand what you mean. If other people do not want the same things you want, why should that stop you from achieving *your* goals? If you are able to create new machines, if your achievement is rationally valuable, you will find people who will appreciate it—as you should have learned from the story of Howard Roark. No man can expect to be an innovator and, simultaneously, expect to find a ready-made audience sharing in advance the values he has not yet produced.

The world can fall apart without anyone's help. But what right have you to expect the world to accept Objectivism without *your* help? If you agree with the philosophy of Objectivism and you know that it is new, how and why do you expect other people to advocate it or teach it or spread it while *you* do nothing about it? Whom do you expect to provide you with the kind of world that you want?

You do not bother to express or advocate your own convictions, yet, somehow, expect the world to share them. You say that you want to quit. How can you quit what you have never started? If you do not fight for your own ideas, you have no right to blame the ideas of others, nor to complain.

You write: "I notice that *The Fountainhead* differs from *Atlas Shrugged* in that Roark fought the creed of the secondhanders by speaking out for the truth, while Galt found it necessary to 'stop the motor of the world.' Is that because conditions have changed, and Roark's way is no longer possible?" No, it is not because "conditions have changed." You seem too eager to believe that "Roark's way is no longer possible." If you studied ideas more carefully, you would observe that Galt "spoke out for the truth"—to the whole world and for three and one half hours, on the day when he achieved the possibility to do it. The political conditions presented in *Atlas Shrugged* are those of an almost total dictatorship. Only when a society reaches that stage is it proper for men to think of quitting. So long as a country has no censorship, it is not yet a dictatorship—and men are free to speak and to fight for their ideas. The strike in *Atlas Shrugged* applies to our present-day conditions only in the following way: it is against the dominant cultural trend of our society, against its philosophy, that one should go on strike. Which means: that one should reject the basic premises of today's culture and start building a new culture on the philosophical foundation of Objectivism. Which means: that one should actively advocate the right ideas, regardless of what other people think. Which is a policy diametrically opposed to the one you suggest.

■ ■ ■

To Vera Glarner

March 2, 1962

Dear Vera:

I was happy to hear from you. Please excuse me for answering you in English—I hope that you can still read it or have it translated for you. As to my French, it is too uncertain to attempt to write it.

I would be delighted to see you, after all these years. I cannot offer to have you stay with me, because New York apartments are extremely small—but would you allow me to be your hostess at a hotel? That is, I would like you to be my guest for the two weeks of your vacation at a hotel in my neighborhood, and I will pay the rent for your room there. Please let me know whether this would be convenient for you and when you plan to come. I have many business appointments outside of New York until May 1st, but will be here after that date.

I like Lisette very much. She impresses me as a very nice and intelligent girl, but I believe that she has certain psychological problems; she needs advice and guidance. I have tried to help her in this respect, but I am not sure that I can do it without a better understanding of her situation. So I would like very much to discuss it with you in person.

■   ■   ■

To David C. Robbins, a fan

March 9, 1962

Dear Mr. Robbins:

I read with great interest the copies of your correspondence on the TV issue, which you sent me.

Your letter to the *Wall Street Journal* was excellent, and it is very interesting indeed that Mr. Minow [Newton N. Minow, chairman of the Federal Communications Commission] sent you a personal answer. Your reply to Mr. Minow is a little too long. Your arguments are good, but you seem to attempt to include the whole case for free enterprise, and this should not be attempted in a letter. It is advisable to limit a letter strictly to the subject under discussion. The paragraph before last in which you invite Mr. Minow to continue the discussion is somewhat inappropriate. It is up to Mr. Minow to decide whether he wishes to continue the correspondence.

It would not be appropriate for me to suggest any further arguments, as you request. You must rely only on your own knowledge and arguments. I observe that you have done a good job of understanding and applying the right theoretical principles to a given issue. You will do very well on your own if you continue to study this subject.

■   ■   ■

To Mrs. John C. Chiles, Jr.

John Chiles was one of the General Electric Co. executives convicted in 1961 of price fixing and defended by AR in "America's Persecuted Minority: Big Business" (reprinted in *Capitalism: The Unknown Ideal*).

March 31, 1962

Dear Mrs. Chiles:

Thank you for your wonderful letter. Please accept my deepest admiration for the spirit and courage that it projected.

If my lecture on "America's Persecuted Minority" made Mr. Chiles feel better about today's situation, if only for a moment—I consider myself well rewarded. He and his six fellow martyrs are the symbol of the battle I am fighting—and to the extent to which I have a public voice, I will continue calling this country's attention to the worst injustice in its history.

I am sorry that I quoted the kind of contemptible distortion which *Time* magazine permits itself, namely the sentence about "bowed his head." Thank you for correcting me. Strangely enough, I was suspicious about that sentence and I omitted it on both occasions when I gave the lecture verbally (and thus it was omitted from the radio broadcasts of my lecture). I included it in the printed version only in order to avoid the use of dots which could suggest that I had cut something relevant. However, I do not want to give further circulation to such a bit of yellow journalism, so I will omit it from the next printing of the lecture.

I am sorry that I cannot send you a transcript of "The Great Challenge"—but I want you to know that the biggest burst of applause in the entire show came from the studio audience when I said that sending businessmen to jail was an example of rule by brute force.

I was happy to learn that you liked *Atlas Shrugged*. You are the kind of reader I hoped it would reach. Thank you for giving copies of it to others. I must tell you (not as a boast, but as a cultural symptom) that it is selling extremely well and is approaching the million copies mark, in the combined hardcover and paperback editions. It will do its part to help counteract the kind of disgusting ideas expressed in the clipping you sent me. It took decades of collectivist philosophy to bring this country to its present state. And it is only the right philosophy that can save us. Ideas take time to spread, but we will not have to wait for decades—because reason and reality are on our side.

Please thank Mr. Chiles for me for the very nice letter he wrote me —and please convey to him my deepest admiration.

■   ■   ■

To Dr. Ronald P. Brown, pastor of Trinity Reformed Church, Grand Haven, Michigan

June 1, 1962

Dear Dr. Brown:

Thank you for your letter of May 2nd. I appreciate the fact that you care to discuss philosophical issues.

I would not say that you are "of no use" to me, as you put it. I respect every human being who has a sincere interest in ideas. But I must say that you and I are *not* fighting the same battle. You seem to see the battle merely in political terms, as an issue of individualism versus collectivism. The battle I am fighting is more fundamental than that: it is the battle of reason versus mysticism.

I realize that there are two contradictory traditions in Christianity: one individualistic, the other collectivistic. But the real issue is epistemological: if you claim that your faith leads you to individualism, the collectivists can claim—with equal validity—that their faith leads them to collectivism. No argument, persuasion or proof is possible to either side since "faith" and "proof" are incompatible concepts.

I suggest that you consider the question of whether today's battle can be fought without a firm stand on the issue of epistemology.

■ ■ ■

To Robert Stack, actor who portrayed Eliot Ness in *The Untouchables* television series

Stack wrote to AR after reading her article "The New Enemies of 'The Untouchables,'" which appeared July 8, 1962, in the *Los Angeles Times* and is reprinted in *The Ayn Rand Column* (Second Renaissance Books).

July 25, 1962

Dear Mr. Stack:

Thank you. I hoped that of all those connected with "The Untouchables," you would see my column. When I received your letter, it was the kind of moment I would have gladly included in one of my novels.

It means a great deal to me that my column pleased you. I am extremely indignant about the vicious injustice of the attacks on "The

Untouchables" and the psychological roots of those attacks—and I intend
to fight that battle by every means open to me.

"The Untouchables" is my favorite TV program, the only one I watch
regularly. The show is actually made by your performance and would collapse without it. You are the only actor I have ever seen who is able to
project heroism and integrity convincingly. The most remarkable part of
your performance is the extent to which you succeed in conveying that
these are *intellectual* qualities.

When I read that you liked *The Fountainhead* and had wanted to play
Roark, I thought—to quote Toohey—that "things like that are never a coincidence."

I am very curious to know what you saw in the character of Roark.
Would you care to tell me why you thought that you were the only one
who could play him? I am asking it because, you see, I agree with you.

I have been approached several times about the possibility of doing a
live TV special of *The Fountainhead*, and I have been saying that the only
man who could play Roark is Robert Stack.

There are very few achievements that I can admire in today's culture;
yours is one of them. So I want to thank you for all the Thursday evenings
I enjoyed.

I would be more than happy to meet you in person. Since, unfortunately, I don't expect to be in California in the foreseeable future, please
let me know when and if you come to New York.

With sincere admiration,

*Stack answered that he "was intrigued as an actor by [Roark's]
uniqueness, his devotion to the purity of his art or craft, and his
unquenchable belief in the right of the individual to fight for that
inner dream."*

■ ■ ■

To Vera Glarner

August 4, 1962

Dear Vera:

Thank you for your letter and for the postcard which you sent me from the
ship.

I was happy to know that everything went well and that you returned
home safely.

The "Little American Dinner" which you gave sounds very charming, and I am delighted if you enjoyed it. I told Lisette about it and she said that it was a new policy on your part, that you were not in the habit of giving large parties. If this new policy was due in some part to my influence, I am very happy to know it. I would love to see you permit yourself to enjoy life a little more than you have in the past. You have certainly earned it.

As to my life, it is as busy and hectic as when you were here, perhaps even more so. My newspaper column is doing well, and so is our *Newsletter*. I am enclosing the August copy of the *Newsletter*. On page 35 you will find a reprint of my first *Los Angeles Times* column, "Introducing Objectivism," which you read here in the original newspaper and wanted to read again.

I miss you very much. To repeat what I told you here, I was happy to find that I feel a deep affection for you, not because you are a relative, but because you are a good person, much better, I suspect, than you give yourself credit for. I hope that I will see you again without waiting many years.

■   ■   ■

To Mrs. John K. Osinga, a fan

August 24, 1962

Dear Mrs. Osinga,

I am glad that you liked my article on Marilyn Monroe ["Through Your Most Grievous Fault," which appeared August 19 in the *Los Angeles Times*], and I appreciate the reaction of a professional newspaperwoman.

I was glad to know that my article helped you to maintain your own views. The statement you quoted from a psychiatrist, that "believing in good, and seeing it in others, is in our time anachronistic," is one of the most contemptible things I have ever heard. It is simply a moral blank check to permit oneself any sort of evil. Does he really believe that there are fashions in morality? If so, who sets them? Is there any reason why we should surrender the world to scoundrels?

I cannot emphasize strongly enough that the most important thing in life is never to surrender one's concept of what is right, what life could be and should be. If your concept of the right is rational, you will be able to achieve it in your own life and, perhaps, influence others to achieve it. But if one abandons one's values, nothing is possible thereafter: it is an act of spiritual suicide. I am glad that you liked *The Fountainhead*, and I can see from your letter why you did. Don't let anyone discourage you.

■   ■   ■

To Rex Barley, executive manager at the Times-Mirror Syndicate

September 7, 1962

Dear Mr. Barley:

I am delighted that the Times-Mirror Company has exercised its option to syndicate my column.

I have found that I enjoy writing the column very much, though it was difficult for me, at first, to get used to the space limit. It is becoming easier now. I will aim at reducing the length further whenever possible, as you suggest.

I am very happy that you like my column. Thank you for the kind things you said about it—particularly for the reference to the "newspaper writing style."

I shall be glad to continue writing the column on the same basis as before, until the syndicate release date.

In December, syndication plans were canceled due to "lack of sales."

■   ■   ■

To Mickey Spillane

September 15, 1962

Dear Mickey:

I am enclosing a little present for you which, I hope, will please you. This is my way of fighting a battle for justice which is as tough as Mike Hammer's.

Will you tell me whether you intend to write a sequel to *The Girl Hunters*? As you probably know, you left us readers dangling up in the air. You build up such an interest in the relationship of Mike Hammer to Velda that one waits impatiently to see their meeting, and it was a little unfair of you not to show it. Also, what about Pat Chambers's love for Velda and his future relationship to Mike? You owe us readers an answer, since it's you who made it so interesting.

Why have you vanished? I was hoping to hear from you when you were in New York, but I understand that you have been rushing in and out of the city and that one can never catch you. If you want me to be a "Spillane Hunter"—take this as part of the pursuit.

With best wishes and love,

■ ■ ■

To Rex Barley

December 5, 1962

Dear Mr. Barley:

In reply to your letter of November 29, I do not question Mr. Nick Williams's [editor of the *Los Angeles Times*] intentions, and I fully believe that it was an honest intention to keep my column up-to-date, as you stated. But this does not change the fact that he had no right to edit my column without my consent.

I have not given you cause to assume that I make statements without reflection—and, therefore, I must repeat that the editing *has* altered the sense or the meaning of my column. a) Its meaning consisted of the full context in which Mr. Kennedy chose to visit the Soviet Ballet. b) I am the only judge of what I *intend* to say under my signature.

I do not understand why Mr. Williams chose not to consult me. There were many ways to bring the column up-to-date, without cutting it.

I must remind you that the most important provision of our agreement, as far as I am concerned, is the provision relating to alterations of my text. I shall, therefore, expect to be consulted about any proposed changes in the text of my column in the *Los Angeles Times*, and I reserve the right of final decision on such changes. If we are unable to reach an agreement, you have the right not to publish that particular column.

I must add that I have noticed small changes before, but they involved one or two words, were purely formal and were obviously dictated by considerations of legal precision—and, therefore, I did not mind them. I trust that this was not taken to mean that I am willing to have my columns edited in content without my knowledge.

I would have preferred to discuss this with you in person, and I tried to reach you by telephone last Friday afternoon, but was unable to do so.

■ ■ ■

To William M. Jones, professor of English at the University of Missouri

February 4, 1963

Dear Professor Jones:

Thank you for your letter of January 28 and for the copy of the comments which you sent me. I should like to ask you to make just one correction in these comments, namely, in the sentence: "In the past few years Miss Rand has become one of the leaders of the New Conservatism that Mr. Justus mentions." I am not a "conservative" and am profoundly opposed to some of the new conservative groups. Besides, I have not read Mr. Justus's essay and do not know his definition of conservatism. I describe myself as "a radical for capitalism." Therefore, please change that sentence to read: "In the past few years Miss Rand has become one of the leaders of a movement advocating capitalism."

I deeply appreciate the rest of your comments—particularly the fact that you note that I am careful in defining my terms.

■ ■ ■

To Vera Glarner

February 4, 1963

Dear Vera:

I am sorry if you thought that I had forgotten you. I used to send holiday greetings to my friends—but have given up the custom years ago, because of my heavy schedule of work, which is usually heaviest at this time of the year.

Of course, I did mean what I told you on the telephone, the day before you left, and I will repeat my invitation: I hope that you will come to New York again, as my guest, and I would be delighted to pay for the passage.

You have expressed very beautifully my own feelings about our meeting: I, too, hope it was not the last event of a dead past, but the beginning of a living future.

I hope that you will visit New York again and that we will have a chance for longer discussions. I know that you do not fully understand my philosophy at present, and I would like to tell you more about it. I believe that it could help you.

I am sorry that Lisette left New York without seeing me, but I know that her time was limited. As I told you, I think that she has serious psychological problems, and I don't think that I can help her to solve them. I hope that you might help her by discussing her problems frankly and openly, as we tried to do it here.

As to Frank and me, we have been as busy as ever. Frank has rented a studio, where he is working on his own paintings and is doing very well. I am busy with various lectures and writing assignments, among them an article about American businessmen which I was commissioned to write for *Cosmopolitan* magazine.*

■   ■   ■

To W. T. Stace, former philosophy professor at Princeton University and author of *The Concept of Morals* and *The Philosophy of Hegel*

February 4, 1963

Dear Professor Stace:

Thank you for your letter of January 21. I appreciate the fact that you chose to comment on my article "The Ethics of Emergencies."

My articles in *The Objectivist Newsletter* are written on the assumption of the readers' familiarity with the Objectivist philosophy. If the subject interests you, you will find its essentials in my book *For the New Intellectual* (Random House).

I am familiar with your work and have looked up the particular passages you mentioned, in *The Concept of Morals.* I disagree with your viewpoint.

In your letter, you write: "There is a real distinction between treating my neighbor's happiness as for me an end in itself, i.e., as giving me pleasure *in itself* apart from any other consequences, and treating his happiness merely as a means to some end which is to bring me happiness."

I maintain: a) that nothing *should* be an end in itself to man except his own life *qua* rational being and his own rational happiness; b) that the

---

* "The Money-Making Personality" was published in the April 1963 issue of *Cosmopolitan* and reprinted in the *Objectivist Forum*, February 1983.

welfare of those one loves is not an end in itself, but a value which contributes to one's own happiness; c) that it is immoral to value anything out
of context, i.e., without considering the consequences and without relation
to oneself.

I believe that I have made this clear even in the text of my article.
Since you are an eminent representative of the ethics of altruism, I would
be very interested to hear your comments on the ethical alternative I discuss
in that article—the example of the husband who has to choose between
saving his wife or ten other women. Would you care to tell me which choice
you would consider morally right?

You write that *correct* English demands a certain use of the words
"selfish" and "unselfish." I do not believe that profoundly controversial
philosophical issues can or should be permitted to slant the meanings of
words. And, in fact, dictionary definitions do not support your assertion. I
believe that correct English demands a precise use of words. "Selfish"
means: "concerned with one's own interests." The question of what constitutes a man's interests and which actions are to be classified as
"selfish" is to be answered by philosophers, not by grammarians or
lexicographers.

However, my use of words is correct even under *your* definitions: you
claim that the word "selfish" applies to the policy of treating one's neighbor's happiness, not as an end in itself, but as a means to some end which
is to bring one happiness. Since that is precisely the policy I advocate in
regard to love or friendship, I comply with *your* definition when I describe
love and friendship as "selfish."

No, I do not "blur a vital distinction." But if one calls love
"unselfish," how does one differentiate between the act of spending one's
money on the welfare of those one loves—and spending it on the welfare
of underdeveloped countries on the other side of the globe? This last is
surely "unselfish." And if both acts are to be called "unselfish," isn't *that*
a vital distinction blurred by the theory of altruism?

As to the issue of psychological egoism which you mention in the first
sentence of your letter, when you write: "Of course it is true that all actions
are motivated by the pursuit of the actor's own happiness"—I must answer: of course it is *not* true, and nothing in my article could have conveyed
the impression that I advocate such an idea.

■　■　■

To Bruce Alger, US congressman from Texas

February 4, 1963

Dear Mr. Alger:

Thank you for your letter and for the material which you sent me: the study on God in Government, the copies of your *Washington Report* and the copies of the *Congressional Record* containing your remarks.

I agree with a large part of your political position and with many of the bills you introduced, as listed in your *Washington Report* of January 12, 1963. I know and appreciate your voting record.

But I am deeply puzzled by your study on God in Government. I cannot understand the purpose you had in mind. I assume that the study is not intended to persuade dissenters, since it is a historical survey, not a theoretical dissertation or argumentation; it merely quotes the views of a number of public figures.

If I understood it correctly, your brief remarks in that study indicate that you seek to prove that the Constitution and the United States government do not deny a belief in God. Of course they do not. It would be as improper for the government to deny a belief in God as to uphold it. The First Amendment means that the government has no right to enter the field of religious beliefs, i.e., to exercise legal force or compulsion over the individual citizen's beliefs, neither on the side of theism nor of atheism.

I regret that on page 2 of your study you chose to be unfair to me. You wrote: "Individual's importance and freedom, which she stresses, results from his accountability to God, his reason for being, which she overlooks." I do not overlook it—I deny and oppose that view, and I have made this explicitly clear in all my books, particularly in *Atlas Shrugged*.

To "overlook" important issues means to *evade* them. I doubt that you would care to accuse me of evasion in view of my public record—and in view of your own estimate of my work, as expressed in your letters and in our telephone conversation.

But the most bewildering statement in your study is on page 14, namely: "ATHEISM, AGNOSTICISM, THEREFORE, IS ILLEGAL." Frankly, I do not know whether you intended that statement to be taken seriously. If you did, how could you send it to *me*? Surely, you realize that I am the first person you would have to send to jail, and my books would be among the first you would have to suppress, under such a doctrine. And surely you could not have intended me to take it as a hint or a threat.

If you did not intend that statement to be taken literally, then don't you think that it is an enormously dangerous thing to play with? If the leftists were to quote you on this, it would destroy your stand and your distinguished record as a defender of freedom and capitalism. You would have no leg (or toenail) to stand on, in defending economic freedom and inalienable rights or in denouncing the dictatorial encroachments of government—*if* you denied intellectual freedom and advocated the government's "right" to prescribe an individual's convictions by law, that is, *by force*. How would you be able to speak of rights or freedom thereafter? And how would you implement such a law? You would have no way to do it except by establishing censorship and a medieval Inquisition.

In accordance with the principles of America and of capitalism, I recognize your right to hold any beliefs you choose—and, on the same grounds, you have to recognize my right to hold any convictions I choose. I am an intransigent atheist, though not a militant one. This means that I am not fighting *against* religion—I am fighting *for* reason. When faith and reason clash, it is up to the religious people to decide how they choose to reconcile the conflict. As far as I am concerned, I have no terms of communication and no means to deal with people, except through *reason*.

If you find that your beliefs do *not* clash with reason and that your political views are rational—then that is the area in which we can communicate. I sincerely hope that we can.

I shall be very interested to hear your answer. And I would appreciate it if you would clarify for me the exact meaning and intent of your statement about the "illegality" of atheism.

Congressman Alger answered that he meant that atheism and agnosticism were "contrary to the spirit of the law, if not the letter."

■ ■ ■

To Ken Guilmartin, a fan

February 4, 1963

Dear Mr. Guilmartin:

I appreciate your invitation, but I cannot appear as a speaker for a religious or church group. Since you know my philosophical views, you must realize that we would have no way to communicate, and that such an attempt would be improper both for me and for the members of the audience.

■ ■ ■

To Renata Adler, staff writer for *The New Yorker* magazine

                                                    April 2, 1963
Dear Miss Adler:

In reply to your letter of March 28, specifically to your explanation of *The New Yorker*'s editorial policy, I should like to point out the following:

(A) Any venture involving the cooperation of two parties, which requires that one party have a discretionary power of choice, while the other party have none and rely only on blind faith—cannot be regarded as practical, rational or moral.

(B) Reviews and interviews are two different kinds of undertaking (although a magazine has to bear responsibility for both): a review does not require the victim's cooperation, an interview does.

(C) When a magazine decides that some person "deserves to be portrayed unfavorably," as you state, it is free to do so on the basis of publicly available material. It should not ask for that person's cooperation. A magazine's attempt to obtain special material which it would not have obtained if it had stated its purposes openly, can hardly be regarded as proper.

(D) If the editor of *The New Yorker* wishes me to consider *his* professional problems, he should, by the same principle, consider mine. The press comments on me are a matter of record. If he realizes the preponderance of smears and does not wish to practice that sort of journalism, then it is up to him to devise a method of cooperation which would protect both my professional integrity and his own. But blind faith or a blank check on one's reputation, is what he should not ask of anyone, least of all of me.

It is not an issue of your personal honesty, which I have no reason to doubt. It is an issue of judging a magazine's policy, which has to be judged by its record. I realize that a magazine may change its policy. But I need factual evidence to balance the evidence of *The New Yorker*'s attitude toward me in the past.

I shall, therefore, offer you a suggestion, as one possible example of how issues of "trust" may be solved. You stated over the telephone that the theme of your proposed article is: the extent of my influence on today's cultural scene and the extent to which the commentators have missed the point. If your editor approves of your theme, I suggest that you write and let *The New Yorker* publish a brief piece on this subject, without interviewing me, basing it only on a study of the public record: of my published works, of their publishing history and of the press comments.

This is not a promise nor a commitment on my part, nor a request for a "bribe." It is merely one way of indicating that *The New Yorker* does not place me in the category of a person who "deserves to be portrayed unfavorably." If this suits your purposes and if you should wish to interview me thereafter, we could then discuss the matter on a more objective basis.

There is no record of a response from The New Yorker. *The article suggested by AR was not published.*

■ ■ ■

To John Herman Randall, Jr., philosophy professor at Columbia University

May 2, 1963

Dear Professor Randall:

I am enclosing a copy of the *Objectivist Newsletter* for May 1963, which contains my review of your book *Aristotle*. Perhaps you will find it of interest.

Although I have to disagree with you on a number of issues, I regard your book as of great value and importance on today's cultural scene. Please accept my compliments.

■ ■ ■

To Joseph A. Stone, a fan

Mr. Stone, a retired brakeman and conductor on the Grand Trunk Railroad, asked AR for an autograph, writing: "You are my best girl. . . ."

May 18, 1963

Dear Mr. Stone:

Thank you for your nice letter. I am glad that you liked my books, and that you cared to tell me about it.

Since you are a former railroad man, I particularly appreciate your saying that I know railroads. I had to do a lot of hard research to acquire that knowledge.

Thank you also for your subscription to *The Objectivist Newsletter*.

No, I have not stopped writing books, and I will write another novel, but I cannot predict its publication date at present.

Cordially,

" *Your first girl* "—

AR

Ayn Rand

. . .

To Elizabeth Mowat, Curtis Brown, Ltd.

June 8, 1963

Dear Miss Mowat:

I am enclosing my copy of the contract for the Spanish language rights to *Anthem*. As you will see, the contract does not grant the Spanish publisher the right to popular reprints.

As we discussed on the telephone, my main problem in regard to Luis de Caralt is his breach of contract on his publication of my collected works.

Please notify Mr. de Caralt that I have written to you as follows and please quote to him verbatim the following three paragraphs:

> I consider the inclusion of unauthorized prefaces and illustrations in the first volume of my collected works in the Spanish language as a flagrant, offensive and damaging breach of contract. My contract with Luis de Caralt specifies that my novels are to be translated and published without any changes of any nature whatsoever. This means that he had no right to include prefaces which argue against the philosophical ideas expressed in my novels. He has no legal or moral right to use *my* novels for the purpose of selling to *my* readers the views of my enemies. In regard to the illustrations, they are in dreadful taste and they contradict the content of my novels, specifically of *Atlas Shrugged* in which I denounce so-called "modern" art in no uncertain terms. Among these illustrations there is a crude cartoon of me, printed apparently *instead* of a photograph; this is self-evidently undignified and maliciously offensive.
>
> Therefore, I demand that Mr. de Caralt eliminate all the prefaces

and all the illustrations from the first volume of my collected works and abstain from any such inclusions in the subsequent volumes. If he wishes to use illustrations in the future, they are to be submitted to me for my approval. As to prefaces, I forbid them altogether: my novels are to be published as they are written, without changes, cuts or additions.

If Mr. de Caralt does not comply with this demand, I shall consider all our contracts void and shall take whatever legal action may be appropriate.

The issue of the popular reprint of *Anthem* will depend on Mr. de Caralt's answer to the above. The contract for *Anthem* gives him exclusive rights to publication in the Spanish language—therefore, I believe that neither he nor I can authorize a popular reprint except by mutual consent. I will not grant my consent unless he complies with the above conditions.

De Caralt answered that although he found neither the cartoon nor the admittedly negative introduction to be offensive, he would eliminate both in future printings.

■　■　■

To Bennett Cerf

July 29, 1963

Dear Bennett:

Here is the synopsis of my screen story *Red Pawn*. If you can judge it in so condensed a form, I will be very interested indeed to hear your reaction.

The commercial history of *Red Pawn* is as follows: I sold it to Universal in 1932, for $1,500. (It was the first thing I ever sold.) About two years later, Paramount bought it from Universal. I heard, at the time, that Paramount got it in exchange for a story they owned which had cost them $20,000. But this was only hearsay, so I cannot be sure whether that was the price.

Paramount bought it for Marlene Dietrich, but her contract expired and she left them, so the story was never made.

As you know, Paramount has now offered (through Mr. Brown of NAL) to pay me a bonus if I would write a novel based on *Red Pawn*. What I want to offer them instead is as follows:

I will write both a novel and a screenplay of *Red Pawn*. They will have the right of first submission on the screenplay—that is, the right to buy it, on terms to be agreed upon. If they do not choose to buy it, they will turn over to me all rights to *Red Pawn* and I will be free to sell the screenplay elsewhere.

The advantage to them will be that the novel will build *Red Pawn* into a major screen property and will cost them nothing, if they buy the screenplay. If they do not buy the screenplay, the cost of the gamble, to them, will be a story which has been lying on the shelf for 31 years, which no one else is likely ever to adapt successfully, and which is thus valueless to them for all practical purposes.

My gamble will be that I will write the screenplay "on spec," since I will have no guarantee that Paramount or anyone else will buy it. But that is a risk I am willing to take. (The minimum I will get out of it will be the novel; the maximum—the novel plus a sensational motion picture.)

This, in rough essence, is the offer I would like to make to them.

Thank you once more for your interest in this project. Your attitude has been truly inspiring to me.

Love and kisses!

Although Cerf and Paramount discussed the project, a deal was never made.

■ ■ ■

To Esther Stone

August 17, 1963

Dear Esther,

I am giving a public lecture in Chicago, at McCormick Place, on September 29. It is entitled "America's Persecuted Minority: Big Business" and deals with the subject of antitrust.

Would you and Burton like to attend the lecture as my guests? Needless to say, I will be delighted to see you. Please let me know, so that I may reserve seats for you.

Also, would you ask Sarah Lipski and Minnie Goldberg [other Chicago relatives of AR] whether they and/or their daughters would like to attend, as my guests? Please make it clear that it is not a "duty" and that

I will not be offended, if they are not interested in political subjects—but if they *are* interested, I will be delighted to have them come.

■ ■ ■

To Ray Dehn, a fan

August 17, 1963

Dear Mr. Dehn:

You ask whether I would consider addressing the Young Republican Clubs of Cleveland. I appreciate your interest, but my schedule does not permit me to accept any speaking engagements at present.

I agree with what you say about the inconsistency of the Republican party and about its desperate need of "intellectual ammunition." But that ammunition cannot be provided by any one speaker or any single speech. What is needed is a consistent political philosophy, which can be achieved only by the work of many individuals advocating the right ideas on any scale open to them, large or small, public or private. If, as I gather from your letter, you agree with the philosophy of Objectivism, I suggest that you train yourself to present a full, consistent case, to answer all rational questions and arguments, and then help others to do the same—by which I mean, those others who have a serious interest in ideas.

■ ■ ■

To Rudolph G. Crute, a fan

August 24, 1963

Dear Mr. Crute:

I sincerely appreciate the fact that you asked me to become your "Pen-Pal." You are quite right when you say that you are not the only one who has asked this, but you are the first "GI" and this does make a difference. So I am willing to try it. You are the first whose invitation I have accepted.

I must warn you that letter writing is extremely difficult for me, because I spend most of my time writing for publication, and letter writing requires a different mental set. Besides, my time is very limited. So, if you are willing to excuse in advance the fact that I will be a very slow and irregular correspondent, I am willing to try. (My secretary, to whom I am dictating this, is grinning—she knows how many hundreds of letters I have left unanswered.) But I feel a deep sympathy for the fact that you will not find much intellectual conversation in the armed services, and if I can help you to bear intellectual loneliness, I will try.

You ask whether *Atlas Shrugged* represents the present or the future. The answer is: both. To be exact, the action of *Atlas Shrugged* takes place in the near future, about ten years from the time when one reads the book. The philosophical and political trends which are destroying the country in my novel, exist today and dominate our culture. Their practical results have not yet reached the stage portrayed in *Atlas Shrugged*, but we are moving in that direction. However, a trend can be stopped and changed. History is determined by men's philosophical convictions. It is philosophy that brought the world to its present state, and it is only philosophy that can save it—a philosophy of reason, individualism and capitalism.

(By the way, Pal, don't write such things as: "About this book I would like an honest answer." I don't give any other kind of answers.)

If what you meant by asking if I'm like the characters I create is: do I really mean the things I write and do I practice what I preach?—the answer is: Brother, and how! No other type of person could have written my books.

With best regards—and waiting for your answer.

■   ■   ■

To Libby Parker, a fan

August 24, 1963

Dear Miss Parker:

If, as you say, you are an advocate of reason, I suggest that you should develop a very strict and independent critical faculty in regard to courses on philosophy. You will find very little rationality in modern philosophy, which is dominated by a revolt against reason. You should be on guard against the influence of modern philosophy which leads you to write such a contradictory sentence as "Einstein's Theory of Relativity does question the objectivity of knowledge." If it does, it would invalidate all theories, including itself; and if so, by what means would you validate it or regard it as knowledge?

But in fact, Einstein's theory does nothing of the kind. Einstein himself objected to the unwarranted distortions of his purely scientific theories by the philosophizing of scientifically ignorant popularizers. The same is true of all modern pseudoscientism: the fact that scientists do not know the cause of a given phenomenon does not give them ground to proclaim that "the universe is based on chance"—any more than the ignorance of primitive savages gave them ground to declare that the universe is ruled by gods and demons.

You mention that you are interested in existentialism. Existentialism is nothing more than oriental mysticism and has no place in philosophy.

You are wrong when you see any parallel between my philosophy and Nietzsche's. Nietzsche was an arch-advocate of irrationalism (see his *The Birth of Tragedy*). If you want a brief indication of my views on all the leading schools of modern philosophy, I suggest that you read and study the title essay of my book, *For the New Intellectual.*

■ ■ ■

To Alan Jay Lerner, playwright and editor of the *New York Times* Sunday theater section

August 31, 1963

Dear Mr. Lerner:

Please accept my enthusiastic congratulations for your article "Illuminate But Don't Eavesdrop" in the *New York Times*, August 25.

It is brilliantly reasoned and written. I wanted to cheer at every paragraph—and did, when I came to the statement that what we need is "a poetic theater, a romantic theater, a heroic theater, a moral theater and *a theatrical theater*" (particularly this last).

■ ■ ■

To Ruth Alexander

September 21, 1963

Dear Ruth:

The enclosed material will give you the information which you requested. It covers the questions of: the sales of my books—the facts about Nathaniel Branden Institute—the schedule of events at Lewis & Clark College [where AR received an honorary doctorate on October 1, 1963]—the list of the universities where I have lectured.

In regard to your question about the comparison between the political views of the faculties and students: I asked this question in almost every university where I appeared and I was told invariably that the faculty is more "liberal" in its political views than the student body; the student body is moving in the direction of free enterprise.

■　■　■

To Robert Stack

September 26, 1963

Dear Bob Stack:

I am delighted that you and Mrs. Stack will be able to have dinner with us.

Please reserve the evening of October 7th for us. I assume that your telephone number is unlisted; therefore, would you call me at the Beverly Hilton Hotel on the morning of October 6th. Or, if you prefer, would you leave your telephone number for me at the hotel, so that I may call you to set the time.

Looking forward to meeting Mr. and Mrs. Eliot Ness in person,

■　■　■

To Rudolph G. Crute

October 27, 1963

Dear Mr. Crute:

Thank you for your letter of September 5. It reached me just as I was leaving for the West Coast for some speaking engagements, so this is the first chance I had to answer you.

"Ayn Rand" *is* my pen name. My legal name is Mrs. Frank O'Connor.

Yes, my husband is very much one of my characters. If you noticed a certain similarity of appearance in Howard Roark, John Galt, Hank Rearden and Francisco d'Anconia—the reason is that my husband was the model. And the same is true of their spiritual resemblance. You may be interested to know that he is an artist.

I do not have any snapshots of myself to send you, so I am enclosing a copy of the photograph which appeared on the jacket of the hardbound edition of *Atlas Shrugged*. It was taken in my publisher's office, but it will have to do.

You say that you want to know what I like and dislike. I will answer you by paraphrasing Howard Roark in *The Fountainhead*: "Don't ask me about my family, my childhood, my friends or my feelings. Ask me about the things I *think*." The only thing that really interests me is *ideas*. And since you asked me to correspond with you because you were lonely for intellectual conversation, it is ideas that we should discuss.

Yes, I would like you to tell me more about yourself. You know a great deal about me from my books, but I do not know you, so tell me whatever *you* regard as important and characteristic of yourself.

You write: "It could be conceit, but I find myself in every one of your works." It may or may not be conceit, depending on what you mean by it. Would you tell me a little more specifically? What characters do you like, what traits do you have in common with them, what particular passages have a personal significance for you, etc.?

You say that you had given up the thing which you loved most and which is art. Why did you give it up, and what career have you chosen instead?

As to the painting which you want to do, and which you want to call "Mind and Ayn Rand"—I must tell you that I cannot allow you to do that. I do not allow my name to be used by anyone for any purpose of his own. I appreciate your intention, but your painting has to stand on your own name and on its own merit.

Yes, I am very much interested in art. I will learn a great deal about you if you tell me which artists or particular paintings are your favorites, and which you dislike most.

As to your request that I refer to you as "Gerard," this is a request that you should not make. Meaning no offense, I am much older than you are and you should leave that up to me. Don't rush things by striving for an artificial informality.

By the way, did you draw the circle of dancing girls on the envelope of your letter, or were they printed there? They are well drawn, but if they're yours, don't you think you'd better put drawings inside the envelope?

None of the above is intended as any kind of reproach or "bawling out." It's all part of the process of getting acquainted.

■ ■ ■

To Bennett Cerf

October 30, 1963

Dear Bennett:

This is in answer to your letter of October 18, 1963.

At our first luncheon, before I submitted *Atlas Shrugged* to Random House, you assured me of the following:

a) that Random House is nonpolitical in its publishing policies, that is, not committed to any specific political philosophy; that you did not always agree with the views of the authors you published, but that such difference of views did not affect you *qua* publisher in your attitude and policy toward a book; and, therefore, that I would never encounter any *political* objections or sabotage at Random House;

b) that the editors at Random House were not an editorial board, but autonomous units, each dealing only with his own authors, none having any authority over or contact with the rest of the Random House list; and, therefore, that I would never have to deal or be concerned with your editors—that I would deal directly with you and Donald, and that your editors would not enter or influence our relationship in any way.

Two months ago, I asked you whether you would be interested in publishing a collection of my lectures and essays with the title-lecture "The Fascist New Frontier," which I gave you. This project was inspired by the fact that there was a growing bookstore demand for that lecture, caused by a favorable mention in Walter Winchell's column.

I did not attempt to "sell" you this project. It was you who "sold" me on it. Your response was enthusiastic; it was you who pointed out to me that the coming election would make the book especially timely; it was you who said that the book would be controversial, sensational and a big seller. Everything you said indicated that you had fully understood the theme and nature of the book. In conclusion, you exclaimed enthusiastically: "*The Fascist New Frontier* by Ayn Rand—what a title!"

The only suggestion you made was that I integrate the various essays into chapters forming a single continuity, to which I agreed. You stated that you would publish the book on your spring list. It was a firm commitment. I so informed my agent, who said he would draw up a contract with you after my return from my trip to the West Coast.

About a month later, just before I left New York, you telephoned me and told me that your editorial staff was raising a violent protest against the publication of my book, sight unseen—and you asked me to send you a dozen copies of the pamphlet "The Fascist New Frontier" (which I did). You said you felt sure that the objections would cease once they had read it. You said that you were shocked and profoundly disturbed by these objections, which were *political* and which you had not expected.

When I telephoned you three weeks later, after my return, your attitude had changed. You were now agreeing with your editors and placing the blame on me, or on certain aspects of my lecture. Your mind was now closed; you had made a decision in my absence, without consulting me, without even giving me a hearing.

As your letter of October 18 indicates, I was not given a hearing even on October 16, when we met in your office. I was not heard. I say this, because your letter ignores everything I said at our meeting.

You write: (1) "The title *The Fascist New Frontier*, as we see it, is wrong for the book you propose. To say that the whole world, including the United States, is drifting steadily in the direction of state socialism, or whatever you want to call it, is your right and we are not making the slightest effort to dispute that right. The title *The Fascist New Frontier*, however, singles out the present administration as the fascist element in America. We cannot accept this."

Do you mean that to criticize the present administration is *not* my right? If you do, you are acceding to a totalitarian viewpoint. If you do not, then you mean that it *is* my right, but you do not wish to publish a book presenting my views on this particular subject. That is a *political* objection.

Now consider please the first part of your statement above. "That the whole world, including the United States, is drifting steadily in the direction of state socialism . . ." is *not* the theme of my proposed book. I am *not* writing about the whole world. I do *not* believe that it is drifting toward state socialism (it is being *pushed* in that direction by statist intellectuals, who are failing—and the trend is changing).

The theme of my proposed book is *an ideological critique of the Kennedy administration*; my central point is to demonstrate that contrary to the popular illusion, *the Kennedy administration's ideology is not socialistic but fascistic.*

I have stated this explicitly and repeatedly at our meeting. I am unable to believe that you have not understood me. I am also unable to believe that my theme is not made unmistakably clear in my lecture-pamphlet. I have, therefore, no choice but to believe that your insistent misstatement of my theme and your refusal to discuss my *actual* proposed book are motivated by an attempt to engineer some sort of compromise between me and my *political* antagonists.

(2) The same is true of the following statement in your letter: "Despite your eloquent arguments to the contrary, we simply will not allow a book published by us to compare excerpts from speeches by Hitler and his henchmen with excerpts from speeches by Kennedy." You can refuse to allow it (if you care to break your word)—but you cannot claim that this is not a *political* objection.

To borrow your style for a moment, I will say that I simply will not allow any publisher to tell me what convictions I may or may not hold and express.

But to return to *my* style, I will say that when you ask me to eliminate the quotations from Hitler, you are ignoring the core and essence of my theme, which is: to denounce the basic principle of any altruist-collectivist-statist system—the principle that the individual should be sacrificed to the "public interest." The Kennedy administration has been using, propagating and stressing that principle as no other American administration has ever done before. Since the public has been conditioned by the liberals to believe that this principle belongs only to the socialist-communist branch of collectivism, it is crucially important to demonstrate how profoundly it belongs also to the fascist-Nazi branch. This demonstration is the most important, novel and original aspect of what I have to say in my lecture.

That is what you ask me to eliminate, and—adding insult to injury—you write: "In asking you to take out these comparisons, I do not feel we are censoring you in the slightest degree."

I cannot believe that you have so low an estimate of my intelligence as to think that I would not know I am being asked to take out the essence of my theme. Nor do I have so low an estimate of *your* intelligence as to believe that *you* would not know it. I have, therefore, no alternative but to conclude that you have closed your mind to the real nature of the dilemma confronting you, and that you yourself are not convinced of the validity of your case.

If you were, you would present your case more openly: you would at least acknowledge my theme—I believe I have earned that much consideration from you—and then discuss it, instead of discussing some book which I never proposed to write. (See the "alternative titles" which you suggest and which are *totally inappropriate* to my book.)

You write: "We have editors here whom I deeply respect, and any publisher who doesn't at least listen to the advice of his editors, is not my idea of a wise or judicious man." That is contrary to your assurance that *I* would not be subject to the "advice" of your editors—of men whom I have never met and who are my political enemies.

At the time you made that promise to me, you knew that apprehension about the political views of your editorial staff was my major objection to Random House, as it was the major objection of my agent, Alan Collins. I took your word for the fact that the political bias of your staff was a thing of the past and that I would have nothing to fear on that score. Now, when my apprehensions have proved to be justified, the situation cannot be solved by trying to call our disagreement "nonpolitical."

To tell you the truth, I do not believe that you are trying to kid me. You are kidding yourself.

By misidentifying the theme of my book, you are trying to convince yourself that the issue involves nothing but some minor changes, and thus to switch the blame to me or to my "stubbornness." But here is the contradiction in your case and in your letter: if those changes *were* minor, you would not insist on them as a precondition of publishing my book; if you so insist, then they are *not* minor—neither in the philosophy of your editors nor in mine.

And it is with an incredulous feeling of unreality that I find it necessary to remind you that the author of *Atlas Shrugged* and *The Fountainhead* is the last person on earth whom one can expect to modify her own convictions under the pressure of a collective—particularly an anonymous collective.

Observe the consequences of your attitude. I know that you have no desire to insult me, and yet you have found yourself forced to do so—to insult me *professionally*, quite apart from the political questions involved. I refer to the issue of a publisher's right to make suggestions. You know fully as well as I do that an author of my standing is not asked to submit a manuscript "on spec" and to accept suggestions in the form of an ultimatum, that is, with the publication conditional upon the acceptance of changes. I never have and never will enter any discussion of changes under such conditions.

I have always been willing to *consider* a publisher's suggestions, but only *after* he had agreed to publish the book, with the final decision on the content of the book remaining exclusively mine.

The last paragraph of your letter states: "I'll await your final decision in this matter. I deeply hope you will agree to make the changes we ask for and will then let us see the rest of the manuscript."

Since this suggestion is an affront to my professional standing, I cannot sanction the implication that you have offered me an alternative and that the final decision is to be mine. *You* have made the final decision. You have done it by breaking your word of the past and of the present—specifically, by rejecting a book you had agreed to publish.

I quote from your note to me of August 28, 1963: "I am sending word around to everybody at Random House that we will have a new nonfiction book by you on the Spring 1964 list called *The Fascist New Frontier*. I think this book will cause a *tremendous* amount of excitement." (Italics yours.)

We had made a firm agreement. I do not intend to hold you to it. But it is you who broke it—and the least you can do is acknowledge that the final decision was yours.

I am sending a copy of this letter to Donald, since you indicated that your letter spoke for both of you.

There is no record of a response from Cerf.

■   ■   ■

To Karen Brady, a fan

December 28, 1963

Dear Miss Brady:

I do not know much about the Unitarians, but I gather that they do not have any specific, clearly defined philosophy. Objectivism is incompatible with any form of mysticism or religion. This does not mean that Objectivists would legally forbid people to hold any beliefs they choose. It means only that if one wants to accept the philosophy of Objectivism, one cannot accept a mystical belief at the same time.

In regard to the question of how you should deal with people who disagree with you, I can only suggest the following general principle: you do not have to argue with people who do not care to discuss an issue; it is sufficient simply to state that you do not agree with them. If they insist on knowing your viewpoint, they cannot accuse you of being rude—provided, of course, that you present your viewpoint clearly, calmly and politely. The way to do this is to discuss the subject, without personal remarks or personal accusations.

No, I do not agree with the John Birch Society. I regard their policy as futile. Our first concern should be to do all we can to establish full, laissez-faire capitalism—and *not* merely to fight Communism.

No, there is no music that corresponds to Richard Halley's Concerto or to "The Song of Broken Glass [from *We the Living*]." These are my own fictional conceptions.

■ ■ ■

To Alan F. Westin, of the Special Committee on Science and Law, New York City Bar Association

March 28, 1964

Dear Mr. Westin:

An issue such as "the invasion of privacy" cannot be discussed without a clear definition of the right to privacy, and this cannot be discussed outside the context of clearly defined and upheld individual rights.

Since individual rights are being evaded, denied, negated and violated by the dominant philosophical theories and political practices of our time, I do not quite know how scientific gadgets can be singled out as the particular offender in the case.

Scientific gadgets or weapons do not put themselves into action; it is men who use them, and men's actions are determined by their philosophical ideas. Therefore, the issue is not what sort of tools science has produced to violate individual rights, but: what sort of philosophy permits men to use these tools.

To answer your specific questions: 1. "Has the theme of protecting privacy from scientific observation and intrusion been a concern of the younger writers since World War II?" I am not an expert on today's younger writers. With very few exceptions, I do not read them.

2. I do not regard "the pressures of mass society, the mass media, the large organization, and conformity pressures beyond the cold war" as the causes of today's invasion of privacy and destruction of individual rights.

If you are interested in my views on the causes of that destruction, the "specific source" I can recommend for your investigation is my novel, *Atlas Shrugged*.

■ ■ ■

To Marjorie Roscam Abbing, a fan

March 28, 1964

Dear Miss Abbing:

You write that you are unbearably bored at school, and ask me whether it is treason not to love every second of one's life. No, it certainly is not treason. One cannot force oneself to feel an emotion contrary to the facts with which one is dealing. There are many things in life which are unbearably boring and, unfortunately, school seems to be one of them everywhere in the world. When you have to deal with the boring or the unpleasant, do it as conscientiously as you can and get it over with, but do not reproach yourself for your own feeling when it matches the facts.

You ask me which books I have enjoyed most and which do not clash with my philosophy. My favorite writer is Victor Hugo whom I admire literarily. I do not agree with his philosophical ideas, but he presents a heroic image of man and that is a very rare value in literature. There are no books with which I agree fully, though I may enjoy some particular aspect of them. Literarily (*not* philosophically), I like Dostoyevsky, O. Henry, Rostand.

I don't mind if you care to write to me again, and I will be pleased to hear from you, but I cannot promise to answer you because, unfortunately, my working schedule does not leave me much time for correspondence.

■ ■ ■

To Thomas A. Bond, a high-school history teacher

May 2, 1964

Dear Mr. Bond:

Please tell your student that I appreciate his intention in designing the "Rand Temple" (provided he understands that I do not advocate such a thing in reality). Speaking symbolically, if the figures are dubbed "John and Dagny," their positions should be reversed, because an ideal woman is a man-worshipper, and an ideal man is the highest symbol of mankind.

Speaking seriously, I was very happy to know your own attitude toward my books. I know the crucial importance of schools in determining the direction of a culture—and I realize the importance of the influence which a man in your position can have on young students and, therefore, on the future.

■ ■ ■

To H. Riga, a Canadian high-school teacher and Estonian émigré

May 2, 1964

Dear Mr. Riga:

I appreciate your interest in my philosophy, and I feel a profound sympathy for all those who chose exile in preference to communist rule.

However, I do not approve of your plan to arrange a contest among students for "the best critical approach" to my philosophy—and, therefore, I cannot grant you permission to use excerpts from my work for this purpose.

My reasons are as follows: I never engage in debates about my philosophy; I do not approve of subjecting a philosophical system to the confusions, misrepresentations and distortions of immature and untrained mentalities; such an attempt can lead only to intellectual chaos—and I can neither sanction it nor have any part in it.

■ ■ ■

To John O. Nelson, philosophy professor at the University of Colorado

Professor Nelson published an article, "The 'Freedom' of the Hippie and Yippie," in the August 1969 issue of AR's journal *The Objectivist*, which described Nelson as agreeing with "the basic principles of Objectivism in ethics and politics."

May 2, 1964

Dear Professor Nelson:

I am sadly astonished by your letter of April 2.

No, there are no "difficulties" in the political philosophy of Objectivism.

The questions you raise in regard to the young mother's statement in *Atlas Shrugged* are the result of an equivocation or a misunderstanding of the term "collective" on your part. My use of that term is made explicitly clear by the context in which it occurs. The full statement reads as follows:

"You know, of course, that there can be no collective commitments in this valley and that families or relatives are not allowed to come here, unless each person takes the striker's oath by his own independent conviction."

This means that no person may assume control of another person's mind and that each person has to arrive at his convictions and decisions individually, by his own judgment.

If the husband's decision were accepted as intellectually binding on his wife, *that* would constitute a *collective* commitment. But if the husband and wife reach the same decision independently, it is a *common* commitment.

The error in your argument consists of the failure to differentiate between these two concepts. The term *"collective"* refers to a group of men regarded as a single unit. The term *"common"* refers to a sum of individual units.

The dictionary definitions of these two terms are as follows: *"Collective,* adj.—pertaining to a group of individuals taken together"; *"Common,* adj.—belonging equally to, or shared alike by, two or more or all in question."

An agreement of independent individuals on a given subject or course of action, is a *common* agreement. A situation in which the decision of *some* men is taken as representing the decision of *all* men in a given group, is a *collective* commitment.

Observe how this applies to your alleged paradox—to your notion that " 'There can be no collective commitments in this valley' is itself a collective commitment." The exact statement, describing the facts in question, is: " 'There can be no collective commitments in this valley' is a common agreement"—*i.e.,* an agreement shared equally and individually by all the residents of the valley, as a logical part of the philosophy each of them has accepted.

To say that a number of men "hold a common commitment to have no common commitments" would be the kind of paradox you have in mind. But this would simply mean that men agree never to agree on anything— which is nonsense.

The fact that a number of men agree on a given subject, does not constitute membership in a *collective* unit, does not extend beyond the specific subject of the agreement, and does not imply the right of a group to supersede the minds, convictions and judgments of its individual members.

Your confusion on these two terms leads you to write a passage which I find truly shocking:

[Nelson contends that in Galt's Gulch there are "collective commitments" to protect individual rights.]

This is totally alien to the philosophy of Galt's Gulch—metaphysically, epistemologically, ethically, politically (and stylistically).

You are right when you say that some such formulation would justify taxation for defense and other purposes. So it would. It would also permit antitrust laws, the military draft, "social gains" legislation, etc., etc., etc.

The notion of justifying a "collective commitment" on the ground of a person's own "self-interest," whether that person agrees or not, is the standard collectivist justification of a dictatorship as acting for its victims' "own good," whether a victim accepts it as the good or not. Surely I do not have to tell you that *this* is the exact opposite of my philosophy.

I must mention that Galt's Gulch is *not* an organized society, but a *private club* whose members share the same philosophy. It exemplifies the basic moral principles of social relationships among rational men, the principles on which a proper political system should be built. It does not deal with questions of political organization, with the details of a legal framework needed to establish and maintain a free society open to all, including dissenters. It does not deal with specifically *political* principles, only with their *moral* base. (I indicate that the proper political framework is to be found in the Constitution, with its contradictions removed.)

■ ■ ■

To Jack Morano, a fan

May 23, 1964

Dear Mr. Morano:

In regard to your inquiry about forming an Ayn Rand Society or Club on Staten Island: such a society must be formed independently, and it must be clearly understood that it has no connection with the Nathaniel Branden Institute or myself—that the society is not a spokesman for me nor an official interpreter of Objectivism—and that neither I nor NBI are in any way responsible for its activities. Since my name is being used, the sole purpose of such a Society must be the study of my works and my philosophy. If the Society engages in any other activity, then its title should be changed and my name should be removed.

The Societies or Clubs to which you refer were all formed by students on college campuses, on the students' own initiative. If, as I gather, you intend to form such a Society for the general public, please be sure to make it a study group and nothing else.

■ ■ ■

To Barry Goldwater

July 14, 1964

Dear Senator Goldwater:

Please accept my sincere admiration for the heroic battle you have fought and are now so deservedly winning.

I want also to express my deep sympathy for the courage, endurance and dignity you have exhibited in the face of your adversaries' contemptibly vicious tactics.

I have no doubt that you can win in November, even though it will be one of the toughest battles in history, and that your victory can bring about a world Renaissance of freedom.

Since you know my political views and my ability to communicate them, I am at your disposal, if you think that my services can be useful to you in your great battle.

■ ■ ■

To Mrs. Milton W. Broberg, a fan

September 3, 1964

Dear Mrs. Broberg:

I hope that you will not find yourself in need of public assistance. But permit me to say that if you do need it, you should not hesitate to call on it, because you are certainly entitled to it—in view of the taxes you have paid and in view of the fact that today's political system makes it impossible for anyone to provide for his own old age. This does not mean that the welfare state is right, but that so long as you oppose the welfare state, you should not be its first victim and should not be made to suffer while your own hard-earned money is being spent to support bums all over the world.

■ ■ ■

To Deborah A. Baker, a fan

September 3, 1964

Dear Miss Baker:

You seem to be mistaken in your approach to [the issue of labor unions]. You ask: "Do you feel these employees are making demands that shouldn't be made? Or do you feel they also are the contributing factor to the success of big business in this country—and are deserving of certain privileges from the company they work for?"

Any competent man, who does his job well, contributes to the success of a business—but that is not relevant to the question of unions and it is not an issue of "privileges." It is an issue of individual rights. All men, whether employers or employees, have the right to earn their own living, to pursue their own interests and to deal with one another by means of discussion, persuasion, bargaining and voluntary, uncoerced agreement, to mutual advantage. Employees have the right to form unions, if they do so voluntarily, and to go on strike. An employer has the right to negotiate with them, if he chooses, or to hire other workers. In case of such disagreements, it is the free market that determines who will win and whether the employees' demands were fair or not.

But today, under our labor laws, both employers and employees are forced to act under government coercion.

Employees are forced to join unions, whether they want to or not—and employers are forced to bargain with unions, whether they want to or not. Therefore, today, the whole field of labor-management relations is unfair and unjust, in basic principle, and violates the rights of all those involved.

You ask whether it is proper for you to represent an employees' union. Since you have no choice about the labor situation, it is proper for you to take part in union activities and to do the best you can under the circumstances—that is, be as fair as you can, always remembering the rights of all parties involved. The principle to remember, in this context, is: just as the employees do not work for the sake of the employers, but for the sake of earning their own living, so the employers are not in business for the sake of providing jobs, but for the sake of earning *their* own living, which means: their profits.

You mention that a representative of Mohawk's management told you that if you agreed with my philosophy, you shouldn't be the "representative of a union arguing the cause of employees." This sounds like the statement of a fool. Apparently, he sees economic relations as a class war in which one must fight either "for businessmen" or "for workers." This is a view which my philosophy rejects and opposes in its entirety. My philosophy upholds the rights of individual men, on any economic level—*not* the special privileges of any "class" or group.

■　■　■

To John R. Cool, a fan

September 3, 1964

Dear Mr. Cool:

Thank you for your letter of August 13th.

I will be glad to autograph a copy of *Atlas Shrugged* for you, if you will send it to the above address.

■ ■ ■

To Michael D. Gill, of Citizens for Goldwater-Miller

AR had written a speech she proposed as the final speech in the Goldwater campaign, but the speech was not used. She later wrote an extensive analysis of Goldwater's defeat ("It's Earlier Than You Think," *The Objectivist Newsletter*, December 1964).

October 28, 1964

Dear Mr. Gill:

I am enclosing the speech which I promised to send you.

It is my understanding that this speech will not be used by anyone other than Senator Goldwater or General Eisenhower.

In case it is General Eisenhower who cares to use it, I strongly urge you to let me reword the passages which will need rewording. This can be done quickly over the long distance telephone. My concern is to guard against possible ideological mistakes if the rewriting is done by someone else.

With best wishes for victory,

■ ■ ■

To Brand Blanshard, philosophy professor at Yale University and renowned critic of contemporary philosophy

March 4, 1965

Dear Professor Blanshard:

I am deeply grateful for the copy of *Reason and Goodness* which you sent me. I have been an admirer of your work for quite some time and I truly appreciate the privilege of receiving an autographed copy of your book.

I know that there are many issues in ethics on which we disagree, but it is always a pleasure to read your manner of approach to philosophical problems. I am reading *Reason and Goodness* with great interest, and I would like to communicate with you when I have finished studying it.

■ ■ ■

To Michael P. Levock, Jr., a fan

March 6, 1965

Dear Mr. Levock:

You are mistaken when you write about "stealing my philosophy." Philosophy is a science that identifies principles which are objectively true. To recognize the truth and to accept it does not constitute "stealing."

My article ["Who Is the Final Authority in Ethics?"] in the February issue of *The Objectivist Newsletter*—which I am enclosing, will make this matter clear to you.

■ ■ ■

To Lee Clettenberg, a fan

March 6, 1965

Dear Mr. Clettenberg:

I was interested to read of the process by which you discovered my novel. The fact that the question "Why does man need a code of values?" arrested your attention, speaks well for your method of thinking. It indicates your ability to think in terms of fundamentals. That *was* the important question.

You are mistaken, however, when you suggest that *The Objectivist Newsletter* should teach my philosophy "in everyday, understandable language." You ask: "Do you have to use such big, fancy words?" Yes, we do. Philosophy cannot be communicated in terms of "everyday" language, which has no words to denote the kind of concepts that philosophy deals with. We do not use "fancy" words—we use the simplest (and most *exact*) ones for the kind of subjects we discuss.

I sympathize with your problem, particularly in regard to modern dictionaries. Perhaps the older dictionaries (of about thirty years ago) may be somewhat more helpful. Or you might learn to grasp the meaning of the words we use by the context in which they occur.

■ ■ ■

To Paul Smith, a fan

March 13, 1965

Dear Mr. Smith:

The sincerity and seriousness of your letter of February 9 prompts me to make an exception and to answer your questions. As a rule, I do not answer questions of this kind, but I do not want you to be victimized by those who raise them.

1) You say you were asked whether "the rape of Dominique Francon by Howard Roark was a violation of Dominique's freedom, an act of force that was contrary to the Objectivist Ethics?" The answer is: of course not. It was not an actual rape, but a symbolic action which Dominique all but invited. This was the action she wanted and Howard Roark knew it. You are correct in your interpretation of the meaning of the dialogue about marble. This is not the only clue to Dominique's psychology. If you re-read the passages pertaining to Dominique before and after the "rape scene," you will find many things to explain her motivation. Needless to say, an actual rape of an unwilling victim would be a vicious action and a violation of a woman's rights; in moral meaning, it would be the exact opposite of the scene in *The Fountainhead*.

2) You quote Karen Andre's line in *Night of January 16th*: "I am capable of murder—for Faulkner's sake," and ask: "Isn't murder a viola-tion of the Objectivist Ethics? Doesn't this statement make Karen Andre an Attila?" The answer is: Yes, murder is a violation of the Objectivist ethics. No, this statement does not make Karen Andre an Attila. It is not to be taken literally, it is merely her deliberate challenge to the moral philosophy propounded by Mr. Flint and an expression of the intensity of her love for Bjorn Faulkner.

3) You ask my opinion of *Night of January 16th* and of its merit relative to my other works. Here, I must point out that you have not read *Night of January 16th*. The published version of this play is an adaptation for the amateur theater (a very poor adaptation) and cannot give you any idea of the full original text of the play. The original version is not available in print. As to my opinion of the original play's merit, it is very high—as high, relative to its scale, as my opinion of any other work of mine.

Now that I have answered your specific questions, let me give you an important suggestion: do not read any statement out of context, particularly when you read fiction. In analyzing the philosophical ideas presented in fiction, you must identify the total meaning of the story, of its plot, its main events and its characters. You must never judge any incident out of context, and this applies particularly to the dialogue. In real life and in fiction, people do not speak in terms of precise, legalistic philosophical definitions. This does not mean that people contradict philosophical principles, but it means that one must learn to distinguish when a particular statement does represent a precise definition and when it is a verbal part of a wider whole. In reading literature, one must learn how to analyze its parts, but one must never forget to put them together again, that is, one must know how to analyze and how to integrate.

With my best wishes to you and your friends of the Honor English IV Class of Broadmoor High School,

■ ■ ■

To a Catholic priest, who requested anonymity

March 20, 1965

Dear Father:

Thank you for your letter. No, I have no desire to "tear it up in disgust" nor to "have a good laugh at an enemy." I found it profoundly interesting and I sincerely appreciate it.

Yes, I was "startled at a clergyman talking like that," but I cannot say that I would have considered it impossible. I have often thought that since religion has been the only field seriously concerned with morality, a religious philosopher should or could be interested in the philosophy of *Atlas Shrugged*. Rather than regard you as an "enemy," I would like to think of you as an honorable adversary. After many disappointments in this regard, I am not certain that such an adversary can exist, but I will assume it as a hypothesis and will answer you on that assumption.

I see that some aspect of my writing appeals to you, but you have not indicated specifically what it is that you do agree with. You indicate that you disagree on the issue of atheism. I do not understand your position on this subject. You write that, according to your concept, God is "the Depth, the Source, the Force, the Love of life." These are metaphorical expressions; I do not know what they mean in this context. You say: "It simply is so, because Life is not a blind force and no contradiction." This is an arbitrary assertion on your part. Life is neither a "blind force" nor a supernatural one; it is a natural fact, which exists and requires no supernatural explanation.

You write: "Am I going to prove my point? Can you prove that contradictions do not exist?" I will refer you to Aristotle's definition of an axiom and to Galt's statement in *Atlas Shrugged* in reference to axioms: "An axiom is a proposition that defeats its opponents by the fact that they have to accept it and use it in the process of any attempt to deny it." The Law of Identity is an axiom; so is the Law of Contradiction. The concept of proof presupposes the existence of axioms from which such proof is derived. The laws of logic are the means by which one proves the truth of one's statements; the demand that one "prove" the laws of logic is a contradiction in terms. But the concept of God is not an axiom.

Your interpretation of the concept of God as "powerless on earth" is highly original, but it is a personal *interpretation*, which does not validate the concept in question and cannot be taken as a fact of reality.

In regard to the meaning of the crucifixion, you must certainly know that your interpretation is not the generally accepted one. There are many interpretations of that meaning, but the prevalent one is that Christ died on the cross as a sacrifice to redeem man from Original Sin. This is the idea I was answering in the *Playboy* interview [March 1964, reprinted in *The Playboy Interviews: The Best of Three Decades, 1962–1992*].

I was astonished by your statement that my answer to *Playboy* was not straightforward, with the implication that I softened the issue in order not to shock the public. Such an implication is unworthy of you. You refer to my courage and seem to understand that courage *was* required to formulate my philosophy and to publish what I have published. If so, then isn't it somewhat preposterous to suspect me of being afraid to speak openly in, of all things, a popular magazine?

I was not "taken aback" by the question about the sign of the cross. It is a question that I have discussed many times. What I did object to was the interviewer's way of presenting the issue in such superficial terms. I considered it offensive on the ground of respect both for my philosophy and for religion. The issue is too serious to hide behind symbolism. A discussion in terms of mere symbols can lead to nothing but misrepresentation and confusion. Since both the sign of the dollar and the sign of the cross are symbols, it is the ideas they symbolize that had to be discussed openly and explicitly. It is the notion of sacrificing the best to the worst, of the ideal to the nonideal, that was essential in this context and that I discussed. I call your attention to my concluding answer on this issue: "If I had to choose between faith and reason, I wouldn't consider the choice even conceivable. As a human being, one chooses reason." Do you regard this as a "softening" touch?

No, I have no desire to "replace the sign of the cross with the sign of the dollar." The sign of the dollar is a symbol introduced by me in fiction to symbolize the cause of the particular group of men in my story. It would be improper to introduce a symbol for *philosophy* in real life, though it is quite appropriate in fiction. Philosophy does not deal in symbols and does not require them.

Perhaps I should add that I am an intransigent atheist, but not a militant one. This means that I am an uncompromising advocate of reason and that I am fighting *for* reason, not *against* religion. I must also mention that I do respect religion in its philosophical aspects, in the sense that it represents an early form of philosophy.

I have the impression that you are a follower of Thomas Aquinas, whose position, in essence, is that since reason is a gift of God, man must use it. I regard this as the best of all the attempts to reconcile reason and religion—but it is only an *attempt*, which cannot succeed. It may work in a limited way in a given individual's life, but it cannot be validated philosophically. However, I regard Aquinas as the greatest philosopher next to Aristotle, in the purely philosophical, not theological, aspects of his work. If you are a Thomist, we may have a great deal in common, but we would still have an irreconcilable basic conflict which is, primarily, an epistemological conflict.

He answered on April 1 with a long, friendly letter. There is no record of a response by AR.

■ ■ ■

To Bennett Cerf

On March 29 Cerf wrote that he was sorry to learn AR no longer wanted Random House as her publisher, but said, "I think you are one of the most wonderful people I ever met in my life, and this decision of yours will not change my feeling in that respect to the least degree." AR and Cerf continued to exchange occasional friendly notes.

April 3, 1965

Dear Bennett:

Thank you for your note of March 29. I sincerely appreciate your good wishes.

After our promising beginning, I deeply regret that the nature of the subsequent events left me no choice but to end our professional relationship.

I, too, wish you well and shall always give you credit for the many good actions you have taken in regard to me.

■   ■   ■

To Mimi Sutton

April 3, 1965

Dear Mimi:

Thank you very much for the two beautiful record albums which you sent us.

I understand your enthusiasm for Elisabeth Schwarzkopf and why you wanted us to hear these particular records. She has a magnificent voice and the way she sings operettas gives them the emotional power of a real opera.

Frank has played the records over and over again and I have seldom seen him enjoy a record so much. I especially thank you for this, in addition to my own pleasure.

■   ■   ■

To Michael G. Moody, a fan

May 23, 1965

Dear Mr. Moody:

I am opposed to the organization known as Young Americans for Freedom. That organization is controlled by, or shares the policies of, the *National Review* magazine and is my avowed enemy.

There can be no cooperation or rapprochement between me and "conservatives" of that type.

Therefore, under no circumstances can I permit a chapter of YAF to be called after me.

If, as you say, you are "Objectivists at heart," I suggest that you check your premises and make a choice. It's either-or.

I am enclosing a copy of "Conservatism: An Obituary" which will tell you why I consider the "conservative" movement an intellectual dead end.

■   ■   ■

To Edward T. Chase, editorial vice president at New American Library, which published most of AR's books

August 21, 1965

Dear Mr. Chase:

Thank you very much for the Shakespeare set which you sent me.

You have good reason to be proud of these books. I think it is the most beautiful publishing job I have ever seen in paperback. I must mention the artist's work on the covers, which is superb.

I have glanced through the copy and I find the handling of the footnote "translations" is excellent. I am happy to have these books, and I know that I will be able to read Shakespeare in English *now*.

■   ■   ■

To John Nicholas, a fan

August 21, 1965

Dear Mr. Nicholas:

I can sympathize with the fact that you feel fear when you look at the present state of the world, but I hope that this is not your chronic emotion. It is too early to feel fear of the future when one is under 30, and too late after that. What I mean is that one must never allow fear to become one's permanent sense of life. The important thing is to prepare yourself intellectually to deal with whatever circumstances you may encounter, which requires that you define your values fully, clearly and rationally—and never betray them.

■   ■   ■

To Diane Schaefer, a fan

August 21, 1965

Dear Miss Schaefer:

In your letter of July 5, you write that you and your history instructor "have found no work on Russian history or theoretical Communism that makes reference to the use of questionnaires to determine who will be the 'true proletariat.' Consequently, would you please send me either the name of your primary sources; or, failing this, enlarge upon this matter."

My primary source is myself. I graduated from the University of Leningrad and had to fill one of those questionnaires myself. This "purge" of Soviet universities took place in the spring of 1924. It was done under the slogan of "We will not educate our class enemies." Thousands of young people were expelled from schools all over the country and were denied an education, in payment for the "sins" of their ancestors. I was not in a position to know, nor care, what particular Soviet official instigated this policy, but it was public and nationwide. Similar questionnaires were used thereafter in regard to employment to determine an applicant's origin.

I do not know what sources you are studying, but they are obviously of a dubious nature if they omit an event of this magnitude. For details, I refer you to my novel *We the Living*, which deals with that period of Russian history and includes, specifically, the "purge" of the Soviet schools. The plot of *We the Living* is fictional, but all the background and political events, including this "purge," are real and exactly as some 200,000,000 people have had to live them. I am astonished that events of such large scale can be kept secret from historians.

■ ■ ■

To Carolyn Riley, assistant editor at *Contemporary Authors*

February 26, 1966

Dear Mrs. Riley:

You asked me for comments on the biographical sketch. I assume that you are acting in good faith, but I must say that I am at a loss to explain the motives of your researcher. He, or she, has apparently failed to read anything I have written, and has relied on press interviews for his summary of my ideas—interviews over whose accuracy I had no control—which is not the place to look for philosophical definitions.

Since, presumably, biographical sketches are intended to be and purport to be objective, I am puzzled by what seems to come close to deliberate malice in the researcher's selection of reviews: he has selected the kind of smears which no civilized publication should care to repeat and which include the opinions of two men who, *self-admittedly*, have not read my works. On the other hand, he has omitted any mention of favorable reviews, even though they appeared in such prominent publications as the *New York*

Times Book Review (review of *The Fountainhead*) and *Newsweek* (review of *Atlas Shrugged*).

Personally, I prefer to omit reviews altogether from any biographical sketch of me—for the following reasons: a. I do not care to give free commercials to my enemies, nor to let them ride on my reputation; b. I do not regard smears and misrepresentations as a mere difference of opinion; c. I do not care to have the public value of my name be used as a means for the further spread of mudslinging. Therefore, to avoid so-called one-sidedness, I am willing to forego quotations from favorable reviews as well.

■ ■ ■

To Elizabeth Smith, of *Cat Fancy* magazine

March 20, 1966

Dear Miss Smith:

You ask whether I own cats or simply enjoy them, or both. The answer is: both. I love cats in general and own two in particular.

You ask: "We are assuming that you have an interest in cats, or was your subscription strictly objective?" My subscription was strictly objective, *because* I have an interest in cats. I can demonstrate *objectively* that cats are a great value, and the charter issue of *Cat Fancy* magazine can serve as part of the evidence. ("Objective" does not mean "disinterested" or indifferent; it means corresponding to the facts of reality and applies both to knowledge and to values.)

I subscribed to *Cat Fancy* primarily for the sake of the pictures, and found the charter issue very interesting and enjoyable.

■ ■ ■

To Stanley Marcus, Neiman-Marcus stores

March 20, 1966

Dear Mr. Marcus:

Thank you for your letter of February 24. I appreciate very much the fact that you included me on your list of your "most favorite people," and I would have been glad to decorate the Easter egg you sent me, if my time had permitted it. But, unfortunately, my schedule is such that this is the first chance I had to answer you, let alone to permit myself the luxury of attempting to paint.

Since you needed the egg by March 15, shall I send it back to you undecorated?

■   ■   ■

To Malcolm K. McClintock, a fan

March 20, 1966

Dear Mr. McClintock:

You ask: "What goods are produced by an attorney? It seems to me that the value of the legal profession is created by man, rather than derived from the needs of man."

The value of the legal profession is derived from the social needs of man. Since men need objective laws in order to live in a free, civilized society, they need the advice of lawyers, that is, of specialists trained professionally in that field.

The practice of the legal profession has been inflated out of proportion and distorted by today's mixed economy. But this is true of most professions today. However, in a proper free society, lawyers have a legitimate and important role to play.

■   ■   ■

To B. Joni Harris, a fan

March 20, 1966

Dear Miss Harris:

The dilemma you describe in your letter in regard to your novel has no solution, since you are guilty of a contradiction in your basic approach.

You write that "Objectivism is the philosophical foundation of the work" and that "the story depicts my heroine as having discovered her 'rational philosophy' on her own." This means that you want to ascribe to your heroine a discovery which in fact is not hers and that, for the purposes of your novel, you want to pretend that Objectivism, in fact, does not exist. You cannot expect me to sanction an attempt of that kind.

If your heroine were a physicist, you could not decide to have her discover the law of gravitation. In the same way and for the same reasons, you cannot write about a heroine who discovers "a rational philosophy," unless you are able to provide her with an original "rational philosophy" of your own.

I suggest that you narrow your theme to your heroine's specific problems and use generalized philosophical ideas, without attempting to make her the discoverer of an entire philosophy.

I cannot give you permission to include in your novel a "notice" connecting it with Objectivism in any way or form. Such a "notice" would imply a sanction which I cannot give to a person I do not know.

If, as you say, you agree with my philosophy, then you must realize that your novel has to stand on your own name, and on its own merit.

You are mistaken when you compare your approach to my attitude towards Aristotle: (1) *Atlas Shrugged* was not a restatement of Aristotle's work and it did not claim that its hero had originated Aristotle's philosophy. (2) Aristotle died over 2,000 years ago, which is not true of me, and his works are in the public domain, which is not true of Objectivism.

■ ■ ■

To Carolyn Riley

April 23, 1966

Dear Mrs. Riley:

Thank you very much for the revised version of your article in *Contemporary Authors*. With the exception of a few minor corrections, which I enclose on a separate sheet, the article is excellent.

To tell you the truth, I was astonished and very pleased. No, I do not doubt your "good faith" now, and I deeply appreciate the work you have done on this.

The best way to express my appreciation is to tell you that your article is one of the very few biographical pieces which I would like to keep. Therefore, I enclose my check for $10 for the volume of *Contemporary Authors* in which it will appear.

■ ■ ■

To Michael L. Haider, chairman of a dinner honoring Lyndon B. Johnson

August 18, 1966

Dear Mr. Haider:

I appreciate your invitation to join the Sponsors Committee honoring President Lyndon B. Johnson, but I believe that some mistake is involved. I am an advocate of laissez-faire capitalism and I am not an admirer of President Johnson's policies. Therefore, in fairness to the views of this Committee, and to my own, I am obliged to decline your invitation.

■ ■ ■

To William C Sage, a fan

August 28, 1966

Dear Mr. Sage:

You ask whether I had a specific piece of music in mind when I described the Halley Concerto. No, I did not. My favorite composer is Rachmaninoff, but even his music does not quite fit what I had in mind for Richard Halley. As to the musical selections you mention, I must say that I do not care for Wagner (with a very few exceptions), nor for *Der Rosenkavalier*.

■ ■ ■

To W. H. Hutt, economics professor at the University of Virginia

August 28, 1966

Dear Professor Hutt:

Thank you for your letter of July 6 and for the copy of *South Africa's Salvation in Classic Liberalism*, which you sent me.

I appreciate your interest and the time you have taken to discuss the issue at length. But, I regret to say, there is a fundamental, philosophical-moral difference between your views and mine.

You do not seem to be acquainted with my views. I regret that in discussing my pamphlet *America's Persecuted Minority: Big Business*, you chose to ignore the crucial passages on pp. 4–5 which define the difference between political power and economic power. If you disagree with me, it is this fundamental distinction that would have had to be discussed. But your letter ignores it and argues in terms of concepts which I have explicitly rejected: concepts equating private actions with governmental actions, and viewing *private* power as *"coercive."*

There is, in fact, only one form of coercion: the initiation of the use of physical force by one man or group against others. I am opposed to the initiation of physical force in any human-social relationships, by anyone, for any purpose whatsoever.

I do not agree with such notions as "contrived scarcity," or "private collusion," or the equation of private agreements with governmental force, or the alleged "rights" of consumers, or the idea that "consumers alone express ultimate economic ends, producers supplying the means," or the idea that "each person should be guaranteed freedom to play off one source of supply against another and one source of demand against another."

All such issues rest on one's views of individual rights and of the nature of government. These, in turn, rest on one's view of ethics—and *that* is where any discussion of such issues has to begin. I do not believe that you are aware of the fact that I am profoundly and totally opposed to the ethics of altruism.

I am enclosing my pamphlet, *What Is Capitalism?* (a small excerpt from which was published in *Barron's*). This may give you a fuller indication of my views on the subject. I call your particular attention to the passages dealing with what I call "the tribal premise."

You are mistaken when you state that "the chaos of interpretations" has caused me "to misunderstand the purpose of laws to prevent the restraint of competition." My opposition to the antitrust laws is based on the text of the Sherman Act, which I have read.

No, the "Austrian approach" has not "helped to mold" my philosophy. It is one of the many approaches to capitalism which I oppose, though I do agree with many of its purely economic ideas.

Yes, I do charge that "capitalism has never had any proper philosophical defenders," and I do not mean "the field of practical politics." I mean the field of philosophy, particularly of ethics and epistemology. I mean that capitalism is incompatible with altruism and epistemological irrationalism. (See the title essay of my book, *For the New Intellectual.*) I was, therefore, shocked to see that you list Hume and Kant among the philosophical ancestors of capitalism. Capitalism cannot exist, nor survive, on a foundation of irrationality—and the two arch-destroyers of reason in modern history are Hume and Kant.

I must mention also, for the record, that I am not connected in any way with Rampart College, and that I do not agree with that College's program, attitude or viewpoint. Perhaps some individual persons there may agree with me on some issues, but if, as you write, they were quoting me in arguments with you, I want it to be clearly understood that they were not speaking for me and were not representatives of my philosophy.

If my viewpoint does interest you, I would be pleased to send you a copy of my forthcoming book, *Capitalism: The Unknown Ideal,* which is to be published in November and which will give you a fuller understanding of my views. Please let me know whether you would care to read it.

Professor Hutt responded: "However much I disagree with you on the matters I have raised, I have read a good deal of your writings with profit and enthusiasm."

■ ■ ■

To Duane Eddy, pop and rock guitarist/singer

June 1, 1967

Dear Mr. Eddy,

Thank you—enormously—for the record of "Will O' the Wisp" which you sent me.

The record is wonderful. The "noise" you mention is so slight that I am not aware of it when I listen to the music. I must tell you that no present can give me a thrill today, only my kind of music can and does. You have given me a powerful source of my personal "benevolent universe." No, it is not a "small thing," it means a great deal to me—and I appreciate it profoundly.

■ ■ ■

To Archibald Ogden

August 24, 1967

Dear Archie:

It was I who asked Bobbs-Merrill to ask you to write an introduction for the 25th Anniversary Edition of *The Fountainhead.* It is I, therefore, who must tell you, with profound regret, that the introduction you wrote is entirely inappropriate and that I cannot accept it.

My basic objection is to its overall spirit and style: it is *flippant.* Flippancy is not a proper approach to the nature of my novel, of my ideas, of my own character, of my career. The events surrounding the publication of *The Fountainhead* were not funny. That a book and an author survived triumphantly the kind of battle I was and still am fighting, is not a humorous subject.

I had always believed that you understood and appreciated *The Fountainhead*. Now I am sadly obliged to conclude that you and I have grown too far apart intellectually and that you have forgotten what you did know about me.

Perhaps the most offensive touch in your Introduction is the following line (in regard to the matter of cutting the character of Vesta Dunning out of the book): "So, out went the Hollywood whore—and every line deleted was like removing one of the author's fingernails with a pair of red-hot pliers."

In your letter to me of July 26, you say: "I may have slightly exaggerated the story of excising the budding actress." What you wrote is not a "slight exaggeration," but an outright fabrication which implies some extremely derogatory things about me. To refresh your memory: it was *I* who decided that Vesta Dunning had to be cut—not for the reasons you state, not because she clashed with the Roark-Dominique relationship, but because her moral treason was a variant of Wynand's, which made her superfluous in regard to the book's theme. I decided this when I was writing Part III—and I told you of my decision in a telephone conversation. Your first reaction was one of regret, but then you agreed with my reasons. I did all the cutting myself, we had no conferences about it, so where were "the red-hot pliers" and who was applying them?

Once I make a decision, either in regard to writing or to any other matter, I do not hesitate, vacillate or suffer over carrying it out. How could I, in reason, decide to delete Vesta, yet suffer over "every line deleted"? This would make me the kind of irrational person who wants to eat her cake and have it, too—a vice of which I have never been guilty. Yet that is what your sentence implies, and more: it implies that the decision was not mine and that somebody had to force me to do it by some tortuous process, line by line.

I do not remember any such thing as a proofreader's query "Who she?" on the page proofs or the galleys of the book. Are you sure you didn't confuse it with some other book? I suppose it is possible that some indirect reference to Vesta might have remained somewhere in the script (though I doubt it), but what you imply is the kind of sloppiness in writing and editing which is the opposite of the way I work. I am not an emotional, "inspirational" writer. So what was the point of building up such a story? Is that the most interesting or significant thing you could find to say about the author of *The Fountainhead*?

(Incidentally, I do not wish to have Vesta Dunning mentioned between the book covers of *The Fountainhead*. She is out, and has to stay out.)

A similarly misleading implication about my character is conveyed by another passage in your Introduction: "my only major contribution to it [the novel], in addition to encouragement and keeping the author's screams to a minimum when proofreaders altered a word, was the title." If I was the kind of person who needed "encouragement," I would not have been able to write *The Fountainhead* nor to survive any of the things that went on before and after its publication. When did you ever see me "*discouraged*" about my writing? As to my "screams"—if you found that interesting enough to report, you should have told the whole story: my refusal to read the galley notes of some pretentious mediocrity who thought she could improve on my lines. Even then, I did not "scream," but I certainly did shout. I am proud of myself in that incident, it was a painful and tragic moment, it was not funny and is not to be treated as a humorous aside.

(Your suggestion about changing the title is presented correctly, only the original title was *Second-Hand Lives* and the title *The Fountainhead* was found by me in a thesaurus.)

The rest of your Introduction contains a great many inaccuracies. I have given a list of the main ones to Mr. Amussen, who is writing to you about it. I shall mention only some personal ones: I did *not* "read the great Russian novelists" as a child; I read only one novel by Dumas (*Monte Cristo*) and hated it* and the only writer I admired profoundly was Hugo. I did not have any "mentors" in literature, no one to be "true to."

As to the meaning and value of *The Fountainhead*, I think it deserves that something more be said about it than that it tells a good story.

You can see from the above that the differences between your attitude and mine are fundamental and that there is no way to bridge the distance. Mr. Amussen said he wanted to let you try another version. I cannot object to that, if you wish to try it, but I must tell you frankly that I do not think

---

* AR had read *The Count of Monte Cristo* at age 11 or 12 and described it in 1960 as her "first big literary disappointment," because it began as a great suspense story and then became just the story of revenge that "comes to nothing important."

it will be possible for you to write an Introduction which would be acceptable to me. You are entitled to your own views about humor. But you know mine, and you chose to ignore them—and there is no meeting ground.

I will not attempt to tell you how sad and painful this is for me.

On September 6, Ogden sent a revised introduction, which he hoped "answers your criticism. I may not express myself very well, but I assure you my sentiments haven't changed over the years." The 25th anniversary edition of The Fountainhead *carries an introduction only by AR herself.*

■ ■ ■

To Pilar and José Manuel Capuletti, a Spanish painter much admired by AR

August 25, 1967

Dear Pilar and Capu,

Thank you for your letter and the beautiful postcards you sent to us—as well as for the lovely sketch of "Poco."

The edited version of the translation of my article ["Capuletti," in *The Objectivist*, December 1966] is excellent, and I agree with Mr. Frank's reasons and explanations. You have my permission to have it published in this version, provided no cuts or changes are made. Please let me know if and when it is published and send me a copy of it.

Mary Ann [Sures, a mutual friend and art historian] has just returned from Europe and gave us a chance to see the paintings which she and others bought from you. These paintings are magnificent. I have the impression that you are growing with every canvas: there is a greater maturity and control in these paintings and a much more complex composition. I'm sorry that your admirers in New York will not have a chance to see those football pictures*—and I hope that you will have more of them in your next show here.

Mary Ann has given us a glowing account of the NBI group's visit to your studio. It was *the* highlight of their tour and they were enthusiastic

---

* Capuletti painted at least two "football pictures," one of New York Giants quarterback Y. A. Tittle and one of the Baltimore Colts' passing combination of Johnny Unitas to Raymond Berry.

about your work, as well as about the graciousness of the reception you gave them.

We are looking forward to your visit to New York in November. Frank asks me to ask you to come in time for Thanksgiving, so that we will have occasion to give thanks.

■ ■ ■

To Gene Shalit, journalist and later movie critic for NBC television

September 27, 1968

Dear Mr. Shalit:

Thank you for your letter and your invitation to participate in an anthology to be called *The Childhood Day I Will Always Remember.*

I appreciate your invitation, and I regret that I am not able to accept it. The reason is that I do not regard any particular day of my childhood as especially memorable. What I regard as significant are certain trends and intellectual developments in my childhood, but not single days or events.

■ ■ ■

To Lloyd Bucher, commander of the *Pueblo*, the US warship captured by North Korea

March 7, 1969

Dear Commander Bucher:

I am enclosing a copy of my magazine, *The Objectivist*, which contains (page 1) my statement in regard to the *Pueblo* case ["Brief Comments," February 1969].

Please accept it as a small token of my profound admiration for your great moral courage and for the rightness of your stand.

If it should become necessary to defend you against injustice, I would be honored and proud to be your Emile Zola. But I believe that this country is still healthy enough not to let it become necessary.

I have read in the newspapers that I am one of your favorite authors. If this is true, I would like very much to meet you some day, when and if possible, at your convenience.

■ ■ ■

To Marjorie Hiss

November 14, 1969

Dear Marjorie,

I was truly happy to hear from you. After all these years, I did not know where to inquire about you. I certainly had not forgotten you. Frank and I have often mentioned you, wondering what had happened to you.

Please let me know how you are and what you are doing. Your mention of my predictions coming true sounds a little ominous. I hope that you are all right and that you were able to get over the influence of the Hiss family.

If you can afford to return the $500, I will appreciate it. But if it is a financial strain, you do not have to return it now. I have not forgotten that you waited when I owed you money.

I will not attempt to tell you all the things that happened to me in all these years until I hear about you. But if you have not read my novel *Atlas Shrugged*, I would like to send you a copy of it.

■   ■   ■

To Michael Collins, astronaut, who was on board the Apollo XI moonshot July 16, 1969. AR was an invited guest to witness the liftoff.

January 2, 1970

Dear Mike,

Thank you for your letter. To tell you the truth, it stunned me—in a happy way. That *you* thought my article [*The Objectivist*, September 1969] was probably the best you have read on Apollo XI, is the best reward I received in my entire writing career.

Yes, of course you may quote from my article any time you wish, any part or all of it. I shall feel very proud if you do.

With profound admiration,

■   ■   ■

To Tammy Vaught, a youngster whom AR met at the time of the Apollo XI liftoff

AR was an avid stamp collector, as she explained in her article, "Why I Like Stamp Collecting," originally published in the Spring 1971 *Minkus Stamp Journal* and reprinted in *The Ayn Rand Column*. In the article, she credits Tammy with rekindling her interest in stamps.

January 30, 1970

Dear Tammy:

Thank you for the snapshot you sent me—you look very pretty and happy. Also, thank you for the First Day Cover with the Christmas stamp.

I am sorry that I am so late in answering, but it's the US stamps that took an awfully long time to sort out. I am not finished yet, I have more of the old regular issues which I'll send you later.

All these new stamps are not from my office correspondence, we don't get letters from the communist countries, such as East Germany or Roumania. But I've asked my friends to save stamps for me, and they've asked their friends— so now I have a network of stamp scouts gathering them from everywhere.

You have influenced me to bring order into my stamp collecting, I bought the Minkus "Master Global Album" and two special albums for US stamps. I find that I really enjoy it enormously.

Tell me how you are getting along with your collection. Are there any particular series or countries that you like more than others? Have you had any luck with trading duplicates?

You ask whether we ever go camping. I wish we could, but the only traveling I do these days is from my bedroom to my desk and back again. I've been terribly busy.

Please give our regards to your family and our best wishes for the new year. Also, say hello for me to Ink Spot Junior.

Love,

■   ■   ■

To Tammy Vaught

May 21, 1970

Dear Tammy:

Thank you for your letter—and for the pretty Valentine. It has been a long time since anyone sent me a Valentine, and it pleased me very much.

You asked which country's stamps are my favorite. It is the US stamps (particularly the old ones), and France, San Marino and Japan.

I am sending you a key ring with a copy of the famous British Guiana 1¢ stamp. As you probably know, it is the most famous and valuable stamp in the world. I am enclosing a clipping from the *New York Times* that tells its history. It was recently sold (for $280,000) at an auction here in New York. I went to that auction, not to bid, but just to see what a stamp auction is like—and these key rings were given to all the guests as souvenirs of the occasion. I thought you might like to have it.

■   ■   ■

To Edward T. Chase

June 16, 1970

Dear Ned:

The matter most important to me *personally*, is the new cover for the reissue of *Atlas Shrugged*. I would like for once, after all these years, to see that novel in a cover I can really like. So I am sending this material directly to you, in order not to delay it.

The Random House ad, which I enclose, will give you the general idea, but it is not well executed. The black circle does not look like a globe, and it is too big. My idea for the cover is to have the face featured and the broken globe (designed as a globe, with the continents, etc.) in the distance, smaller (or no larger) than the face—as if Galt had shrugged and the world broke, rolling away into space. I suggest that the picture be done in color, as a picture (i.e., as a separate rectangle with lines of demarcation from the rest of the cover) and that it be the full size of the cover, except for the lettering of the text.

I am enclosing two photographs of that portrait (one is a color transparency). The portrait part has to be kept as is, but the background has to be redrawn by your artist. These are my only photographs of the portrait, so please return them to me as soon as the Art Department has made copies. (It's a portrait of my husband. I neither hide nor publicize this fact.)

I am sending a list of the articles for my proposed new book (*The New Left: The Anti-Industrial Revolution*).

■   ■   ■

To S. S. Peikoff, M.D., fellow stamp collector and father of Leonard Peikoff

October 5, 1970

Dear Sam:

Thank you enormously for the marvelous stamps you sent me. Please forgive me for my delay in answering—this is the first chance I've had to write privately instead of publicly (that is, letters instead of articles).

I am returning the Hungarian, New Zealand and Spanish stamps which I did have. Most of the stamps were new to me, and I was thrilled to get them.

I am returning also the block of four Canadian stamps of the Tokyo Exposition, because you sent me such a block the previous time. I looked and looked, but could not observe a difference. If I am wrong, it's because I am not yet expert enough—but I am struggling to learn.

The more I work with stamps, the more I love it. I guess it's an incurable addiction. You ask how I can find the time for it. I find that stamps help me to work: it is the only thing that gives me mental rest. If I take an hour off for my stamp albums, I can go on writing for hours.

I hope you can use the stamps that I am enclosing.

■　■　■

To José and Pilar Capuletti

October 5, 1970

Dear Capu and Pilar:

Thank you very, very much for your letters and for the wonderful stamps you sent me.

The Spanish stamps were very beautiful. I liked particularly the 1969 series with copies of paintings by Alonso Cano. I am returning two stamps which I had—you gave them to me here.

Since you like horses, I am enclosing a new series of Chinese stamps. They are reproductions of a painting of the XVII–XVIII century, called *One Hundred Horses*. The long strip (which should not be separated) is supposed to have that number of horses, all of them different. (I did not try to count them.) The two single stamps are magnified details of the strip.

I am enclosing also some new US stamps.

The sketch (in your letter) of the additions to your house looks magnificent. It is growing into a castle. I hope it will not delay for too long your visit to New York. Mary Ann told me that you are not coming in

652 LETTERS OF AYN RAND

October. I was afraid of that, remember? Please prove me wrong and do come in the not too distant future.

What happened in your interview with Dali? You mentioned that you would tell me.

■ ■ ■

To S. P. Wang, director general of posts, Taiwan

December 14, 1971

Dear Mr. Wang:

Please accept my sincere gratitude for the publication of my article "Why I Like Stamp Collecting" in your magazine of October 1971.

I felt pleased and honored to see my work translated into the Chinese language.

Allow me to express my profound sympathy for the Republic of China. I feel a great indignation against the foreign policy of President Nixon, which I regard as a grave injustice to your country, and I shall continue to express my opposition to it. This is the voice of only one American citizen, but there are many who feel as I do.

AR expressed her opposition in a three-part article on Nixon and China beginning in the March 27, 1972, issue of The Ayn Rand Letter.

■ ■ ■

To William M. Magruder, special assistant to President Nixon

December 14, 1971

Dear Mr. Magruder:

Thank you for your letter. I am very pleased that you found my articles helpful.

Yes, of course, I shall be delighted to see you again, this month or next, at your convenience. I found our conversation very interesting indeed. I have great sympathy for your cause [a "science defense league" to show how science contributes to our standard of living], as I understand it—and I hope that you can succeed. I look forward to hearing about your progress.

Please convey our thanks to Mrs. Magruder for her *sweet* thoughtfulness.

■ ■ ■

To W. F. Carter, director of posts, Papua New Guinea

December 14, 1971

Dear Mr. Carter:

Thank you very much for your letter, for the kind things you said about my article "Why I Like Stamp Collecting," and for the attractive Presentation Folder which you sent me.

The stamps of Papua New Guinea are very beautiful and I shall give them a place of honor in my collection.

■ ■ ■

To S. S. Prilkoff, M D

December 14, 1971

Dear Sam:

Thank you very much for the 8¢ Queen Victoria stamp, which I am returning.

There was nothing wrong with the first one you sent me: when I took it out of the Showguard, I discovered that I had inadvertently folded some of the perforations and that the stamp is not damaged at all.

Thanks once more for the enormous avalanche you gave me when you were here. I have just finished sorting them out. Please let me know whether you want me to hold them here until you move, or to mail them back to you now.

■ ■ ■

To Lloyd Laury, a fan

December 15, 1971

Dear Mr. Laury:

I deeply appreciate the fact that you understood my article on "Racism" in *The Virtue of Selfishness* and that you liked *The Fountainhead*. I hope that you will continue to find my philosophy helpful.

What you say about the faults of the black leadership is true, but the same is true today of the white leadership. It is not an issue of race, but of the wrong philosophical influence on all groups in our society.

If you understand my philosophy, as I think you do, you know that you must never allow the actions of others to be a reflection on you. Every man has to judge himself and be judged only by his own actions and character.

Do not allow anyone ever to make you feel ashamed of being black. That would be an acceptance of the vicious racist premises of other people. The best way to fight racists of any color, black or white, is never to allow their ideas into your own mind.

In regard to my article "The Age of Envy" [reprinted in *The New Left: The Anti-Industrial Revolution*], observe that the white groups I mention, particularly Women's Lib, are much worse and much more guilty than the black movement.

You should be proud of your intellectual achievement, which your letter demonstrates, and I urge you to continue along the road of individual, intellectual independence.

■ ■ ■

To Yoav Dror, a fan

December 15, 1971

Dear Mr. Dror:

I am glad that you liked my books and that you find my philosophy helpful.

I am particularly impressed by your attitude because you were raised in a "kibbutz" and had to rise out of it on your own.

With my best wishes for your success in this country,

■ ■ ■

To Wesley S. Hartley, a high-school English teacher

December 15, 1971

Dear Mr. Hartley:

I am enclosing a copy of my article "The Goal of My Writing" (from my book *The Romantic Manifesto*), which you may find of interest to your students.

As to your question: "How important to Miss Rand was her high school education, and is college experience necessary for creative writing?" I cannot say that my high school and college education were important to me in regard to my writing, but knowledge and proper education were certainly important. No, college experience is not necessary for creative writing, but an enormous amount of independent thinking is.

■ ■ ■

To Grace L. Hardy, a fan

June 20, 1972

Dear Mrs. Hardy:

I appreciate the honesty of your intention, but you are mistaken if you think that your original letter "sounded whiny," as you say. I was prompted to send you a gift subscription to *The Ayn Rand Letter* precisely because your letter was *not* whiny. I admire your spirit of independence and your active interest in ideas at the age of 78. As you probably have observed, many people give up thinking much earlier than that (or never even begin it).

So please accept the gift subscription as a kind of tribute to your character—and not as "charity." I am glad if your financial circumstances have improved, but regardless of these circumstances, you are not obligated to pay for my *Letter*. Please consider it as an answer to the fact that I liked yours.

As to the comment of your son, I do have a secretary, but my secretary never signs mail in my name. I am unable to maintain philosophical correspondence, which is why she often answers for me, but in such cases she signs her own name.

■ ■ ■

To Anthony Swerling, a fan

November 6, 1972

Dear Mr. Swerling:

In answer to your letter of October 24, I must say that I have not read enough of August Strindberg to form a full opinion of his work. But the little that I have read has not aroused my interest to read more—which, I suppose, *is* an opinion.

■ ■ ■

To David L. Baker, Marine Corps captain and instructor in the behavioral science department, US Naval Academy

November 22, 1972

Dear Captain Baker,

I am very pleased that you liked my talk on national unity [delivered at the Ford Hall Forum, October 22, 1971] and that you want to use it in a course at the Naval Academy. I am enclosing a copy of this talk which, as you will see, was published in my periodical.

Would you let me know in what form you consider using it? Do you intend to use excerpts? If you intend to use the article in full, it will be necessary to formally request permission to reprint it—which, of course, I would be pleased to give you.

■　■　■

To E. W. Birch, M. G. Morisette, and E. M. Swarthout ("Three Concerned Americans" aboard the USS *Mauna Kea*)

December 1, 1972

Gentlemen:

In regard to your letter of November 14, I have not read *None Dare Call It Conspiracy* by Gary Allen. But I can say that I am deeply suspicious of any book alleging conspiracies. It would take an almost impossible job of research to check on the documentation of such a book, a job which I cannot undertake.

I am profoundly opposed to the so-called conspiracy theory of history. The conclusions of its advocates are usually unproved, arbitrary and out of context. They raise more questions than they attempt to answer.

As to the John Birch Society, I regard it as a futile organization because it is unphilosophical, anti-intellectual, and is not an advocate of capitalism, but is merely opposed to Communism.

In order to fight any issue, it is necessary to fight *for* something, not merely *against* something.

■　■　■

To Nora Drobyshev, the younger of AR's two sisters

Until Nora's letter, AR had not heard from her sister since the late 1930s. The three letters to Nora in this book were translated from the handwritten Russian, except for material in italics, handwritten in English.

May 5, 1973

Dear Nora!

I cannot express how glad I was to receive your letter. It was so unexpected that I laughed and cried and was very, very happy.

Thank you for not forgetting me. A long time has passed, but I was hoping that you would know or feel that I have not forgotten you and never will. I have always dreamt that I would see you some day.

Your letter was on its way for almost two months, but it reached us. I hope that my answer reaches you faster.

I won't tell you all the details of my life. I will only say that I have achieved everything I wanted to achieve in my youth. Frank and I have been very happy all this time, as well as now.

I have not changed at all, except, of course, for having aged. But I feel like a young woman. I love everything and everyone I loved when I was twenty.

Dear, dear Norochka, I love you very much. Please write about yourself in detail. How is your husband, Fedya? It is somewhat difficult for me to write in Russian, so please forgive me if you find errors in this letter. I will learn to write more correctly.

Passionate kisses—and *Love from both of us to both of you.*

Alisa

■　■　■

To Doris Gordon, a fan

May 30, 1973

Dear Miss Gordon:

In your letter of April 2, you ask me why I am opposed to amnesty.

My views on this issue are as follows. I *do* oppose the draft because it is a violation of an individual's right to his own life (as I have written in "The Wreckage of the Consensus," *Capitalism: The Unknown Ideal,* paperback edition). But there are so many different motives among the men who opposed the draft, that each case has to be judged on its own merits.

If a man objected on the ground that the draft represents a violation of his rights, he would deserve amnesty. So would any man who objected on the ground of his convictions, even if they were religious ones.

But those who objected neither to the draft nor to war, as such, but to this particular war, do not deserve amnesty, because their motive was not one of principle but of sympathy with the enemy. The most outrageous examples in this category are the men who expressed sympathy with North Vietnam and publicly carried the Vietcong flag—at a time when Americans were being killed in Vietnam. Such men are never to be forgiven.

One is free to disagree with the government of one's country on any issue, including its foreign policy, but one has no right to express one's sympathy with the enemy in wartime, because this amounts to sanctioning the killing of one's countrymen.

■ ■ ■

To Marilyn Van Derbur, a businesswoman and Miss America of 1958

Van Derbur asked AR for biographical incidents she could use in a project she described as "working with high-school students in the classroom regarding motivation."

May 30, 1973

Dear Miss Van Derbur:

I am glad to answer the questions in your letter. I agree with you that it is very important to teach high-school students "how much work is involved in accomplishment."

The Fountainhead was rejected by twelve publishers. I do not know all their names, because the submissions were handled by a literary agent, but I can tell you the names I know: Macmillan (who had published my first novel, *We the Living*); Doubleday; Knopf; Simon & Schuster; Random House; Little, Brown. An editor of this last company told me that although their editorial board's appraisal of the book was very favorable, it was their unanimous opinion that the book would not sell. Finally, Bobbs-Merrill published *The Fountainhead*; I learned later that one of their editors had said that it was a bad book which would sell, and another that it was a good book which would not sell.

I remember reading in the literary columns that Pearl Buck's first novel, *The Good Earth*, was rejected by twenty-one publishers.

It took me seven years to write *The Fountainhead*, and thirteen years to write *Atlas Shrugged*. There is no page in either book that I did not rewrite many times. On *Atlas Shrugged*, I used a ream of paper (500 pages) for every 100 pages of manuscript—i.e., it amounted, on the average, to my every page being rewritten five times.

I have never met a good writer who claimed that writing came easily or that he wrote "inspirationally"; all those I met, said that writing required excruciating effort (e.g., Sinclair Lewis).

I recommend to your attention a very interesting book on this subject: *How to Think Creatively* by Eliot D. Hutchinson, which is a summation of his interviews with hundreds of writers, artists and scientists. The author is a psychologist; his thesis is: "Inspiration comes only to those who deserve it." (This book is available in paperback.)

As to articles written about me personally, most of them contain so many misrepresentations that I cannot recommend them. One of the few that I liked was by Rex Reed, in the *New York Sunday News* of February 25, 1973. I am not sure, however, that this article is relevant to your theme.

■ ■ ■

To Judge Reuben L. Lurie

June 1, 1973

Dear Judge Lurie:

Thank you for your letter of April 27 and your invitation to speak at the Ford Hall Forum. So long as you are there, I shall always be delighted to accept.

Please excuse my long delay in answering your previous letter, in regard to the invitation to speak for the Free Market Conference Committee. I do not know anything about this group and they did not write to me until some time after I received your letter. I regret that they took it upon themselves to invite you to act as moderator without the courtesy of informing me about it or obtaining my consent to speak. I deeply appreciate the fact that you considered their invitation, but I cannot agree to speak for them. It is my policy not to appear under the sponsorship of any group representing some specific viewpoint (especially if it is a "conservative" one) —because, as you probably know, there is no group whose ideas I would agree with or support.

One of the reasons I enjoy speaking at the Ford Hall Forum is the fact that it is an open, nonpartisan organization.

■　■　■

To Larry Cole, host of a radio show on WRVR in New York City

July 5, 1973

Dear Mr. Cole:

The following are the conditions under which I agree to appear on your program *Growing Up in New York*. If you find them acceptable, please sign the enclosed copy of this letter and return it to me.

1. The program on which I will appear will be a serious discussion of ideas between the host and myself, followed by a telephone question period.

2. There will be no debate, no engaging in personalities, no attacks on me, and no remarks of an offensive, insulting or derogatory nature (i.e., any disagreement is to be expressed politely and impersonally).

3. There will be no quotations from or references to any of my critics, or to any secondhand reports about me, my writing or Objectivism.

4. If the program is taped, it will be broadcast exactly as recorded without any cuts or changes of any kind. This applies also to future re-broadcasts of the program, if any.

5. The exact wording of how I will be introduced and/or referred to on the program, and how my appearance will be announced prior thereto, will be submitted to me for my prior consent.

6. If I will be asked to sign a release, or any other documents in connection with my appearance, I will receive same from you at least a day prior thereto.

■　■　■

To Nora Drobyshev

August 6, 1973

Dear Nora!

Thank you very, very much for your letter—and, especially, for your offer to visit us. You don't know how glad I am. I did not dare to hope that it was possible but, nevertheless, I was hoping silently.

When I received your letter, I immediately applied for a request for the documents issued by the American government for a visa to the United States. I have just now received them and am sending them to you with this letter.

They told me here that you must send these documents to the USSR government to the Department of Visas and Registrations (OVIR), with a request to issue the passport for you to visit the United States. If you want to come in November or December, you have to send the request now. (If it is inconvenient to you now, you may delay it until it is convenient.)

No matter when it happens, Frank and I will be very, very happy if you come. When you receive the passport, please send me a telegram at once.

Can Fedya come with you? I would like very much to meet him. Please ask his physician and, if his health allows, I hope that you both are able to come. If it is possible, I will immediately send a request and the documents for him. Give me his name and his patronymic: Fyodor _____ Drobyshev?

Dear Fedya (since you are my brother-in-law, I shall not address you formally), I really hope you are able to come and visit us, so that we can see you. If it is impossible, I am very grateful that you are willing to let Nora go; at least, for a short while. I understand how you both feel: Frank and I also cannot part for long.

Nora, write me your telephone number in Leningrad. I have found out that I can telephone you and talk to you. I want to call you when you return from the cottage. Please give me your number when you come back to Leningrad and what time (according to your time) you are usually home.

Now, about the other news in your letter. Thank you for writing about Daddy, Mama and Natasha. I know that it was difficult to write—and read. I am very, very glad that Fedya has recovered from his disease and can now live a normal life. I have always thought that the hardest and the worst part of life is the illness of those whom we love, and I feel deep respect for you because you have endured such suffering. *I wish you both all the happiness that you deserved and have earned. Happiness and courage can keep people alive and well for a long, long time.* Everything you wrote about your feelings for Fedya, I can say (and often have said) about my feelings for Frank, even using the same words. For example, "we are one, and I do not know where I end and he begins." Just like you, we think in the same fashion, and everything one of us likes or dislikes, the other always likes or dislikes as well—even music. Our friends say that we have an *"ideal marriage."*

Now, if you want to practice reading English, I will write a bit in

English. It is remarkable that Frank and I resemble Fedya and you in temperament! I am tense, aggressive and very articulate, Frank is calm, gentle and silent. But, inside, he is tougher than I am—and if we ever disagreed, I wouldn't be able to budge him, and nobody would. I call him "my rock of Gibraltar." When I am unhappy or discouraged, which is not often, he is the only one who can give me the strength.

We often talk about you. We both hope that you will soon come. We are waiting for you in great impatience—*impatiently and enthusiastically.*

Passionate kisses—*and love from both of us to both of you.*

Alisa

■ ■ ■

To Nora Drobyshev

September 12, 1973

Dear Nora!

With this letter I am sending you the documents for Fedya (the invitation to the United States).

I won't write a long letter so as not to delay the sending of these documents. I will only say that Frank and I will be very, very happy if you both come to visit us.

I was very glad to speak to you over the telephone. When I hear your voice, I feel as if we were near each other, as if you were here, in my room.

We will be waiting impatiently—but will force ourselves to wait patiently—for the moment when we see you both.

Love from both of us to both of you
Passionate kisses—
Alisa

Nora and her husband visited AR but chose to return to the USSR, despite AR's urgent arguments. The visit was a bitter disappointment to AR, who found her sister a totally changed and unlikable person.

■ ■ ■

To Nathalie Rivard, a fan

November 8, 1973

Dear Nathalie:

Your question is a very broad one, and I am not certain which aspect of it you had in mind. You ask "why mental children always have so much money spent on them when the bright ones need it much more." If you want to know the motive of the people who practice such a policy, then the brief answer is: the morality of altruism, which makes them resent the able and intelligent people (or children).

■ ■ ■

To Herman V. Ivey, lieutenant colonel and professor of English at the US Military Academy, West Point

March 20, 1974

Dear Colonel Ivey,

I want to thank you for your help and guidance, and for arranging my lecture at West Point ["Philosophy: Who Needs It," later the title essay of a book]. After all the time and effort which you gave to the task of briefing me, on your visits to New York, I am delighted that the occasion was so successful.

I believe that the cadets enjoyed it—and as for me, it was the most interesting and enjoyable of my lecture appearances. As you might have gathered, I do admire rational military efficiency, and you stand in my mind as one of its best symbols.

I hear that my lecture did stimulate the cadets to philosophical discussions. If you can, let me know a little about it, I would be most interested. If you have played the tape of my lecture for other departments, please let me know the response.

And please don't forget to send me a program of the West Point band concerts. All of us are anxious to see West Point again and to hear your band.

■ ■ ■

To Mrs. William Maethner, a fan

June 20, 1974

Dear Mrs. Maethner:

You have good grounds to be concerned.

Please tell your daughter that I am profoundly opposed to today's so-called libertarian movement and to the theories of Dr. Murray Rothbard. So-called libertarians are my avowed enemies, yet I've heard many reports on their attempts to cash in on my name and mislead my readers into the exact opposite of my views.

Please call to your daughter's attention my article "The Nature of Government," in my book *Capitalism: The Unknown Ideal*.

■ ■ ■

To Ethan C. Mordden, assistant editor at *Opera News*

Opera News asked AR to write an article on the nature of heroism in Richard Wagner's *Ring* cycle.

June 20, 1974

Dear Mr. Mordden:

I appreciate your interest, but I cannot participate in your project.

It is true that my schedule does not permit me to undertake any outside writing assignments, but this is not the only reason in this particular case. Wagner's idea of heroism and his image of the hero are not mine. In fact, they are the opposite of mine.

■ ■ ■

To James Michener, author

March 11, 1975

Dear Mr. Michener:

Thank you for your letter of February 7 inviting me to become a member of the National Society of Literature and the Arts.

I appreciate your invitation, but I cannot accept it because I am profoundly opposed to the intrusion of force, i.e., governmental power, into the fields of literature and the arts—in the form of censorship or subsidies or special political pull or "the creation of a Secretary of the Arts in the President's Cabinet."

■ ■ ■

To Robert F. Anderson, philosophy professor at the University of Nebraska

February 14, 1977

Dear Mr. Anderson:

You say "I find I am not quite clear on whether you hold that the proper life for humans is a life of productive work or a life of rational activity." I do not understand what you mean by the words "rational activity" in such a context. Does this mean that you regard productive work as an irrational activity?

If, by "rational activity," you mean thinking, or mental work, or intellectual work, then you are totally outside my context. I do not recognize the mind-body dichotomy. I hold that intellectual work is the root of any other kind of work, and that every kind of productive work includes both an intellectual and a physical component.

■ ■ ■

To Flora Reekstin, a former employee

February 16, 1977

Dear Flo:

Thank you for the most thrilling present [of a stuffed animal resembling Morris the Cat] I have received in many, many Christmases.

As you know, it is my principle not to accept presents, but a superior value such as Morris takes precedence over lesser issues.

THANKS again!

■ ■ ■

To Richard P. Ford, a fan

March 14, 1978

Dear Mr. Ford:

I am glad that you found my philosophy helpful and that it has put you on the right road, if I judge by your letter.

I realize that you are an individual in your own right, not merely "Gerald Ford's nephew," but I cannot resist the temptation to tell you that

I like your uncle very much, even though I do not agree with all of his policies. I hope he will run in the next presidential election—I would be happy to vote for him again.

■   ■   ■

To John E. Marshall, television producer

October 18, 1980

Dear Mr. Marshall:

Thank you for your letter of August 6, and for your invitation to take part in a television series dealing with "Cultural Conservatism."

I appreciate your interest, but I'm *not* a Conservative as the term is used today. I am an Objectivist, which is quite a different thing. In politics, I call myself a radical for capitalism.

This year in particular, I would be ashamed to be connected with the so-called Conservatives in any way. Their anti-abortion stand is outrageous—and so is their mixture of politics with religion.

As you can see, I cannot accept your invitation.

■   ■   ■

To Whom It May Concern

Leonard Peikoff had asked for a reference as an academic teacher of philosophy.

November 21, 1980

To Whom It May Concern:

I am happy to comply with Dr. Leonard Peikoff's request for a reference. I have known Dr. Peikoff since the 1950s. I have attended lectures he has given on my philosophy, Objectivism, and on other subjects. For eight years, I employed him as an Associate (later Contributing) Editor of my publications *The Objectivist* and *The Ayn Rand Letter* (1968–1976).

Dr. Peikoff has a superlative understanding of the philosophy of Objectivism, and is able to communicate it expertly. He grasps not only its well-known ideas in ethics and politics, but also their base in the Objectivist epistemology. In particular, he has a detailed grasp of my theory of the role of mathematics in concept-formation, and of the implications of this theory for the analytic-synthetic, a priori-a posteriori dichotomy. I am often asked for an endorsement by aspiring teachers of my philosophy, but I know of no philosopher who is Dr. Peikoff's equal on this subject.

Dr. Peikoff is an outstanding teacher. His material is well-structured, his examples colorful and arresting, his pace lively, his emphases definite. At the same time, his lectures are deliberate enough to encourage his students to think, to understand, and to evaluate for themselves the ideas presented. I once saw Dr. Peikoff explain Kant's Transcendental Deduction to a class of undergraduates; I marvelled at his ability to include a wealth of technical elaboration, to convey it with full clarity, and to retain the unflagging interest of the students. I was also impressed by the balance he struck between student and teacher participation; the students were active in volunteering questions or comments, but the class did not dissolve into random discussions or side issues.

I have recently written an Introduction to Dr. Peikoff's forthcoming book, *The Ominous Parallels*. I regard this work as an extremely important intellectual achievement, which deserves—and may well gain—a wide influence, when it is published next year. One day soon, I think, Dr. Peikoff will have a national reputation in the field of the philosophy of history.

■ ■ ■

To Charles S. Smallman, a fan

March 11, 1981

Dear Mr. Smallman,

To answer your questions:

The *Ruff Times* has nothing in common with Objectivism and, if anything, is antagonistic to it.

No, my next book will not be the complete presentation of Objectivism.

No, I am not "somewhat satisfied with the returns of last November's election." I did not vote for any of the Presidential candidates. I do not approve of Mr. Reagan's mixture of capitalism and religion. Mr. [Alan] Greenspan [a member of the President's Economic Policy Advisory Board and former contributor to AR's periodicals] hopes to influence him in economics—and I hope he can succeed, but—?

No, I have not become a "second assistant bookkeeper"—and I would write for the *New York Times* sooner than for the *Wall Street Journal*, which

I despise. Incidentally, the article, a copy of which you sent me, is *not* good. No student of mine would quote such vicious junk as "religion in America . . . must be regarded as the first of their political institutions." (And no Objectivist would accept de Tocqueville as a philosophical authority.)

■ ■ ■

To Mimi Sutton

December 22, 1981

Dear Mimi,

This is to help you with the burden of holiday guests.

I think you are a very brave girl—and I don't like you to be depressed, if it can be helped.

Give your guests something nice for dinner, without worrying about the cost.

Merry Christmas and a Happy New Year—to you and the family.

Love,

This is AR's last letter, written just over two months before she died.

■ ■ ■

APPENDIX
A LETTER FROM AYN RAND
"TO THE READERS OF
THE FOUNTAINHEAD" (1945)

To the Readers of *The Fountainhead*:

I am glad and grateful when readers wish to know what kind of person wrote *The Fountainhead*—but I find it extremely difficult to answer, because the answer is contained in the question. There is nothing of any importance to be said or known about me—except that I wrote *The Fountainhead*.

When I am questioned about myself, I am tempted to say, paraphrasing Roark: "Don't ask me about my family, my childhood, my friends or my feelings. Ask me about the things I think." It is the content of a person's brain, not the accidental details of his life, that determines his character. My own character is in the pages of *The Fountainhead*. For anyone who wishes to know me, that is essential. The specific events of my private life are of no importance whatever. I have never had any private life in the usual sense of the word. My writing is my life.

I decided to be a writer at the age of nine—it was a specific, conscious decision—I remember the day and the hour. I did not start by trying to describe the folks next door—but by inventing people who did things the folks next door would never do. I could summon no interest or enthusiasm for "people as they are"—when I had in my mind a blinding picture of people as they could be.

I decided to become a writer—not in order to save the world, nor to serve my fellow men—but for the simple, personal, selfish, egotistical happiness of creating the kind of men and events I could like, respect and admire. I can bear to look around me levelly. I cannot bear to look down. I wanted to look up.

This attitude has never changed. But I went for years thinking that it was a strictly personal attitude toward fiction writing, never to be discussed and of no interest to anyone but me. Later I discovered I had accepted as the rule of my life work a principle stated by Aristotle. Aristotle said that fiction is of greater philosophical importance than history, because history represents things only as they are, while fiction represents them "as they might be and ought to be." If you wish a key to the literary method of *The Fountainhead*, this is it.

I left home when I was quite young and have been on my own ever since. My life has been "single-tracked," or anything anyone wishes to call a life consciously devoted to a conscious purpose. I have no hobbies. I have few friends. I do not like to "go out." I am unbearable—to myself and to others—when I stay too long away from my work. Nothing else has ever mattered to me too much.

The only exception to that last line is my husband, Frank O'Connor. *The Fountainhead* is dedicated to him. He is my best proof that people such as I write about can and do exist in real life.

I have never studied writing nor taken any formal course in literature. I did have a college education, but whatever I learned I had to learn by myself and in my own way. I did not attempt to write professionally until I knew what I was doing and felt that I was ready. I sold the first screen story, the first stage play and the first novel I ever wrote. The screen story was called *Red Pawn* and was bought by Universal Pictures. The play was *Night of January 16th*, which ran on Broadway in the season 1935–36. The novel was *We the Living*, published in 1936.

Yes, I've had a hard struggle before, between and after these jobs. I had to earn my own living before I could start writing. After I started, I had to earn my living whenever the money I made by writing was exhausted. I did all sorts of odd jobs: I have been a waitress, an office clerk, a reader for film companies. I could not concentrate on a business career, but had to take such jobs as could be held temporarily and would leave me free to write in my spare time.

At present, I live in California where I have bought a small ranch. My home is a modern house—glass, steel and concrete. I am now working part of my time as a screenwriter for Hal Wallis Productions. Film rights to *The Fountainhead* have been bought by Warner Brothers; the picture will go into production soon. I am now starting to work on my next novel.

There has been a steady stream of letters from readers of *The Fountainhead*—more, I regret, than it was possible to answer. I shall attempt here to answer the questions asked most often.

The Fountainhead started in my mind as a definition of a new code of ethics—the morality of individualism. The idea of individualism is not new, but nobody had defined a consistent and specific way to live by it in practice. It is in their statements on morality that the individualist thinkers have floundered and lost their case. They had nothing better to offer than vulgar selfishness which consisted of sacrificing others to self. When I realized that that was only another form of collectivism—of living through others by ruling them—I had the key to *The Fountainhead* and to the character of Howard Roark.

The key statement to the whole conception of *The Fountainhead* is in Roark's speech: "I wished to come here and say that I am a man who does not exist for others. It had to be said. The world is perishing from an orgy of self-sacrificing." All the rest of the book is a demonstration of how the principles of egoism and altruism work out in people and in the events of their lives.

I have been asked why I chose to present a philosophy of ethics in fiction form. I am interested in philosophical principles only as they affect the actual existence of men; and in men, only as they reflect philosophical principles. An abstract theory that has no relation to reality is worse than nonsense; and men who act without relation to principles are less than animals. Those who say that theory and practice are two unrelated realms are fools in one and scoundrels in the other. I wanted to present my abstract theory where it belongs—in concrete reality—in the actions of men.

Readers have asked me whether my characters are "copies of real people in public life" or "not human beings at all, but symbols." Neither is true. My characters are *not* copies of real persons. No serious writer ever "copies" people in that naïve, journalistic way. What I did was to observe real life, analyze the reasons which make people such as they are, draw an abstraction and then create my own characters out of that abstraction. My characters are persons in whom certain human attributes are focused more sharply and consistently than in average human beings.

Readers have asked me whether there is a real prototype of Howard Roark. Literally—no. Essentially—yes. Every man who has an innate sense of independence and self-respect, and a spark of the creative mind, has that much of Roark in him.

One reader wrote to me saying that Roark "could not possibly be a human being." Actually, Roark is the one genuine *human* being in the book—because he embodies precisely those qualities which constitute a human being, as distinguished from an animal. Keating is subhuman—

because he has no independent existence, no mind of his own, no moral quality.

If Keating were the typical representative of humanity, we would never have risen out of the swamp and the cave. It was not the Keatings who got us out. Never mind about there being more Keatings than Roarks. It's the Roarks who count.

Readers have asked me why I chose architecture as the background of my book. Was my choice motivated by any previous knowledge of architecture or architects? No. When I made my first notes for *The Fountainhead* I knew nothing whatever about architecture, had never dealt with it in any way, and had never met an architect. I chose it deliberately as the background best suited to my thesis. A builder is one of the most eloquent representatives of man's creative faculty.

Once I chose that background, I had to face the somewhat terrifying task of learning something about it. I did two years of reading and research, then got a job in the office of a New York architect. I enjoyed the job tremendously. Nobody in that office knew my real purpose in working there, except the head of the firm. I shall always be grateful to him for taking a chance on me—he had no idea of what kind of book I might write. He never questioned me about it. He was extremely helpful and generous in giving me information. Professional etiquette doesn't permit me to give his name in print; but it is a prominent name. After I left his office, I did not see him again for five years—until I came back and put the galley proofs of *The Fountainhead* on his desk. I am glad to say that he liked the book, even though he was a bit shocked by it.

How long did it take me to write the book? Seven years. I spent the last and final year writing steadily, literally day and night; once I wrote for thirty hours at a stretch, without sleep, stopping only to get some food. It was the most enjoyable year of my life.

The Fountainhead owes its appearance in print to the courage of one publishing house and of two men: Richard Mealand, story editor of Paramount Pictures, who read the manuscript and recommended it to the Bobbs-Merrill Company; and Archibald G. Ogden, who was editor of Bobbs-Merrill at that time. They were men who had the integrity to form an independent judgment and the courage to act upon it. I mention their names here in token of my gratitude.

The success of *The Fountainhead* has demonstrated its own thesis. It was rejected by twelve publishers who declared that it had no commercial possibilities, it would not sell, it was "too intellectual," it was "too unconventional," it went against every alleged popular trend. Yet the success of *The Fountainhead* was made by the public. Not by the public as an organized *collective*—but by single, individual readers who discovered it of their own choice, who read it on their own initiative and recommended it on their own judgment.

I did not know that I was predicting my own future when I described the process of Roark's success: "It was as if an underground stream flowed through the country and broke out in sudden springs that shot to the surface at random, in unpredictable places."

To every reader who had the intelligence to understand *The Fountainhead*, the integrity to like it and the courage to speak about it—to every one of you, not in mass, but personally and individually, I am here saying:

Thank you.

Ayn Rand

INDEX

NOTE: A **bold face number** indicates a letter *to* that person or organization.

· A NOTE ON THE TYPE ·

The typeface used in this book is a version of Times Roman, originally designed by Stanley Morison (1889–1967), the scholar who
supervised Monotype's revivals of classic typefaces (Bembo) and
commissioned new ones from Eric Gill (Perpetua), among others.
Having censured The Times of London in an article, Morison was
challenged to better it. Taking Plantin as a basis, he sought to produce a typeface that would be classical but not dull, compact without looking cramped, and would keep high readability on a range
of papers. ''The Times New Roman'' debuted on October 3, 1932,
and was almost instantly in great demand; it has become perhaps
the most widely used of all typefaces (though the paper changed
typeface again in 1972). Given its success, it is noteworthy that it
was Morison's only original design. Ironically, he had pangs of
conscience, writing later, ''[William] Morris would have
denounced [it].''

B
RAND

Rand, Ayn

The letters of Ayn
Rand

87571

$34.95

DATE			